PARALLEL PROCESSING AND ADA

Yehuda Wallach

Syracuse University
and
Wayne State University

Prentice Hall
Englewood Cliffs, New Jersey 07632

Library of Congress Cataloging-in-Publication Data

Wallach, Y. (Yehuda)
    Parallel processing and ADA / Y. Wallach.
      p.   cm.
    Includes bibliographical references.
    ISBN 0-13-650789-1
      1. Parallel processing (Electronic computers) 2. Ada (Computer
    program language)   I. Title.
    QA76.5.W247 1990
    004'.35--dc20   89-23176
                                                                  CIP

Editorial/production supervision
  and interior design: *Jacqueline A. Jeglinski*
Cover design: *Wanda Lubelska Design*
Manufacturing buyers: *Kelly Behr and Susan Brunke*

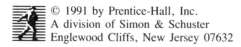 © 1991 by Prentice-Hall, Inc.
A division of Simon & Schuster
Englewood Cliffs, New Jersey 07632

The publisher offers discounts on this book when ordered
in bulk quantities. For more information, write:
  Special Sales/College Marketing
  Prentice-Hall, Inc.
  College Technical and Reference Division
  Englewood Cliffs, NJ 07632

Printed in the United States of America
10 9 8 7 6 5 4 3 2 1

ISBN 0-13-650789-1

Prentice-Hall International (UK) Limited, *London*
Prentice-Hall of Australia Pty. Limited, *Sydney*
Prentice-Hall Canada Inc., *Toronto*
Prentice-Hall Hispanoamericana, S.A., *Mexico*
Prentice-Hall of India Private Limited, *New Delhi*
Prentice-Hall of Japan, Inc., *Tokyo*
Simon & Schuster Asia Pte. Ltd., *Singapore*
Editora Prentice-Hall do Brasil, Ltda., *Rio de Janeiro*

To Aaron Wallach
my father and grandson

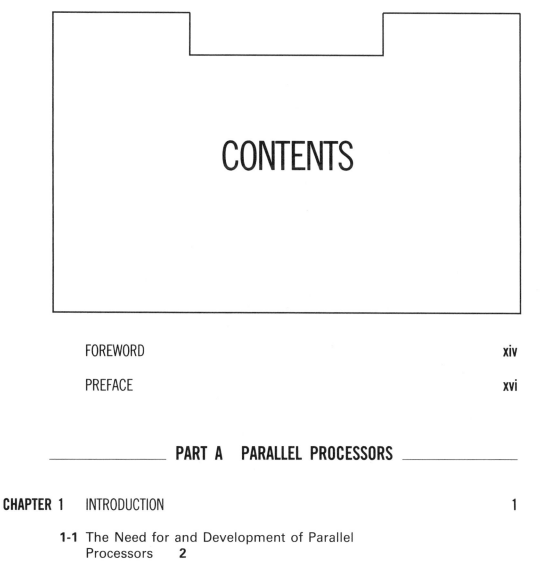

CONTENTS

_____ **PART B   PARALLEL PROGRAMMING AND ADA** _____

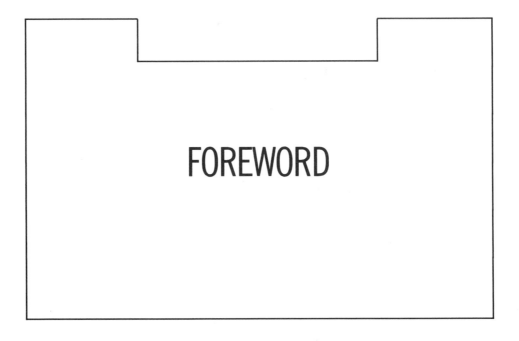

FOREWORD

'Panta rei' (Πάντα ῥεῖ), old Greek philosophers say, and there is no doubt that all things are going on simultaneously or 'in parallel.' This 'Panta rei' is also apparent in Analogue Computers—in particular in those of the mechanical type—where all wheels are running at the same time to solve a Differential Equation. These turning wheels reflect the real world which is parallel in nature.

First Digital Computers—beginning in the thirties—seem nevertheless to be instruments where a lonely 'one' is going up and down in wires, tubes, and resistors. Theorists developed—nearly at the same time—a model with very elementary sequential operations called the Turing-Machine. The machine prints a 'one' on a particular space of a tape at a certain time and clears a 'one' on this tape at another time. The tape of a Turing-Machine is stepping back and forth, following the elementary operations, which are executed quite sequentially.

Parallelism has come up in this context only in a very simple variant in the fifties. The classical von-Neumann-Computer has been called a ''Parallel Computer'' with respect to the processing of one parallel word at a time. Nevertheless the whole control mechanism still works as a sequential device, shifting a few binary entities back and forth. By hindsight the von-Neumann-Computer was a sequential concept. At the time of its birth, however, it had been a most ingenious idea created by K. Zuse, J. V. Atanasoff, J. von Neumann and others. The essential sequentiality at that time was also based on the fact that hardware was extremely expensive regarding costs.

With the upcoming semiconductor-technology and even more with the technology of integration (mainly VLSI) the scene changed considerably. Since then hardware became the cheaper part—compared to software. At the same time devices became smaller and smaller. The question then rather was what could be shifted into hardware from what originally had been a matter of software.

The physical limits in hardware nevertheless remained, in spite of the fact that switching elements became faster and faster. The speed of light as well as the 'size' of elementary particles were given as final bounds. The limits regarding one processor were characterized by the fact that only one program could be processed at a time. With the concept of a pure von-Neumann-structure one could not overcome the boundary. So considerations came up to multiply elementary units. Processors which in the context of integration have become chips of a barely five-to-five-mm space may in this sense be considered elementary units.

But what to do with a multitude of processors? This question proved to be the key-problem of parallelism. The difficulties of programming (sometimes called software crisis) with respect to one processor were fairly attacked when a new problem came up as a challenge: to do it for an orchestra of processors, communicating via a network, synchronizing with respect to the need of distributed tasks and mainly partitioning algorithms for being processed in parallel.

There is now a general consensus that in the near future the requirements in performance can be reached only by parallel devices. The upcoming new degree of complexity casts nevertheless a deep shadow. Experts doubt, theorists write abstract papers, user-programmers refuse to think in parallel, and sometimes the scene becomes confused.

On the other hand some interesting concepts are realized today, computers of a real 'parallel type' are in operation. Parallel Programming tools are developed. Interesting operational experience can be derived from parallel computers and in particular from multiprocessors.

The new book of Yehuda Wallach *Parallel Processing and Ada* is highly topical. It offers an insight into the most promising approaches of the field and also shows a very pragmatic way where to go.

The book is an important step not only regarding a new practice of parallel processing but also in the direction of a new 'thinking in parallel,' while thinking has been caught up to now by the ingenious but sequential analysis of Newton's age.

Wolfgang Händler

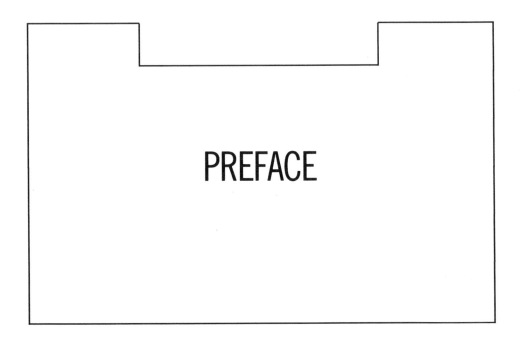

PREFACE

Parallel processing is not a new idea. In 1848, it had already been mentioned by Manabrea, and ENIAC—the venerated pioneer of modern computers—included some parallel processing features. Since the 1960s, a number of hardware architectures were developed and assembled. The advantages sought were speeding up the computations, increasing the fault tolerance and availability of computers, increasing their modularity and scalability, and decreasing their cost.

Despite of all these advantages, the development of parallel processing systems proceeded rather sluggishly, until recently. The reasons are believed to be: The *cost* of a parallel system is high if the research, design, marketing, and software costs must be paid for by only few supercomputers sold, the massive amount of hardware makes the parallel systems *unreliable, algorithms* have to be developed, and all programs have to be rewritten in new computer *languages.*

The sluggish development may also be charged to the supply/demand situation. Until recently, industry supplied ever cheaper and faster computers while the demand for speed and reliability did not increase commensurately. Lately, applications such as high-speed data-gathering, computer-aided design, various military simulations, etc., require speeds that single computers cannot offer. On the other hand, large quantities of inexpensive Processor-Memory chips are now marketed. Because of high volume, both the hardware and the basic software (compilers, assemblers, etc.) are becoming comparatively inexpensive. Engineering and nonrecurring costs can be kept low relative to the amount of hardware involved. Likewise, since nearly all of the hardware of most types of parallel processing systems is contained in a number of identical elements, the reliability problem is tractable. Most faults occur in the elements and element failures can often be tolerated. It may even be said that by producing chips on a massive scale, industry is now pushing the development of at least some types of multiprocessors.

The fact that the hardware has been available for some time, but parallel processing systems are seldom used, must be explained by looking at the software problems. Completely new, sometimes rather esoteric languages were developed for them. The industry is as yet unwilling to completely switch from Fortran, and is even less willing to make a huge investment by reprogramming in languages that are completely different and whose longevity is doubtful.

This state of affairs is now changing too. Recently, a new language, *Ada,* was developed by the U.S. Department of Defense, and this book demonstrates that it can be used for describing algorithms to be run on various parallel processing systems. The industry will probably switch to Ada anyway, so there is every reason to write parallel programs in Ada. Moreover, only few extensions to Ada will be necessary in order to describe all algorithms, except those for array computers in which it is the compiler that changes the sequential into a parallel program.

To sum it up. The VLSI revolution drives the industry in the direction of employing the Processor-Memory chips, while Ada provides a vehicle for algorithmic developments (like rewriting of numerical programs). The time for parallel processing has arrived.

There are a number of books on parallel processing. In order to justify another one, the following reasons are given:

A. HARDWARE

1. The present book includes not only pioneering projects like the C.mmp or DIRMU, but also modern architectures, e.g., the RP3, the Connection Machine, Butterfly, MPP, and Hypercubes.

2. The author has advocated since the early 1970s the use of so-called ''Alternating Sequential-Parallel'' or ASP Systems. These are described in Chapter 5 and one of them, the ''Topps,'' to the point of supplying complete diagrams. It is hoped that this will remove the last doubts as to the ease of assembling an ASP by any good engineering staff.

3. *Local Area Networks* are normally treated separately, but are basically parallel processing systems or can be used as such. These systems are included and it is shown how to use a LAN as an ASP. Moreover, they can also be used as Hypercubes [Fea89]. The importance of this cannot be overstated: It really means that every office that has a LAN (and which doesn't have it?) will be able to do the labor-intensive, computationally heavy tasks when the mainframe is off.

B. PROGRAMMING

4. To present a balanced picture, *programming has to be discussed*. This should not be done in an ad-hoc way, i.e., by combining various snippets of algorithms written in various language extensions. This book unifies programming for various parallel systems by writing all programs in Ada.

5. *Ada is important by itself* and a review of its traditional features is given. Ada is based partially on Pascal and the reader is assumed to know it. The discussion of the sequential part of Ada is therefore short. Additionally, Ada has the multitasking feature which allows the writing of programs for various parallel processing systems. Finally, reliability is not only a hardware feature. Various Ada features, e.g., exceptions, will facilitate software reliability.

6. Algorithmic approaches have matured enough for a separate treatment. The algorithms used in this text, namely numerical, sorting, and searching algorithms, are not too complicated and are all explained in Sections 6-1 and 6-2. Each of these subjects is extremely diversified and we will discuss only a very small subset of known methods. For instance, no time will be devoted to the extremely important topics of accuracy or stability of the algorithms for solving linear sets of equations.

C. NOTES ON THE FEATURES OF THE BOOK

1. Whenever there is a good text available, the presentation has been shortened, e.g., Interconnection Networks, the Connection Machine [Hil85], or Hypercubes [Fea88], but especially Systolic Arrays [Kun88], which are not discussed at all.

   Some books try to describe *all* parallel systems, some deal with a single system; this text tries to describe a few systems in some detail.

2. Simple examples are preferred to proving theorems, etc. The reader will find it easy to add the mathematical treatment, having grasped the main points of the algorithms.

3. Part A is descriptive and therefore the problems at the end of chapters 1 to 5 are used as a review of the various systems. On the other hand, Part B deals with programming and some of the problems should be considered projects.

4. Algorithms are best understood and followed as programs. For a long time no Ada compiler was available whose use I would advocate. Lately a number of them appeared and programs can finally be written and run. In the worst case, they can be viewed as simulators of programs running concurrently on a number of processors.

5. A local area network can simulate Hypercubes [FHC89] and Alternating Sequential-

Parallel systems [YaW88]. (Vector Processors can run simulations on commercially available machines.) The advantages of this approach are that before committing themselves to a particular parallel system, organizations can simulate their programs on the LAN, and that every unit on the system has an I/O (mostly screen).

6. The programs developed in this book are not production programs (for such programs an entire book would be necessary). The programs have only one aim: *to describe parallel algorithms.*

7. Almost all programs were run, but since they were rewritten many times, they probably have bugs.

8. In some cases a picture (''worth a thousand words'') was considered self-explanatory.

9. Not much is written about evaluating the performance of various systems. I believe that this would mostly reflect only my biases and that readers can use a simulator or a laboratory companion to find for themselves which system they need.

D. USE OF THE BOOK

Not much mathematical background is necessary and for ease of explanation, even the material needed is not reviewed rigorously (in some cases including some intentional simplifications). The level of the book is about that of college seniors in engineering or computer science. Parallel processing is normally taught at the graduate level, but—as with so many other subjects—it may migrate to the senior level. This may in fact be the major difference: *This is not a research monograph—it is a textbook and can be used:*

a. As a textbook for seniors enrolled in either Computer Science, Computer Engineering, or other areas of engineering, e.g., Electrical Engineering. The prerequisites required are a course on computer organization and knowledge of a high-level computer language, for example, Pascal. I am a strong believer in learning by examples, and have explained all the examples to be programmed in Sections 6-1 and 6-2. Some may think that the examples are oversimplified and they are, but I think that readers can add mathematical depth later; all I want is to discuss the fundamentals. This is also why questions are added to the Hardware part and projects to the Programming part. I have used chapters 1 to 5 and the appendices for a course in ''Parallel Processors,'' and chapters 6 to 11 for a course on ''Parallel Programming and Ada.''

b. As a book to be used by scientists and engineers working on parallel processing or Ada, especially if connected in any way with embedded systems, e.g., for the Department of Defense.

c. By libraries and by the general public.

ACKNOWLEDGMENTS

It is a pleasure to acknowledge friends and students who helped me throughout the time I developed this book. I am thankful to Professor Harpreet Singh, who convinced me to write this book in the first place. My thanks go to Professor D. Agrawal, Professor R. Brandt, Professor G. Frieder, Mr. F. Keebler, Mr. J. Silva, and Mr. B. Baas for reading the text and making suggestions. I also wish to thank Prentice Hall and Springer Verlag for the permission to quote from my previous books; I quoted extensively without each time mentioning the sources.

OFTEN USED ACRONYMS

(Add an s for plural items, e.g., MB is a memory bank, MBs are a number of them. Prefix M stands for million, e.g., MIPs.)

ALU	=	Arithmetic Logic Unit
AP	=	Associative Processor
ARP	=	Array Processor
ASP	=	Alternating Sequential Parallel Processor
Bps	=	Bytes per second
CPU	=	Central Processing Unit
CU	=	Control Unit
Cube	=	Hypercube computer
FLOP	=	Floating-Point Operations per second
IN	=	Interconnection Network
I/O	=	Input/Output
IP	=	Instructions Per second
LAN	=	Local Area Network
LM	=	Local Memory
MAR	=	Memory Address Register
MBR	=	Memory Buffer Register
MB	=	Memory Block
MIMD	=	Multiple-Instruction, Multiple-Data stream
MIN	=	Multistage Interconnection Network
MP	=	Message Passing multiprocessor
PAP	=	Peripheral Array Processor
PE	=	Processing Element (a generic term used for CPU, ALU, etc.)
PaM	=	Processor-and-Memory (chip)
PPS	=	Parallel Processing System
SIMD	=	Single-Instruction Multiple-Data stream
SM	=	Shared Memory Multiprocessor (MIMD)
VLSI	=	Very-Large Scale Integration
VP	=	Vector Processor

NOTATION

d is the diameter (of a Hypercube)

$i\Sigma$ means "the summation index i"

log is a logarithm on base 2

ln is a "natural" logarithm (on base ϵ)

mcs = microseconds

mls = milliseconds

nns = nanoseconds

O = the "order" of the (number of) operations

pcs = picoseconds

p = the number of processors in a PPS

q = is their running number, i.e., $q = 1, \ldots p$ or $q = 0, \ldots, (p - 1)$

sec = seconds

t = time

α = the time for a single addition

δ = degree of concurrency

ϵ = accuracy

ϕ = the time to compute a function

η = efficiency (speedup divided by p)

μ = the time for a single multiplication

ν = utilization factor

π = penalty (ratio of communication to calculation times)

σ = speedup

ρ = time ratio (the inverse of speedup)

ω = the time for a single "operation" ($\alpha + \mu$)

ψ = overrelaxation factor

ζ = the time for (bus) synchronization

K = overhead (mostly communication) time

Φ = "empty" set

Ω = overall computation time

** = raised to power of . . .

$>>$ = much larger than

$<<$ = much smaller than

[] used also for vectors

{} used also for sets

CHAPTER 1

INTRODUCTION

The objectives of this chapter are:

Establish the need for faster computers.

Sketch the developments leading to Parallel Processing Systems. These systems will be denoted by PPS in singular and PPSs in plural.

Classify various parallel architectures, from the point of view of hardware, programs, and the type of problems they can handle.

Discuss characteristics of PPSs, for example, the speedup, efficiency, or communication penalty.

Preview the material in chapters 2 to 5 of the book.

It is assumed that the reader knows the general organization of digital computers given in [Man79, Wak89, Mot85].

1–1 THE NEED FOR AND DEVELOPMENT OF PARALLEL PROCESSORS

Since the advent of digital computers in the late 1940s and early 1950s, their organization remained essentially the same. The computer as shown in Fig. 1-1(a) consists of:

1. Memory which holds both instructions and data.
2. A control unit, CU, which fetches a stream of instructions IS from memory, decodes them, and issues commands to the Arithmetic and Logic Unit, ALU. The ALU performs operations on data fetched from memory (the data stream DS) and returns the results to the memory. The addresses of the operands and of the result are supplied by the CU. (The CU and ALU form the Central Processing Unit, CPU. We will use PE as a generic term for a Processing Element like a CPU or an ALU.)
3. Input and Output (I/O) equipment is connected to the memory through *channels* or *ports* (a channel is an I/O device able to run a program independently).

One of the earliest attempts at a computer was the ''Analytical Engine'' proposed by Babbage in 1821. It used a ''store'' (the memory), a ''mill'' (ALU), punched cards (I/O device), and a card-controlled CU. Unfortunately, the technology of the day allowed only the use of gears and wheels instead of currently available Very Large Scale Integrated (VLSI) circuits. But even with VLSI, there are shortcomings; they can be summarized as follows:

1. When von-Neumann and his colleagues developed their computers, they used relatively fast CPU components, such as vacuum tubes, whereas the memories were made of relatively inexpensive but slow components, such as delay lines. The speed of computers was limited primarily by the large *memory access latency*, which is defined as the delay from when the processor puts an address into the Memory Address Register (MAR), to when the data is returned into the Memory Buffer Register (MBR). Because the MAR and its decoder point to only one address, *only a single word can be accessed in the memory at any given time*. The CPU is idling while waiting for the data; this slows down the computer.
2. Most computers use a *bus* for passing information and for Input/Output (I/O). The use of the bus is time-consuming. Time could be saved by the use of *cache memory*, but these memories are expensive.

2

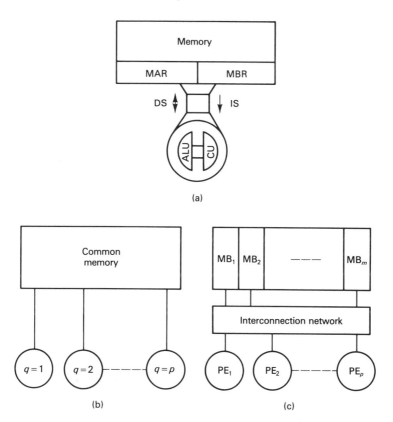

Figure 1-1   (a) A digital computer (b) A shared memory multiprocessor (c) Paracomputer

A program stored in the memory of a computer such as the one of Fig. 1-1(a) sequences the instructions so that only a single instruction is processed at a time. This is usually called the von-Neumann paradigm or model of computation and it forces any algorithm to fit the sequential operation of the machine. The time has come to ask: Wouldn't it be better if computers were adapted to the (possibly nonsequential) nature of some algorithms? In other words, instead of forcing all algorithms to be sequential, wouldn't it be better to assemble machines that match parallel algorithms? The usual answer is that the known algorithms of numerical analysis are sequential, so why bother? This approach is putting the cart before the horse. In nature, many interrelated processes occur simultaneously. The fact that the human thought process and the numerical procedures developed up to now both seem to be sequential may be responsible for the fact that no traces of parallelism remain in current algorithms. Computers can work in parallel, so why not use this fact in order to adapt them closer to nature and make them work faster?

One of the reasons for the lack of parallel algorithms seems to be that, until recently, no need for them was felt. If a faster computer was needed, industry supplied it.

Unfortunately, because of basic physical laws, we seem to be approaching the upper limit of the speed at which a digital computer can transfer information. To show this, let us compare the (hardware) speeds in the past to those possible in the future. An addition of two 32-bit words required about 300 milliseconds (mls) in 1944 (on a computer using electromagnetic relays), 300 microseconds (mcs) in 1954 (using electronic tubes), and 300 nanoseconds (nns) in 1964 (using Integrated Circuits). The speed increase was 1000 or 10^3 every ten years. Suppose a computer is to be built with another speed increase of 10^3, that is, with an addition time of 300 picoseconds (pcs). Since the speed at which an electrical signal travels in silicon is 0.003 cm/pcs, it would propagate ≈ 0.9 cm during the entire time of executing the instruction. The distance between the memory and the CPU will probably be larger; this limits the speed of any future computer.

Very small chips are now produced. They include a Processor-and-Memory (we will call them chips or PaMs). A chip of 3 cm would propagate a signal in about $1/10^9$ seconds. During this time, a single floating-point operation (one FLOP) can be performed, so that altogether this small chip can support no more than 10^9 FLOPs, or 1 GFLOP (Giga-Flop). This is then the highest speed at which today's chips can perform sequentially. Microelectronics experts do not expect computers to exceed 1 GFLOP with the present technology. To increase the speed further requires an attempt to find other solutions rather than incrementally reducing the execution or propagation time.

Computer practice implies an unwritten rule: *A sequential solution is slow and inexpensive, but a parallel solution is fast and expensive*. If speed is to be increased then parallelism should be used.

The speed of computers has increased by leaps and bounds since their introduction in the 1940s. Do we need even higher speeds? The answer is "yes" as can be seen from an example of fluid dynamics. Suppose we have to calculate the flow through a cube of 1,000 points to an edge for 1,000 times and each point requires 1,000 FLOPs. Altogether we have $10^9 * 10^3 * 10^3 = 10^{15}$ FLOPs, which the 10^9 FLOP computer could do in 10^6 seconds or in about 11.5 days.

For some computations, especially in "real-time" applications, the need for speed is even more significant since slowly produced results may be useless (e.g., if to calculate the time when a missile will hit your town takes longer than the flight time of the missile, then this calculation is certainly useless).

The reason behind the drive for parallel processing can also be formulated as follows: If a given algorithm can complete on a $1000 computer in, say, 8 minutes, it should be possible to complete it in 4 minutes on a $2000 computer and in 1 minute on an $8000 computer. Conventional computers do not have such linear price/performance characteristics since to achieve greater speeds it is not enough to add more components; instead, the components must be faster. This leads to line 1 in Fig. 1-2, with a saturation point *a* when all components reach the theoretical performance limit of the technology upon which they are based. Little speedup is achieved above *a*, i.e., for higher prices.

A PPS could be assembled as shown in Fig. 1-1(b). Since the memory is shared by all PEs, it is called a Shared-Memory PPS or SM. Such systems do not have the linear price/performance characteristic because only a single PE may access the shared memory at any given time. Therefore, some processors will have to wait; this is called *memory*

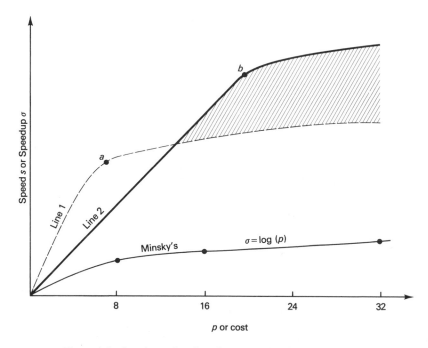

Figure 1-2   Speed as a function of cost or p (number of processors)

contention or interference. Because of memory contention, the speed will increase less than p, but the price will increase by p and the solution may be counterproductive. At some point (b of Fig. 1-2), adding processors will increase the interference between them so much that the performance levels off. The shaded area (relatively high prices and high speeds) in Fig. 1-2 shows where to expect an advantage from parallel processing.

No matter how large the shared memory is, no more than a single word is accessed at any given time. Hence, no matter how a *utilization factor* v is defined, it is low for the shared memory. Increasing the size of the memory will not increase v; on the contrary, since it is still a single word that is being accessed, the utilization will drop further. The bigger we build the shared memory, the worse it gets.

A proposed solution to both the speed and utilization problems is to assemble a PPS as in Fig. 1-1(c). This is known as the "Paracomputer" [Sch80]. It consists of p PEs, and m Memory Blocks, MBs, each with a separate MAR and MBR register. To allow each CPU to access every MB, an Interconnection Network (IN) is included in Fig. 1-1(c). The idea is that m MBs can be accessed simultaneously, increasing the utilization of the memory, while at the same time p CPUs can work concurrently, providing a p-fold (linear) increase in speed—or at least a *speedup* approaching p. No matter how fast a serial computer operates, a Paracomputer, which consists of many fast serial CPUs, should be faster; no advance in sequential processing can eliminate this advantage.

What is a fast computer? The speed of computer components is normally measured by the number of bits passing some point in the system—the *bandwidth*. When hardware designers refer to speed, they mean a higher bandwidth. When computer-center managers refer to it, they mean a higher *throughput* so that more jobs can be processed in a given time. What a user means is *turnaround time*, that is, the time the user has to wait for the results. Throughput and turnaround time are not the same: the throughput may be doubled by employing two stand-alone computers instead of a single machine, but the turnaround time is probably the same.

Another term used in connection with parallelization is that of *multiprogramming*. The idea is to process a number of jobs in a single CPU and at the same time have a number of I/O devices executing in an overlapped fashion. Thus, if a running program "A" encounters, say, a "read" instruction, it transfers A to an input device and switches to process job "B". I/O devices are electro-mechanical and very slow compared to electronic devices. It may take a long time until job A is again ready to be processed and re-enters the job queue. In the meantime, jobs B, C, and so on, have been partially processed and are running on other I/O devices. Since a number of I/O devices and the CPU are working concurrently, multiprogramming increases the throughput. Since only a single CPU is used and multiple programs are executed, it is not parallel processing.

Definitions: *Parallel processing hardware* and *concurrent programs* are ways to reduce the time it takes to put *a single program through p processors*. *Interleaving* is the execution of a number of programs in an interleaved fashion. The names show that concurrency and parallel processing is when p PEs work simultaneously, while in interleaving, the single CPU works simultaneously with a number of I/O devices.

In the case of PPSs we do not use bandwidth, throughput, or turnaround time, but define the speedup σ as

$$\sigma = t(1)/t(p); \sigma > 1 \qquad (1\text{-}1)$$

where $t(1)$ is the time needed on a single computer, $t(p)$, the time on p PEs. If $\sigma > 1$, the time $t(1)$ is σ times longer than $t(p)$. Dividing σ by p yields the *efficiency* η:

$$\eta = \sigma/p; \eta < 100\% \qquad (1\text{-}2)$$

One aim of parallelization is to have a (large) speedup which approaches p and an efficiency of nearly 100%.

Even more important advantages of PPSs are their high availability and good fault diagnosis. *Fault diagnosis* is defined as the ability to identify and remove a faulty unit. *Availability* is defined as the capability to proceed working despite this removal.

Fault diagnosis is related to the *reliability* of the system. A machine with a large number of PaMs cannot reasonably be expected to operate reliably without some form of fault diagnosis. Each PaM needs the ability to test its neighbors, and if necessary, remove them.

In some applications, for example in process-control, a failure can endanger the staff, result in costly damage, and loss of vital data. This explains why it is important to have a reliable system that is up at all times. Unfortunately, a single computer is no more reliable than the weakest of its parts. When a single computer is used, its failure is catastrophic.

Sometimes a part of a PPS must be removed for maintenance or because a fault was detected in one of its components. The system should nevertheless be available and continue its service at only a slightly slower pace. Moreover, this continuity of service should—if possible—be achieved without expenditure on redundant components, as is done in some "fault-tolerant" systems such as in certain systems on the space shuttle. In these systems, the hardware is triplicated and the results constantly compared. Majority voting (two out of three) ensures fault diagnosis, but this is expensive; the price is three times higher, but the performance remains the same as for a single unit.

Hardware reliability can be studied by estimating the probability for system reliability in terms of component reliability. This approach uses the "mean-time between failures" of components, as published by the U.S. air force. There is also the question of program reliability which refers to run-time errors. For example, suppose that in a program we have $a := b/c$. If, because of a particular set of data, c is 0, then the division should not be carried out. In a computer-center environment, the operating system would stop the program and indicate a "division by zero" error. In real-time environments, the program should transfer to an *exception-handler*, may print a warning, make object a the largest number available (on this particular computer), and go on with the job, but probably not with the particular task in which the error in $a := b/c$ was detected.

There are other errors which may occur because of a particular set of input data. The language should include features that will detect all such errors, but until recently no computer language had either exception handling or other features for dealing with errors. In fact, *algorithm development*, *programming language*, and operating system development lag the pace of hardware advances. This state of affairs is changing because government agencies and industry recognized that software is more expensive than hardware.

To sum up: PPSs are needed to achieve higher speed and reliability. Hardware reliability of PPSs is higher than that of single computers; their availability is much higher. Languages for parallel processing which support fault detection are needed.

The idea of parallel processing is not new. In 1842, Manabrea described the lectures by Babbage and wrote: ". . . the machine can . . . give several results at the same time, which will greatly abridge the whole amount . . ." of time. This statement refers to parallelism.

In the 1970s, a number of various PPSs were assembled. These were mainly small, laboratory machines; commercial PPSs entered the market in the 1980s. The reasons for the delay are as follows:

1. Parallel algorithms rely on one simple yet crucial observation: *Independent computations may be executed simultaneously*. For instance, the "Parallel Ensemble of Processing Elements" (PEPE) [EaT73], tracked a number of targets (rockets). Each PE had a single target assigned to it. It worked independently of and in parallel with other PEs. Another example is payroll processing, since paychecks and files of different employees may be processed simultaneously and independently on p PEs. Such algorithms are called *inherently parallel*.

Inevitably, the question was asked whether many inherently parallel problems exist; there is no need for PPSs if there are only a few problems to be solved in parallel. A review of numerical analysis was disappointing since most algorithms seemed to be purely sequential. Whether our mind works so that we do not do "B" until having finished "A," or we are taught to solve problems that way, is immaterial. The fact remains that few problems seemed to be inherently parallel.

Computer programs consist of instructions operating on data. Large programs have tens of thousands of instructions operating on maybe millions of data elements. Inherently parallel programs imply mostly *data-parallelism* in which a massive number of PEs work on an even larger set of data elements, performing the same operation on all of them. There also exist problems in which independent parallel instruction streams can be identified. This is *instruction-parallelism*.

According to various references, high-performance is required in a large number of problem areas. Most of these applications, e.g., the fluid dynamics problem mentioned earlier, process immense data sets; some of them are even data-parallel.

To sum up this point: there are many problems in which a speedup in achieving the solution is important. Moreover, we will find that some problems are indeed *inherently parallel*, and "massively parallel" machines can be used (Sec. 3-5) to solve them.

2. Another reason for the delay was in doubts about the achievable speedup. Before many PPSs were built, "Minsky's conjecture" [MaP71] was pronounced. It implies (Fig. 1-2) that $\sigma = \log(p)$ [$\log(p)$ means logarithm with base 2]. This overly pessimistic conjecture may have delayed the development of PPSs. If a PPS costs p times more than a single PE while its speedup is only $\log(p)$, there is little reason to build PPSs. If Minsky's conjecture is correct, $p = 4$ leads to $\sigma = 2$, but $p = 64$ only leads to $\sigma = 6$ and an efficiency of $\approx 10\%$. Thus, p should not be above 4 or 5.

To show what this conjecture means, suppose that we have to add 16 numbers: $y = \Sigma x(i); i\Sigma - 1, \ldots, 16$ ($i\Sigma$ means "with i of the summation from 1 to 16"). If we do it on two PEs ($p = 2$), we have two steps: In the first, $z(1): = x(0) + \ldots + x(7)$ and concurrently $z(2): = x(8) + \ldots + x(15)$, and in the second, $y: = z(1) + z(2)$. For $p = 3$ we would need three steps:

1. $z(1): = x(0) + \ldots + x(4)$; $z(2): = x(5) + \ldots + x(9)$; $z(3): = x(10) + \ldots + x(14)$

2. $z(4): = z(1) + z(2)$; $z(5): = z(3) + x(15)$, and in step 3. $y: = z(4) + z(5)$.

In the first case, the two steps required 7 and 1 additions respectively, in the second case, 4, 1, and 1 were needed. The "time" was reduced from 8 to 6. In the same way, $p = 4$ and 8 would require times 5 and 4 respectively. This is summarized in Table 1-1. As seen, the speedup increases with p, but the efficiency decreases and we should use $p = 2$ and not more.

Consider the utilization defined as $\nu = \sigma * \eta$. In Table 1-1 it is highest for $p = 4$ so that Minsky's conjecture does not apply. Additionally, it will be shown in Chapter 4 to apply to only some SM multiprocessors. Others do provide high speedups for larger numbers of PaMs; they *scale* well. Finally, if a number of programs are run, then each can run on a few out of p PEs, thus improving the efficiency.

TABLE 1-1 SPEEDUP, EFFICIENCY,
AND UTILIZATION OF A PPS

p	$t(p)$	σ	η	ν
1	15	1.00	1.00	1.00
2	8	1.88	0.94	1.76
3	4	2.50	0.83	2.08
4	5	3.00	0.75	2.25
8	4	3.75	0.47	1.76

At about the same time that Minsky announced his conjecture, "Grosh's law" [Kni66] came into vogue. It says that the cost of a (single) computer is proportional to the square root of its speed. Therefore, if a speed increase of, say 9 is required, it might be best to use a bigger computer that will cost only three times as much. In a PPS, we would need at least p computers with a cost $p = 9$ times higher. This "law" was disproved recently [KMP86] by finding that, when computers are grouped according to their power and size, Grosh's law holds *within* the groups, but *it does not hold among the groups.* Moreover, it was found that "all being equal, an IBM or IBM-compatible CPU will cost more" and that "at least for one class of computers (minicomputers), Grosh's law is no longer valid." Moreover, Fig. 1-3 compares single with supercomputers and it can be

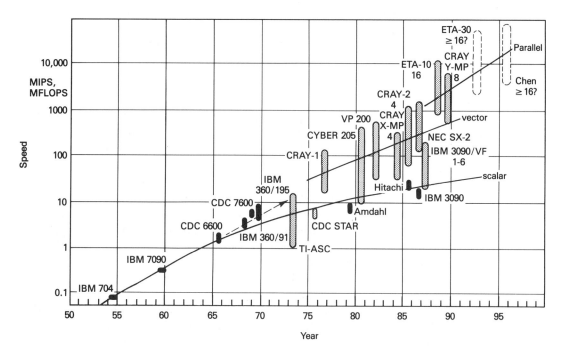

Figure 1-3 Power of computers from 1950 to 1989. Courtesy of F. Hertweck, Vector- und Parallel-Rechner, Informationstechnik, 31 (1989) Oldenburg Verlag, W. Germany.

seen that for larger PPSs, the price increases linearly with p, thus disproving the law. Finally: ''VLSI processors are 10 to 100 times more cost effective than the semiconductor technology currently used in conventional supercomputers. Thus, Grosh's law is not applicable to Parallel processing systems in the VLSI era because powerful single processors tend to be custom made, whereas slower but inexpensive processors are mass-produced'' [Dig 86].

To sum up this point: The two ''laws'' may have been applicable, but not anymore (except for some PPSs).

3.   Mathematicians define a theoretical model, leaving the worry of building it to engineers. The ''Paracomputer'' of Fig. 1-1(c) consists of an *unbounded* number of CPUs all of which may access the common memory at the same time, without interference. The Paracomputer enables the study of inherent, total parallelism in an algorithm and indicates its optimal performance. This is a standard by which to measure the effectiveness of other architectures. Unfortunately, it suffers from not being practical for the following reasons:

(a) The model assumes that all p CPUs are connected to the shared memory and, whenever two or more CPUs request the same word from it, they obtain the word instantaneously. This is clearly not achievable because of contention.

(b) The number p of CPUs was assumed to be unbounded. The multiplication of two n-by-n matrices on the Paracomputer would require n^3 processors. Therefore, a rather ''lean'' matrix of $n = 100$ would require a million processors. Presently, even when using VLSI techniques, this seems a bit too much. Only in the late 1970s was microelectronic technology mature enough so that commercial computers of thousands of CPUs could be contemplated.

To sum up this point: The number of processors may be rather large; the problem of how to connect the computers is discussed in Chapter 2.

4.   A primary reason for the failure of early PPSs like the ILLIAC-IV was that they were based on unattractive technology. This has changed dramatically in the 1980s. The cost of gates with VLSI technology has diminished to the point that it is economical to use, say, 1,000 times as many gates per computer system in 1988 compared to what was practical in 1978. Since reducing the time of gate-delay is now very expensive, but gates are inexpensive, it seems logical to build PPSs.

Miniaturization of electronic components may have been one of the most important factors in the present, as yet unnamed, technological revolution. It has already produced not only the processor-on-the-chip, but also a chip that includes a Processor-and-Memory, the *PaM*. The building blocks of PPSs are the PEs (ALUs or CPUs), the MBs, and the PaMs. The issue is how to operate the p PaMs on a single problem to achieve a speedup that approaches p in a practical way.

To sum up this point: The technology (the VLSI chips), and in particular the PaMs, are available. As a matter of fact, we may have more models of good PPSs than we can digest. Moreover, they seem to be appearing at an ever faster pace. This is leading to chaotic conditions. (This should not be surprising because most revolutions are usually preceded by chaos. There was starvation and chaos in both France in the 1780s and in Russia in the 1910s.)

5. To achieve a parallel solution, we must first identify a problem that lends itself to concurrency, develop the algorithm, and map it into a suitable architecture. Whether a program should be executed on a single processor or on a PPS depends on the following questions:

(a) What is the ratio of Input/Output (I/O) operations to computations? I/O normally require a high overhead in a PPS, so only compute-intensive jobs seem candidates for parallelization.

(b) Can the job be divided into independent tasks? If so, then these tasks can be run efficiently in parallel. If tasks are highly dependent on other tasks, parallelization may be inefficient. In this case, a different algorithm should be developed.

(c) How do we coordinate the activities of the many PaMs? How do we program the new hardware to execute the parallel algorithm?

Software transforms a computer from a conceptual tool that can solve a problem in principle to one that does so in practice. As mentioned above, hardware advances alone will not do; the speed at which PPSs will penetrate and transform industrial, service, and scientific enterprises depends on progress in software technology. Progress will come from better algorithms and more powerful languages. First we discuss the *algorithms*.

There is a need for a "parallel numerical analysis" that is a theory which would prove what can be achieved by "maximal concurrency" and how best to take advantage of PPSs. It may indicate that some of the older algorithms are better than certain "modern" algorithms.

To sum up this point: We should put more effort into *programming* and less into producing more and more hardware models. Programming (PPSs) will be the theme of Part B (chapters 6 to 11) of the book.

6. Until recently, each PPS required a special computer *language*. This means that all programs would have to be rewritten. The resistance of the industry to the rewriting of Fortran programs into other languages is well known, and therefore, rewriting all of them in special languages was an insurmountable obstacle to the use of PPSs.

Few, if any, of the high-level computer languages implement *multitasking* by which a job can be divided into p tasks and processed by p CPUs. In 1983, the Department of Defense introduced the Ada-language [DoD83]. This language is expected to replace other languages. It will be shown in this book that it includes exceptions, multitasking, and so on, so that PPSs can be programmed in Ada.

To sum up this point: Ada has the features necessary for concurrent programming; it can even serve as a unifying language for parallel PPSs.

7. It was once stated [BaS76] that parallel processors are not being installed despite their apparent advantages primarily because of inertia, namely:

• "The basic nature of engineering is to be conservative. This is a classical deadlock situation: we cannot learn how to program multiprocessors until such systems exist; a system will not be built before programs are ready.

• The market does not demand them. Another deadlock: how can the market demand them since the market does not even know that such structure can exist? IBM has not yet blessed the concept." (It will be shown in Chapter 4 that IBM has blessed the concept.)

Parallel processing systems are being produced now, because the bleak picture painted in the preceding points 1 to 7 has changed considerably, and because two revolutionary trends—VLSI-chips (PaMs) and Ada—are driving the industry in this direction. The PaMs have reduced the price so that connecting thousands of them is conceivable. Ada enables the (unified) development of algorithms and software. As a result, after a period of extreme skepticism, some designers now have an unlimited faith in the possibilities. It seems better to differentiate between hopes and reality, to assemble models, verify them by measurements, to debunk myths and biases and replace them by numbers and theorems, and to finally start programming them.

An advantage of PPSs is that they are built from p modules (*modularity*) so that when the power of the PPS is considered to be inadequate, additional modules can be installed. A single computer would have to be replaced by a larger, faster computer.

Contrary to Minsky's conjecture, some PPSs are *scalable* (that is, they allow significant increases in their size with almost no redesign of their components). Additionally, the same software should run on any number of PaMs. Since software often costs more than hardware, a system with a high number of PaMs would appear to be more economical. Scalability often becomes bounded due to inefficient use of additional elements. There are attempts to build PPSs which are unbounded extendible, but until they prove themselves we assume bounded scalability [LaM87].

In summary: At present, parallel processing systems are being built by a number of companies. (I know of Alliant, Ametek, BBN, CDC, Cray, DEC, Encore, Floating Point Systems, IBM, Intel, NCube, and Thinking Machines.) They bring the promise of being:

- faster
- more economical
- more reliable, available, and capable of fault detection
- programmable in Ada
- modular and scalable

1–2 CLASSIFICATION OF PARALLEL PROCESSING SYSTEMS

Flynn [Fly66] helped initiate an organized study of PPSs by showing that computer systems fall into certain classes. His and other classifications lead to a review of the properties of various types of PPSs. Therefore, next we introduce a number of classification schemes. Also, a classification of jobs and the relationship between real-time and parallel processing is discussed. The classification of PPSs is introduced step of step using different approaches.

1-2.1 A Gasoline Station

Suppose that a gasoline station is situated at a road as shown in Fig. 1-4. The most basic parallelism is evidenced by the gas attendant servicing a single car. His left hand may wipe the windshield, at the same time his right hand is opening the battery for inspection,

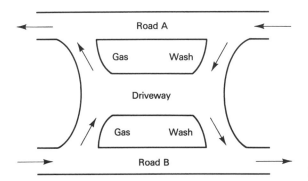

Figure 1-4 A gasoline station

his leg is kicking the tire, and gasoline is flowing into the tank. This is parallelism at the lowest level similar to various registers of a single CPU working in parallel. It corresponds to the way the single computer of Fig. 1-1(a) works and thus will not be discussed any further.

Suppose next that there is a steady stream of cars to be serviced during the day by two attendants. At any moment, two independent tasks may be performed by the two independent attendants. This case simulates two stand alone computers that may work simultaneously. The two processors must be able to do entire jobs by themselves and each must have its own resources (disks, tapes etc.). Such systems are called symmetric, independent "duplexes." If they stay out of each other's way, no overhead is incurred; the price paid for the duplex is double the cost of hardware and salary of the personnel. Cars are also serviced at a double rate (throughput) and the availability is higher (that is, even when one of the attendants is sick, the station does not have to close down). Duplexes do not work in parallel on the same jobs, so they are not PPSs and will not be discussed further.

Suppose that a single attendant slices his time so that he accepts payments from one owner while a second car is being filled. There is interleaving so that the attendant is doing one job and the pump as an I/O device is working at the same time. This case simulates multiprogramming, with the processor attending to one job while a previously interrupted job has its input or output serviced by a channel. Since there is only a single CPU, this case is not a PPS.

Suppose two attendants work independently on one car in order to finish the job earlier. This corresponds to the definition of a PPS. One problem is that if they both need the same tool simultaneously, one attendant will have to wait. Interference and a time loss results. In computers this would be equivalent to a number of CPUs accessing the (common) shared memory at any time and is known as *memory contention*. Scarcity of resources leads to a time loss, but is less expensive (since there is only one memory), so that the total cost-performance is probably higher. Such computers are called *Shared-Memory Multiprocessors* or *SMs*.

Suppose that every car requires two different services, say filling and washing. In this case it may be wise to let two attendants work in an assembly line, or *pipeline* fashion, each doing one of the two jobs again and again. This will reduce the time spent servicing the cars, but unless the time of the two jobs is equal, unless they are synchronized, and the "pipe" is always full of cars, there will be times when one of the attendants is idle. Since one job is processed by two attendants, this is a PPS. In such pipelined processors, an instruction or operation is broken down into a series of simple functions to be executed as segments by application of assembly line techniques.

Assume that one person owns the station and only organizes the work of a large number of attendants. The work might be organized so that the boss waves his hands in a way which indicates to *all* of the attendants what to do at any given time. The attendants do not need the same intelligence as the boss—they just follow his orders in "lock-step" synchronization. Still, some of them will be idle for lack of work while others are busily obeying the boss's whims.

As an example, suppose the boss decides that it is "cleaning time." All workers do the same job, possibly in synchronism, but on different parts of the station (different data). No communication between the workers is needed. This is called *data-parallelism* and simulates an ARray Processor (*ARP*) in which a single master (CU) directs all the slaves (ALUs) to do the same job on different data (cars). Since the slaves are simple ALUs and there is only a single CU, the cost should be lower. On the other hand, the availability suffers. When the boss is sick, who knows if the attendants will work?

It would improve the situation if one of the slaves could take over while the boss is sick. For this to occur, the attendants have to be as intelligent as the boss (each having a CPU consisting of both a CU and an ALU); the system is one with a *roving master*. Since the slaves are capable of independent work, there is no reason why the boss should decide on every single move—he just distributes the cars for different service to different attendants and makes a new decision when they have finished. This is called *Alternating Sequential Parallel*—ASP—processing because when the master makes the decision and distributes the work, all slaves are idle, but while they work all in parallel the master is idle. The master is a single person and represents the sequential part of the program, but there are p attendants and they work in parallel. The two phases alternate.

1-2.2 Customary Classifications

To translate the previous examples into computer diagrams, we first employ the classification of Flynn [Fly66].

A conventional computer [like that of Fig. 1-1(a)] fetches instructions from memory to the control unit, CU, operands to the ALU, executes the instructions, and stores the results in the memory. For the program in Fig. 1-5(a), this is shown in Fig. 1-5(b). Note that both instructions and data reside in the same memory and that there is only one stream of data *DS* and one stream of instructions *IS*. Such a machine [Fig. 1-5(c)] is called a "Single Instruction, Single Data" or *SISD* computer.

An array processor (ARP) uses a single control unit CU to send a single instruction stream to all its slaves which obey every order in lock-step synchronization, but each works on its own data. The ARP of Fig. 1-5(d) executes the same instruction $a(i):=d(i)*f(i)$ in all six Local Memories (LMs); hence, multiple-data streams. The system of Fig. 1-5(d) is called a "Single Instruction, Multiple Data" or *SIMD* computer.

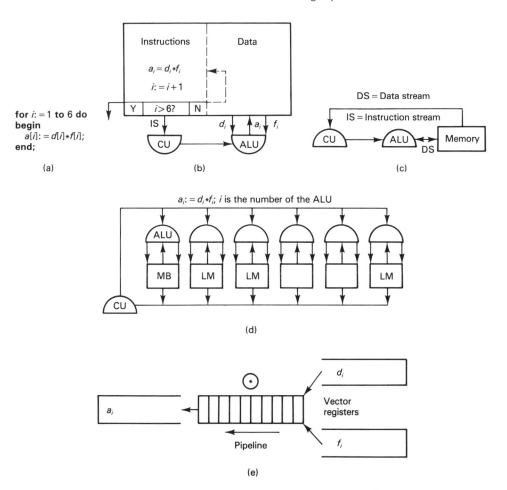

Figure 1-5 (a) A program (b,c) Its execution on a single computer (d,e) Its execution on an Array and Vector Processor

In SIMD, the CU broadcasts instructions to the ALUs. Each of the p ALUs has the *option* of either executing or ignoring it. Thus, although every ALU is presented with the same instruction sequence, only active ALUs execute the same instruction at the same time. Nonactive ALUs must "wait out" the active ones.

SIMD systems can be compared to a bingo game. In bingo, one person calls out numbers one at a time in succession. Each number call is an instruction to check the cards for the called number. If the number appears, cover it, if it doesn't, do nothing. The single instruction given by the "control unit" (the number caller) causes all "logic units" (the players), to do nothing or to take the same action as the other players. The numbers on a player's card are the data. The cards are the local memories, *LMs*, accessible only to their owners.

SIMD machines exploit the inherent parallelism of data-parallel tasks such as image processing. They process many different image elements simultaneously with the same operation.

A modified pipeline or *vector* computer, *VP*, works as shown in Fig. 1-5(e). Assume vectors **d** and **f** are stored in vector registers. Vector machines use vector instructions for cases in which the same operation (here *) is performed on many sets of operands. Only a single instruction fetch is necessary for many data operations in executing a vector instruction. These machines (for instance, CRAY-1) depend heavily on pipelining of their PEs, and faster vector registers to obtain high performance. Unfortunately, programs also include scalar operations that slow down the performance of vector computers.

The paracomputer of Fig. 1-1(c) shows p independent CPUs sharing the same memory. Each of the CPUs follows its own program; thus, there are multiple instruction streams. Each CPU fetches its own data on which to operate; thus, there are multiple data streams. These PPSs are called "Multiple Instruction, Multiple Data" (*MIMD*) computers or *SM multiprocessors*. In the case of Fig. 1-1(c), the MIMD computer has to access the program in the common (shared) memory, and execute it on data stored in the m MBs. If the instructions are independent of each other, like in the program of Fig. 1-5, they may be done at the same time without conflicts and a substantial speedup is achieved. Note, however, that if the instructions depend on each other, it is possible not to have any speedup. *Instruction parallelism* may be hampered by *memory contention*.

Because each CPU of an MIMD system executes its own program, the CPUs operate *asynchronously* with respect to each other and not in lock-step synchronization as in SIMD machines. The inputs to the system arrive independently (that is, asynchronously).

Actually, the difference between SIMD and MIMD systems is one of the degree of centralization: In ARPs, each instruction is centrally controlled; in multiprocessors it isn't.

Even in an MIMD multiprocessor the calculations are seldom run completely asynchronous (at their own speed). In many cases, the larger tasks of an MIMD have to be coordinated, i.e., started simultaneously. Instead of the lock-step synchronization of an ARP, we need *barrier synchronization* of the tasks: this is similar to the ASP-mode.

Feng [Fen72] classifies systems according to the number of bits in a word and the number of words being processed in parallel. A computer structure is represented by a point in the plane of Fig. 1-6 where the x-axis is the word length and the y-axis is the number of words processed in parallel by p processors. For example, C.mmp, which has 16 CPUs and words of length 16, is represented by (16,16) and the rectangle bound by (0,0) and (16,16) indicates the "amount of parallelism."

Flynn's classification scheme does not represent pipelining or ASPs. Feng's classification does not distinguish between autonomous processors that execute programs (CPUs) and ALUs that execute only operations. Therefore, there is no distinction between array and multiprocessors. The ASC (Advanced Scientific Computer of Texas Instruments) would be represented by (64,2048). The number 2048 is obtained from 4 pipelines, each consisting of 8 stages with 64 bits. However, 2048 can also be obtained

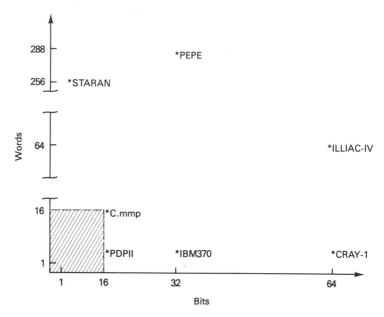

Figure 1-6 Classification of parallel processors

from 8 pipelines, 8 stages, and 32 bits, and so on. Thus, this classification cannot unambiguously represent a multiple pipeline structure such as the ASC. PEPE (Sec. 3-4) is characterized as (288,16) because it has 288 PEs with 16 bits in a word. There is no indication that each PE consists of three CPUs.

In the *Erlangen Classification System* [Han77] a PPS can include c CUs, each of which controls a ALUs, each of which performs the same operation on b bits (the length of the word). For pipelining, multiply parameters c, a, b by the number of "pipelines" PEs, "chained" ALUs, and the number of "segments," respectively. A computer is thus characterized by a triple $<c*c',a*a',b*b'>$.

Next are some examples of the Erlangen classification: The simplest computer with a single CU, a single ALU, and wordlength of 1 bit is defined by $<1,1,1>$. An IBM 370 computer is represented by $<1,1,32>$, Illiac-IV by $<1,64,64>$, and the C.mmp by $<16,1,16>$. Note that the C.mmp has 16 ALUs, one for each of its 16 CUs. The ASC is represented by $<1,4,64 \times 8>$ since it has 1 CU, 4 ALUs, and the arithmetic is done by 8 pipelines on words of length 64. In PEPE, a data set is processed sequentially on three different processors. Therefore, the PEPE is characterized by $<1 \times 3,288,32>$.

The Erlangen classification scheme gives no indication of whether local memories were used. Other than that, it can be used for the organizations to be discussed in this book.

With the appearance of the PaMs, the PPSs can be classified into *multicomputers* and *multiprocessors*. Multiprocessors like the paracomputer of Fig. 1-1(c) share the memory, while if the building blocks are PaMs, the memory is distributed; they are multicomputers. If a PaM needs access to the memory of another PaM, it can get it only through an interaction with the second PaM; the PaMs communicate only by sending (and receiving) messages. We will name these two groups the "Shared Memory Multiprocessors," SMs, and "Message Passing Multiprocessors," MPs.

As an example of an MP consider a Hypercube (*Cube* from now on). It consists of $p = 2**d$ nodes (*d* is the dimension) at the corners of a Cube as in Fig. 1-7(a), each connected by a special high-speed network over which messages are exchanged; it is a *message based system*. The difference between SMs and MPs is in the position of the IN, as can be seen by comparing Fig. 1-1(c) with Fig. 1-7(b). An advantage of MPs is that they require less additional logic circuits and fewer support chips on a per-node basis than do MSs; they cost less.

1-2.3 Societal Classifications

From the beginning, the driving motivation for developing parallel processing has been that if one processor can do a certain amount of work in a given time, then two can do the same work in half the time, and so on. The situation is analogous to building a house. If one worker can do it in a year, then two should be able to do it in half a year, and every so often one sees on TV the population of an entire village putting up a house in a few hours. Multiplicity of effort is the idea behind some of civilization's great achievements: how many worked on the pyramids or the great wall?

Since a PPS may be viewed as a society of computers, study of various organizations of human societies can lead to a better understanding of PPSs which combine to do a job faster than one member alone could do. As in human societies, an organization is needed to ensure that the members work toward the same goal. The more intelligent and independent the individuals are, the more easily the group will achieve its goals. Unfortunately, the problems of coordination may be increased so much as to make a society of independent computers almost ungovernable.

As in human societies, parallel processor organizations may be classified into the following types:

1. *Autocratic, centralized systems*: The elements are slaves and as such follow their leader blindly. Since each operation is completely prescribed by the master, the only freedom the slaves enjoy is to be idle. These systems are exemplified by array processors, ARPs.

2. *Democratic, decentralized systems*: The members know how to do their jobs and are motivated, say, by income. Each chooses a job with the government enforcing only loose control ("don't kill" laws). In terms of computers, if the units (CPUs) are very intelligent complete units with a CU and an ALU, then there is no need for central control. Each unit seeks its own tasks, secures the resources required (memory, etc.), and makes the connections. This organization (*multiprocessors*) is flexible, but may be too liberal for computers with a large number of CPUs which are sometimes bogged down by interference (that is, constant and voluminous transfer of information); communication between processors and any other re-

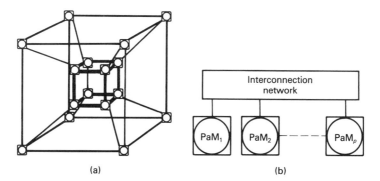

Figure 1-7   (a) A Hypercube (b) A Message Passing Multiprocessor

sources can become a bottleneck. A solution to the interference problem might be to dispense with shared memory and transfer information by links (MP—multiprocessors of Fig. 1-7).

3. *Hierarchical systems*: In a hierarchical system, the scheduling of "slaves" is done by a "master," but the master does not prescribe how the jobs are to be done. In short, the slaves are as intelligent as the master—only their jobs are different.

These three societies may be exemplified by orchestra ensembles. Consider first a string orchestra playing, for example, Dvorak's string serenade. The conductor gives the beat and other directions to all players. The players can either play or not play a particular part. This is similar to a system that includes a single control unit (CU) and p Arithmetic-Logic Units (ALUs). The CU decodes an instruction and broadcasts the corresponding microsequence to all p ALUs. If (and this is a big if) all p ALUs work simultaneously, then the speedup is $\sigma = p$. This is an ARP (only the conductor has the score ("program") and all slaves play in unison or lock-step synchronization).

The way multiprocessors work resembles a chamber orchestra. No conductor (master) is needed, but the (players) *processors have to synchronize* their tempi *and exchange some information*. This is done in the SM-multiprocessors by sharing memory (the same score), in MP-multiprocessors by exchanging messages (winks, beat, etc.).

The hierarchical system would have the conductor bring the scores from backstage and distribute them among the musicians prior to playing the concert. After the piece starts, the conductor only signals when to start or stop playing, but the musicians have different scores and each plays his or her part. These two steps would repeat themselves for every piece of the concert. This is similar to an ASP.

The societal difference could also be explained in terms of *autonomy*. SIMD or centralized systems allow no autonomy at all. MIMD or democratic systems offer complete autonomy. Hierarchical systems offer no autonomy on the coarse, task level, but complete autonomy on the fine (instruction) level.

1-2.4 Classification of Programs by Granularity

As indicated earlier, PPSs could also be classified according to the number of PEs: the massively parallel PPSs have hundreds or thousands of them, while the SMs have $p < 20$. In the first case, the PEs are very simple and can perform only very simple jobs controlled from the common CU, while in the SMs they are fairly powerful, so that each PE may be performing a different type of task at any given time.

Suppose we repeat the payroll example mentioned earlier, but assume that, for statistics, *data are to be exchanged*. For 10,000 employees, if the PPS has $p = 10$ PEs, 1,000 files may be processed before data are exchanged. If $p = 10,000$ data have to be exchanged after every file is processed. The first represents *coarse*, the second, *fine granularity*.

Grain size is the time between synchronizing PEs (of SMs) or nodes (of MPs). Synchronization is necessary in PPSs to initialize a task, parcel out the work, and merge results. Even numerical values were given, for example, that fine-grained, medium-grained, and coarse-grained algorithms have synchronization intervals of less than 20 instructions, 20-200 instructions, and over 200 instructions, respectively.

The memory of PPSs used for fine-grained algorithms currently has about 1,000 bytes per node. They are used in such machines as the MPP and Connection Machine (Sec. 3-5). The Connection Machine CM-1 consists of 65,536 very small CPUs, each having a one-bit ALU and 4096 bits of storage. It is clearly not feasible to store a large program in such small memories. These machines solve the problem by having the program stored in the CU (called the "host"); they are SIMD systems. We see a connection between *small-grained programs and SIMD systems*.

From now on we will use the name *cellular systems* for SIMD machines like the CM-1 and abbreviate it to *CM*. "The brain may be an example of a cellular computer. Each element is a neuron which (in a very oversimplified fashion) we can consider to be repeatedly executing the simple instruction 'if sum of inputs is greater than my threshold and no inhibitions are set, then output a spike' " [Fea88].[†]

Computers for coarse-grained problems have enough memory so that the problem can be solved in large "chunks." These are SM machines and we see the connection—*SM machines solve coarse-grained problems*. This indicates that Minsky's conjecture holds for SMs and coarse granularity. As will be shown in this book, Vector and ARray Processors (VPs and ARPs) should be used for fine-grained and data-parallel, ASPs and MPs for medium-grained, instruction-parallel algorithms.

1-2.5 Real-Time and Parallel Processing

Parallel processing systems can also be classified according to their suitability for various applications.

In control and military applications, PPSs are used in order to speed up the solution

---

[†]Fox/Johnson/Lyzenga/Otto/Salmon/Walker, SOLVING PROBLEMS ON CONCURRENT PRO-CESSORS, Volume I, (c) 1988. Reprinted with permission of Prentice Hall Inc., Englewood Cliffs, N.J.

time and achieve what is termed "*real-time*" performance. Another group of applications where real-time processing is essential are Bank-of-America On-Line Inquiry, an automated quotation system, an In-House Time-Sharing System [LaC85], a savings bank, warehouse control, a large stockbroker company, an airline ticket reservation system [Gla83], and the manager of an investment association [Org83], or a small bank [OaW83].

The "real" in "real-time processing" shares with art the characteristic that those acquainted with it can recognize it immediately, but are unable to provide a formal definition of what it is. It seems easier to recognize processing that is not real-time. If the design of equipment will be the same no matter whether it is done at 8 A.M. or 3 P.M., then it is not real-time processing. On the other hand, tracking enemy missiles is certainly a real-time job with results needed in a rather short time. The first characteristic of real-time systems is that the response time must be short.

How short is short? The teller in a bank should not keep a customer waiting for more than a few minutes; otherwise, the customer will be unhappy. The inquiry in an airline ticket-reservation system is usually obtained in a matter of seconds; again, it should not take longer than the arrival rate of the customers. The control circuit of a rocket must adjust its flight plan almost immediately to external influences such as differences in wind direction or velocity. In all these cases, *the time must be short compared to changes in the "state" of the system.*

The input data arrive mostly at unpredictable times (asynchronous processing). If data are not read immediately, they may be lost, and this in turn may lead to incorrect results and incorrect conclusions. A second characteristic of real-time systems is that they must respond to *asynchronous inputs or events.* In the cases of a bank, ticket-reservation, and control of a rocket, the inputs were asynchronous.

The third characteristic is *concurrency*, exemplified, for instance, by the existence of a number of (parallel) queues in a bank. Generally, the inputs may occur simultaneously and the system must respond so that all inputs are accepted and processed simultaneously and concurrently.

There are two groups of applications with the characteristics of short response time, asynchronous inputs, and concurrency. The first group may be termed the *inquiry system* and is exemplified by the airline ticket-reservation system. The other group may be termed *process-control*: automobiles, refineries, intensive-care units, power-station control centers, flight-control systems, space shuttle, aircraft avionics, all kinds of military applications, etc. These so-called embedded systems incorporate hardware and software into larger systems. They must respond in real-time to, say, the wind velocity change for a missile, or to halt the movement of the robot as it handles some equipment. The differences of the two groups are:

1. Process-control systems operate on the order of milliseconds; dialogue systems on the order of seconds or minutes.

2. The principle task of the computer in process-control is to monitor and control a time-critical *process* (task) whose own logical sequence is asynchronous to that of the computer itself. In inquiry systems, the task is to manage a large *database*.

3. In process-control, the computer is "dedicated" and the system is called an *embedded system*. In dialogue systems, this is not necessarily so.

Parallel processing systems are needed for both types of applications. In inquiry systems (Sec. 8-1), a number of computers are needed to service the large number of customers asking for information from different locations. It might be better to have the computers and the common database distributed geographically. In process-control it is vital that the information is on-time and since the problems may be mathematically complex, a single computer will not suffice.

Years ago, control circuits used feedback to correctly operate a single element. For process-control, the number of controlled elements is increased. As an example, consider traffic lights. It is easy to control the sequence green-yellow-red by measuring the traffic density of the four directions of a single intersection, and using a feedback circuit. A slightly more complicated problem is to coordinate the lights so that they form a "green lane." Simple feedback will not suffice when the traffic density is sensed and the traffic lights are controlled for overall optimization of traffic flow. The same applies to an instrument vs. an entire factory, or control of energy distribution in an electric energy system.

In the above examples, computers replaced the automatic feedback circuits because they are less expensive (their cost may be lower than installing a digital or analog controller), can be reprogrammed and tuned to include decision-making capabilities, and are well suited for the control sequence of process-control: data acquisition from sensors, data processing, and output to actuators or displays.

The use of a microprocessor centralizes a number of autonomous processes. This reduces the reliability and availability since when the microcomputer fails, the control system becomes inoperative. This is another reason to use parallel (and distributed) processing systems.

For process control, the computer is connected as in Fig. 1-8. Data or a status report is sent by the process to the computer. The computer then activates a particular program and sends the results (for example, new set-points) to the process. The computer *monitors* the process (through *sensing* of its status and accepting of alarms) and in turn *controls* it by the output of control signals. For the computer to be able to monitor and control a process, it must be able to sequence its operations in time, or it must operate in *real-time*.

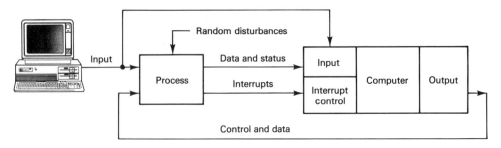

Figure 1-8 Computers in process control

While processing a particular algorithm, the process may indicate by an interrupt that a more urgent task is to be activated. The higher-priority job is done and then the interrupted job can be resumed.

Real-time systems get their inputs from external, sensor devices. These *external events* occur at arbitrary times of its execution. For example, the programmer cannot predict at what time a sensor pulse will occur. It may occur in the middle of an arbitrary instruction. Since these events occur asynchronously and often simultaneously, concurrent execution is required even if only one CPU exists.

The normal solution is to divide the program into a set of separate processes (to be called tasks), each handling a class of events which occur in some sequence. Each *task* can then be programmed without concern for the unpredictable order of events just as a sequential program dealing with a deterministic set of inputs does.

Each task is sequential; its activation is not. For example, one task might deal only with the sensor pulse and recording a single event which occurs over and over. A second task might deal with an analog-to-digital converter which would handle a repetitive cycle of two deterministically ordered events, the start-conversion and read-results.

The order in which these tasks execute is unpredictable, since the underlying real-time events as a group are unpredictable. There are three problems that must be solved in order to build the set of tasks into a useful system. First, a mechanism must be available to execute a task when an event (an *interrupt*) from the class it handles, occurs. Second, a mechanism must be available to allow the tasks to *communicate* with each other, since the control of real-time devices depends on other signals occurring *asynchronously*. Third, the task structure must be designed so that the execution of one task does not interfere with other tasks going on simultaneously and *concurrently*.

1–3 CHARACTERISTICS OF PPSs

The most important property of real-time systems should be *predictability* which means that the output should be the same for different timing of inputs. Testing the equipment does not insure predictability as was evidenced in the space-shuttle program. For all the laborious testing and simulations, a timing bug delayed its first flight despite the fact that there was only a 1 in 67 probability that a transient overload will desynchronize redundant CPUs during initialization (which is what happened). In order for a PPS to provide predictability and speed it should be well matched to the application. Otherwise, the PEs and the communication subsystem may not be able to handle the load in a deterministic and timely fashion [AaG89].

The speedup σ and efficiency η of PPSs were defined in Eq. (1-1) and Eq. (1-2) as $t(1)/t(p)$ and σ/p, with $t(1)$ being the time needed on a single, $t(p)$ the time on p processors. This definition of σ can be misleading since algorithms that may be appropriate for a single processor (have good convergence rate) may be totally wrong for a PPS. It therefore makes sense to use the *fastest* sequential algorithm for a single CPU and compare it with the parallel algorithm used for the PPS.

Actually, this definition is not fair to the concurrent algorithms because the sequential program often has had the benefit of years of fine tuning, code optimization, efficient use of registers, and the like. It is not to be expected that the same effort has been spent on tuning an experimental concurrent code. In particular, if some PEs are idle, the efficiency, which essentially measures the fraction of time the PEs are usefully employed, is lowered. Another difficulty is encountered when the amount of data is such that it will not fit a single PaM, so that the concurrent algorithm has to use more input/output. As a result of all these considerations, some kind of an "equivalently best" (but not too good) serial code should be used.

The two times $t(1)$ and $t(p)$ are seldom measured. Traditionally, the timing of algorithms is evaluated by an operation count called *computational complexity*. It simply states that the time is "on the order of" some function of a dimension "n" e.g., $\mathbf{0}[g(n)]$. For instance, if the Fourier analysis has n samples, then it may be said that its time-complexity is $\mathbf{0}(n^2)$, while the time complexity of the Fast Fourier Transform is only $\mathbf{0}(n*\log n)$. Specifically, if $n = 1024$, and each step takes 1mcs, then the first requires $(1024)^2$ or 1,048,576 mcs, while the second requires only $1024*\log(1024)$ or 10,240 mcs.

A PPS running a program requires times for:

1. *Computation*: This is the useful time, Ω.
2. *Communication*: The PEs inform each other about the state of the calculation and possibly exchange data. Communication time is κ.
3. *Synchronization*: The PEs may have to wait for each other as the order of the computation is followed. Synchronization time is ζ.
4. The *overhead* is the sum of communication and synchronization times.

Calculating the speedup by using the $\mathbf{0}$-count may be misleading. If the choice is between an algorithm which has a very high count, but no need for synchronization and overhead (so that all p PEs are used all the time), and an algorithm with low count but high overhead, the first will be preferred. Thus, it is the *degree of concurrency* or the relative amount of computation which can proceed concurrently that is important. Mathematically, if δ is this degree of concurrency, i.e., the fraction of work in the algorithm that can be processed in parallel, and if the time $t(1)$ has been normalized to unity, then the fraction δ of the algorithm can be speeded up by a factor of p, but the remaining part $(1-\delta)$ must proceed sequentially on one of the PEs. The time on a PPS would be $t(p) = (1-\delta+\delta/p)*t(1)$ and the speedup therefore would be

$$\sigma = 1/[(1-\delta)+\delta/p] \qquad (1-3)$$

Figure 1-9 shows σ as a function of δ (for $p = 4$ and 16). It is seen that in order to achieve a reasonable speedup, the fraction of work done in parallel must be high, i.e., δ must tend to 1. In extreme cases, if all work is done in parallel, $\delta = 1$ and $\sigma = p$; in a sequential computer: $\delta = 0$ and $\sigma = 1$. For $\delta = p/(p+1)$, we have $1/\sigma = 1-p/(p+1)+1/(p+1)=2/(p+1)$. For $p = 9$, the speedup is only five!

Suppose that 80 out of 100 operations proceed concurrently ($\delta = 4/5$). If $p = 80$, the time is still that of 20 operations to be done *sequentially* and one concurrently. The

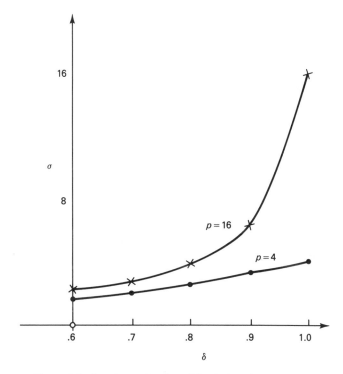

Figure 1-9   Speedup as function of the degree of concurrency

speedup is only 100/21 ≃ 5. In short, if p is very large, then $\delta/p \simeq 0$ and $\sigma \simeq 1/(1-\delta)$. A "law" attributed to G. Amdahl states this by: "The maximum performance gain of any parallel program is equal to the reciprocal of the fraction of the program which is inherently parallel." In our case, $\delta = 0.8$, and the maximal speedup is only 5, *no matter how many PEs work in parallel*. This indicates that p should be low, but the assumption applies most to VPs [Her89] for which the x-axis is interpreted as the fraction of work that can be vectorized. Since in VPs "the fraction δ is only 70% to 80%, speedups of only 3 to 4 are achieved, and such programs run with an efficiency of only 25% to 35% of the maximal vector part." On the other hand, for other PPSs, "there are numerous computational problems for which δ decreases to zero as the size of the problem increases, and Amdahl's law is not a concern" [BaT89].†

For multiprocessors, a *communication penalty* π is defined using the overhead (mostly communication) time κ and the computation time Ω:

$$\pi \;=\; \kappa/\Omega \tag{1-4}$$

In MPs, mostly because of data-dependencies, the PaMs are not equally loaded.

---

†Bertsekas, D.P. and Tsitsiklis, J.N. *"Parallel and Distributed Computations"* Prentice-Hall, Englewood Cliffs, NJ, 1989. Reprinted by permission.

Load-balance strongly influences the speedup with σ reduced whenever the load is unbalanced (in an extreme case, if $p-1$ PaMs are not working, we have no speedup).

We need to include the cost of the system in our considerations. For instance, it is shown in [Man 79] that the bit-sequential adder is very inexpensive and very slow, whereas the parallel adder is expensive but fast. It seems like an unwritten law that the product of speed and time is constant, say c. On the other hand, to achieve a higher speed, we must pay more, i.e., speed $= k*$cost. (One would expect that a system that costs twice as much will also be twice as fast.)

The product of power (or cost) and time is sometimes [LaM87] called the "energy." Using the two constants k and c from above, it is seen that the energy is also constant: time*cost $= (c/$speed$)*($speed$/k) = c/k$. We will not use the term energy and note that it is the aim to have a low time*cost product which implies high utilization and low overhead.

In most cases, efficiency η measures the ratio of the effectively used energy to the applied energy. Because of energy losses, it is less than 100% (otherwise it would be a "perpetuum mobile"). As we will see later, the efficiency of an algorithm can also depend on data and an apparent efficiency of over 100% [WHB81] can be achieved in PPSs.

Next we define the *time-ratio*:

$$\rho = t(p)/t(1); \; \rho < 1 \qquad (1\text{-}5)$$

The time to do a job with p PEs includes the times $t(1)$ and $\kappa = p*t'$ for overhead, for example, for communication between the p PEs. Since the total time $t(p) = t(1) + p*t'$ is split among the p PEs, the ratio is $\rho = [(t(1)+p*t')/p]/t(1)$.

and with $\pi = \kappa/t(1)$:

$$\rho = 1/p + (\kappa/p)/t(1) = 1/p + [\pi*t(1)/p]/t(1);$$

or

$$\rho = (1+\pi)/p \qquad (1\text{-}6)$$

Once π is known, ρ can easily be calculated.

As can be seen, ρ includes the overhead time, κ, and *can be easily computed*, after which the speedup σ is simply calculated, as $\sigma = 1/\rho$. The division needed in order to calculate σ is difficult. *We will therefore use the ratio whenever possible* since it accounts for communication and synchronization overheads as well as the degree of concurrency, and is easier to compute.

Ideally, $\rho = 1/p$, but in fact $\rho > 1/p$. Sometimes $\rho - 1/p$ is called the "deterioration," $t'/t(1)$. This definition is not correct. For example, if $p = 10$ then ρ of $1/9$ would yield $1/9 - 1/10 = 1/90$ or about 1.1%, while for $p = 100$ and ρ of $1/90$, $t'/t(1)$ should be the same, but is $1/90 - 1/100$ or about 0.11%. It is better to use $\pi = p*t'/t(1)$ for it yields the correct result of 11% in both cases. The communication penalty π should be as small as possible for ρ to be small, or for σ to be large.

1–4 ADDENDUM

1-4.1 Review of Material Covered in the Book

The design of a PPS should start from the application and lead to the organization [Wal82]. This would produce an efficient, but "special purpose" PPS. We will not deal with such systems, not even with the "systolic arrays," because they are well covered in other books, for example [Kun88]. As the name indicates, special purpose computers cannot deal with a large number of different applications. We must be willing to pay more to get a system that will solve a large subset of our problems, even if they are less efficient than a system that solves very efficiently only a few problems. This is merely a question of approach, and those who disagree are not less right.

In Chapters 2 to 5, we will cover the following material:

1. The Interconnection Networks (INs) are important parts of any PPS, so much so that PPSs are sometimes classified according to the INs they use. In particular, it should be noted that if a connection is to be made, or a message transmitted between a PE and MB, but the connection is "blocked," these units are idle and the utilization decreases. Single-stage and multiple-stage INs will be discussed in Chapter 2. We will then discuss the following systems.

2. The "pipeline" systems run programs in the same way cars are assembled—on a conveyor belt or an assembly line. Suppose a job takes an hour to do. If it is split into $p = 10$ stages on the line, each of which is done in exactly 6 minutes, then a job is leaving the assembly line every 6 instead of every 60 minutes. The "speed-up" is $\sigma = p = 10$.

   • It should be noted that a pipeline computer consists of a single processing unit with pipeline execution of instructions, or arithmetic operations. Since pipeline computers are best at applying the same operations to whole streams of data (vectors), they are also called vector-processors, VPs, and some of them will be discussed in Chapter 3. They are mainly used to increase the throughput—not speedup.

   • Recall the *ARray Processors*, ARPs. If they have a different type of memory, they are called *associative* computers. Both ARPs and associative PPSs will be included in Chapter 3.

   • The ILLIAC, an ARP, was not successful. There are a number of reasons for this, e.g., each of its 64 PEs was rather expensive, and had too little memory. The reason for the high price was that ILLIAC was assembled before the appropriate technology (VLSI chips) was available. With this new technology and some other improvements, the ideas of ILLIAC were revived in the (cellular) machines of Chap. 3.

3. Consider again Fig. 1-1(c). This is called a (shared-memory) SM multiprocessor. Examples of multiprocessors will be discussed in Chap. 4. They use much more powerful computers than the ARPs. Their memory must store a copy of the program

and is used for synchronization. In ARPs, the synchronization is automatic and the LMs are small. SMs, though, can be used over a broader range of applications.

4. We have indicated that the frequency, cost of communication and of synchronization among processors is crucial to the performance of an algorithm on any PPS. SMs not only waste synchronization and communication time, but also can become "deadlocked." Because of these disadvantages, ways were thought for reducing synchronization and communication time as well as eliminating the danger of deadlock. The Alternating Sequential-Parallel or ASP systems (Sec. 5-3) do it by way of hardware, MPs (Sec. 5-1), mostly by way of software.

   • In MPs the memory is distributed among the p processors. Examples of MPs are the "Hypercubes" discussed in Secs. 5-1 and 5-2.

   • Consider the way we eat. We use both hands (concurrently) to put the food into our mouths, but we swallow it piece by piece (i.e., sequentially). The parallel and sequential activities alternate until the meal is finished. In computerese: Assemble a master/slaves system such that the master directs sequentially the slaves which work in parallel, independently on different data. ASP systems can be thought of as a generalization of being purely sequential and purely parallel; these systems can be obtained by removing either the parallel or the sequential parts. ASP systems are discussed in Secs. 5-3 and 5-4.

   • "Local Area Networks" of computers called LANs are normally not used as PPSs. It would be nice to be able to do it, since every office that has a LAN (and which doesn't) could use it for compute-intensive jobs at nights or on weekends. It will be shown in Sec. 9-2 that they can be connected to work as ASPs.

It would be impractical to describe all architectures ever proposed. Instead only the pioneering, the commercially available, and/or those that (in my opinion) have a good chance to survive will be discussed.

The architectures to be dealt with are the following:

(a) Array, Pipeline, and Vector Processors, VPs (Chap. 3).

(b) SM multiprocessors (Chap. 4).

(c) MP multiprocessors and ASPs as well as other PPSs, such as (DIRMU) systems with "restricted interconnections" (Chap. 5).

No apologies are given for including the ASP systems or DIRMU [Erl86]; on the contrary, because they are less well known, but fill a need and were assembled, it is even more important to deal with them.

The top speeds of various PPSs were collected from later chapters and are shown in Fig. 1-3 and Table 1-2. It is to some degree a summary of developing PPSs. The reader can clearly see that great strides have been achieved. On the other hand, this picture may be misleading from two points of view: first, it relates to "peak" speeds and is thus not as indicative as benchmark program running times, and second, it does not take into account the software, i.e., the programs that were actually run. Still, it is impressive.

The usefulness of any PPS depends on the availability of appropriate algorithms,

TABLE 1-2 COMPUTER POWER (MFLOPS) THROUGHOUT THE YEARS 1970–1987

Name	ASC	STAR	ILLIAC	CRAY-1	HEP	MPP	X-MP	VP200	S-810	N/10	iPSC/2	CM2
Year	70	70	70	77	82	83	84	85	85	86	86	87
MFLOPs	15	16	20	128	128	200	300	533	840	500	640	625

computer languages, and ultimately, the efficiency of the programs written for these machines. In Part B (chapters 6 to 11), we discuss the algorithms, languages, and programming of PPSs.

Chapter 6 introduces both sequential and parallel algorithms, Chap. 7, the conventional features of the Ada language, and Chap. 8, the use of Ada for various PPSs. Chapters 9 to 11 use Ada as a unifying language for writing programs to be run on various PPSs.

1-4.2 Matrix Operations

To demonstrate the operation of several PPSs, we need simple problems. For this, we introduce next some *MATRIX OPERATIONS*.

An n-by-n matrix is a collection of n^2 numbers ordered in n rows and n columns. (The matrix will be denoted by a boldface, upper-case letter, say **A**, its elements will be identified by the indices e.g., $A(i,j)$, meaning the element in row i, column j.)

To add two matrices, every element of one matrix is added to the corresponding element of the other matrix. Thus, $\mathbf{C} := \mathbf{A} + \mathbf{B}$ means:

$$C(i,j) := A(i,j) + B(i,j) \text{ for } i = 1, \ldots, n \text{ and } j = 1, \ldots, n \qquad (1\text{-}7)$$

Subtraction of matrices is identical with " $+$ " replaced by " $-$ ".

In the case of matrix problems, the actual number of operations Ω can be easily calculated. There are n^2 additions or operations in Eq. (1-7) (one for each combination of indices i and j). If the time of an operation (i.e., of an addition, subtraction, multiplication, or division) is denoted by ω, the result is

$$\Omega = n^2 * \omega \qquad (1\text{-}8)$$

Multiplication of n-by-n matrices **A** and **B** yields matrix **C** as follows:

$$C(i,j) = \Sigma A(i,k) * B(k,j); \ k\Sigma = 1, \ldots, n \qquad (1\text{-}9)$$

This rule can be explained using the following full matrix notation:

$$
\begin{vmatrix}
C(1,1) \ldots C(1,n) \\
C(2,1) \ldots C(2,n) \\
\cdots\cdots\cdots\cdots \\
\cdots\cdots\cdots\cdots \\
\cdots\cdots\cdots\cdots \\
C(n,1) \ldots C(n,n)
\end{vmatrix}
=
\begin{vmatrix}
A(1,1) \ldots A(1,n) \\
A(2,1) \ldots A(2,n) \\
\cdots\cdots\cdots\cdots \\
\cdots\cdots\cdots\cdots \\
\cdots\cdots\cdots\cdots \\
A(n,1) \ldots A(n,n)
\end{vmatrix}
*
\begin{vmatrix}
B(1,1) \ldots B(1,n) \\
B(2,1) \ldots B(2,n) \\
\cdots\cdots\cdots\cdots \\
\cdots\cdots\cdots\cdots \\
\cdots\cdots\cdots\cdots \\
B(n,1) \ldots B(n,n)
\end{vmatrix}
\qquad (1\text{-}10)
$$

An element $C(i,j)$ accumulates the products of elements in row "i" of **A** with corresponding elements in column "*j*" of **B**. This is a "scalar product" of the row and column vectors. In detail:

$$C(i,j) = A(i,1)*B(1,j) + A(i,2)*B(2,j) + \ldots + A(i,n)*B(n,j) \qquad (1\text{-}11)$$

For each element $C(i,j)$, there are $(n-1) \simeq n$ additions and n multiplications. Since matrix **C** has n^2 elements, there are $\simeq n^3$ multiplications and additions. The number of operations is

$$\Omega = 2*n^3*\omega \qquad (1\text{-}12)$$

If matrix **B** has a single column, i.e., is a *vector*, we have the product **A*****b** which will be used repeatedly in the text.

1-4.3 Comments

The classification as given in Sec. 1-2 is not sufficiently precise. There exist computers, e.g., PAX [Hos89] which are sometimes classified as SIMD, sometimes as MIMD. The author had the same experience with ASP systems, with the reviewers claiming "it is a SIMD (or MIMD) machine". Even in [Hos89], the PAX is claimed to be MIMD on p. 10 and SIMD in other places, but then this is not that important. To the claim that "PAX is essentially an ILLIAC-IV, which was a failure. The level of originality is low," the author replied that "PAX is not an ILLIAC-IV. Originality is not the same as effectiveness."

The ASP systems were criticized on the account that the synchronization they employ is very time-consuming. The TOPPS and PAX computers demonstrate that it can be done simply and efficiently.

Having introduced matrix multiplication, $C(i,j) = \Sigma A(i,k)*B(k,j)$, we can discuss granularity again. Calculation of each product $A(i,k)*B(k,j)$ on one of the n^3 PEs, or the accumulation of each $C(i,j)$ on n^2 PEs, is fine-grained concurrency. If **A**, **B**, **C** are block-matrices we may consider the calculation to be coarse-grained. A sequential part of a parallel program is an individual grain, which can be as small as a single instruction or as large as a task.

The example of matrix multiplication shows the need for parallel processing. It requires over n^3 operations, and for "average" matrices of $n = 1,000$, this is over 10^9 operations. Even if an operation takes only 300 nns, this amounts to 5 minutes.

1–5 PROBLEMS

1. Explain what is meant by the "memory bottleneck." Give the reasons that limit the speed of SISD computers. Explain the meaning of speedup, time-ratio, and efficiency. Enumerate the items included in the ratio. Discuss the communication penalty π.

2. Enumerate the reasons for the delay in developing efficient PPSs and list their advantages. In what way were they influenced by the fact that different PPSs are needed for algorithms that have different grain size?

3. Classify all PPSs according to a gasoline station, to societal considerations, and in the traditional way. Define the CDC6600 and the MPP of Chap. 3 using the Erlangen classification system. Define the two types of "real-time" systems. Describe which characteristics of real-time systems are difficult to implement on some PPSs.

4. Sometimes the opinion is voiced that the two groups of applications may be better served by different classes of parallel processing systems: multiprocessors for process-control and the others for inquiry systems. This is so because in all cases of a master-slaves architecture, *the slaves cannot accept the interrupts* being isolated from the outside world by the master. If and when the master accepts an interrupt, it can ask *all* the slaves to do a new job, but not a particular slave (it can only "download" the job). Therefore, the array, pipeline computers or the ASP systems are suitable for speeding up the solution of problems for a host computer, which accepts the interrupts. This type of job activation may be called "hierarchical scheduling."

In multiprocessors, the scheduling processor can assign the job to any one of the p independent processors even to the point of interrupting them. This may be called "liberal scheduling." Note that in this case all three problems mentioned above: an interrupt mechanism for handling events, a mechanism for communication between the processors and a structure for eliminating the interference must be provided. Is this correct? Should only multiprocessors be used for process-control?

5. Modern operating systems (OSs) are multiprogrammed. Execution of OS code often accounts for a large percentage of the processing time for context switching and so on. Show how PPSs can use multiprogramming to their advantage.

6. A very useful and important algorithm is that of *Fast Fourier Transformation*, FFT. It is described in many books; for special-purpose computers in [Kun88]. Write a program for FFT using the assembly language of [Wak 89]. After having learned the Ada language, you will be able to change it into parallel programs for various PPSs and develop appropriate algorithms.

CHAPTER 2

INTERCONNECTION NETWORKS

The objectives of this chapter are:

Classify the interconnection networks (INs) and describe their characteristics.

Describe the time-shared bus, the multibus, the crossbar, the multiport, the Local Area Networks (LANs) and the token ring.

Describe various multistage INs, the MINs.[†]

Summarize the performance, indicate the choices, and provide problems.

[†]Since an extensive literature exists especially on MINs, this chapter is comparatively short particularly when discussing the most often used MINs.

2–1 INTRODUCTION

2–1.1 Classification

In the broadest sense, the term "Interconnection Network" (IN) could mean a nationwide network of computers linked by telephones or satellites, it could mean a few switches interconnecting microcomputers, or anything in between. Here, it will mean a network capable of providing rapid data transfer among the various units (e.g., CPUs, MBs, I/O ports, etc.). The distance between these units should not be large—they should all be housed in the same room or building. The delay should not be greater than a few microseconds (mcs).

The simplest IN is a single bus [Fig. 2-1(a)], a common path connecting all units. All of the information must go through the bus, but only a single message can be passed at any given time among the Processing Elements (PEs). Hence, if two messages are to be passed, the time is divided between the two messages so the second message waits until the processing of the first is completed. This time-multiplexing is the reason for a bus also being called a *time-shared bus* or a *common bus*. When more than one CPU is connected to the bus, whenever a CPU tries to access memory, it must first get permission from the other CPUs. Arbitration among them leads to contention and to longer waiting times. Adding more and more CPUs will make the problem worse and may lead to a bottleneck.

One way to reduce traffic congestion on the bus is to add local memory (LM) to each PE (making it into a PaM defined as a Processor-and-Memory) or to add a cache. For instance, if 90% of the time, a PE accesses a local memory, then ten times as many PEs can share the bus with the same previous contention.

A second way to reduce traffic congestion is to use simultaneously up to b buses instead of a single bus [Fig. 2-1(b)].

A third way to reduce bus congestion is to use $p*m$ buses for p PEs and m memory blocks MBs. This interconnection method is known as a *crossbar switch* and is shown in Fig. 2-1(c). In principle, it will allow m PEs to access the memory simultaneously as long as each PE accesses a different MB. In most cases, the crossbar switch allows simultaneous access only to a majority of the m MBs; if two PEs try to access the same MB, one will have to wait. This contention reduces the speedup.

Some contemporary problems such as image processing or weather computations require an execution rate of one billion instructions per second (10^9 IPs). Suppose that the PEs have an execution rate of $10^4 = 10,000$ IPs; this means that 10^5 PEs have to be connected into a PPS. For such a large number of PEs, a single bus would be hopelessly overloaded and only one processor at a time could use it. It would be inefficient and unreliable. Using a fully connected crossbar will be too expensive already for a PPS of over $p = 20$ CPUs and $m = 20$ MBs.

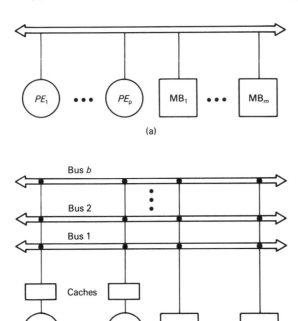

(a)

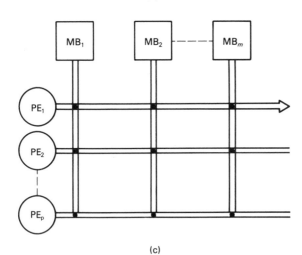

(b)

(c)

Figure 2-1 (a) Single bus (b) Multibus (c) Crossbar switch

It is particularly difficult to design an efficient IN for a large number of units. For example, if it becomes greater than 100 (which is certainly less than 10^5), the choice of interconnection organizations becomes quite a challenge.

Can it be met? The advances in Very Large Scale Integration (VLSI) technologies enabled designers to integrate thousands of IC chips on a single wafer, so the answer is "yes" but not if the bus or crossbar are used. A shared, time-multiplexed bus is the least complex IN, but it does not allow more than one PE to access the shared memory at any time. A large number of PEs usually means a long wait for the bus and a low efficiency. On the other hand, a crossbar can connect every PE with every MB simultaneously. However, its cost is $\mathbf{0}(p*m)$ and for a large number of units it would be prohibitive. It is more common to use INs between these two extremes of cost and performance. They are known as *Multistage Interconnection Networks—MINs*.

These are based on the same idea as telephone networks. There are millions of telephones around and we can talk to almost any station despite the fact that they are not all connected by wires. Instead, groups of telephones are connected through local switching stations each responsible for some area. When a connection is requested (by dialing a phone number), the request propagates by way of several such switching stations until the particular phone is reached.

The latency (time delay) of access to memory increases for MINs, since each request must travel through a number of switching stations. As is the case with telephone networks, there may be times of peak activity, like on Mother's Day, when the network becomes saturated. A considerable advantage of these MINs is that, as in telephone service, they can effectively connect large numbers of processors among themselves or to memory.

MINs are built from primitive switch elements, SEs. The simplest SE of interest has two switching states, s, corresponding to the two switching modes of Fig. 2-2(a) (i.e., through or cross), depending on a single control signal. Another SE of four states may either send its inputs through, cross [Fig. 2-2(a)], or broadcast one of the inputs to both outputs [Fig. 2-2(b)]. It is not permissible to switch two inputs to the same output.

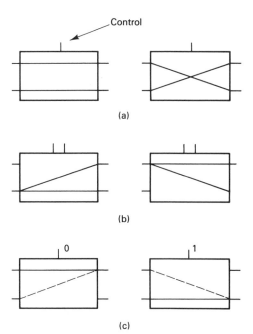

Figure 2-2   Switching elements (SEs)

Finally, an SE may send the input to the upper or lower output port [Fig. 2-2(c)]. The number of control bits (shown as vertical lines above the SE) is log(s).

In order to switch data through the network, each element in the MIN is set to one of the above states (not necessarily the same state) and then the data are allowed to pass from the input ports of the MIN to its output ports.[†] The SEs correspond to telephone switching stations.

There are a number of variations of MINs depending on the functional requirements, the control scheme, and many other factors. As mentioned, and especially for very large p and m, the connective logic is organized into several stages of SEs interconnected in some regular pattern, through connection links. From a geometric point of view, stages are normally represented by columns of SEs.

A MIN is usually capable of connecting arbitrary input terminals to arbitrary output terminals. Various MINs will be reviewed in this chapter. In most of these networks, there are $p = 2**d$ (where d means *dimension*) input/output ports, and log(p) stages of switching elements. Each stage uses $p/2$ SEs and is connected to the next stage by at least p paths. For example, Fig. 2-3(a) shows a network with dimension $d = 4$, $p = 2^4 = 16$ ports, log(p) = 4 stages, each of which uses $p/2 = 8$ SEs.

Another example is the Benes networks as proposed for telephone switching [Ben65]. For $p = 2**d$, a p-by-p Benes network consists of $2*d - 1$ stages of 2-by-2 SEs and $p/2$ switches per stage as illustrated for $p = 16$ in Fig. 2-3(b). It can perform all possible permutations, as can a crossbar, while reducing the cost from $0(p^2)$ to $0[p*\log(p)]$. The major disadvantages of the Benes network are its complicated routing algorithm and the long time required to set the control and send the message since it needs a large number ($2*d - 1 = 7$) of stages.

Figure 2-3(a) showed the ''Omega'' MIN in which 2-by-2 SEs connect 16 PEs and 16 MBs in four instead of seven stages. Its latency is log16 = 4, its complexity is $0[p*\log(p)]$. The factor log(p) corresponds to the number of stages, and p to the number of ports.

Suppose, we assume $p = m = 2^{10}$ (is 1024, much lower than 10^5 mentioned earlier). We are thus comparing the cost of the MIN (109 stages$*2^5 = 5120$) with the cost of a crossbar ($p = m = 2^{20} = 2^5*2^{15} = 5120*32K$). The conclusion is that for larger p and m, only MINs should be used.

2-1.2 Characteristics

Two measures characterize a MIN: its complexity and diameter. The *complexity* of the SE is the number of links per SE (node) and reflects the cost of the SE. The *diameter* of the MIN is the longest distance a message ever has to travel. The network in Fig. 2-3(a) has a complexity of 4 and a diameter of 4. Additionally, we next deal with switching methodology, timing, control, and interconnection topology.

There are two major methodologies comparable to telephone and mail service: they are called *circuit and message switching* respectively. In circuit switching, a path is

---

[†]In all figures of Chap. 2, MBs are also drawn as circles and PEs and MBs are simply considered Input and Output ports.

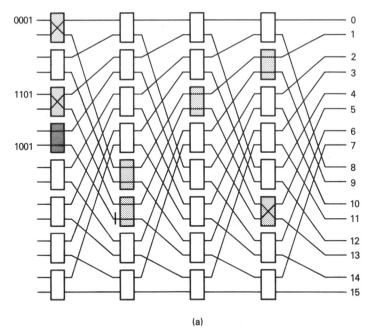

(a)

Figure 2-3a An Omega switching network. Courtesy of F. Hertweck, Vector- und Parallel-Rechner, Informationstechnik, 31 (1989), Oldenburg Verlag, W. Germany.

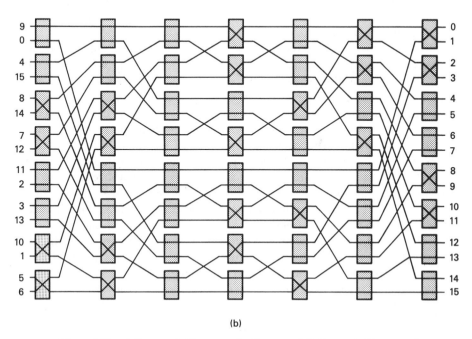

(b)

Figure 2-3b A Benes switching network. Courtesy of F. Hertweck, Vector- und Parallel Rechner, Informationstechnik, 31 (1989), Oldenburg Verlag, W. Germany.

physically established between input and output ports. In message switching, the message is routed through the IN without establishing a physical connection path. When the message is split into constant-length units, this is *packet switching*.

The phone company uses circuit switching to transfer your calls; the post office uses message switching to send your letters. In a circuit-switched system, two users establish a connection and talk over the phone for as long as the connection is not interrupted. The "routing" algorithm is rarely executed (i.e., only when a new connection is sought). In a message-switched system, a new route is chosen each time a message (letter) is transmitted; thus, the same SEs may be used for different routes at different times.

A packet consists of a "header" with the destination address and a sequence number for reforming the entire message in the correct order of packets, the actual content of the packet, and error-checking codes. The packets are sent across the network, which like the postal service reads the addresses and delivers the packets. There is no circuit setup delay because no circuit is set up and no individual path was reserved. A small percentage of the communication capacity, however, is used for routing information, headers, and other control data. The receiver must acknowledge the reception of the packet, which doubles the traffic on the MIN.

Once a circuit-switching path is established, the SEs in the path retain their position until the path is released. In packet switching, the data is put into a packet and routed through the MIN without establishing a physical connection path. The packet makes its way from stage to stage releasing switches and links immediately after using them. In this way, only one switch is used, at a time, for each packet.

Often the entire message is stored at some switching point until a possible path is found; this mode of operation is called *store and forward*. There is never a solid path between the input and the output.

In *circuit-switching* networks, data can be transferred more rapidly, because the rate does not depend on other communications taking place in the network—as is the case for packet switching. Unfortunately, as anybody who makes frequent long-distance calls may attest to, it takes considerable time to establish a connection. Such a delay would be intolerable when interposed between the rapid, staccato bursts of data that often take place between the computers. In telephone networks, to reduce the delay, paths could be leased as dedicated circuits. This could be very wasteful for PPSs. It could be compared to leasing a freeway. If you wanted to drive, you would call the highway system and ask them to close one lane on the entire stretch to all other traffic. The result would be a large, reserved but empty highway, and many traffic jams on the "free" parts of the freeway.

The size of the packet is important. "If packets are large, then it is sensible to establish a complete path from sender to receiver before transmitting the data. The machine would then have a circuit-switching architecture. However, if the packets are small, then it is sensible to send the data in a series of short jumps, *buffering* it at intermediate points. This yields a packet-switching scheme" [St187]. Using a circuit-switching system with short messages will be inefficient because time will be wasted to establish the circuit for each short message and π will be large. On the other hand, using message switching with long messages may result in inefficiency if the messages are longer than the size of the intermediate buffers, which would necessitate breaking the message into several packets. Circuit switching is better for coarser grained algorithms.

and must be used in networks constructed from combinational logic, since such networks do not include buffers to store delayed data.

Once a path is established in a circuit-switching system, the only delay in the network is the propagation delay. In packet switching, the overhead of routing, of buffering packets, and of potential conflict increases the delay. However, packet switching reduces contention since no fixed paths are required. Thus, in general, circuit switching should be used when the connections, once established, seldom change, while packet switching should be used when they change frequently.

In SIMD systems, we are interested in sending a set of messages in the shortest possible time, for example, if we wish to perform an operation on a vector of data. In MIMD systems, we are interested in minimizing the average delay or in maximizing the throughput. Therefore, most SIMD systems should use circuit switching, while MIMD machines should use packet switching. The MIN connects PE-to-PE in ARPs, PaM-to-PaM in MPs, or PE-to-MB in SMs. The main advantage of the first two INs is fast *local* memory references, and those of the third approach is ability to share large blocks of data and to vary the amount of memory used by individual processors.

The *timing may be synchronous or asynchronous*. Synchronous systems are characterized by a central clock which broadcasts its clock signal to all elements connected by the IN so that they operate in lock-step synchronization. Asynchronous systems do not have a common clock and operate independently.

Based on the overall control of the network, an IN may be classified as *centralized* or *decentralized*. A central controller receives all messages and distributes them on the IN. In decentralized control, the messages are handled independently by the SEs which make up the IN. A central controller may be complex, may create a system bottleneck, and directly affects the performance and reliability of the entire system. Distributing the control to the SEs avoids these drawbacks.

A packet-switching MIN consists of simple SEs that provide communication paths among the units of a PPS. Each packet identifies a particular destination port. This information is used by the switches to route the packet to the proper port: The control of packet movement through the IN does not require a centralized controller.

Computational speed is measured by the Bandwidth BW defined either as the amount of traffic that can be handled by the MIN or as the number of memory requests accepted per cycle. In a crossbar, since all nonconflicting requests are accepted, the BW is high. In a MIN, the BW is lower because of the conflicts in the network (two PEs trying to use the same link). The computational speed can only be increased by reducing the propagation delay in the IN. Since the switch delay increases with the number of stages, the fewer stages the better.

The *throughput* of a packet-switched IN is defined informally as the number of packets that it can pass per unit of time. *Delay* is defined as the average time required to route a single packet. Because several packets can be in motion simultaneously through a network and packets can collide at an internal stage, the delay does not generally equal the reciprocal of the throughput. Instead, it is proportional to the number of SEs through which the signal must pass between an input and output. Each SE is assumed to have the same time delay and the connections are supposed to have no delay. The delay in the network of Fig. 2-3(a) is the distance d (which is four).

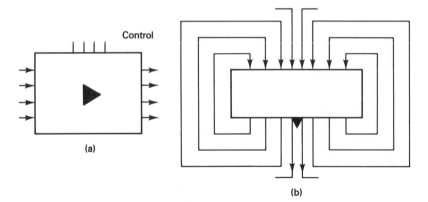

Figure 2-4   (a) A four-port SE (b) A recirculating switching network

A four-port SE [Fig. 2-4(a)][†] would produce 16 (instead of four) different connections. This would require fewer switches, fewer stages, and would result in a shorter delay. The obvious question is "why not use an eight-port switch?" It was determined that four is probably the best compromise between price and time.

A single-stage MIN could pass the outputs into the inputs a number of times (the number of stages in a MIN). Such a single-stage network may also be called a recirculating network [Fig. 2-4(b)], because the data items may have to recirculate through the single stage several times before reaching their final destination. A recirculating MIN must include buffers so that a blocked message can be temporarily stored. Since the exact size of the messages is not known, the buffers are designed for the largest message size.

The difference between a "normal" and "recirculating" MIN is that the MIN can be used both in the circuit-switching and in the packet-switching mode. The recirculating MIN can be used only in the packet-switching mode since it does not establish a fixed connection.

2–1.3 Topology

An IN can be illustrated by a graph in which nodes represent SEs and links represent communication paths. The overall graph representation is called network topology. The topology determines which connections can be established, and the limitations and capabilities of the various INs, and it is closely related to the capabilities of various node types (SEs).

Many topologies have been proposed and implemented for INs. They can be grouped into two broad categories: *static* and *dynamic*. In static INs, links between the ports are passive and cannot be reconfigured for changing the interconnections. Dynamic INs can be reconfigured during communication. The primary advantage of static topologies is their simplicity. For cases in which the topology matches the natural topology of the problem (e.g., in image processing), static topologies are also faster. However,

---

[†]Since information may go both ways, no arrows on SEs will be shown.

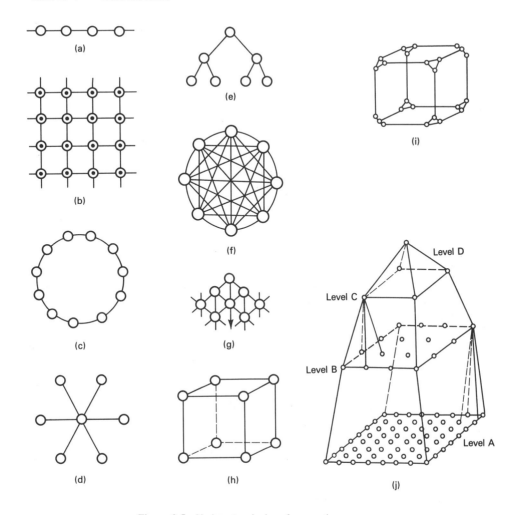

Figure 2-5 Various topologies of connecting processors

when the topology changes (as in symbolic processing), dynamic topologies are better. (The CM of Sec. 3-5 uses dynamic topologies set up in software.)

Figure 2-5(a) shows a one-dimensional static topology as used by pipeline computers. Fig. 2-5(b) shows a two-dimensional static topology known as nearest neighbor (or mesh), which is used by arrays of processors. Often, the opposite edges of the two-dimensional mesh network are interconnected, thus producing a "torus" network (similar to a doughnut). Other two-dimensional topologies include: ring, star, tree, the completely connected ring, and systolic array [Fig. 2-5(c–g)]. Three-dimensional topologies include the Cube, the cube-connected cycles, and a pyramid [Fig. 2-5(h-j)]. Even higher dimensions can be set up by Cubes. In all these INs, each processor can communicate directly only with a small subset of processors, and communication with other nodes involves the transfer of information through one or more intermediate processors.

2–1.4 Interconnection Functions

From an analytical point of view, an IN may be viewed as a set of interconnection functions. Each such function is a *permutation* on the set of input addresses marked as an ordered list of integers 0 to $p - 1$. Function f permutes the list into $f(0), f(1), f(2), \ldots, f(p - 1)$.

Mathematically, if i is the address of an element connected as a source of an IN, and $f(i) = j$ is the address of an element connected as a destination of an IN, then the function connects PE(i) with PE(j).

The following are descriptions of some often used functions (permutations).

The *perfect shuffle* of Fig. 2-6(a) is so called because it can be affected by cutting the set of numbers in half and interleaving the two subsets in a way similar to the shuffling of a deck of cards. If the numbers are written in binary, then the permutation corresponds to a circular left-shift or rotation as indicated in Fig. 2-6(b), namely:

$$\{b(p), b(p-1), \ldots, b(1)\} => \{b(p-1), b(p-2), \ldots, b(1), b(p)\} \qquad (2\text{-}1)$$

The *Exchange* permutation is shown in Fig. 2-6(c) and can be described by complementation of a single bit:

$$\{b(p), b(p-1), \ldots, b(i), \ldots, b(1)\} => \{b(p), b(p-1), \ldots, b'(i), \ldots, b(1)\} \qquad (2\text{-}2)$$

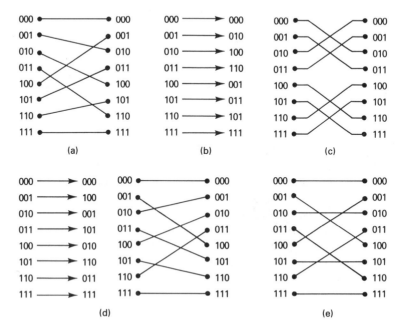

Figure 2-6 Various interconnection functions

A very useful permutation is the *Shuffle-Exchange* in which each perfect shuffle (Eq. 2-3) is followed by an exchange (Eq. 2-4):

$$\{b(p),b(p-1), \ldots ,b(i), \ldots ,b(1)\} => \{b(p-1), \ldots ,b(i), \ldots ,b(1),b(p)\} \quad (2\text{-}3)$$

$$\{b(p-1), \ldots ,b(i), \ldots ,b(1),b(p)\} => \{b(p-1), \ldots ,b'(i), \ldots ,b(1),b(p)\} \quad (2\text{-}4)$$

The *inverse shuffle* of Fig. 2-6(d) applies a right-circulate:

$$\{b(p), \ldots ,b(i), \ldots ,b(2),b(1)\} => \{b(1),b(p), \ldots ,b(i), \ldots ,b(2)\} \quad (2\text{-}5)$$

The *Butterfly* permutation of Fig. 2-6(e) exchanges the first and the last bits:

$$\{b(p),b(p-1), \ldots ,b(2),b(1)\} => \{b(1),b(p-1), \ldots ,b(2),b(p)\} \quad (2\text{-}6)$$

2–1.5 More on Characteristics of MINs

Control strategy.   The interconnections are realized by properly setting the control of the SEs. Two distinct types of control have emerged: centralized control and distributed control. Most existing SIMD interconnections use the centralized control on all SEs; whereas MIMD computers normally use the distributed control scheme.

Networks may be classified by their ability to establish desired connections between an input and an output. Basically, if a new path is required and an existing connection is in the way, the new connection may be either *blocked* (kept waiting) or the network will allow a new connection to be established (through some other links and SEs). Therefore, the MINs are divided into the following classes:

- In *blocking* networks, simultaneous connections of more than one input/output pair may result in conflicts for the use of network communication links. In other words, a network is said to be blocking if there exist connection sets that will prevent some additional desired connections from being established between unused ports even with the rearrangement of the existing connections.
- A network is called (strictly) *nonblocking* if any desired connection between unused ports can be established immediately without being blocked by some already existing connection.
- A network is called a *rearrangeable* nonblocking network if it can perform all possible connections between inputs and outputs by rearranging its existing connections so that a connection path for the new input-output pair can always be established. In other words, a network is said to be rearrangeable when a desired connection between unused ports may be temporarily blocked, but a connection can be established if one or more existing connections are rerouted.

Blocking can be exemplified by the omega MIN of Fig. 2-3(a). For connecting port 4 with port 13, the SEs would be connected cross, twice through and cross again. Suppose that port 7 is to be connected to port 9. The connection "through" in the second stage cannot be effected because the SE is already busy; the omega network is *blocking*.

The Benes network is a rearrangeable (and thus nonblocking) MIN. If *all* desired connections are specified *a priori*, then every input port can be connected to every output port, but if a connection is required while "in flight," some of the connections have to be rearranged.

The optimum network for a particular application depends on the requirements. Thus, a blocking network may be used in networks like the telephone system, where not all of the inputs and outputs are used simultaneously, and delays in making a connection are acceptable. A blocking network may also be used in a PPS, provided that the most often required connections can always be established, and the blocking is confined to connections that are seldom, if ever, used.

The SEs of a packet-switching network may contain data buffers. These are registers organized as first-in-first-out queues. The size (length) of a buffer is the maximum number of packets it can hold. For the MINs, either all SEs have buffers or none of them do. Moreover, the lengths of all buffers will be equal. These buffers serve as temporary storage to hold packets that have been blocked by a switch. Thus, a packet that has progressed through the MIN and is blocked at an SE in one of the later stages can wait in a buffer at an input port until it is unblocked. However, buffers can also block packets; if the buffer at a port is full, then a switch cannot pass a packet to that port.

Buffers increase the throughput of a MIN by enabling different switches on a path to operate on different packets at the same time. Sometimes, instead of two, four buffers are installed in an SE.

Reliability: It is necessary to include some fault tolerance into the MINs so that at least a single fault in a switch or a link can be tolerated. MINs can achieve fault tolerance either by adding hardware redundancy or through multiple passes. Algorithms can be devised to detect and remove faulty elements.

The IN represents a large part of the PPS's cost, most of its power dissipation, most of its wiring, and some of the performance limitations. *An IN should be efficient, reliable, and cost effective*. Additionally, *the performance and fault tolerance* of multiprocessor systems depend on the properties of the INs, and for many algorithms, the total *time* required to move data to the appropriate PEs is as large or larger than the time required for the completion of the computation. Therefore, as the component density of integrated circuits continues to increase, computer designers will be as concerned with the interconnection of the processors as with the processor design itself.

Having classified various MINs, let us specify how they are chosen. The combination of advantages we are seeking include the following:

1. A small diameter and short wires so that the communication time is reduced.
2. Extendability so that an arbitrarily large network can be built.
3. A fixed node complexity so that one SE type can serve all MINs.
4. Redundant paths allowing even a partially defective network to continue to function, thus increasing availability. Also, if a path is blocked by traffic, a message can be directed along another route.

5. A simple routing algorithm, because it can be locally controlled, thus keeping down the cost.

As always in the design of any system, these wishes are contradictory and a compromise is needed. As I wrote in another book: *"The scientist seeks the truth, the engineer seeks the compromise."* In the present case, the engineer may have to settle for what the present technology offers, disregarding other advantages.

To sum up: Because of their structure, MINs are capable of supporting a large number of computing units and a large number of simultaneous connections using a reasonable number of SEs. With proper design, a MIN can provide connections with reasonably short delays and with a relatively simple control strategy. Many MINs have built-in flexibility and redundancy which can be utilized for fault tolerance with graceful degradation in the computational speed.

The next sections deal with various INs: Bus-based INs in Sec. 2-2, and MINs in Sec. 2-4.

2–2 BUS-BASED INTERCONNECTION NETWORKS

2–2.1 The Time-Shared Bus

The bus is described in almost any book on microcomputers (see [Cle 82] and [Wal 82]). For parallel processors, the following are of interest.

Data transfer is controlled by the interfaces of the sender and receiver. The sender must make sure that the bus is available and then that the receiver is ready for the transfer. The receiver recognizes its address and acknowledges the request. Due to bus contention, arbiters must resolve a possible conflict. *Such asynchronous "handshaking" requires considerable time.* Moreover, the bus is reserved for a single CPU. The connection when established is asynchronous in the sense that it may last any integer number of memory cycles. When the protocol is over, the "End of Transmission" EOT signal from the "talking" processor interrupts the connection and permits other units to use the bus. This is why it is called a time-sliced bus.

Each message put on the bus must contain the data to be transferred and the address of the destination. It is not possible for multiple messages to arrive simultaneously at a unit since only one message can be on the bus at any time and a transmitter has to wait until the bus is free to place its message on the bus. Each unit connected to the bus must contain the circuitry necessary to recognize its address in a message and respond correspondingly.

Transmission can be synchronous and asynchronous. In *synchronous* transmission, time slots can be assigned to devices on either a dedicated or nondedicated basis. Dedicated time slots are permanently allocated to a device regardless of how frequently that device uses them. Each device on the bus is allowed to communicate on a rotational (time-division multiplex) basis. The only way that any priority can be established is by assigning more than one slot to a device. Time is wasted, since not all devices will want to transmit at the same time and some may not even be implemented. Also, faster devices will have to wait for slower devices, and if the time-slot rate is made as fast as the fastest device on the bus, (sometimes, quite large) buffers must be included for the slower devices.

Another approach is to run the bus slower than the fastest device and assign multiple time slots to that device. This complicates the control and wastes bus bandwidth if that device is not always transferring data.

For reliability, it is desirable, even in synchronous control, that the receiving device verify and acknowledge correct arrival of data. If the time slot is wide enough to allow a reply for every word, then data transmission will be slow because the time slots rely on the slowest device connected to the bus. One solution is to use verification by default. If an error occurs then a signal is returned to the source sometime later. The destination has enough time to test the validity of the transmission without slowing the transfer rate; however, the source must retain all words which have been transmitted, but not yet verified.

A memory block MB receives a request to read and the bus is released for use by another PE. When the MB is ready, say in 100 nns, it reacquires the bus and sends the data to the requesting PE. In synchronous control, the bus would have been idle and the time (100 nns) would have been wasted. With the many faults of synchronous control, it is no wonder that *an asynchronous bus is often chosen for parallel systems*. With such control this time can be used to access an MB that is not busy. The asynchronous mode, however, requires additional hardware for bus control.

The *control of the bus* may be either centralized or decentralized. In centralized bus control, the hardware used for passing bus control from one unit to another is called the *Bus-Control Unit*, BCU. All messages are first transmitted to the shared BCU, which retransmits the messages over the bus to the proper destination. The BCU can be within a particular microcomputer or it can be a dedicated unit. In decentralized bus control, the bus-control logic is distributed throughout the PEs connected to the bus. Usually, centralized control is used for buses along with the following schemes: Daisy chaining, polling and independent request [Wal82].

The bus can be totally passive, in which case transfer operations are controlled completely by the bus interfaces of the sending and receiving units. As seen, the transfer process can be simplified by the use of a centralized bus arbiter. In both active and passive buses, the cost of adding or removing functional units is quite low. Usually all that is required is to physically attach or detach the unit. This is not true for other interconnections, such as shown in Fig. 2-5. For some of these INs, the removal of a node incapacitates a large part of the IN.

The bus may transfer either *blocks of data or single words.* In the case of parallel systems, a block transfer will be essential since large amounts of data will have to be transferred, at least at the start of every job. Moreover, the block size must be variable, sometimes using a single word as the block size. This method for transfer of single words or variable-length blocks is the most expensive but also the most flexible and efficient method of those available.

The reliability of the bus is low because any break in the bus removes a large part of equipment. One technique for reliability enhancement is to bypass the bus [Hol76] as in

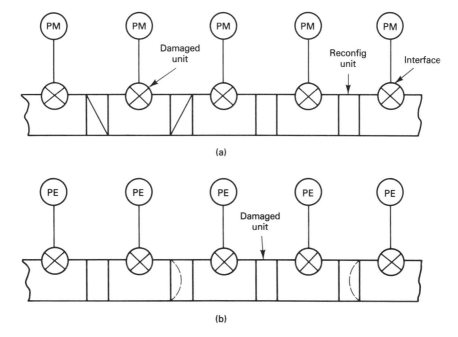

Figure 2-7   Enhancements of bus reliability

Fig. 2-7(a). (Note that two buses are used.) Here, the traffic is routed around a number of malfunctioning interfaces so that the connectivity of the bus is maintained. Unfortunately, it offers no help whatsoever if the reconfiguration unit itself is faulty.

A second technique shown in Fig. 2-7(b) is based on a bidirectional, double-bus structure [Hol76]. By using this *self-heal* technique, complete connectivity can be maintained when any number of adjacent terminals or reconfiguration units fail. When two nonadjacent nodes or reconfiguration units fail, the sections of the bus on either side of the failure are isolated. Unfortunately, if more than a single reconfiguration unit fails, the bus disintegrates into a number of disconnected parts. This method is highly reliable when a limited number of devices is connected to the bus.

2–2.2 Multibus Structures

A single time-shared bus is not sufficient for most PPSs, because it is often desirable to allow a number of CPUs to send data *simultaneously*. Ideally, each CPU should be linked directly to every other CPU via a dedicated path, as in Fig. 2-5(f). Unfortunately, these INs are too expensive. Moreover, since only one out of $p*(p-1)$ lines is busy at a time, utilization is very low.

One way to increase the capacity of the system, and at the same time its fault tolerance, is to increase the number of buses. The PPS is then connected, as in Fig. 2-1(b). There are b buses with $b \leq \min(p,m)$, each connected to all p PEs and m MBs. Thus, b PEs may be simultaneously working with b MBs. Since there are now b buses, whenever a PE needs access to the common memory, it can choose to do it through any of the *b* available buses. If a bus is defective, it can be removed, thus providing availability with slightly degraded service.

The complexity or cost (*c*) of the multibus IN is $0[b*(m+p)]$; its bandwidth is the average number of memory accesses in a cycle.

One of the problems with the multibus system is that (with $p > b$) the possibility exists that more CPUs will try to access the common memory than buses are available. This problem can be solved by using hardware arbiters [PFL75, LaV82]. (An arbiter allocates cyclically a bus to an MB that has an outstanding request.) This adds to the cost of the multiprocessor, but if the system consists of not more than 25 CPUs, the cost increase can be tolerated.

Multibus structures sometimes use *cache memories*. We will discuss caches in Chap. 4. For the present, view the cache as a local memory that is faster, more expensive and whose hardware decides when to transfer data. When data are accessed in a cache, the time it takes is 10 to 30 times lower than if they are accessed in the main memory. If all the data were stored in caches, all memory access would be much faster. When the requested data is not in the cache (a *cache miss*), an entire block, which includes the required data, is transferred from the memory to the cache.

The effective access time of the computer as a whole is

$$t(eff) := m*t(\text{main}) + h*t(\text{cache}); \; m = 1 - h; \tag{2-7}$$

where *m* and *h* are the probabilities of a miss (miss ratio) or a hit (hit ratio) respectively. Suppose that we install a cache 20 times faster than the main memory and that $t(\text{cache})$ is a single cycle. Then we have

$$t(eff) = [20*(1-h) + h] \tag{2-8}$$

If the hit ratio $h = 99\%$, then $t(eff)$ is only 1.19. In other words, the computer behaves as if its access time were 1.19 that of the cache. Unfortunately, if the hit ratio drops to 89%, the effective access time increases to 3.09. This shows that the ratio $t(\text{main})/t(\text{cache})$ should be as large as possible, or the speed of the cache as high as possible, and that *h* has an extremely large influence on the effective time.

The importance of the caches in multibus systems is that they reduce the bus traffic, allowing the number of buses *b* to be relatively low. In this case, the cache does not have to be very fast (and is thus less expensive), since it is installed for the sole purpose of reducing the traffic on the buses. This will avoid the potential performance degradation associated with having to wait for the shared resources. The policy of when to overwrite a cache is also important.

Two sources of conflict resulting from memory requests are present in the multibus system. First, more than one request may be made to any particular MB. Second, the number of buses may be insufficient. Therefore, the allocation of a bus to a CPU with a memory request is done according to fixed policies (see Problem 4).

The multibus can be message or circuit switched. In circuit switching, once a device is granted the use of the bus, it will occupy the bus for the entire duration of data transmission. For example, a CPU in a read operation will occupy the bus during the time of sending its request, performing the memory operation, and receiving the requested data. This will result in a significant fraction of bus bandwidth being wasted because of mismatch between the speeds of the PEs, bus, and memory. Packet switching, as used for instance in the Multimax computer of Encore, is better.

2–2.3 Crossbar Switches

In order to avoid contention on the single bus, $p*m$ buses for p CPUs and m MBs could be used [Fig. 2-1(c)]. (As shown later, $p = m$ in most cases.) Since each MB has its own bus, m PEs could be simultaneously connected to them. Therefore, the highest number of simultaneous transfers is limited only by the number of MBs and on how fast the buses are rather than on the number of possible paths. It will, in principle, allow all PEs to access memory simultaneously as long as each PE accesses a different MB. If two PEs try to access the same MB, one will have to wait—as was the case in the single bus.

The crosspoint connections in Fig. 2-1(c) include extensive hardware: Not only must each crosspoint be capable of switching independent transmissions, but it must be able to resolve multiple requests for access to a particular MB, which occur during the same memory cycle. A predetermined priority and a selector are normally used for this. Because a large number of PEs are connected to the switch, multiplexer modules are also needed. Thus, even with VLSI and a reduction in the size of the switch, each crosspoint is expensive, and the cost of a crossbar switch of p*m crosspoints is considerable.

The expansion of a system can be effected by adding crosspoints. The control of these crosspoints may be very complex and the reliability of the system will depend crucially on the reliability of the crossbar switch. There is only one path between a PE-MB pair. If a crosspoint fails, an MB becomes unreachable from the corresponding PE.

The single-stage crossbar is the only IN with a true uniform delay of one time-unit, since there is only one switching node between any input and output. Communication time is independent of the number of PEs.

2–2.4 Multiport Structures

If the control, switching, and priority arbitration logic are transferred to the interface of the memory blocks (MBs), a Multiport scheme such as that of Fig. 2-8 results. Each processor PE has access through its dedicated bus to all MBs, but none is connected to another PE. Access conflicts are resolved by memory ports. Note that this scheme is not identical to the connection of Fig. 2-5(f) since not all units are connected [e.g., PE(0) is not connected to PE(1)].

Since each processor has access to all memory blocks, it is possible to have a very high transfer rate in the system. Unfortunately, the maximum configuration of this system is limited by the number of ports available on memory units. The necessity to resolve the conflicts that occur in accessing these units by hardware makes this switch almost as expensive as the crossbar switch. In addition, multiport memories have the following characteristics:

- They are costly in terms of line selection logic and line driving circuits, the system has a large number of interconnections between processors and memories, and puts

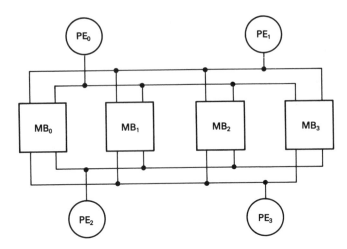

Figure 2-8   A multiport switch

limits on its flexibility since conflicts are resolved through priorities implemented in hardware.

- Since only one unit of information can be transferred over a line at a time and the processors cannot deal simultaneously with a number of messages, most of the lines are idle and the circuitry associated with these lines is not being effectively used. Assuming $p = 4$ and $m = 4$ for Fig. 2-8, each CPU and each MB has four connections, but uses only one at a given time. A heavy price was paid, but neither the lines nor the circuitry was used efficiently.

- As mentioned earlier, it would be an advantage if the topology of the IN would adapt itself to the topology of the problem. The multiport structure lends itself to such adaptive strategy (with the number of units in the tens instead of in the thousands).

2–2.5 Local Area and Token Ring Networks[†]

Decreases in the cost of semiconductor devices and corresponding dramatic increases in the number of computers has facilitated communication between them, eased data exchange, and simplified information flow in the form of messages and programs. Local Area Networks (LANs) are an example of a path by which computers can communicate. LANs have become extremely popular, with several hundred thousand installed worldwide. They enable members of the same organization to send messages to one another, to access the same databases and programs, and to share expensive memories and I/O equipment. Although their first use was in sharing peripherals, other applications may be found, such as parallel processing. In particular, in Chap. 9, a LAN will be used as a Parallel Processing System.

LANs may be defined as geographically confined communication systems sharing

---

[†]Yaprak, E., *Use of Local Area Networks as Alternating Sequential-Parallel Systems*, Ph.D. Thesis, Wayne State University, 1989; by permission.

transmission media. Because the distances are short, they can operate at high speeds and reliability. The main parts of a LAN are:

1. the transmission media (its wiring and network)
2. the access protocols that govern access to the shared media
3. the interface (''adapter'') that controls the access to the media and implements the access protocols
4. the communication protocols needed once the access is achieved

The telephone network can serve as an example: The media are the wires, dialing a number initiates the access protocol and establishes the connection. The phone itself is the communication interface and the protocol is the spoken language converted to electrical form. In telephones we use circuit switching. Computers tend to communicate in ''bursts,'' i.e., periods of high activity followed by lulls. During this period of inactivity, the LAN's capability would be wasted. Therefore, in LANs we use packet switching and the stations have exclusive access to the medium only while they are sending a packet. During the lulls, other nodes will have an opportunity to transmit. The problem of sharing access is reduced to that of providing some rules (*protocol*) that will periodically, and in a fair manner, allow each node on the network to send a packet.

The two most commonly used LANs are the Ethernet and the ''token ring'' from IBM. The *Ethernet* is one of the earliest LANs; it was designed at Xerox Palo Alto Research Center in 1976. The Ethernet consists of a single channel to which units are connected by interfaces [Fig. 2-9(a)]. The channel, the ''Ether,'' is a coaxial cable that serves as the bus to which all stations are connected.

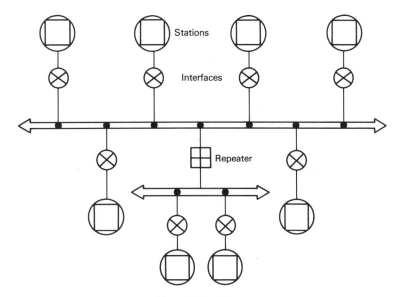

Figure 2-9   Ethernet

The interface is both a receiver and transmitter: It splits the messages into packets and sends them over the cable or scans the cable for packets addressed to its units and re-assembles the messages.

A node wishing to transmit first listens to the medium to determine if another transmission is in progress. If the medium is in use, the node backs off and tries again after some time. If the channel is idle, a node may transmit. Collisions may occur because other nodes may have also detected that the channel is idle and send data. In Ethernet, if the channel is busy, the node continues to listen in order to detect a collision. If a *collision* was detected, the transmission is aborted and rescheduled; thus, there are variable delays in transmission. This method of accessing the bus is called ''Carrier sense multiple access with collision detection.'' The sender must always be notified that its message was rejected. Because there may be a collision, a node waits a reasonable amount of time after transmitting for an acknowledgment, taking into account the maximum round-trip propagation delay. The node assumes that a collision has occurred and retransmits if there is no acknowledgment. After a transmission is established, it continues without interruption. There is no controller on the bus; the control of the network is distributed throughout the network nodes.

It is easy to extend an Ethernet. Hardware can protect the system from node failures, but a break in the transmission medium could be catastrophic. Reliability can be improved by using connections similar to those of Fig. 2-7.

The sending of many short packets reduces the efficiency of the network; therefore, the network will not function for packets smaller than a minimum packet size. For further reading see [HTW86 and Ta088].

The IBM token ring was developed at the IBM Zurich Laboratory and is based on the ''permission token principle.'' The computers are attached to the ring through interfaces [Fig. 2-9(b)]. The messages are transferred over the ring in the time-division, multiplexed way.

In a token ring, data are sent in the form of addressed blocks called *frames*. These variable-length frames, each bearing a source and destination address, are transmitted whenever a unit sends a message. The ring itself [Fig. 2-9(b)] is a high-speed, unidirectional digital communication channel such as a pair of twisted wires or a fiber-optics link. It uses a *token* to signify the availability of the medium for the transmission of data. A token circulates continuously on a free ring. Any station that has a frame to transmit may do so only after it captures this token. This guarantees that there will be no conflicts with other stations that also want to transfer data. Upon completion of its transmission, the station regenerates and transmits a new token.

Successful exploitation of a LAN requires that nodes involved in data transfer must agree to adopt the same conventions for exchanging information. These conventions, the *protocol*, are usually reserved for the diplomatic service, e.g., when presenting the accreditation papers, an ambassador has to doff the hat, bow three times, extend the hand, etc. Such protocols only determine the *manner*, not the substance, of the communications. As the LANs became popular, standards were needed to define how to implement the protocols. These standards simplify the interconnection of (partial) networks produced by different manufacturers and allow a customer to install a single network and attach to it equipment from different vendors. In addition, a standard supported by different vendors increases the competition, and makes the development of inexpensive VLSI chips feasible, all of which contribute to lower cost to the customer.

Standards divide the architecture of LANs into different levels of service built on top of each other. Each level provides a service for the level above it, and relies on the services of the layer directly below it. These services are called primitives and will typically contain a request to transmit a frame, establish a connection, or give an indication that a frame was received or that an error occurred. Each layer behaves as if it is communicating with the corresponding layers on the other sites. The guidelines for such virtual communication are the *protocols*. To the user, at the top of the hierarchy, the conversation with another user appears to be via a direct link. Actually this virtual connection uses all of the network layers. The direct link is at the bottom layer where there is an actual physical transmission medium connecting the nodes of the network.

The International Standards Organization's reference model for "Open System Interconnection" (OSI) defines the interconnection of devices in nonhomogeneous environments. The OSI model consists of seven layers of protocol of which the two important here are:

- *The physical layer* contains the physical interface between devices. It includes a specification of the mechanical and electrical characteristics of the physical connection and defines the manner in which bits are passed.
- *The data link layer* provides the means to activate, maintain, and deactivate the link. The control information contained in a packet is used by this layer to control access to the communication medium.

These two levels were adapted for the ring in the IEEE Standard 802.5. The data link level was split into the Logical Link Control, and Medium Access Control.

Addressable blocks of data are called frames. A frame is shown in Fig. 2-10(a). The information field of the frame is of variable length (up to a maximum) and contains the data to be transferred. The header consists of the two addresses and three bytes: a Starting Delimiter *SD*, which identifies the start of the frame, an Access Control, *AC*, to the transmission medium, and the Frame Control, *FC* byte. [Str87]†

The trailer consists of three subfields. First is a four-byte Frame Check Sequence (FCS) that is calculated by the source node and used for detecting errors that occur during transmission. The Ending Delimiter (ED) identifies the end of the frame. The Frame Status (FS) byte contains bits that are set by the destination node to indicate when it recognizes a frame addressed to the station, and whether or not it copied the frame.

The FCS uses the bit string as representing a polynomial, e.g., if it is 10110010, then the n-th degree polynomial is $x^7 + x^5 + x^4 + x^1$. The FCS is the remainder of dividing this polynomial modulo-2 by a predetermined generating polynomial. On receipt of a frame, the data stream is used to compute the FCS: If the computed checksum does not agree with the one received, the frame is discarded and no acknowledgment is returned.

In particular, the following bits are shown in Fig. 2-10(a):

†N.C. Strole, "The IBM token-ring network—a functional overview," *IEEE Network Magazine*, Vol. 1, No. 1, Jan. 1987, pp. 23–30 (© IEEE, 1987). Reprinted by permission.

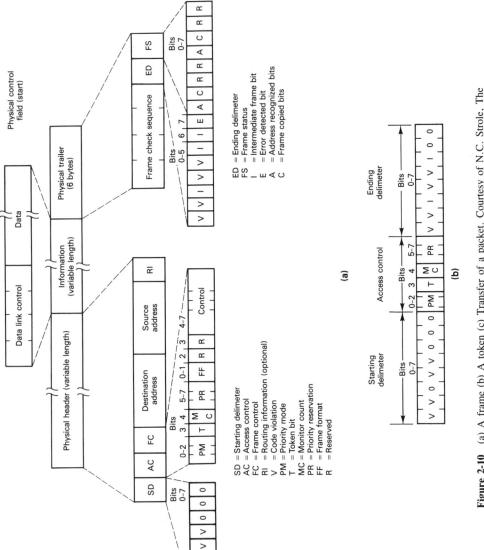

Figure 2-10 (a) A frame (b) A token (c) Transfer of a packet. Courtesy of N.C. Strole, The IBM Token-Ring Network. . . , IEEE Network Magazine, Vol.1, No. 1, pp. 23–30 (© 1987 IEEE)

SD = Starting delimeter
AC = Access control
FC = Frame control
RI = Routing information (optional)
V = Code violation
PM = Priority mode
T = Token bit
MC = Monitor count
PR = Priority reservation
FF = Frame format
R = Reserved

ED = Ending delimeter
FS = Frame status
I = Intermediate frame bit
E = Error detected bit
A = Address recognized bits
C = Frame copied bits

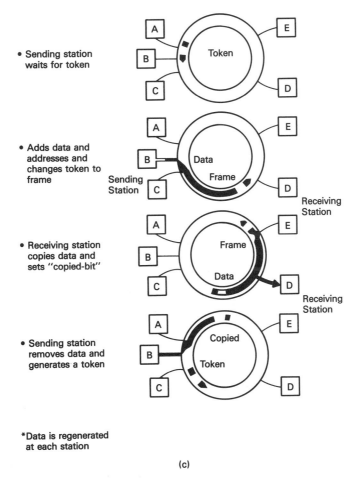

- Sending station waits for token

- Adds data and addresses and changes token to frame

- Receiving station copies data and sets "copied-bit"

- Sending station removes data and generates a token

*Data is regenerated at each station

(c)

Figure 2-10 *(cont'd)*

1. Priority mode bits (*PM*) indicate the priority assigned to the token, thereby providing multiple levels of access to the ring.

2. A Token bit (*T*) provides a mechanism for accessing the ring so that only one station can transmit at any given time.

3. A Monitor bit (*MC*) is used to detect errors associated with the token access protocols.

4. Reservation bits (*PR*) allow stations to request a higher priority token, thereby providing an interrupt mechanism associated with the different levels of access.

5. Frame Format Indicator bits (*FF*) enable the receiving node to determine whether the data is control (FF = 00) or user data (FF = 01).

6. An Error-Detected bit (*E*) provides a mechanism for isolating segments of the ring that have high transmission error rates.

7. An Address Recognized bit (*A*) allows a transmitting station to detect whether the intended receiver is currently active on the ring.

8. Frame Copied bits (*C*) allow a transmitter to detect whether the receiver is presently too busy.

The token is a combination of signals which no data message contains. It consists of three bytes [Fig. 2-10(b)], with the token bit set to zero. A station changes the token to a one to start transmission.

To allow collision-free communication, a token is passed around the ring. A node must accept the token before it can transmit data. Possession of the token gives permission to transmit, instead of having stations contend for this privilege as in the Ethernet.

The interface of the sender forms the frame, inserts into it the address of the destination, and sends it onto the ring followed by the token. Each interface checks the address and retransmits the message "downstream" if the address is not its own. Otherwise, it is received by the interface and sent to the attached processor (node).

In LANs, a node "sees" all passing traffic, but copies only those packets that contain its address. The sender's address is included so that the receiver will know where to send an acknowledgment, and the sender will know when to remove a frame.

With the token-access control scheme, a token circulates on the ring [Fig. 2-10(c)] giving each node, in turn, an opportunity to transmit data. Such a node would change the token to indicate it is now a frame, immediately following the AC byte, append the FC byte, the addresses, the RI field, the information field, and the trailer. The same node will remove the frame and send a token into the ring. Therefore, a node cannot transmit more than one frame, and all nodes have equal chances to transfer; when the load is heavy, each node in turn will send a frame. If a node completes the transfer of a frame before it receives its header, it will transmit 0s until it recognizes the header. This ensures that only one token or frame is on the ring at any time.

The *A*-bits are set when an address is recognized by a station, the *C*-bits, when the frame is copied by a node. If only the *A*-bits are set, the destination node is active but did not copy the frame.

The token is a part of the frame and travels with it around the ring. If the token is "on," this means that it is used; otherwise it is "off," which means that all fields of the packet are invalid and the transmission may occur. When an interface has a message to transmit, it checks the tokens until it finds one that is "off." The interface then sends the frame including an "on" token. When an interface has a message to receive, it checks the frames until it finds one with its address and accepts it. When an interface has neither a message to receive nor to send, it checks the frames for messages, and sends them on to the next interface. Obviously, collisions cannot occur, but variable delays can, and it may take longer than usual for a token to pass a station. The way a packet is sent by *B* to *D* is shown in Fig. 2-10(c), and is as follows: When *B* receives the token, it transmits its frame, which circulates around the ring until it reaches node *D*. This station will receive the frame by copying the data, mark it as "correctly received," and send it downstream.

When the frame arrives back at *B*, station *B* will interrogate the bits in the trailer of the frame, namely the Error-Detected (*E*), the Address-Recognized (*A*), and the Frame-Copied (*C*) bits to detect possible errors. The frame is then removed and a new token sent by *B*. The function of error recovery from lost frames is handled by the logical link control functions within the stations, or by higher level protocols. Otherwise the station could have only one frame outstanding at any given time. Queues are used to enable handling of priority requests.

The connections of a typical ring are shown in Fig. 2-11. It can be seen that the topology is that of a star-shaped ring. Physically, a number of interfaces are combined in *distribution panels*. The signals flow from a panel and back to it. The path traced by the signal is called a *lobe*, and the network is made up of a number of panels. The distribution panels have taps that provide a bidirectional link for the connection of "ring adaptors"

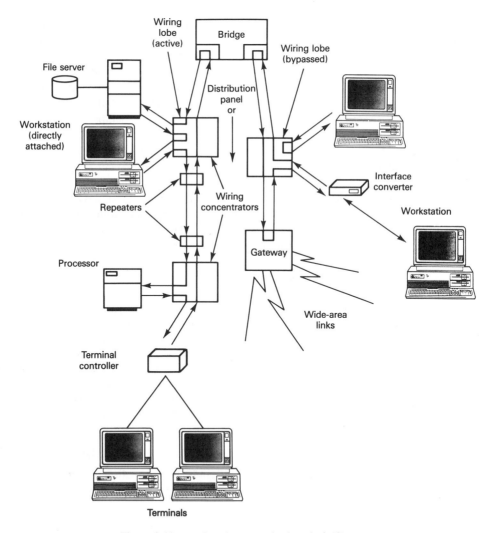

Figure 2-11   A token-ring network (© as in 2-10)

(interfaces). These adaptors may connect or disconnect a station by setting of relays. The primary functions of these adaptors are data transmission, token recognition, frame recognition, token generation, address decoding, error checking, buffering of frames, and link fault detection. Advances in VLSI technology make it possible to concentrate all functions in the adaptor, freeing the node itself for processing.

The panels provide points within the network that facilitate reconfiguration and maintenance, thus enhancing the reliability of the ring. A panel needs only enough power to activate the connection relays; otherwise it is a passive element of the ring. Fig. 2-11 also shows the "repeaters" needed to redrive the signals to the next downstream node, and a bridge used to connect two rings. Such a connection is needed when the distances between data processing centers are too large or when the number of stations on a ring are too large.

Each line in Fig. 2-11 depicts a transmission cable which supports full duplex communication; that is, information can be propagated in both directions at the same time. This means that there are two wire pairs or two fiber pairs in each line. The system is similar to the double-bus used to increase the reliability in Fig. 2-7.

If a device (which is connected to an adaptor) wants to be inserted into the ring, a relay in the distribution panel is activated to make the link. An adaptor contains the circuits necessary to control the exchange of data by manipulating the low-level token protocol.

The *misconceptions* about the ring are that it is not fast enough, cannot extend to enough distance, and most important, that it is unreliable. Let us discuss these points one by one.

Delays may result because on the average in a ring, a message travels through half of the nodes, reading of messages by stations introduces wait periods for stations downstream, and messages are purged by their senders. Also, if a node cannot find anything to keep itself busy while it is waiting for data to arrive, its resources will be idle. If data from other PaMs are often needed, then a large amount of computing power will be wasted. Despite this, R.C. Dixon points out that:

> The full duplex interface to each station on the ring allows stations to monitor the information being received from the upstream station and at the same time to modify the contents of the information before it is forwarded to the downstream station. This characteristic of a ring provides for a number of logical control channels paralleling the transfer of data. These are supported on the token ring through use of control bits located in the header and trailer portions of a frame. As a consequence, delays within each station to recognize control fields within a frame are not required. Furthermore, the token is released by the transmitting station when it has completed its transmission and has verified the source address in at least one received frame. [Dix87][†]

The new technology of optical fibers can be used in rings, but cannot be used with buses. The reason is that optical fibers can relay information only in one direction. While buses have a bandwidth of less than five Mbps (Mega-bits-per-second), if light-emitting

---

[†]R.C. Dixon, "Lore of the token ring," *IEEE Network*, Vol. 1, No. 1, Jan. 1987, pp. 11–18 (© IEEE, 1987). Reprinted by permission.

diodes are used as light sources, fibers can provide up to 150 Mbps, and if laser diodes are used, even higher speeds are possible. With time, these speeds will probably be increased; in short, the ring is fast.

Other characteristics of optical fibers of interest in LANs are as follows. A defective node in a ring should be bypassed. In systems using copper media, this can be done using a simple and inexpensive relay. Fiber optic bypass relays, however, are still under development and are still expensive. One of the major advantages of optical fibers over other media is their complete immunity to noise: because light is used, electromagnetic waves have no influence on it. As a side effect of this, optical fibers are almost impossible to tap.

With a single bus, a system failure can occur as the result of a malfunction in any part of the bus. Failure of a LAN can take two forms. First, an individual node can malfunction. As we have seen, it should then be bypassed. The second reason the ring is not considered a reliable IN is because any break or loss of power causes the ring to stop functioning. This is not so in the double ring since the ring does not disintegrate into two parts. Moreover, two ways of improving the reliability of the bus were shown in Fig. 2-7 and can be used in a ring. As seen next, reliability of a ring can be improved by other means as well.

There is always a single monitor station which has overall control of the ring and the token. At ring startup or when the ring loses its monitor station for any reason, the adaptor with the highest ring address takes over as the new monitor station. The monitor station generates the initial token, and provides the clock signals for the ring and some buffer functions.

One of the problems inherent in the token-passing access method is that of a continuously circulating packet. To solve it, a monitoring station inspects and sets bit *MC* as the packet passes at it. If the bit is already set, the packet must have gone around the ring more than once. This is an error indication and the monitor station will remove the packet and issue a new token.

The monitor function is always active in a single node of a ring. It can be performed by the ring interface adaptor of any node on the ring. It initiates the error recovery procedure if normal token operation is disrupted. A distortion of the receiver's address will either result in a message being delivered to the wrong receiver or the distorted message will keep circulating around the ring. The central monitor could remove such a circulating message. It can also deal with a broken cable (see below). A node may seize the token, transmit a frame, and then fail to remove it. Such a frame would then circulate for all times around the ring, making it unavailable to any of the nodes on the ring. Another type of error is where the token is destroyed. Both of these errors are handled by the monitor. We have already seen that the *MC*-bit prevents a frame from continuously circling around the ring. The monitor also maintains a timer which is reset by the passing of either a frame or a token. If the token is lost because of either interference or noise, then the timer expires and the ring is reinitialized by issuing a free token.

There are other faults which may be corrected. If noise produces an additional token, two stations could start transmitting simultaneously. Each of these stations would, however, detect a wrong source address and not re-issue a token and follow the same procedure as when the token is lost. If a frame is returned to a sending station, it is known whether it was copied by the receiver from the Address (*A*) and the Frame Copied (*C*) bits. The former informs the station that the destination exists on the ring and that it recognized its address in the frame. The latter tells whether the node received it. If there is a transmission error because of noise, etc., the Frame Checking Sequence (FCS) will detect it. The node that recomputed the FCS and found that it does not match the FCS in the frame will set the Error Detected (*E*) bit.

A break can occur either in the wiring lobe between a node and a panel or in the wiring between two panels. The failure of the receiver and/or transmitter of an active node can also cause a total disruption of the signal path. A hard fault is detected immediately by the next active node downstream from the fault as a loss of signal transitions at its receiver. This is corrected by *beacons*.

> When the cable used in a ring network is severed, a one-way connection path still exists between the nodes. One can take advantage of this fact in finding the location of the fault. If a station, by monitoring its input, detects a serious problem, it will employ a technique called beaconing. This involves repeatedly transmitting a network management packet addressed to all stations which contain the address of the node immediately upstream of it (i.e., the defective node/segment). In this way, the location of the fault can be determined and isolated. [Ta088]

The node that detects a fault transmits a unique frame known as a beacon. It includes the address of the beaconing node as well as the address of the active node immediately upstream. Since each node knows the address of this neighbor, all the active nodes except the beaconing node can receive and transmit normally. The adaptor that recognizes its address as being the beaconing node will remove itself or the node upstream from the ring.

> Once the general location of a fault (hard or soft) has been determined, some action is necessary to eliminate the faulty segment(s) from the ring so that normal operation can resume. The wiring concentrators provide centralized points for bypassing such faults. Alternate backup links are normally available between the wiring concentrators in parallel with the principal links (Fig. 2-12). If a fault occurs in the ring segment between two wiring concentrators, wrapping of the principal ring to the alternate ring within the two wiring concentrators restores the physical path of the ring. The concentrator's "ring in" and "ring out" connectors will wrap back to the alternate ring if the segment to the next upstream or downstream concentrator is disconnected. Figure 2-12 shows three wiring concentrators as they would be configured with both a principal and an alternate ring. The signals on the alternate ring propagate in the direction opposite to those on the principal ring, thus maintaining the logical order of the nodes on the ring. Consequently, configuration tables associated with the network management functions do not have to be altered. In addition to the procedure for bypassing faults, each node can perform self-diagnostic tests of its own circuitry and wiring lobe to ensure that it does not disrupt the signal path when it is inserted into the ring. If these tests indicate a potential problem, the node is not inserted into the ring until after the situation is remedied. [Str87]†

---

†N.C. Strole, "The IBM token ring network—a functional overview," *IEEE Network*, Vol. 1, No. 1, Jan. 1987, pp. 23–40 (© IEEE, 1987). Reprinted by permission.

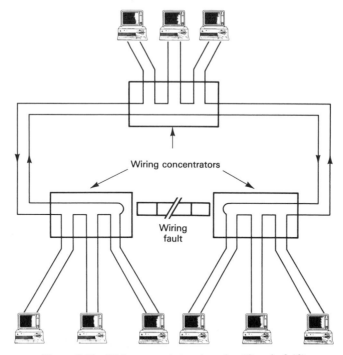

Figure 2-12   Wiring concentrators in a ring (© as in 2-10)

There are advantages in using the ring instead of the bus:

1. The speed is increased by having the interfaces instead of the computers pick up the messages and by using fiber optics. These lead to much higher speeds: Cable LANs have a transmission rate of 8Mbps; optical fiber technology may increase this to about 100 Mbps.

2. Optical fibers provide more security and safety, immunity to electromagnetic interference, and have reduced weight and size. Also, the use of optical fiber has significantly reduced the size, cost, and complexity of the hardware required by a LAN, except for the relays, which are more expensive.

3. The ring provides broadcast with every interface picking up the same message (one of the addresses means "every node"). A bit within the RI field of the frame is set whenever the frame must be broadcast. Broadcast will be shown to be very important for some parallel systems.

4. Blocks of data of up to a maximum size may be transferred by sending the messages in a train, with the destination removing them one by one, and sending the token so that the next message may be sent.

5. The physical addition or removal of stations from the network is relatively easy, since each link is an independent connection. Automatic failure isolation and

reconfiguration ensure that the ring is operative even while the connections are changed.

6. The routing algorithm is extremely simple.

2–3 MULTISTAGE INTERCONNECTION NETWORKS

2–3.1 Introduction

Several MINs for dynamically connecting input and output ports have been proposed. They are mostly asynchronous, decentralized, and use packet switching. A dedicated link exists between any two neighboring SEs that communicate with each other. A message generated at a source port may go through a number of intermediate stages of SEs before reaching the output port. The latency (transit time for a packet) increases in proportion to the number of stages. The routing control, so simple in a time-shared bus, may be very complicated in a MIN.

All processors can access memory simultaneously and in parallel provided that not more than one CPU is trying to take the same branch or link. This is somewhat more constraining than the condition that each CPU access a different MB, as required in the crossbar switch. Therefore, at least potentially, the contention in the MIN is more of a problem. However, since the price of the MIN grows linearly with p, while the complexity of the crossbar is $0(p^2)$, extra paths are used to reduce the contention. In this case, when two or more memory references collide at the output of a node, one can proceed while the others take alternate routes. By adding a single switching column (as will be done in Sec. 3-5), two independent paths are provided between every input and every output port. The overhead of providing alternate paths is minimal, so that whenever $p*m$ is large, a MIN is used.

Complexity of the network is directly proportional to the number of SEs used and the number of external links in the network. Accordingly, if the size of the SE is increased, then the number of SEs per stage will decrease. The larger size SEs with appropriate interconnection patterns can reduce the number of stages for the same number of ports. Reduction in the number of stages will reduce the number of external links. Altogether, it is beneficial to use larger size SEs. The Butterfly uses such 4-by-4 SEs and connects them in $\log_4$ stages each with $p/4$ switches per stage. Let us compare the two cases for $p = 16$. With 2-by-2 SEs, we need $\log(p) = 4$ stages each with $p/2 = 8$ SEs, so that 32 SEs are used. With 4-by-4 SEs, there are two stages with four SEs each, so that only eight SEs are used. If we assume that a 4-by-4 SE costs about twice as much as a 2-by-2 SE, the cost was decreased by 100% through the use of 4-by-4 SEs. So was the delay. As mentioned, the maximum size used is four. Even in this case, fewer messages pass a 4-by-4 than two 2-by-2 SEs.

2–3.2 The Ring

The simplest MIN for MP multicomputers is the ring. A single, unidirectional ring has a complexity of 2, a diameter of $p/2$, but a single fault may disable the ring. In the same way, as shown for buses in Sec. 2-2, the addition of a second ring will improve the

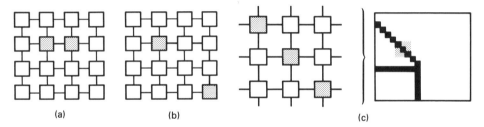

Figure 2-13 Mesh switching networks. Courtesy of C. Stanfill: "Communication Architecture in The Connection Machine (TM) System," Thinking Machine Corp., Technical Report Series, HA87-3, March 17.

availability, but the performance stays low because of bus interference. Even a multibus system cannot efficiently connect a large number of PMs.

2–3.3 Meshes

Figure 2-13 shows a mesh (called also a nearest-neighbor grid). It

has several advantages. First, it is easily laid out on two-dimensional boards and chips. Second, it allows very fast local communications [Fig. 2-13(a)]. Third, it scales indefinitely: It is practical to build a grid machine of nearly unlimited size. The disadvantage of a grid structure is that communication between nonadjacent processors may have to pass through a large number of intermediate processors [Fig. 2-13(b)].

Many algorithms have highly localized communication patterns: If the problem is embedded in a two- or three-dimensional grid, then a given computation will only need to access data in a small region of the grid. Algorithms for computer vision, such as line detectors, are particularly likely to exhibit this behavior. For example, if an image is represented as a grid of dots (pixels), lines may be detected by finding all dark pixels which have exactly two dark neighbors [Fig. 2-13(c)]. [Sta87][†]

The mesh is especially suitable for SIMD computers since, in a SIMD system, all active PEs must use the same connections at all times. It will be shown in Sec. 3-5 that for the "Massively Parallel Processor," the mesh was preferred to all other MINs.

2–3.4 Cubes

The most widely used MINs for MPs are the *Cube networks*. A three-dimensional ($d = 3$) *Binary-Cube* IN (*b*-cube) with $p = 2**d$ nodes is shown in Fig. 2-14. Since the longest distance between any two nodes of a Cube is d (distance), the longest distance a message must travel is only $\log(p)$. Note that each node is connected to d other nodes. For $d = 4$ or a Cube with $2^4 = 16$ nodes [Fig. 2-14(b)], each node is connected to four other nodes and the longest distance to another node is 4. Note also that the numbers assigned to two nodes differ by exactly one bit if and only if they are connected by a link and that every dimension of the Cube corresponds to a bit position in the address. In Fig. 2-14(a),

---

[†]C. Stanfill, "Communication Architecture in the Connection Machine™ System," Thinking Machine Corp., Technical Report Series, HA87-3, March 17, 1987. Reprinted by permission.

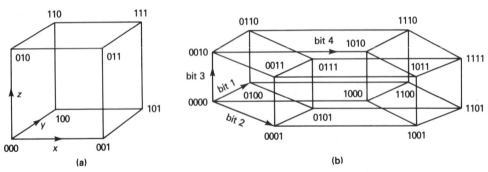

Figure 2-14 Hypercube switching networks. Courtesy of D. P. Bertsekas, J. N. Tsitsiklis, PARALLEL and DISTRIBUTED COMPUTATION (© 1989 Prentice Hall).

dimension x corresponds to the rightmost bit, dimension y corresponds to the leftmost bit, and dimension z corresponds to the middle bit. This correspondence can be generalized to any number of bits (any dimension), so that from the point of view of permutations, it is

$$\{b(p-1), \ldots, b(i), \ldots, b(1)\} => \{b(p-1), \ldots, b'(i), \ldots, b(1)\} \quad (2\text{-}9)$$

In a multicomputer, the average internode distance, the message traffic density, and the fault tolerance are dependent on the diameter and the complexity of a node. There exists a tradeoff between the two. The lower the complexity the higher the diameter, meaning that reducing the cost will increase the time delay in transferring the messages between the nodes. For instance, a completely connected structure with $p-1$ links per node has distance 1 between any two nodes, and no matter how many nodes fail it still remains connected. However, the high cost of $0[p*(p-1)]$ links and multiport connections limits the size of the PPS. This MIN, and the ring, remain extreme solutions, while the b-cube may be a reasonable balance between the two requirements. For the MIN of Fig. 2-14(b), both the complexity and the diameter are four.

B-cube MINs feature a simple algorithm for calculating the path of a message. The routing algorithm is as follows. First, for every message, find the *relative address* by taking the exclusive OR of the addresses of the sending and receiving nodes. Second, send the message over any unused link corresponding to a 1 in the relative address. If no such link can be found, put the message in a buffer. If no buffer is available, send the message over any free wire. Third, whenever a message passes the link, the corresponding bit in the relative address is inverted. Finally, when the relative address contains all 0's, the message has reached its destination. If a message is to go from 000 to 110 in Fig. 2-14(a), the number of bits in which they differ and the distance is 2. Moreover, since there are a number of ways for this, the b-cube is highly fault-tolerant. The route would be $000->100->110$ and the relative address would be $110->010->000$.

An advantage of the b-cube network is that it can be partitioned so that each of its subnetworks is independent of the others. The requirement for this is that the addresses of all the ports in a partition of size $2**i$ agree in $s-i$ of their bit positions. For example, the network of size eight of Fig. 2-14(a) can be partitioned into two subnetworks, each of size four. The division corresponds to two b-cubes, each of four nodes. Group A consists of ports 0 to 3. Group B consists of ports 4 to 7. All ports in group A or group B agree in the high-order bit position (it is 0 and 1 respectively). Two other ways of partitioning this network into two independent networks of $p = 4$ are based on setting other bits. Each subnetwork is a b-cube network and can be subdivided further (see Problem 15).

To summarize, the b-cube has the advantages of a short delay [log(p)], efficient work with a partitioning corresponding to the "knee" in Fig. 1-2, high reliability if alternate routes are provided, and a simple and decentralized routing algorithm. However, if a cube is assembled and is to be expanded later, additional links are needed. Changing from dimension d to $d + c$ requires additional c links; therefore, old boards (chips) would have to be replaced. By comparison, to expand a mesh, all that is necessary is to add units to the perimeter without replacing those in the old mesh. Another disadvantage is that the number of ports in a b-cube is log(p). Both the cube-connected cycles and the trees are helpful in eliminating this disadvantage.

The Cube-connected cycles network (*c-cube*) is similar to the b-cube except that each node of the d-dimensional cube is replaced by a cycle (ring) of i nodes [Fig. 2-5(i)]. With d split as $d = s - r$, the p PaMs are arranged in 2**d rings of 2**$r - 1$ nodes. As r becomes larger or smaller, the number of connections per node decreases or increases, and the scheme becomes more b-cube-like or ring-like. The cycles are numbered 0 to $j - 1$ and the nodes are numbered from 0 to $i - 1$. Each node has the same number of connections, namely three (generally i). Let us take two examples. In the figure $s = 5$ and $r = 2$, so $d = 3$ and there are eight rings of size 3 each, or 8*3 = 24 nodes. If $s = 6$ and $r = 2$, then the dimension of the cube is $d = 4$; there are 16 rings of size 3 each.

Performance analysis yields a running time of $0(s - r) + 0(2**r)$. Since a c-cube of p nodes performs a computation in time $0(p)$, the first term corresponds to the b-cube, the second to the ring. r should be chosen to allow a good c-cube performance and reduce the interconnection complexity. If s, r are chosen so that $(r - 1) + 2**(r - 1) \leq s \leq r + 2**r$, then the first $\leq$ ensures the efficient c-cube performance of $0(s)$ and the second $\leq$ ensures that enough processors are on each ring. Therefore, only one connection per processor is needed to connect the ring to the cube and the number of connections per processor is less than four.

The Dual-Cube MIN, d-cube proposed in [Sin87][†] warrants a closer look despite the fact that it is basically a blocking network. However, it has full-access capability which guarantees connectivity between all the input and output ports and uses a 4-by-4 SE like the Butterfly, and especially because it has very good fault tolerance properties.

There are four Input and four Output ports, and two control lines, C(1) and C(2). Fig. 2-15(a) shows the input/output mappings for different control settings.

When the C_1 and C_2 control lines are connected together (i.e., if the same input is given to both control terminals), this SE is transformed into two separate 2-by-2 SEs as shown in Fig. 2-15(b). Terminals (0,3) and (1,2) act as two separate SEs which are connected through when $C(1) = C(2) = 1$. This is why the name "Dual SE" (DE) was coined for it. However, the use of a DE as two units of 2-by-2 SEs is neither advisable nor advocated as this will increase the number of stages required, and thus the advantages of increase in computational speed and reliability will be lost.

[†]Kuldip Singh, "DCMIN—A new interconnection network topology for parallel processing," Ph.D. Thesis, Roorkee (India), April 1987. Reprinted by permission.

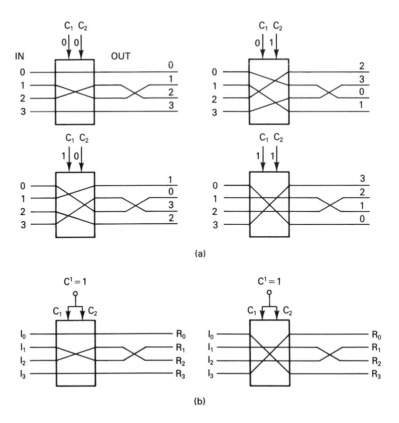

Figure 2-15 Dual-cube switching networks. Courtesy of Dr. K. Singh from his Ph.D. Thesis.

One possible gate level realization of a DE is shown in Fig. 2-15(c). Because of the circuit symmetry and regular structure, it can be represented in terms of multiplexers, etc. The following are the features of a DE:

1. The circuits connecting gates are repetitive in nature.

2. The conventional 2-by-2 SE has two levels of gates whereas DE has three levels. To achieve 4-by-4 connections using 2-by-2 SEs, one would need 4 levels of gates. However, due to the increased component density of integrated circuits, the individual gate delay becomes an insignificant fraction of the total module-switching delay. Thus, in general the module-switching delay is considered as a single parameter to model the delay of the SE.

3. Any arbitrary input can be connected to any arbitrary output by changing the control signal combinations of C_1, C_2 (i.e., by changing the control signals to appropriate mode).

4. The use of DEs in the conventional IN will reduce the total number of modules required. Also, incorporation of 4-shuffle permutations with DEs reduces the number of stages and external links for networks of any size p.

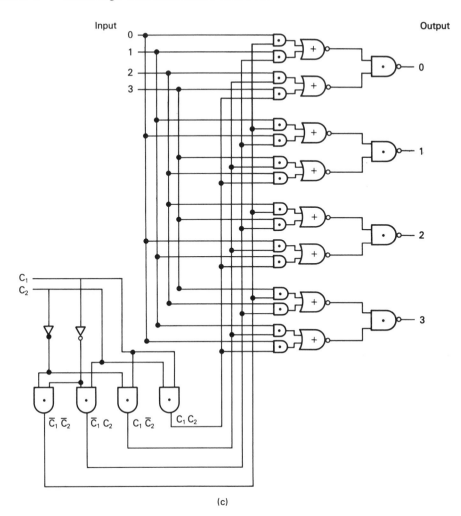

(c)

Figure 2-15   (*cont'd*)

Thus, DE is a potentiaı alternative to 2-by-2 SEs which should improve reliability and reduce complexity (of the MIN). [Sin87]

The design of a *d*-cube using DEs will be developed using an example shown in Fig. 2-16 to which the following observations are made:

1. This *d*-cube has $p = 16 = 4^2$ ports and the dimension and number of stages equal 2. Generalizing, we postulate that $d = s = \log(p)$ on base 4.
2. Each stage has $p/4$ DEs.
3. Since a DE is a 4-by-4 network, the following steps are involved in developing a 16-by-16 *d*-cube from a 4-by-4 *d*-cube:

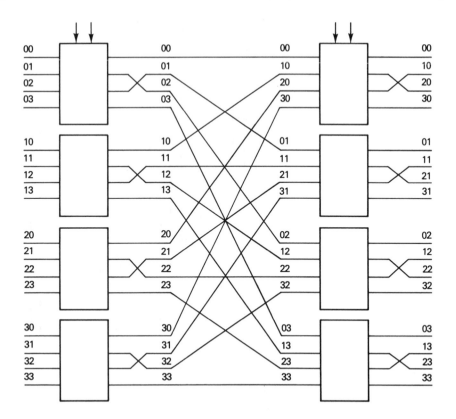

Figure 2-16 Dual-cube switching networks. Courtesy of Dr. K. Singh from his Ph.D. Thesis.

(a) Four single-stage *d*-cubes are stacked one over the other.
(b) In addition, 4**(2 − 1) DEs are stacked one over the other and connected as an additional stage.
(c) The two stacks of step 1 and step 2 are connected through a four-to-four shuffle permutation.

The above observations on Fig. 2-16 can be readily used to develop a network of size $p = 4^3 = 64$ in the following steps:

1. $p = 64 = 4^3$ suggests that the network should have three stages.
2. Each stage should have $p/4 = 16$ DEs.
3. Four units of 4-by-4 *d*-cubes should be stacked one over the other.
4. Sixteen DEs should be stacked to form the last stage.
5. Stacks of step 3 and 4 should be connected through a four-shuffle permutation of size 64-by-64.

One of the advantages of *any cube network* is that it can be changed into other networks. Imbedded in a *b*-cube is a ring with additional links (as illustrated in Fig. 2-17(a) for $p = 8$). Another imbedded MIN is the two-dimensional *mesh* network shown in Fig. 2-17(b). The network allows PE(i) to send data to any one of PE($i - 1$), PE($i + 1$), PE($i + k$), and PE($i - k$) where $k = \sqrt{p}$ and the arithmetic is done in modulo p (k is assumed to be an integer).

2–3.5 Other MINs

The Omega network.   Lawrie [Law75] introduced a network [Fig. 2-18] for ARPs and in particular for ILLIAC. An *n*-by-*n* Omega network consists of *d* identical states, where each stage is a perfect shuffle or inverse shuffle followed by a column of $n/2$ 2-by-2 SEs under independent control. The SEs say f and g in Fig. 2-18 may be interchanged without changing the links connecting them.

In the Omega network, broadcasting is possible because each SE can broadcast its input to both its outputs. For instance, input 2 can be broadcast to all outputs by setting SEs e and f to lower broadcast and c, i, j, k, and l to upper broadcast (see the solid lines in Fig. 2-18).

As noted, the Omega network has an efficient control scheme. Entering from any input, the bits of the desired output port (in binary) are used to control the successive stages of the MIN. If the bits are 00, then the upper output of the SE is taken; if they are 11, then the lower output is taken. This applies even if two-function SEs are used.

The Omega network is highly blocking: any single path immediately blocks many other connections. From a hardware standpoint, the limited capability results in a lower cost since fewer SEs are needed. It is a very useful MIN since the relatively few connections it can make are precisely those that are needed. Even though not all permutations are possible, any output can be reached from any input. Finally, the control algorithm mentioned above allows the connections to be established very fast (time $= \mathbf{0}[\log(n)]$).

The Butterfly network.   It was already mentioned that 2-by-2 SEs are not the only ones in use; the Butterfly (Fig. 2-19) computer uses 4-by-4 switches implemented by custom VLSI chips. Since they yield 16 instead of four I/O combinations, fewer stages are required; this in turn reduces the delay of transferring a packet. The switch as used in the Butterfly computer is described in more detail in Sec. 4-3.

The Baseline network.   This network was introduced in [Wu978] and shown to be equivalent to the Staran network, the Omega network, the indirect binary *n*-cube, the SW banyan network, and the modified data manipulator.

The topology of a Baseline network is generated in a recursive way. Initially, we connect a *p*-by-*p* block with two ($p/2$)-by-($p/2$) subblocks through a perfect shuffle. Next, these subblocks are divided in the same way into two ($p/4$)-by-($p/4$) blocks each. After $[\log(p) - 1]$ such steps, only 2-by-2 SEs result and the network consists of $\log(p)$ stages.

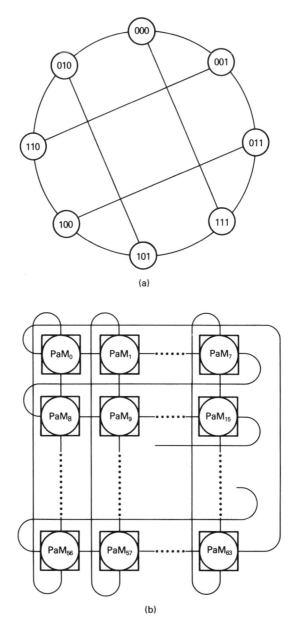

Figure 2-17 A Hypercube changed into a mesh or ring

2–3.6 Trees

In a directed graph, for any node v, the number of arcs that have v as their initial node is called the *outdegree* of node v. The number of arcs that have v as their terminal node is called the *indegree* of v. A tree is a directed graph such that every node (except one, called

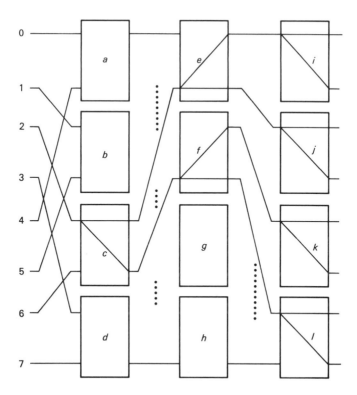

Figure 2-18   An Omega switching network

the *root*) has exactly one arc incident on it (indegree = 1). A node that has outdegree 0 is called a *leaf*. The *level* of any node is the length of the path from the root to this node, with the level of the root being 0.

The tree is normally drawn as in Fig. 2-20 with the root up in the sky and all nodes of a given level on a horizontal line. Borrowing terminology from family trees, we call every node reachable from a node its *descendant*; if a single arc is connecting them, its *children*. If the outdegree of every node is m, the tree is called an m-nary (complete) tree. For $m = 2$, it is a *binary tree* defined as follows:

1. A binary tree is either empty or consists of the root with possibly two children, the "left" and "right" child, each of which can be the root to a subtree.
2. A binary tree with $2**k - 1$, $(k > 0)$ nodes and k levels is called a complete tree, if all leaf nodes appear on level k.

All internal nodes of a binary tree have two children and one parent and thus a constant complexity of three. The complexity of the root is two, and of the leafs it is one.

The advantage of the tree topology is its constant *fanout*. Fanout is defined in combinational circuits as the number of signals leaving a gate. If the fanout should not be above ten, but more signals have to be sent, gates can be added to a tree-like structure.

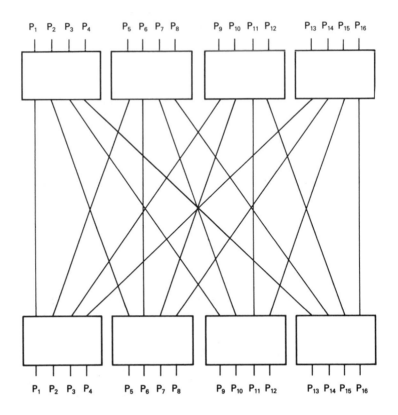

Figure 2-19 A Butterfly switching network

One gate can drive ten buffers, each of which drives ten more, and so on, until the desired fanout is achieved.

Consider the tree of Fig. 2-20(a). It has $L = 2**d = 8$ leafs, $2*L - 1 = 15$ nodes $(8 + 4 + 2 + 1 = 2^3 + 2^2 + 2^1 + 2^0 = 2^4 - 1 = 16 - 1 = 15)$, and $2*L - 2$ or 14 links. Note that each node needs to handle at most two messages, and that the size of the

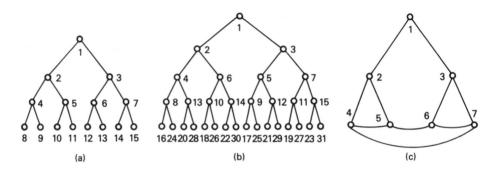

Figure 2-20 Tree-connected switching networks

nodes (PaMs) need not be too large. The disadvantages of the tree are that the internal structure has to be stored, thus "wasting" memory space. They also waste time: A node must send data through the tree before the data can be communicated to the connected nodes. This internal communication latency requires $\mathbf{0}[\log(d)]$ message transmission steps, where d is the degree of the nodes (a balanced tree is assumed). If a link fails, two subtrees are produced with PEs communicating only inside a subtree. Binary trees are very useful as INs since, as was noted in [MaC80], the chips forming it can easily be manufactured. They are also important for some parallel algorithms (Sec. 6-4).

Other advantages are mentioned on pp. 140–143 of [DeC89]. In terms of the IN, the most important feature is how messages can be routed through the tree. Many algorithms have been proposed for moving a packet from the root down. For (the more difficult) routing between two nodes i and j ($i/=j$), two algorithms were defined in Horowitz and Zorat:

> Node i compares the destination address of the message (j) to its own address (i); if they are equal, the message is "consumed" at node i. Otherwise, the message is transferred to a neighbor of i, on its way to the final destination j.
> The neighbor of i to which to send the message is selected by checking if j is in the left [right] subtree of i, in which case the message will be sent to the left [right] child of i. If j is not in the subtree rooted in i, the message will be sent to the parent of i. [HaZ81]†

The nodes are numbered so that the left child of node i is numbered $2*i$, the right child is $2*i+1$. Such a tree is shown in Fig. 2-20(a) and each node should be numbered in binary with p, and q being the number of bits necessary to express the node numbers. Then, j is in the left [right] subtree of i *iff* the following conditions are all satisfied.

1. $p < q$
2. Binary i equals binary j divided by $2**(q-p)$
3. The bit in position $q-p-1$ of j is 0 [is 1]

The division may be done by shifting the number $q-p$ bits to the right. Suppose that $i = 7 = 0111$ sends a message to $j = 12 = 1100$. For i, only $p = 3$ bits, but for j, $q = 4$ bits are needed. $12/2 = 6$ does not equal 7 so the parent of i, node $i = 3 = 0011$ is chosen. Next, $p = 2$, and $12/4 = 3$ so that 12 is in the left subtree of 3; it is even in the left subtree of node 6.

An alternate numbering scheme for binary trees [HaZ81] does not require the shifting of the value of j before the comparison.

> Starting at the root as one, we interpret going left as replacing the high-order bit by zero, while going right is interpreted as leaving it at one. Then, a new high-order bit of one is

appended. For example, the binary tree with five levels would be numbered as in Fig. 2-20(b). If $i = [x(p-1), \ldots, x(0)]$ as before, then $x(p-1) = 1$ for all nodes and

$$\text{parent}(i) = [1, x(p-3), \ldots, x(0)], \text{ left}(i) = [1, 0, x(p-2), \ldots, x(0)]$$
$$\text{and right}(i) = [1, 1\ x(p-2), \ldots, x(0)].$$

We call this numbering scheme even-odd numbering because of its obvious effect of splitting the even- and odd-numbered nodes into two separate subtrees.

Under the even-odd numbering scheme, j is in the left [right] subtree of i if and only if the following three conditions hold.

1. $p < q$
2. $[x(p-2), \ldots, x(0)] = [y(p-2), \ldots, y(0)]$
3. $y(p-1) = 0\ [y(p-1)=1]$ [HaZ81]

As an example, compare $i = 9 = 1001$ [Fig. 2-20(b)] with $j = 17 = 10001$ and $j = 25 = 11001$. Since $p = 3$ and $q = 4$, we have $p < q$ and the rightmost bits are 01 for both, the first two conditions check. Since $y(3) = 0$ for 17, but 1 for 25, the first is on the left, the second on the right of 9.

A route from a node i to node j is unique in a tree. Therefore, any fault along a path will cause some nodes to be unreachable. Various schemes for adding links were proposed. One of them is the *completely linked* binary tree [Fig. 2-20(c)]. It "is a graph produced by taking a full binary tree, connecting all leaf nodes to their neighbors and connecting the first and last node on the bottom level to each other." [HaZ81]

It is shown in [HaZ81] that in such trees when the degree of each node is 3 (including the root, if the connection to the host is also counted), that it can be produced on a single chip and that two trees can easily be combined into a single, larger tree. An algorithm for processing a message is also given.

Tree networks have the least number of links for interconnecting a given set of nodes, can be used for both circuit and packet switching, have a low diameter and fixed degree, and a good internode distance. However, any fault at the root disables the system; hence, the structure is highly vulnerable to system failure. There is also a high traffic density at the root. Various INs sporting additional links or roots (e.g., the fat trees or the Banyan trees) were suggested to improve their performance.

Because the root may become a communication bottleneck, we sometimes use *Fat Trees* [Fig. 2-21(a)]. They add

extra communication paths at the higher levels of the tree. For example, the first and second levels might be connected by single wires, the second and third levels by double wires, the third and fourth by quadruple wires and so forth. All computation takes place at the leafs of the tree. The interior nodes switch signals between the various channels connecting them. One advantage of fat trees is that, by varying the number of wires at each level, a family of architectures suitable for a variety of different applications can be generated. [Sta87][†]

[†]C. Stanfill, "Communication Architecture in the Connection Machine™ System," Thinking Machine Corp., Technical Report Series, #A87-3, March 17, 1987. Reprinted by permission.

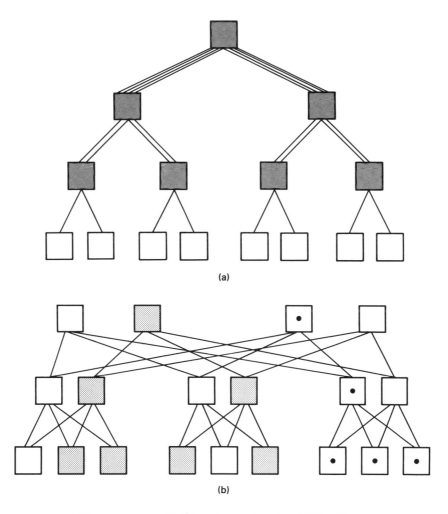

(a)

(b)

Figure 2-21   (a) A fat tree (b) A Banyan tree. Courtesy of C. Stanfill: "Communication Architecture in the Connection Machine (TM) System," Thinking Machine Corp., Technical Report Series, HA87-3, March 17.

The fat tree has a cost of $p*\log(p)$ and an average time of $\log^2(p)$.

Another solution to the bottleneck problem is to use multiple roots. Trees with multiple roots do exist; they are called "Banyan trees" [Fig. 2-21(b)]. A Banyan Interconnection Network (a BIN) is a generalization of a tree having multiple roots but retaining the property that it can create subnetworks that are trees. It also retains other desirable properties of tree INs.

All BINs have the property that for any root $R(i)$, the subgraph leading to all leafs $L(j)$s is a tree and vice versa. Thus, trees provide movement control for packets and a minimum path for circuit switching. Also, a disjoint set of trees can be created in a BIN by a very efficient algorithm [GaL73] that is capable of avoiding faulty nodes. There is a rich

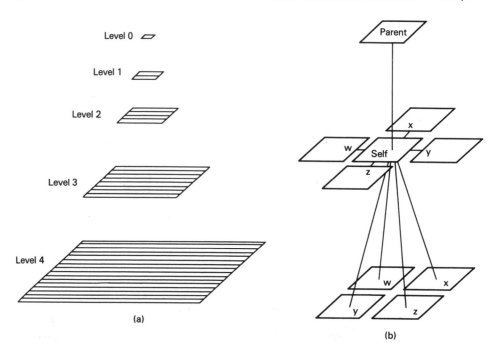

Figure 2-22 The GAM pyramid. Courtesy of D. H. Schaefer et al: "The GAM Pyramid," on pp. 15–42 of L. Uhr (Ed): "Parallel Computer Vision," Academic Press, Inc.

literature on graphs and trees. A good summary of it can be found in [LaM87]. The best known tree-structured PPS is the HM^2p [SLS82].

2–3.7 Pyramids

The pyramid-like IN [Fig. 2-5(j)] was first proposed for the EGPA [Bea85] to be used for numerical simulation. The lowest A-level of nodes is connected as a mesh with each four nodes connected to a higher level by links.

As an example of a pyramid topology used for image processing, the GAM pyramid [Sea87][†] as built at George Mason University is shown in Fig. 2-22. The nodes chosen at the lowest level were the same as used by NASA for its MPP computer (Sec. 3-5) and commercially available chips were used for higher levels. Altogether it uses 341 nodes in a pyramid of five levels with the dimensions 1x1, 2x2, 4x4, 8x8, and 16x16 respectively. Each node has nine connections to its neighbors [Fig. 2-22(b)] as follows: one parent, four siblings (north, east, west, and south), and four children.

Generally, the location of each node is defined as a triple $<k,i,j>$ such that k is the "level," i is the "row," and j is the "column." The number of nodes in a level is $4**k$. Level 0 consists of only the "root" at $<0,0,0>$. Each node has neighbors on three levels: on its level k, on one level above $(k-1)$, and one below $(k+1)$. This excludes the root,

---

[†]D.H. Schaefer et. al., "The GAM Pyramid," in [Uhr87], pp. 15–42 (© Academic Press, 1987). Quoted by permission.

but if "dummy" nodes are added at the highest level [0 of Fig. 2-22(a)], then it does apply to this level as well. Each cell $<k,i,j>$ may have up to 13 neighbors as follows:

$$<k-1,\lfloor i/2 \rfloor,\lfloor j/2 \rfloor> \quad <k,i-1,j-1> \quad <k,i-1,j> \quad <k,i-1,j+1>$$

$$<k,i,j-1> \quad <k,i,j+1> \quad <k,i+1,j-1> \quad <k,i+1,j> \quad <k,i+1,j+1>$$
$$<k+1,2i,2j> \quad <k+1,2i,2j+1> \quad <k+1,2i+1,2j> \quad <k+1,2i+1,2j+1>$$

Each node has three siblings. These siblings are the remaining children of the common parent node. To find them, either bit i or bit j has to be complemented. This means that (i,j) has the three siblings: (i,j''), (i',j), and (i',j'). These expressions can be used for control.

2–4 PERFORMANCE AND COMPARISON

Several terms are needed in order to discuss the performance of INs. Memory bandwidth BW is the average number of active MBs in a transfer cycle of a synchronous IN. By active we mean that a PE successfully performs a memory operation (read or write). The bandwidth BW takes into account the connection for the MBs. In asynchronous operation, the throughput T is defined as the average number of packets delivered by the IN in unit time, or the mean number of memory access completions per unit time. Processor utilization υ is defined as the expected percentage of time that the PE is active, i.e., is computing without having to access the global memory. Summing the utilization of all PEs yields the processing power of the PPS; υ is therefore a good measure of performance. It was computed as

$$\upsilon = B/(p*\lambda*t) \text{ and } \upsilon = T/\lambda \tag{2-10}$$

for synchronous and asynchronous operation with λ being the memory request rate and t the time of a read or write operation [BYA89].

The bandwidth of a crossbar switch was computed in [BYA89] as

$$B = m*[1-(1-P/m)^p] \tag{2-11}$$

where a PE generates a request to each MB with probability P.

A simple explanation of this formula is the following: Since P/m is the probability that a PE requests a particular MB, $(1-P/m)**p$ is the probability that none of the p PEs requests the MB in a particular cycle. Subtracting this term from one gives the probability that at least one request to this MB is issued. Multiplying by m yields the expected number of distinct MBs being requested in a cycle, and hence the bandwidth. The maximum percentage of error with this approximation is limited to 8% for $m/p > 0.75$ [BYA89]

and is therefore widely used for predicting the performance of crossbar switches.

The performance of multibus INs is usually based on the assumption that a PE addresses any one of the MBs with the same probability. It is shown in [DaB85] that, in that case, the multibus has almost the same performance as the crossbar switch for $b < p$.

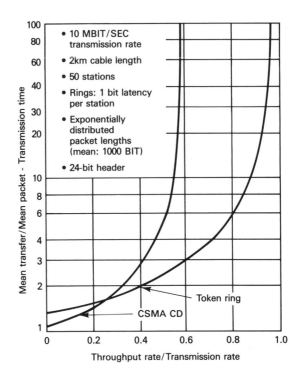

Figure 2-23 Transmission time as function of transmission rate. Courtesy of N. C. Strole, The IBM Token-Ring Network . . . , IEEE Network Magazine, Vol. 1, No. 1, pp. 23–30 (© 1987 IEEE).

Comparing the prices, the number of arbiters should be included. A crossbar switch requires m 1-of-p, MINs require $p*\log(p)$ 1-of-2 arbiters, while multibus switches require a single b-of-m and m 1-of-m arbiters. Again, the multibus is less expensive than the crossbar.

The performance comparison between an Ethernet and a token ring are discussed in [Str87] and summarized in Fig. 2-23.

> . . . the overall token ring throughput characteristics are superior to contention bus protocols for a wide range of frame sizes and physical transmission distances. Specifically, the token ring is not susceptible to collisions, and therefore bandwidth loss, as is the contention-based protocol. This allows a token ring to span a larger distance at greater speeds. . . . The throughput of the token ring and the other protocols are comparable for large frames, but the Ethernet protocol is very sensitive to the ratio of the frame transmission time to the network propagation delay. Thus, their efficiency is reduced for small frames and relatively long propagation delays. [Str87][†]

[†]N.C. Strole, "The IBM token ring network—a functional overview," *IEEE Network*, Vol. 1, No. 1, Jan. 1987, pp. 23–30 (© IEEE, 1987). Reprinted by permission.

The performance and reliability of bus-based INs are discussed in Sec. 3-2 of [DeC89]. Comparison of INs leads to the following.

The *time-shared bus*:

1. Is the most inexpensive and least complex.
2. With many PEs, when a PE attempts to access the bus, it must get permission from other PEs. Arbitration among the PEs leads to contention and the more PEs there are, the worse it gets; the bus becomes a bottleneck. Still for ASP, both a bus [TaW78] and a ring can be used (for $p < 20$).
3. Units can be added (modifying the system configuration), but scalability is limited by contention for the bus.
4. As shown, the reliability can be enhanced by adding a second bus.

The *multibus network* is:

1. More expensive than a single bus but much less than a crossbar.
2. Well suited for modifying system configurations (e.g., adding units).
3. The contention is low, and its performance is almost the same as that of the much more expensive crossbar switch.
4. Its reliability is sufficiently high.
5. Its control is very simple.
6. Originally it was using circuit-switching, but it was later determined that message switching is more appropriate for it.

The *crossbar switch*:

1. Is the most complex and the most expensive interconnection system. It is cost-effective only for multiprocessors.
2. May usually be expanded without reprogramming. Expansion is limited only by the size of the crossbar switch which itself may be expanded within engineering limits.
3. Has potentially the highest transfer rates, but a number of problems developed in PPSs that used them.
4. Is as reliable as the switch (which is not much).

Crossbar switches are a good choice in cases like the C.mmp where a relatively small number of rather powerful CPUs and MBs are interconnected (say $p < 20$). In such cases, it may even be less costly than some of the MINs. For higher numbers of PEs it is the most expensive IN, so much so that other switches are used in most multiprocessors.

The multiport system:

1. Uses the most expensive memory units, but is still less expensive than the crossbar switch.

2. Is limited in size and configuration by the number and type of memory ports.

3. Has the potential for high transfer rates.

4. Requires no special switching circuitry but requires a large number of cables and connectors. Its overall reliability is not as high as that of the multibus, but is higher than the other two INs.

Based on this comparison, the following choices are advocated: A single or dual ring may be used in an ASP, and a crossbar switch or multibus switch may be used in shared-memory multiprocessors. Pyramids are especially suitable for image processing. DIRMU attempts to adapt its topology to the problem at hand and uses multiport MBs. If the changing of the topology could be effected by software, it would be an excellent choice for SMs with $p \leq 30$. For higher p, fat trees, Butterflies, and Cubes are a good compromise between escalating cost and deteriorating performance: Their cost per PE grows as $p*\log(p)$, and their latency increases as $\log^2(p)$. The choice is governed by engineering and board layout concerns. In practice, Butterflies are used in SMs, while Cubes are used for MP-multiprocessors. The Omega network was designed for ARPs, but mostly meshes are used, at least for data-parallel applications (MPP). The reasons are that a mesh is a good choice whenever the problem is also regular, e.g., in image processing, that it is relatively inexpensive and that both meshes and trees can be extended to arbitrary sizes, but their topology limits the communication patterns to either local or some regular patterns. The maximum latency of the mesh is high: $\sqrt{p}$. Cubes are used for the CM.

2–5 PROBLEMS

1. Give the reasons why a bus, crossbar, and MINs are normally used for p less than or equal to 6, 20, and 10^5 respectively.

2. What control schemes of a bus do you know and what are their advantages and disadvantages?

3. Describe the various rings. How do you improve their reliability?

4. The policy of bus allocation in a multibus IN according to [MHW87] is:
   "(a) Memory conflicts are resolved first by m 1-to-p arbiters, one per MB. Each 1-to-p arbiter selects one request from up to p requests to get access to the MB.
   (b) Memory requests selected by the memory arbiters are then allocated a bus by a b-of-m arbiter. The b-of-m arbiter selects up to b requests from the m memory arbiters."
   Run (paper) simulations to convince yourself that this policy works.

5. Design the digital logic circuit for the arbiters of problem 4 as used by multibus INs of Sec. 2-2 according to [PFL75] and [LaV82].

6. What SEs do you know and how are they controlled? Write down the various permutations and networks using set-theoretical considerations. Define degree and diameter of a MIN. Calculate it for known cases.Characterize the various MIN networks. List the advantages and disadvantages of circuit vs. packet switching.

7. Draw the Benes and Omega MINs. What are the differences? What control schemes of MINs do you know and what are their advantages and disadvantages? How do you control the MINs of Fig. 2-3, so that inputs 0 to 3 are transferred to outputs 0 to 3?

8. You are working at a company that has a ring network connecting 16 computers. The network supports broadcast (sending a message to all computers at once). The exchange of data between

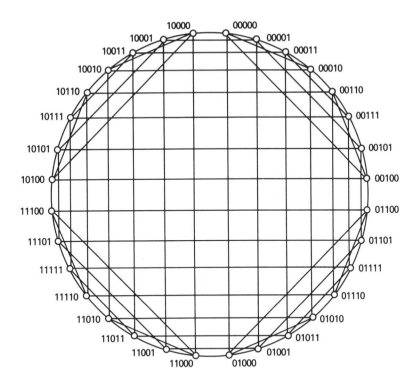

Figure 2-24 A ring-connected switching network

nodes is by messages. You have several algorithms that work using a b-cube IN. Describe how you would implement these b-cube algorithms on your company's network, without changing the computation part.

9. Assume that your company just doubled the number of computers on the network. You now receive complaints about the response time. What solutions would you suggest to eliminate this problem?

10. Why are buffers needed? Draw two possibilities of utilizing them. Extend the buffers to a 4-by-4 SE such as used in the Butterfly.

11. Change a three-dimensional and four-dimensional cube into corresponding meshes. Why is the first more difficult? Draw the connections of the SEs for the two MINs.

12. A cube can be changed not only into a mesh but also into an "extended ring" like the one shown in Fig. 2-24 for $d = 5$. The multiport connection can also be made into an extended ring. Using the fact that in DIRMU each CPU and each memory of a node may be connected to seven other nodes, redraw Fig. 2-24 so that use is made of all seven (instead of only five) cables. How do the cube and multiport MINs compare?

13. Compare the cube, tree, and pyramid MINs. Connect a b-cube using 2-by-2 SEs (see [SaM81]). Do the same for the c-cube.

14. Divide the cube of Fig. 2-14(b) into three- and two-dimensional cubes.

15. Draw a Hypercube with $p = 2**6 = 64$ nodes as a two-dimensional picture (eight rows and eight columns of nodes are to be connected as a Cube).

CHAPTER 3

ARRAY
PROCESSORS

We have now discussed the elements of Parallel Processors (PPSs) and will review the simplest of them, the Array Processors (ARPs) in more detail. The objectives of this chapter are therefore to review:

The supercomputers, especially the CRAY-1, classified previously as Vector Processors (VPs).

Peripheral Array Processors, PAPs, especially the AP120B.

Some Array Processors, ARPs, and associative processors, APs.

Cellular Computers: the MPP and the Connection Machine (CM).

There is a tradeoff between the number and size of the Processor Elements (PEs), as well as in terms of granularity. The conservative approach (Minsky) is to use only a few, large PEs (SMs); the ARP approach is to achieve as much parallelism as possible by using a large number of very simple PEs (the cells of cellular machines). The SMs are best applied to coarse, the ARPs to fine-grained algorithms.

To indicate why VPs and ARPs are discussed in the same chapter, we use the following example: Suppose that 100 workers have to do 100 identical steps of a job. They could work on an assembly line, each doing a different step of the job, or all of them could do step-1, step-2, . . . , step-100. The first is pipelining, the second is ARP-like. In both cases, *data parallelism* is used, i.e., the same operation is performed on many sets of operands: either interleaved in time (pipelining) or in space (ARPs).

3–1 PIPELINE AND VECTOR PROCESSING

3–1.1 Pipelining

This book was started in Detroit, so inevitably an assembly line comes to mind, and in fact, pipelining is the application of assembly line principles to computers (Fig. 3-1).

If a dozen workers assemble a car along a line with the first fastening the chassis, the second putting the first four bolts in, . . . , mounting the engine, . . . , putting on the tires, . . . , driving out the car, and each such job requires exactly five minutes, then each car is on the assembly line for one hour, but a car is leaving the line every five minutes. The speedup is therefore 1 hour/5 minutes = 12 or exactly equal to the "length" of the pipe.

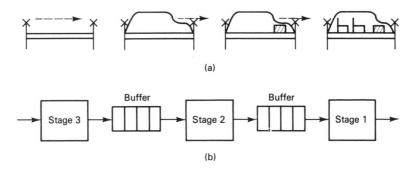

Figure 3-1 (a) An automobile assembly line (b) Buffers in a pipeline

This being so, we might be tempted to make the pipe as long as possible and divide the job into as many tasks as possible. Even in a car this has a limit, since some tasks cannot be divided (e.g., fastening a bolt). Moreover, there are some precedence relations (e.g., the chassis must be on the conveyor before the seats can be installed). If a task takes longer to complete than others, all will have to wait for it to finish; for example, if in the previous example, the first worker needed ten minutes, only six cars would leave the assembly line in an hour, and the speedup would drop from 12 to six.

A computer pipeline consists of processing "segments." Each segment executes part of the processing and the result appears as the output of the last segment. Full speedup is achieved by having p data items at the same time in the p-segment pipeline. Buffers [Fig. 3-1(b)] are used to separate the segments and keep the information for the next stage.

A segment should access a buffer only after making sure that the buffer contains the required data. To this effect, the data is tagged; the speedup and efficiency will be reduced because checking and changing tags wastes time. Since the speed of the pipeline is determined by its slowest element, the segment delays should be made as equal as possible.

One of the first examples of pipelining was the look-ahead or *instruction pre-fetch*. An instruction is normally executed as follows:

1. Instruction Fetch—IF (say of MOVE.W A,D0 as below):
   Increment the program counter (cycle 1).
   Initialize the fetching of the instruction (cycle 2).

2. Instruction Decode—ID:
   Transfer the instruction to the Instruction Register (cycle 1).
   Generate the microword that corresponds to it (cycle 2).

3. Address Calculation—AC:
   Calculate the effective address of the operand (A) (cycle 1).
   Calculate the physical address by adding an offset (cycle 2).

4. Operand Fetch—OF:
   Read the physical address (cycle 1).
   Transfer operand (A) to a register (cycle 2).

5. Execution of the Instruction—EI:
   It will be assumed that it too takes two machine cycles.

6. Store Result—SR (needed only after adding):
   Calculate the address (cycle 1).
   Store the result (cycle 2).

Consider next a sequence of instructions for calculating repeatedly C: = A + B (in the assembly language of MC68000, see [Wak89]).

```
MOVE.W A,D0; Clear register D0 and add to it the value of A (CLA).
MOVE.W B,D1; Clear register D1 and add to it the value of B (CLB).
ADD D0,D1  ; Add A to B and place the result in register D1 (ADD).
MOVE.W D1,C; Store the result D1 = A+B in location C (STO).
```

Since each of these operations consists of the six steps above, the execution on single and pipeline computers is as shown in Fig. 3-2(a) and (b).

The following conclusion may be drawn from the picture of the execution of the "program" in Fig. 3-2(b): in the initial $(p-1)$ steps, only some of the stages are working (water has to flow into the pipe). The same happens in the final $(p-1)$ stages (water has to flow out of the pipe). For $m+p-1$ steps, the total amount of "work" is $m*p$ ("straighten" the figure into an m-by-n rectangle). For part of this time, the pipeline is underutilized; a *setup time* $s*\omega$ is wasted.

There are p stages. Each operation takes time ω and there are m pairs of operands. In the case of a sequential computer, the time is $t(1) = m*p*\omega$; for the pipeline, it is $s*\omega = p*(p-1)*\omega$ and $(m-p+1)*\omega$. Thus:

$$\rho = (p*p+m-2*p+1)/(m*p)$$
$$= (p*(p-2)+m+1)/(m*p) = 1/p + p/m - 2/m + 1/(m*p) \qquad (3\text{-}1)$$

For long vectors (large m), we have $\rho \simeq 1/p + p/m$. The speedup and efficiency are therefore

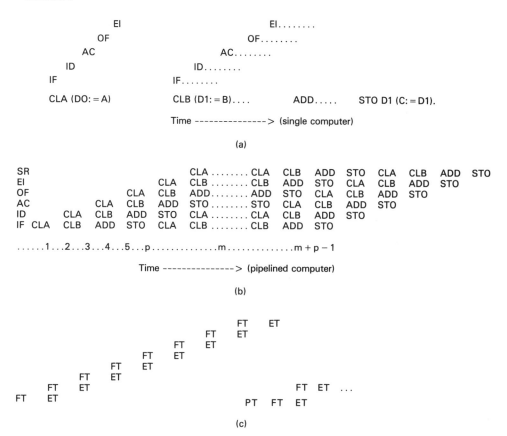

Time ---------------> (single computer)

(a)

Time ---------------> (pipelined computer)

(b)

(c)

Figure 3-2   (a) Single computer (b,c) Pipeline execution of code

$$\sigma \simeq (m*p)/(m+p*p); \quad \eta \simeq m/(p*p+m) \tag{3-2}$$

The efficiency is less than 100%. The initialization time, also called start-up time, reduces the efficiency and speedup. Note that only in cases where the start-up time is significantly smaller than the length of the vector m will the speedup approach p.

Since the times of instruction fetch "I" and execution "E" of the operations depend on the particular instructions, the following conditions must be imposed:

$$I(k) < E(k); \; I(k) < I(k+1); \; E(k) < E(k+1) \tag{3-3}$$

where "$<$" means "should be done before." The total time will be

$$T = \Sigma[t(I(k)) + t(E(k))]; \; k\Sigma = 1, \ldots, m \tag{3-4}$$

Equation (3-4) shows that the speedup depends on the two times. If $t[E(k)] = t[I(k)]$ for all k, then the speedup will be 2. If, on the other hand, $t[E(k)]>>t[I(k)]$, then $T \simeq \Sigma t(E(k))$ and the speedup of only 1 can be achieved ($>>$ means "much greater"). Thus, instruction pre-fetch can supply at most $\sigma = 2$; to achieve higher speeds, we try execution.

The *execution* of an arithmetic instruction usually entails a number of consecutive suboperations. Two floating-point numbers,

$$a = c*10**d = 0.25*10^2 \text{ and } b = e*10**f = 0.25*10^1,$$

will be used to exemplify it. When multiplying them, the processor has to go through the following stages.

1. Multiply the mantissas (i.e., $0.25*0.25 = 0.0625$).
2. Add the exponents (i.e., $2+1 = 3$).
3. Normalize the results (i.e., shift $0.0625*10^3$ to be $0.625*10^2$).

Three circuits could perform these stages. If done sequentially, only one circuit is working at any given time—the other two are idle. Pipelining consists precisely of making all three stages work all the time. *Execution pipelining* is the simultaneous execution of different stages of instructions in an assembly-like fashion. The maximum $\sigma = 3$.

We will have the following stages for adding $a+b$:

1. Compare the two exponents, i.e., form $d-f$ (here $2-1 = 1$).
2. Shift a with respect to b by $d-f$ places ($2.5*10^1$) in order to align the decimal points (normally the binary points).
3. Add the two mantissas (here $2.5+0.25 = 2.75$).
4. Normalize by shifting the result to the left until the leading nonzero digit follows the decimal point ($2.75*10^1 = 0.275*10^2$).

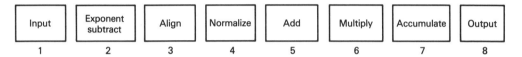

Figure 3-3 A floating-point pipeline

It has already been established that σ could be increased by subdividing the operation into more segments. Since floating-point operations are longer than fixed-point operations, pipelining will be more effective for it. If an eight-segment pipeline is used for floating-point addition and multiplication (Fig. 3-3), then σ increases.

Note that only four segments are needed for multiplication, six for addition. The execution of a multiplication and addition proceeds therefore at different times.

By the early 1960s, pipelining was used in a variety of computers, both for speeding up instruction fetch and arithmetic execution. Some microprocessors, e.g., the MC68020 ([Mot85]), are pipelined. The advantages of pipelining were mentioned; its disadvantages are:

1. The speedup at most equals the length of the pipe. Consequently, it is relatively low (less than ten).

2. The maximum speedup is achieved if all segments work. Even for floating-point addition, segments 6 and 7 of Fig. 3-3 are not used. In other cases, the speedup will be reduced even more.

3. The speedup of a PPS (here Pipelined Parallel System) is determined by the speed of its slowest segment. The speedup will be reduced further because of the following:

4. The equalization of times of the segments is very often impossible and buffers are used. Buffers average the delay; tag processing wastes time.

5. In the instruction/execution overlap, the memory was common and only a single word can be accessed at a time.

6. If the assembly line analogy is recalled, these systems could have a high overhead. In the program for C: $= A + B$, only the ADD was useful; the rest was overhead. Such communication overhead may reduce the speedup (see Code 3-1).

7. Normally, when an interrupt occurs, the status is saved and work resumed later. With a full pipe, the "water must be removed" first. To do this, a point in the program must be selected such that program execution will not pass it. "Filling" and "draining" the pipe occurs when work begins and ends, at each interrupt, and some goto's. This further reduces the speedup and complicates control.

8. Suppose we have to multiply two matrices with a large number of zero elements spaced at random. Multiplication by zero is a wasted effort and reduces the speedup.

3–1.2 Vector Processors

In many computation-intensive applications, a large percentage of the execution time is spent on executing the same operations again and again on many elements of the data streams. For instance, the loop

$$a(i) := b(i) + c(i); \; i = 1, \ldots n \qquad (3\text{-}5)$$

would be translated into Code 3-1 (without indexing).

```
   MOVE.W   R,D0;   Move the counter R (is 0) to register D0.
   ADD      N,D0;   Add the value of n to D0.
L: MOVE.W   B,D1;   Move value of b(i) to (accumulator) D1.
   MOVE.W   C,D2;   Move value of c(i) to register D2.
   ADD      D1,D2;  Add the two and place the result in register D2.
   MOVE.W   D2,A;   Store the result in a(i).
   SUB      #1,D0;  Subtract 1 from D0.
   BNE         L;   Branch to label L if D0 not equal zero.
```

Code 3-1

A single computer has the following "overhead" inside the loop:

1. Six instructions have to be removed from memory.
2. Addresses of $b(i)$, $c(i)$, and $a(i)$ have to be calculated.
3. The values of $b(i)$ and $c(i)$ have to be removed from and $a(i)$ stored in memory.
4. The loop control instructions SUB, BNE introduce additional overhead.

If done in a single computer, the add operation is decoded n times. There exist computers, the *vector processors*, VPs, in which the data arrives at the pipelined arithmetic units contiguously, as in Fig. 3-4, with every segment of the pipeline performing useful work except at the beginning and end of processing the two vectors. *Only a single vector instruction is fetched* and $n-1$ decode-times are saved. Operations 2 and 3 above are also shortened. This makes very efficient use of the circuitry employed, at a cost of some start-up time. The overhead was reduced considerably.

A vector hardware instruction initiates the flow of operands to the pipeline. Assuming the instruction involves two source vectors, each segment of the pipeline accepts two elements, performs the arithmetic suboperation, passes the results to the next segment, and receives the next two elements from the stream of operands. Thus, in loops like that of Eq. (3-5), the source operands would be added n times, with every addition done by different stages of the pipeline. Altogether, several pairs of operands are being processed simultaneously in the pipeline, each pair being in a different stage (segment) of the

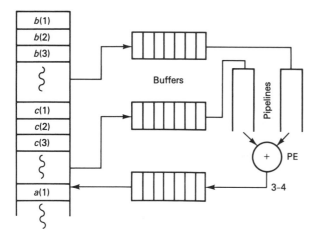

Figure 3-4 Operation of a Vector Processor

computation. The instruction might be $a(1..n): = b(1..n) + c(1..n)$ and the speedup comes primarily from pipelined execution. VPs have been able to execute such vector operations in time comparable to the addition of two numbers, say, $a: = b + c$. Thus, as far as the user is concerned, VPs behave as if the vectors were operated on concurrently; the VP is considered a PPS.

If we denote by FT the time to feed the two operands into the functional units, by ET the execution time, and PT, the time to "empty" the pipeline, then the picture of execution follows Fig. 3-2(c).

If the length of the vector is n, then only the time of $n + 3$ is required if the delay is four clock pulses. Thus, for $n = 4, 16, 64$, and 128, the number of clock times needed per vector component is 1.75, 1.19, 1.05, and 1.02, respectively. The longer the vector, the better.

Given a declaration: array A(8,8), array **A** could be considered two vectors of length 32 each or eight vectors each of length 8. At least theoretically, in the last case all eight vectors can be accessed simultaneously, and the memory-to-memory bandwidth increases. Additionally, four (instead of one) pipelines are kept busy. Unfortunately, the vectors are of length 8 and the start-up time will decrease the speedup. As noted, the vectors should be as long as possible—we prefer two vectors of length 32 each.

A *vector computer* consists of a control unit CU which fetches and decodes instructions in the customary way, a vector processor which executes vector instructions in a way explained above, a separate scalar processor to execute scalar instructions, and the memory to store programs and data. For scalar instructions, the operands are accessed directly in the memory. [To reduce memory contention in vector computers, the pipelines should be supplied with arguments from different memory blocks, MBs, like in the Paracomputer of Fig. 1-1(c).] The memory usually includes some secondary memory (disks, etc.). In this way, both speed and capacity are provided.

3–1.3 An Example of a VP: The CRAY-1

The block diagram of CRAY-1 [Rus78][†] is shown in Fig. 3-5. The maximum size of its main memory is $2^{20} = 1,048,576$ words of 64-bit length. It has an access and cycle time of 50 nns and is organized in 16 MBs of 72 modules per block. Since the clock rate of the machine is 12.5 nns, an MB will be busy for four clock periods after it accepts a request (to read or write). Other requests can be made during this time to the remaining blocks so that every 50 nns, a word can be delivered from one of the blocks, provided there is no contention. This leads to a memory bandwidth of 320 Mwords/second, of which, incidentally, only a quarter that is 80 Mwords/second are used.

Most instructions fit in a 16-bit long *parcel*. Some of the branch instructions and memory reference operations require two parcels.

There are four instruction buffers (bottom left of Fig. 3-5) each holding 64 instructions of length 16 bits each. Each buffer is connected to the main memory by a 64-line bus. Each bus can transfer four words per clock period supplying a bandwidth of 320 Mwords/sec to match exactly the bandwidth of the memory. Again, this applies only in the case that there is no interference between memory blocks.

Associated with each instruction buffer is a "Base Address Register" which is used in order to determine if the buffer contains the current instruction. Since the buffers are rather large, substantial parts of programs can be stored in them and, often, the branching can be made inside the buffers. If a "goto" leads outside the buffer, or if the current instruction is not found in one of the buffers, then a buffer is filled from the main memory. This will be the buffer which was least recently accessed. A parcel counter register P points to the next parcel to exit from the buffer. Prior to issuing, parcels are held in the Next Instruction Parcel, NIP, Lower Instruction Parcel, LIP, and Current Instruction Parcel, CIP registers.

The basic registers of CRAY-1 are:

The eight address *A registers* of 24 bits each are used primarily as address registers for memory references and as index registers, but they are also used for shift counts, loop control, and I/O operations. They provide a base address for scalar operations and both the base and an index address for vector memory references. The addresses may be incremented, decremented, and even multiplied by a factor in the integer functional unit.

Data (mostly addresses) can be transferred directly from the main memory to the A registers or be placed for some time in the B registers. This allows buffering of data between the memory and the A registers. Data can also be transferred between A and S registers and from an A to the vector length registers, VL.

The 64 Address-save *B registers*

> . . . are used as auxiliary storage for the A registers. The transfer of an operand between an A and a B register requires only one clock period. Typically, B registers contain addresses and counters that are referenced over a longer period than would permit their being retained in A registers. A block of data in B registers may be transferred to and from memory at the rate of

---

[†]R.M. Russell: "The CRAY-1 Computer System," Comm. ACM, Vol. 21, No. 1, pp. 26–35. Copyright 1978, Association for Computing Machinery, Inc., reprinted by permission.

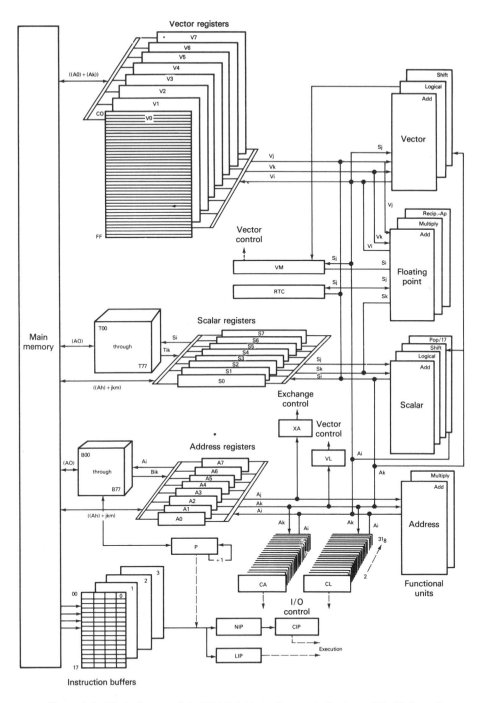

Figure 3-5 Block diagram of the CRAY-1 Vector Processor. Courtesy of R. M. Russell: "The CRAY-1 Computer System," Comm. ACM, Vol. 21, No. 1, pp. 26–35. Copyright 1978, Association for Computing Machinery, Inc.

one clock period per register. Thus is it feasible to store the content of these registers in memory prior to calling a subroutine requiring their use. [Rus78]

The eight scalar *S registers* of 64 bits each are the main data-handling storage for scalar operations. They store the two operands and the result of the scalar or logical operation. Logical, shift, fixed- and floating-point operations may be performed on data residing on the S registers. They also store scalar data which are used in some vector operations.

The 64 scalar-save *T registers* serve as buffers for the S register. In one clock period, data can be transferred between T and S registers.

Typically, T registers contain operands that are referenced over a longer period than would permit their being retained in S registers. T registers allow intermediate results of complex computations to be held in intermediate access storage rather than in memory. A block of data in T registers may be transferred to or from memory at the rate of one word per clock period. [Rus78]

The main super-registers are the eight vector *V registers* of 64 words of 64 bits each. If the data in a V register occupies successive locations, it may be considered a vector. Vector instructions operate identically on all elements of any two V registers to produce a result to be stored in another (or one of these) registers. There is a vector mask VM register which can indicate (by a 1 and 0) the elements of the two vectors which participate in the operation. The vector-length or VL register stores the length of the two vectors to be processed.

The A, S, and V registers are called "primary," whereas the B and T registers are considered to be "intermediate." This makes for a total of 4,888 bytes of high-speed (6 nns) register storage space. Additionally the following supporting registers are briefly mentioned:

A *BA register* monitors the bounds of the memory area used by the program. All instructions of a program which reference the memory must do so with relative instead of absolute addressing. An *LA register* supplies a limiting address. Any attempt to reference memory outside of the limits given by the BA and LA registers will lead to a "range error" and an interrupt.

The *XA register*

contains the upper eight bits of a 12-bit memory address. The lower four bits of the address are considered zeros. Because only 12 bits are used, with the lower four bits always being zeros, exchange addresses can reference only every sixteenth memory address beginning with address 0000 and concluding with address 4080. Each of these addresses designates the first word of a 16-word set. Thus, 256 sets (of 16 memory words each) can be specified. Prior to initiation or continuation of a program's execution, the XA register contains the first memory address of a particular 16-word set or exchange package. The exchange package contains certain operation and support register's contents as required for operations following an interrupt. The XA register supports the exchange sequence operation and the contents of the XA register are stored in an exchange package whenever an exchange sequence occurs. [Rus78]

A nine-bit *F register* indicates, by its bits (flags), if an interrupt condition exists for: normal or error exit, I/O interrupt, uncorrected memory error, program range error, operand range error, floating-point overflow, real-time clock, and console interrupt. Each of these nine interrupts initiates an exchange sequence.

Finally, a mode register (M) supports the interrupt sequence, and a channel address register (CA) along with a channel limit register (CL) support the input/output operations through the channels.

Instructions other than simple assignment or control operations are performed by hardware in the *functional units* of Fig. 3-5 (right). These functional units of CRAY-1 are organized in four groups: address, scalar, vector, and floating-point units.

A functional unit receives operands from (A, S, and V) registers and upon getting the result, delivers it to a register; CRAY-1 is considered a "register-to-register" VP. The units need three addresses: two for the source operands and one for the result register. These addresses are short because the number of registers is limited. For instance, to specify one of the eight address registers, only three bits are needed (000, . . . ,111). The B and T registers help with scalar operations. Temporary scalar values can be accessed from and delivered to the A and S registers in two clock periods.

The units perform their operations in a fixed amount of time. There are no delays once the operands are in the units. The amount of time that is used by the operations is called "functional unit time" and is measured by a multiple of clock periods.

All functional units are pipelined and may accept new operands every clock period. In other words, a new set of operands for an unrelated computation may enter a functional unit each clock period even though the functional unit may still be processing other operands.

A vector operation may use either two vector registers (V) or one scalar and one V register as the input. Vectors exceeding 64 elements are processed in 64-word segments. Thus, Eq. (3-5) would be executed as the "program" of Code 3-2.

```
MOV A0,N;       -- Move the length n into register A0
MOV VL,A0;      -- Put n into VL (it cannot be done directly from memory)
MOV V1,B1;      -- Load addend
MOV V2,C1;      -- Load augend
ADD V1,V2,V3;   -- Add the two into V3
MOV V3,D1;      -- Store result (A1 could not have been used)
```

Code 3-2

Code 3-2 shows that in a vector addition, once the registers are loaded, no memory accesses are needed until their content is exhausted; this saving of memory accesses increases the speed.

The vector registers not only facilitate vector operations, but enable *chaining*, which requires the storage of intermediate results in the V registers. Chaining takes advantage of the independence of the functional units (FU) and the large number of registers. The results of one operation are stored in a register as they move out from an FU (at the rate of one per clock period) and are used immediately as input to another FU. This happens simultaneously with the result being stored in the destination register. In other words, no intermediate results need be stored in the memory and results can be used even before the vector operation which computed them is itself completed. The delay suffered is only the FU time plus two clock periods. As an example, take a scalar product of two vectors. For $x = \Sigma v(i)*w(i)$, we need one pipe to perform the multiplication, one to accumulate the result by adding the products. The advantage of chaining is that we can start accumulating the second product while the first is not yet ready. In the same way, chaining can be used among three or more FUs leading to a significant speedup, at least for repeated vector operations.

There are 12 input and 12 output channels on the CRAY-1. Some or all of them may be active at the same time, with each 16-bit channel being able to transfer up to 160 Mbps. Higher rates could be achieved, but the slow peripheral devices will limit the speed anyway. Also, since I/O share access to the memory with the CPU, their speed is limited.

When an interrupt occurs, instruction flow is terminated by the hardware. All memory activity as well as any vector operation are allowed to complete and an *exchange sequence* is initiated. During this sequence, the Operating System will determine the cause of the interrupt and proceed to perform remedial actions. The exchange package includes all eight address (A) registers and eight scalar (S) registers. During the exchange sequence the B, T, and V registers must be saved. Being quite large, they are saved in the "Job Table Area" of the user.

Vector computers must have vector operands of considerable length to be efficient. It is claimed [Rus78] that in CRAY-1 this length is only two to four elements, and that the start-up times of CRAY-1 are very short.

3–2 PERIPHERAL ARRAY PROCESSORS, PAPs

Supercomputers achieve high processing efficiencies only if the data to be processed can be rearranged into relatively long vectors [Eq. (3-2)]. The use of a scalar unit leads to a decrease of efficiency for all programs in which the scalar part is substantial. Additionally, they are very expensive. For many applications it is better to acquire a *Peripheral Array Processor*, or PAP. It is similar to a vector computer but it works with a *host* and costs less, except for the cost of the host (front-end) computer. The host downloads the programs for faster, parallel execution. Since the host is used for other computations anyway, not including it in the evaluation of the cost is justified.

An example of the effectiveness of PAPs was provided in [KaC81]. The problem solved was that of nonlinear filtering for which about 83,000 FLOPs were required in each iteration. The problem was programmed in Fortran for a number of computers. The AP-120B (a PAP) was outperformed only by the supercomputers. If the price is also taken into account (i.e., the hardware cost is divided by the number of FLOPs) then the AP-120B was about seven times more cost-effective than its nearest competitor, the CRAY-1. On the other hand, a long development effort was needed in running the problem on the PAP, since it had to be microcoded.

The cost-effectiveness of the PAP depends on its architecture, which optimizes certain tasks at the expense of others. PAPs were designed to do signal processing jobs efficiently. However, in performing some general-purpose operations, including bit, byte, and string computations, they were rather slow.

There are now a number of PAPs on the market. The market for PAPs is first of all the universities which lack funding, but have not-fully-utilized host computers and an inexpensive labor force (the professors are paid anyway, graduate students are not paid at all).

One of the designers [Cha81] of AP-120B mentions eight design guidelines; they are summarized next.

1. Optimize *both* scientific and signal processing. The PAPs evolved from applications which are dominated by the FFT algorithm and solving sets of linear equations. For these algorithms, the absolutely necessary functional units are an adder and a multiplier. No separate division unit was designed, so that it is programmed by a small table look-up and a Taylor series expansion involving multiplications and additions. It was found that division was 43% as fast as the vector add and multiply operations.

2. In order to have more accuracy than 32 bits could provide, a 38-bit word was chosen. The accuracy is less than that offered by supercomputers, but is sufficient for scientific calculations.

3. It is reasonable to expect an overall vector fraction δ of about 75% for typical scientific problems. According to Amdahl's law for PAPs: $\delta/(1-\delta) = 0.75/0.25$, and this yields a balanced vector/scalar performance ratio of 3:1. The capabilities of vector and scalar calculations can be thus balanced.

4. "Given a moderate vector/scalar performance ratio, a vector processor also performs well on short vectors and sequential operations. Therefore, we adjusted the cycle time of our machine to shorten the functional unit pipelines to only two and three stages" [Cha81].† VPs with longer pipelines perform relatively poorly on short vectors.

5. Supercomputers have separate hardware for scalar and vector operations. In the PAPs, *only scalar hardware is provided*, and vector operations are constructed by software loops. This results in significantly lower price—a virtue mentioned earlier for all PAPs.

6. No multiprogramming was used because the system is used to run off-loaded programs. Only a single processor is needed.

7. "Much more than conventional computers, parallel processors are burdened by complicated control logic, which is needed to synchronize and coordinate concurrent activities. We shifted most of this burden to the programmer or compiler. The programmer or compiler explicitly codes all parallelism into the program only once,

---

†A.E. Charlesworth: "An approach . . . AP120B . . . ," Computer, Sept., Vol. 14, No. 9, pp. 18–27 (© 1981, IEEE). Reprinted by permission.

so that the hardware need not detect it millions of times per second'' [Cha81]. *Programming is done in microcode.*

8. Only *standard hardware* was used. "Extra hardware is devoted to parallel data paths and multiple functional units rather than to large amounts of extra control and synchronization logic. Thus, a conscious trade-off balanced hardware and software complexity and kept the price of PAPs substantially below that of supercomputers'' [Cha81].

Built from a design based on these guidelines, the highly successful AP-120B had about 1,600 machines in use by 1980.

Peripheral Array Processors, PAPs, are generally designed to speed up multiplication and addition operations by providing a pipelined adder and multiplier. Since these operations are relatively time consuming, especially for wide words and floating-point formats, the two units should work in parallel, delivering their results simultaneously. For the same reason, the system should be able to simultaneously fetch in one cycle both the instruction to be executed and the data for the arithmetic functional units FUs of the AP-120B (Fig. 3-6) that provide the basic parallelism (all units working simultaneously). A maximum of two data computations, two memory accesses, an address computation, four data register accesses, and a conditional branch may be initiated in a given CPU cycle, for a total of ten distinct operations. Paths for the transfer of all these data must be provided, and the circuitry required for address computation, loop counting, and other operations must be supported in parallel.

Since the operations of the adder, multiplier, and memory are inherently more time consuming than those of the registers and addressing units, they were pipelined. The pipelines have only two or three stages, enough to enable all units to initiate a new operation every 167-nns cycle. This allows a balanced performance.

Sequential computers store both data and instructions in the same memory, while PAPs not only provide *separate memory units* for instructions and data, but frequently distinguish several varieties of data. Since instructions use wide words (64 bits), the separation of memory units is almost mandatory. Starting at the top of Fig. 3-6, the memories of the AP-120B memories are: a *control memory* for storing the program; a *scratch-pad* memory for storing addresses and indices; a *table memory* for storing frequently used constants; two *data pads X and Y* for storing temporary floating-point results; and a *main memory*.

Both the addition and multiplication require two input operands. For concurrency, they are fed from the two data pads. The table memory stores constants needed for such jobs as the Fast Fourier Transform. Typically, these table and program memories can be modified only by the host; as far as the PAP is concerned, they are "Read-Only" memories. As with any other computer, a PAP includes a large shared memory in which data are stored. It can also serve as the main buffer for communication with the host computer and other devices outside the PAP.

To run at full speed, each of the ten functional units needs its own subinstruction on every cycle. The 64-bit instruction word (Fig. 3-7) contains a separate subinstruction parcel for

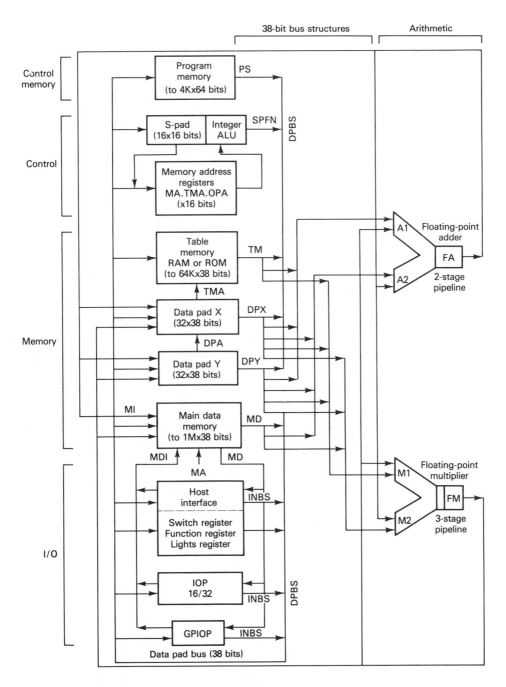

Figure 3-6 Block diagram of the AP-120B Peripheral Array Processor. Courtesy of A. E. Charlesworth: "An approach . . . AP120B . . . ," Computer, Sept. 1981, Vol. 14, No. 9, pp. 18–27 (© 1981, IEEE).

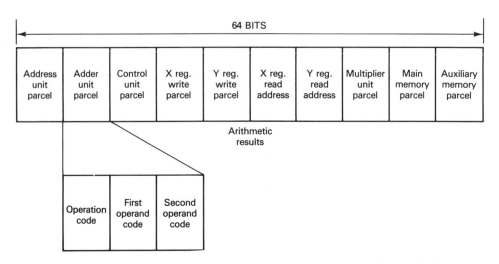

Figure 3-7 The instruction word of the AP-120B. Courtesy of A. E. Charlesworth: "An approach . . . AP120B . . . ," Computer, Sept. 1981, Vol. 14, No. 9, pp. 18–27 (© 1981, IEEE).

each of the 10 functional units. This solution is similar to the wide control words used by the microprocessors that implement most conventional computers. Using the ten parcels, a program can specify a new operation for each of the ten functional units on every CPU cycle.

The parcels are analogous to the individual instructions of conventional computers. The adder parcel, for example, specifies an operation (e.g., subtract) and selects two operands—register contents, memory outputs, or previous results—to be subtracted. The ten parcels allow a single instruction to add, multiply, fetch numbers from each memory, decrement a loop counter, and test for loop completion. A complete vector loop is possible in a single instruction. [Cha81]

The microcode is "horizontal," controlling all ten FUs (if each word only controlled a single unit, it would be called "vertical"). Instructions are processed at the speed of six MIPs, but since each instruction controls a number of operations the real speed is higher.

The scratch-pad (S-pad) contains an additional ALU which can add integers, subtract them, perform logical, and shift operations. Each of the operations takes one clock period. It is used for address calculations and loop counters. It has 16 registers each of 16 bits—the length of an address.

Input and Output are performed by an I/O Port (IOP) through the host interface. The IOP is connected to the main data memory through "direct memory access" devices and "steals" cycles for data transfer. It can accommodate up to 256 external devices.

Because it uses multiple functional units, the AP-120B requires a dense interconnection network. Six individual results: from the adder, the multiplier, the two register units, and the

ᶠA.E. Charlesworth: "An approach . . . AP120B . . . ," Computer, Sept., Vol. 14, No. 9, pp. 18–27 (© 1981, IEEE). Reprinted by permission of the IEEE.

two memories are produced according to Fig. 3-8. These results must be connected to the eight individual inputs: the four arithmetic operands, the two register units, and the two memories.

A full crossbar would have 6x8 connections to be switched simultaneously. Instead, a partial connector which makes 30 of the possible 48 connections was chosen. It uses four buses to supply operands to the arithmetic units and two to carry results. An additional bus links the register and memory units.

The densest portion of the interconnect (Fig. 3-8) is centered on the two register units, which are connected to all seven buses. They act as temporary buffers for arithmetic results, especially when another unit cannot immediately use a result. The register bandwidth is limited to two reads and two writes per cycle. If both memories and both arithmetic units are active at once, then a total of six reads and four writes are required.

The programmer overcomes the gap between the register bandwidth of four accesses per cycle and the maximum requirement of ten accesses per cycle by bypassing the registers

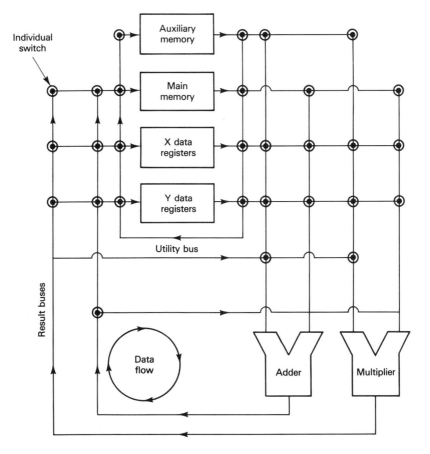

Figure 3-8 The crossbar of the AP-120B Peripheral Array Processor. Courtesy of A. E. Charlesworth: "An approach . . . AP120B . . . ," Computer, Sept. 1981, Vol. 14, No. 9, pp. 18–27 (© 1981, IEEE).

and using the direct connections between the memories and the arithmetic units. Each of the four memory and arithmetic results are connected directly to one of the two inputs of the adder and multiplier. Data can flow directly from memory into the arithmetic unit and back into memory without using the registers. Each time a direct connection is used, a cycle of delay is saved. Without these direct connections, the pipelines would effectively be one stage longer.

The partial crossbar of Fig. 3-8 represents a tradeoff between implementation constraints and maximum execution speed. [Cha81].

Programming in a high-level language is independent of the particular architecture of the computer, its registers, data paths, etc. On the other hand, in the case of the PAPs, programming manuals usually include the architecture of the computer. This is necessary in order to know which operations share which buses or other equipment, since sharing prevents concurrency. The programmer must also know how the registers are interconnected and some other details on the machine level. In summary: The PAPs are usually programmed by *microprogramming*, thereby maximizing the performance and using every drop of concurrency. This means that the convenience of high-level or even assembly language is not available, and the programming time is much longer. Mathematical libraries of microcode (and Fortran) are available from the manufacturers and may be of some help. Freezing the architecture at the time of the design prevents the upgrading to a better architecture because the users have by then a considerable investment in microcode. This is a distinct disadvantage of using microcode.

The problem of programming is particularly difficult outside of the linear equations and conventional signal processing for which the PAPs were originally designed. For such cases, the implementation is quite different from standard signal processing, for three reasons [KaC81]:

1. Simulation programs for complex dynamic systems tend to be long. Often, many hundreds and sometimes thousands of Fortran statements are required when using sequential digital computers.
2. The data to be processed can rarely be structured in vector form to facilitate pipelining.
3. Processing frequently involves conditional looping (decisions to determine data flow). This makes efficient pipelining virtually impossible.

Clearly, PAPs cannot become an effective simulation tool if users are required to microprogram; software programming aids are a necessity.

3–3 PIONEERING ARRAYS OF PROCESSORS, ARPs

ILLIAC-IV was the first array processor to become operational for the benefit of a large user community when it was installed at the NASA Ames Research Center in the early 1970s. Although it was removed from service in 1981 (mainly because of maintenance problems), it provided probably the most computational experience with such computers.

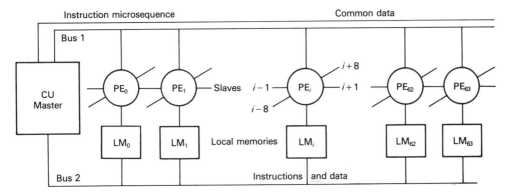

Figure 3-9   The architecture of the ILLIAC-IV

It was already mentioned that a way of speeding up the calculation is by replicating the arithmetic units (called here PE for Processing Element) and forming an array out of them (Fig. 3-9). All PEs are under the control of a single instruction stream performing at any given time the same operation on different data in their local memories (LMs).

Let us compare execution of the loop in Eq. (3-5), using various SIMD systems. In an ARP (Fig. 3-9), many essentially scalar processors are used to run the loop instruction by performing it on different elements of vectors b and c in different PEs, all controlled by a single control unit, CU. The instruction is performed by reading the elements of $b(i)$ and $c(i)$ from the LMs, executing the arithmetic addition, and sending the result back to the LM (an IN may be used to transfer the three words). If the number p of PEs is less than the number of additions in Eq. (3-5), then the first $p<n$ pairs of elements $b(i)$ and $c(i)$ can be sent to the p processors and the p results are obtained in the time α of a single addition. The next group of p pairs is then sent, added, and so on. Assume that $k = n/p$ and k is an integer; then a time of $k*\alpha$ is needed and the speedup is

$$\sigma = t(1)/t(p) = n*\alpha \; / \; (n*\alpha/p) = p \tag{3-6}$$

In the case that k is not an integer, it is rounded up to one and the speedup is reduced slightly.

In principle, array and vector computers (ARPs and VPs) are similar, which is why we deal with them in the same chapter. A VP overlaps the operations on an array of operands by means of pipelining. An ARP replicates the number of PEs and applies them simultaneously to an array of operands. The speedup of ARPs can be higher than that of pipeline computers because the number of units in an ARP can be higher than the number of segments in the VP (as seen previously, it seemed to be $p\leq10$).

To compare vector and array computers, let us review the addition of two floating-point numbers as part of the loop in Eq. (3-5). The addition entails four suboperations. In a single computer, the four suboperations [Fig. 3-10(a)] must be completed on $b(1)$ and $c(1)$ to produce $a(1) = b(1)+c(1)$, before the second element pair $b(2)$ and $c(2)$ enters the arithmetic unit. For n elements of a loop, this may result in a rather long execution time [Fig. 3-10(c)] of $p*n*\omega$, where $p = 4$ is the number of suboperations (only four in this

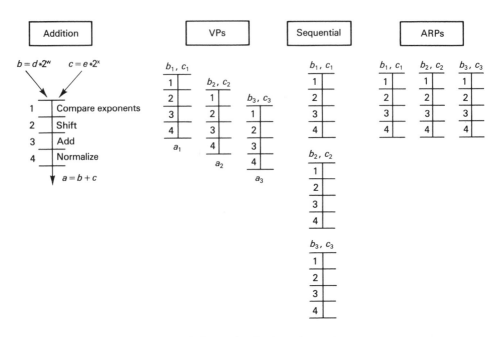

Figure 3-10   Adding floating-point numbers

case) and ω is the time to complete each suboperation. It is instructive to note that the segments are only active one-fourth of the total time. This in itself represents an inefficiency since three-fourths of the segments are always idle.

Figure 3-10(b) shows the speedup to be achieved by vector operations. The time to perform the loop of length n is $[s+(n-1)]*\omega$, where $s*\omega$ is the start-up time and other overheads, and p is the number of stages (here 4). The speedup is therefore

$$\sigma = (p*n*\omega)/[(s+n-1)*\omega] \simeq p \qquad (3\text{-}7)$$

where the overhead and one ω were neglected. As can be seen in Fig. 3-10(d), the speedup of an array-of-processors is higher than that of a VP because its p is larger and there is no start-up time.

Figure 3-9 shows one quadrant of ILLIAC. It has the following principal features:

1. An array of 64 ALUs (PEs) controlled by a single control unit (CU).
2. Sixty-four local memories, LMs, of 2048 words of 64 bits each.
3. The PEs were connected by an omega MIN and later by an 8x8 mesh—both discussed in Chapter 2 and not shown in Fig. 3-9. The mesh is better suited for image processing and other data-parallel problems.
4. Information can be broadcast from the CU to all PEs.
5. Information can be exchanged between neighboring PEs.
6. There is very little local control at the PE level.

The single control unit CU fetches instructions on bus "2" from the local memories LM(i), decodes them, and then broadcasts the same instruction to all 64 PEs, on line "1." Data are transferred to the LMs in the form of vectors of p or fewer words. The results of the computation are transferred back to the LMs by the MIN.

At the time the ILLIAC was developed, the control logic was much more expensive than arithmetic units. Therefore, it was thought that having a single CU for all 64 Arithmetic Logic Units (the PEs) and producing them devoid of most control circuitry will save a large percentage of the cost. At present, microchips include a CU and little is saved.

ILLIAC was designed to work on scientific problems which require not only high speed but also high accuracy. Special hardware for arithmetic operations was therefore provided. There are four kinds of floating-point and two of fixed-point arithmetic on words which are 64-bits long. No wonder the floating-point add, multiply, and divide need 350, 450, and 2750 nns, whereas fetch and store, only 350 and 300 nns and a register-to-register transfer, only 50 nns. The PEs and the CU are connected through a memory logic unit. In the present technological environment, this hardware would raise the price very much.

An ARP is normally connected to a *host* computer (not shown in Fig. 3-9). The host contains the operating system, controls program loading and I/O operations, supports such system programs as compilers, assemblers, etc; it works with a database on the disk, and acts as a resource manager. Being a single (nonreplaceable) unit, it adversely affects the fault detection and the reliability of the system.

Data can be distributed to the PEs from outside or from the host either through the data bus or via the CU by being broadcast on the control bus. The control unit has limited arithmetic capability.

The PEs operate synchronously, in lock-step fashion, but each has its local memory, LM, so that no memory interference occurs. Every PE has the following registers: an accumulator "A," an operand "B," a carry "C," a routing "R," and a (temporary) storage S register. The MAR is the address register, the X register is a local index register, D is a data register, and F is an activity flag register. Register R is wired directly to four adjacent PEs forming the mesh Interconnection Network. In addition to two enable bits, there are six other bits in the mode register "E" which handle fault and test results.

The PEs have a degree of freedom through register X. An address $a(i)$ in LM(i) is the sum of the address broadcast by the CU and the content of X. (The addition is computed in an "address adder" provided with each PE.) Thus, if the content of X(i) is "c," of X(j) is "b," and the address broadcast by the CU is "a," then PE(i) will process address $a + c$ while PE(j) will "see" $a + b$ as the address. It will be shown below that the use of the index register X is quite effective in some problems.

Every PE has a local memory LM with 2048 words of 64 bits. The LMs are independently accessible by their PE, the CU, and by the I/O devices. From Fig. 3-9 it can be seen that a PE can fetch or store operands only in its own LM. The CU can fetch instructions from any of the 64 LMs.

Since each PE has its own memory, it can get data locally much faster than the SM-multiprocessors, which have to access a common address space. On the other hand, if some PE(i) requires data stored in LM(j), where $i \ne j$, then it gets the data by way of *routing*. The data is first transferred to register R of PE(*j*), from there to the R register of PE(*i*) and, stored in LM(*i*), if required. If the "distance" *i* to *j* is $+1MOD64$, $-1MOD64$, $+8MOD64$, or $-8MOD64$, then only $\simeq 100$ mls are needed for the routing of the data, but the distance can be as high as seven links. Considerable time ($\simeq 700$ mls) is wasted especially if one considers that 63 PEs may have to wait idly until PE(*i*) receives the data it requested. This in turn leads to a *software problems*: The programmer must not only think in terms of the algorithm, but must also allocate memory to minimize routing. This may lead to rather complicated data structures.

The CU receives its instructions from the LMs also through bus 2 (Fig. 3-9). The CU produces a microsequence for each instruction in the same way that a control unit of a conventional, microprogrammed computer does. Thus, all PEs receive the same sequence and work in lock-step synchronization. If PE(*i*) multiplies, then all PEs multiply.

Well, not necessarily; *any slave can be turned off* either by the CU or by its own data by having a mode bit set to zero. Thus, the CU may first broadcast (on bus-1) a word of, say, 32 zeros followed by 32 ones with one bit being stored in each PE as the mode bit. Only PEs 32 to 63 in which the mode bit was set to 1 will process later instructions; the other PEs must first be turned on (by the CU). This shows that conditional branches of conventional computers are accomplished in ARPs by tests which enable or disable local execution of subsequent commands in the instruction sequence.

Another case is exemplified by the CU issuing a command to be obeyed only if the data in an accumulator is, for example, positive. All PEs for which this is not true will turn their mode bits off and do nothing for as long as the mode bit is not turned on again (probably by the CU.)

The control unit has the following *functions*:

1. Decode the instructions; broadcast the corresponding microsequence.
2. Generate and broadcast common addresses and data to all PEs.
3. Receive and process interrupts from the PEs, I/O devices, and the host.

The control unit has the following main *components*:

1. A program look-ahead buffer PLA which can hold 64 words each of 64 bits. They constitute a *queue* of 128 instructions (of 32 bits each), so that the CU can go on decoding for a long time before it needs to fill the buffer. The CU will fill the buffer when it finds that the next group of eight words (there are eight such groups) is not yet in the PLA. The transfer of a new group will destroy the "oldest" group. This queuing reduces the waiting time for the instructions.
2. There is a local data buffer of 64 words which is connected to all PEs and their local memories.
3. The arithmetic unit of the CU is rather simple and restricted to logic operations and fixed-point additions/subtractions on data from the data buffer.
4. There are four 64-bit registers used for indexing, logical operations, and broadcasting.

5. The instructions are held in a "final queue" and broadcast as data or as an instruction microsequence. Local instructions (indexing, jumps, etc.) are executed by the arithmetic unit of the PE.

Information transfer between the CU and the 64 PEs is effected in several ways:

1. The CU broadcasts a word to all PEs. It is stored in the same register of every PE.
2. The CU broadcasts a word such that one bit is transferred to every PE. In this way some PEs are enabled, some are disabled through their mode registers.
3. The PEs can form a 64-bit word and send it through bus 2 to the CU. The CU thus senses a single bit of all 64 PEs and if this bit is the *mode bit*, then the word describes the state of the entire system.
4. The CU can fetch a single or a block of eight consecutive words from the local memories. The latter requires only slightly more time than fetching a single word and is used to feed the instruction buffer.

Algorithms must be designed so that all PEs obey the same commands. Suppose we have an area of n-by-n points and want to replace the value in each one of them by the average of its four neighbors (including border values). The program in ILLIAC might have been as in Code 3.3.

```
S : = 0.0;                -- Assign 0.0 to all S-registers.
S : = S+R((i-1) mod 64);  -- Shift all values "east" and accumulate.
S : = S+R((i+1) mod 64);  -- Shift all values "west" and accumulate.
S : = S+R((i+8) mod 64);  -- Shift all values "north" and accumulate.
S : = S+R((i-8) mod 64);  -- Shift all values "south" and accumulate.
p(i)  : = 0.25*S;         -- Replace all n² points by the values of S.
```

Code 3-3

This was a simple *data-parallel, fine-grained* algorithm. To exemplify other problems, we use an algorithm for matrix multiplication $Z := X*Y$. In particular, it illustrates the problem of memory allocation and shows how *code-parallelism* is achieved in ILLIAC.

Matrices **X**, **Y**, and **Z** may be stored as in Table 3-1. In this table, an element is stored in a local memory cell of a particular PE according to the column and row headings, respectively. For instance, element X(3,2) is stored in location 13 of local memory LM(2).

The "program" may be summarized in a mixed English and Pascal language (for 4-by-4 matrices) as in Code 3-4.

TABLE 3-1 STORAGE OF THE MATRICES IN THE ARP

PEM$_i$	loc				loc				loc			
	11	12	13	14	21	22	23	24	31	32	33	34
PR 1	X_{11}	X_{21}	X_{31}	X_{41}	Y_{11}	Y_{21}	Y_{31}	Y_{41}	Z_{11}	Z_{21}	Z_{31}	Z_{41}
PR 2	X_{12}	X_{22}	X_{32}	X_{42}	Y_{12}	Y_{22}	Y_{32}	Y_{42}	Z_{12}	Z_{22}	Z_{32}	Z_{42}
PE 3	X_{13}	X_{23}	X_{33}	X_{43}	Y_{13}	Y_{23}	Y_{33}	Y_{43}	Z_{13}	Z_{23}	Z_{33}	Z_{43}
PE 4	X_{14}	X_{24}	X_{34}	X_{44}	Y_{14}	Y_{24}	Y_{34}	Y_{44}	Z_{14}	Z_{24}	Z_{34}	Z_{44}

```
for i := 1 to 4 do begin          --- symbols start a pseudoinstruction.
  --- Copy row i of X from the LMs into the control unit.
  --- An instruction, like "transfer the contents of location
  --- 11 to the CU", would transfer the entire first row of X.
  for j := 1 to 4 do begin
    ---  1. Broadcast X(i,j) from the control unit to all
    ---     A-registers.
    ---  2. Fetch row j of Y into the B-register. This can be done
    ---     as "Fetch element K from local memory to the B-register",
    ---     and will be denoted by k => B. For instance 22 => B
    ---     transfers Y(2,1), Y(2,2), Y(2,3), and Y(2,4) into the
    ---     B-registers of the four processing elements.
    ---  3. Multiply the A and B registers (in all four PEs).
    ---  4. Add the result to the S-register of every PE. This
    ---     effectively accumulates the inner product by S:=S+A*B.
  end;
  --- Store S as the new Z. A row will be stored by one command
  --- Z => k in the same location k of all elements PE.
end;
```

Code 3-4

To understand how the algorithm works in parallel, follow the first few steps in Table 3-2, using the data of Table 3-1. At the end of these few steps, the first row ($i = 1$) of **Z** is stored as the accumulated sum in registers S. It is easily verified that this is

$$Z(1,j) := \Sigma[X(1,k)*Y(k,j)]; \; k\Sigma = j\Sigma = 1, \ldots ,4 \qquad (3\text{-}8)$$

This is indeed the first row of $\mathbf{Z} = \mathbf{X} * \mathbf{Y}$. The entire row is stored by the single command "Register S => 31."

TABLE 3-2 THE INITIAL PART OF EXECUTING MATRIX MULTIPLICATION

I = 1	Element-1	Element-2	Element-3	Element-4	
J = 1	X_{11}	X_{11}	X_{11}	X_{11}	stored in register A
	Y_{11}	Y_{12}	Y_{13}	Y_{14}	k → B is here 21 → B
	$X_{11}Y_{11}$	$X_{11}Y_{12}$	$X_{11}Y_{13}$	$X_{11}Y_{14}$	stored in register S
J = 2	X_{12}	X_{12}	X_{12}	X_{12}	in A registers
	Y_{21}	Y_{22}	Y_{23}	Y_{24}	22 → B
	$X_{12}Y_{21}$	$X_{12}Y_{22}$	$X_{12}Y_{23}$	$X_{12}Y_{24}$	increments to S; Z + S → S
J = 3	X_{13}	X_{13}	X_{13}	X_{13}	in A registers
	Y_{31}	Y_{32}	Y_{33}	Y_{34}	in B registers
	$X_{13}Y_{31}$	$X_{13}Y_{32}$	$X_{13}Y_{33}$	$X_{13}Y_{34}$	increments to S
J = 4	X_{14}	X_{14}	X_{14}	X_{14}	in A registers
	Y_{41}	Y_{42}	Y_{43}	Y_{44}	in B registers
	$X_{14}Y_{41}$	$X_{14}Y_{42}$	$X_{14}Y_{43}$	$X_{14}Y_{44}$	increments to S

Next, i is increased to $i = 2$ and row 2 of **X** [i.e, X(2,1), X(2,2), X(2,3), and X(2,4)] is transferred into the CU. Thus, for $j = 1$, all four A registers will store X(2,1) and after execution of 21 $=>$ B, the B registers will hold Y(1,1), Y(1,2), Y(1,3), and Y(1,4). The S registers will therefore start accumulating the next sums from X(2,1)* Y(1,1), X(2,1)*Y(1,2), X(2,1)*Y(1,3), and X(2,1)*Y(1,4), respectively, If j is increased to 2, 3, and then to 4, the second row is calculated. In the same way, rows 3 and 4 are calculated.

Note that row i of **X** is copied into the control unit from the LMs; column j of **Y** is fetched into the B registers also from the LMs of the respective PEs. Thus, *there is no memory contention (interference)*.

The speedup, ratio, and efficiency were defined in Chapter 1. For the matrix multiplication example, if it is assumed that the number p of PEs equals the size of the matrix n, these can be calculated by counting the operations in the inner loop (on j): Two transfers $(2*\tau)$, one addition α, and one multiplication μ are required for each $i-j$ pair (i.e., n^2 times altogether). The outer loop requires n synchronizations and thus the time of $n*\zeta$. The ratio is therefore (with $\omega = \alpha + \mu$)

$$\rho = [n^2*(a+\mu)+2*n^2*\tau+n*\zeta]/[n^3\omega] = 1/n+2*\tau'/n+\zeta'/n^2 \qquad (3\text{-}9)$$

$$\eta = 100/(1+2*\tau'+\zeta'/n) \simeq 100/(1+2*\tau'); \ \tau'=\tau/\omega; \ \zeta'=\zeta/\omega \qquad (3\text{-}10)$$

For $\tau' = 0.5$, an efficiency of only 50% would be achieved. Actually, $\tau' = \tau/\omega$, $\zeta' = << 0.5$, but if $n /= p$, then the efficiency will decrease again.

With an interconnection network that can connect all m LMs to a given PE, it is very desirable to be able to access not only rows, but also columns, diagonals, subdiagonals, etc., *without conflicts*. This cannot be achieved if the matrix is stored as a vector, or in the "natural order," Fig. 3-11(a).

For a 4-by-4 matrix (n = 4), and 5 (a primary number) instead of 4 LMs, the storage could be "skewed" [Law75] as in Fig. 3-11(b). Suppose that row and column 3 is to be accessed. The row is indicated in Fig. (b) by circles, the column by squares. The main diagonal cannot be accessed simultaneously in all LMs, but if the storage is arranged as in Fig. 3-11(c), then it also can be accessed concurrently.

In general, data must be arranged efficiently for computations on ILLIAC. This rearrangement is to be done ahead of the actual computation and may take more time than the calculation proper or, for that matter, than some sequential calculations. For not completely inefficient use of ILLIAC, rows and columns must be equally accessible (i.e., skewed storage must be provided). It is not easy to modify the "natural" arrangement of data. As an example of the difficulties encountered, the data arrangement for eigenvalue calculations as shown in [KaS72] are mentioned. This paper shows that even without a basic change in the algorithm, a complete layout of data is required and that it is by no means easy to secure data for each PE in its own or in its four neighboring LMs.

In summary, the major objections to the use of ARPs are:

1. One reason for using PPSs is *availability* and *fault detection*. The meaning of availability is that even if any of the units is faulty, the system should be available and function properly (maybe somewhat slower). In ARPs there will be a way to

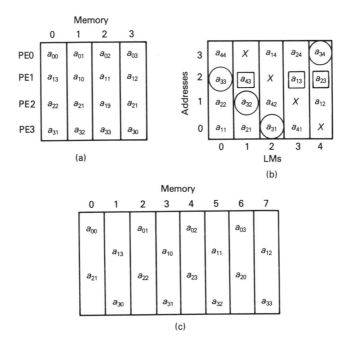

Figure 3-11 Skewed storage of matrices

substitute for the PEs, but the entire system is down if the controller (or host) is down. By fault tolerance we understand that the system should periodically check itself, amputate faulty parts and proceed working. It is difficult to check the CU of an ARP.

2. The speedup of matrix multiplication was high for dense matrices. The matrices of most practical problems are very large and extremely sparse (size 2,000-by-2,000 with only 10–20 nonzero terms in a row is considered average). In an ARP, a PE is either following CU-orders or is doing nothing. Hence, for sparse matrices, most of the PEs will do nothing most of the time and the machine will not be utilized efficiently. Our matrix multiplication program is then very inefficient.

3. It was seen that memory assignment for matrices is rather difficult and that there is a lot of waste in memory usage. Since memories cost as much as the CPUs, this increases the price even more.

4. The interconnection network may be rather complicated and costly.

5. Most important, routing was seen to be complicated and inefficient. With a fixed topology, *ARPs are efficient only for data-parallel problems*. On the other hand, if the topology could adapt itself dynamically to the problem, the efficiency would be higher (e.g., instead of going through a number of PEs in a mesh, make them into neighbors). This will be used in the CM of Sec. 3-5.

6. Data-parallel, small-grained problems are solved efficiently using loops. Unfortunately, not all programs can use loops and not all loops fit exactly the number p of

PEs. For instance, to run an 8x9 problem on an 8x8 ARP would increase the time by 100% compared to the time of running an 8x8 problem. On the other hand, a 16x8 problem could be solved easily by asking each of the 64 PEs to do two operations instead of one.

3–4 ASSOCIATIVE PROCESSORS

3–4.1 The General Idea

In 1945, Dr. V. Bush discussed the problem of accessing the ever-increasing amount of information. Data-retrieval was in its infancy, but it was pointed out by Bush that selecting it by a subclass (as in telephones) or sequentially (as in computer addressing) seemed to be inefficient. We have seen that the access to memory (or bus) limits the performance of PPSs (by contention) especially since much of the traffic sends information merely to calculate the effective address. Moreover, Bush asserted that the mind does not work in either way but "associatively" and that "*selection by association, rather than by indexing, may yet be mechanized.*"

Let us give an example of what "selection by association" means. Suppose that we have a list of student files each containing a student's name, age, social security number, courses taken, grades obtained, etc. Next, suppose that a teacher has submitted grades for a course and these have to be entered into the files of the students who took the course. Checking the entire list starting with the first and ending with the last student, asking each time if the particular student has taken this particular course, would be extremely inefficient. On the other hand, if we could broadcast the names of the students who took the course and get a "tag" for matching student files we could insert the grades into the tagged files only. Instead of searching sequentially the files of *all* students at the university we could locate each time a small number of persons and update their files.

This was an example of an "exact match." Next are examples of "comparative match." We do not usually care for what the Germans used to call an "ewiger Student," which is loosely translated as "lifelong student." We could ask who are the students enrolled for more than, say, ten years. All students for which this is true would "raise their hands" (actually, the so-called activity registers). By broadcasting a letter that it is time to leave the university, and writing it only to students who raised their hands, we have solved the problem in a one-two punch. The same difference between associative and vector memories (indices used for addressing) can be exemplified by a professor asking the students if they have a certain book. Vector addressing means to ask every student *in turn* according to his/her seat. Associative addressing means to ask the students to raise a hand if they have the book, and then look at the response. In the second (parallel) case, the process will be definitely shorter.

Associative search is also called *search by content*. The content we were looking for in the three examples was who took the course, who is enrolled for longer than ten years, and who has the book.

3–4.2 Associative Memories

Associative processors are ARPs, except that they access and manipulate their memories through content instead of by a vector address. Using such memories, Associative Processors, APs execute very efficiently operations on many sets of data with a single instruction (i.e., in parallel). These are exemplified by searching, but they are also capable of performing traditional serial computations at reasonable speeds.

Figure 3-12(a) shows words partitioned into three segments. The left segment shows if the location is used and if so the type of information stored (data or code). It was seen that in order to retrieve data by content, it must be possible to match items with a search-key word (the files). The middle field is used for this. If a part of a word, a *field*, has to be matched, other parts of the key have to be "masked out." The right segment holds the information to be returned or modified. Hence, the middle field could be as shown in Fig. 3-12(a), where a 10-word, 12-bits per word memory is searched for "1101" in its inner four bits. The result would be stored in ten "tag flip-flops" (the hands of the students). The outer eight bits of the words are "masked out" by the 0's of the mask and are not compared with 1101 at all. The comparisons are made by the statement:

$$\text{if (key and mask) then tag} := 1; \tag{3-11}$$

The correlation is done sequentially by bits (i.e., bit-5, then bit-6, bit-7, and finally bit-8)—it is called a *word-parallel, bit-sequential* search. All words are processed simultaneously, but bit-by-bit, one bit at a time. A single time unit is required for every bit, so that the search will take the time of b time units.

Bit "slices" are defined as follows: If the memory is visualized as in Fig. 3-12(b), then word i includes $B(i,1)$, $B(i,2)$, . . . , $B(i,m)$, and *bit slice j* includes $B(1,j)$, $B(2,j)$, . . . , $B(n,j)$. The slice is a binary vector which includes the j-th bit of every word that was selected and the "don't cares" for all those words that were not selected (tagged).

The collection of all tag bits is called the *response store*. The Control Unit (CU) should be able to set all tags to 1 by a single command SET; broadcast a word that is in its comparand to all words; or send a part of the comparand for which the mask bits are 1. If the CU issues a COMPARE instruction then all words that do not match the unmasked part of the comparand will reset their tags to 0. The CU can also READ or WRITE into bit positions of words whose tags are on.

Signal $R(i)$ of word i in Fig. 3-12(c) is

$$R(i) := \Sigma M[(j)*(C(j)*B'(i,j) + C'(j)*B(i,j)]; \; i, \, j\Sigma = 1,2, \ldots, m \tag{3-12}$$

where m is the number of bits in a word and summation or multiplication are understood as Boolean "OR" and "AND" respectively. Thus, if the masking flip-flop is off, $M(j) = 0$ and the tags will not be reset. If the masking flip-flop is on, the tag $T(i)$ will be reset if

$$\text{we look for } C(j) = 1, \text{ but } B(i,j) = 0 \text{ or}$$

$$\text{we look for } C(j) = 0, \text{ but } B(i,j) = 1 \tag{3-13}$$

i.e., when $B(i,j)$ does not correspond to the comparand $C(j)$.

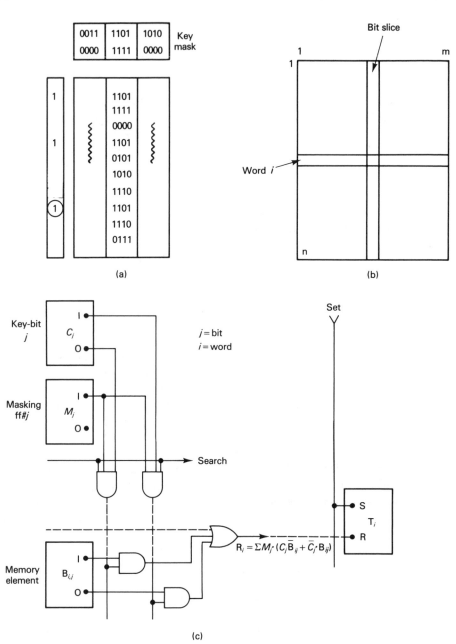

Figure 3-12 Associative storage, bit slices, and switching circuit

The first associative memories were special (e.g., cryogenic memories) and very expensive. Even for the memory as depicted in Fig. 3-12(c), the amount of hardware [Fos76] is approximately 50% higher than that needed for vector (index) addressed memories. (A hash table could be used in place of the associative memory, but not when speed is essential.)

Suppose that the largest of n words, stored in memory, is to be determined. First, all tag bits are SET (i.e., made 1). Then, with the mask of "100 . . . 0," the most significant (left-most) bit of all words are compared with 1. Following the first comparison, r words for which $T(i)$ remains 1 have in fact a 1 in their most significant bit, the $n-r$ words which have a 0 cannot compete for being largest. Next, the same is done for bits 2,3, . . . , m of the memory, each time either updating the corresponding bit in the key register or leaving a "1" there. With all m bits processed, the key register stores the largest word (or k words, if k of them are identical).

Comparison is an area of applications in which associative processors excel. Let us see how arithmetic could be done.

If every word is viewed as composed of fields F1, F2, . . . Fk, and each field has b bits, then the following operations may be performed:

$$Fk := Fj\char`^Fj; \quad \text{in all words with } T=1,$$

$$Fk := C\char`^Fj; \quad \text{between the comparand C and all words, and}$$

$$Fk := Fi\char`^Fj; \quad \text{between different words.}$$

The operator "`^`" is an addition, subtraction, multiplication, division, comparison $(>, \geq, =, \leq, <)$, etc. Using these operators, we can for instance calculate $\mathbf{s} := \mathbf{a} + \mathbf{b}$ where $\mathbf{s}$, $\mathbf{a}$, and $\mathbf{b}$ are vectors of b bits of a field in a word. Addition of two bits is based on the following Boolean equations:

$$s(i) := a(i) \oplus b(i) \oplus c(i) \tag{3-14}$$

$$c(i+1) := a(i*b(i) + a(i)*c(i) + b(i)*c(i) \tag{3-15}$$

where s and c are the sum and carry bits, while $*$, $+$, and $\oplus$ denote "and," "or," and "exclusive or," respectively.

3–4.3 PEPE [EaT73, MaH78, VaC78][†]

PEPE was assembled for Ballistic Missile Defense applications (i.e., for inherently parallel problems). The applications include multiple target tracking, discrimination, etc. Such problems require:

1. Matching real-time data with independent targets.
2. A large amount of scientific calculations (e.g., Kalman filters).
3. High reliability because of the nature of the problems.

[†]A.E. Evensen, J.L. Troy: "Introduction to . . . PEPE," Sagamore Conf. on Parallel Processing, 1973, p. 162–168 (© IEEE, 1973); M.P. Mariani, E.J. Henry: "PEPE—a user's viewpoint . . .," Nat. Comp. Conf., 1978, pp. 993–1002; and C.R. Vick, J.A. Cornell: "PEPE Architecture . . .," Nat. Comp. Conf. 1978, pp. 981–992 (© IEEE, 1978). All three by permission of the IEEE.

For matching data with targets, PEPE uses *associative memories* and is an ARP, with a large number of PEs under global control. The global control units and the *Control Console* interact with a *host* computer to reduce its computational load by ''offloading'' all parallel tasks.

A general block diagram of PEPE is shown in Fig. 3-13. The host is a CDC7600, and each of the 288 Processing Elements (PEs) is composed of three processors sharing a common memory. The Correlation Unit (CU) correlates input with stored data by association. The Associative Output Unit (AOU) orders and outputs data. It is designed to perform complex, multidimensional searches rapidly and efficiently. The Arithmetic Unit (AU) is used for large-scale scientific calculations; it is similar to a conventional general-purpose computer with fixed-point and floating-point operations, loads, stores, etc.

PEPE (Fig. 3-13) can be viewed as showing three ARPs: a correlation, an arithmetic, and an associative-output unit. Each of the three systems is driven by a separate control unit, namely by CCU for the correlation, ACU for the arithmetic, and AOCU for the associative-output unit. All three CUs are combined into a control console.

PEPE is an associatively addressed ensemble of parallel processing elements. The key words are ''associative,'' ''ensemble,'' and ''parallel.''

PEPE is *associative* because data storage or retrieval is based on data content rather than data location. By avoiding the inefficient search conducted through vector address-ing, very high correlation of input and output operations can be achieved.

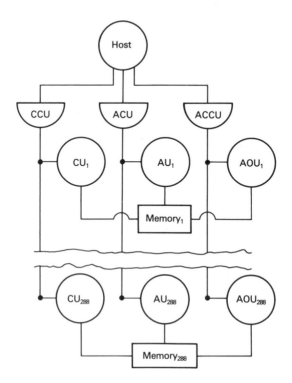

Figure 3-13   The architecture of PEPE

PEPE is called an *ensemble* because it is unstructured and there is no lock-step synchronization as in other ARPs. PEPE was one of the first PPSs to be based on prospective VLSI chips or *PaMs*. The advantage of modularity is that the hardware is simple and inexpensive. Reliability is enhanced by the fact that a PE can fail with no impact on the calculations, in progress, in other PEs. Moreover, for BMD problems, data are continuously being updated, so that if a PE fails it can be disconnected and the job transferred to another PE. A new file is started in the latter PE so that only the file in the disconnected PE is lost.

Several tradeoff decisions were made in assigning functional capabilities to different parts of PEPE. These tradeoffs were made to improve the response of PEPE for BMD. The design decisions were:

1. *No interelement communication*. The PEs cannot communicate directly, but only through the Control Console (i.e., sequentially). The lack of a parallel interelement data transfer capability limits the speed of PEPE on problems with interrelated data sets (e.g., in most numerical problems). Since the BMD application involves independent data sets, this is of no major concern. For such *data parallel* problems, each independent data set (e.g., a file on a missile or an aircraft) is assigned to a PE, and each PE performs identical operations on different files—it is an ARP.

2. *Floating-point vs. fixed-point arithmetic*. PEPE has six different processor types: three sequential control units and three parallel slaves. All of them are capable of simultaneous, overlapped operation. It had to be decided which operations require floating-point and which require only fixed-point arithmetic. The control units are of standard design with each being equipped with its own data and program memory. These control units are used mainly for comparison, branching, control of program flow, and supervisory operations which need only integer, branching, load, store, and logic operations, but no floating-point hardware. The scientific calculations are done in the Arithmetic Units—AUs—so they were provided with a full, powerful repertoire of floating-point arithmetic operators, in addition to the conventional and associative operators. The CUs and AOUs are mainly used for input and output of data, to perform associative comparisons, matches, searches, and ordering functions; all of which can be handled with logical and integer-arithmetic operations. However, they are occasionally used for some subroutines which also require floating-point operations. Instead of providing the CU and the AOU with floating-point hardware, it was decided to let the respective CUs interrupt the ACU, which then asks one or more AUs to interrupt their neighbors. This was indicated by saying that there is no direct connection between the three units. Simulations proved that the performance degradation due to lack of floating-point hardware in the CUs and AOUs is insignificant, while the reduction in price of these units is considerable.

3. A *parallel instruction queue* is needed and was provided for the parallel instruction streams of the ACU because the program memory of the ACU is larger and slower than the other memories.

4. A *common data memory*. Instructions are broadcast to all PEs from the control units; the data are stored in a common memory. This would lead to contention (recall Sec.

1-3) and conflicts incompatible with real-time processing, except if there is a *fixed priority* of access. Since it is less important if a given calculation is done on time, while it is extremely important to correlate all the incoming information with the data files, it was decided that the priorities should be CU first, AOU second, and AU last. Simulations have indicated that with these priorities, the AU will execute at only a 5% reduction of speed compared with the case when it had exclusive access to the memory.

The ACU and CCU, together with the host, store and control the programs specifying the operations of the AUs and CUs. The ACU broadcasts one instruction at a time simultaneously to all AUs. The same is done by the ACU for all the CUs—remember it is a SIMD system. The AU and CU in each PE share the 1024 word, 32-bit memory (RAM) on a cycle-stealing basis and the correlation of these two instruction streams is maintained by the host.

As in other APs, each PE contains an activity, tag flip-flop (register). When a CU broadcasts an instruction, all active PEs respond while nonactive PEs do nothing. At most then, $3*288 = 864$ instructions can be executed simultaneously.

There are two types of parallelism in PEPE—macroscopic and microscopic. In the first, all 288 PEs work in parallel; in the second, data is handled on a bit-sequential but word-parallel basis.

3–5 CELLULAR MACHINES

The two machines of this section process massive amounts of data. One of them is called the Massively Parallel Processor, the *MPP*, and the other is the Connection Machine (*CM*). The description is almost completely based on [Bat80][†] for the MPP and on [Thi87][‡] for the CM.

> In this decade, NASA will orbit imaging sensors that can generate data at rates up to 10^{13} bits per day. A variety of image processing tasks such as geometric correction, correlation, image registration, feature selection, multispectral classification, and area measurement are required to extract useful information from this mass of data. The expected workload is between 10^9 and 10^{10} operations per second. [Bat80]

The MPP of Goodyear Aerospace Corp. processes such vast amounts of data.

The CM was also built with image processing applications in mind. As indicated in [Hil85]:

> In image processing, for example, we know that it is possible to perform two-dimensional filtering operations efficiently using a two-dimensionally connected grid of processing

[†]K.E. Batcher: "Design of a Massively Parallel Processor," Trans. IEEE, Vol. C-29, No. 9, Sept., pp. 836–841 (© 1980, IEEE). Reprinted by permission of the IEEE.

[‡]Thinking Machines Corp.: "Connection Machine CM2, Summary," Technical Report HA87-4. Reprinted by permission of Thinking Machines Corp.

elements. In this application it is most natural to store each point of the image in its own processing cell. A 1000x1000 point image would use a million processors. [Hil85]

The calculations normally requested can be done locally, e.g., to compute the average value for each point as in Code 3-3. The calculation consists then of five steps: in the first four the data are shifted up, down, right, and left; then in the fifth step, the average is taken. This requires eight operations (four shifts, three additions, and one multiplication). For 16K points, a single computer would need $16K*(3*\alpha + \mu)$, so that

$$\sigma = 16K*(3*\alpha + \mu)/(4*\tau + 3*\alpha + \mu)$$

and, if we neglect the transfer time of $4*\tau$, $\sigma \simeq 16{,}384$. The speedup seems to be extremely high except that addition and multiplication are done bit-by-bit and thus slowly.

The above method of solving a problem was called *inherently or data-parallel* programming and may be summarized by saying that the programmer has *a large number of conventional processors* operating within a *uniform address space* in a *synchronous execution mode*. This last was the case above since the same operations were done on all *cells* of the CM.

3–5.1 The Massively Parallel Processor, MPP

The major components of MPP are shown in Fig. 3-14(a).

> The array unit (ARU) processes arrays of data at high speed and is controlled by the array control unit (ACU), which also performs scalar arithmetic. The program and data management unit (PDMU) controls the overall flow of data and program through the system and handles certain ancillary tasks such as program development and diagnostics. The staging memories buffer and reorder data between ARU, PDMU, and external (host) computer. [Bat80]

These units will next be discussed in more detail, starting with the *ARRAY UNIT*, ARU.

The 16,384 cells of the ARU are organized as a 128-by-128 mesh. This topology matches the two-dimensional nature of satellite imagery, and the reformatting of data between the ARU and the outside world is handled in a "staging memory."

Since the edges of the mesh had to be sometimes connected and sometimes left open,

> edge-connectivity was made a programmable function. A topology register in the ACU defines the connections between opposite edges of the cell array. The top and bottom edges can either be connected or left open. The connectivity between the left and right edges has four states: open (no connection), cylindrical (connect the left cell of each row to the right cell of the same row), open spiral (for $1<n<127$) connect the left PE of row n to the right PE of row $n-1$, and closed spiral (like the open spiral, but also connect the left PE of row 0 to the right PE of row 127).
>
> The spiral modes connect the 16,384 cells together in one long linear array. One can pack several linear arrays of odd sizes (e.g., lines with thousands of image pixels per line) in the ARU and process them in parallel. [Bat80]

In order to enhance *reliability*, there are 132, instead of 128 columns, with the additional four columns used for availability. The 132 columns are divided into 33 groups of four columns each. When a faulty cell is discovered, its entire group is disabled and the additional group connected in its place. Because the data cannot be trusted, the program is restarted from the last checkpoint or from its starting point. Thus, there are always 128 columns working.

Processing is done in a *bit-serial* mode. This has the advantage of processing words of varying length.

> Conventional computers typically use bit-parallel arithmetic units with certain fixed-word lengths such as 8, 16, or 32 bits. Operands of odd lengths are extended to fit standard word sizes of the machine. Some of the hardware in the memory and the arithmetic unit is wasted storing and processing the extensions.
>
> Bit-serial processors can handle operands of any length without any wasted hardware. Their slower speed can be counteracted by using a multitude of them and processing many operands in parallel. [Bat80]

Each *cell* of the MPP has a full adder and a shift register, as well as six 1-bit registers [A,B,C,G,P, and S of Fig. 3-14(b)], a random-access memory, a data-bus (D), and some combinational logic.

Logic and Routing: The P-register is used for logic and routing operations. A logic operation combines the state of the P-register and the state of the data bus (D) to form the new state of the P-register. All 16 Boolean functions of the two variables P and D are implemented. A routing operation shifts the state of the P-register into the P-register of a neighboring cell (up, down, right, or left).

Arithmetic: The full adder, shift register, and registers A, B, and C are used for bit-serial arithmetic operations. To add two operands, the bits of one operand are put into the A register, one at a time, least significant bit (LSB) first. The corresponding bits of the other operand are put into the P register. Then the full adder adds the bits in A and P to the carry bits in the C register to form the sum and carry bits. Each carry bit is stored in C to be added in the next cycle and each sum bit is stored in B. The sum formed in B can be stored in the random-access memory and/or in the shift register.

> Two's complement subtraction is performed by adding the one's complement of the operand in P to the operand in A and setting the initial carry bit in C to 1 instead of 0.
>
> Multiplication is a series of addition steps where the partial product is recirculated through the shift register, register A, and register B. Appropriate multiples of the multiplicand are formed in P and added to the partial product as it recirculates. Division is performed with a nonrestoring division algorithm. The partial dividend is recirculated through the shift register, register A, and register B, while the divisor or its complement is formed in P and added to it.
>
> Floating-point addition compares exponents; places the fraction of the operand with the least exponent in the shift register; shifts it to the right to align it with the other fraction;

adds the other fraction to the shift-register; and normalizes the sum. Floating-point multiplication is a multiplication of the fractions, a normalization of the product, and an addition of the exponents.

The G register can hold a mask bit such that the operations are performed only in those cells for which the G-bit is 1. A masked routing operation can be combined with an unmasked arithmetic operation or vice versa. We are dealing with the tag bits again.

Storage: The random-access memory stores 1,024 bits per cell. Standard RAM integrated circuits are used to make it easy to expand storage as advances occur in solid-state memory technology. The ACU generates 16-bit addresses so ARU storage can be expanded to 65,536 bits per cell. Thus, the initial complement of 2 MBytes of ARU storage can be expanded 64-fold if technology allows it. A parity bit is added for error detection.

Input/Output: The S register is used to input and output ARU data. While the cells are processing data in the random-access memories, columns of input data are shifted into the left side of the ARU, and through the S registers [Fig. 3-14(b)] until a plane of 16,384 bits is loaded. The input plane is then stored in the random-access memories in one 100 nns cycle by interrupting the processing momentarily in all PEs and moving the S register values to the memory elements. Planes of data are output by moving them from the memory elements to the S registers and then shifting them out column by column through the right side of the ARU. The shift rate is 10 MHz; thus, up to 160 Mbytes/s can be transferred through the ARU I/O ports. Processing is interrupted for 100 ns for each bit plane of 16,384 bits transferred—less than 1 percent of the time.

The *Array Control Unit*, ACU: Like the control unit of other parallel processors, the ACU performs scalar arithmetic and controls the cells. It has three sections that operate in parallel: cell control, I/O control, and main control. Cell control performs all array arithmetic of the application program. I/O control manages the flow of data in and out of the ARU. Main control performs all scalar arithmetic of the application program. This arrangement allows array arithmetic, and input/output to be overlapped for minimum execution time.

The basic clock rate is 10 MHz. Due to the massive parallelism, very high speeds were achieved. Table 3-3 shows some of these, measured in Million Operations per second (MOPs). Note how much slower it processes floating-point-data—but then the MPP was built to process integers.

3–5.2 The Connection Machine, the CM

For applications mentioned earlier, the PPS seems to require an unlimited number of PEs. Since the CM has no infinite resources, compromises will have to be made.

The first compromise is to have a large but not unlimited amount of memory in every cell. Second, since large numbers of cells are to be used, they must be as small and as simple as possible so that we can afford to have as many of them as we want. The cells

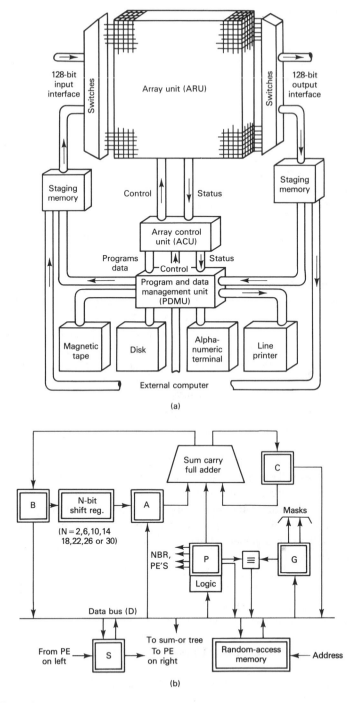

Figure 3-14 The architecture and components of the MPP. Courtesy of K. E. Batcher: "Design of a Massively Parallel Processor," Trans. IEEE, Vol. C-29, No. 9, Sept. 80, pp. 836–41 (© 1980, IEEE).

TABLE 3-3 EXECUTION SPEEDS FOR THE MPP

Operations	Execution speed[†]
Addition of Arrays	
8-bit integers (9-bit sum)	6553
12-bit integers (13-bit sum)	4428
32-bit floating-point numbers	430
Multiplication of Arrays	
(Element-by-Element)	
8-bit integers (16-bit product)	1861
12-bit integers (24-bit product)	910
32-bit floating-point numbers	216
Multiplication of Array by Scalar	
8-bit integers (16-bit product)	2340
12-bit integers (24-bit product)	1260
32-bit floating-point numbers	373

[†]Million Operations per Second

K. E. Batcher: "Design of a Massively Parallel Processor,"
Trans. IEEE, Vol. C-29, No. 9, Sept. 80, pp. 836–841 (©
1980, IEEE) by permission.

of the CM are so small that 16 of them fit on a single chip of 1 cm^2 together with a router for the MIN and a decoder.

The CM uses message, and not circuit switching. For a very large number of cells, the connections will be done better by software. We may then tailor the routing for each application separately to avoid "traffic jams." The combination of fine granularity and software communication is especially adapted to the "symbol crunching" of the CM, as distinguished from the "number crunching" of, say, CRAY-1.

A shared bus, ring, or crossbar switch are not feasible INs for the large number of nodes. The CM should handle nonlocal and nonregular communication patterns, which rules out the meshes and trees. For the CM, a Cube was chosen for the following reasons:[†]

First, a Cube has redundant data paths. This, it was felt, would reduce delays in routing due to contention for wires. Second, a Cube has only computational nodes, rather than a mixture of computational and switching nodes; this reduces the number of different component types. In addition, it makes the computational facitilies of the individual nodes available to assist in the routing of messages. Finally, every node in a Cube is topologically equivalent; this means that only one type of node, and one type of board to carry those nodes, is ever needed. Based on economic and engineering limits, a Cube with 4096 (2^{12}) nodes was chosen.

There are advantages to placing more than one cell at each node of a Cube. First, for the regular pattern alluded to above, it is optimal to have one cell attached to each wire of a node. Second, for nonregular patterns, doubling the number of cells at each node causes the communication time to increase by a factor of less than two. This effect is due to the efficient utilization of the interconnecting wires. A Cube has sufficient bandwidth to route messages in

[†][Sta 87].

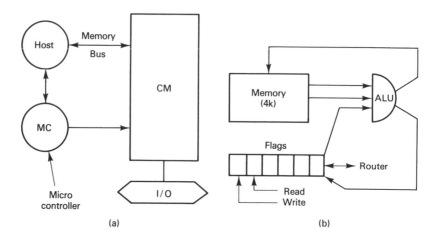

Figure 3-15 The architecture and elements of CM

$\log(p)$ time. However, because it is impossible to keep all wires busy all the time, the actual communication time is $\log^2(p)$. Putting several cells at each wire and queuing messages waiting to use the wire increases the utilization of the system's raw bandwidth. Partly on the basis of these considerations, each node was given 16 cells. This gives a total of 65,536 (2^{16}) cells. [Sta87]

The CM consists of 64K cells, connected in a Cube of dimension 12 each with 512 bytes of memory, a *host* computer which stores data in much the same way that a conventional machine stores them in memory, the I/O, and the microcontroller. Its block diagram is shown in Fig. 3-15(a).

The host may ask each cell to multiply two values locally, provided the status is "on," or transfer some information through the IN. Thus, a single command from the host can result in tens of thousands of multiplications and a permutation of data that depends on the pattern of connections. Since all these operations happen in parallel on all cells, the CM is a *data-parallel system*. It not only reduces the time by parallelism, but also makes the programming very easy—it follows the natural parallelism of a problem.

The CM-2 has floating-point operations—the CM-1 does not. Custom Weitek chips serve as floating-point coprocessors. Each is shared by 32 PaMs, so that in a CM-2 with 64K PaMs, there are 2K FP-chips. According to [Thi87][†]: "When 64K processors are operating in parallel, each performing a 32-bit integer addition, the CM-2 parallel processing unit operates at about 2,500 Mips." With the floating-point chip, 3,500 MFlops (single precision) or 2,500 MFlops (double precision) can be achieved.

In addition to the programmable IN, the CM-2 has a NEWS (for North, East, West, and South) grid which can connect the 64K cells into a 256x256, a 1024x64, a 16x16x16x16 mesh, and other meshes. The advantage of the mesh over the router is that there is no need to specify the destination addresses; it is either all N, or E, or W, or S.

[†]Thinking Machines Corp.: "Connection Machine CM2, Summary," Technical Report HA87-6. Reprinted by permission of Thinking Machines Corp.

A small crossbar, the *Nexus*, interconnects the front ends with the PPSs. Reconfiguration time of the Nexus is counted in seconds. For every group of 8K data processors there is one I/O channel. The CM has eight "*Data Vaults*," each of which consists of 39 individual disk drives. A Data Vault holds 5 Gbytes of data, expandable to 10 Gbytes, and transfers data at the rate of 40 Mbytes/sec. Since the eight vaults may operate in parallel, a combined rate of 320 Mbytes/sec can theoretically be achieved.

The host provides program development and execution environment. All CM programs execute on a host; during the course of execution the host issues instructions to the CM-2 parallel processing unit. In effect, the CM-2 parallel processing unit extends the instruction set and I/O capabilities of the front-end computer.

To the user, the CM appears to be an extended version of the host computer. There are several direct benefits to maintaining program control only on the host. First, programmers can use the same programming language, debugging facilities, and operating system of the host with which they are familiar. Second, only the part of the code that pertains specifically to the data residing in the CM processors needs to use any extensions to the language of the host. Finally, parts of the program more suited for the host, e.g., file manipulation, can be done on the host, while the part of the program that runs efficiently in parallel, namely the "inner loops" that operate on the data set, can be done on the CM. In this way, the individual strengths of both the serial front-end and the CM processors can be exploited.

The block diagram of a cell is shown in Fig. 3-15(b). It consists of an ALU, 4K (or in CM-2, 64K) bits of memory, flags, an optional floating point accelerator, a router, NEWS, and I/O interfaces. The basic operation of the PE is to read two bits from the external memory and one flag, calculate the two bits of the result and to write the resulting bits into the external memory and an internal flag, respectively. This sequence of operations requires three clock cycles, one for each reference to the external memory. During these three cycles, the microcontroller specifies two 12-bit addresses (the first bit and result as well as the second bit), three 4-bit flags for reading, writing, conditionalizing, and 1 bit for sensing the condition, eight bits for specifying which of the 256 Boolean operations is to be done, which computes the flags, and two bits for specifying in which direction data is to move through the NEWS network. The (65,536) set of instructions on the CM includes not only the usual arithmetic and logical operations, but also thousands of useless operations. In the future, this set will probably be optimized, the speed of the PE increased, and the width of its microcode reduced.

Each cell of the CM-2 contains one router node, which serves the 16 data processors on the chip. The router nodes on all the processor chips are wired together to form the Cube MIN. Each router node is connected to 12 other router nodes. Specifically, router node i (serving data processors $16i$ through $16i + 15$) is connected to router node j if and only if $|i - j| = 2^k$ for some integer k, in which case we say that routers i and j are connected along dimension k.

Each message travels from one router node to another until it reaches the chip containing the destination cell. The router nodes automatically forward messages and perform some dynamic balancing. For example, suppose that cell 117 (which is cell 5 on router node 7, because $117 = 16*7 + 5$) has a message M whose destination is cell 361 (which is cell 9 on router node 22 because $361 = 16*22 + 9$). Since $22 = 7 + 2^4 - 2^0$, this message must travers dimensions 0 and 4 to reach its destination. In the absence of congestion, router 7 forwards the message to router 6 ($6 = 7 - 2^0$), which forwards it to router 22 ($22 = 6 + 2^4$), which delivers the message to cell 361. On the other hand, if router 7 has another message that needs to use dimension 0, it may choose to send message M along dimension 4 first, to router 23 ($23 = 7 + 2^4$), which then forwards the message to router 22, which delivers it.

A *Microcontroller* occupies an intermediate position between the host and the nodes. The host specifies higher level macroinstructions, which are interpreted by the microcontroller to produce nanoinstructions, which are then executed directly by the nodes. The instructions executed by the microcontroller that specify how this interpretation is to take place are called microinstructions. The bit-at-a-time nanoinstructions are executed very fast.

As already mentioned, software can change the connections of the CM. In Fig. 3-16 we show the $2**n$ PEs and $2**n$ LMs. The address field of any LM(i) points to a PaM(k). Assuming a fixed displacement, this connects Data(i) to Destination(k). The microcontroller may change these pointers, thereby changing the underlying topology.

Summary: Cellular arrays are ARPs. They are more expensive because their memories are associative, and provide a very high speedup only for data-parallel problems. The CM can also use its dynamically changing topology for solving logic problems such as needed in artificial intelligence.

Note: After this book was written, the author had a chance to work with a CM and found it can be used in many more applications than indicated here.

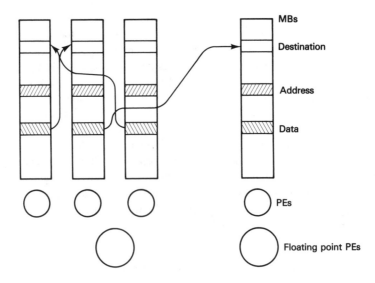

Figure 3-16   Addressing in the CM-2

3–6 PROBLEMS

1. Explain start-up time and instruction pre-fetch, and the need for and problems of adding buffers between stages. Explain how a vector computer works and why the speedup is reduced.

2. What is the speedup of pipeline computers and why is it so seldom achieved? Write a ''program'' for matrix-addition and a program similar to the matrix-multiplication program for ILLIAC (Sec. 3-3) but for a vector machine. Assume that the length of the pipelines is much shorter than the order n of the matrices. Remember that VPs work efficiently only if loops on long vectors can be performed. Calculate the speedup and efficiency of both your programs. Write a ''program'' for matrix addition for APs and PAPs.

3. Compare a single CPU to a pipelined computer and to an array of processors for execution of a loop.

4. Explain how an associative processor finds in which memories a word is stored (say, such that there is 0011 in the least significant bits). Draw one bit of an associative memory and explain how it works.

5. Explain how the CRAY-1 and the ILLIAC work. Which IN does each use?

6. Draw the skewed storage of a 16-by-16 matrix in a 17-MB memory.

7. Explain why different types of memories are needed in a PAP. Explain why the crossbar is needed for the AP120-B and what is special about it. List the design guidelines of the AP120-B and justify them.

8. Write the two ''programs'' of problem 2 but now for the AP120-B. (If needed, compare with the program described in [Cha81].)

9. Describe an associative memory and the connection between bit-slice processing and the speedup. Describe the overall architecture of PEPE and its advantages, as well as the design considerations of PEPE and their influence on its design.

10. Sometimes division is not supported in the hardware but the reciprocal is. Show how the reciprocal can be used for division.

11. CRAY-1 as described in Sec. 3-1 uses a hierarchy of memories including the two buffers T and B. These memories could be compared to a cache except that they are not managed automatically. Data are moved in and out of these buffers by program instructions. Discuss the advantages and disadvantages of this arrangement as compared to a possible use of a cache instead. How does it influence the overall speed? Is programming made easier or more difficult? Is the type of programming used in vector processors more or less adaptable to a cache? Do we need it?

CHAPTER 4

SHARED-MEMORY MULTIPROCESSORS

The objectives of this chapter are:

Describe the organization of Shared-Memory Multiprocessors (SMs) and Message-Passing Multicomputers (MPs). Example systems are included in order to discuss briefly the problems of multiprocessors, namely (memory) contention, synchronization, and scheduling.

Introduce commercially available and university-sponsored SMs.

Discuss hardware solutions, namely the use of local and cache memory, synchronization by the F&A operation, and the combining switch.

Derive the bounds of speedup for SM Multiprocessors.

4–1 ORGANIZATION OF PIONEERING SM SYSTEMS

4–1.1 Communication Methods

All MIMD systems work with larger tasks (larger granularity) than the SIMD systems. Since there is no lock-step synchronization, the tasks must first be *scheduled* (spawned). Since the execution time of these tasks is unequal and sometimes unpredictable, they must be coordinated, *synchronized*. Finally, for these tasks to proceed, they must *communicate*. The way to communicate depends on the hardware: Multiprocessors may communicate either by sending messages or by using the common memory.

The shared memory scheme may be compared to a bulletin board in a student union. Users post information about merchandise they wish to sell or buy on the board [Fig. 4-1(a)]. The information on the board can be read and updated by anybody: It is *shared* among the ''users.'' This scheme is referred to as a *shared-memory multiprocessor,* the SM.

Message-Passing (MP) multiprocessors communicate by *messages*. This scheme is similar to the mail service [Fig. 4-1(b)] where letters and mailboxes represent the message communication and the buffers, respectively. The sender usually needs an acknowledgment, so we assume that only ''return signature'' letters are sent. This is a type of *protocol* usually required for explicit communication between the sender and receiver of the message.

To cooperate in running a single program, the processors must share data. Some values computed by one of them will be needed by another. The two communication methods for multiprocessors are shown in Fig. 4-1(c) and Fig. 4-1(d): for SMs (or bulletin board), all memory is accessible to all PEs through the Interconnection Network (IN), for MPs any specific memory can be accessed *directly* by one and only one node (a PE and Local Memory, LM). A value produced by one node and needed by another has to be sent by the *producer* to the *consumer*. Like in the mail service, *send* and *receive* primitives are supported by the MP. In SMs, data are sent by the producer executing a *write* to a shared location (the board) and the consumer reads it by executing a *read* on the same address.

In MPs, the communication (letters) is initiated by the producer as soon as it has produced it, so as not to let the consumer wait for it too long. In SMs, the communication is mostly initiated by a consumer looking for some data in the shared memory. The producer sends the data not to any particular consumer, but to an address in the shared memory.

The producer and consumer have to *synchronize,* i.e., the consumer cannot read a message that was not yet produced; it sometimes has to wait. The consumer must be ''told'' that the message exists and the producer has sent it. Additionally, if several messages are sent from a producer to the same consumer, the order must be preserved. In

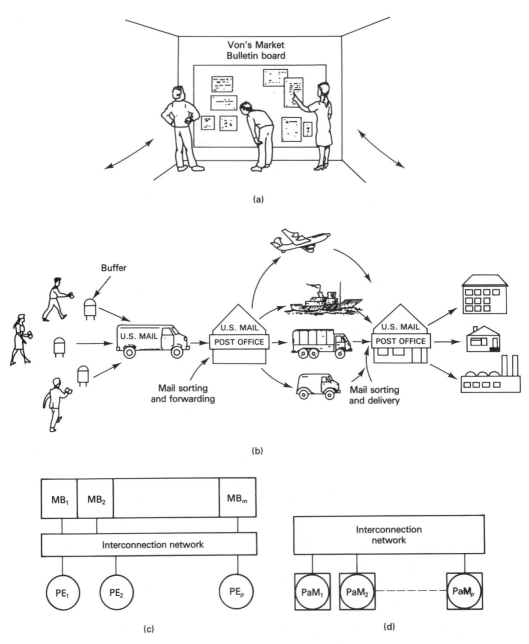

(a)

Buffer

Mail sorting
and forwarding

Mail sorting
and delivery

(b)

| MB₁ | MB₂ | | MBₘ |

Interconnection network

PE₁ PE₂ PEₚ

(c)

Interconnection
network

PaM₁ PaM₂ PaMₚ

(d)

Figure 4-1 The two types of multiprocessors. Courtesy of C. Weitzman: "Distributed Micro/Minicomputer Systems," Prentice Hall (**a** and **b** reprinted by permission).

SMs, the synchronization will be explicit, with the producer informing the consumer that it has sent it a message. In MPs, the synchronization is implicit, since the producer has sent the message with some indication which address should receive the message. This is like in Fig. 4-1: The producer must first post the message for everyone to see; the mail will be delivered only if it was sent to a specific address.

To transfer a message to another node of an MP, the IN has to be activated. If the receiving node is not a direct neighbor, then the message has to go through a number of nodes. Such message passing may be slow if it is implemented in software and requires the cooperation (acknowledgments, etc.) of the receiving node. It may also require buffers (like the mailboxes of Fig. 4-1(b) for multiple messages). We will find in Sec. 4-4 that some Switching Elements of the MIN (mailboxes) may be overloaded and constitute ''hot spots.'' Finally, it must be determined which message is for which consumer.

Recall the granularity (Chap. 1) which could have been defined as the amount of computation that can be done independently by the PEs before required to communicate. Since MPs also show an overhead, they should be used only for algorithms in which message passing is assumed to be infrequent compared to the amount of computations. This means that MPs should be used for medium- or coarse-grained programs. Other mechanisms (ARPs) were used for fine-grained programs.

Equal access is provided by SMs for all processors (PEs) to all of the shared memory. Any PE can write a message to the common memory for any other PE to read. The data is placed in the shared memory where it remains and can be accessed by any PE. SMs do not require protocols (acknowledgments, etc.); communication through direct, shared memory is faster. There is usually no path connecting the PEs, but when MBs are used, a special, costly IN is required (e.g., a crossbar switch). We will see later in Chap. 4 that SMs should apply an even coarser granularity than MPs; otherwise Minsky's conjecture applies.

An advantage of SMs is the relative ease of programming (in the familiar sequential language with only synchronization primitives added). One of the disadvantages is *memory contention*.

Mainframe computers use very large memories in order to apply multiprogramming techniques and increase the throughput. Multiprocessors cannot increase their speed by adding to the common memory since a memory can read or write one unit of data at a time. Returning to our bulletin board example, if only one person can view the board, all others have to wait in a queue. Similarly, if many processors access the same shared memory, serialization of the requests results and nothing is gained. It is better to divide the memory into blocks [Fig. 4-1(c)] and add blocks whenever CPUs are added. Another disadvantage of SMs is that they need specific synchronization. The problems of contention and synchronization will be discussed in Sec. 4-2.

To sum up: In MPs, data sharing is initiated by the producers, synchronization is implicit, addressing is by node/local address, efficiency is gained by the producer sending the message as soon as it is produced, and medium- or coarse-grained algorithms should be used. In SMs, data sharing is initiated by the consumer, synchronization and addressing are explicit, and the consumer waits for the message to arrive. We will discover even more differences, but first let us discuss some SM multiprocessors (MPs are discussed in Chap. 5).

4–1.2 The C.mmp—Carnegie-Mellon Multiprocessor

The C.mmp is an example of an SM. Its design started in 1971, the machine was assembled in 1975, and it remained operational until 1980. The planned architecture is shown in Fig. 4-2, in which p Central Processing Units (PEs) are connected through an interconnection network, IN1, to the m MBs and through IN2 to d I/O channels (e.g., to the disks). The controllers manage secondary memories and I/O devices. The shared primary memory consists of 16 blocks, MB(i), with up to 64K-bits each.

The control of IN1 can be by any of the PEs, but one PE is always assigned to be the monitoring processor. The crossbar IN1 connects p PEs to m MBs, and has $p*m$ crosspoints. The routing of memory requests from the PEs to the MBs is effected by costly, and not very reliable, hardware (within IN1).

A memory block can satisfy only a single request at a time. Hence, if two or more PEs attempt to access the same MB, the resulting conflict is arbitrated by the crossbar switch. If $p>m$, the contention will be too high; if $m>p$, the utilization of the PEs is too low. To avoid memory conflicts or at least to reduce their rate, m is usually made equal to p (in the case of C.mmp, both are 16). This ensures that if each PE is connected to a different MB, no access conflicts exist.

The crossbar switch is not only complicated and expensive, but because of conflicts in access, its computational power can be wasted. To avoid this, local memory LM(i) may be added with the objective of directing most of the memory accesses to it rather than to the main memory. This increases the bandwidth, allowing completely independent operations. The *Map* attached to each PE translates its addresses into physical memory addresses. Usually, the LMs store the kernel code and operating system tables, which are the most commonly used code.

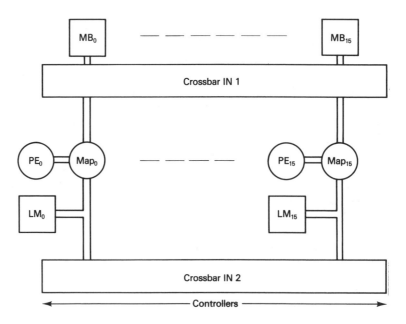

Figure 4-2   The planned architecture of the C.mmp

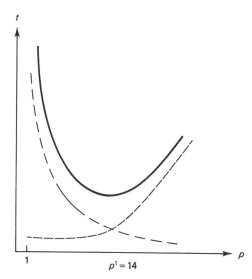

Figure 4-3 Time as function of p, the number of PEs

There are problems with using LMs, e.g., code or data used in common by a number of processes cannot be placed in an LM, but placing it in the main memory will lead to performance degradation due to contention for it (see Sec. 4-2). To reduce conflicts and use better local memory, a cache memory between the Map and the IN was suggested. This would allow programs to migrate into the cache, thereby diminishing the number of requests for a single memory, providing faster access. The problems of using a cache will be discussed in Sec. 4-4.

An additional crossbar (IN3) could be added for handling interrupts. It would permit each PE to direct an interrupt to any other PE. Synchronization between processors may then be effected by such a network. Such an IN3 could also be used by a failing PE to broadcast a hardware-initiated alarm to the functioning PEs.

The assembled C.mmp is different from that of Fig. 4-2. It has no caches, only one crossbar switch (IN1), and the I/O devices are connected to specific PEs on a permanent basis. Since the LMs are only used for interrupts and error-recovery, only the common memory is available for programs resulting in severe memory contention.

A test case was run on the C.mmp with $p = 1,2, \ldots$ It was found (Fig. 4-3) that when $p \geqslant 14$, the more PEs, the more time is needed (i.e., that adding processors is counterproductive). The program itself is running in less time, but the more PEs that are connected, the more contention there is, therefore increasing the overall time.

The operating system of the C.mmp, the Hydra, helped in error detection and recovery. It employed a "watchdog mechanism" which checked every four seconds if any of the PEs was in an endless loop or had stopped working. Another PE was chosen at random to check the "suspect" PE. If it confirmed the suspicions, the suspect PE would be removed; otherwise, more extensive tests are conducted. This recovery scheme was inefficient in that it took about two minutes for the system to restart, and because only the PEs, but not the MBs, or software were checked.

*4–1.3 The Carnegie-Mellon Star—the Cm**

There are two variants of an SM: tightly coupled and loosely coupled SMs. In tightly coupled systems, the main memory is common and the access time for any PE is the same. In loosely coupled systems, the main memory consists of all the Local Memories (LMs) of the p PaMs; the PaMs share the entire address space. Examples of the first are the C.mmp, the Multimax (Encore Corp.), the FX (Alliant) or the Balance (Sequent Corp.), of the second, the Cm*, the Butterfly (BBN), and the RP3 (IBM). The C.mmp and Cm* are discussed in this section, and the Butterfly and the RP3 in later sections of this chapter.

Shared-Memory Systems, SMs, are costly and unreliable because of the crossbar. Hence, this switch is used only for small p ($p = m = 16$ of the C.mmp). Multistage Interconnection Networks (MINs) are cheaper but not as fast. On the other hand, addition of local memories, LMs, to the C.mmp would have increased the throughput, reduced memory interference, and in general improved the performance. It is therefore only logical that Carnegie-Mellon University used the idea of adding LMs to assemble a system based on even more independence between the modules, and reduced coupling between them; this is the Cm*. This subsection will offer a summary of its design and implementation based on [JaG80].[†]

Cm* consists of 50 nodes called computer modules, CMs, connected by a tree structure (Fig. 4-4). At the lowest level, a "Local Switch," called *Slocal,* connects a CM through the Map Bus to other CMs. Up to 14 CMs are grouped together into clusters whose parents are high-speed microprogrammable communication controllers, the *Kmaps.* A Kmap provides the mechanism for CMs to communicate with each other and cooperate with other Kmaps to service requests for accessing CMs in nonlocal clusters. Since Kmaps are microprogrammable, it is usual to implement the key operating system functions in the microcode of these processors. All communication uses *message switching* and is mediated by a Kmap. The Kmap of each cluster has two bidirectional ports, each of which may be connected to a separate *intercluster bus* to implement a variety of interconnection schemes. The availability of Cm* is increased since most units are replaceable and decreased because the Kmap is a scarce unit.

The fundamental computational unit of Cm* is the computer module CM. Each CM contains a processor (PE), local memory (LM), a combination of mass-storage and I/O devices, and the local switch, *Slocal.* The PE is an LSI-11 microprocessor produced by the Digital Equipment Corporation. Each LM may have 64 or 128 Kbytes divided into 4K pages as required by the Slocal. The PE and its LM were separate units in Cm*, but the idea was that PaMs will be built in the future (and they are in 1990).

The Slocal [Fig. 4-4] is a controller for the PE's local bus. It acts as a switch when the PE presents it with an address. If this address "A" is in the LM, the value stored at A is immediately available. If A is not in the LM, the Slocal maps the physical address provided by the PE to a virtual address and passes it through the "map bus" to the Kmap. Receiving memory references from the Map bus to the LSI-11 bus is similar.

[†]Reviewed from A. K. Jones, E. F. Gehringer (Eds.), "The Cm* Multiprocessor Project . . .," Carnegie-Mellon University, Computer Science, July 1980, CMU-CS-80-131; by permission of A. K. Jones.

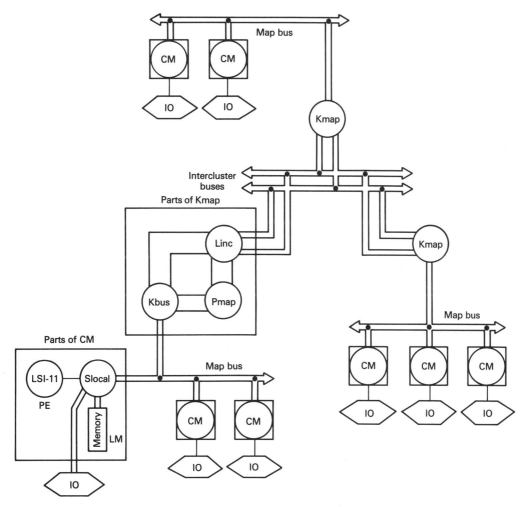

Figure 4-4   The block diagram of the Cm*

The LSI-11 bus is 16 bits wide and the LM of each CM is divided into 4K byte page boundaries. The Slocal uses the four most significant bits of the PE's generated address [Fig. 4-5(a)] along with the eXternal Processor Status Word (XPSW) register to form a pointer to an entry in the relocation table of the Slocal. The table contains the address of the referenced page, a bit that indicates the address is ''Read-Only,'' and a map bit to signify a nonlocal reference when appropriate. The result is an 18-bit address reference for local requests or an 18-bit wide virtual address plus CPU number for a nonlocal reference.

The Kmap is a fast (150 nns cycle) horizontally microprogrammable (80-bit wide) microprocessor that provides the basic address mapping, communication, and synchronization functions of the system. It consists of three coupled processors [Fig. 4-5(b)]. The

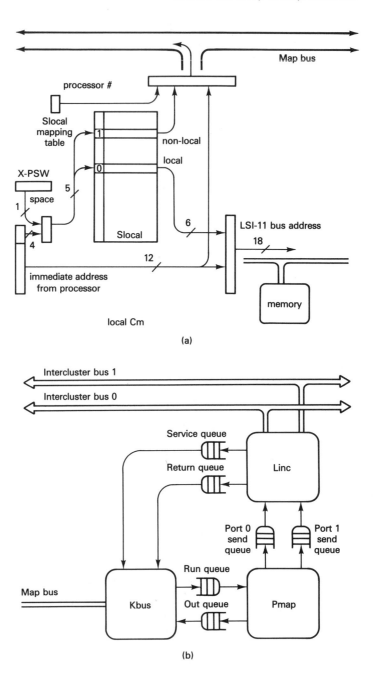

Figure 4-5 (a) The Slocal (b) The Kmap of the Cm*. Courtesy of A. K. Jones, E. F. Gehringer (Eds.): ''The Cm* Multiprocessor Project: A Research Review,'' Carnegie Mellon University, Computer Science, July 1980, CMU-CS-80-131.

bus controller or Kbus acts as the arbitrator for the bus that connects the CMs in the local cluster to their Kmap. The Linc manages communication to and from the Kmaps. The mapping processor or Pmap responds to requests from the Kbus and Linc performing most of the actual computation for a request for service. The Pmap also directs the Kbus and Linc to perform any needed operations on behalf of the request being processed. Since the Kmap is much faster than the main memory, most of the time for a simple reference is spent in accessing memory and relatively little time is spent within the Kmap. As a matter of fact, for each memory access the Kmap could execute up to eight operations.

When the Kmap receives a request for nonlocal memory from any of the Slocals in its cluster, it passes the request to the proper CM. The Slocal, of the target CM, acknowledges the request and returns the needed data. If the desired memory reference is outside of the local cluster, the Kmap will send its request on the intercluster bus in the form of a *message*. The Kmap of the target cluster will receive the message and pass the request on to the proper CM.

Since requests for memory can come from any PE at any time, the Kmap handles the overflow by entering each request in a queue and servicing each in sequence [Fig. 4-5(b)]. When the Kbus receives a request from an Slocal, it is put into the Run Queue of the Pmap. The Pmap will use a table in its memory to map the request to its final destination. If the request is an intracluster request, then the address is sent to the Out Queue, then to the Kmap, and ultimately to a CM.

When a request to the Pmap cannot be mapped to a CM within the Kmap's cluster, the result will be a request sent to the Linc on its two Send Queues, depending on which intercluster bus the desired memory is found.

The Linc will send the request to its destination and wait for a reply. When the reply is received, it is placed into the Return Queue to be picked up by the Kmap and then sent to the requesting CM. The Kmap that was the target of the request in the above example processed the request through its Linc and passed the request along via its Service Queue. The response made its way back to the requestor in the same way as the original request. A total of eight concurrent requests may be serviced. The Kmap's cycle time is much faster than that of the CM it is servicing; therefore the time spent in a queue is not long.

Local memories form a common store shared by all CMs so that each CM "sees" the same address space. Each PE in the Cm* system understands the memory to be shared and uniformly addressable. This is why the *Cm* is considered an SM,* albeit loosely coupled and using message instead of circuit switching. The number of connections it needs is minimized far below what was needed in a crossbar switch. Any memory block or I/O device can be accessed by a PE without regard to its physical address. The only difference in accessing local and nonlocal memory is that the delay is longer for the nonlocal memory. Typical times for memory accesses were 3 mcs for local, 9 mcs for intracluster, and 26 mcs for intercluster access. The underlying assumption made was that of *program locality* [i.e., that a PE(*i*) will seldom require information from outside of LM(*i*)]. Because more time is needed for transfer of information between CMs of different clusters, partitioning and allocation of program segments and data play a crucial role on the overall performance of an application program.

As in C.mmp, each I/O device is bound to a single CM and any CM can initiate I/O on a device attached to any other CM. However, interrupts can only be serviced locally, so that if a CM is lost, then all the I/O devices attached to it are also lost. This is undesirable for reliability, especially since the address space is common.

4–1.4 The Pluribus

The Pluribus [Hea73] is an almost forgotten SM which greatly influenced present-day PPSs. It was used as a dedicated system in the ARPA network of interconnected computers. This network consists of a large number of sites with the "host" computer at each site connected to the network through a small communication processor, the IMP (for Interface Message Processor). When a message from a line arrives at the IMP, it should receive (and buffer) it, perform error checks; when it is short enough, process it directly; otherwise, route it to another line or to the host. In order to be able to perform all these jobs, the IMP must be fast and possess enough memory for both programs and buffers. It was the demand for speed that led the designers of the IMP to the idea that a PPS would achieve the required bandwidth (speed) and reliability, and would have the added flexibility that no single, fast and powerful machine could provide. The design of the system as shown in the block diagram of Fig. 4-6 followed an "implicative" reasoning which leads from a particular application to a system design and therefore is of interest for the design of multiprocessors in general.

According to [Hea73], the design principles of Pluribus were as follows:

- Since requests arrive at unpredictable times, (seven) buses with asynchronous access were used. The experience of Cm* may have convinced the designers to use two local memories (LMs) per PE. The system includes two buses for the memory units. Each bus has 16K of memory. There is a single I/O bus.

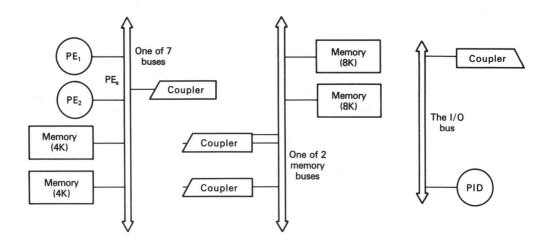

Figure 4-6   The elements of the Pluribus

- Out of fear that the buses cannot handle all the traffic, they were provided with bus couplers which formed the "switching arrangement" interconnecting all the buses. For reliability and availability all PEs were identical, and able to perform any system task. The buses were connected allowing all PEs and I/O devices to access all shared memory. Each of the PEs was also able to control the operation of any I/O unit.

- Access of shared memory through the switching system will incur time delays. In most applications, some parts of a program are executed frequently while others are executed far less. This naturally leads to the use of LMs to allow fast local access to the frequently used code. All LMs typically contain the same code. For Pluribus it was found that the ratio of local vs. shared memory was better than three to one.

- The number of CPUs is 14 and since they work in parallel, an increase in speed is assured. Therefore, slow but inexpensive CPUs were chosen. One bus could then service up to four such CPUs, but in simulation studies, serious degradation due to bus contention occurred at three CPUs per bus (Minsky's conjecture). Two CPUs were connected to each bus. Because of slow memories, two LMs were connected to a bus with almost no interference. Since I/O devices are even slower, a single bus is used for all I/O devices.

Various interference delays caused a slowdown of the system as follows: because of contention for a processor bus, for the shared memory buses, and for the shared memories, the slowdowns were 5.5%, 3%, and 5%, respectively. Because of the contention for a single systemwide software resource, assuming each processor wants the resource for six out of 120 instructions, the delay was 10%. An additional 2% slowdown was also reported. At that point there was a 25.5% slowdown, which would be unacceptable for process-control applications.

In the Pluribus system, PEs on different buses access each other through the I/O bus. The couplers are bidirectional so that the possibility exists that the buses of two PEs may try to get hold of each other through the I/O bus. They may never get it. This is an example of a hardware deadlock, since two computers are waiting forever for the resources the other is holding. In Pluribus it is easily detected and removed by preemptive switching every 500 mcs.

The IMP employs a reliability scheme in which the system is aware, at all times, of the state of affairs and if something seems to be wrong a "diagnostic" is run and the "bad" unit amputated.

4–2 PROBLEMS OF SHARED-MEMORY MULTIPROCESSORS

4–2.1 Contention Problems

Every address of a shared-memory multiprocessor (SM), say C.mmp, consists of a block number (0..15 MBs) and a *local* address. Two ways to choose the block numbers are shown in Fig. 4-7: by the most or least significant positions of the address word. The first

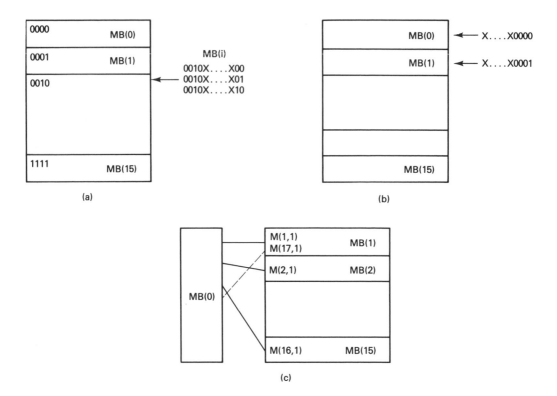

Figure 4-7   (a) Banking (b) Interleaving (c) Scattering

case is sometimes called *Memory Banking* and the second is called *Memory Interleaving*. Since a program occupies consecutively numbered addresses, this leads to two ways of storing a program: either all in one memory block (MB) or distributed among all (16) MBs. In case (a), up to 16 programs could be executing simultaneously with each CPU addressing another MB. In case (b) of Fig. 4-7, every program uses all 16 MBs and only one program can access, at any given time, a particular MB. Therefore, if two processors are trying to access the instructions in a given MB, one of them must wait.

Suppose an MB is faulty. In the first case the programs that use this MB cannot be run and must be transferred to one of the healthy MBs. In the second case, each program uses all 16 MBs and therefore all programs would have to be abandoned. It seems that for the sake of reliability, memory banking is better.

Let us discuss data storage by the example of matrix multiplication as per Eq. (1-9). Each $C(i, j)$ is to be calculated for all n^2 elements (i.e., for $i, j = 1, \ldots, n$). If executed in parallel, n^2 CPUs could compute n^2 elements $C(i,j)$. If the matrices **A** and **B** are stored in a single MB, then this MB must provide $2n^2$ values. It handles $2*n^3$ reads or *data access* requests. This can lead to enormous memory contention. Even if more MBs are used, n processors require the same row (column) of **A** or **B**. Interleaving of memory accesses as in Fig. 4-7(b) will reduce contention, and increase parallelism.

The contradiction is sometimes resolved by scattering the data (of an n-by-n matrix) across m MBs as shown in Fig. 4-7(c). A list of pointers, say in MB(0), point to a row (or slice of rows), each in a different MB. It uses $p+1$ MBs but reduces contention by a factor of p and provides the full memory bandwidth. Because to access any MB(i), also MB(0) must be accessed, this memory management technique increases the required time. The spreading of data across all MBs should be transparent to the programmer.

Memory interleaving is efficient in PPSs with a bus as an IN where the MBs can work in parallel responding to a series of read requests. Memory banking works best with crossbar switches, but they are very expensive. If the cheaper MINs are used (e.g., the Banyan in HEP), they introduce an unavoidable delay. Moreover, access to memory may be blocked not only in the MBs but contention can be in the MIN too.

Another solution to memory conflict problems is to buffer elements (Paracomputer) or to remove all but one of the conflicting requests and let the others try later (Butterfly).

4–2.2 Scheduling Problems

As shown in Chap. 1, a multiprogrammed Operating System, OS, divides a program into a number of tasks in order to facilitate I/O on a single computer.

Definition. A *task* is a sequence of instructions which exchanges information with other tasks and a parallel program is a set of concurrently executing tasks (*multitasking*).

An entire chapter will be based on multitasking. As an introduction we discuss first scheduling (assigning jobs to CPUs) in time-sharing multiple-process Operating Systems. Three levels of scheduling are used. Long-term or job-scheduling selects a subset of submitted jobs to compete actively for various computer resources. Each active job may create one or more tasks. Intermediate-term scheduling may temporarily activate or swap a task out of memory and place it on the disk or drum to achieve smooth and efficient operation. Short-term scheduling determines the next ready task to be assigned to the CPU for some time (quantum).

The scheduler of the OS controls all tasks in the system. As shown in Fig. 4-8 (for a single CPU, $q=2, \ldots, p$ are devices), a job enters at left and a number of tasks which constitute the job are created. All such created tasks are initialized and put into the job queue. The scheduler then puts the task in the *ready* queue, where it waits together with other tasks until the scheduler attaches it to a processor or device. This transfers the task from the ready state to the *running* state. If the task is to be blocked, then it is put into the *blocked* queue waiting for an *event* to happen. When the expected event occurs, say an input, the scheduler inserts the task again into the ready queue. Its execution is then resumed until it is completed. Having circled around the diagram for a number of times, the task is completed and leaves the system. Initialization and termination are part of the state diagram of Fig. 4-8, which also shows how tasks "flow" through devices, CPUs, and other units of a *multiprocessor*. The tasks are: compute(j), Input, Output, or use a library routine.

The task at the head of the ready queue is allowed to run until (a) it completes, (b) it

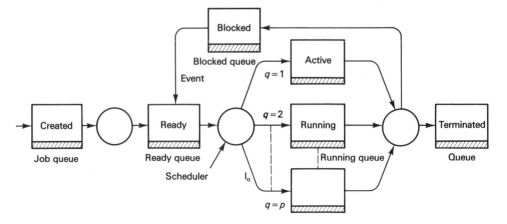

Figure 4-8 States of tasks (processes) and jobs

is blocked, (c) it calls the OS, or (d) it is interrupted, say by a timer. If the task is blocked, then the task at the head of the ready queue is run. Timer interrupts do not change the fact that the task is still ready to run and it is therefore returned to the ready queue, albeit at its tail.

Since some tasks are more time-critical than others, they must contain a specification of their relative priorities. Tasks with higher priorities may interrupt the execution of the lower priority tasks. (In a real-time system, a task handling an emergency message should have priority over ''normal'' tasks.) If a number of tasks with the same priority are at the head of the queue, scheduling them could proceed according to the round-robin strategy. When a program is interrupted, the currently running task is in one of the states of Fig. 4-9. As seen, systems that manage tasks must be able to create, destroy, block,

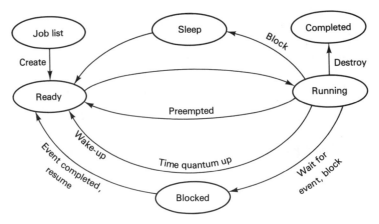

Figure 4-9 Task movement through a system

resume, wake up a task and change its priority. Creating a task involves many operations including its naming, insertion in a queue, setting its initial priority, and so on.

In multiprogramming, the tasks use *resources* (e.g., each I/O request is a task using an I/O device). The computational task releases the CPU (resource) while the I/O process uses the device. In multiprocessors, the division into tasks competing for resources is even more important because there may be more programs, more tasks, more than one CPU, a number of MBs, etc., and the software modules are also shared and should be considered resources. Some tasks *should not be preempted*: If a line printer is asked to mix jobs, then the printout will be gibberish.

Single processors have a single level of control even when multiprogrammed. In multiprocessors, we define three levels of control for programs: job, task (process), and instruction. On the job level, several programs can be executed in *parallel* (by multiprogramming) or sequentially (by batch or interactively). Each job or program consists of one or more tasks and each task can at a given time be assigned to a CPU. Each task is a sequence of instructions executed on a single CPU and can be treated as an indivisible unit with respect to processor allocation. At run-time, the OS puts all the active tasks in a queue. The queue can be accessed by all p CPUs through the IN. Whenever a CPU becomes idle, the OS gets a new task from the front of the queue and executes it sequentially. This is called parallel-serial control. As seen, *a task is a sequential program that exchanges information with other tasks*.

Scheduling can be *static or dynamic*. In static scheduling, tasks are allocated to CPUs during the algorithm design by the user. For instance, in the Occam language (Appendix A1-3), programmers specify the instruction execution sequence and compilers allocate registers and bind instructions to specific functional units at compile time. The disadvantage of static scheduling is that if the times are guessed wrong, a time loss occurs because some CPUs have to wait idly.

Dynamic scheduling by the machine at run-time offers better utilization of the CPUs, at the price of additional scheduling time. The dynamic scheduling algorithm can be centralized as in HEP or distributed as in the Ultracomputer. (In the HEP machine, there is a division of labor: The programmer defines (statically) the tasks, and the OS uses self-scheduling to balance their execution time.) In a distributed algorithm for self-scheduling, tasks are specified by the programmer at algorithm time and put into a central queue in the privileged memory of the OS at run time. Each processor requests the first task from the queue and executes it whenever it becomes idle.

4–2.3 Synchronization Problems

Synchronization is studied in courses on multiprogrammed operating systems. It should be studied also in the context of SMs, since their performance is influenced by synchronization. For instance, suppose one task selects all students who took an exam and the second calculates the average grade. The second starts when the first has completed. Synchronization is when PEs are waiting for other PEs to catch up and resources are used in a prescribed sequence.

Synchronization of SMs leads to the *critical section* problem. For example, when two or more CPUs try to access the same MB to change the contents of common data, they should not be allowed to do it even in an interleaved fashion. This may be exemplified by Mr. and Mrs. X requesting simultaneously but in different branches $100 each from their joint bank account. Each teller accesses the common database and finds a balance of $120. Each then pays out $100 and updates incorrectly the balance to $20. The common database, called the critical section, should be modified by only one teller at a time and be in his/her exclusive possession until it is updated. Update is by *mutual exclusion*. If used in the present context, the second teller will find the balance is only $20 and will refuse to pay $100.

Definitions.   A critical section is an instruction sequence which can be modified (exclusively) by only one process at a time; it involves mutually exclusive access to shared variables. Mutual exclusion ensures that the sequence is treated as an indivisible operation.

Another example of the same problem is in the C.mmp where sharing of data in the main memory occurs if two addresses are translated into the same physical location. This may lead to contention and wrong results, as evidenced by a program to sum the elements of a vector. Suppose that two PEs are used and each accumulates half the sum. For a vector of length 32 this may be written as sum: $= \text{sum} + a(i)$; $i = 0, \ldots, 7$ for the first and $i = 8, \ldots, 15$ for the second PE.

In assembly language, the steps inside the loops are as in Code 4-1.

CPU-1	CPU-1
1. MOVE.W (A0),D0	4. MOVE.W (A1),D2
2. ADD.W (A0),D0	5. ADD.W (A2),D2
3. MOVE.W D0,(A1)	6. MOVE.W D2,A(1)

Code 4-1

According to [Wak89], MOVE.W (An),Dn means ''Move a word from memory as pointed to by address register An (*n* is its number) to data register Dn,'' and ADD.W Dn,Dm means ''Add contents of Dn and Dm with the result in register Dm.'' It is assumed that the address of a(0), a(8), and that of the SUM are pointed to by address registers A0, A2, and A1, respectively. Obviously, the value of SUM in (A1) and registers D0, D2 would be started with zero.

If the calculation is done in the order given above, then the results will be correct. Note though that the order provides for mutual exclusion, since CPU-2 starts working on the critical section (i.e., the common variable SUM) only after CPU-1 has completed its update.

In a parallel processing system like C.mmp, *the order is unpredictable* and may have been 1,4,2,3,5, and 6. This yields the following result: Accumulator ''D0'' is loaded with zero. Accumulator ''D2'' is loaded with zero. The value a(0) is added to D0 making it a(0). This result is stored in location SUM. In step 5, CPU-2 adds the value of a(8) to its D2, but since it is still zero, the result is D2 = a(8). In step 6, CPU-2 stores this value in location SUM. As a result, SUM is a(8) instead of being a(0) + a(8)—it is wrong. To maintain data consistency, access to shared variables must be controlled by mutual exclusion.

Mutual exclusion is a type of *synchronization* since the second CPU starts working when the first has finished and the first starts when the second has finished. Mutual exclusion has guaranteed that the resource (e.g., the balance or the SUM) is held indivisibly.

As in the examples of Ms. X and Mr. X, or summation shown, the critical section must be protected or *locked* while being updated. In the assembly language locking may be done by a "Test and Set" TAS instruction as in Code 4-2.

```
LP: TAS L       ; This instruction will simultaneously test L, set the
                ; condition code Z in the Program Status Word
                ; accordingly and set the highest bit of L to 1.
    BNE LP      ; Branch on a non-zero condition code back to label LP.
                ;
                ; This is where the critical section is processed.
                ;
    SUB #1,L    ; Subtracting 1 unlocks the critical section.
```

Code 4-2

The locking effected by this program proceeds as follows:

- Suppose L = 0 (i.e., the lock is open and the critical section is not used). The TAS instruction tests L, sets the condition code bit Z to 1, and simultaneously sets L to 1. If from now on another CPU tests L, it finds L locked. In the BNE instruction, since Z was made 1 (i.e., L was Zero), no branch is taken, the critical section is entered, and until it is re-opened, no other CPU can interfere. (In the cases mentioned earlier, the balance of X was reduced to $20 or the SUM was updated.) Once the processing of the critical section is complete, the lock L is made zero so that other CPUs can access the critical section.
- Suppose L is 1 and a CPU is executing TAS L. Since L is 1, the condition code is made Z = 0 and L is set to 1 (this does not change L since it was 1 to begin with). At the BNE instruction, the program branches back to TAS L since Z indicates that L was not zero. The processor (CPU) is in a loop which it can leave only when another CPU makes L = 0. The loop is called *busy-waiting* since the CPU is busy doing nothing while waiting. It reminds me of a cat chasing its own tail; the cat is extremely busy, but all it does is loop around.

When the time for mutual exclusion is short, "busy-wait" is appropriate. Since the CPUs wait doing nothing, time is lost.

Locking must be done in an "indivisible" or "atomic" way (i.e., by disabling the interrupts before TAS L is executed); otherwise an interrupt could change the condition code, resulting in havoc.

As seen above, the task does not relinquish the processor while it is waiting for a lock to be unlocked by another task. This has the advantage that once the lock is unlocked the processor may enter its critical section very quickly. However, this may create quite severe problems for the error-recovery mechanism if the processor that is currently executing the locking operation fails. The second processor will wait forever doing nothing but waiting. This is called *starvation,* (the first processor starved the second).

Next, suppose two processors enter their respective TAS instructions with $L = 1$. Both will therefore busy-wait forever. This is called *indefinite blocking* since there seems to be no way in which the two CPUs can escape looping forever in the busy-loops.

An example of a *deadlock* is if in C.mmp, CPU(1) works on MB(0) to MB(7) and at the same time CPU(2) works on MB(8) to MB(15). If both ask for one more block without releasing the MBs they already hold, there is a deadlock since none will be able to proceed on its own and the system does nothing. The operating system is supposed to come to the rescue, but as usual this involves a considerable time loss.

One of the best examples of the problems of mutual exclusion, starvation, and deadlock is that of the *five* (Chinese) *philosophers* proposed by E. Dijkstra. The philosophers alternate between thinking and eating. Each philosopher has a plate and chopstick numbered as in Fig. 4-10(a). In order to eat, two chopsticks are needed—the chopsticks are therefore the resources and access to them is by *mutual exclusion*: no two philosophers can use the same chopstick at the same time and it is in their *exclusive* possession. If all five sit down at the table simultaneously and each picks up the right chopstick, they will wait forever for the left chopstick and a *deadlock* results. (Note the circularity: each philosopher needs the left chopstick.) If two philosophers hate the philosopher seated between them, they could alternate eating and by this ruse, literally *starve* the hated philosopher. *The problem is to devise a management strategy* (in the form of a program) that will let them use the chopsticks but ensure mutual exclusion, freedom from deadlocks and from starvation, and yet let them eat as much *simultaneously* as possible, to speed up the process of eating. Such management policies are discussed in Sec. 8-1.

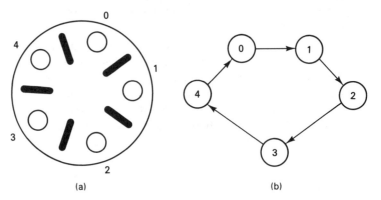

Figure 4-10 (a) The five dining philosophers (b) Resource allocation

We have used mostly memory as the resource to be shared, but devices, controllers, MBs, and even PEs are all resources that can be shared. They represent an item which has a state that can be sensed (read) or modified (written) by a number of tasks. The examples above show that deadlock occurs when a number of tasks compete for resources held by each other. In a more general way, consider Fig. 4-10(b), where each resource i is allocated to task $T(i)$ for $i = 0 \ldots 4$. Suppose that simultaneously $T(i)$ requests resource $T(i + 1)$ for $i = 0, \ldots, 3$, and $T(4)$ requests 0. This leads to a deadlock, since each of these resources is used by another task which is unwilling to part with it, but also requires the use of an additional resource held by another. The circularity of requests is reflected by the cycle in Fig. 4-10(b).

Notes.   The two examples of Fig. 4-10 are similar. If each chopstick in Fig. 4-10(a) is a node and each arc indicates a philosopher holding a chopstick, we get the cycle of Fig. 4-10(b). Also note that had we given two chopsticks to each philosopher, no critical section would exist. It is the sparsity of resources that leads to all the woes.

Having discussed blocking and deadlock in an informal way, we next deal with them more formally. Any computer system that supports interleaved or concurrent computation is in danger of entering a state where some subset of the tasks of the system cannot progress. This is known as *indefinite blocking*. Indefinite blocking can take three basic forms: indefinite blocking because of programmer's error, starvation, and deadlock.

An example of the inability to make progress because of programmer's error is if the programmer forgot to initialize the locks correctly before entering the critical section. An example of starvation is if a task has low priority and all tasks coming into the system have higher priority. This task is indefinitely blocked as a result of the conditions, and yet there are no errors in the system. Deadlock is a system state when the following four necessary conditions are true at the same time:

1. *Mutual exclusion:* Each task claims exclusive right to use the resources allocated to it.
2. *Non-preemption:* A task will first complete the job before it releases the resources it holds.
3. *Wait condition:* A task holds resources already allocated while waiting for additional resources.
4. *Circularity of requests:* A set of tasks $\{T(1), T(2), \ldots, T(n)\}$ exists such that $T(1)$ requests a resource held by $T(2)$, $T(2)$ requests one held by $T(3)$, $\ldots$ and $T(n)$ requests a resource held by $T(1)$.

If any of the conditions do not appear simultaneously in the system, then there is no deadlock. This leads to a method of preventing deadlocks. It assures that deadlock cannot occur by preventing one of the above conditions from possibly happening. The wait condition can be prevented by guaranteeing that if a task requests a resource then it does not control any other resources. The non-preemption condition can be prevented by requiring that if a task requests a resource and it cannot obtain it, then it must release all other resources it is controlling. The circularity of requests condition can be prevented by assigning a linear ordering to all resource types: whenever a task requests a resource, it must be a higher numbered resource. Unfortunately the scheduler must be able to predict the future behavior of all tasks to provide mutual exclusion. Therefore, prevention is difficult to achieve.

Deadlock Avoidance is when the OS checks to see if a deadlock is possible. If it is possible then the OS does not assign the requested resources; otherwise it does assign them. Multiprocessors will use the OS to schedule tasks so as to use advance information about future requests in order to avoid a deadlock. For instance, in Fig. 4-10(b), the scheduler knows that T(4) will request resource "0" thereby leading to deadlock. It may refuse this request and either ask task T(4) to wait or give it another resource which it might use profitably.

Detecting and recovering from a deadlock is the simplest policy from the point of view of the scheduler: It allocates resources as soon as they become available. When and if a deadlock occurs, it will be detected and the scheduler "breaks" the cycle by forcing de-allocation of resources in order to recover from the deadlock. To detect deadlocks, the OS measures how long a task remains in the waiting state and if it is too long, it is considered being deadlocked. This policy would detect any deadlock within the time of its occurrence, but it would also label some healthy situations as deadlocks.

Access to data by a number of PEs may generate *inconsistent* data areas. Some mechanism must be employed to ensure that data areas, when changed, preserve the integrity of the stored information (see Sec. 4-4). Finally note that locking will not help in understanding a concurrent program or prove its correctness. For this, a so-called "axiomatic approach" should be taken, but this is outside our scope.

Three basic problems were identified in multiprocessors, namely how to *partition* a program into tasks, how to *schedule the execution* (i.e., how to assign each task to one or more processors for execution), and how to synchronize them. *Synchronization* is also needed for the OS to assure an order of execution that will lead to correct results.

In SM systems, it should be possible to include synchronization and scheduling in the programs themselves. This is why the actual software policies to be followed are relegated to Part B of the book, where more examples of mutual exclusion, starvation, or deadlock problems will be discussed. To be able to discuss hardware solutions, we next discuss some commercially available or university-sponsored SM Multiprocessors.

4-3 ASSEMBLED SM MULTIPROCESSORS

4-3.1: The Butterfly [BBN87][†]

This system consists of a number (originally 128, later 256) of Processor-and-Memory modules (PaMs) connected by the Butterfly switch. Each PaM is located on a single board; all PaMs are identical. The PaM and additional hardware will be called a *node*. Collectively, the memory of all PaMs forms the shared memory. The Butterfly is an

---

[†]By permission of BBN Advanced Computers Inc., from their Technical Reports.

MIMD system with each PaM being able to access nonlocal memory through the Butterfly switch (will be abbreviated to "switch" below). The only difference between access to local and nonlocal memory is that local access is shorter (2 mcs) than nonlocal access (5 mcs). Local data are allocated locally, but shared data structures are scattered uniformly across the PaMs by interleaving.

The Butterfly operates as a satellite for a front-end machine (the "host") which provides program development facilities through a UNIX Operating System (OS). The Butterfly connects to the host either by an Ethernet connection or a serial line. I/O is very flexible since it can be effected by any of the PaMs. To reduce memory and switch contention, copies of code exist in each PaM.

The Butterfly products include the Butterfly Plus (an enhancement to the original Butterfly computer), and the Butterfly 1000 family, comprising the GP1000 and RT1000 parallel processors. The Butterfly Plus represents a major improvement in the processing power of each PaM, while the two 1000's use the same hardware and extend the OS, language repertoire, etc. We will deal with a generic Butterfly and discuss first its elements.

Figure 4-11(a) illustrates a 16-PaM Butterfly system with each node "cut" so that it appears on both sides of the *switch*. Each switching node is a 4-by-4 switching element (SE) implemented by a custom VLSI chip. The transfer of messages through a node is controlled by two bits which designate outputs by 00, 01, 10, and 11. For example, suppose that PaM-0 sends a message to PaM-6 or to address 0110. The first bits (01) transfer the message to output 1 of SE(1), bits 10 then transfer the message through SE(6) to output 2, or to PaM-6. Notice that it is immaterial which PaM is sending the packet; it will be routed by the destination address (to 6).

The communication capacity of the switch grows linearly, its complexity remains manageable [i.e., the number of SEs grows as p*log(p) (on base 4) and is thus considerably lower than p^2 required by a crossbar]. For $p = 100$ nodes, the number of connections amounts to about 350, while the crossbar requires 10,000.

> Because the switch eliminates the need for a dedicated path between each pair of PaM nodes, messages *can conflict* in frequently referenced memory. However, unlike some architectures, the Butterfly does not buffer messages. Rather, an unsuccessful transmission retreats and leaves the network free. This allows other messages to use the intermediate paths, and immediately clears the switch. Messages are automatically retransmitted after a short delay over the first available alternate path. [If desired, the switch can also efficiently transfer entire *blocks* of data between any pair of nodes—and we will see later that this is important.]
>
> The contention in the switch is application dependent. It was small in all programs run up to now—typically only 1% to 5% of the total time. If the configuration is such that the probability of message collision within the switch is low, then the transit time required for a message to pass through the switch is effectively that of the bit-serial transfer through the nodes.
>
> [The original node of the Butterfly [Fig. 4-11(b)] used a Motorola 68000 with at least 1 Mbyte of main memory, a microcoded coprocessor, called the Processor Node Controller (PNC), memory management hardware, an I/O bus, and an interface to the switch. In later architectures, each node contains a] Motorola MC68020 microprocessor with MC68881 floating-point coprocessor and MC68851 Paged Memory Management Unit (PMMU), a PNC

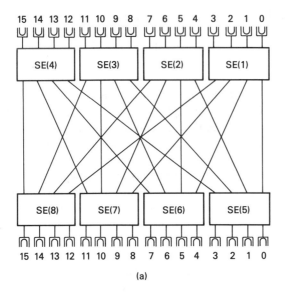

(a)

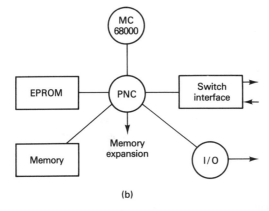

(b)

Figure 4-11 (a) The Butterfly switch
(b) The node of the Butterfly

with 32 KByte control store, address-decoding logic, four megabytes of main memory and a memory controller, 128 kilobytes of programmable read-only memory, interface to the Butterfly switch, an I/O bus adapter, a dual-channel [serial port for diagnostic I/O, and the power supply [BBN87].

[The Motorola MC68020 and MC68881 are] running all Butterfly application programs. The PMMU translates the virtual addresses used by both processors into the physical addresses used by the PNC, memory, switch and bus adapters [BBN87]. Each PaM is capable of executing 0.5 MIPs and is usually configured with 1 MByte of memory (it may be expanded up to 4 MBytes per PaM).

[All user application software is run on the MC68020 with the program (code) normally stored locally. Note that this does not apply to data.]

The PNC consists of a 32 KByte microcode sequencer, a static RAM control store, an interrupt-service-routine address generator, and a bit-slice processor. It provides many functions required for parallel processing and not found in the MC68020; it initiates all messages sent over the Butterfly switch, and processes all messages received from the switch. It is involved in every memory reference made by the MC68020. It uses the PMMU to translate the virtual addresses used by the MC68020 into physical memory addresses [BBN87].

When the PaM makes a write reference, its local PNC gains control and uses its memory management hardware to transform the virtual into a physical address. If this address is included in the PaM's memory, it is satisfied in 2 mcs. Otherwise, the PNC sends a packet addressed to a remote PaM through the switch. The remote PNC receives the packet, reads the given location, and writes the packet into it.

For reading data from remote memory, a slightly higher level transaction takes place (Fig. 4-11). Upon receiving a command such as *MOV 2000,D1*, the local MC68020 processor tells the PMMU to translate logical address 2000 to a physical address, for example 41000. The local PNC then recognizes that this address requires a remote reference, and sends a message to the processor that owns that memory address. The message goes through the switch to the remote PNC, and from there to the remote memory module. This operation does not use the remote MC68020 or its associated MC68881, leaving both components free to do other work. The remote PNC then sends the data value back to the first PNC, which passes it back to the MC68020. To the MC68020 it looks like a normal local-memory reference, taking only slightly longer [BBN87].

The PNC performs a variety of indivisible *atomic* operations which were shown earlier to be essential for *mutual exclusion*. On the Butterfly systems, atomic operations are shared-memory operations that are enacted without interruptions. Setting an atomic *lock*, for example, means that a processor will be allowed to perform the two steps of testing the value of a lock variable and changing the value, without any other processor being able to step in between the actions. Using an *atomic-add* means that a processor can access and add to some constant or variable, while all the other processors are blocked from reading, writing, etc., on the same data. Other similar functions are available, such as *atomic-and* and *atomic-or* . . . In the Butterfly products, atomic operations and microcode for incrementing (decrementing) the value of a memory location, and performing an "inclusive-or" or "logical-and" of a memory location with a mask value are provided by the hardware. Also provided are atomic operations for inserting and removing elements from a dual queue. It is the PNC which provides "atomic" instructions for the locking necessary in a MIMD computer (introduced in Sec. 4-2) by implementing in microcode a collection of operations required for synchronization, namely: test-and-set, queuing, and event-processing operations [BBN87].

The Butterfly design reduces *contention* in the switch as follows. It may add an

extra switching column, so that there are two independent paths between every input and every output port. The switch therefore has two possible binary addresses for the same destination. [The contention is also reduced by employing 4x4 SEs, since there are fewer] columns through which the data must pass, and therefore fewer opportunities for conflict. A single SE can handle as many as four messages simultaneously, provided that each of the four accesses a different output port [BBN87].

There can also be contention among multiple PaMs that all need to read from the same memory module. The Butterfly is spreading or interleaving data uniformly throughout the shared memory. Thus, for example, the numbers from a matrix row are dispersed to many different memory modules, and no build-up in references occurs.

The contention by several processors for a specific memory location is resolved by using *atomic operations* that allow the user to *lock* the data ensuring mutual exclusion in the way described in Sec. 4-2.

The *I/O system* is distributed among the nodes, with I/O boards attached to any PaM. Two types of I/O boards are available: the Butterfly Multibus Adapter (BMA) board and the Butterfly (Serial) I/O-board (BIO). The BMA provides efficient data exchange between a PaM and a multibus to which compatible devices such as I/O devices, memory, or PEs may be connected. The BIO board supports four asynchronous interfaces and four synchronous lines. Terminals can be interfaced using either the BIO or the BMA; other devices such as Ethernet interfaces and disk storage units can be interfaced only through the BMA.

Whenever the bandwidth requirement exceeds the I/O capacity of a single PaM, a bus adapter (BVME) may be added. It has a higher peak data transfer rate than the rate of the PaM, so a higher bandwidth path has to connect the bus adapter to the Butterfly system.

The Butterfly computer is connected to the host by Ethernet. Editing, compiling, and linking a program on the (UNIX) OS is done on the host. The program is then downloaded to the Butterfly, where it is debugged and run.

The Butterfly runs under the supervision of its own kernel, the "Chrysalis" OS. It is designed to provide a UNIX-like environment that supports programming in a high-level language. It also includes application libraries which manage many of the resources such as allocating memory and setting up tasks. An application is structured so that tasks are created on as many PaMs as are available. Each task runs the user's application tasks on a subset of the data as stored in the common address space. The OS provides procedures for efficiently allocating the data, for managing the buffers required for communications, for stream-oriented I/O interface, etc.

> The kernel's main functions are system configuration and initialization, process support, memory management, and implementation of primitives for parallel processing and interprocess communications. Some kernel services are written in microcode on the PNC for better speed; most of the remainder are written in the C language. All kernel functions are called from the user's programs as subroutines or macro invocations [BBN87].

The GP1000 supports the Butterfly Ada language. "Butterfly Ada features a production-quality compiler that fully complies with ANSI/MIL STD-1815A" [the standard, and] . . . an efficient run-time system for full-featured *tasking*, exception-handling, and I/O support" [BBN87]. This is important because we intend to use Ada for various

PPSs and the above statement disproves the widely held view that Ada, and in particular its multitasking facilities, are very inefficient for SM multiprocessors.

The general characteristics of the Butterfly architecture are:

1. The Butterfly is an *MIMD* system with each PaM executing its own sequence of instructions but with data both in the local and nonlocal memory. The Butterfly is a shared-memory system (*SM*) but uses packet switching (whereas C.mmp used circuit switching). This permits efficient interprocessor communication and allows each PaM to access all system memory efficiently.

2. The Butterfly uses *message-passing* for communication and synchronization, so that tasks send and receive messages instead of reading from or writing into shared variables. Communication is achieved because a task obtains a message from another task which sent it. Synchronization is obtained, because a task cannot receive a message unless it was sent and only after it was sent. A channel of communication between tasks is needed.

3. The Butterfly is *scalable* over a wide range. Each node contributes processing power, memory, switch bandwidth, and possibly also I/O capacity; therefore, all four characteristics scale in the same proportion. Furthermore, the complexity and cost of its MIN remain at an acceptable level, which is not true for the bus, multibus, and the crossbar switches used in other SM systems (e.g., in the C.mmp, the Pluribus, or the Cm*). The I/O capacity and the switch should be expanded with the number of PaMs to maintain overall system balance and to prevent possible bottlenecks. The processing power is achieved by a large number of inexpensive PaMs working in parallel. The main reason for Minsky's conjecture was contention for information, mainly code. In the Butterfly, the code (programs) are distributed and accessible in the local memories of the nodes.

4. *The Butterfly is cost-effective* being a *homogeneous system* (although I/O may exist on some PaMs and not on others). As a result, every PaM is capable of performing any application task.

5. *Fault detection and availability* of the Butterfly are relatively high. Since all components are identical, they can be interchanged and the loss of a few PaMs can be tolerated. Since 4-by-4 SEs are used, we remove four PaMs whenever one PaM is faulty. As a matter of fact (see Appendix 2), the loss of say 3 PaMs reduces its performance by only 2%.

> Butterfly computers can be built with redundant paths available between every pair of processor nodes. By adding one more "column" of switch nodes than the minimum necessary configuration, there are two possible paths for every transaction. Not only does this improve overall system reliability, permitting continued operation even with several failed switch nodes, but the additional paths reduce the effect of contention at any given junction. Messages are automatically rerouted within fractions of a microsecond [BBN87].

A switch with alternate paths is used primarily in larger configurations (over 16 PaMs) in order to make the MIN *fault-tolerant* to SE failures.

6. The shared-memory architecture of the Butterfly, together with its firmware and software (OS), provide a program execution environment in which tasks can be distributed among the processors with little regard to the physical location of the data associated with those tasks. This greatly simplifies programming of the machine—a very important characteristic according to the Preface (you must have read it by now).

Multiple Instruction, Multiple Data execution is natural for the programmer since no additional effort to locate data is required. The programs run efficiently in a wide range of applications. It was even found that in many cases simple uniform scattering of data over the memory is very efficient so the programmer is free from data distribution functions.

The uniformity of the architecture, OS, and locking simplify *programming* since the programmers need not concern themselves with allocating tasks to specific PaMs. "Programs written on small Butterfly systems, will run unchanged on large configurations, and software intended for large systems will still run on configurations reduced by unavailable components" [BBN87].

4—3.2 The Ultracomputer and the RP3

The Ultracomputer is a general-purpose, shared-memory (SM) system designed at the Courant Institute of New York University [Gea83]. The design was for 4096 PEs connected to the common memory via an Omega MIN. The largest Ultracomputer apparently assembled consisted of eight PEs (the MC68010 with a floating-point processor) and 8 MBytes of shared memory. The distinguishing features of the Ultracomputer are that message switching is used, that locking of a new type—the fetch-and-add, F&A—is used for synchronization, and that messages are "combined."

The block diagram of the Ultracomputer is shown in Fig. 4-12(a). It includes $p = 2**d$ autonomous PEs connected through the IN to p MBs. Each PE is connected to the IN through a "Processor Network Interface," PNI, and each MB is connected through a "Memory Network Interface," MNI. The PNI performs translation of virtual addresses to physical addresses, assembly/disassembly of memory requests, cache management, and enforcement of the memory pipelining policy so that a request is issued before the previous one is acknowledged. The MNI performs only requests for assembly/disassembly and supports the F&A operation. The memory is interleaved to reduce contention, cache memories are used to reduce latency, queues are used in the SEs to reduce message collisions, and combining and adders at the memory are used for the F&A instruction.

The MBs are standard, off-the-shelf memory chips. The PEs, however, were slightly enhanced by characteristics needed for synchronization. In particular, to fully utilize the bandwidth of the IN, a PE must continue the execution of the instruction stream immediately after executing a request to fetch a value from central memory. The PEs can be used for I/O, but since the design does not require homogeneous PEs, special-purpose processors can also be used.

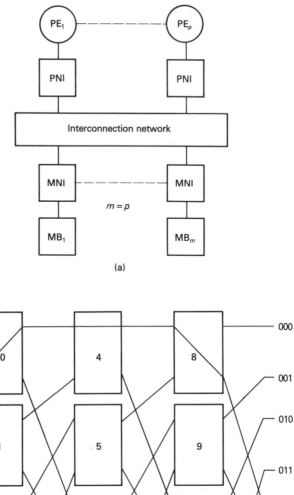

(b)

Figure 4-12 The block diagram and the MIN of the Ultracomputer

Contention for memory may exist in the Ultra. A hashing function for translation of virtual addresses to physical locations is supposed to ensure that unfavorable situations occur with probability approaching zero as p increases. Another improvement used in the design was to implement the local memory as a cache. This effectively shifts the burden of managing a two-level memory from the software to the hardware.

The Interconnection Network [see Fig. 4-12(b)] is an Omega network with 2-by-2 SEs, with the routing controlled by the binary address of the destination and the following characteristics and enhancements:

1. Its bandwidth is $\mathbf{0}(p)$. It includes $p*\log(p)/2$ SEs.

2. "The network is pipelined, i.e., the delay between messages equals the switch cycle time, not the network transit time. (Since the latter grows logarithmically, nonpipelined networks can have bandwidth at most $\mathbf{0}[p/\log(p)]$.) The latency is logarithmic in p." [Gea83]

3. The network is message switched, i.e., the switch settings are not maintained while a reply is awaited. (The alternative, circuit switching, is incompatible with pipelining.)

4. A queue is associated with each switch to enable concurrent processing of requests for the same port.

5. So as not to be a bottleneck in routing messages and be efficient in routing short messages, the control is local to each SE.

It may appear that since message switching is used,

both the destination and return addresses must be transmitted with each message. We need, however, transmit only one *d*-bit address, an amalgam of the origin and destination: when a message first enters the network, its origin is determined by the input port, so only the destination address is needed. Switches at the *j*th stage route messages based on memory address bit $m(j)$ and then replace this bit with the PE number bit which equals the number of the input port on which the message arrived. Thus, when the message reaches its destination, the return address is available [Gea83].

As an example, suppose that a message is sent from port 1 ($=001$) to port 4 ($=100$) of Fig. 4-12(b)]. In the first stage, while the message is transferred to the upper terminal of SE(0), the address is changed into 000. In SE(4) the address is not changed, but in SE(8) it changes to 001.

The IBM Research Parallel Prototype Processor [Pea85] or *RP3* was assembled in cooperation with the Ultracomputer group and assumed many of its characteristics. It consists of 512 PEs with 512 MBs of 2-4 MBytes, 64 I/O microprocessors with an aggregate capacity of up to 192 MBytes/second, and two MINs. Figure 4-13 shows the overall organization. Next we will discuss some of its units.

Each *Processor-and-Memory, PaM,* contains a 32-bit microprocessor, local memory, a 32-Kbyte cache, a floating-point unit FPU, an interface to an I/O-and-Support-Processor, ISP, a monitor, and an IN interface. The PaM was not designed for use by a

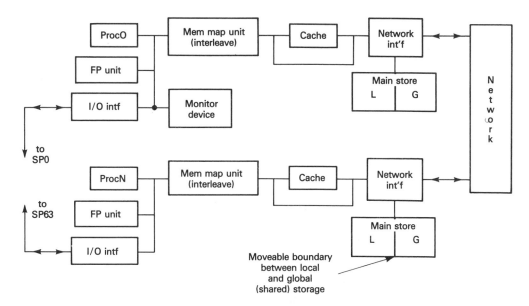

Figure 4-13 The block diagram of the RP3. Courtesy of G. Pfister et al: "The IBM Research Parallel Prototype (RP3) . . . ," Proc. of 1985 Int. Conf. on Parallel Processing, Chicago, Aug. 1985, pp. 764–71 (© 1985, IEEE).

PPS and its instruction set was expanded to deal with multitasking, synchronization, and control of the cache.

> The processor has the ability to prefetch; i.e., issue a memory request and then continue execution until the datum is needed. The prefetch ability provides a performance enhancement since the average effective latency of a shared-memory access is reduced. It is further reduced by acknowledging stores immediately rather than waiting until they are serviced at a memory. [Pea85]*

The floating-point unit, FPU, provides operations on 32-bit and 64-bit operands.

> A floating-point operation is initiated by the processor. The processor loads the FPU with the operation to be performed, the (starting) address of the operands, and, if a vector operation is to be performed, a stride and length. Once the FPU has been initiated, the FPU fetches and stores operands and performs the arithmetic function independently and asynchronously to the processor. When an operation is completed, the FPU can signal the processor via an interrupt or by setting a completion flag in the FPU-status register which the processor can monitor [Pea85]. [The FPU is pipelined.]

*G. Pfister et al., "The IBM Research Parallel Prototype (RP3) . . . ," Proc. of 1985 Int. Conf. on Parallel Processing, Chicago, August, pp. 764–771 (© 1985, IEEE). Reprinted by permission of the IEEE.

The performance of the FPU is governed by several factors:

1. Operand location: operations on vectors resident in the cache execute several times faster than operations performed on operands stored in shared memory [Pea85].
2. Control-register reload: scalar-operation time can be dominated by the number of internal FPU parameters (e.g., operand addresses) that must be changed by the processor between successive operations [Pea85].
3. Vector length: this has minimal effect, since little pipelining is performed; typically, a vector length of less than 20 is sufficient to reach 90% of peak performance.
4. Peak bus-bandwidth: the FPU, processor, and I/O interface device share a common bus. Therefore, the contention can limit performance. Without contention, the bandwidth limits peak performance to 1.5 MFLOPs/PE for single precision (768 MFLOPs for 512 PEs) and to 0.9 MFLOPs/PE for double precision. The FPU can also move blocks of data asynchronously with processor operation.

RP3 allows all of primary memory to be partitioned between global (i.e., shared memory) and local memory. Figure 4-14 shows how the global address space is distributed. Memory contention is reduced by memory banking (Sec. 4-2) and hashing of addresses. The rest of the memory is considered local (i.e., belonging to particular nodes).

The boundary between the local and global memory may be moved right or left. Moving it all the way to the right makes it into an SM system; moving it all the way to the left makes it into a loosely coupled MIMD system. In the mixed mode, shared-memory oriented applications can allocate private data locally, thereby gaining efficiency, while message-oriented applications can use global memory to aid load-balancing. The code may reside globally or locally.

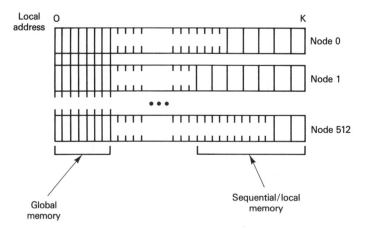

Figure 4-14 Addressing in the RP3. Courtesy of G. Pfister et al: "The IBM Research Parallel Prototype (RP3) . . . ," Proc. of 1985 Int. Conf. on Parallel Processing, Chicago, Aug. 1985, pp. 764–71 (© 1985, IEEE.)

The I/O organization uses the ISPs which are the same PaM as the rest. Each ISP supports eight PaMs through an independent bus and can drive a standard channel to which a disk storage unit is attached.

4–4 HARDWARE ELEMENTS

4–4.1 Caches and Local Memories—LMs

A cache as the one we introduced in Sec. 2-2.2 is normally placed between the memory and the CPU. It does not have a fixed set of addresses, but duplicates a small set of *lines* from the main memory. If this set includes frequently used information, this increases the overall speed of the computer (its hit ratio is then high).

A cache [Fig. 4-15(a)] has a memory address and memory buffer register (MAR and MBR). When an address appears in the MAR, the cache is searched *associatively* (see Sec. 3-4) for the address: If it is found then its content is transferred to the MBR; if it is not found, a line has to be transferred from the main memory replacing one line in the cache. Since a line in a cache includes a number of items, the last digit of the address indicates which of the items is to be read. (Often, instead of an associative, a "Direct-Mapped" cache is used, to save money [Wak89].)

We do not know normally which information will be used most frequently and often use the Least Recently Used (LRU) policy of replacing the line which was accessed farthest in the past. In order to be able to determine when a line was used, we keep a counter for each line.

A number of caches can keep a copy of a line from the shared memory. With no special mechanism, one of the PEs could change the line in its cache while all other copies of the same line remain as they were. One of these PEs can later access an "old" copy of the line. This would make the data *incoherent*.

When a line in the cache is replaced by a line from the memory, the question is what to do with the old line. If it was changed in the cache earlier, then it should first be transferred back to the memory—but this reduces the speedup. We could have asked that whenever the line was changed it should have been written into the memory right away. When replaced by a new line, it will not have to be written into memory, but this solution is counterproductive. It is better to add logic to the cache so that it will be able to decide whether the line was changed and has to replace the old line in the memory.

In Sec. 4-2 we used locks to prevent two persons updating data. The reason this was required was that otherwise the second teller found the "old" value. This situation is even worse if caches are used, since the teller may hold the "new balance" for a very long time—maybe even indefinitely—in its cache.

Another case is when PE(1) updates the value both in its cache and in the main memory, but PE(k) uses a "stale" value stored in its cache. Thus, there are two ways for the data not to be coherent: if the data is updated only in the cache, but not in the main memory, and second, if it was updated in both, but another PE keeps a "stale" copy in its cache.

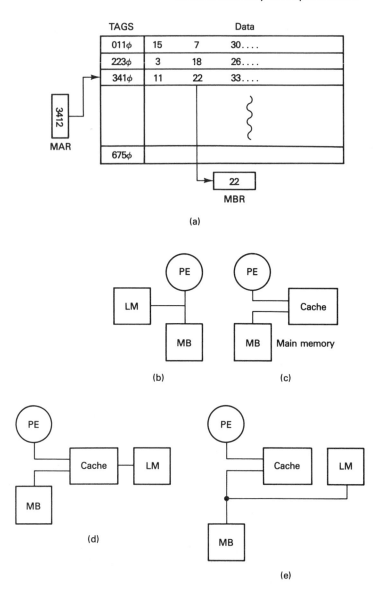

Figure 4-15 The cache and possible positions of memories and of the cache

One simple solution would be never to use shared values in a cache, but how does the system know which information is shared? Tracking all memory activity would be quite expensive. Various solutions were proposed in [CaF78, DaB82, KaW73, Pat82, and Smi82] and summarized in [AaB86]. Another solution as proposed in [Sto87] is formulated as follows.

"Here are the basic operations that must take place to maintain cache coherence:

1. If a READ operation for a shared datum misses in cache, then all caches in the system must be interrogated for a copy of the datum.
2. All WRITE operations to a shared datum, whether they are hits or misses, force all caches in the system to be checked for a copy of the datum. A possible exception to this rule is if the datum is tagged as being the only cached copy of the data in the system, in which case no external broadcast is necessary.'' [Sto87]

In this case, data should be tagged by the compiler as *cacheable* and *noncacheable*. For instance, locks should never be cached.

Assume that each of the p PEs accesses every one of the MBs equally often and that the coherency problem is solved. The (automatic) transfer of lines may follow the "Buffered Write Back" strategy, namely: A line is changed in the main memory only when it is transferred to it from the cache. When a miss occurs, a line from the cache is first buffered, a new line is moved from main memory to the cache, and then the old line is moved from the buffer into the main memory.

Consider the cache of the RP3 (Fig. 4-13): approximately 80%–90% of the data traffic can be intercepted by it, so that only 10%–20% of the total data traffic is managed by the IN. If a reference to memory has passed around the cache, the network interface decides if it is to its own memory or to another node. In the last case, the reference is sent over the network, where another node's interface responds to it, altering or retrieving the appropriate information. In either event, a response is returned through the IN to the initiating node. There the response is treated as if it had been generated by the Local Memory, LM.

The memory organization is very important to SMs because memory is used not only by the PEs and I/O devices, but also for communication between its different units. As seen in Sec. 4-1, the SM may or may not possess local and/or cache memory. It can therefore be connected in one of the five ways [BaF88] [See Fig. 4-15(b) to (e)].

a. No local memory or cache is used. Only Main Memory, MM, exists.
b. Only local and global memories are used.
c. The cache stores lines from MM. Transfers are automatic.
d. Both a cache and LM are used. The lines stored in the cache can come only from the local memory.
e. A cache and LM are used. The lines can also come from MM.

The following conclusions were reached in [BaF88]:

1. A cache with the ability to store lines from the shared memory (cases c and f) increases the capacity considerably.
2. The miss access rate of a cache is defined as the probability of a PE requesting data not present in the cache. The capacity of an SM increases even more if the miss access rate is reduced.
3. The best organization for direct INs is d.

4. It was noted that the caches are more important to bus-connected (multibus INs of Sec. 2-2) than to other SM systems.

5. For MINs and single buses as INs, LMs should be used as well. Even if the miss ratio of the cache is low, the LM will increase the capacity so much as to warrant the higher complexity of scheme e.

4–4.2 The F&A Operation and the Combining Switch

To make precise the effect of simultaneous access to the shared memory, a "*serialization principle*" was defined in [Gea83] as follows: The effect of simultaneous actions by the PEs is as if the actions occurred in some (unspecified) serial order.

To facilitate concurrent applications and provide a simple yet effective means of synchronization, a "Fetch-and-Add," F&A, operation was added in the Ultracomputer, the RP3, and in the Butterfly computers. The format is $w := F\&A(v,e)$ where v is an integer variable and e is an integer expression. The operation is indivisible (atomic); it fetches the old value of v from memory and replaces it with the sum of $v + e$; in short, it means that the following two instructions happen as if they were one: $w := v$; $v := v + e$. (The instruction obviously takes two memory cycles.) Thus, if v is a shared variable and many F&A operations use it simultaneously, the effect is the same as if all e's were added in any order. For two F&As, $x := F\&A(v,e)$ and $y := F\&A(v,f)$, if they are executed in the order stated, the result is first $x := v$, $v' := v + e$ then $y := v + e$, $v'' := v + e + f$, but if the order is reversed, first $y := v$, $v' := v + f$ then $x := v + f$ and $v'' := v + e + f$. In both cases, the end value of v is $v + e + f$. (Note that the returned values of x and y were different.)

The F&A operation is performed at the memory. If done at a PE, other PEs must be prevented from accessing the common variable for the two cycles of the F&A. Add to it one processor cycle and one round trip through the MIN, and a sizeable delay results. Done at the memory, it takes two cycles.

The $F\&A(v,e)$ operation can be written with braces { and } indicating an atomic (indivisible) operation:

$$w := F\&A(v,e) = \{w := v; \; v := v + e\} \tag{4-1}$$

Since the Test and Set, TAS, operation was defined as

$$TAS(v) := \{temp: = v; \; v := TRUE\} \text{ return temp;}$$

it can be produced by a "Fetch and OR" operation F&O(v,TRUE), namely as

$$F\&O(v,e) = \{temp: = v; \; v := v \text{ OR TRUE } = \text{ TRUE}\} \text{ return temp;} \tag{4-2}$$

which are precisely the same actions as were described for TAS.

The F&A instruction provides parallelism with multiple PEs accessing multiple MBs, provided that the MBs are distinct. For the case that the references are to the same memory (e.g., accessing a lock), these references will be *combined*. For this the F&A operation uses adders in the Memory Network Interfaces, MNIs, of the Ultracomputer [Fig. 4-12(a)]. When $F\&A(x,e)$ reaches the MNI associated with the MB in which x is

stored, the addition $x + e$ can be performed, the sum is stored in x, and the
is returned to the requesting PE.

> The combining switch is able to identify fetch-and-add operations and combi
> all processors so that the memory location is accessed only once. In addition, the switch
> distributes to the various processors the different values for the result of the fetch part of the
> operation and in this way allows parallel execution of the fetch and add. The disadvantage is
> cost: Adders and buffering must be integrated into the switch. However, as the cost of
> hardware is driven down, this approach may become more attractive. [Gea83]†

Parallel F&As directed at the same location are combined. If two messages arrive at
an SE and should be directed to the same output port, one of them is stored temporarily in
a queue and transferred later. When two F&As referencing the same shared variable, say
F&A(x,e) and F&A(x,f), meet at a switch, the switch forms the sum $e+f$, stores e (in the
wait buffer), and transmits the combined request F&A($x,e+f$). When the value y is
returned to the switch in response to F&A($x,e+f$), the switch transmits y to satisfy the
original request F&A(x,e) and transmits $y+e$ to satisfy the original request F&A(x,f).

Assuming that the combined request was not further combined with yet another
request, the values returned by the switch are x and $x+e$, thereby effecting the serialization order "F&A(x,e) followed immediately by F&A(x,f)." The memory location x is
also properly incremented, becoming $x+e+f$. If other fetch-and-add operations updating
x are encountered, then the associativity of addition guarantees that the procedure gives a
result consistent with the serialization principle. Stated differently, since combined
requests can themselves be combined, any number of concurrent memory references to
the same memory location can be satisfied in one memory cycle.

There are two MINs in the RP3. Both are based on an expanded Omega MIN with
an extra stage to improve performance and fault tolerance. The "noncombining" MIN
has four stages of 4-by-4 SEs with extensive buffering which provides low latency. The
"combining" MIN has six stages of 2-by-2 SEs with buffers and with logic for combining
requests and recombining responses. Contention is reduced in RP3 by buffering, while an
alternative memory path was provided in the Butterfly.

Both MINs use a mixture of circuit-switching and message-passing. A message is
pipelined across the stages of the IN as if circuit-switched, but when blocked, some or all
of the message is queued within a switch stage much like in packet switching. The transfer
of information is only between the nodes and MBs and not between the nodes alone. The
fetch-and-add operations are sent to the combining IN with all other requests being
handled by the noncombining IN. Requests from different PaMs to the same memory
location are combined before they get to the memory, that is within the combining MIN.

The SE of the combining switch is shown in Fig. 4-16. It consists of two units: one,
in the forward direction, combines two messages and forwards them, the other supplies
broadcast by providing replies to two addresses. The forward direction subnode is a
standard 2-by-2 crossbar with output queues and the following characteristics:

†A. Gottlieb et al., "The New York University Paracomputer . . . ," Trans. IEEE, Vol. C-32, No. 2,
Feb., pp. 175–189, (© 1983, IEEE). Reprinted by permission of the IEEE.

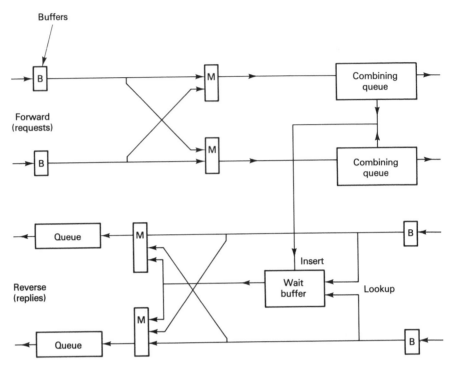

Figure 4-16 The SE of the combining switch of the RP3. Courtesy of G. F. Pfister, V. A. Norton: "Hot spot contention . . . ," Trans. IEEE, Vol. C-34, Oct. 1985, pp. 943–48 (©1985 IEEE).

1. A message is queued only if the succeeding stage cannot accept it; otherwise, the message is forwarded with a single delay time.
2. Only messages in the queues are combined, so there is no combining if the traffic is low and the queues are empty.
3. Two messages may be destined for the same output and are enqueued simultaneously.
4. An additional buffer able to hold one complete message is associated with each input. It is used to hold a message in the event that the destined output queue is full. Without it, each node would have to signal to both its predecessors that it cannot accept input if either queue had less than two message slots free. With it, the signal that a message cannot be accepted on a given input is identical to that input's buffer being full. The buffer therefore allows greater output queue utilization; and since combining is done only in the output queues, this greater utilization implies that more opportunities for combining are available.
5. Saved information about combinations made in both input queues is held in a single wait buffer. Replies arriving from either reverse-direction port are de-combined

using information in that wait buffer. The output queues in the reverse direction are assumed to be able to accept up to four inputs simultaneously: two messages from the two reverse direction inputs, and two ''de-combinations.''

6. A message can combine only with one other message in a given node. A combined message can combine again at a later node. [PaN85]†

   It will be shown presently that this is undesirable.

7. The entire operation is pipelined so that one message may leave while two are being combined.

When F&A is used simultaneously by p PEs, the following conditions should be imposed:

1. A shared location is read only once and written only once no matter how many requests occur simultaneously.

2. Sequentialization of requests means that the values returned are the same as would be returned by sequential processing.

3. Each request must have exclusive access to the location while it is updating it.

As an example of using the SE of Fig. 4-16, consider what happens if three PEs add 1, 2, and 3 to a common location L which is initially 0. If done sequentially, the result is $L = 6$. If F&A instructions are used, we have

$$L := F\&A(L,1);\ L := F\&A(L,2);\ L := F\&A(L,3);$$

If done concurrently [Fig. 4-17(a)], a tree-like procedure is followed. The first combining switch adds $1 + 2 = 3$, stores 1 and transfers 3 to the second switch. The second switch adds $3 + 3 = 6$, stores 3 and transfers 6 to the memory location. On the ''return trip'' from the memory, the ''second'' switch receives from the memory location the previous value 0, adds it to the stored 3, returns 3 and transmits back the 0. Now, 3 happens to be the value before 3 was added to the sum (and in the order we are using represents the sum at this point of accumulation). While this is happening, the ''first'' switch receives the 0, adds $0 + 1$ to return 1 and 0 to its two inputs. The result in memory is 6 (as it should be).

As seen, the F&A uses a tree of SEs and executes in time of $\mathbf{0}[\log(p)]$ while the TAS locking executes in time of $\mathbf{0}(p)$. Additionally, the F&A instruction does not force a completely sequential execution, as TAS does. The F&A is faster and enables greater parallelization.

Combining requests reduces communication traffic and thus decreases the length of the queues mentioned above, leading to lower network latency (i.e., reduced memory access time). Since combined requests can themselves be combined, the network satisfies the key property that any number of concurrent memory references to the same location can be satisfied in the time required for just one central memory access. It is this property,

---

†G. F. Pfister, V. A. Norton, ''Hot spot contention . . . ,'' Trans. IEEE, Vol. C-34, Oct., pp. 943–48, (© 1985, IEEE). Reprinted by permission of the IEEE.

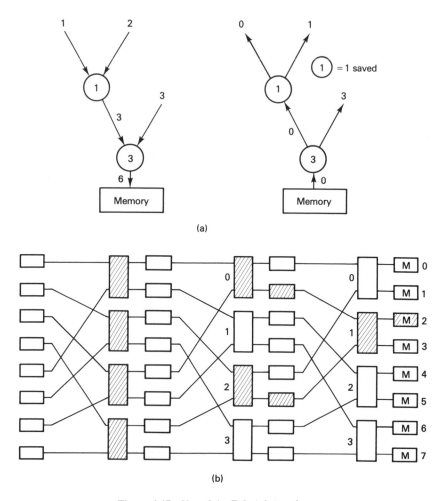

Figure 4-17   Use of the F & A instruction

when extended to include F&A operations, that permits bottleneck-free implementation of many coordination protocols.

Although the preceding assumed that the requests arrive at the switch simultaneously, the actual design can also combine an incoming request with requests already queued for output to the next stage.

An experiment for evaluating the performance of the combining switch was reported in [PaN85]. In order to determine the optimal length of the queue, a number of runs were simulated with an assumed uniform distribution of memory references. Under those circumstances, virtually no combining occurred since the probability that references to exactly equal addresses are queued in the same switch node at the same time is negligible. To account for locks, a spike was added to this uniform distribution. The fraction of total references during a spike to one particular location was varied from 0.5% to 32%. It was found that the latency increased considerably, not only for the locked location but for all memory locations. The reason is as follows. The spiked, "hot" MB is accessed with a probability h, all other MBs with equal probability $1-h$. Therefore, when the p PEs produce "a" accesses per cycle to the memory, the hot MB is accessed at the rate

$$r = a*(1-h) + a*h*p \qquad (4\text{-}3)$$

where the first part accounts for the uniform share of the load, the second for the hot MB being slightly overloaded.

Since only one access per cycle is possible, $a \le 1$. Therefore, the maximum rate of generating accesses is that for which $a = 1$:

$$R = 1/[1 + h*(p-1)] \qquad (4\text{-}4)$$

This function depends very much on the spike height h. Thus, for $h=0$ and $p = 1024$, we have $R = 1$, but for $h = 0.01$ we have $1/11.24 = 0.088968$. As seen, a 1% change in h leads to a 91% decrease of rate R.

This is made even worse by the following issue discussed in [PaN85]. Suppose that MB(2) at output of the IN in Fig. 4-17(b) is the "hot" MB. When it is accessed, SE(0) and SE(2) of the middle segment are used by the two inputs (shading an SE shows that it is used). At the leftmost stage, all four SEs are used. This is called "tree saturation" because all queues in the tree of SEs rooted at the "hot" memory location are full and cannot accept more messages.

Simulations were run on noncombining switches. It was found that with 1000 CPUs, a hot-spot traffic of only 0.125% would limit the speedup to only 500 (efficiency of 50%) and thus the *conclusion* was reached in [PaN85]:

> By considering nonuniform hot-spot memory reference patterns, we have demonstrated that multi-stage blocking networks have an unfortunate property: A sufficient concentration of references to one server—a "hot spot"—can degrade the response of the network to all references, not just those of the hot-spot server; and the potential degradation is sufficient to cripple system performance. The "tree saturation" effect causing this requires only that the network be multistage, blocking, and controlled by distributed routing. The presence of the cache is of little help since none of the references to a globally accessed lock can be cached.
>
> A number of simulations with a combining switch were also run, and the conclusion was reached that *message combining is adequate to deal with the effect of hot-spots.* [PaN85]

Therefore, despite the fact that a combining switch is more expensive, its use was advocated.

4–5 SPEEDUP OF MULTIPROCESSORS

4–5.1 Speedup of Coarse-Grained Algorithms

The efficiency of multiprocessors depends on the degree of concurrency in the algorithm and on the required overhead for scheduling-and-synchronization. For high efficiency, as much concurrency and as little overhead as possible is sought; both of these factors depend on the granularity of the problem. Figure 4-18(a) shows a graph of a computation with eight vertices and ten links representing computations and dependencies, respectively. Since each vertex has to be scheduled and each link synchronized, a penalty is to be paid for such *fine granularity*. There is parallelism in this graph (e.g., the tasks represented by vertices 2, 3, 4, and 5 can proceed in parallel). Suppose we combine [Fig. 4-18(b)] vertices 2 and 3, 4 and 5, as well as 6 and 7. The synchronization penalty will be reduced but there will be much less concurrency left. Merging vertices 6 and 7 into vertix Z forces the sequential execution of 5 and 6 since Z is executed after Y.

Clustering combines several operations into a task reducing the overhead of scheduling and synchronization, but also its concurrency. Partitioning a program into more tasks increases the efficiency.

Figure 4-19(a) describes a possible scheduling for computing

$$\mathbf{G} := \mathbf{f(A)} * (\mathbf{A} * \mathbf{B} - \mathbf{A} - \mathbf{B}) \tag{4-5}$$

on a multiprocessor. Upper-case boldface letters represent n-by-n matrices and **f** is a (vector) function. (SMs should process coarse-grained algorithms and thus the matrices and function in Eq. (4-5). If these were scalars, the granularity would have been too fine for an SM.)

The scheduling should obey some precedence relations (e.g., that **E** cannot be computed until and unless **C** and **D** are first calculated).

Let two processors be scheduled to calculate **G**. They may compute first the intermediate matrices **C** and **D,** and then **H** and **E** in parallel. When this step is complete, one processor is idle while the second yields the result **G**. Waiting for some calculation to be completed is denoted by Φ. Under these assumptions, the Gantt chart is shown in Fig. 4-19(b).

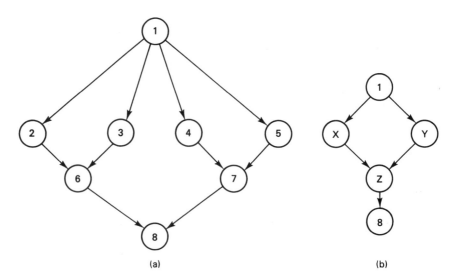

(a)   (b)

Figure 4-18   Two possible schedules of a job

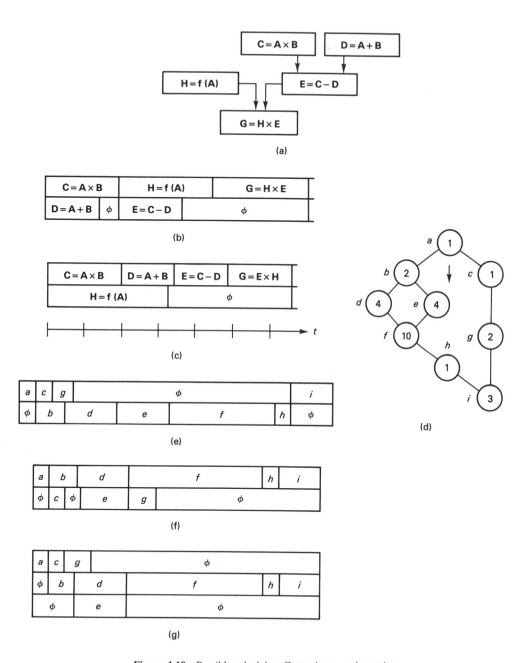

Figure 4-19   Possible schedules, Gantt charts, and speedups

The speedup can be computed as follows: Let us assume that computing the sum or the difference of two n-by-n matrices $[0(n^2)]$ requires the time of 10 units, but the multiplication $[0(n^3)]$ requires 100 time units. The function f may be quite complicated, so it requires, say, 200 time units. If done on a single computer, the time required would be $100 + 10 + 200 + 10 + 100 = 420$ time units. With $p = 2$, the time would be 400 time units. The speedup and efficiency are therefore

$$\sigma = 420/400 = 1.05; \quad \eta = 50.25\% \tag{4-6}$$

The same calculation can be scheduled also according to the chart of Fig. 4-19(c) and in this case, the speedup and efficiency would be

$$\sigma = 420/300 = 1.40; \quad \eta = 70.0\% \tag{4-7}$$

As can be seen, *the proper scheduling can drastically improve the efficiency* of multiprocessors. The second scheduling is called "biggest task first" or "packing" as in packing a knapsack. As most hikers know, given the objects to be packed are of different sizes (say, from a knife to a blanket), the *largest* items should be packed first. This type of scheduling means to compute longer jobs first.

Minsky's conjecture implied that multiprocessor algorithms should be run on not more than two processors. Thus, in the previous example, if there were three processors scheduled, they could have produced **C, D,** and **H,** but only one could be used for calculating **E** and finally **G**. The time is again 300, so that the speedup and efficiency are only $\sigma = 420/300 = 1.4$ and $\eta = 1.4/3 = 46.7\%$, respectively.

Figure 4-19(d) shows a program graph. The number in each node in the task graph represents the execution time of that task. Figure 4-19(e) and Fig. 4-19(f) give two schedules for the graph using two processors. Note that a better schedule is achieved by keeping a processor idle while process g could be active. The total execution time $t(1)$ of the task graph in Fig. 4-19(d) on a uniprocessor is the sum of the numbers (weights) associated with each node. Hence, $t(1) = 28$. From Fig. 4-19(e) and Fig. 4-19(f), the execution time on the two-processor system is $t(2) = 25$ and 21, respectively. Therefore, the speedup and efficiency are

$$\sigma = 28/25 = 1.12; \quad \eta = 1.12/p = 56\% \tag{4-8}$$

$$\sigma = 28/21 = 1.33; \quad \eta = 133/2 = 66.7\% \tag{4-9}$$

By increasing the number of processors to three, the speedup will not increase (proving Minsky's conjecture for SMs). In fact, Fig. 4-19(g) shows that $t(3) = 21$, which is the same as $t(2)$ and the efficiency therefore decreases to 44.4%. Hence, the execution of the task graph in Fig. 4-19(d) is most cost-effective on a two-processor system.

4–5.2 Bounds of Speedup for Fine-Grained Algorithms

For calculating the *bounds of the speedup,* multiprocessors may be represented by the Paracomputer of Fig. 1-1(c). Assume its processors execute binary operations (e.g., additions, multiplications, comparisons, etc.). Each operation is performed on two operands and yields a single result. Next, suppose that the sum of 16 operands is to be calculated. If performed sequentially, this would require the time of 15α, or in general $n-1 \approx n$ addition times "α".

The same problem can be performed on a multiprocessor with $p=2**(r-1)$ in a manner exemplified by Fig. 4-20, for which $p=2^3=8$ or $r=4$. The first eight additions yield eight partial sums, when these are added they yield four partial sums, when these are added they yield two partial sums which when added yield a single result: the same sum arrived at sequentially.

In Fig. 4-20, the program terminates after c time steps. The final scalar result is the outcome of a binary operation on two operands performed by a single CPU at time c; the remaining $p-1$ CPUs do nothing at time c. Backtracking, at time $c-1$, at most two CPUs are usefully employed, namely those which produce the two operands for the addition at time c (we say "at most" since one of the two operands may be ready from a previous step). Since at c only one CPU is used, at $c-1$ at most two CPUs are used, and at $c-2$ at most four CPUs are working, it follows that at time $c-(r-1)$ at most $2**(r-1)=2**r/2=p$ processors work.

The number of operations that were needed in the last step was one addition, two additions in the one before last, four and eight additions in the previous steps respectively. Altogether, the number of additions is

$$1 + 2 + 4 + 8 = 15 \approx 2**r \qquad (4\text{-}10)$$

At the beginning of the process (time $c-r+1$), the number of working CPUs was $p=2**(r-1)$ $[2^3=8]$ or $p=2**r/2$ and $2**r=2*p$ $[2^4=2*8]$. If the log of both sides is taken, then

$$r = 1 + \log(p) \qquad (4\text{-}11)$$

A (sequential) uniprocessor executes a single instruction in time ω, where ω is the time of a single operation like addition, so that:

$$t(1) = 2*p*\omega \qquad (4\text{-}12)$$

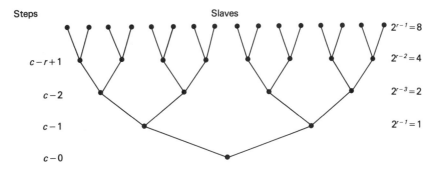

Figure 4-20   Calculation of a sum of 16 number on multiprocessors

Since on a multiprocessor there were r stages $(c-0, c-1, c-2, \ldots, c-r+1)$ the time on p processors is

$$t(p) = r*\omega \qquad (4\text{-}13)$$

and the speedup is

$$\sigma \simeq (2*p*\omega)/(r*\omega) = (2*p)/r \qquad (4\text{-}14)$$

Inserting $r = 1 + \log(p)$ yields the following result:

$$\sigma \leq (2*p)/(\log p + 1) \qquad (4\text{-}15)$$

If p is large, say 1024, then 1 can be neglected and the speedup is

$$\sigma \simeq [2/\log(p)]*p \qquad (4\text{-}16)$$

At the top of Fig. 4-20, all p CPUs are working. In the next step, only half of them are working, in step k only $p/2**(k-1)$ are working, and so on until at the last step, r, only a single processor works. This reminds the author of Joseph Haydn's "Farewell Symphony." To impress upon Count Esterhazy that it was time to let them depart for Vienna, each musician in turn bowed and left the stage. Finally, only the conductor (Mr. Haydn) remained and Count Esterhazy was convinced. This *Haydn effect,* as shown in Fig. 4-20, reduces the maximally possible speedup. The reduction was calculated to be

$$\sigma = [2/(1 + \log p)]*\sigma^M; \qquad (4\text{-}17)$$

where σ^M is the maximal speedup.

This shows that in multiprocessors the equipment often is not used efficiently. There is a lot of redundancy. The equipment is underutilized and the utilization factor ν can be calculated as follows:

$$\nu \simeq 2/[1 + \log(p)] \qquad (4\text{-}18)$$

Equation (4-15) provides the justification for Minsky's conjecture. For $p = 2$, $\sigma \leq 2$ and $\eta \leq 100\%$, for $p = 4$ we have $\sigma \leq 8/3$ and $\eta \leq 66.67\%$, and for $p = 16$, we have only $\sigma \leq 32/5$ and $\eta \leq 40\%$. This conjecture does not apply to utilization (Table 1-1). The speedup will also increase substantially if the granularity is made coarse.

4–5.3 How to Design an Algorithm for SMs

To show how the speedup of Eq. (4-17) can be achieved, consider matrix multiplication. If the size of the matrices are n-by-n, then each of the n^2 elements of $\mathbf{C} = \mathbf{A} * \mathbf{B}$ is calculated as

$$C(i,j) = \Sigma \, A(i,k)*B(k,j); \ k\Sigma = 1, \ldots, n \qquad (4\text{-}19)$$

In the Paracomputer model, there are as many processors as needed and they calculate the n^2 products $C(i,j)$. Each requires $n*(\mu + \alpha)$ operations, where α and μ are the time of a single addition and multiplication respectively. The times of addition and multiplication on microcomputers with floating-point operations are approximately the same (ω), so that altogether $2*n^3*\omega$ are needed, but if there are n^3 PEs, than all n^2 *products* are calculated in the time of μ. The number of *additions* is $n-1$, and they require time of $1+\log p$ being calculated as in Fig. 4-20 (i.e., the calculation is delayed by the Haydn effect). Thus, $t(p)$ and $t(1)$ are, respectively

$$t(p) \geq \mu + (1+\log n^3)*\alpha \simeq \mu + 3*\alpha \log(n) \simeq 3*\omega*\log(n) \qquad (4\text{-}20)$$

$$t(1) = n^3 * (\alpha+\mu) = 2*n^3*\omega \qquad (4\text{-}21)$$

The lower bound of the speedup will be

$$\sigma \leq 2*n^3*\omega/[3*\omega*\log(n)] = (2/3)*[n^3/\log(n)] \qquad (4\text{-}22)$$

For $n = 1024$ this would be only $\eta = 200*1024^3/30 \simeq 6.67\%$ of the optimum efficiency but would be achieved by a very high number of CPUs. For $n = 1,000$ ($\simeq$ 1024), the enormous number of 1,000,000,000 CPUs is required.

The *conclusion* is that for matrix multiplication, SMs require a very large number of PEs but provide only a very moderate speedup—*if this fine-grained algorithm is used.* Let us try other algorithms.

A method of multiplying 2-by-2 matrices was suggested by V. Strassen in [Str69], and is as follows:

$d(1) = [A(1,2)-A(2,2)]*[B(2,1)+B(2,2)];$
$d(2) = [A(1,1)+A(2,2)]*[B(1,1)+B(2,2)];$
$d(3) = [A(1,1)-A(2,1)]*[B(1,1)+B(1,2)];$
$d(4) = [A(1,1)+A(1,2)]*[B(2,2);$ $C(1,1) = d(1)+d(2)-d(4)+d(6);$
$d(5) = [B(1,2)-B(2,2)]*[A(1,1);$ $C(2,2) = d(2)-d(3)+d(5)-d(7);$
$d(6) = [B(2,1)-B(1,1)]*[A(2,2);$ $C(1,2) = d(4)+d(5);$
$d(7) = [A(2,1)+A(2,2)]*[B(1,1);$ $C(2,1) = d(6)+d(7); \qquad (4\text{-}23)$

Counting the operation symbols in Eq. (4-23) leads to

$$\Omega = 7 * \mu + 18 * \alpha \qquad (4\text{-}24)$$

Strassen proved that for large $n = 2**k$, *if additions are not counted* then the count of operations is $\Omega = k*n**(\log 7) = k*n**(2.81) = \mathbf{0}[n**(2.81)]$ instead of $\mathbf{0}(n^3)$. This indicates that this is a more efficient method of matrix multiplication, except that:

It does not take into account the time to access the elements.

It does not count the number of additions.

It is very inefficient for sparse matrices.

There is no numerical error control.

The computation of the d's and C's is not independent of each other and it may be very difficult to parallelize the calculation.

As shown next, notwithstanding the Haydn effect, a high speedup can be achieved by block-decomposition. In Eq. (4-25), all $A(i,j)$, $B(i,j)$, and $C(i,j)$ represent $(n/2)$-by-$(n/2)$ *block matrices*.

$$\left| \begin{matrix} A(1,1) & A(1,2) \\ A(2,1) & A(2,2) \end{matrix} \right| * \left| \begin{matrix} B(1,1) & B(1,2) \\ B(2,1) & B(2,2) \end{matrix} \right| = \left| \begin{matrix} C(1,1) & C(1,2) \\ C(2,1) & C(2,2) \end{matrix} \right| =$$

$$\left| \begin{matrix} A(1,1)*B(1,1)+A(1,2)*B(2,1) & A(1,1)*B(1,2)+A(1,2)*B(2,2) \\ A(2,1)*B(1,1)+A(2,2)*B(2,1) & A(2,1)*B(1,2)+A(2,2)*B(2,2) \end{matrix} \right| \qquad (4\text{-}25)$$

If $p = 4$, then each processor could compute a block submatrix $C(i,j)$ in a time of $(n/2)^2*\alpha + 2*\mu*(n/2)^3$ and need $\tau*n^2/4$ and ζ:

$$t(p) \simeq 2*n^3*\mu/8 + n^2*\alpha/4 + \tau*n^2/8 \simeq 2*n^3*\mu/8 + \tau*n^2/8 \simeq 2*n^3*\mu/8 \quad (4\text{-}26)$$

$$\rho \simeq 1/4; \quad \sigma \simeq 4; \quad \eta \simeq 100\% \qquad (4\text{-}27)$$

This is the optimum speedup. It was achieved by using submatrices instead of scalar elements, i.e., by making the algorithm coarse-grained. Complications appear when $pl = 2**k$.

The *conclusions* are:

1. In order for SMs to be able to solve fine-grained problems efficiently, their synchronization must be efficient. If adding two matrices (Eq. 1-11) requires less time than synchronization, using a single PE is more efficient than using an SM. In general, an *SM-Multiprocessor is inefficient for fine-grained algorithms*. Therefore, making an algorithm coarser, and dividing jobs into tasks (not operations) is beneficial.

2. Seek as many independent jobs as possible; as shown above, scheduling is then also easier.

4–6 COMPARISON

In order to achieve a speedup in a multiprocessor, the tasks that constitute the program must be executed in parallel. The scheduler that effects the concurrency is designed as a mutually exclusive program which can be executed by only one task at a time. This shows that the problem of mutual exclusion has to be solved not only because of parallel algorithms, but also because of the scheduler, and that an additional delay may be incurred in parallel algorithms because of it.

When programming multiprocessors, it is not enough to outline an algorithm; as shown, the programmer must consider how to schedule the independent processors. Normally this is the job of the operating system. Scheduling has a definite influence on σ and η. Recall that in addition to a task having to wait in a queue because there is no CPU available, it also may have to wait for another CPU to finish.

During the execution of a task on a CPU, external events such as interrupts may occur, demanding urgent service. Usually, such an interruption is permitted and the scheduling is called ''preemptive.'' It increases the time required to complete the algorithm because the state of the interrupted task must be preserved (i.e., the values of all registers, the allocated memory boundaries, etc.). This process is known as context switching. The overhead of context switching is then again incurred when the task is reactivated.

It is customary to compare the MIPS and/or MFLOP figures of the systems discussed. In the case of SM-Multiprocessors we can do better. Programs were run and the speedups or efficiencies measured. For the Butterfly computers, the results in [BBN87] show rather convincingly that the speedup is high and repudiate all kinds of ''laws'' and ''conjectures''; as a matter of fact $\sigma \approx c*r$, (c = constant).

In computing, and especially in scientific computing of today, two unmet demands are the need for new techniques and the need for a cheaper supercomputer. The supercomputers are simply too expensive for university and frequently even industrial laboratories. (Supercomputers carry a price tag of millions of dollars.) On the other hand, even if these computers were affordable, the speedup that can be achieved is, to many users, too limited.

Researchers therefore find themselves at the horn of a dilemma: They can reduce their problem size in order to accommodate the computer, thus solving only part of the problem, or they can solve the entire problem, but at the cost of too much time, frustration, and often monopolizing the time of the computer for very long periods.

In this chapter, SMs were used to solve the dilemma. Another possibility is to connect a large number of PaMs (nodes) to a minicomputer—a ''host.'' Such computers, namely the ''Cubes'' and the ASPs, are discussed in Chap. 5.

4-7 PROBLEMS

1. Explain the difference between shared-memory and message-passing (SM and MP) multiprocessors.
2. Describe the general organization of the C.mmp, Cm*, Pluribus, Butterfly, and RP3.
3. List the design principles of Pluribus and explain them.
4. List the advantages and disadvantages of the two types of addressing used in SMs.
5. Describe the problem of critical sections and its solution.
6. Explain how a deadlock can happen and give an example of one.
7. Explain in as much detail as you can both coarse and fine granularity. In which multiprocessors are they applied?
8. Given the equation $G := (A*B - A - B)*f(B) + f(A)*A*B + A + B$ and p either 2 or 3, draw the Gantt charts and show whether $p = 3$ yields a higher efficiency and how scheduling improves the efficiency.
9. Draw the Gantt chart for matrix multiplication using 2-by-2 blocks.
10. If you were given a program and told to draw a precedence graph, how would you determine what can be done in parallel?

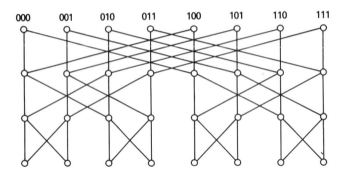

Figure 4-21

11. Write a "program" in English and mathematical notation for adding two *n*-by-*n* matrices: **A** := **B** + **C** in an SM-Multiprocessor. Check how the speedup depends on granularity and *p* as the number of PEs.

12. Schedule calculation of **C** = **A** * **B** by Strassen's method, Eq. (4-23).

13. The Butterfly network consists of $(d+1)*(2**d)$ PaMs, where *d* is some integer. The PaMs are arranged in $d+1$ rows and $2**d$ columns (Fig. 4-21). Show that if the PaMs of the top row and the corresponding incident links are removed, we obtain two identical Butterflies of $d*[2**(d-1)]$ PaMs [BaT89].

CHAPTER 5

OTHER
PARALLEL
SYSTEMS

The *objectives* of this chapter are:

Reiterate the reasons for developing the Message Passing, MP, Multiprocessors. Describe in general the Hypercube (*Cube*)—the best-known MP.

Describe some of the commercially available Cubes.

Describe the Alternating Sequential-Parallel (*ASP*) System and calculate the bounds of speedup it can achieve. This leads then to conditions for designing an efficient ASP.

Discuss the hardware organization of an assembled ASP, namely the TOPPS.

Describe additional PPSs, discuss characteristics of various PPSs, compare them, and present problems.

5−1 INTRODUCTION AND HYPERCUBES

Let us start by reviewing the reasons for developing MPs.

The name "Supercomputer" seems to have been appropriated by the vector processors (VPs) of Chap. 3. The VPs are "super" when processing vector or array problems which frequently occur in large-scale scientific and engineering problems. A portion of any code will also include *scalar* parts. For "super" performance, the VPs must handle both the vector and scalar operations very fast. Unfortunately, the maximum speedup is achieved when the vector content of the program approaches 100%, but when the scalar part predominates, the speedup is very low. The super-VP has become scalar bound or not so super. It does not handle scalar operations any faster than mainframes.

Additionally, pipelining presents a programming problem: Either the programmer must manage the time dependencies in the code or rely on a sophisticated compiler to do it. Even if such a compiler is available, some hand-tweaking of the code will be required.

Arrays of processors (ARPs of Sec. 3-5) execute instructions in lockstep synchronization. They efficiently execute data-parallel programs (e.g., image processing). For "number crunching" problems of the instruction-parallel type these computers are not too efficient. Associative processors of Sec. 3-4 add the high cost of their memories to the above disadvantages.

SM-Multiprocessors have the disadvantages that they limit the number of CPUs and are efficient only for coarse-grained problems. They support familiar programming, but suffer from contention, require synchronization, scheduling, and are always in danger of being deadlocked. The Butterfly and RP3 scale well, but the address-switching interconnection network permits reading and writing in someone else's memory with all the hazards this entails.

The enormous advances of VLSI circuitry have made it possible to connect a large number of complete *PaMs,* Processor-and-Local-Memory (*LM*). We depict them by a circle inside a square. In this chapter a single PaM or a number of PaMs may be combined in a *node*.

Vector and array processors use high-speed, but custom-designed components. Because of limited demand their prices are very high. VLSI components (in particular the nodes) are physically compact and are produced on a huge scale, making them widely available; they are 10 to 100 times more cost-effective than the components used currently in conventional supercomputers. Hypercubes (to be called *Cubes*) use such nodes and as a consequence have a high performance/price ratio.

Cubes were first proposed in [SaB77]. For some time there was little interest in them until they were assembled as the "Cosmic Cube" [Sei85] at CalTech. Other cube-connected computers are listed in Table 5-1.

TABLE 5-1 SOME ASSEMBLED HYPERCUBES AND THEIR CHARACTERISTICS

Computer	Developer	Year	p	m	es/p	es/r
Cosmic Cube	Caltech	1983	64	128	0.025	0.7
Mark II	Caltech	1985	64	256	0.035	1.0
iPSC	Intel	1985	128	512	0.035	1.0
N-Cube/TEN	NCube	1986	1024	128	0.400	2.0
iPSC-VX	Intel	1986	64	1.5K	5–20	1.0
T-Series	Floating Point	1986	16384	1.0K	15–20	7.0
Connection Machine	Thinking Machine	1986	65536	0.5	—	0.015
Mark III	Caltech	1986	1024	4.0K	20	1.0

Column headings
p is maximum number of nodes
m is maximum memory per node (in K bytes)
es/p is estimated performance (in Mega-Flops) of a node
es/r is estimated node instruction rate (in Mega-Ips)

The name "Cube" indicates that the topology can be thought of as a multidimensional cube, with a node computer at each corner. In a Cube, if the dimension is d, then there are $p = 2**d$ nodes, with each node connected to d neighboring nodes. Figure 5-1(a) illustrates Cubes from $d = 1$ to $d = 3$. In particular, $d = 1$ represents two node computers connected by a bus, $d = 2$ represents four nodes connected as a mesh, $d = 3$ is the familiar three-dimensional Cube, and $d = 4$ would be two such Cubes interconnected [Fig. 2-14(b)].

The actual physical connections are made by wires, conducting layers, or a backplane. If wires are used then the Cube of each dimension is obtained [Fig. 5-1(b) and (c)] by connecting corresponding nodes of Cubes of the next lower dimension. (For $d \geq 4$ it is better to show the connections as a two-dimensional picture.) One of the advantages of the Cubes is that as the number of nodes increases, the number of connecting wires per node grows only by adding one wire for an extra dimension so that very large numbers of nodes become feasible.

A node can communicate only through the links. For instance, if $d = 7$, there are 128 nodes and each is connected by links to seven neighbors. A simple and efficient algorithm for routing a message through intermediate nodes was described in Sec. 2-3. The path length for sending a message between any two nodes is precisely the number of bit positions in which their binary tags differ. If a node sends a message to a neighbor, the time τ may be short, but if the message is sent to more remote nodes, it could take up to $d*\tau$ in a Cube of dimension d. This indicates that the algorithm cannot be too fine-grained since the communication time may be too high.

Note that in an SM every PE has access to every location, in a Cube a node has access *only* to its own Local Memory, LM; the system is one with distributed memory. The nodes include control so that control too is distributed. The activities of the nodes are coordinated by sending messages among themselves through an IN of communication channels. The Cube's IN is dense enough to support efficient communication between arbitrary nodes, yet sparse enough to be relatively simple and inexpensive to build. To

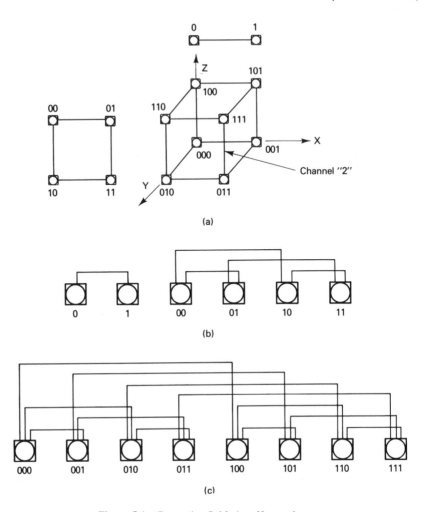

Figure 5-1 Connecting PaMs into Hypercubes

access a memory residing in another node requires *communication*. Cubes are thus classified as *distributed memory, message-passing* PPSs; we called them MPs.

Are there any problems that could be solved on such computers without too much communication between the nodes? The answer is positive: In problems originating in physical sciences, engineering, and numerical analysis, the problems are modeled by regular structures with subparts communicating by *messages*. The same is true for string searching, sorting, event-driven simulation, and artificial intelligence. In all of these applications, the nodes operate independently on a subsection of a larger problem according to instructions and data resident in their LMs. This data originates either from other nodes or from the *Manager* of the Cube.

This type of concurrency denotes *independent* operation of a number of simultaneous computing activities, rather than the lock-step or shared-memory synchronization. In fact, this type of concurrency is based on *asynchronous* operation of the nodes. It is not an SIMD system since the nodes operate with multiple instruction streams. Since p different instruction streams are active at the same time on p different data sets, it is Multiple-Instruction, Multiple-Data. The systems use message passing instead of shared storage for communication between the nodes—they are MPs.

The local memory (LM) approach has the important advantage of scaling well. So, at the most basic level, the Cubes are MIMD systems with LMs and a large number of nodes that operate independently and cooperate by sending and receiving messages.

Message-passing is used to execute the basic unit of computation, the *task*. A task is defined as a sequential program which sends and receives messages. In fact, tasks may communicate *only* by sending and receiving messages. Since more than a single task will be run on a node, the nodes need a multiprogrammed OS, the *kernel*. If they constitute an entire program (complete locality), then no communication is needed and $\tau = 0$. (Some of the tasks may be I/O tasks.) The number of tasks in a node is limited by the amount of local memory in a node.

It has been shown that some SMs are suitable for a limited number of CPUs because of memory and bus contention, scheduling or synchronization problems. The fact that Table 5-1 mentions 1024 processors and even larger Cubes are being planned rests on the high communication capabilities of MPs. Moreover, the advantages of the Cubes increase with higher dimensions. Thus, a Cube with the dimension $d = 8$ or $p = 256$ nodes has twice the computational capacity of a Cube with $d = 7$ or $p = 128$, but has a communication capability of $8*256 = 2,048$ compared to $7*128 = 896$ channels for $d = 7$. The communicational capacity has increased by a factor of $2*8/7 = 2.3$. The largest communication delay also increases more slowly than its capacity; in this example, from 7 to only 8.

Any IN introduces some delay in passing the messages but there is no delay as long as the messages reside in the LM of the node or a small delay if they reside in the LM of an adjoining node. To get as small a delay as possible, communicating tasks should be placed in adjoining nodes to take advantage of "communication locality." The result will be a message system that is faster, simpler, and scales up much better.

Interprocess communication is performed through "channels." There is no synchronization between tasks (processes) when a channel is established. One task communicates with another task simply by opening the channel between them and initiating send and receive requests.

These requests are system calls. Send and receive calls merely *enable* message transmission—if the action is not satisfied, the request for it will be pending until activated. During this waiting time, the processor is not idle, but may continue executing programs.

The choice of communication protocols is important for simplicity, correctness, reliability, and speedup of concurrent algorithms. Basically, there are two kinds of protocol style:

1. In synchronized message-passing, a sender is blocked until a corresponding receive request has been issued, and a task initiating a receive request is waiting until a message has been received. This synchronizes the sender and receiver; therefore it makes indefinite blocking of the same kind as discussed in Sec. 4-2 possible.

2. In asynchronous message-passing, the sender proceeds to compute while the message it has sent is waiting to be received. In the same way, the receiver proceeds with computations (if they are independent of the message) until the message arrives and even after it arrives. At a pause of computation, the buffers are polled and messages transferred. This minimizes waiting and facilitates easily understood algorithms, eliminating indefinite blocking.

Because message-passing among tasks is *asynchronous,* there is no guarantee that a task is ready to receive a message when it arrives. Therefore, messages that are received by a node before a receive request is issued are *buffered* by the kernel. Whenever the receive request is issued, the message is passed to the buffer of the receiving task.

Once a channel has been opened, a send and its corresponding receive may occur in any order. In order not to let messages be buffered for a long time, it is better if the receive is executed before a message arrives at the node. The receive is therefore delivered to the task rapidly, without occupying a system buffer for any extended period.

A single node may contain one or more tasks. All tasks execute simultaneously either by virtue of being activated in different nodes or by being interleaved in a single node. Each task has a global ID Number (Identification) which serves as an address for sending and receiving messages. All messages have headers which include the ID of both sender and receiver (and the message type and length). Messages may be queued in transit from one node to the other, but their order is preserved.

The static task structure is a snapshot of the dynamic task structure. It can be represented as a number of task vertices (we can't again use "nodes") connected by arcs (we can't again use "links"), which represent the communication facilities. An example is shown in Fig. 5-2. The arcs represent virtual communication channels.

The mapping of the problem structure onto a particular machine is the embedding of the task graph into the machine graph. For instance, in Fig. 5-2, the task graph was embedded into a machine with four nodes (the figure may represent only a sub-cube). Note that the number of simultaneous tasks should be at least as high as the number of nodes.

For high efficiency and utilization, a Cube should *balance the load* between the nodes with each node solving a part of the job. The distribution of the tasks does not influence the computed results, but it does, through load-balancing and message locality, influence the achieved speedup by using more than one PaM for this task.

The hardware model of a Cube is quite similar to the task model of a computation. Hence, instead of formulating a problem so that it fits the hardware graph of the machine (its nodes and links), the problem is better formulated in terms of tasks and virtual communication channels which connect the tasks. It appears that many highly parallel programs can be so expressed (see Chap. 10, [Fea88] or Proceedings of "Hypercube Conferences").

Because they have only local memory, the Cubes necessarily employ a distributed

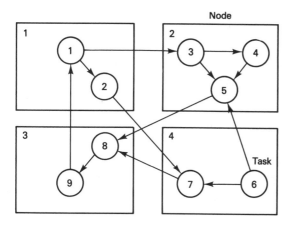

Figure 5-2 Mapping of a task-graph into a Hypercube

operating system (*OS*). Task programming with interprocess messages for communication are common to many multiprogramming OSs for single computers. A copy of such a system *resides in every node*. It is called the *kernel* and all kernels can work in parallel.

A kernel performs construction of messages, decodes message headers, splits up long messages into standard size packets, performs task management, spawns and kills tasks within its own node, schedules their execution (normally by simple round-robin policy with tasks running a fixed amount of time), supervises the tasks, provides physical memory management, queues and routes the messages for its own node and those that are only passing through. Usually, if a task is instantiated in a node, the kernel ensures that it is not relocated to another node. Hence, the node number can be included in the ID of the process. Some Cubes have a separate coprocessor which handles all this, freeing the main PaM of the node from much of the communication overhead.

The lowest level of software usually includes the instruction set of the PaM in a node, its I/O communication with channels, a bootstrap loader, and diagnostic programs. These are normally stored in a read-only memory of the node. When a start-up packet arrives from the host, an initialization process sets the node number, checks the functions of all communication channels, and loads the kernel.

It is convenient to have a separate computer, the *manager* (not shown in Fig. 5-1). The manager is connected to all the nodes, or to a subset of them, by a global bus that is used only for manager/host, manager/nodes but not node/node communications. The role of the manager is to initiate a computation, collect results upon completion, and serve as the link to the outside world. It permits the Cube to operate either as a stand-alone system or as a computational server with programs downloaded from a host computer. The manager compiles user programs and loads the tasks into the nodes. Once the manager initiates a computation, the manager and the nodes proceed asynchronously, synchronized by exchanging messages.

The OS of the host should treat the Cube as a resource that can be allocated in "Subcubes." Programs can be written for different sizes of the Subcube allocated to them. This is important because, as shown in Fig. 1-2, every problem has an efficiency which tapers off at a certain number of CPUs; adding more and more processors is wasting computing power. By using the Subcube allocation by the OS, a user can tailor the size of the Subcube to the program and leave the remaining nodes for other users. Each user thus works in the optimum fashion with a large number of nodes on large problems and a small number of nodes on small problems, all working presumably below the "knee" of the curve with high overall efficiency. The variable "granularity" of the allocation ensures that the programs work near their optimum points. It also affects a compromise between those who want more storage per node and those who want more nodes for the same amount of money.

The programming supported by the two operating systems is *medium grain* which means that each node has a significant task; the tasks are synchronized by passing messages; and the messages are small compared to the computation required by the task. As shown earlier, fine-grained programs where the messages are equal to the computation are inefficient, while large-grained programs where the messages are relatively very small do not scale well to a large number of nodes. It appears from various experiments that for Cubes and ASPs, the medium-grained approach is well conceived. For ARPs and SMs, small-grained and coarse-grained algorithms respectively may be used.

The partitioning of problems for parallelization is very important for running Cubes efficiently. The objectives are to *balance* the load among the PaMs and reduce the amount of interprocessor *communication*. If the load is unbalanced, some nodes are underutilized. If the ratio of communication time to computation time increases, more time is wasted on communication. Both reduce the speedup. They will be discussed at length in Chap. 10.

As indicated in Chap. 2 and above, the Cube topology has the following advantages:

1. Its communication properties of high data-bandwidth (growing as $p*d$) and low message latency (time delay) of d increase the efficiency compared even to loosely coupled SM multiprocessors.
2. The distributed memory lessens contention, deadlock, etc., which was difficult to handle in the SM multiprocessors of Chap. 4.
3. Cubes can and are built with hundreds or even thousands of nodes (see Table 5-1); they scale well.
4. Their topology can be changed into a ring, a tree, and two- or three-dimensional meshes and thus adapted to any particular problem.
5. Cubes are homogeneous (i.e., all nodes are identical), except for the manager. Because of reliability considerations, one of the nodes may be chosen to act as the manager with the additional advantage of faster communications between the manager and the nodes.
6. The *reliability* of the Cube is high because there are many ways (Chap. 2) to transfer a message from any node to any other node.
7. By splitting the Cube, the overall *efficiency* is increased.

5–2 SOME ASSEMBLED HYPERCUBES

5–2.1 CalTech Cubes

The "Cosmic Cube" assembled at CalTech was an experimental computer for finding out the benefits of Cube architectures. It used the 8086 processors of Intel, because at that time, it was the only single-chip instruction processor for which a floating-point coprocessor, the 8087, was available, and floating-point performance was considered essential for the type of scientific programs to be run. The dimension was $d = 6$, so that $p = 64$ such processors were connected through bidirectional, asynchronous, point-to-point communication channels to six neighbors. It operated at 5 MHz although it could have run at 8 MHz were it not for the slower coprocessor. The amount of storage in a node was 128 KBytes.

Based on simulation studies, fairly slow channels (about 2 Mbps) were chosen. Queues for 64-bit "hardware packets" were added to each sender and receiver. The processor overhead for dealing with each 64-bit packet was found to be comparable to its latency.

The Cosmic Cube was programmed in either Pascal or the C-language with extensions effecting the sending and receiving of messages. The programs were compiled first on the host, or on other available computers, and then loaded into the nodes.

Having successfully tested the cosmic Cube, the scientists at CalTech developed the Mark Cubes (Table 5-1). Since there are now commercially available Cubes, these will be discussed next.

5–2.2 The iPSC (Intel's Personal Supercomputer)

The iPSC consists of two major functional elements: the *Cube* and the *Cube Manager*. Cube hardware consists of an ensemble of one, two, or four computational units each consisting of 32 nodes. Nodes contain Intel 80286 CPUs coupled with 80287 numeric processing units and 512 KBytes of local memory. Cube manager hardware consists of an Intel 286/310 microcomputer which is linked to each node over a global Ethernet communication channel [see Fig. 5-3(a)].

Cube software consists of a monitor and kernel residing on each node board. The monitor is in PROM and the kernel is loaded into node RAM after successful initialization. Cube manager software consists of a Unix-based programming and development environment with FORTRAN, C, cube control utilities, and communications, and complete system diagnostics. [Int85][†]

The basic computational unit is the "task": a sequential program that sends and receives messages. For processing tasks, the system software is also divided among the nodes and the manager. The *kernel* OS residing in the node supports message-passing, process creation/destruction, provides input/output, and debugging services. The software

---

[†][Int85], Technical Reports by the Intel Scientific Computers. By permission.

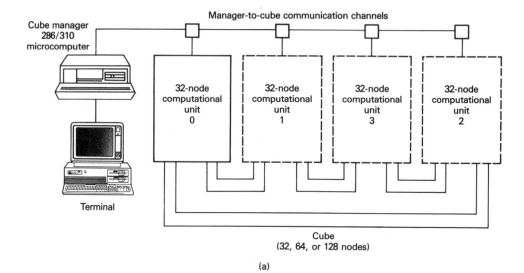

(a)

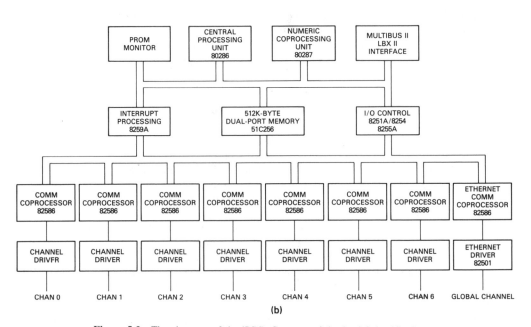

(b)

Figure 5-3 The elements of the iPSC. Courtesy of the Intel Scientific Computers.

includes the Xenix operating system, program development tools, and a support system to manage the Cube and monitor its status.

Before any processing can occur, the CPU reads the program for node initialization. During this phase, it executes the Node Confidence Test and, if successful, loads the kernel into the RAM. Then, processing can begin in the customary way.

Memory management is maintained by the kernel. Processes are packed into high memory and messages into low memory with a movable partition between them which is used as buffer space for the kernel.

Interrupt Processing is handled by two controllers. Each accepts interrupts from up to eight sources. They resolve priority and then interrupt the CPU identifying the source of the interrupt.

The block diagram of a node is shown in Fig. 5-3(b). Its components will next be described one by one.

The *CPU* is the Intel 80286 with a 16-bit external data path. It operates at a clock rate of 8 MHz, so it should achieve about 0.78 MIPs. Intel claims that a five-dimensional unit executes approximately 25 MIPs.

The 80286 operates in protected virtual-address mode. Memory protection ensures that the kernel is isolated from node processes and that one node process does not overwrite another one in memory.

The CPU has four independent processing units that operate in parallel. This allows a pipelined fetch-decode-execute instruction cycle to provide maximum throughput and efficiency.

The *Numeric Processing Unit* (NPU), an 80287, will handle 32-, 64-, and 80-bit floating-point data types for the CPU. It monitors the instructions as they are fetched by the CPU and executes those that involve floating-point data types. The data are transferred between the CPU and the NPU by direct memory access asynchronous to the processing going on in the CPU.

The *Programmable Read-Only Memory*, PROM, of 32 KBytes contains the software that allows the CPU to execute the "Node Confidence Test," loads the kernel into the PROM in case it passes the test, provides other diagnostic support, etc.

The *Dual-Port RAm Memory* of 512 KBytes contains the kernel for the node, its tasks, and space for the buffers. It has two ports in order to be able to handle requests from both the processor and the I/O bus.

The *bus* generates the address, data, and command signals for the access to the memory and provides I/O control. In its "free" time, the bus looks ahead and pre-fetches instructions from the memory. These instructions are stored in a six-byte queue for later use by the CPU. As a result, there should be less idle time in the CPU.

Functionally, the *I/O Control* consists of a LAN I/O contained in the programmable peripheral interface and the Diagnostic I/O.

The *Local Bus Extension*, LBX-II, was provided for future expansion to serve as an interface between the iPSC and customer-designed hardware.

The *Memory Address Space* consists of the PROM located at the upper 128 Kbytes, of the RAM located at the lowest 512 Kbytes, with the rest provided for future system enhancements. The *I/O Address Space* provides access to programmable peripheral controllers. The system can handle both vectored and nonmaskable interrupts, interval timers, LAN control, and other diagnostic and hardware control functions.

Each node contains eight bidirectional communication channels managed by dedicated 82586 communication coprocessors (the "drivers"). Seven of these channels physically link the nodes together and serve as dedicated point-to-point communication channels. The eights channel is a global Ethernet channel that provides direct access to and from the cube manager for program loading, data input/output, and diagnostics. [Int85]

Communication is by means of asynchronous message transfer through communication channels. Each node is completely independent and communicates with its neighbors by *queued message-passing*.

The drivers are activated by the CPUs to send messages to other nodes, and are connected so that driver ''i'' is connected to terminal ''i'' of its neighbors. There are seven terminals, which is enough for a seven-dimensional (128 node) Cube. For five- and six-dimensional Cubes, one or two terminals are not used.

When a node has a message to *send*, the following sequence occurs:

1. The CPU determines which driver will send the message; then it writes the message into the RAM and directs the driver-I/O to start the communication coprocessor, the ''driver.''
2. This driver reads the message from the RAM and sends it over the serial link.
3. Finally, the driver initiates an interrupt to report to the CPU that the message was sent.

When a node has a message to *receive*, the following sequence occurs:

1. A message arrives at one of the drivers, which writes it into the RAM. The driver interrupts the CPU to give it the address of the message.
2. The CPU reads the message.

When a node has a message to route, the two sequences—read and write—are performed in turn. Between reading and writing, the CPU determines to which node to route the message and how best to do it.

Routing and protocol of the iPSC is based on the ISO model discussed in Chap. 2.

Messages are automatically routed from node to node, if necessary, to reach the destination process.

The *Cube Manager* is a multibus-based microprocessor, called System-310. It includes the 80286 CPU, the 80287 NPU, a 40 Mbytes disk, a 320 Kbyte floppy disk, and a 2 Mbytes RAM memory. It is a desktop station that provides both management and programming support. Normally, the iPSC will be used as a stand-alone system, but it may also be used as a node of a geographically distributed system. An Ethernet interface in the manager provides communication facilities for the latter case.

There are two manager-to-cube communication channels: the global and the diagnostic channel. The global channel connects each node to the global Ethernet communication link, which is the main connection between the manager and the nodes of the Cube. The diagnostic channel is a separate path which, in the event of a failure, can be used to determine if the fault is within a node or within the global communication channel. It is used to reset the nodes, initiate on-board diagnostics, and monitor the results.

The global link of the node-to-manager channel enables the processes in the manager to communicate with the processes in the nodes. It also handles the I/O functions between the nodes and the manager. It loads node processes from the manager to the nodes and collects the results from the nodes in the manager.

5–2.3 The N-CUBE/TEN

The first distinguishing feature of the N-CUBE/TEN system is that it uses a custom-made VLSI computer. In a single chip, it integrates a general-purpose 32-bit processor (including high-speed 32-bit and 64-bit floating-point arithmetic), an Error Correcting Memory interface (ECM), and 22 independent Direct Memory Access (DMA) communication links: 11 inbound and 11 outbound. Two of the channels are used for Input-Output and 20 for connecting the node bidirectionally to the ten possible neighbor nodes. The minimum system has $p = 16$, the maximum system has $p = 1024$ such nodes (highest dimension d is 10 which explains the "TEN" in the name of N-CUBE/TEN). Each node has 128 KBytes of physical memory organized into two 64-KBytes blocks.

Each node is connected to its neighbors through the DMA channels controlled by the processor. This facilitates not only the sending and receiving of messages between neighboring nodes, but also the more powerful *broadcast* of data by an interrupt-driven message system. Thus, the processor may continue its processing while the DMA transfers information to the memory by cycle-stealing. When the transfer of data by the DMA channel is completed, it sends an interrupt to the processor. The processor therefore does not have to waste time polling.

Each node executes its program out of its local memory with data normally supplied from the same memory. Its instruction set includes a full and symmetric set of arithmetic and logical operations on single, double, and even four-byte integers. It also has floating-point operations on two- and four-byte words. Each node processor has 16 general-purpose registers, each 32 bits long, and a set of addressing modes which include support for vector and matrix operations.

The performance of a single processor is in the supermini range and the performance of the Cubes starts with 8 MFLOPs and 30 MIPs and increases up to 500 MFLOPs and 2,000 MIPs which is in the supercomputer range. The memory of the largest system has 160 MBytes. Thus, the N-CUBE/TEN can compete with supercomputers except that it is suitable only for medium- to coarse-grained algorithms, while supercomputers process fine-grained algorithms. The reliability of the N-CUBE should also be high.

A large N-CUBE provides massive computational power. However, for a computer to be useful, its number-crunching must be balanced by an equally powerful Input-Output system (I/O). The N-CUBE has eight I/O channels for transferring of programs and data from disks or other such devices into the Cube and for transferring of results back to these devices. Each channel can move data at 720 Mbps in each direction. As already mentioned, two of the 22 DMA channels are used for I/O.

At least one of the I/O boards must be a host board. This board runs the "user interface," which includes the OS, all editors and translators. It also controls the standard peripherals. Each host board has an 80286/80287 Intel processor with four MBytes of memory that runs a UNIX-type OS and compilers for Fortran, the C-language, and an assembler. This board controls up to four disk drives; has eight serial channels for terminals and other devices; and a parallel port for a high-speed printer; a number of miscellaneous units such as a real-time clock and temperature sensors for automatic shutdown in the case of overheating. There is also the capability of graphics, of communication between two N-CUBE/TEN arrays, etc.

The OS consists of two parts: *Axis* runs on the Manager, while *Vertex* is the kernel running on each of the nodes.

Axis is a virtual-memory, multi-tasking, multi-user system. It has a full set of UNIX utilities including a debugger and a fast backup facility for its tapes, a multi-window screen editor, and compilers for Fortran or C extended with communication facilities. Axis treats the N-CUBE as a device to be allocated in subcubes and provides for loading, running, communicating with, and debugging of programs in the nodes.

The kernel has facilities for message-handling, for process loading, and for its debugging. A program sends a message to a node or broadcasts it to a set of nodes by executing a send system call with the following parameters: a set of destination nodes (or a single node), the length and type of the message, and a pointer to this particular message. Programmers need not specify the channel numbers or worry about the locality of calls since the kernel will automatically route the message through the shortest path to its destination.

The following advantages are claimed for the N-Cube:

1. A potential raw performance of 500 MFLOPs or 2 billion integer OPs. This is complemented by an I/O potential worthy of a supercomputer: eight I/O channels, each with a bandwidth of 180 MBytes/second.
2. The operating system permits the Cube to be optimally subdivided among the users and provides automatic routing of messages. It works with large p, small LMs or fewer PEs of more memory each.
3. A very high reliability with a Mean Time Between Failures of more than six months for the largest-sized Cube. They are easy to repair. System diagnostics isolate a defective board and remove it, ensuring fault detection and availability. Failures should be rare because only seven chips per computing node exist, all memory is error-corrected, and all communication has error detection with retry.
4. The implemented languages are Fortran-77, C, and an assembly language.

5–2.4 The iPSC/2

The iPSC/2 is quite different from its predecessor, the iPSC. We will concentrate on two aspects, namely the node and the communication facilities as described in [Int85, Int88].

The CPU of the node is a high-performance, 32-bit, off-the-shelf commercial microprocessor, the 80386. It has a rating of 4 MIPs and is thus faster than the 80286 used in iPSC, but is software-compatible with the 80286. The 80386 has separate 32-bit data and address paths. The bus can sustain a throughput of 32 Mbytes/sec. The 80386 can respond to an interrupt in 3.5 mcs. The overhead for task switching—saving the state of the interrupted task, loading the state of the new task, and resuming execution—is not much longer.

The coprocessor is often the 80387 which extends the opcode set to deal with floating-point, extended integer, and BCD data types. The 80387 instruction set also includes a number of transcendental and arithmetic functions such as sine, arc tangent, and logarithm.

With the Vector eXtension, VX-unit, the 80386 is *pipelined* (recall Chap. 3) so it can perform instruction fetching, decoding, execution, and memory management functions concurrently. Because it pre-fetches instructions and queues them internally, it rarely has to wait for an instruction fetch. The VX combines the benefits of a Cube with pipelining. The arithmetic section of the VX contains both a floating-point adder and a floating-point multiplier. These elements can execute in parallel, and after filling the pipeline, are able to produce a result on every cycle. The capability to perform overlapped floating-point add and multiply operations is particularly useful for efficient execution of inner product operations which we will use repeatedly beginning in Chap. 6. Each VX vector-extended iPSC/2 node has a peak performance that exceeds 6 MFLOPs double precision and 20 MFLOPs single precision. The aggregate peak performance for a 64-node system is 424 MFLOPs double precision, and 1280 MFLOPs single precision.

The local memory has up to 8 Mbytes Dynamic RAM (DRAM). A fast static Random Access Memory (RAM) of 64 Kbytes may be used as a data and code *cache*. An Erasable Programmable Read-Only Memory (EPROM) of 64 Kbytes as installed on each node contains a ''Node Confidence Test'' and the boot loader. Memory accesses from the node processor and floating-point units are buffered by a 64-Kbyte fast cache memory.

Data transfers across the routing interface are controlled by a DMA controller. Two DMA channels are provided for the in and out directions. While both channels share the same bus, transfers in and out of the node can be interleaved, occurring concurrently.

The communication facilities of iPSC/2 are based on circuit switching (and not on packet switching). This should improve the ratio of computation to communication times. A self-contained hardware unit in every node, the Direct-Connect-Module, DCM, routes messages. When interconnected to form a Cube network, the routers are used to pass messages of arbitrary size between pairs of nodes.

The DCMs form a circuit-switched synchronous path, from a source to a destination node, which remains open for the duration of transferring a message. The path is composed of a series of channels and may pass through a number of intermediate DCMs associated with other nodes. When more than one DCM lies in the path, this is referred to as a ''multi-hop'' route. The system is shown in Fig. 5-4 with the DCMs depicted by $\otimes$.

The router allows messages to route through intermediate nodes without interrupting processes on those nodes. Messages encounter minimal delays in routing through intermediate nodes and so the transit time of a multi-hop message is only marginally longer than a single hop. As a result the details of the network topology are virtually invisible to the user. It appears to be a fully interconnected network and consequently the mapping of applications is greatly simplified. [Nug88]

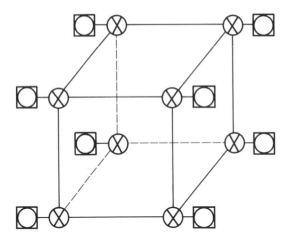

Figure 5-4 The routers of the iPSC/2

In a circuit-switching network:

> When one node wants to communicate to another, a series of switches are closed and the communication path established. Once the path is built, messages proceed at the full hardware speed of 2.8 Mbytes/second. Only the sending and destination processors are involved in the communication. The other processors in the path continue with their normal activities. Since it takes only a few mcs per node to build the path, the additional overhead for multi-hop communications is insignificant. Single-hop and multi-hop message transmittal is almost uniformly fast. [Arl88]

The routing algorithm uses naming conventions shown for a three-dimensional Cube in Fig. 5-1(a). The nodes are assigned unique addresses so that the address of any two neighbors differs in one bit as mentioned earlier. The channels that connect nearest neighbors are named as follows: Take the XOR of the two node addresses, e.g., for the channel connecting nodes 7 and 3 we have $111 + 011 = 100$. Since the 1 appears in position "2" (out of 0, 1, 2), that channel is called "2."

The nodes use the routers (DCMs) for high-speed message-passing within the systems communication network. In addition to the seven full duplex communication channels used to connect up to 128 nodes, each DCM provides an eighth channel for high-speed external communication. Each DCM

> . . . supports eight full-duplex serial communication channels operating at 2.8 Mbytes/sec in each direction and is capable of simultaneously routing up to eight messages. One Kbyte first-in, first-out (FIFO) buffers smooth the transmission and reception of messages between the router and the node, and allow simultaneous transmission and reception.
>
> The ensemble of DCMs that create the Cube network are capable of routing and relaying messages throughout the system without the assistance of the nodes. The only time a node is involved with a message is as the source or the final destination of that message. [Nug88]

The node's DCM contains all the necessary hardware for building the circuits and moving the data. Each DCM contains eight routing units along with the necessary inbound and outbound FIFOs, serializer and deserializer, plus multiple arbitration units. The routers are connected in a partial crossbar to enable all eight to be operating.

Once NX/2, the OS of the node, moves a message from its local memory to its outbound FIFO, the hardware takes over. The destination address information at the front of the message is used to form the circuit. A header is sent first to the destination address and sets the gates on each DCM at each node in the path until the destination node is reached. Following the acknowledgment from the destination node, a hardware signal indicates the circuit is open and data starts to flow at full speed.

As the last bits of the message move through the router, it releases its portion of the circuit and makes itself available to other message traffic. When the message is received at the destination, hardware verifies a check-sum on the message and causes an interrupt if there is an error. The message is deposited in the destination FIFO and then moved into the node's local memory. A circuit is released a link at a time, as the end of a message moves through each node along the path. Other circuits waiting to be formed automatically grab the free links as they become available.

Direct-Connect communication is fast and efficient. The time to build an end-to-end circuit is very short—just a few mcs per node in the path. Once built, messages move between sender and receiver at the full hardware speed of 2.8 MBytes/sec.

The iPSC/2 is programmed in FORTRAN, C, and LISP. A precompiler optimizes performance of the VX. The high-performance OS, the NX/2, resides on each node. It supports multiple tasks per node, dynamic memory management, and UNIX-compatible file I/O. A System Resource Manager provides access to standard disk, tape, and graphics peripherals and to an Ethernet LAN. For more intensive I/O applications, each node can be configured with an interface to a bus.

The distinguishing feature of the iPSC/2 is that it uses circuit switching. The advantages that this brings include hardware routing decisions, bidirectional message traffic, any length of messages, the elimination of the store and forward mode, and a fixed, small set-up time for data transfer so that, as long as the granularity is not too fine, the communication penalty is relatively low.

5–3 ALTERNATING SEQUENTIAL-PARALLEL SYSTEM

5–3.1 The mode of operations [Wal82]

The hierarchical system discussed in Chap. 1 is "translated" into a Parallel Processing System (PPS) with a master and p slaves. The slaves will be intelligent enough to execute rather complicated tasks independent of the master. For this they will need their own programs and data (i.e., the slaves each have both a control unit and Local Memory, LM). The system that evolves along these lines is shown in Fig. 5-5 and its characteristics are exemplified by an orchestra.

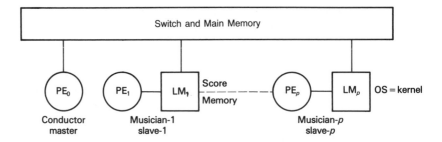

Figure 5-5   An Alternating Sequential-Parallel System, the ASP

1. There is no common address space. The slaves access main memory only through the master. In the orchestra example, the conductor distributes the score prior to the start of the concert. He/She does not run around in order to start different sections of the orchestra; hence, no multiprogramming is used. The slaves have their scores which they play. The score of the conductor is not more complicated; it only mentions when the various sections should start playing and what they are supposed to play.

2. It will be shown below that *no deadlock can ever occur.*

3. One of the claims made for PPSs vs. uniprocessors is that their availability is higher because the loss of a single processor does not incapacitate the entire system. In Fig. 5-5 this is only true if the master is identical to all the slaves. In this case, if the master (conductor) is sick, one of the musicians takes over the baton (every slave can be the master). The symmetry slightly increases the cost, but improves the availability. Actually, the master could even read new data while all the slaves are working on their respective memories. This could (but will not) be done. (I have seen the English Chamber orchestra play with the pianist simultaneously functioning as the conductor.) Thus, a symmetrical PPS with a dedicated controller, the master, was chosen. (It is not the assistant conductor Mr. Bernstein replacing the sick Mr. Walter, but an orchestra in which every musician is a possible conductor.)

4. Each slave should have its own local memory (LM) in order to enable the slave to work in parallel and autonomously. The master should be able to access both the main memory and the local memories of the slaves. The slaves only have access to their own local memories. In terms of the orchestra, the conductor has access to the scores prior to distributing them among the musicians. During the performance each musician has access to his/her score. Obviously the string player does not even look at the score of the percussionist. In terms of the system shown in Fig. 5-5, the LMs should be accessed by the slaves and the master at different times.

5. Cost-effectiveness is assured because $p + 1$ PaMs, each complete with a CPU and an LM, cost less than specially built hardware. As we will see, software is simple, making ASPs even more cost-effective.

6. Since message transfer is simple, a time-shared bus is sufficient to be used as a switch. It even may be better to connect it as a *ring*.

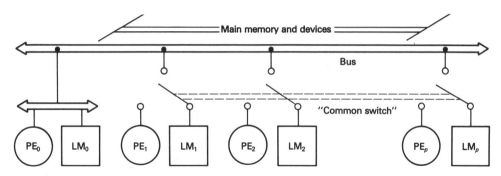

Figure 5-6 Block diagram of the ASP

These points lead to the block diagram of the system in Fig. 5-6. The "Common Switch" is not a hardware switch but is added to better explain how the system works. Assume that it can be in only one of two positions: horizontal (down) or vertical (up). With the switch in the up position, all LMs are part of the memory space of the master. With the switch in the down position, $LM(q)$ is connected only to slave q for $q = 1, \ldots, p$. Local Memory $LM(0)$ as well as the main and secondary stores are connected to the master. Thus, either the master has access to all memories or each LM is used by the slave to which it "belongs."

The diagram of Fig. 5-7 indicates the *mode of operation*. All programs must start with an "initialization" step I [or $S(0)$] during which the programs and data for the slaves are transferred to their LMs. If done by the single master, this would take too much time. It is therefore advisable that all slaves each have their own I/O devices, so that the input can be transferred simultaneously to all p slaves in a time that is only the p-th part of the previously mentioned time. The input data will probably be on a disk-pack and may therefore be transferred in parallel. The program is the same for all slaves and will be broadcast by the master during $S(0)$. In terms of the orchestra, p servers instead of the conductor distribute the scores to all musicians.

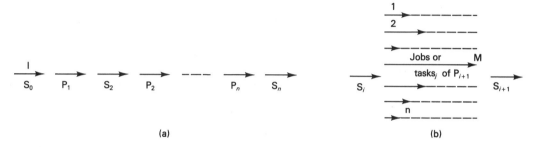

Figure 5-7 The mode of operation of an ASP

With the common switch in the down position, each slave works on its own LM; this is a parallel step P(i) in Fig. 5-7. Note that in Fig. 5-7(b) *all* parallel tasks have to finish for a sequential task to commence. After all slaves have completed their parallel assignments, the common switch changes to its vertical position and the master takes over. Since there is only one master, whatever it does is considered a "*Sequential Step*" (during which all p slaves are idle). The master transfers data among or into the LMs and then starts another parallel step. The sequential and parallel steps alternate as in Fig. 5-7(a) until the job is completed and a new job is initialized by the master.

With the switch in the down position, there is no common address space—each musician plays his/her score. During every break, the conductor transfers messages (sequential step); during the concert, the orchestra plays every piece concurrently (parallel step).

At the end of every sequential step, the master *broadcasts the starting address of the first instruction to the program counters of all slaves* and WAITs (this instruction exists in most microprocessors and effectively removes the master). When *all* slaves complete their tasks [as shown in Fig. 5-7(b)], a signal is sent to the master, activating the master from the next point in the control program, as stored in its program counter. The slaves WAIT. Since in both cases a message (bit-write) changes the WAIT into a GO command, no interrupt handling is necessary and the time of the switchover is extremely short; this may be termed read/write bit handshaking. It is important to note that it is the mode of operation and not the hardware that makes ASP different from SMs.

A *deadlock* can occur in a parallel system if some resources are requested simultaneously and cyclically (Fig. 4-10) by a number of tasks. In ASP, only the LMs are shared. They are used in a mutually exclusive manner: by the master during the sequential and by the slaves during the parallel steps. Since the intersection of the access to the shared resources is null, *there can be no deadlock in ASP*. We could say that two neighboring philosophers never eat at the same time.

Scheduling is shown in Fig. 5-8(a), with S(k) processed by the master, P(1), . . . , P(p) by the slaves. The aim for ASP is to write the programs so that the "idle" times Φ of the Gantt chart [Fig. 5-8(b)] are negligible. This means that S(k) should be as short as possible and the duration of P(1), . . . ,P(p) as nearly equal as possible.

Recall that in SMs nondeterministic scheduling was used, so that the last CPU which finished its job assumed the role of the manager or master. The ASP mode is completely *deterministic*. An analogy will illustrate the difference. Suppose a bus brings a number of farm hands to a field. If the bus driver *waits* until they all have finished working the field and *then* drives them to the next field, this is the ASP mode. If, on the other hand, they were driven to the field by one of the workers and the last who finishes working in the field drives all of them to the next field, this is an example of an SM. In both cases, the workers work concurrently on parallel tasks.

A method similar to the ASP method of synchronizing completely the starting and stopping the parallel steps (and called "barrier synchronization") is used by the Digital Equipment Corporation [Dig86] in its VAX8300 and VAX8800 multiprocessors. The reason for the name is that if it is drawn as in Fig. 5-9, there is a barrier to be crossed

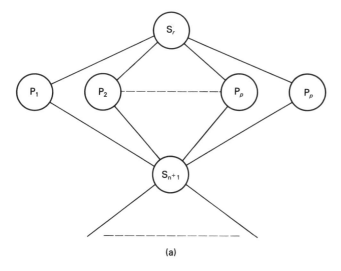

(a)

(b)

Figure 5-8 The scheduling of tasks in an ASP

whenever the code changes from the single-stream, *main* code to the *parallel* code or vice versa.

This mode of operations is different from ASP in that the number of tasks are variable (in ASP it was constant, namely p), that scheduling is required to provide work for the CPUs, and that synchronization is provided by software (in ASP it is provided by hardware).

If barrier synchronization is used on a tightly coupled MIMD system, the parallel section can be started by "busy-waiting" employing a user-created flag residing in the shared memory. It has already been discussed and can be summarized as the command:

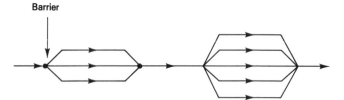

Figure 5-9 The scheduling of tasks by barrier synchronization

```
label: if not flag then goto label;
```

In this way, the tasks can commence only when the main process has set the flag to TRUE. Care should be taken because the continual testing consumes a significant amount of time.

Another way of starting the parallel step is to use *event flags* which are provided by the OS. This method is less error-prone, but each time an event flag is used, the OS is called using many machine cycles (in [Dig86], 500 are mentioned). Therefore, if the sequential step is short (say, 50 instructions), it would be inefficient for the tasks to execute that many instructions by calling the OS whenever the main code signaled a changeover. The cutoff time is about 500 machine cycles; if the average time of the main code streams is longer, then the use of event-flags is recommended; otherwise the busy-wait is more efficient.

The advantages of the busy-wait are that it is easy to implement and that it allows the use of a separate flag for every event—all of them stored in the shared address space. The disadvantage is a potentially long wait. Another problem is that of the "sticky-flag." When a CPU is completing a job it is looking for another; this means that it transfers back to the previous "label" or goes to the next flag-testing position. Since the flag is still TRUE (otherwise the CPU could not have been working on the previous job), it would repeat the same task. To solve the problem, two flags are used to activate the parallel tasks and a third one to signal the main code that all tasks have completed their jobs.

According to [Dig86], "There are essentially two methods by which tasks within a parallel section can be scheduled: the *task identifier* number and the *worklist*. The first is particularly applicable where tasks are similar; the second where tasks are very different."

In both cases, a unique number is assigned to a task. In the case of "direct" scheduling, the number represents the specific task to be executed (e.g., $i = 15$ means that task 15 has to be computed). In the "indirect" method of scheduling, $i = 15$ means that a function $g(i)$ indicates the task to be run. No matter how the scheduling is done, i has to be locked and this means additional time loss.

In a hardware ASP, scheduling is simple: Each parallel step runs on all p slaves. With barrier synchronization, the number of tasks is not necessarily p and a *task assignment* is required. The disadvantages of task-scheduling are that it is initially more difficult to program than by ASP assignment, it is more difficult to debug, and the mechanics of task scheduling creates some program overhead.

5–3.2 Bounds of speedup for ASP systems

Let us return to ASP, where from now on we mean that *synchronization is done by hardware and not by software.*

Figure 5-7 will be used to calculate the bound of the speedup in an ASP. Note that there are p tasks, the longest of which lasts $t(m) = M$. The sum of $t(q)$ for $q = 1, \ldots, p$ is the useful work of step $P(k)$. Since the data stored in the LMs are different and mostly independent of the program, the time of each task may be different. The next sequential step $S(i+1)$, should start only after the longest task M has completed. (This is not a necessary condition—a slave could ask for a new task as soon as it finishes one, but it is easier to operate the ASP mode as in Fig. 5-7.) Speedup depends upon the difference in task times. To ensure the highest speedup the algorithms will be designed so that the execution time of the slaves is nearly equal and startup time of the slaves is insignificant. Since the master costs no more than a slave, not using it all the time is tolerable.

The following simplifying assumptions are made initially to calculate the bounds of speedup σ that can be achieved:

a. The overhead and inequality of task times is neglected.
b. The sequential and ASP algorithms are the same.

With $j(i)$ as the time required for the i-th parallel job, and n as the number of jobs or tasks, the P and S steps of Fig. 5-7 would be executed on a uniprocessor in the time of

$$t(1) = s + \Sigma j(i); i\Sigma = 1, \ldots, n \tag{5-1}$$

This equation is not strictly correct, since in a single processor the sequential time s used to transfer information among memory locations would be insignificant. The difference will be disregarded.

The first case to be discussed is that of $n \leq p$ (i.e., the number of tasks is less or equal to the number of slaves). In most cases $n = p$ because we want all slaves to work. With M being the longest of the parallel tasks $j(i)$, an ASP will complete an S and a P part in time

$$t(p) = s + M \tag{5-2}$$

The speedup is therefore

$$\sigma = [s + \Sigma j(i)]/(s + M) \tag{5-3}$$

In Fig. 5-7(b), the solid lines are the actual times, the broken lines represent the case of all tasks of equal length M. Since $n*M$ would include the time nothing is done (broken line), we have

$$n*M > t(1) - s = \Sigma j(i); i\Sigma = 1, \ldots, n \tag{5-4}$$

$$M > [t(1) - s] / n \tag{5-5}$$

$M = [t(1) - s]/n$ would make all jobs equal. The bound of speedup is therefore

$$\sigma \leq (s + n*M) / (s + M) \tag{5-6}$$

Complexity theory demands that s, the time for a sequential step, be strictly zero and thus $\sigma \le n$. In ASP, s is not zero, but should be made as small as possible. The "parallelization principle" is: *Design the algorithm so that the sequential parts s are relatively as small as possible, and the granularity is not too fine.*

In a strictly sequential program executed on a single computer, we have $M = 0$ and $\sigma = 1$. Even in the best case, $\sigma \le n$. Therefore

$$1 \le \sigma \le n \qquad (5\text{-}7)$$

It was assumed that the changeover from a P-step to an S-step is instantaneous, but it is not. First, the ASP has to wait for all slaves to complete their tasks and then "wake up" the master. Ways will be found to do it fast, but not instantaneously. *The waiting time plus the wake-up time will be called bus synchronization time ζ.* Obviously, this time must be made as short as possible.

In the second case for $n > p$, the time $t(1)$-s is divided into more tasks than there are slaves. For simplicity, assume that the tasks are of equal length and that each slave executes k such tasks (say $n = 2*p$). The total time $k*[t(1)$-$s]$ is less than or equal to the time which would be required if each slave were to execute the task of maximum length M. Thus:

$$k*[t(1) - s] \le n*M \qquad (5\text{-}8)$$

Substitution of $k*[t(1)$-$s]$ for $n*M$ in Eq. (5-6) yields

$$\sigma \le \{s + k*[t(1) - s]\}/(s+M) \ = \ \{s*[1 - k] + k*t(1)\}/(s+M) \qquad (5\text{-}9)$$

This expression attains its maximum for $k = 1$. The conclusion therefore is: *In order to achieve a high speedup, k should be 1 or the number of tasks n should equal the number of slaves p.*

As a result of the expressions we got for speedup, we may state the following conditions for building an efficient ASP:

a. The sequential steps $S(i)$ consist of synchronizing the system and the subsequent transfer of information from the master to all slaves. Information may be transferred through the bus either by single words or by blocks of words.

In the first case, the program in an assembly language is Code 5-1:

```
    MOVE.W SAD, A0        ; Move the starting address SAD to register A0.
    MOVE.W TAD, A1        ; Move the target address TAD to register A1.
    MOVE.W NMB, D0        ; Move the number of words to register D0.
XR: MOVE.W (A0)+,A(1)+    ; Move the word addressed by A0 into the memory
                         ; as addressed by A1 and increment the values
                         ; in A0 and A1 by 1. + indicates auto-increment
                         ; Next, decrement the number of words to be
    SUB #1, R2           ; transferred by 1. As long as the number
    BNE XR               ; of words is not 0, return to XER.
```

Code 5-1

Assuming the block of data to be transferred is large, the three instructions ahead of label XR may be disregarded when compared to those in the loop. Inside the loop three instructions have to be removed from the memory, one data word removed and one inserted into the memory—altogether five memory cycles are required for transferring a single word. If this is done by hardware, for instance with a DMA Device, the same transfer would require only two memory cycles, because while the word is being moved all three registers are updated simultaneously. Therefore, a loop with a block transfer is faster ($5/2 = 2.5$ times) than without it. The conclusion may therefore be drawn that *block transfer of data over the bus is essential*.

b. It will be shown that most algorithms will compute data (a single word) in a slave and then have to transfer it to the remaining p-1 LMs. Without broadcast the word will have to be transferred first to the master and then from the master to the p-1 slaves. If the time to transfer a word is τ then the overall time is $(p\text{-}1)*\tau + \tau = p*\tau$. If there is broadcast, then the time for transferring a word from the master to all p slaves is τ; altogether only time $2*\tau$ is needed. The time decreases by a factor of $p/2$. The conclusion is that *broadcast capability reduces sequentialization*.

c. The maximum duration M is in the denominator of σ, so that the lower it is the higher the speedup. To decrease M, try to *divide the parallel calculations into equal tasks*.

d. A single bus is normally thought to be the bottleneck of a system, but in an ASP it is used only for block transfers and the broadcast of data. As a matter of fact, it has been measured and in some algorithms the bus is used for less than 2% of total time. Therefore, bus interference is a minor problem and the bus is not a bottleneck in ASP systems. *A time-shared bus or a ring might be sufficient for ASP*. [TaW 78]

e. Since during the P-steps the master is idle, it would be possible to divide the tasks so that the shortest of them can be done by the master. This would effectively increase the number of "slaves" to $p+1$ and reduce the idle times, Φ, in the Gantt chart of Fig. 5-8(b). As indicated, this is not done since simplicity is considered more important than adding another CPU to the already existing p CPUs.

The design rules of ASP and the reasons for them are:

1. For reliability, it should be *symmetric,* with a roving master.

2. For speed, *each slave should have its local memory,* LM, and also its own I/O devices (to the disk).

3. The switch may be *a single or dual bus* or a ring.

4. In order not to be too expensive, standard *off-the-shelf* equipment should be used.

5. In order to achieve a high speedup, *the sequential steps must be short*. This means that *block transfer and broadcast are essential*.

6. The Gantt chart leads to the same conclusion, but additionally it shows that the *slave tasks should be of equal duration if possible*.

7. The bound of speedup is higher if the number of tasks is not higher than the number of slaves. *In most cases, n will equal p*.

8. Conditions 6 and 7 show that *algorithms for ASPs should exhibit medium to coarse granularity.*

5—4 AN ASSEMBLED ALTERNATING SEQUENTIAL-PARALLEL SYSTEM

The Siemens Company of West Germany introduced *two ASP-systems,* the SMS101 and the SMS201 (SMS stands for Structured Multimicroprocessor System) [Kob76, KKK76, Kob77, Kuz77, KaK79].

The following were the disadvantages of the SMS systems and in particular that of the SMS201 (which was used by the author).

1. Two of the aims of PPSs mentioned in Chap. 1 were availability and fault detection. Availability depends crucially on the symmetry of the system, but the SMS201 is asymmetric (i.e., the master is not identical to the slaves and cannot be replaced by a slave). In fact, it is a rather large minicomputer whereas the slaves are small microcomputers. This makes the SMS201 less suitable for on-line, process-control problems.

2. The operating system of the master is an extension of the operating system of the minicomputer. Therefore, it is too big.

3. The language used was Fortran. For transfer of information between the various units, the operating system has to be invoked and this means a very large time loss. Transfer of information should really be part of the language, but at the time the SMS systems were built no language had such facility. Since the development of the SMS201, Ada has been implemented and it supports data transfer.

We next discuss the TOPPS [Ten82].[†]

5—4.1 Hardware layout

The architecture of ASP systems is such that every processor, be it master or slave, is identical. Each module of the Tristate-Operated PPS, or TOPPS, consists of the parts indicated in Fig. 5-10: One Motorola 68000 CPU, a number of status registers, one dynamic address decoder, DAD, four sets of tri-state, or bilateral switches, TS (hence the name), 64K (expandable to 16 megabytes) of random access memory MEM, parallel I/O, real-time clock, mode-control PROM, and associated logic.

There are four buses in the unit, each consisting of 44 lines, except for the master bus, which has 50. Bus 1 is the master bus, common to all CPUs but only used by the processor that is the master at any given time. This bus is connected to a module via TS2, TS4, and DAD. Buses 2, 3, and 4 are internal buses of the units. They form the so-called "Nodal Switching Network," NSN. Bus 3 connects TS3 and TS4 to the memory, I/O and real-time clock board. Bus 2 connects TS1 to the CPU.

[†]By permission of J. Tenenbaum from his Ph.D. Thesis.

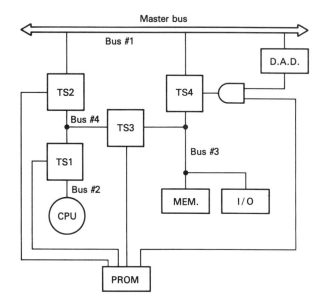

Figure 5-10 The block diagram of the TOPPS. Courtesy of the thesis by Dr. J. Tenenbaum.

System components. *The CPU* used was the Motorola 68000 [Mot83]. This section deals with the additional hardware installed.

Status registers. In order to prevent a CPU from simultaneously reading from or writing to the same register, each of the eight outside registers associated with each CPU was designed so that:

a. It is "read-only" to its CPU and "write-only" to the master, or

b. It is write-only to its CPU and read-only to the master, or

c. It can be cleared only by its own CPU and loaded only by the master, or

d. It can be loaded only by its own CPU and cleared only by the master.

These addressable and unclocked registers are: (1) Slave done/busy, (2) Slave wait/go, (3) Slave subroutine number, (4) Master/slave, (5) Program number, (6) Mode number, (7) Processor number, and (8) Number of processors.

Four of the registers, namely 1, 2, 3, and 6, are addressable by the master via two addresses. The master may address all the slaves by issuing a single address, *broadcast,* or it may address a single slave. These addresses are set via (DIP) switches prior to system initialization. So are registers 5, 7, and 8, which are read-only. Register 4 is read-only and depends on the processor number register.

A short explanation of these registers follows (with letters referring to parts of Fig. 5-11):

The output of the done/busy register in part (a) is OR'ed with the disable line of the CPU and the master/slave line. The output of this OR-gate is transferred to an open-collector buffer which drives the done/busy line on the master bus. If the CPU is disabled

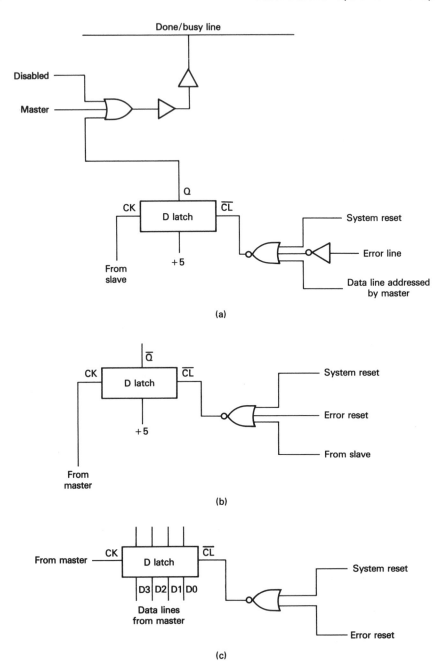

Figure 5-11   The registers of the TOPPS. Courtesy of Dr. J. Tenenbaum.

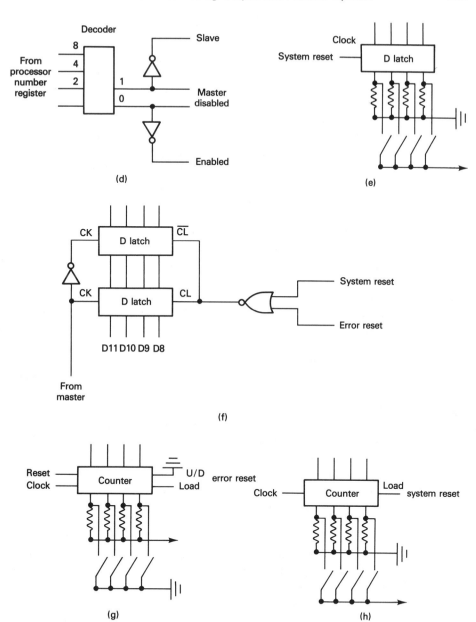

Figure 5-11   (*cont'd*)

or if it is a master, the output will stay high to prevent pulling down of other CPUs. Only the master may clear this register.

The Slave Wait/Go register of Fig. (b) may be asserted by the master but negated only by a slave. The slave is always in a software loop when attempting to read the status of this register. In the sequential mode, when all slaves are cut off from their memory, the DTACK signal is never asserted, forcing a continuous wait by the CPU—as it should.

The Subroutine Number Register of Fig. (c) is a 4-bit register. It is write-only to the master and read-only to a slave. When the master indicates that a task is to be performed, it writes the number of the subroutine to this register. When the slave reads it, it calls the corresponding routine and executes it. This is basic to ASP-mode.

The register shown in Fig. (d) defines whether the unit is the master or a slave. It is read-only and has an input coming from the number register of the CPU through a decoder.

The register of Fig. (e) is a 4-bit, read-only register. At system initialization, the CPUs read this number and transfer to the appropriate starting points in the software.

The mode register of Fig. (f) is a 4-bit, write-only to the master register. Its output is tied to the mode-control decoding logic.

The Processor-Number register of Fig. (g) is a d-bit register ($p = 2**d$). It is a counter which may be read by all CPUs. Before system initialization, the user must set this number; the system may change it during system deallocation or system recovery.

The Number-of-Processors register of Fig. (h) is also a d-bit, read-only counter tied to the error sequencing logic.

Internal buses. Data lines are on pins 1 to 16, address lines on pins 17 to 39 (see [Mot83]). Other pins are: 40 => AS, 41 => UDS, 42 => LDS, 43 => READ and 44 => WRITE. Pin 45 is connected to the done/busy line, pins 46 to 49 to the error lines, and pin 50 to the reset line. The last six are the only signals that are not related to the MC68000. As long as any CPU is busy, line 45 is negative, and as long as any CPU asserts an error line, the error line of the CPU is held low.

The Nodal Switching Network, NSN. Each of the four switches, TS1 to TS4, that form the NSN consists of quad-bilateral switches as in Fig. 5-12. These are 4066 CMOS devices acting as electronic relays which connect or disconnect bus lines.

One control line from each group of these switches is connected to the Programmable Read-Only Memory, the mode control PROM or mode-control decoder. There are separate control lines for the quad-bilateral switches of TS2 and TS3. During the broadcast mode, the Read/Write lines from the master determine the source and destination of data flow. For enhanced reliability, only the upper data strobe, the lower data strobe, the read and the write lines are controlled.

Memory. Theoretically, it would be possible to have 16 Megabytes of main memory connected to each CPU. In the actually assembled system, 64K bytes of random access and 32K bytes of PROM memory were installed.

TOPPS is a memory-mapped system and the concept of ports does not apply. Memory is mapped in two ways: Each CPU identifies by buses 2 and 3 its memory, including some status registers as starting at the same location. If the CPU is the master, it sees all slave memories via the master bus through their TS4 and DAD. Each DAD will

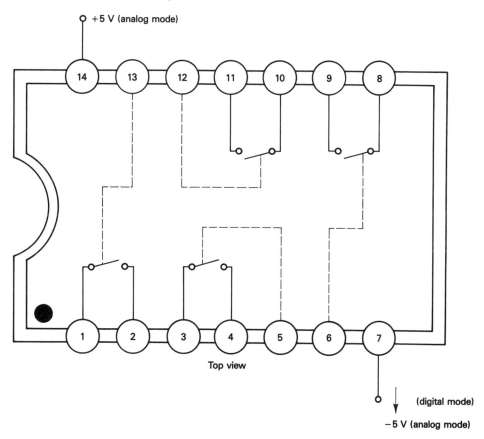

Quad digital or analog
bilateral switch

+3 TO +15 V (digital mode)

+5 V (analog mode)

Top view

(digital mode)

−5 V (analog mode)

Figure 5-12   The Nodal Switching Network of TOPPS. Courtesy of Dr. J. Tenenbaum.

allow the memories of the CPUs to be seen by the master as a different memory segment. The master may also read from and write to specific status registers via the master bus. The nodal switching network allows flexibility when it comes to accessing memory and I/O through different routes in the system.

The memory addressing of TOPPS is unique in that *each* address of the master can be mapped to *each* address of *each* slave. This allows for transparent segmentation of the entire memory space. Total memory addressing, as seen by the master, is then $(16*10^6)$ bytes. Although this capability exists, it would not be practical since 16 million slaves would be needed to implement the configuration. On the other hand, nobody has ever asked for, nor would they hardly need this much address capability. For a practical case, e.g., 128 slaves as in SMS201, the address space would be 128*16 megabytes, which certainly is large enough. This proves the point that each slave has the ability to act as an intelligent peripheral controller.

The Dynamic Address Decoder, DAD (Fig. 5-13) is connected to the master bus and acts as a partial controller for TS4 and as a memory management unit preventing unauthorized memory access by comparing the address seen from the main bus with the high and low addresses given to the comparators within a DAD. If the address is within the range, the DAD activates TS4. If not, then the Address Strobe line may never pass into Bus 3, thereby disabling the usage of that memory.

The DAD consists of two sets of comparators, both tied to the address lines of the master bus. The lower set is wired so that its (cascaded) output of "A>B OR A=B" form the lower, and the other output "A<B OR A=B" form an upper address boundary. The output Y(out) = [(A>B OR A=B) AND (A<B OR A=B)] is AND'ed with the address strobe and PROM output line to form the TS4 control.

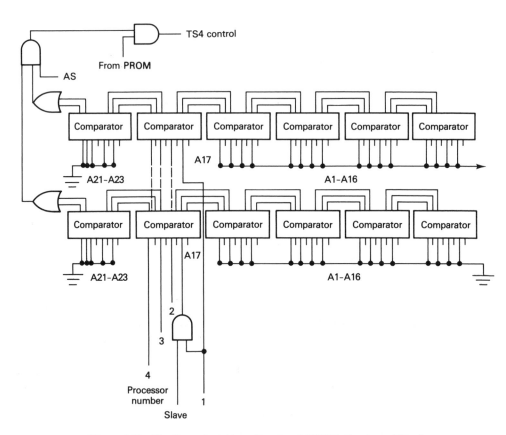

Figure 5-13 The Dynamic Address Decoder of TOPPS. Courtesy of Dr. J. Tenenbaum.

The comparators are wired so that the master "sees" the memory of each processor in the sequential mode as

```
P1(master)  =  000000 to 01FFFF (H=hexadecimal)
P2(slave)   =  100000 to 10FFFF H
P3(slave)   =  110000 to 11FFFF H
```

Addressing in this unique hardware fashion has three advantages:

1. All processor addressing depends on a single variable—the processor number. Since this number is initially set by the user and otherwise forgotten, there is no software overhead to worry about.

2. Normally, the master would see in the sequential mode all the memory of the slaves, including their EPROM. With this memory allocation, the master sees only its own EPROM (lowest 64K segment), with all the remaining RAM of the slaves seen as one contiguous block of memory. This leads to easier software development.

3. Even though the master sees only one 64K-word segment of RAM on each slave, it does not restrict the slaves from seeing a full 16 megabytes of their own memory in the parallel mode. This allows sophisticated memory management techniques to be applied should the need arise. The decision to use 64K word boundaries as the size of each segment was arbitrary; any reasonable size would do.

Control of modes. A PROM is used to switch the bus routing from one mode to another [Fig. 5-14(a)]. This is a rather simple method and proceeds at a very high speed (related to the access time of the PROM). Each CPU in the system has one mode-control PROM which acts as a programmable switch. This PROM may be replaced by a decoder and a few gates as shown in Fig. 5-14(b).

The PROM is arranged as a 256*8-bit memory device which has eight inputs and eight outputs, of which only five outputs were used. Each one of them enables/disables one set of bilateral switches. The eight inputs are tied directly to the status registers: AS, R/W, Master/Slave, Enabled/Disabled, Mode1, Mode2, and Mode3. The PROM is preprogrammed to enable the correct bilateral switches.

To switch from one mode to another, the master addresses these status registers and writes into them the code for the new mode. The modes may also be set from the front panel. In the case of the ring and broadcast modes for which the physical memory locations are different for a read and a write access, the R/W line on the PROM routes automatically the correct sequence of bilateral switches. This is transparent to the CPU and keeps the system software and hardware overhead to a minimum.

Timing and I/O.   The only hardware device that is clocked and used for handshaking or data transfer is the CPU. Its clock is not common to any other piece of hardware in the system. This is done because the handshaking of the MC68000 with the outside world (reading and writing) is done asynchronously. The CPU will wait for the

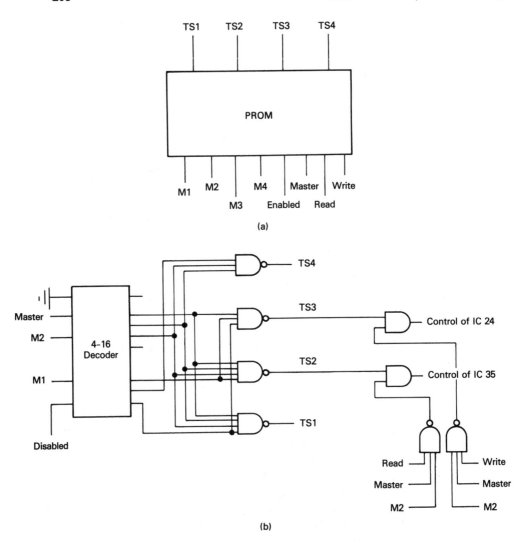

Figure 5-14 The control of modes in the TOPPS. Courtesy of Dr. J. Tenenbaum.

read/write access to finish, no matter how many clock cycles it takes. When the device has finished reading or writing data, it lowers then raises the DTACK signal line on the CPU (Fig. 5-15). By taking this asynchronous concept several steps further, the creation of a totally event-driven system is possible.

For simplicity of the model, the I/O of each CPU consisted of one 8-bit parallel output port connected to eight light-emitting diodes. This I/O, like any that the system might eventually contain, is memory mapped and addressed through TS3 or TS4. For user

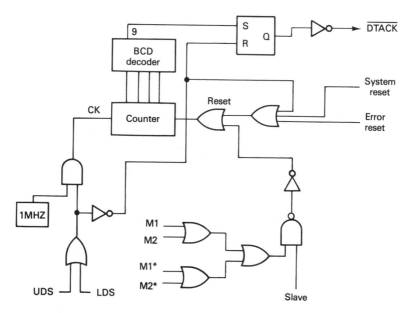

Figure 5-15   The timing of modes in the TOPPS. Courtesy of Dr. J. Tenenbaum; by his permission.

codification purposes, the software of the system may be accessed by a combination of the master bus and the front panel.

5–4.2 Operating modes

The basic modes are shown in Fig. 5-16. In the *parallel mode* shown in (a), the master is connected to its memory via TS1, TS2, the DAD, and TS4. The slaves access their memories through TS1 and TS3. Each slave sees the same virtual starting and end addresses (the physical addresses are different), while the master sees its memory through the DAD which may be set at any location the master wishes.

In the *sequential mode* shown in (b), the slaves are in a HALT state and are cut off from their memories. The master views the entire memory of the system as its address space. All memory is seen through the DADs which are set at different segments in the system memory space. The master sees the memories of the slaves through each DAD and TS1, while it sees its own segment of memory through TS1, TS2, TS4, and the DAD.

In the *broadcast mode* shown in (c), the master transfers data from its memory to all slaves simultaneously. It is a "bucket-brigade" action which is completely transparent to the master, thereby eliminating any software protocol. For the duration of the broadcast, the master's data, address, and AS lines of TS1, TS2, and TS3 are enabled. If the CPU is a slave, all lines of TS2 and TS3 are enabled during a read or write cycle. If the master

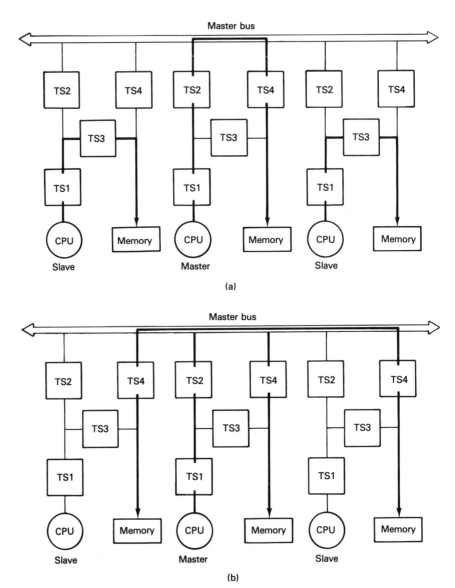

Figure 5-16   The operating modes of the TOPPS. Courtesy of Dr. J. Tenenbaum.

asserts the READ line, the UDS, LDS, READ, and WRITE lines of TS3 are enabled. If the master asserts the write line, the UDS, LDS, READ, and WRITE lines of TS2 are enabled.

In addition to the two basic modes, parallel and sequential, TOPPS also has a third basic mode (again the "tristate" in its name). In this *ring* or *pipeline* mode, the switches

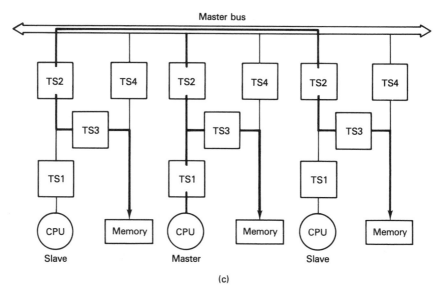

(c)

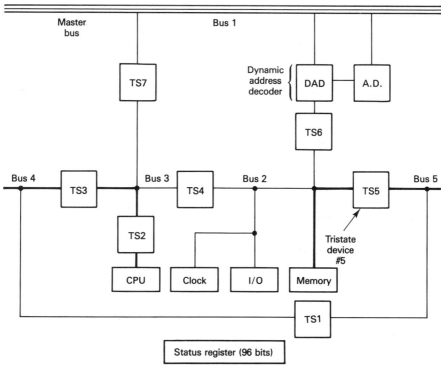

(d)

Figure 5-16   *(cont'd)*

TS2, TS3, and TS5 of Fig. 5-16(d) in every unit are set. Thus, each CPU, say CPU(i), has access to the local memory of CPU(i-1). The master may be part of the ring, in which case it may be considered to be slave 0.

5–4.3 System operation

When the application program is set to run, the slaves must have some data to work with. There are two ways they could obtain data:

1. Through the master by broadcast.
2. Loading it through the parallel ports of all the slaves.

The master starts the operation by transferring to the starting point of the program. If the slaves need a special starting point, the master can write it into the slave subroutine register. During this time, the slaves have been waiting in a loop by checking constantly their wait register. The master then writes a number (02H) to the mode register which sets the system in the broadcast mode. When all data has been sent, the master writes 00H to the mode register which transfers the system into a parallel mode. The master loads a 0 into the slave/wait registers in order to activate the slaves and waits for the slaves to finish. As soon as the slaves accept the "GO" bit, they reset that bit. This protects them from running the same program twice. The slave subroutine register is read and the routine executed. When the slaves complete, they assert the done/busy line and return to the wait-loop of the slaves. If and when the master recognizes that the slaves have completed, it clears the done/busy line and changes the mode to sequential. After the master accepts the data, the program may be completed or another procedure may be initiated.

The only difference in the way data is input is seen to be in one additional step using the broadcast mode. Since this step may take a considerable amount of time, the second mode was used.

Since all system registers, including the mode register, are modified by writing to a memory location, it takes only one write cycle to effect a mode change. The cycle speed depends directly on the clock rate of the PE used, and is not limited by the additional hardware of TOPPS.

5–4.4 A comparison

Two of the aims of parallelization stated in Chap. 1 were higher reliability/availability and higher speed. It should again be stressed that the first is considered rather important and that it depends crucially on the symmetry of the system. The SMS201 is asymmetric because the master is different from the slaves and cannot be replaced by any of them. In TOPPS, all units are identical.

SMS systems have a single bus. This decreases substantially the reliability. In TOPPS, if a part of the bus is defective, this part can be removed and the system can proceed working.

Another fundamental difference is in the operating system. SMS systems are built for off-line, TOPPS for on-line jobs.

For transfer of data among the various units, the SMS uses the Operating System. This slows down the operation very much. TOPPS uses assembly language and transfers data very fast.

Each unit of TOPPS has its own I/O. Thus, instead of collecting data in the main memory and block-transferring it through the master bus, data is transferred individually and simultaneously to all slaves. I/O is therefore done in the parallel instead of in the sequential mode.

Notes.   This section proves how easy it is to assemble a small-scale ASP system. Additionally, a "token ring" of IBM can be modified to work as an ASP. This in turn means that any office which has a LAN (and which hasn't?) can use it as an ASP, at least in the off-hours or when the main computer is down. We discuss such a system in Sec. 9-2.

5–5 OTHER SYSTEMS

In this section we will discuss systems that combine the advantages of multiprocessors with pipelining, HEP, pyramids, and the Distributed Reconfigurable Multiprocessor.

5–5.1 Systems that combine pipelining and shared-memory characteristics

The Cray systems.   The systems to be discussed below evolved from earlier PPSs, e.g., the CRAY X-MP evolved from CRAY-1 and combines vector processing with multiprocessing. The original X-MP introduced in 1982 consisted of two processors, the next one introduced in 1984 had up to four processors, as did the last X-MP introduced in 1985. At the same time, the sizes of the memory were increased to four, eight, and sixteen million words respectively, and the clock cycle times were decreased to 9.5 nns. The throughput of the last X-MP model is supposed to be up to ten times that of CRAY-1.

Another model, the CRAY-2, introduced in 1985, is a multiprocessor with four processors, working with a shared memory of 256 million words, a clock cycle time of 4.1 nns, and a throughput of up to 12 times that of CRAY-1. The speed of others, e.g., the Y-MP, were shown in Fig. 1-3. The block diagram of CRAY-X-MP is shown in Fig. 5-17.

The intercommunication section is composed of five (on X-MP/4) or three (on X-MP/2) clusters of shared registers for interprocessor communication and synchronization—as required in a multiprocessor. Each cluster of shared registers consists of eight 24-bit shared address (SB) registers, eight 64-bit shared scalar (ST) registers, and 32 one-bit synchronization (SM) registers.

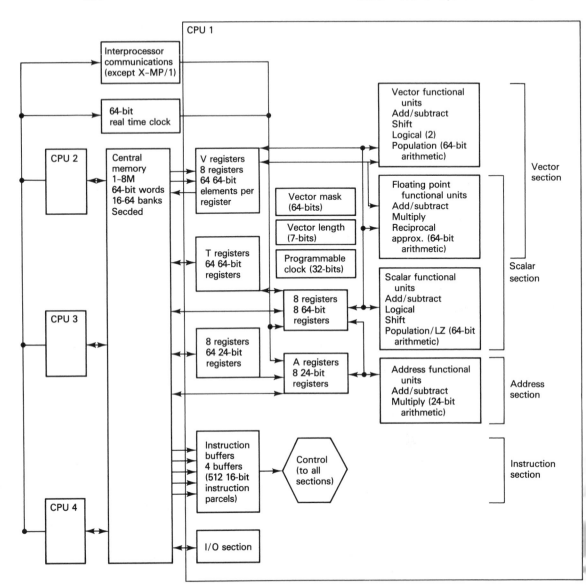

Figure 5-17 The block diagram of CRAY-XMP-4. Courtesy of J. J. Dongarra, A. Hinds: "Comparison of the CRAY-X-MP-4, Fujitsu VP-200 and Hitachi S-810/20," Simulation 47:3, pp. 93–107. Reprinted by permission of the Simulation Council.

Depending on the configuration, a cluster of registers may be assigned to one, two, three, four processors or to none. Each processor in a cluster can execute scalar and vector operations of the user program in an asynchronous way.

There are two modes of operation: the user and system mode. A processor in the system mode can interrupt any other and cause it to switch from the user to the system mode. A register cluster may be accessed by any number of processors to which it was allocated both in the user and system mode. The hardware provides built-in detection of a system deadlock within the cluster.

The HEP computer.   The overall speed of a computer is influenced by the hardware type and the amount of parallel activity possible in a given organization. HEP is implemented with a conservative technology and increases the speed primarily by combining pipelining with multiprocessing. To be able to process fine-grained algorithms, the HEP uses a pipelined PE and one-word message passing (for synchronization.)

The HEP system [Kow85, Smi81] consists of up to 16 processors (*PEs*) connected to as many as 128 data memory modules through a *packet switching network*. This makes it a shared-memory multiprocessor, *SM*. Each PE has one million words of program memory, and each memory module has 128 million words of 64 bits each.

Multiprocessors have a hard time dividing the problem so that the amount of communications is reasonably low. As indicated in Chap. 4, the number of PEs in a multiprocessor is limited and their speedup decreases because of memory latency, contention, and synchronization. The advantages of multiprocessors are its modularity, fault detection, availability, and the use of existing high-level languages.

Each PE of Fig. 5-18(a) consists of the CPU or ''Instruction Processing Unit'' and program memory of up to 8 Mbytes. As mentioned, the CPU is pipelined with the HEP executing multiple instruction streams over multiple data streams. Instructions are fetched from the memory every 100 nns with concurrent decoding and execution of previously fetched instructions. Each PE has an added memory reference pipeline (the Scheduler Function Unit, SFU), an execution pipeline and a process queue. The SFU is used for memory access and synchronization. Instead of using a Program Counter, the PE uses special hardware to operate the task queues. Synchronization among tasks uses message passing. The instruction-level, *fine-grained* task switching is fast. The combination of multiprocessing and pipelining works as follows.

Suppose there are p PEs and p tasks. Each task can be active on a different PE for some time [see Fig. 5-18(b)]. The tasks are waiting in the queues: memory latency is hidden by concurrency. As long as the queues keep the instruction pipelines busy, memory references do not cause the PEs to wait longer than for other instructions. The queues grow and shrink with the change in the frequency of memory references.

The problems of branching in pipeline computers are eliminated by allowing only one instruction of a given task to be in a pipeline at a time. Since problem switching occurs after each instruction, rapid task switching is accomplished by the task queues mentioned above.

An active task in a PE has a tag in the queue. The hardware injects tags of *different*

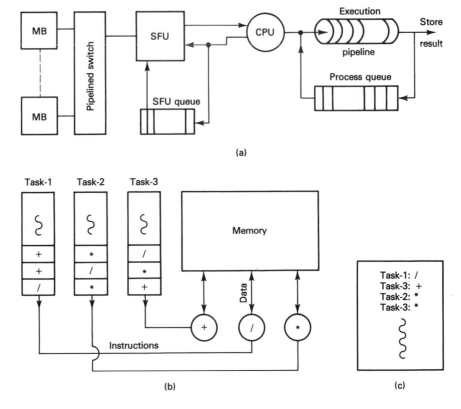

Figure 5-18   The queues of the HEP computer

tasks into the execution pipeline. The process may be viewed as fine-grained multitasking and because it is achieved by hardware, it is fast.

To see how HEP works, consider the main execution pipeline [Fig. 5-18(c)], which interleaves instructions from a number of tasks. Independent instructions (including their operands) flow through this pipeline, each requiring eight steps for completion. The instructions of a task are still processed in a strict sequence, with one being executed only after the previous one was completed. But, once this happened, the next instruction may be from another task and may have been already started in the pipeline. Therefore, instructions accompany their operands into the pipeline in order not to mix data from different tasks. Independence of activity is achieved by alternating instructions from various tasks (instead of processing corresponding elements of a vector in a VP). The entire strategy leads to fine-grained parallelism.

A full/empty bit associated with each memory location or register, is used for synchronization. When a task updates a location, it must wait until its state is 0; following the update, the status bit is set to 1 (meaning "full"). The reverse is done when reading.

Both actions are indivisible and thus can be used to implement locking: the 1 and 0 states correspond to the lock being closed and open respectively.

In order to guarantee mutual exclusion, an ''asynchronous'' variable must ''wait for full and set empty'' if it appears on the right-hand side of an assignment statement, and must ''wait for empty and set full'' when it appears on the left-hand side. The synchronization is usually fast, despite the fact that busy waiting is used.

There are four types of memory in a HEP system: program memory, register memory, constant memory, and data memory. The first three are local to a PE. The constant memory may not be changed by a user process. There are 2048 general purpose registers and 4096 constant registers, so that, even if many processes run in parallel, each has access to some private working storage.

The mass-storage of HEP consists of a large memory, an I/O, disk storage modules, and I/O channels (they couple the disk storage modules to the I/O cache and are controlled by an I/O control processor).

The system provides almost unlimited addressing and eliminates data dependent delays by direct internal data forwarding through the shared data memory modules. Synchronization is done by the hardware.

Figure 5-19(a) shows an example of a system configuration with four PEs, four data memory blocks, a shared memory, an I/O-control processor, and node connection to four other devices. This example configuration has 28 switching nodes.

The HEP has a banyan IN [Fig. 5-19(a)]. This packet switching network is synchronous and pipelined. It consists of an arbitrary number of nodes. Each node, which consists of three full duplex ports, is connected to its neighbors. These neighbors may be process execution modules, data memory modules, subsystems, or other nodes.

A switching node is shown in Fig. 5-19(b). It receives three message packets on each of its three ports every 100 nns and attempts to route the messages so that the distance from each message to its addressed destination is reduced. For this purpose, each node has three routing tables (one per port) which are recording the actual system configuration. The node is thus capable of deciding which port should be used to get to the destination in the shortest route. This also allows the system to isolate a faulty node and to reroute messages around it.

A unique feature of this switching network is that there is no queue to let the packets wait. The packets are instead routed by the switch nodes every 50 nns regardless whether there is port contention or not.

Table 5-2 compares HEP with ARPs reviewed earlier. It could also be compared to the PAX-computer. This latest is described fully in [Hos89] and can be treated here as a combination of ARP with an ASP. Like an ILLIAC, it has a mesh of 8×16 or 128 PEs connected to a single control unit which itself is connected to a host. Like any of the ASPs, it has a global bus which provides broadcast from the CU to all PEs. Its mode of operation is between that of an ARP like the ILLIAC and an SM like the HEP. In an ARP synchronization is performed on every instruction, in HEP synchronization is prescribed only by the algorithm; it can be programmed to execute completely asynchronous tasks in parallel and to synchronize any parallel tasks at any moment. Compared with the lack of

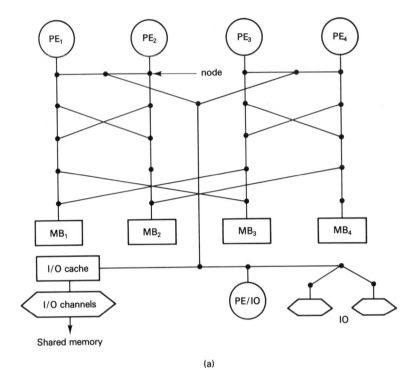

(a)

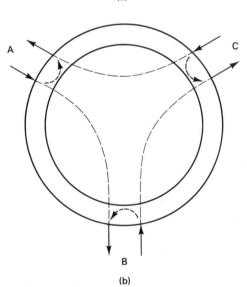

(b)

Figure 5-19 The elements of HEP and a switching node

TABLE 5-2 COMPARING CHARACTERISTICS OF ARPS

Name	MPP	CM-2	HEP
Number of PEs	16K	64K	16
Topology	mesh	mesh	tree
Word length bit	1	64	64
Clock rate MHz	10		
Memory/node RAM	1 KB	512 MB	128 MW
Performance MIPs		2,500	
Performance MFLOPs		3,500	100

flexibility of ARPs, and the over-flexibility of HEP, in PAX, like in ASPs, the PEs (slaves) can perform substantial procedures between synchronization points. They use the global bus for program loading, for diagnostic tests, and for global synchronization.

5–5.2 Pyramids

Pyramid-connected PPSs are used for "parallel computer vision" [Uhr87]. It is normally suggested that in order to get enough computational power for processing a digital image, one should assign a node to each picture element ("pixel") and allow the nodes to communicate with their neighbors. This means an extremely large number of nodes, but they can all be on level A [see Fig. 2-5(j)]. On the other hand, if only plane A exists, no global (nonlocal) characteristic of the image would be captured.

Suppose we have a mesh of $2**n$-by-$2**n$ pixels (size $2**n$). Averaging each level and putting the result into the parent of four PEs would result in an image with size $2**n/2$, $2**n/4$, etc. Counting the number of pixels in each level yields: $2**(2*n) = m$, then $m/4$, $m/16$, and finally sizes 16, 4, and 1. Adding, we get with $r = 4**n$, the sum $r + r/4 + r/16 + \ldots + 16 + 4 + 1$ or $r(1 + \frac{1}{4} + \frac{1}{16} + \ldots + 16/r + 4/r + 1/r)$. If n were an infinite number, the term in the parenthesis would be $1/(1\text{-}1/4) = 4/3$ and the number of PEs on all levels of the pyramid only $4/3*r = 4/3*(4**n)$. This is only one-third more than there are pixels on level A.

Additional advantages claimed for pyramid-connected PPSs are:

1. Since in most of these algorithms the amount of data is so large that a secondary storage (disks) is absolutely necessary, the number of channels must also be large and the number of local memories to which they connect the disks should also be large in order to keep the nodes busy. The mesh at level A fits this requirement admirably.

2. The locality of the operations allows local synchronization techniques (see Sec. 4-2). Therefore, a closely coupled multiprocessor with a mesh connection of nodes is provided on level A.

3. Computations on coarse and fine grid structures lead to a varying number of grid

points. Therefore, a hierarchy of at least two levels of connected arrays that decrease in size is available.

4. The nodes within the IN work on their own control (no SIMD control). This can be important for local refinements.

5. By selecting a suitable interconnection pattern, the PPS can be well fitted to the computational structure of the application. This leads to a good balance for the load of the system components.

6. In pyramids, the largest distance is $0[\log(n)]$ (where n is the linear size of the mesh at level A). This is fast, matches the data-driven model, and supports hierarchical processing modes required by graphic applications.

[Parallel arrays (for meshes) of] large numbers of serial computers are extremely fast at computing functions of information stored locally; but they can be very slow at moving this information around and computing global functions. Pyramids superimpose a good global interconnection network over the basic array topology. Thus they combine the virtues of arrays with those of trees, at the same time eliminating most of the drawbacks of each . . . The essence of a pyramid appears to lie in its integration of massively parallel arrays of potentially any size with logarithmically converging tree links that pull distant parts of these arrays close together. The computers in the array can all work in parallel . . . The tree-like structure that links arrays together can be used, as desired, to converge (transform, combine, compute interactions) and to diverge (pass along, broadcast) information. [Uhr87][

In short, the pyramid, through its hierarchical structure, will retain most of the advantages of one node per pixel while adding capability for global computations. Pyramidal structures that are simultaneously parallel and serial allow gradual formation of more and more global description of image data, in parallel [Uhr87]. It is interesting to note that the same concept that is useful for a very large number of nodes was successful with up to 20 nodes in ASPs. In both cases, the SIMD mode is not used despite the fact that pyramids have a hierarchical structure while ASPs employ a master and a number of slaves.

5–5.3 The Distributed Reconfigurable Multiprocessor

The block diagram of a node of the DIstributed Reconfigurable Multiprocessor (DIRMU) is shown in Fig. 5-20(a). It consists of a processor module (P-Module) and a multiport memory (M-Module). The P-Ports of any P-Module can be connected (by plugged-in cables) to the M-Ports of other PaMs to provide *shared-memory access* to the M-Modules.

The internal structure of a PaM is shown in Fig. 5-20(b). The P-Module includes an Intel 8086 16-bit microprocessor and an 8087 coprocessor to provide the required arithmetic operations. The two CPUs can access a local memory (320K bytes of RAM and 16K of PROM) which stores code and private data (constants, etc.). Also provided are I/O interfaces for terminals, printers, disks, etc. The I/O interface and the local memory

[L. Uhr (Ed.): "Parallel Computer Vision," Academic Press, Inc., Boston. Reprinted by permission of Academic Press, Inc.

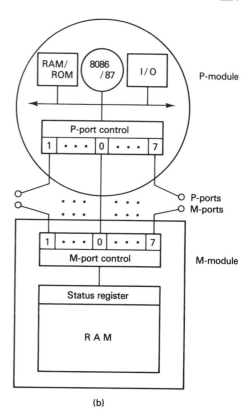

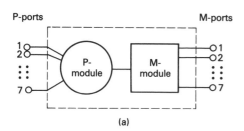

Figure 5-20   The node of DIRMU Courtesy of Prof. W. Händler.

cannot be shared because they are connected to the CPUs by a bus; the shareable memory is in the M-Modules.

Each M-Module includes 64K bytes of memory. Each CPU is connected to its M-Module through a port. The access to the other M-Modules is achieved by connecting any one of the remaining six P-Ports to an appropriate M-Port. All M-Modules form the common address space.

All data paths are 16 bits wide. The memory cycle times are 800 nns for the local memories and 1.2 mcs for the multiport memories (provided there is no access conflict). The RAM chips are slow and there are delays due to the P-port and M-port controls. It should be emphasized that all multiport memories connected to any particular PaM are accessed at the same time no matter which PaM is making the request.

If more than a single processor is trying to access a multiport memory at the same time, an *access conflict* occurs. It is resolved by the M-port control as follows: A requesting PaM has to wait until it is serviced; no PaM gets two accesses to an M-Module while another PaM is attempting to access the same M-Module.

Measurements have shown that the higher cycle time of the M-Module as well as delays caused by access conflicts have only a very small influence on the total execution time of

typical application programs. The reason is that only shared data are stored in the M-Modules. The majority of memory accesses however refer to program code and data in the private
memories.

A PaM can lock the multiport memory for more than one memory cycle. This is
required for some synchronization primitives (e.g., EXCHANGE instruction). Interprocessor
communication is further supported by two registers in the address space of the multiport
memories. By setting appropriate bits in these registers, two PaMs sharing a common
M-Module can send interrupts to each other.

Another status register supports fault diagnosis of neighboring PaMs. If an error is
detected within a building block by some detection logic (e.g., power failure, illegal HALT
instruction, etc.), a corresponding bit is set in the status register and an error interrupt is sent
to all neighbors. Neighborhood diagnosis is an important prerequisite for fault-tolerant
DIRMU configurations. [Han86]

Figure 5-21 shows some typical examples of DIRMU interconnections. One of
them, the pyramid, was discussed above and in Sec. 2 in conjunction with its possible use
for image processing. DIRMU and its predecessor, the EGPA, were pioneering efforts in
this area. Note that the number of PaMs used in DIRMU is not limited. However, each
PaM can be connected to at most seven neighbors—this accounts for the "Restricted"
neighborhood in the DIRMU name.

Two basic characteristics required for a DIRMU type machine were:

1. The nodes of the network should be commercially available computers-on-the-chip
   (the initial system uses Intel 8086 and 8087).
2. The coupling is through a common though distributed memory. This was the reason
   for using multiport units.

As for the first point, note that using a von-Neumann architecture means that the
languages used will be those standard today. The language used in this particular case is
Modula-2, which is very easily changed into Ada. The communication primitives between
the modules can also be done by extending Ada (see chapters 7 to 11).

The prototype of DIRMU has the following characteristics:

1. A single PaM consists of two CPUs and a multiported memory (hardware complexity therefore minimal).
2. Scheduling of memory access by a fair strategy.
3. A high transfer rate (word length of processors).
4. Additional hardware for interprocess communication and synchronization is minimal.
5. The hardware assists in fault diagnosis (see Appendix 2).
6. Almost free-form interconnection of various types by simple cable connections. The

W. Handler: "Multiprozessoren: Effizienz und Fehleztolezanz," NTG Fachberichte, No. 92, pp. 7–29
(in German). By permission.

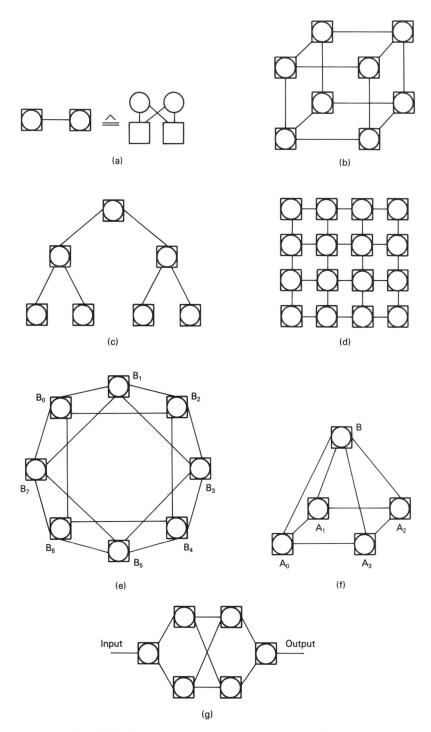

Figure 5-21 The interconnections possible in DIRMU Courtesy of Prof. W. Händler.

TABLE 5-3   EFFICIENCY OF DIRMU FOR A FEW
ALGORITHMS

Matrix inversion by Gauss-Jordan (200 × 200)	0.950
Matrix multiplication (200 × 200)	0.975
Solution of linear sets by Gauss-Seidel .... almost	1.000
Solution of differential equations by relaxation	0.875
Topographical representation	0.900
Lighting of topographical models	0.600
Vectorizing gray-colored matrices	0.925
Distance transformations	0.850
Minimization of multidimensional functions	0.800
Graph-theoretical investigation	0.875
Text formatting	0.650

fanin-fanout is not wide enough—7 at present. There is no reason why it cannot be made larger in future systems.

DIRMU systems do not require complicated communication primitives, since each PaM can directly access data in all of its neighbors. In those systems that used buses or crossbars, the data is copied from other memories by special I/O routines. This means that "send" and "receive" instructions are required. The fact that data are so easily accessible leads to high efficiencies, as indicated above.

The partitioning of the programs and data can only be done up to a certain *granularity*; otherwise the efficiency will suffer. It is therefore often the case that a problem will be solved on less than the full complement of p nodes; this is space sharing. In most cases though, the efficiency is rather high (see Table 5-3). For such efficiencies, appropriate interconnection of the nodes was used.

The efficiency, important as it is, is not the only characteristic that is of interest. Others are program-friendliness, synchronization, modularity, and fault diagnosis or fault tolerance. It is important also that the programming aspect is solved satisfactorily—but this is the subject of chapters 7 to 11 (on Programming and Ada).

5—6 PROBLEMS

1. Draw the wiring connections for a 64-node Cube.
2. Add material of the T-Series Cubes of Floating-Point Systems.
3. Design an algorithm for matrix multiplication along the lines of Sec. 4-5.3.
4. Provide two algorithms, one more suitable for the iPSC and the other for the iPSC/2.
5. What are the characteristics of ASPs? Compare TOPPS with the SMS systems.
6. As a project, redesign the TOPPS using the MC68020.
7. Read on HEP in [Kow85] and rewrite Subsection 5-5.1.
8. The CRAY X-MP and two other VPs, the Fujitsu VP-200 and the Hitachi S-810/20 are described and compared in [DaH86]. Read it and form your own opinion.
9. This is the end of Part A on Parallel Processors. Draw your conclusions about which PPSs are suitable for which jobs.

CHAPTER 6

ALGORITHMS

Various hardware systems were discussed in the first five chapters. In this chapter we begin to discuss how to program them. In particular, the *objectives* of this chapter are:

Present in sections 6-1 and 6-2 sequential algorithms which can be used throughout the rest of the book as examples.

Discuss the approaches to parallel programming in section 6-3, and the methods of ''divide-and-communicate,'' ''reordering,'' and other methods in sections 6-4 to 6-6.

In the next chapter we will describe briefly the traditional features of Ada. Therefore, projects using the algorithms discussed in this chapter will appear at the end of the next chapter.

6-1 ORGANIZATIONAL PROBLEMS

The main activity in various inquiry systems is sorting and searching. We search for the account number or for the quotation (or number of seats available on a particular flight), etc. One way to make the frequent search more efficient is to have the data sorted.

A number of sorting and searching algorithms will be used throughout the book. The mechanics of solving them will be discussed in this section, and in particular it will be shown that a speedup can be achieved if sorting is executed in parallel, even on a single computer.

Consider a telephone list. Each subscriber has a "record" with the fields of the record being:

```
Family name, First name, Second name, if any
House number, Street name, Zip code, Phone number.
```

Suppose someone's phone number (his/her name will be called the "key") is to be looked up. In most cases, a list is ordered by the letters of the subscriber names. The simplest method is to perform a *linear search*, which is as follows: Check if the first subscriber has the name of the key. If so, then the search is complete, otherwise, check the second name. Proceed in the same way to the third name, fourth name, and so on. If the end of the list is reached, without having found the key, the name is not on the list.

In comparing various algorithms, an important factor is the expected solution time of each alternative. Sometimes, like in matrix multiplication this time can be computed, sometimes this depends on the data at hand. For instance, if the search is conducted for a key (a name) which begins with the letter "A," not many *comparisons* will have to be done, but if the name begins on a "W," the number of comparisons will be large. In such cases, it is very helpful to know the *Operations Count* 0 (see Sec. 1-3). In the case of the search for a name, it would be helpful to know how the search-time depends or grows with the length n of the telephone list.

Suppose that the time grows with the square of n. Thus, if sorting names in a list of say ten names requires one second, sorting a list of n = 20 requires not 2, but $2^2 = 4$ seconds and for n = 100 or 1,000 the number would be $(100/10)^2 = 100$ and $100^2 = 10,000$ or approximately three hours. Finally, 10,000 records, which corresponds to a telephone book of a small town, would require almost two weeks.

The most common operation counts are $\log(n)$, n, $n*\log(n)$, n^2, and 2^n or *logarithmic, linear, n-log, quadratic,* and *exponential*, respectively.

To get some idea of the computation time, assume that the time required for a list of length $n = 1$ is 1. Then the times for the various orders of magnitude would be as in Table 6-1.

TABLE 6-1 OPERATION COUNT FOR VARIOUS
SEARCH METHODS

n	$\log(n)$	$n \times \log(n)$	$n ** 2$
1	0	0	1
2	1	2	4
4	2	8	16
8	3	24	64
16	4	64	256
32	5	160	1024
64	6	384	4096
128	7	896	16384
256	8	2048	65536
512	9	4608	262144
1024	10	10240	1048576
2048	11	22528	4194304
4096	12	49152	16777216
8192	13	106496	67108864
16384	14	229376	268435456
32768	15	491520	1073741824

On the average, it may be assumed that the name will be found in the middle of the list. An estimate of the operations count is therefore:

$$t(\text{linear search}) = 0.5*n = \mathbf{0}(n) \tag{6-1}$$

Since telephone books are quite voluminous, this is a large number (see Table 6-1); therefore, a faster procedure is required.

Such a faster algorithm, the *binary search*, consists of the following steps:

1. Divide the list in half and compare the key with the name in the middle. If the name is the key, the search is complete.
2. If the name begins with a letter that is earlier in the alphabet, disregard the higher part of the list; if it begins with a letter later in the alphabet, disregard the lower part of the list.
3. Repeat steps 1 and 2 for the remaining half of the list.

Eventually, either the key is found or the list was divided so many times that the remaining list shrank to one item and cannot be divided any more. In the last case, the key was not found. (Note: more than one letter is required for the algorithm to work.)

To calculate the order of magnitude for this algorithm, assume that the length of the list is a *binary number*, that is, that $n = 2**m$ (e.g., $n = 2^8 = 256$). In the worst case, this list is divided m times (i.e., at 128, then at 64, at 32, . . . , 2 and finally at 1). Thus, the upper bound on the number of tries is 8, or, in the general case:

$$t(\text{binary search}) = \mathbf{0}[\log(n)] \tag{6-2}$$

(As earlier, the base of the logarithm is 2, if not otherwise mentioned.) As can be seen from Table 6-1, the order of magnitude compared to the linear search has decreased markedly.

Sometimes, the *Fibonacci search* is used to calculate the new element for comparison. The Fibonacci numbers form the sequence

0, 1, 1, 2, 3, 5, 8, 13, 21, 34, 55, 89, 144, . . .

If they are stored as elements of a vector, say "fibel" (for Fibonacci element), then starting with fibel(3), each new term of the sequence is

$$\text{fibel}(i+1) = \text{fibel}(i) + \text{fibel}(i-1) \qquad (6\text{-}3)$$

i.e., each is a sum of the preceding two fibels. This is a *recursively* generated sequence because fibel(i) depends on fibel ($i-k$); $k = 1, 2 \ldots$. The search in a list of 144 elements can therefore be conducted as follows:

Determine if the key is at 89.

If not, determine if it is in the lower or higher "half."

Repeat the two steps for the remaining "half," each time using a lower Fibonacci number (here, 55).

Next, we discuss *sorting*—a very important field of study because so much of the processing time of computers is spent on sorting long lists of records. Entire books were devoted to this subject. Here, only the material needed for parallelization is discussed.

In all that follows, it is assumed that either the list is small enough or the memory is large enough so that the list fits into the memory in its entirety. This is called *internal sorting*. It is also assumed that a long list of records is to be sorted according to one of its "fields." This field contains a numerical "key" or in the simplest case, an integer. For example, sort a small list, say 3, 8, 6, 5, 1, 4, 9, 7, 2 in ascending order.

The first algorithm is the following: Compare the key in position 1 to the keys in positions 2,3, . . ., n in sequence, and if necessary exchange them. In the above case, 3 would be exchanged, *swapped* with 1, and 1 would be in position 1. The list after one iteration is

```
Positions 1 to n:  1, 8, 6, 5, 3, 4, 9, 7, 2
```

Starting with the second element (8) we would exchange 8<−>6, and since now 6 is to be compared with 5, also exchange 5<−>6. Finally, 5<−>3 and 3<−>2 are exchanged. The list and later lists are

```
Positions 2 to n:   2, 8, 6, 5, 4, 9, 7, 3
Positions 3 to n:      3, 8, 6, 5, 9, 7, 4    Note:  The already sorted
Positions 4 to n:         4, 8, 6, 9, 7, 5           keys are not shown.
Positions 5 to n:            5, 8, 9, 7, 6
Positions 6 to n:               6, 9, 8, 7
Positions 7 to n:                  7, 9, 8
Positions 8 to n:                     8, 9
```

As can be seen, the number of comparisons is $n - 1$ in the first iteration, then $n - 2$, $n - 3, \ldots, 2$ and finally a single comparison. Altogether $(n - 1) + (n - 2) + \ldots + 2 + 1$ comparisons are required.

This is a geometric progression and equals $n*(n - 1)/2 = (n^2 - n)/2$. For a large n, say $n = 1,000$, n^2 is so much larger than n that approximately n^2 is the number of comparisons, or the "time of work":

$$t(\text{selection sort}) = \mathbf{0}(n^2) \tag{6-4}$$

The program for the selection sort is discussed later. In order to show why parallel processing is advantageous, suppose the same list is to be sorted by selection sort on *two* processors working in parallel:

```
Positions 1 to 4 and 5 to 9:   3,8,6,5   and   1,4,9,7,2
Positions 2 to 4 and 6 to 9:     5,8,6   and     2,9,7,4
Positions 3 to 4 and 7 to 9:       6,8   and       4,9,7
Positions 8 to 9 in processor No.2:                  7,9
```

The lists are 3,5,6,8 and 1,2,4,7,9.

For the final list, *merge* these two sublists by comparing their leftmost keys and sending the lesser key to the common list:

```
3,5,6,8....3,5,6,8. ,3,5,6,8..5,6,8. ,5,6,8. ,6,8..8....8...φ...φ
(1,2,4,7,9.(2,4,7,9.(4,7,9...(4,7,9.(7,9..(7,9.(7,9.(9..(9....φ
(1,.......(2,......(3,......(4,.....(5,.....(6,..(7,..(8,.(9....
```

Every key was compared to every other key so that n comparisons are needed. For 1, 2, and 4 CPUs working in parallel, the orders are

$$0.5*n*(n - 1) + n = n^2/2 + n/2;$$
$$0.5*(n/2)*(n/2 - 1) + n = n^2/8 + 3*n/4$$
$$0.5*(n/4)*(n/4 - 1) + n = n^2/32 + 7*n/8 \tag{6-5}$$

Table 6-2 shows this for various values of n. Multiplying the last rows by 2 and 4 yields the operation count for a single CPU. Thus, even for a single CPU, it would be more efficient to divide the sorting into parts. Two or more CPUs lead to a speedup.

The time of the selection algorithm can be reduced if the number of swaps is reduced as follows: In a list 6,8,3,5,2,4,9,7,1, the procedure exchanges first 3 with 6, then 3 with 2, and finally 2 with 1. The list is reordered into 1,8,6,5,3,4,9,7,2. Instead of exchanging 6 with 3, key 3 is stored with its index (here 3) in an auxiliary variable

TABLE 6-2 OPERATION COUNTS FOR PARALLEL SORTING

		20	50	100	200	500	1000
	n	20	50	100	200	500	1000
1	CPU	190	1225	4950	19990	124750	499500
2	CPUs	65	350	1325	5150	31625	125750
4	CPUs	30	122	400	1425	8250	33375

(sindex). Then key 3 is compared with the remaining list, and sindex will change to 5 and then to 9. The key in position 1 is then exchanged with the key in position 9 to yield the list: 1,8,3,5,2,4,9,7,6. Only one exchange instead of three was needed.

In the second "pass," sindex starts as 2 and changes into 3 and 5, when keys 8 and 2 are exchanged to produce the list: 1,2,3,5,8,4,9,7,6. In the third pass, no exchange is made, in the fourth pass 5 is swapped with 4 and the list is: 1,2,3,4,8,5,9,7,6. In the same way, the lists are consecutively:

```
1, 2, 3, 4, 5, 8, 9, 7, 6
            6, 9, 7, 8
               7, 9, 8
                  8, 9
```

In this procedure, only a single swap was done in every pass. The time complexity is still $O(n^2)$, but the overall time will generally be shorter because only one exchange is made in every pass.

Another algorithm with an order of n^2 is the so-called *bubble-sort*. It is based on comparing *adjacent* keys: A(1) with A(2); then A(2) with A(3); and so on until A($n-1$) is compared with A(n). This is called a *sweep*. Whenever A(i) > A($i+1$) the two are swapped.

If the list is sorted, no exchanges are necessary. This can be used in the sort procedure as follows: At the start of every sweep, make a Boolean variable "swapped" FALSE. Whenever a swap is made, set it to TRUE. If at the end of the sweep "swapped" is still FALSE then the list is ordered, otherwise another sweep is necessary.

This procedure is exemplified by the list below, where the list is shown vertically, for a reason to be explained in the next paragraph.

39	39	39	39	39	39	39	(41)
3	20	20	20	20	35	(41)	39
20	14	14	18	35	(41)	35	
14	8	18	35	(41)	20		
8	18	35	(41)	18			
18	35	(41)	14				
35	(41)	8					
(41)	3						

The original list of 41,35,18,8,14,20,3,39 was sorted into the list 3,8,14,18,20,35,39,41. In the way in which it was printed, the key 41 "floats" to the top like a bubble in water—hence, "bubble" sort.

The number of swaps can be determined as follows: In the case that the list is ordered to begin with, only a single sweep is necessary and the time is $O(n)$. The worst case is when the list is in exactly the reverse order since then only one element changes its position in every sweep. The number of sweeps is therefore n and the time is $0(n^2)$. Since the average case is somewhere in between, it follows that

$$0(n) < \text{the average time(bubble sort)} < 0(n^2) \tag{6-6}$$

A very similar algorithm is the *cocktail shaker*. It differs from the bubble-sort only in that the sweeps are alternating between "down" and "up." For the list above, this results in

39	39	41	41	41	41
3	20	39	39	39	39
20	14	20	20	35	35
14	8	14	14	20	20
8	18	8	18	14	18
18	35	18	35	18	14
35	41	35	8	8	8
41	3	3	3	3	3

This algorithm has a time complexity of $0(n^2)$ in the worst case, but in most cases will require less work than the bubble-sort. In the present case, the number of sweeps was reduced from 8 to 6.

A much better algorithm is *Quicksort*. In the worst case, it is still $0(n^2)$, but from a large number of experiments it was found that in the average case:

$$t(\text{quicksort}) = 0[n*\log(n)] \tag{6-7}$$

If the original list of keys is 20 35 *18* 8 14 41 3 39, then the algorithm proceeds like a candle to be "burned" from both sides simultaneously. Choose first an element, say 18 (from the middle) and compare all keys with it from the left. When an element is found that is higher than the chosen element 18, its index is noted, say as i. The same is done from the right, but now a key that is less than 18 is noted by say j. In the present case, $20 > 18$ so that $i = 1$, and $3 < 18$ so that $j = 7$. Next, the elements in positions i and j are swapped and the list is

3 35 *18* 8 14 41 20 39

What happened was that key 3, which is lower, was placed on the left, whereas key 20, which is higher than 18, was transferred to its right. If this is done until the indices i and j "cross," all keys i which are less than 18 will be on its left, all larger keys on its right. As a result, 18 will be in its "final position," as evidenced by

i = 2, key = 35 > 18; j = 5, key = 14 < 18; list: 3, 14, 18, 8, 35, 41, 20, 39
j = 4, key = 8 < 18; the list is now: 3, 14, 8, *18*, 35, 41, 20, 39

and all keys smaller than 18 are on its left, and keys larger than 18 are on its right—18 is in its final position.

The two parts, left-of-18 and right-of-18, can be dealt with in the same way. For parallel processing, this means that if two processors are available, both can work simultaneously. Moreover, in the next stage, there will be four sublists, so that *the number of processors that could work in parallel is* 2, 4, . . . *p*.

To exemplify this, here is the quicksort for 16 keys with the "pivot" key italicized.

$12, 5, 6, 16, 15, 1, 2,\ \ 9,\ \ 8, 4, 3, 10, 13, 11, 7, 14.$ key (i) = 12,   key (j) = ⌐

$7, 5, 6, 16, 15, 1, 2,\ \ 9,\ \ 8, 4, 3, 10, 13, 11, 12, 14.$ key (i) = 16,   key (j) = ⌐

$7, 5, 6, 3, 15, 1, 2,\ \ 9,\ \ 8, 4, 16, 10, 13, 11, 12, 14.$ key (i) = 15,   key (j) = ⌐

$7, 5, 6, 3, 4, 1, 2,\ \ 9,\ \ 8, 15, 16, 10, 13, 11, 12, 14.$ key (i) = 9,   key (j) = ⌐

The two lists can be sorted separately as follows:

$7, 5, 6,\ \ \ \ \ 3,\ \ \ 4, 1, 2, 8$ $9, 15, 16, 10,\ \ 13,\ \ \ 11, 12, 14$

$2, 5, 6,\ \ \ \ \ 3,\ \ \ 4, 1, 7, 8$ $9, 12, 16, 10,\ \ 13,\ \ \ 11, 15, 14$

$2, 1, 6,\ \ \ \ \ 3,\ \ \ 4, 5, 7, 8$ $9, 12, 11, 10,\ \ 13,\ \ \ 16, 15, 14$

$2, 1,\ \ \ \ 3, 6,\ \ \ 4, 5, 7, 8$

Next the four sublists are sorted:

$1,\ \ 2,\ \ 3\ \ \ 6, 4,\ \ 5,\ \ 7,\ 8$ $9, 12,\ \ 11,\ \ 10$ $16,\ \ 15, 14$

$1, 2, 3\ \ \ \ \ \ \ 4, 5, 6, 7, 8$ $9, 10, 11, 12$ and $14, 15, 16$

For quicksort to perform well, even on sequential machines, it is essential that the italicized keys should be chosen with some care, so as to make evenhanded splits of the list. Otherwise, quicksort may behave poorly, the usual example being the quadratic time that quicksort takes on almost-sorted lists.

Next we introduce *radix sorting* by quoting from [Knu73]:[†]

> Readers who are familiar with punch card equipment are well aware of the efficient procedure used on card sorters, based on the digits of the keys . . . Suppose we want to sort a 52-card deck of playing cards. We define A < 2 < 3 < 4 < 5 < 6 < 7 < 8 < 9 < 10 < J < Q < K, as an ordering of the face values, and for the suits we may define
>
> $$\clubsuit < \diamondsuit < \heartsuit < \spadesuit$$

"One card is to precede another if either

(i) its suit is less than the other suit, or

(ii) the suits are equal but its face value is less . . . Thus

$$\text{A} \clubsuit < 2 \clubsuit < \cdots < \text{K} \clubsuit < \text{A} \diamondsuit < \cdots < \text{Q} \spadesuit < \text{K} \spadesuit$$

It is natural to sort the cards first by their suits into four *piles*, then to fiddle with each of the individual piles until they are in order.

But there is a faster way to do the trick. First deal the cards face up into 13 piles, one

[†]Donald Knuth, The Art of Computer Programming, vol. 3, © 1973, Addison-Wesley Publishing Co., Inc. Reading, Massachusetts. Reprinted with permission.

for each face value. Then collect these piles by putting the aces on the bottom, the 2's face up on top of them, then the 3's, etc., finally putting the kings (face up) on top. Turn the deck face down and deal again, this time into four piles for the four suits. By putting the resulting piles together, with clubs at the bottom, then diamonds, hearts, and spades, the deck will be in perfect order.

The same idea applies to the sorting of numbers and alphabetic data. Why does it work? Because (in our playing example) if two cards go into different piles in the final deal, they have different suits, so the one with the lower suit is lowest. But if two cards have the same suit (and consequently go into the same pile), they are already in the proper order because of the previous sorting. In other words, the face values will be in increasing order on each of the four piles as we deal the cards on the second pass.'' [Knu73]

The number of different cards is 13, and therefore the radix of the above ''program'' was 13, but since computers work in the binary system, we will use it. Suppose we consider the list of numbers discussed earlier, namely: 6,8,3,5,2,4,9,7,1 written in binary as:

0110, 1000, 0011, 0101, 0010, 0100, 1001, 0111, 0001.

According to the previously described algorithm, only two piles are needed: into the first go all numbers ending on a 0, into the second those ending on a 1. This provides the two piles:

0110, 1000, 0010, 0100   0011, 0101, 1001, 0111, 0001

Next, combine the piles and order them by the third, second, and the first bit. This yields the three lists, the last being sorted

1000, 0100, 0101, 1001, 0001   0110, 0010, 0011, 0111
1000, 1001, 0001, 0010, 0011   0100, 0101, 0110, 0111
0001, 0010, 0011, 0100, 0101, 0110, 0111   1000, 1001

6–2 NUMERICAL PROBLEMS

A number of numerical examples will be used throughout the book. The mechanics of solving them will be discussed next. The first examples deal with the *direct solution of a set of linear equations:*

$$\mathbf{A} * \mathbf{x} = \mathbf{b} \qquad (6\text{-}8)$$

Matrix **A** and the two vectors **x** and **b** are usually very large. Since it is clearly impossible to exemplify the solution method using too many equations, four equations will be used as an example:

$$
\begin{aligned}
20*x(1) + 2*x(2) - 4*x(3) + 2*x(4) &= 20 \\
2*x(1) + 10*x(2) - 2*x(3) + 1*x(4) &= 20 \\
-4*x(1) - 2*x(2) + 8*x(3) - 2*x(4) &= 8 \\
2*x(1) + 1*x(2) - 2*x(3) + 2*x(4) &= 6
\end{aligned}
\qquad \text{or } \mathbf{A} * \mathbf{x} = \mathbf{b} \qquad (6\text{-}9)
$$

Elimination (Algorithm by Gauss), which is probably remembered from high school, proceeds in the following steps:

To eliminate $x(1)$ from the second equation, multiply the "*pivot*" row 1 by $A(2,1)/A(1,1) = 2/20 = 0.1$. Multiplying any row by a nonzero value does not change it. Row 1 is now $2*x(1)+0.2*x(2)-0.4*x(3)+0.2*x(4) = 2$. Subtracting the pivot row from row 2 yields $0*x(1)+9.8*x(2)-1.6*x(3)+0.8*x\ (4) = 18$. Since $x(1)$ is multiplied by 0, it is eliminated from the second equation—hence the name of the procedure.

To eliminate $x(1)$ from the third equation, multiply row 1 by $-4/20 = -0.2$ and subtract it from row 3. Row 3 is now: $0*x(1)+2.4*x(2)+7.2*x(3)-1.6*x(4) = 20$. (The calculations here are rounded to one place of accuracy only.) Similarly, multiplying row 1 by $2/20 = 0.1$ and subtracting the resulting row from row 4 yields $0*x(1)+0.8*x(2)-1.6.*x(3)+1.8*x(4) = 4$.

The original and the set of equations after eliminating $x(1)$ are

$$\begin{vmatrix} 20 & 2 & -4 & 2 \\ 2 & 10 & -2 & 1 \\ -4 & 2 & 8 & -2 \\ 2 & 1 & -2 & 2 \end{vmatrix} * \begin{vmatrix} x(1) \\ x(2) \\ x(3) \\ x(4) \end{vmatrix} = \begin{vmatrix} 20 \\ 20 \\ 8 \\ 6 \end{vmatrix} ; \quad \begin{vmatrix} 20 & 2.0 & -4.0 & 2.0 \\ 0 & 9.8 & -1.6 & 0.8 \\ 0 & 2.4 & 7.2 & -1.6 \\ 0 & 0.8 & -1.6 & 1.8 \end{vmatrix} * \begin{vmatrix} x(1) \\ x(2) \\ x(3) \\ x(4) \end{vmatrix} = \begin{vmatrix} 20 \\ 18 \\ 20 \\ 4 \end{vmatrix} \quad (6\text{-}10)$$

Next, element $A(3,2)$ is eliminated by subtracting the pivot row 2, multiplied by $A(3,2)/A(2,2)$ from row 3. Then in the same way, $A(4,2)$ is eliminated by subtracting row 2 multiplied by $A(4,2)/A(2,2)$ from row 4. Finally, element $A(4,3)$ is eliminated. The original and transformed matrices are

$$\begin{vmatrix} 20 & 2 & -4 & 2 & 20 \\ 2 & 10 & -2 & 1 & 20 \\ -4 & 2 & 8 & -23 & 8 \\ 2 & 1 & -2 & 2 & 6 \end{vmatrix} \begin{matrix} \rightarrow \\ \rightarrow \\ \rightarrow \\ \rightarrow \end{matrix} \begin{vmatrix} 20 & 2.0 & -4.0 & 2.0 & 20.0 \\ 0 & 9.8 & -1.6 & 0.8 & 18.0 \\ 0 & 0.0 & 7.6 & -1.8 & 15.6 \\ 0 & 0.0 & 0.0 & 1.4 & 5.6 \end{vmatrix} \quad (6\text{-}11)$$

Note that the method can be generalized by subtracting from row j, the pivot row i whose elements were multiplied by $A(j,i)/A(i, i)$. All elements of row j are therefore replaced according to

$$A(j,k) := A(j,k) - A(j,i)*A(i,k)/A(i,i); \quad k = 1, \ldots, n \qquad (6\text{-}12)$$

The resulting matrix **U** is upper-triangular with non-zeros on the diagonal. Having produced matrix **U**, the solution is calculated in the order $x(n)$, $x(n-1)$, $\ldots$, $x(2)$ and finally $x(1)$. Because the order is from n to 1 (i.e., "backwards"), this part is called the *back-substitution*. In the present case, $x(4)$ is computed from the last equation: $1.4*x(4) = 5.6$ to be 4. If this value of $x(4)$ is used in the third equation: $7.6*x(3)-1.8*x(4) = 15.6$, then $7.6*x(3) = 22.8$ and $x(3) = 3$. Then $9.8*x(2)-1.6*x(3)+0.8*x(4) = 18$ or $9.8*x(2) = 19.6$ is solved for $x(2) = 2$, and if $x(4)$, $x(3)$, and $x(2)$ are used in equation 1: $20*x(1)+2*2-4*3+2*4 = 20$ or $20*x(1) = 20$, then $x(1)$ is 1. The general equation for the back-substitution is (for $i = n, n-1, \ldots ,2,1$):

$$x(i) := [b(i) - \Sigma A(i,k)*x(k)]/A(i,i); \quad k\Sigma = i+1, \ldots , n \qquad (6\text{-}13)$$

A matrix **A** can be *factored* into a lower (**L**) and upper (**U**) triangular matrix, i.e., written as

$$\mathbf{A} = \mathbf{L} * \mathbf{U} \tag{6-14}$$

where the diagonal entries of either **L** or **U** are ones. For a 4-by-4 set:

$$
\begin{vmatrix}
L(1,1) & 0 & 0 & 0 \\
L(2,1) & L(2,2) & 0 & 0 \\
L(3,1) & L(3,2) & L(3,3) & 0 \\
L(4,1) & L(4,2) & L(4,3) & L(4,4)
\end{vmatrix}
*
\begin{vmatrix}
1 & U(1,2) & U(1,3) & U(1,4) \\
0 & 1 & U(2,3) & U(2,4) \\
0 & 0 & 1 & U(3,4) \\
0 & 0 & 0 & 1
\end{vmatrix}
=
\begin{vmatrix}
A(1,1) & A(1,2) & \dots \\
A(2,1) & A(2,2) & \dots \\
A(3,1) & A(3,2) & \dots \\
A(4,1) & A(4,2) & \dots
\end{vmatrix}
$$

L*U is the original matrix **A**. The equations for computing the elements of **L** and **U** are

$$L(i,k) := A(i,k) - \Sigma[(L(i,m)*U(m,k)]; \qquad m\Sigma = 1, 2 \dots k \tag{6-15}$$
$$U(k,i) := [A(k,j) - \Sigma(L(k,m)*U(m,j)]/L(k,k); \quad m\Sigma = 1, 2 \dots k \tag{6-16}$$

The order must be such that first, column 1 of **L** then row 1 of **U**, then column 2 of **L**, etc., are computed. Obviously, since these matrices are triangular, only the non-zero, non-one elements are computed.

Having completed the factorization, **A** = **L** * **U**, the solution to **A** * **x** = **b** proceeds by first computing **L***(**U*x**) = **b** or with **z** = **U*x** as

$$\mathbf{L} * \mathbf{z} = \mathbf{b} \tag{6-17}$$

This so-called "Forward substitution" yields vector **z**, which is used in the "Backward substitution" to calculate **x**:

$$\mathbf{U} * \mathbf{x} = \mathbf{z} \tag{6-18}$$

Suppose that a "unitary" matrix **I** with 1's on the diagonal and 0's everywhere else replaces the "right-hand vector" **b**. Proceeding in the same way as before yields:

$$
\begin{vmatrix}
A(1,1) & A(1,2) & A(1,3) & A(1,4) \\
A(2,1) & A(2,2) & A(2,3) & A(2,4) \\
A(3,1) & A(3,2) & A(3,3) & A(3,4) \\
A(4,1) & A(4,2) & A(4,3) & A(4,4)
\end{vmatrix}
\begin{matrix}
\rightarrow \\ \rightarrow \\ \rightarrow \\ \rightarrow
\end{matrix}
\begin{vmatrix}
Y(1,1) & Y(1,2) & Y(1,3) & Y(1,4) \\
Y(2,1) & Y(2,2) & Y(2,3) & Y(2,4) \\
Y(3,1) & Y(3,2) & Y(3,3) & Y(3,4) \\
Y(4,1) & Y(4,2) & Y(4,3) & Y(4,4)
\end{vmatrix}
$$

Viewing matrix **Y** as four independent vectors, four back-substitutions would produce four solution (column) vectors which if combined into a matrix is the *inverse* of the original matrix.

In the algorithm of *Jordan*, the original matrix **A** is not changed into an upper triangular **U** but instead into a diagonal matrix **D**. In this case, not only elements in column i below the diagonal, but also those above the diagonal of pivot row i are eliminated. The result is

$$\mathbf{D} * \mathbf{x} = \mathbf{b} \tag{6-19}$$

Every $x(i)$ is computed from $\mathbf{D}*\mathbf{x} = \mathbf{b}$ by $x(i) := b(i)/D(i,i)$; $i = 1, \ldots, n$.

The algorithm by Gauss requires $\simeq n^3/3$ operations for solving $\mathbf{A}*\mathbf{x} = \mathbf{b}$ and n^3 for inverting a matrix. Jordan's algorithm requires $\simeq n^3$ operations for each one of them. Since the algorithm by Jordan is easily parallelized whereas the algorithm by Gauss is not, Jordan's algorithm should be used—at least for inversion in parallel.

The amount of required storage is $2*n^2$, since we need both the original matrix and its inverse. For conserving storage, an inversion *in situ* [Wal86 and Ott87] is used. It overwrites the original matrix with its inverse. It can be defined as the following steps:

1. Search the n rows "r" and columns "c" for the largest absolute value $A(pr,pc)$ in pivot row pr and pivot column pc. Initialize permutation column and row vectors cv and rv respectively to 0.

2. Set $cv(pc) := pr$, and $rv(pr) := pc$.

3. Invert the pivot element $A(pr,pc) := 1.0/A(pr,pc)$

4. Change the entire pivot column, except in row pr through:
   $A(i,pc) := -A(r,pc)*A(pr,pc)$

5. Change all elements of A outside the pivot row and column:
   $A(r,c) := A(r,c) + A(r,pc)*A(pr,c)$

6. Set elements of the new pivot row to $A(pr,c) := A(pr,c)*A(pr,pc)$

Steps 1 to 6 are repeated n times and then the resulting matrix $\mathbf{B}$ has to be sorted according the the permutation vectors cv and rv. If $\mathbf{B}$ is the inverse of $\mathbf{A}$ then this can be written as:

$$B(r,c) := B[cv(r),\ rv(c)] \tag{6-20}$$

This algorithm is next exemplified on a 3-by-3 matrix from [Ott87]:

$$\mathbf{A} = \begin{vmatrix} 2.00 & 7.00 & 3.00 \\ 4.00 & 1.00 & 9.00 \\ 6.00 & 8.00 & 5.00 \end{vmatrix} ; \quad \begin{array}{l} pr = 2,\ pc = 3;\ A(2,3) := 1/9 = 0.11 \\ vr = [0,3,0];\ A(1,3) := -3*0.11 = -0.33 \\ vc = [0,0,2];\ A(3,3) := -5*0.11 = -0.55 \end{array}$$

$\begin{array}{ll} A(1,1) := 2 - 0.33*4 = 0.67; & A(3,2) := 8 - 0.55*1 = 7.45 \\ A(1,2) := 7 - 0.33*1 = 6.67; & A(2,1) := 4*0.11 = 0.44 \\ A(3,1) := 6 - 0.55*4 = 3.80; & A(2,2) := 1*0.11 = 0.11 \end{array}$

The second step is as follows:

$$\mathbf{A} = \begin{vmatrix} 0.67 & 6.67 & -0.33 \\ 0.44 & 0.11 & 0.11 \\ 3.80 & 7.45 & -0.55 \end{vmatrix} ; \quad \begin{array}{l} pr = 3,\ pc = 2 \\ vr = [0,3,2]; \\ vc = [0,3,2]; \end{array} \quad \begin{array}{l} A(3,2) := 1.00/7.45 = 0.13 \\ A(1,2) := -6.67*0.13 = -0.90 \\ A(2,2) := -0.11*0.13 = -0.02 \end{array}$$

$\begin{array}{ll} A(1,1) := 0.67 - 0.9*3.80 = -2.72; & A(2,3) := 0.11 + 0.02*0.55 = 0.12 \\ A(1,3) := -0.33 + 0.9*0.55 = 0.16; & A(3,1) := 3.8*0.13 = 0.51 \\ A(2,1) := 0.44 - 0.02*3.8 = 0.38; & A(3,3) := -0.55*0.13 = -0.07 \end{array}$

The third step is as follows:

$$\mathbf{A} = \begin{vmatrix} -2.72 & -0.90 & 0.16 \\ 0.38 & -0.02 & 0.12 \\ 0.51 & 0.13 & -0.07 \end{vmatrix}; \quad \begin{matrix} pr = 1, \ pc = 1 \\ vr = [1,3,2]; \\ vc = [1,3,2]; \end{matrix} \quad \begin{matrix} A(1,1) := -1/2.72 = -0.37 \\ A(2,1) := 0.38*0.37 = 0.14 \\ A(3,1) := 0.51*0.37 = 0.19 \end{matrix}$$

$A(2,2) := -0.02 - 0.9*0.14 = -0.14; \quad A(3,3) := 0.19*0.16 - 0.07 = -0.04$

$A(2,3) := 0.12 + 0.13*0.16 = 0.14; \quad A(1,2) := 0.9*0.37 = 0.33$

$A(3,2) := 0.13 - 0.19*0.90 = -0.03; \quad A(1,3) := 0.16*0.37 = -0.06$

The matrix **A** is shown below and if rows 2,3 and columns 2,3 are interchanged then the final result, the inverse matrix **B**, results.

$$\mathbf{A} = \begin{vmatrix} -0.37 & 0.33 & -0.06 \\ 0.14 & -0.14 & 0.14 \\ 0.19 & -0.03 & -0.04 \end{vmatrix}; \quad \mathbf{B} = \begin{vmatrix} -0.37 & -0.06 & 0.33 \\ 0.19 & -0.04 & -0.03 \\ 0.14 & 0.14 & -0.14 \end{vmatrix}$$

Matrices are usually much larger than those discussed thus far, but they are extremely *sparse*. A "typical" matrix would be 2,000-by-2,000 but on the average a row would have ten nonzero and 1,990 zero elements.

A matrix may be represented by a graph so that a branch exists between nodes i and j if and only if $A(i,j) / = 0$ (A not equal to 0). If there is no branch between nodes i and j, then $A(i,j) = 0$. Additionally, the diagonal elements $A(i,i)$ are always nonzero. Thus, the graph and matrix of Fig. 6-1(a) are equivalent (x depicts a nonzero element).

Elimination of element $A(2,1)$ introduces a nonzero in elements $A(2,3)$, $A(2,4)$, and $A(2,5)$ which were originally zero. This is called *fill-in* and should be avoided if at all

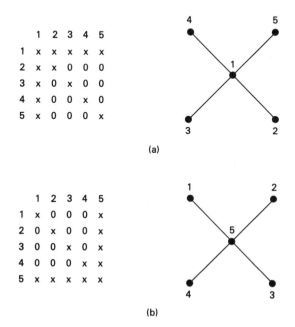

(a)

(b)

Figure 6-1 Matrices and their graphs

possible because it not only increases the storage demand, but also because fill-in leads to a higher operations count. The six zeros under the diagonal will all fill-in and therefore will have to be subsequently eliminated.

There will be fewer fill-ins if the equations are ordered in a particular way. The best ordering can only be determined by checking all possible orderings—an intractably time-consuming process. Instead of using it, a heuristic algorithm is normally used. Heuristic means that it was found to work in a great many cases, but that there is no theoretical foundation for it ("rule of thumb").

A "static" algorithm would order the matrix according to an increasing number of nonzero elements. In the case of the matrix above, the first row has 5, all other rows have 2 nonzeros. Thus, the algorithm consists of renumbering row 1 as 5, which leads to Fig. 6-1(b).

The elimination of this matrix produces no fill-in elements. Unfortunately, this case is very simple and the static policy as given is seldom the best. Instead, a "dynamic" policy of reordering is used. It consists of determining at every stage which of the not yet eliminated rows has the fewest number of nonzero elements and choosing it as the next pivot. The policy is dynamic because it takes into account that fill-in changes the number of nonzero elements.

Only the nonzero elements should be stored so that the matrix of the graph in Fig. 6-2 is stored as in Table 6-3.

Suppose that the value of the element $A(2,7)$ is required. The first index is $i = 2$ and the first step is to determine $ip(i)$ and $ip(i+1) - 1$. In this particular case: $ip(2) = 2$ and $ip(3) - 1 = 6 - 1 = 5$. Next, a search for the second subscript of **A**, namely $j = 7$, is made in vector *adj* for indices 2 to 5. It is found located in position 5, so that element $A(2,7)$ is in location 5 of vector "**v**."

Note that row "i" is stored between elements $ip(i)$ and $ip(i+1) - 1$. If a vector is to be multiplied by it, only the elements in the corresponding positions of vector *adj* have to be multiplied.

The next solution of a set of linear equations goes under the name of "*Gauss-Seidel.*"

First, every equation i is divided by $A(i,i)$ so that elements $A(i,i) = 1.0$. This is called "normalization." Next they are rewritten so that row i starts by $x(i) = \ldots$ For Eq. (6-9) the result is:

$$
\begin{aligned}
x(1) &= 1.0 - 0.1*x(2) + 0.20*x(3) - 0.10*x(4) \\
x(2) &= 2.0 - 0.2*x(1) + 0.20*x(3) - 0.10*x(4) \\
x(3) &= 2.0 + 0.5*x(1) - 0.25*x(2) + 0.25*x(4) \\
x(4) &= 3.0 - 1.0*x(1) - 0.50*x(2) + 1.00*x(3)
\end{aligned}
\tag{6-21}
$$

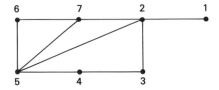

Figure 6-2 A network

TABLE 6-3 STORAGE OF A SPARSE MATRIX

The actual values of $a(i, j)$ = vector "**v**".																				
adj vector:	2	1	3	5		7	2	4		3	5	2	4	6	7	5	7	2	5	6	0
ip vector:	1	2	6	8		10				14	16		19								
index vector:	1	2	3	4		5				6	7		8								

The method starts by assuming a solution vector for the set, say that they are $x(i) = i \pm 0.1$, for instance $x(1) = 0.9$, $x(2) = 2.1$, $x(3), = 3.1$, and $x(4) = 3.9$. Inserting $x(2)$, $x(3)$, and $x(4)$ into the first equation yields a new value for $x(1) = 1.02$. Inserting this $x(1)$ and the previously assumed $x(3)$ and $x(4)$ into the second equation yields $x(2) = 2.026$. In the same way, the third equation yields $2.0 + 0.5*1.02 - 0.25*2.026 + 0.25*3.9 = 2.9785 = x(3)$. The last equation yields $3.0 - 1.020 - 1.013 + 5.9785 = 3.9455 = x(4)$. This is called an *iteration* and a new one may be started next. The iterative procedure is stopped when $\Sigma r^2 \leq eps$, with $r = x(\text{new}) - x(\text{old})$ being the "residual" and *eps* being a predetermined "accuracy." Note that the "distance" (**d**) of the computed values from $\mathbf{x} = [1,2,3,4]^T$ was originally $\mathbf{d} = [-0.1, 0.1, 0.1, -0.1]^T$, but was reduced to $\mathbf{d} = [0.02, 0.026, 0.0215, 0.0545]^T$. (Superscript T transposes the row into a column vector.) The errors and the distance will decrease until, in a few iterations, the result is correct to within *eps*.

The way this algorithm is formulated seems to be completely sequential: It is impossible to compute $x(i)$ without earlier having computed all $x(j)$ for $j = 1, 2, \ldots, i-1$. As will be shown later, this algorithm may and was in fact parallelized.

The form of Eq. (6-21): $\mathbf{x} = \mathbf{r} - \mathbf{A}*\mathbf{x}$ is the same as a *linear recurrence*, which will be discussed later.

The solution of the partial differential equation of Laplace:

$$\partial^2 u / \partial x^2 + \partial^2 u / \partial y^2 = 0 \tag{6-22}$$

is required very often in computation of electrostatic fields, temperature distributions and the like. In most cases, the problem is to solve the above equation for a given area, with the potential u prescribed on the border of the area (Dirichlet's problem).

For example in, Fig. 6-3 the potential u is prescribed on the border and is to be calculated for points 1 to 8. The basic equation for any point on the inside can be written as the average of the potentials of its four neighbors, whether they are inside or are boundary points (e, n, w and s are east, north, west and south).

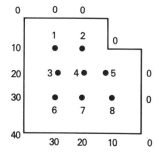

Figure 6-3 The area for which to solve the Laplace equation

$$4*u(j)^{i+1} = u(e)^i + u(n)^i + u(w)^i + u(s)^i \tag{6-23}$$

where i is the iteration number. If this is done for every one of the 8 inside points, we get:

$$4*u(1) = u(2) + u(3) + 10; \quad 4*u(2) = u(1) + u(4); \quad 4*u(3) = u(1) + u(4) + u(6) + 20;$$
$$4*u(4) = u(2) + u(3) + u(5) + u(7); \quad 4*u(5) = u(4) + u(8);$$
$$4*u(6) = u(3) + u(7) + 60; \quad 4*u(7) = u(4) + u(6) + u(8) + 20;$$
$$4*u(8) = u(5) + u(7) + 10.$$

In matrix form, and with "$-$" substituting for -1, this is

$$
\begin{bmatrix}
4 & - & - & & & & & \\
- & 4 & & - & & & & \\
\hline
- & & 4 & - & & - & & \\
& - & - & 4 & - & & - & \\
& & - & & 4 & & & - \\
\hline
& & & - & & 4 & - & \\
& & & & - & - & 4 & - \\
& & & & & - & - & 4
\end{bmatrix}
*
\begin{bmatrix}
u(1) \\ u(2) \\ u(3) \\ u(4) \\ u(5) \\ u(6) \\ u(7) \\ u(8)
\end{bmatrix}
=
\begin{bmatrix}
10 \\ 0 \\ 20 \\ 0 \\ 0 \\ 60 \\ 20 \\ 10
\end{bmatrix}
\tag{6-24}
$$

As seen, the equations are not really tridiagonal, but rather *block tridiagonal* since the elements are submatrices—or blocks. In cases like the "spline" approximation method, the elements are scalars. To satisfy all these problems, the set is written as follows:

$$
\begin{vmatrix}
b(1) & c(1) & & & & \\
a(2) & b(2) & c(2) & & & \\
& a(3) & b(3) & c(3) & & \mathbf{0} \\
& & \multicolumn{4}{c}{- - - - - - -} \\
& & & a(k)\ b(k)\ c(k) & & \\
\mathbf{0} & & & \multicolumn{2}{c}{- - - - - - - - -} \\
& & & a(n-1)\ b(n-1)\ c(n-1) \\
& & & a(n)\quad b(n)
\end{vmatrix}
*
\begin{vmatrix}
x(1) \\ x(2) \\ x(3) \\ - - - \\ x(k) \\ - - - \\ x(n-1) \\ x(n)
\end{vmatrix}
=
\begin{vmatrix}
r(1) \\ r(2) \\ r(3) \\ - - - \\ r(k) \\ - - - \\ r(n-1) \\ r(n)
\end{vmatrix}
\tag{6-25}
$$

For symmetry, it is assumed that $a(1) = 0$ and $c(n) = 0$ so that every equation has exactly three elements.

Usually, Eq. (6-25) is solved iteratively. If the equations are first normalized, this means $b(k) = 1$ and a new value of $x(k)$ called y is

$$y := r(k) - a(k)*x(k-1) - c(k)*x(k+1) \tag{6-26}$$

The old value of $x(k)$ is replaced by $x(k) := y$, after the residual was calculated for every index k and iteration i as

$$e := y - x(k) \tag{6-27}$$

In the *Overrelaxation method*, every $x(k)$ is computed from

$$y := x(k) + \psi*e = x(k) + \psi*[y - x(k)] \tag{6-28}$$

For $\psi = 1$, this is again the Gauss-Seidel method. It was found that in most cases, $1.5 < \psi < 2.0$ will speed up the solution.

The set is considered solved whenever $\Sigma e^2(k)$, $k = 1, \ldots, n$ in an iteration, is less than a predetermined accuracy, ϵ.

We discuss next the problem of calculating the zero of a function (Fig. 6-4) or the ordinate x where a given function f obeys

$$f(x) = 0 \qquad (6\text{-}29)$$

Probably the most often used method to solve Eq. (6-29) is that of *Newton-Raphson*. It starts with a rough approximation, say $x(1)$. The slope through the point $x(1)$, $f[x(1)]$ in Fig. 6-4 yields a better approximation of x where $f(x) = 0$ or where $f(x)$ crosses the x-axis.

$$\tan(\alpha) = f(1)/[x(1) - x(2)]; \ f(i) = f[x(i)] \qquad (6\text{-}30)$$

$f[x(i)]$ is the value of the function (or of y) for $x(i)$. The slope, $\tan(\alpha)$, is also the derivative f' so that

$$x(2) := x(1) - f(1)/f'(1) \qquad (6\text{-}31)$$

or with x on the left being a "new" value:

$$x := x - f/f' \qquad (6\text{-}32)$$

As an example of using this formula, let us calculate $x = \sqrt{n}$. If we write $f(x) = x^2 - n = 0$ then the derivative is $f'(x) = 2*x$ so that

$$x := x - (x^2 - n)/(2*x) = 0.5*(x + n/x) \qquad (6\text{-}33)$$

The Newton-Raphson method has quadratic convergence (i.e., is very fast) and has replaced older methods which are not as fast. Still, for parallel implementation, some of these older methods may be very useful such as the *bisection* method based on the following (see Fig. 6-4).

If $f(i)*f(i-1)$ is negative, this means that $f(x)$ must have crossed the x-axis between $x(i)$ and $x(i-1)$. We then evaluate $f(x)$ at a midpoint $x(i+1) = 0.5*[x(i) + x(i-1)]$ and

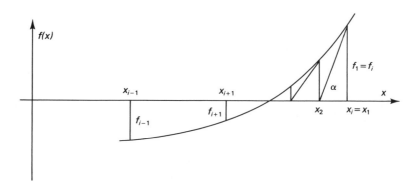

Figure 6-4   Determination of the zero of a function

check the two products $f(i)*f(i+1)$ and also $f(i-1)*f(i+1)$. The zero must be between $x(i+1)$ and either $x(i-1)$ or $x(i)$ depending on which of the products was negative.

This method has only "linear" convergence, but has none of the pitfalls of the Newton—Raphson method. Additionally, if the initial distance from $x(1)$ and $x(2)$ is "d," then at each iteration the distance is exactly halved; after i iterations, the distance shrinks to $d/(2**i)$. For instance after only ten iterations, the distance shrinks by the factor 1024. Therefore, it is known how many iterations are needed for a given accuracy.

Consider next the calculation of an integral (an area bounded by $f(x)$ and the x-axis between a and b). If the function to be integrated is that of Fig. 6-5(a) then it can be computed by summing the k strips, each of which is a rectangle. Each such strip has a height h and an area of

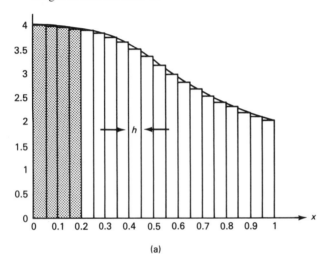

(a)

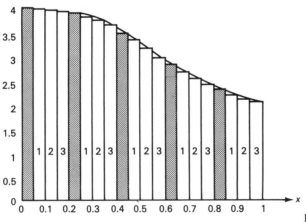

(b)

Figure 6-5   Integration of a function (calculation of an area)

$$h: = (b-a)/n; \; \text{sum} := h*\Sigma f(x+0.5*h); \; i\Sigma = 1, \ldots, n-1 \qquad (6\text{-}34)$$

Suppose that the function to be integrated is $4/(1+x)^2$. The integral for $a = 0$, $b = 1$ equals $\pi = 3.14 \ldots$ Computing it to 12 decimal places requires about 10^6 rectangles, and this is too much; we need to develop better algorithms. For trapezoidal strips

$$r[x(i)]: = 0.5*h*f[x(i)] + f(x(i+1))] \qquad (6\text{-}35)$$

is the area of a strip. Summing up all trapezoids yields

$$\text{sum} := r[x(1)] + r[x(2)] + , \ldots, + r[x(k)]; \; k = n-1; \qquad (6\text{-}36)$$

Inserting into Eq. (6-36) shows that each $f[x(i)]$ except for $i = 1$ and $i = n-1$ appears twice, so that the sum is

$$\text{sum} := h*\{0.5*\{f[x(1)] + f[x(n-1)]\} + \Sigma f[x(i)]\}; \; i\Sigma = 2, \ldots, n-2 \quad (6\text{-}37)$$

A rich source of numerical algorithms is provided by image processing. Some of them, presented below, deal with the values of picture elements, "pixels," in an area inscribed into x-y coordinates.

The algorithms are usually classified into *point* and *area* processes. In the first, the change in the value at a pixel depends only on it, in the second, it also depends on neighboring values.

Point processes may be used to enhance a picture (e.g., when a constant value is added to each pixel, the picture will be brighter). Area processes use neighborhood information to modify pixel values or assert the existence of some property of the image. They can sharpen an image, find some objects, measure image properties, remove noise in the picture, etc. For example [Daw87], if we measure how many pixels in a remote sensing (satellite) image of the earth have a certain range of values, and know that wheat corresponds to these values, the image can be classified into wheat and nonwheat areas. The machine might then be able to recognize these fields in the image.

Convolution is a classic algorithm for finding image features. If a pixel is located at point (x,y), then a 3-by-3 convolution means to set:

$$p(x,y) := \Sigma w(i,j)*p(i,j); \; i\Sigma, j\Sigma = N, \; NW, W, SW, S, SE, E, NE \qquad (6\text{-}38)$$

Figure 6-6 shows that this is a weighted average. It is similar to the solution of the Laplace problem except that in the latter only four points are taken and all weights are one.

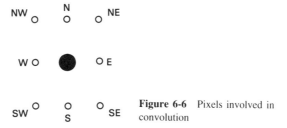

Figure 6-6   Pixels involved in convolution

Equation (6-38) is applied to every point, but this is not a point operation; every point requires the pixel values of its nine neighbors.

Repeating this operation for an area of a-by-b points requires $a*b*9$ additions and multiplications; for the usual 256-by-256 screen, this amounts to 589,824 operations. Thus, convolution may be a rather simple algorithm, but there are a number of issues to be taken care of:

1. The number of operations is so large that it is clearly a candidate for parallelization and a "new" algorithm should be developed.
2. The value $p(x,y)$ computed above *cannot replace the old value* since the old $p(x,y)$ is needed for calculating p of the neighbors of (x,y). An additional area of memory has to be declared and each new p put into it. As will be seen later, this actually helps in developing the parallel algorithms.
3. The operation should not be applied when (x,y) is a border-point.
4. The computed values may either be too large for the number of bits per pixel, or be negative and we cannot display negative intensity.

Therefore, some additional processing is needed.

Note. *The* numerical problem to be parallelized is the Fast Fourier Transform. Since there is an abundance of literature on it and it may be mathematically outside of our scope, we don't deal with it.

6–3 ON PARALLEL ALGORITHMS

An algorithm is the description of a calculation by a sequence of primitive subcomputations ("instructions"). It consists of the specification of these instructions and their sequencing. Algorithms differ in the nature of instructions and type of sequencing them.

A *sequential program* executes its instructions as a step-by-step sequence in the order in which they are written. IFs, LOOPs, etc., do not change it, because in any given case, there is only one path (thread of control) from the start of the program [Fig. 6-7(a)] to its end.

A parallel program consists of p ($p>1$) sequential programs to be executed at the same time; the result is that there are p threads of control. We thus define a *parallel algorithm* for a multiprocessor as a collection of tasks that *may* operate simultaneously to solve a given problem. A *task* was defined earlier as a sequential program which communicates with other tasks by sending and receiving messages. The collection of p tasks may be called an algorithm with p tasks, and a sequential algorithm is an algorithm with a single task.

In a multiprogramming system, there is only one CPU, but many I/O devices may be working simultaneously with it. If devices are considered as CPUs, then p is larger than 1. Multiprogramming shows also more than a single thread of control.

Multiprogrammed tasks share memory and/or communicate between themselves. They have the *potential* to be parallel, but if there is a single CPU, the program is

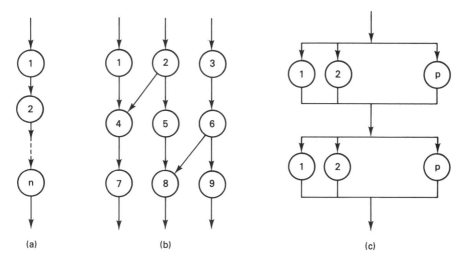

Figure 6-7   Thread of control in various algorithms

executed in an interleaving fashion. In true PPSs, the programs or tasks of a program are executed concurrently. As seen, concurrent and interleaved programming are similar— only the implementation is different.

Communications between the tasks of a program are necessary for it to work correctly and efficiently or to work at all. The points in a concurrent algorithm at which the tasks communicate with each other are called interaction points. They divide the tasks into stages. Thus, at the end of each stage, a task may communicate with other tasks; it cannot do that while processing a stage. For instance, in Fig. 6-7(b), the processes or tasks must *communicate* to *synchronize* their activities (e.g., task 4 is synchronized to start only after tasks 1 and 2 have indicated their completion). As seen, concurrent algorithms are different from sequential in that the following are required: (1) Task scheduling, namely the breakdown of the job into smaller tasks assigned to different PEs, (2) Synchronization, namely waiting for the completion of tasks when they are interdependent, and (3) Communication, namely the transfer of information between the PEs.

The algorithm of Fig. 6-7(c) would run on an ARP provided each circle of a group is the same instruction, with the control unit (CU) sending the microcode corresponding to this instruction to *all* ALUs which execute the same microcode. If the circles represent identical tasks, but different data, then the program would run on an ASP system.

We repeat next the definitions of speedup and communication, and discuss consistency and different approaches to parallelization of algorithms.

The *speedup*, as mentioned in Sec. 1-3, is $\sigma = t(1)/t(p)$ where $t(1)$ is the time required to solve the problem on a single computer using the fastest sequential algorithm and $t(p)$ is the concurrent algorithm used on p processors. If the concurrent algorithm is inefficient, the speedup may be relatively low.

It is more the algorithm than the hardware which determines the speedup. Unfortunately, whereas sequential algorithms are very well understood, parallel algorithms are not. This deficiency may be termed the software barrier. As mentioned in [Den86], "it is not a brick wall that can be broken down with a heavy ram. It is a deep, thick jungle through which slow progress will be achieved by constant chopping and hacking." The challenge before us is to devise algorithms and organize the computations so that the features of any particular machine are used to best advantage. In doing this, it may be found that an old algorithm is better for a given PPS than the best available algorithm.

Algorithms are classified according to the numerical techniques used, the data-distribution methods applied, and the communication demands. If they pose no communication demand at all, they are called "inherently parallel" algorithms, mostly based on *data* being *partitioned* among the processors. Each processor works on its own data, but all have identical programs. There exists also *task partitioning* in which processors work on different tasks, but probably identical data. In both cases it is the *communication* between the units that is to be as efficient as possible.

To show the two types of partitioning, we discuss the example of cartography (image processing). In cartography the objects (heights, streets, roads, railways, etc.) are to be extracted out of a "grey" matrix by applying various functions to each point. Data partitioning applies when the area is divided into subareas and each CPU processes all objects of a single subarea. Task partitioning applies when each processor computes a different function but in the entire area.

It is important to note that even in the case of data partitioning, some data have to be exchanged between the CPUs. Thus, in the cartography example, the values on the border between the subareas are of interest to both neighboring CPUs and have to be exchanged whenever they are recomputed by one of them.

In some algorithms (especially for ARPs), a serial computation requiring $O(n)$, where n is the "problem size," will be replaced by a parallel algorithm which requires $O(n*\log n)$ operations. *If* there are n PEs (i.e., $p = n$), then the speedup will be $n/[n*\log n/p] = p/\log(p)$. However, as pointed out in [LaV75], for Vector Processors, VPs, the total number of operations is important, so that even though vector operations can be used, at some point the $n*\log(n)$ term will dominate and the "parallel" algorithm will require more time than the scalar case. This leads to the following definition: "An implementation of an algorithm for solving a problem of size n is said to be *consistent* if the number of arithmetical operations required by this implementation as a function of n is of the same order of magnitude as required by the usual implementation on a serial computer." [LaV75]

There are two approaches to solve problems on PPSs: either to modify existing, sequential algorithms or to develop new algorithms. In both cases, the problem is that we cannot follow classical numerical analysis, since each parallel hardware organization seems to require a different algorithm, and each algorithm, a different language to express it. Thus, VPs require only the re-structuring of sequential algorithms, the "vectorization" (i.e., enabling the use of (long) vector registers). On the other hand, in multiprocessors, it is the communication and synchronization aspects that can determine the speedup and must be handled by the algorithm in an efficient way. In this chapter, we will discuss various approaches to algorithm development.

Let us exemplify this by simple numerical problems. Some general methods may be

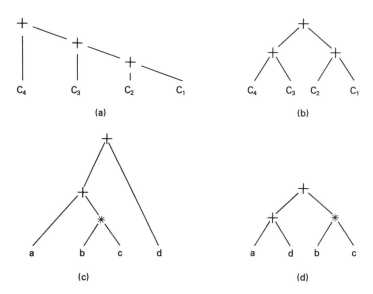

Figure 6-8   Using associativity and commutativity for concurrency

applied using the graph of the computation (called Directed Acyclic Graphs in [BaT89]). For instance, suppose that the simple first-order linear recurrence $x(i) := c(i) + x(i-1)$, $i = 1, \ldots, n$ is to be calculated. For $n = 4$, we have $x(4) := c(4) + \{c(3) + [c(2) + c(1)]\}$. This can also be written as $x(4) := [c(4) + c(3)] + [c(2) + c(1)]$. The two trees of Fig. 6-8(a) and (b) show that the use of associativity has made the depth d of the tree lower. Since each level of the tree corresponds to a time unit, the speedup is higher for lower d. It is shown in [BaT89][†] that d is the time needed by the algorithm for an unbounded number of PEs, and that if $p = \mathbf{O}(t(1)/d)$, then $t(p) = \mathbf{O}(t(1)/p)$.

> This suggests a methodology whereby we first develop a parallel algorithm as if an unlimited number of processors were available, and then adapt the algorithm to the available number of processors. . . . as long as $p = \mathbf{O}[t(1)/d]$, the availability of p processors allows us to speed up the computation by a factor proportional to p, which is the best possible. We thus see that for a number of processors nearly equal to $t(1)/d$, we obtain both optimal execution time and optimal speeding up of the computation (within constant factors). [BaT89]

The commutativity can also be used, e.g., if $a + b*c + d$ is executed as written, $d = 4$ in Fig. 6-8(c), while if it is rewritten as $(a + d) + (b*c)$, $d = 3$ of Fig. 6-8(d) results. It is obvious that $(a + b)*(a + c)$ has lower d than the equivalent $a^2 + a*c + a*b + b*c$.

The definition of an algorithm is hierarchical since an instruction can itself be seen as an algorithm to be executed by microinstructions. Generally, the *granularity* of an algorithm is a continuum from *coarse* to *fine* according to the nature of the algorithm and

---

[†]D. P. Bertsekas, J. N. Tsitsiklis: "Parallel and Distributed Computation," Prentice Hall, 1989. Quoted by permission.

its "instructions." A fine-grained algorithm is such that communication or synchronization is done on a low level (e.g., the fetch/execute cycle), while coarse-grained algorithms may use entire procedures as "instructions." Array Processors (ARPs) use fine-grained algorithms, SM multiprocessors use coarse-grained algorithms, while ASPs and MP multiprocessors use medium-grained algorithms.

That the acceptance of parallelization depends on software can be seen from sequential processing; only hardware manufacturers that have succeeded in developing a good software environment have done really well. It might be wise to take it a little slower in the hardware area and concentrate efforts on the software. As seen in Chapters 3 to 5, there are enough basic organizations and, barring a sensational new concept, it is better to spend the time developing algorithms, writing programs, and verifying the speedup. Next is a discussion on the types of algorithms suitable for various PPSs.

Communication and synchronization are achieved in multiprocessors either by the use of *shared memory* or by sending *messages*. In multiprocessors, the PEs communicate through the shared memory (so theoretically in SMs no time is wasted), through the master and broadcast (so little time is wasted in ASPs), and in Cubes the nodes communicate directly, indirectly, or through an intermediate "host." The use of shared memory results in a faster mechanism but limits the number of processors p. The message system has a higher overhead for message transfer but can be used for a larger number of processors.

We have seen in Chap. 1 that there are two types of real-time systems: the process control and the inquiry type. Process control was introduced there; next we introduce a brokerage house as an inquiry case. This is an example of a problem normally *solved on an SM*.

Consider each of the *nb brokers* of the company sitting at the phones and accepting calls from any number of customers. Obviously, up to *nb* calls may occur simultaneously, so that we certainly are dealing with a parallel processing example. The number of *customers* is not known, and in any case, a new customer may always open a new account. It is even more important to note that the company has no control over the "arrival time" of the customers; the system is asynchronous. Any of the brokers services the customers on a first-come, first-serve basis. For this, the brokers ask for the account number, a password, and the right to purchase stock, sell stock, and get a quotation. Once a call is accepted, the broker will first probably verify the data by interrogating a *common database*.

The customers are "producers" (of calls), the brokers are "servers." It often happens that a number of calls arrive almost simultaneously, but at other times the brokers wait empty-handed. To average it out and accept all calls, the computer puts arriving calls "on hold" ("he/she will be with you in a moment"). The activities of the brokers are *asynchronous* in the sense that the brokers don't know when to expect a call, they are *independent* since there is no connection among the customers and are *interacting* through the database. It corresponds to the definition of "real-time" systems given in Sec. 1-2.

The waiting customers are put on hold in a *queue* which is normally arranged in a circular way, as shown in Fig. 6-9, that is, the "tail" points to the next call to be taken "off-hold." The "head" points to where the data of the next caller is to be inserted and

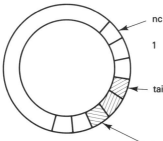

Figure 6-9   A circular queue

the number of waiting calls is head-tail. Since the queue is circular, the entry following the maximum number of callers nc is 1. Increasing the head or tail pointer will be done by tail $:= $ (tail $+ 1$) mod nc. (mod is the "modulo" function which counts up to nc and then starts from 1 again).

The system therefore has five major *components*:

1. An unknown number of customers, each with a separate account.
2. A fixed number of brokers: nb.
3. A circular queue for each of the nb brokers.
4. A number of tasks, e.g., investigations, buy or sell decisions or opening of a new account.
5. A single, common database.

Similar components exist in other parallel systems, e.g., in an airline ticket reservation system with the system searching not for a quotation but for the number of seats available on a particular flight.

For simplicity, it is assumed that the company sells stock of one type only—if you change this type into "money," the brokerage company is changed into a bank, with the brokers replaced by the tellers. Having waited in your bank in one of the nb queues, you certainly appreciate that the problem is that of parallel processing, except if the bank has only a single "sequential" teller—but who would want to stay in a bank like this?

The activities of the brokers are organized as a collection of *servers and requestors*. In the present case, customers normally request the services of the brokers. Sometimes, though, the roles are reversed, as when brokers interrogate the database. In this case the broker is the requestor, and the database is the server. In all cases, the requestor is active, the server is passive.

Having mentioned SM programming, we deal with the methods used to *solve problems on MPs*. The simplest scenario for running a program in a Cube is:

1. A problem is formulated as a graph structure of vertices (processes or tasks) and arcs (communication paths) and embedded in the graph of the Cube—its nodes and links.

2. The host downloads the (mostly identical) code into the nodes and initializes the workspaces of the nodes.

3. The code in each node is then activated. Cooperation among the nodes is achieved by exchanging messages. Message transmission to a neighboring node is not very costly, but to a distant node is costly both in the resources of the nodes and in time. Therefore, the algorithms should exhibit strong locality, i.e., messages should be transferred if possible only to neighboring nodes—if at all.

4. Intermediate and final results, as well as some status information, are accumulated in the host which then kills the node processes and terminates the computation.

As seen, communication between the units of a Cube is an integral part of the algorithm; we pay a *penalty* π for excessive communications. The penalty was defined as $\pi = K/\Omega$ or $t(\text{overhead})/t(\text{computation})$.

The performance issues to be determined for a Cube are as follows:

1. The degree to which all nodes are active depends on the *load balance* (in a completely unbalanced case, some PaMs would be idle). The more active the PaMs, the higher the efficiency. The conclusion is that we require balanced loads.

2. The higher the *penalty* ratio π, the more time is wasted on communication and less remains for calculation. The conclusion is that we strive to achieve as low a penalty as possible.

3. Since all nodes must *synchronize* at the same point in the computation, the last PaM to synchronize determines the overall speed. All PaMs waiting for the last PaM are under-utilized, the load is not balanced, and the efficiency is lowered.

To improve load balance, we could decrease the grain size since more chunks of smaller size can be distributed in a more even fashion. We could also increase the degree of multiprogramming (per node). To improve the ratio π we should increase the grain size since this means there will be relatively more calculations to be done between communication periods. *As seen, load balance and reducing the penalty π require opposite actions.* We could also restructure to have fewer, larger messages (e.g., it is better to deal with one long message instead of having to transfer four short messages, see Fig. 6-10(a)]. Another way to reduce the penalty π is to combine multiple "logical" messages into single messages as in Fig. 6-10(b). To improve the synchronization, we should send needed values as soon as possible, and reorder or modify the algorithm to eliminate synchronization where not needed.

As an example, suppose a Cube of 1024 nodes is used to solve the Laplace problem (Sec. 6-2). The programmer may divide the entire area into 32 segments of 32 points each. Each node calculates the solution inside its segment and, as the system of equations converges to a solution, periodically communicates its results to nodes simulating neighboring segments. The entire area could also have been left as one segment of 1024 points. This case is data partitioning; the first was task partitioning and is treated in the next section. The communication penalty π depends on how the area was divided and in turn determines the efficiency. It would be different for the two algorithms.

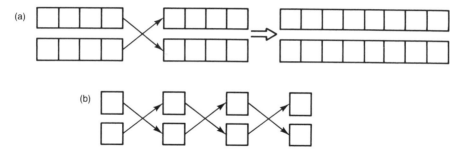

Figure 6-10   Restructuring of algorithms for running them on Cubes

Having discussed parallel algorithms in general, let us next deal with the best-known paradigm of parallel computation.

6–4 DIVIDE-AND-COMMUNICATE ALGORITHMS

The *Divide-and-Communicate* paradigm (I don't like divide-and-conquer and will use *DaC*) can be briefly summarized as follows: Divide the problem into p tasks. Solve these tasks separately and concurrently, and then combine the solutions into a solution of the original problem.

The DaC method is used for both SM and MP multiprocessors. Each complex system is assumed to have associated with it a domain of objects or data. The first step in concurrent computation consists of *decomposing this domain into several grains*. In an SM one must decompose the algorithm over the CPUs, but the data can be left undivided in the shared memory. In the case of Cubes we must make the domain decomposition explicit and divide the domain into "chunks" of one or more grains to be associated with each node of a Cube. Each chunk will be controlled by a separate computer program, a *task*. The "chunks" communicate through the nodes via *message passing*. Making the chunks relatively large will reduce π, but requires a sizable amount of memory for each chunk.

A number of algorithms will be used to exemplify the DaC method. The first simple DaC algorithm is to calculate the sum

$$z = \Sigma \sin[x(i)]; \; i\Sigma = 1, \ldots, 1000 \tag{6-39}$$

where $p = 10$. The *divide* part is to calculate 10 sums (one per CPU):

$$y = \Sigma \sin[x(k)]; \; k\Sigma = (q-1)*100+1, \ldots, q*100 \tag{6-40}$$

where $q = 1, \ldots, p$ is the number of the CPU and therefore $k\Sigma = 1 \ldots 100, 101 \ldots 200, \ldots, 901 \ldots 1000$. These sums can be computed completely independently. The *communicate* part of the algorithm consists of sending the nine partial sums from nine CPUs to CPU No.10 (or to the master) and summing these y's into the required result z.

The ratio can be computed easily for this algorithm. Using ϕ for the time to calculate the (sine) function, α to add two numbers, τ to transfer a word, and ζ for (bus) synchronization, leads to

$$\rho = (100*\phi + 100*\alpha + 10*\tau + \tau + \zeta)/(1000*\phi + 1000*\alpha) \qquad (6\text{-}41)$$

Neglecting the additions as compared to the rest, we get

$$\rho = 1/10 + \tau/(100*\phi) + \zeta/(1000*\phi) \qquad (6\text{-}42)$$

The time ϕ to calculate the sine functions is not large but assumed to be higher than the transfer of a single word between the CPUs (τ) or their synchronization (ζ). Therefore, the time for communication and synchronization to be added to $1/p$ is small. In general, the larger the granularity or the ratio of times ϕ/τ and ϕ/ζ, the higher the speedup. In order to decrease the ratio of communication to computation, *granularity should not be too fine*.

The load is not balanced since the PaM that computes the 100 sine values near zero has very little to do: the Taylor series has only a few terms. The PaM that calculates the 100 sines near 90 degrees has to account for a long series. To improve the load balance, the summation could proceed for $q = 1$ as in Eq. (6-43):

$$y(1): = \Sigma \sin[x(1)] + \ldots + \sin[x(10)] + \ldots + \sin[x(901)] + \ldots + \sin[x(910] \qquad (6\text{-}43)$$

instead of per Eq. (6-40), and similarly for $q = 2. \ldots p$. Note: If the same problem is solved with $p = 5$ PaMs, i.e., by a coarser algorithm, the chunks are larger, and π may be reduced.

To increase the granularity of ϕ/τ and ϕ/ζ, let us replace the sines by more complicated functions $f(x)$. The summation may calculate the area bounded by $f(x)$ and the x-axis between 0 and 1 in Fig. 6-5(a):

$$s := h * \Sigma f[x(i)]; \ i\Sigma = 1, \ldots, k \qquad (6\text{-}44)$$

Figure 6.5 shows the area divided into 20 strips each of width h. Assume $p = 5$. In (a), each node computes four consecutive strips, in (b) every fifth strip (the black strips are calculated on node "0"). The values of s have to be accumulated. Such a summation suffers from the Haydn effect, but for balancing the load the schedule in Fig. 6-5(b) might be better because if the function is irregular, i.e., it takes different amounts of time to compute it at various $x(i)$, the load will stay approximately balanced. This is a case of *static load balancing*. In Pascal, these two cases are shown in Code 6-1.

```
procedure sm (pi: VAR REAL; h: REAL);      -- The same for this one.
begin                                      begin
  s,x : REAL;                                s,x : REAL;  j : INTEGER;
  s := 0.0;                                  s := 0.0;  j := me+1-p;
  for i := me+1..me+4 do begin               for i := 1 to p do begin
    x := h*(i-0.5);                            j := j+p;  x := h*(j-0.5);
    s := s+f(x);                               s := s+f(x);
  end;                                       end;
  pi := h*s;                                 pi := h*s;
end;                                       end;  -- of procedure sm;
```

Let us follow the two cases for node *me* = 0 and a few strips.

```
x=h*(1-0.5)=0.5*h;  s=0+f(0.5*h);      x=h*(1-0.5)=0.5*h;   s=0+f(0.5*h);
x=h*(2-0.5)=1.5*h;  s=s+f(1.5*h);      x=h*(5-0.5)=4.5*h;   s=s+f(4.5*h);
x=h*(3-0.5)=2.5*h;  s=s+f(2.5*h);      x=h*(9-0.5)=8.5*h;   s=s+f(8.5*h);
x=h*(4-0.5)=3.5*h;  s=s+f(3.5*h);      x=h*(13-0.5)=12.5*h; s=s+f(12.5*h);
```

The rectangular formula has an error of $O(h)$. If we use the trapezoidal rule, the global error will be $O(h^2)$. To reduce it, we might use the very popular Simpson's rule (see also problem 7-3):

$$\text{area of two strips} := h*[f(i) + 4*f(i+1) + f(2)] \tag{6-45}$$

which has an error of $O(h^4)$. For $h = 0.1$, the error would be reduced from 0.1 to 0.01 to 0.0001.

To calculate the area by Simpson's rule [Fig. 6-5(a)], the summation is

$$\text{area} = h*[f(0) + 4*f(1) + f(2)]/3 + h*[f(2) + 4*f(3) + f(4)] + \ldots \tag{6-46}$$

In this case, the even values of $f(x)$, except for $x=0.0$ and $x=1.0$, are computed in every one of the PaMs and then transferred to the ''next'' PaM. The transfer can proceed simultaneously like in a pipeline.

Suppose two PaMs calculate the area. The ''chunks'' in Fig. 6-5 will then be larger, the penalty π will decrease, but at the same time the load may be unbalanced because more function values are to be computed and the times on the PaMs may be different. Better examples for showing the contradictory requirements are given later.

The summation of n numbers discussed in Chap. 4 while dealing with the Haydn effect is almost the same as the above algorithm. Each CPU bears the k-th number. The tree of computations is shown in Fig. 6-11(a) (with *i-j* representing the sum of elements i to j).

Comparing with summation of the sines, the speedup has decreased because instead of the time of ϕ, we need only α. Recall that the speedup is reduced by a factor of $O(\log p)$. In order to increase it we need to have lower p and coarser granularity, and for this to *distribute tasks—not single operations*. This was exemplified at the close of Chap. 4.

Suppose we change this example into that of computing all partial sums of an array of numbers. It could be used to balance a checkbook. Put into an array the initial checkbook balance, followed by the amounts of the checks as negative and deposits as positive numbers. Computing the partial sums produces all the intermediate balances and the final balance.

In a single computer this is obviously a very sequential algorithm, since each balance requires the previous one. Because of the Haydn effect in a parallel algorithm [Fig. 6-11(a)] most of the CPUs are idle most of the time: During iteration i, only $p/(2**i)$ processors are active, and indeed half of the processors are never used. Note that the sum from i to m can be written as the addition of a sum from i to k plus a sum from $k+1$ to m. On a PPS this can be used as a parallel algorithm [Fig. 6-11(b)], which will replace each $x(k)$ by the sum from 0 to k (i.e., the entire sum up to this point). Overall, many more

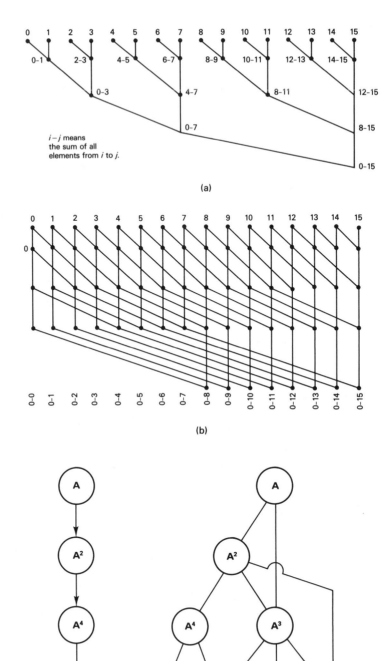

Figure 6-11 Computational trees for various algorithms

254

calculations are performed, but the process will complete in the same time it took to calculate the first sum; sequentialization is avoided by performing logically redundant additions. The algorithm keeps more processors busy: during step j, $p - 2**(j-1)$ CPUs are in use. The speedup though is higher only if all partial sums are actually required.

Another case is when the powers of a matrix are to be calculated. If only the binary powers are required, then they may be calculated as in Fig. 6-11(c), where each circle squares or multiplies matrices. If other powers of **A** are also of interest, the PEs can be used as in Fig. 6-11(d).

The solution of the Laplace problem can also use the DaC paradigm. In Fig. 6-12, the entire area is split into p "slices" with each slice processed by another of the p CPUs. At the start of every iteration, a time κ is needed for exchanging results for the boundary points and for synchronization. One of the advantages of this algorithm is that the number of slices was chosen to be p. Another advantage is that the slices may be chosen so as to balance the communication between the units, which also will increase the efficiency of the program.

Some search and sort algorithms also use DaC methods. Divide the list into p sublists and process each separately. Then exchange results.

In the Introduction, so-called inherently parallel problems were mentioned. From the above, it can be seen that *an inherently parallel program is a divide-and-communicate algorithm for which synchronization and communication times are negligible*. If the times are neglected, the speedup will be p. Therefore, inherently parallel algorithms yield either an ideal speedup, or it can be claimed the PPS has the same throughput and response time, but at a fraction of the cost of a single CPU (thus disproving Grosh's law).

The following algorithms can be classified as inherently parallel:

1. *All point processes for image processing.* This is so because in all of them the function to be computed at point (i,j) depends only on the pixel value $p(i,j)$. Therefore, nothing has to be communicated.

2. *The convolution algorithm.* If in each iteration an additional area of memory is set

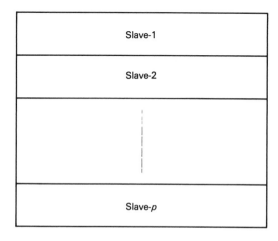

Figure 6-12 Division of an area for solving the Laplace equation

aside for the new values, then the original values are not changed, and only at the end of an iteration, the areas are swapped. $\kappa = 0$ if this swapping requires no time.

3. The Ballistic Missile Defense and other "associative problems" as discussed in the first part of this book.

Obviously, no other algorithms fit all types of PPSs as well as inherently parallel methods, but the numerical properties and stability have to be rechecked. In short, the algorithms have to be rediscovered; currently, there is a substantial amount of work in this area.

We complete this section by discussing a divide-and-communicate algorithm that is not only inherently parallel but seems to have an efficiency above 100%. It is the algorithm for *least-squares estimation* and can be described in the following simplified form [Wal86].[†††]

Suppose we intend to estimate the values of z as a function of y [Fig. 6-13(a)]. In order to get a functional relationship, a number of measurements are taken. The pairs of values $[z(i), y(i)]$ of these measurements are not on a straight line, mostly because of measurement errors. However, we may draw a straight line $z = a + b*y$ that passes through some "center" of the measurements, i.e., so that the deviation of the measured points from the line is in some way minimal.

If we have made the measurements, then the m equations

$$e(i) = z(i) - [a + b*y(i)]; i = 1, \ldots, m \tag{6-47}$$

define the errors $e(i)$, $i = 1, 2, \ldots, m$. Eq. (6-47) may also be written as

$$\begin{vmatrix} z(1) \\ \cdot \\ \cdot \\ z(m) \end{vmatrix} - \begin{vmatrix} 1 & y(1) \\ \cdot & \cdot \\ \cdot & \cdot \\ 1 & y(m) \end{vmatrix} * \begin{vmatrix} a \\ b \end{vmatrix} = \begin{vmatrix} e(1) \\ \cdot \\ \cdot \\ e(m) \end{vmatrix} \tag{6-48}$$

or, using an m-by-2 matrix $\mathbf{M}$ of 1's and m known $y(i)$'s

$$\mathbf{e} = \mathbf{z} - \mathbf{M} * \mathbf{x} \tag{6-49}$$

The "true" values should yield $\mathbf{e} = 0$. We seek therefore the best estimate of $\mathbf{x}$, say $\mathbf{x}'$, such that $\mathbf{e}$ is a minimum.

If we define $\mathbf{x}'$ so that $\Sigma e(i)$ is minimal, then we may have many large positive deviations reduced to zero by an equal number of large negative deviations. Thus, despite the large deviations, the algorithm would detect nothing. It seems better to use the criterion *minimize* $\Sigma e^2(i)$ for $i\Sigma = 1, \ldots, m$. This sum may also be written as the *scalar product*:

$$\mathbf{e}^T * \mathbf{e} = [e(1), \ldots, e(m)] * [e(1), \ldots, e(m)]^T \tag{6-50}$$

with T as "transpose." The scalar product yields as a result a scalar:

†††Y. Wallach. *Calculations and Programs for Power System Networks*. Prentice Hall, 1986. By permission.

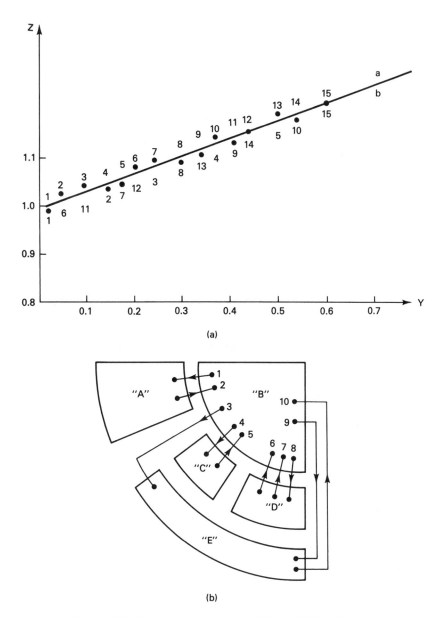

Figure 6-13 Least-squares estimation (a) Linear (b) Network case

$$U(x) = \mathbf{e}^T * \mathbf{e} = (\mathbf{z} - \mathbf{M}*\mathbf{x})^T*(\mathbf{z} - \mathbf{M}*\mathbf{x}) = (\mathbf{z}^T - \mathbf{x}^T*\mathbf{M}^T)* (\mathbf{z} - \mathbf{M}*\mathbf{x}) \quad (6\text{-}51)$$

$$U(x) = \mathbf{z}^T*\mathbf{z} - \mathbf{z}^T*\mathbf{M}*\mathbf{x} - \mathbf{x}^T*\mathbf{M}^T*\mathbf{z} + \mathbf{x}^T*\mathbf{M}^T*\mathbf{M}*\mathbf{x} \quad (6\text{-}52)$$

Since U is a scalar, each of its summands is a scalar. Any scalar "c" equals its own transposed values $c^T = c$ (if $c = 2$ then $2^T = 2$) so that the second and third product in Eq. (6-52) are equal:

$$\mathbf{z}^T*\mathbf{M}*\mathbf{x} = (\mathbf{z}^T*\mathbf{M}*\mathbf{x})^T = \mathbf{x}^T*\mathbf{M}^T*\mathbf{z} \quad (6\text{-}53)$$

Inserting yields

$$U(x) = \mathbf{z}^T*\mathbf{z} - 2*\mathbf{x}^T*\mathbf{M}^T*\mathbf{z} + \mathbf{x}^T*\mathbf{M}^T*\mathbf{M}*\mathbf{x} \quad (6\text{-}54)$$

The differentiation of the last term (with x^2) yields $2*\mathbf{M}^T*\mathbf{M}*\mathbf{x}$, of the second term yields $-2*\mathbf{M}^T*\mathbf{z}$, and since $\mathbf{z}^T*\mathbf{z}$ does not depend on $\mathbf{x}$, its derivative is zero. The condition for a minimum is $2*\mathbf{M}^T*\mathbf{M}*\mathbf{x} - 2*\mathbf{M}^T*\mathbf{z} = 0$

$$(\mathbf{M}^T*\mathbf{M})*\mathbf{x} = \mathbf{M}^T*\mathbf{z} \quad (6\text{-}55)$$

Since matrix $\mathbf{M}$ and the vector of measured values $\mathbf{z}$ are known, the right-hand side is constant, while $\mathbf{M}^T*\mathbf{M}$ is a known matrix, say $\mathbf{A}$. To calculate the vector $\mathbf{x}$ we have to solve a set of linear equations, the so-called *normal equations* of (again) Gauss. In the particular case of Eq. (6-48), the solution can be written explicitly as

$$a = (f*d - c*g)/(m*d - c^2); \quad b = (g - c*a)/d$$

where $c = \Sigma y(k)$; $d = \Sigma y^2(k)$; $f = \Sigma z(k)$; $g = \Sigma y(k)*z(k)$

Let us return to the estimation of a linear function, Fig. 6-13(a). A concurrent algorithm would solve p subproblems each with m/p measurements instead of solving the original problem with m measurements.

Assume that $m = 15$ and $p = 3$. Two cases are indicated in Fig. 6-13(a):

a. Use points {1,2,3,4,5}, {6,7,8,9,10}, and {11,12,13,14,15}, or
b. Use points {1,4,7,10,13}, {2,5,8,11,14}, and {3,6,9,12,15}

This problem was run and it was found that the sum of squares of errors in case **a** was $(5.5113 + 3.9011 + 4.9531)/10^4$, whereas in case **b** it was $(2.3255 + 1.2618 + 1.7775)/10^4$, or about three times lower; the second algorithm is better. The reason is that in case **b**, the slopes are closer to an average slope.

Usually, the error vector includes a nonlinear vector function $\mathbf{f}(\mathbf{x})$. In that case, in order to estimate $\mathbf{x}$, an initial value $\mathbf{x}(0)$ is assumed and a Taylor expansion approximates the function near this point:

$$\mathbf{f}(\mathbf{x}) = \mathbf{f}[\mathbf{x}(0)] + \mathbf{f}'[\mathbf{x}(0)]*\Delta\mathbf{x} + \mathbf{f}''[\mathbf{x}(0)]*\Delta\mathbf{x}^2/2 + \ldots \quad (6\text{-}56)$$

Disregarding higher than linear terms and using vectors and matrices, we have $\mathbf{f}(\mathbf{x}) \approx \mathbf{f}(0) + \mathbf{J}(0)*\Delta\mathbf{x}$, where the Jacobian matrix is defined through $J(k,m) = \partial f(k)/\partial x(m)$ and $\mathbf{J}(i)$ and $\mathbf{f}(i)$ are a shorter notation for $\mathbf{J}[x(i)]$ and $\mathbf{f}[x(i)]$.

Inserting $\mathbf{f} = \mathbf{f}(0) + \mathbf{J}(0)*\Delta\mathbf{x}$ into $\mathbf{e} = \mathbf{z} - \mathbf{f}$ and letting $\Delta\mathbf{z} = \mathbf{z} - \mathbf{f}(0)$ yields

$$U(\mathbf{x}) = \mathbf{e}^T * \mathbf{e} = [\Delta\mathbf{z} - \mathbf{J}(0) * \Delta\mathbf{x}]^T * [\Delta\mathbf{z} - \mathbf{J}(0) * \Delta\mathbf{x}] \tag{6-57}$$

Comparing with Eq. (6-51) shows that $\Delta\mathbf{z}$, $\Delta\mathbf{x}$, and $\mathbf{J}(0)$ replace $\mathbf{z}$, $\mathbf{x}$, and $\mathbf{M}$ respectively, and the resulting equation can be obtained from Eq. (6-55) as

$$\mathbf{J}^T(0) * \mathbf{J}(0) * \Delta\mathbf{x} = \mathbf{J}^T(0) * \Delta\mathbf{z} \tag{6-58}$$

Defining a *normal matrix* $\mathbf{A}$ we have the final form

$$\mathbf{A} * \Delta\mathbf{x} = \mathbf{b} \text{ where } \mathbf{A} = \mathbf{J}^T(0) * \mathbf{J}(0) \text{ and } \mathbf{b} = \mathbf{J}^T(0) * \Delta\mathbf{z} \tag{6-59}$$

This is a set of linear equations. If higher order terms of the Taylor expansion of $\mathbf{f}(\mathbf{x})$ were really negligible, the solution would yield the correct $\mathbf{x}$. Since this is not so and additionally the Jacobian $\mathbf{J}$ is itself a function of $\mathbf{x}$, we must view Eq. (6-59) as a prescription for an iterative procedure which in a finite number of steps will compute $\mathbf{x}$ to a certain degree of accuracy. Vector $\mathbf{x}$ should therefore be changed according to:

$$\mathbf{x}^{n+1} := \mathbf{x}^n + (\mathbf{J}^T * \mathbf{J})^{-1} * \mathbf{J}^T * [\mathbf{z} - \mathbf{f}(n)]; \tag{6-60}$$

where $\mathbf{J}$ is the Jacobian at iteration n. Eq. (6-60) is followed until convergence is achieved.

This method was parellelized for electric power networks in [Wal86] as follows: a network as the one shown in Fig. 6-13(b) is "cut" into subnetworks, each of which is then solved (under certain mathematical conditions) on a separate CPU. Assuming that the initial number of variables is n, that the number of CPUs is p, and that each subnetwork has n/p variables, in each iteration we solve concurrently p linear sets each of dimension n/p. Since the operation count for solving linear sets is $\mathbf{O}(n^3)$, each subproblem requires $\mathbf{O}(n^3/p^3)$. On a single computer we have an operations count of $\mathbf{O}(n^3)$. The resulting speedup is

$$\sigma = n^3/(n^3/p^3) = p^3 \tag{6-61}$$

This is too good to be true. It would mean for a network of $n = 1,000$ that $\sigma = 1,000^3 = 10^9$ or 1,000,000,000—a budgetary number. In reality, the speedup was measured to be more like n^2, but this still is an extremely high value. It shows that the efficiency can be higher than 100%. (The reason is that we had $\mathbf{O}(n^3)$ for the sequential algorithm and no communication penalty π.)

The conclusion of this section is that the divide-and communicate paradigm is an efficient method indeed.

6–5 REORDERING METHODS

Another method of parallelization is based on changing the sequence of operations in order to increase the percentage of those computations which proceed in parallel. Such reordering is known as "diakoptics" in electrical engineering and "substructuring" in structural engineering. For example, suppose the network of Fig. 6-14(a) is torn (diakoptics means tearing in Greek) on the circled nodes and numbered so that these nodes are numbered last. This will produce a "block-bordered, diagonal" matrix of Fig. 6-14(b),

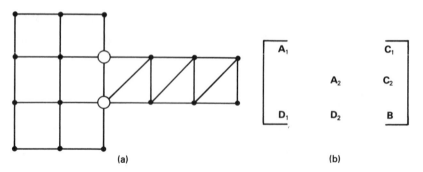

(a)   (b)

Figure 6-14   Diakoptics: Tearing and the resulting matrix

where the **A** matrices represent the two parts of the network, the **B** matrix represents the interface points, and the **C** and **D** matrices represent the dependencies between the interface nodes and the two regions. It is easy to parallelize the inversion of such matrices [Wal86].

We next discuss in more detail how to parallelize the Gauss-Seidel procedure of Sec. 6-2 by reordering the computations. To remind the reader, in order to solve $A*x = b$, the sequence of vector approximations x^m for $m = 0,1,2,\ldots$ is formed. A general equation for row i is

$$A(i,1)*x(1) + A(i,2)*x(2) + \ldots + A(i,i-1)*x(i-1) + A(i,i)*x(i)$$
$$+ A(i,i+1)*x(i+1) + \ldots + A(i,n)*x(n) = b(i)$$

Suppose next that this equation is divided by $A(i,i)$ and written as

$$x(i) := b(i) - A(i,1)*x(1) - \ldots - A(i,i-1)*x(i-1)$$
$$- A(i,i+1)*x(i+1) - \ldots - A(i,n)*x(n) \qquad (6\text{-}62)$$

where the elements $A(i,j)$ were changed because of division by $A(i,i)$.

The so computed $x(i)$ is called y. It is considered a new and better approximation to $x(i)$. A still better approximation can be calculated by $x(i) := \psi * (y-x(i))$. The *overrelaxation factor* $\psi = 1$ represents the Gauss-Seidel method with $x(i)$ on the right as the "old," and a "new" and improved value of $x(i)$ on the left. Old is the value of $x(i)$ before, new is the value of $x(i)$ at the end of the current iteration.

As "everybody" knows (Sec. 6-2), the Gauss-Seidel method is "purely sequential" since it computes or iterates strictly according to the sequence: $x(1), x(2), \ldots ,x(n)$ and again from $x(1)$. For any $x(i)$, the values of $x(i-1), x(i-2), \ldots ,x(1)$ are needed. For starting the calculation that is for computing $x(1)$, old values for $x(2), \ldots x(n)$ have to be either known or assumed.

It will next be shown how to parallelize this strictly sequential method, but for clarity it will also be exemplified on a very small set of six equations Eq. (6-63):

$$A(1,1)*x(1)+A(1,2)*x(2)+A(1,3)*x(3)+A(1,4)*x(4)+A(1,5)*x(5)+A(1,6)*x(6)=b(1)$$
$$A(2,1)*x(1)+A(2,2)*x(2)+A(2,3)*x(3)+A(2,4)*x(4)+A(2,5)*x(5)+A(2,6)*x(6)=b(2)$$

$$A(3,1)*x(1)+A(3,2)*x(2)+A(3,3)*x(3)+A(3,4)*x(4)+A(3,5)*x(5)+A(3,6)*x(6)=b(3)$$
$$A(4,1)*x(1)+A(4,2)*x(2)+A(4,3)*x(3)+A(4,4)*x(4)+A(4,5)*x(5)+A(4,6)*x(6)=b(4)$$
$$A(5,1)*x(1)+A(5,2)*x(2)+A(5,3)*x(3)+A(5,4)*x(4)+A(5,5)*x(5)+A(5,6)*x(6)=b(5)$$
$$A(6,1)*x(1)+A(6,2)*x(2)+A(6,3)*x(3)+A(6,4)*x(4)+A(6,5)*x(5)+A(6,6)*x(6)=b(6)$$

First, two temporary vectors z and t are defined and a row i of Eq. (6-62) is rewritten as

$$z(i) := \Sigma A(i,k)*x(k); \ k\Sigma = 1, \ldots ,i-1 \tag{6-64}$$

$$t(i) := b(i) - \Sigma A(i,k)*x(k); \ k\Sigma = i + 1, \ldots ,n \tag{6-65}$$

$$x(i) = y := t(i) - z(i) \tag{6-66}$$

Equation (6-66) can be used for a parallel version of the algorithm because $z(i)$ is computed at iteration m, but $t(i)$ at iteration $m-1$.

In an ASP, all $A(i,j)$ are transferred during an initial step to the slaves so that each slave's memory holds a slice of $h = n/p$ rows of $\mathbf{A}$. In the same way, slices of vector $\mathbf{b}$ are transferred. The master assumes an initial vector $\mathbf{x}$, calculates initial vector $\mathbf{t}$ and transfers the entire vector $\mathbf{x}$ and slices of $\mathbf{t}$ to the slaves. Additionally, all elements of vector $\mathbf{z}$ are made zero.

The iterations consist of sequential and parallel steps which alternate.

In the sequential step, the master calculates a new value of $y = x(i)$, a value of the residual r, and accumulates an error e, as follows:

$$r := y - x(i); \ e := e + r*r \tag{6-67}$$

Having done this, y replaces $x(i)$ by the Gauss-Seidel method, or by the Successive Over-Relaxation (*SOR*) method. In both cases, the sequential step ends with the residual r and the new value of $x(i)$ transferred by the master to *all* p slaves.

In the parallel step, the slaves update vectors $\mathbf{z}$ and $\mathbf{t}$ through

$$z(i) := z(i) + A(j,i)*x(i) \text{ for } i \text{ in a range of the slice} \tag{6-68}$$

$$t(i) := t(i) + A(j,i)*r \text{ for } i \text{ in a range of the slice} \tag{6-69}$$

Equation (6-69) when expanded yields $t(i) := t(i)+A(j,i)*[y-x(i)]$, which means that the new value y has replaced the old $x(i)$ in $t(i)$.

Recall that $\Sigma A(i,j)*x(j) = b(i)$ can be rewritten as

$$x(i):=[b(j)-\Sigma A(i,j*x(j)]-\Sigma A(i,k)*x(k); i\Sigma=1,\ldots,6; \ j\Sigma=1,2,3; \ k\Sigma=4,5,6,$$

so that $x(i):=t(i)-z(i)$. For Eq. (6-63), assume values for $x(1),\ldots,x(6)$, and set $\mathbf{z}:=0$. Note that $z(1) = 0$ and $t(6) = b(6)$ will not change. Initialize also vector $\mathbf{t}$.

For $p = 2$ and the two tasks inside braces, we then have:

```
Compute y := t(1) - z(1); r(1) := rr = |y - x(1)|; x(1) := y;
        {z(2) := z(2) + A(2,1)*y; z(3) := z(3) + A(3,1)*y;}
        {z(4) := z(4) + A(4,1)*y; z(5) := z(5) + A(5,1)*y;
                                  z(6) := z(6) +A(6,1)*y;}
```

```
Compute y := t(2) - z(2); r(2) := rr = |y - x(2)|; x(2) := y;
       {t(1) := t(1) + A(1,2)*rr); z(3) := z(3) + A(3,2)*y;}
        {z(4) := z(4) + A(4,2)*y; z(5) := z(5) + A(5,2)*y;
                                  z(6) := z(6) + A(6,2)*y;}

Compute y := t(3) - z(3); r(3) := rr = |y - x(3)|; x(3) := y;
       {t(1) := t(1) + A(1,3)*rr); t(2) := t(2) + A(2,3)*rr);}
        {z(4) := z(4) + A(4,3)*y; z(5) := z(5) + A(5,3)*y;
                                  z(6) := z(6) + A(6,3)*y;}

Compute y := t(4) - z(4); r(4) := rr = |y - x(4)|; x(4) := y;
       {t(1) := t(1) + A(1,4)*rr); t(2) := t(2) + A(2,4)*rr);
                                   t(3) := t(3) + A(3,4)*rr;}
        {z(5) := z(5) + A(5,4)*y; z(6) := z(6) + A(6,4)*y;}

Compute y := t(5) - z(5); r(5) := rr = |y - x(5)|; x(5) := y;
       {t(1) := t(1) + A(1,5)*rr); t(2) := t(2) + A(2,5)*rr);
                                   t(3) := A(3,5)*rr;}
       {t(4) := t(4) + A(4,5)*rr; z(6) := z(6) + A(6,5)*y;}

Compute y := t(6) - z(6); r(6) := rr = |y - x(6)|; x(6) := y;
       {t(1) := t(1) + A(1,6)*rr); t(2) := t(2) + A(2,6)*rr);
                                   t(3) := t(3) + A(3,6)*rr;}
       {t(4) := t(4) + A(4,6)*rr; t(5) := t(5) + A(5,6)*rr;}
```

This completes one iteration for which the error is $\Sigma r(i)*r(i)$. The following possibilities to proceed exist:

1. The *Jacobi method* results if another vector **x** is computed by

$$x(i) := t(i) - z(i); \; i = 1,\ldots,n \qquad (6\text{-}70)$$

where the **x** on the left is yet another new value. Since the slices of the two vectors **t** and **z** reside in the slaves, this step is a parallel step. Unfortunately, in order to begin a new iteration, the values of **t** have to be updated, because the most recent values of **x** must substitute for the old ones. This can be done in parallel, if the master first collects the most recent **x** and broadcasts it to the slaves. Since the convergence of the Jacobi method is not as high as that of the Gauss-Seidel or the SOR methods, and since the amount of work in preparing for a new iteration is considerable, the Jacobi method will not be used.

2. If the updating of the vector **t** is removed, it is possible to follow an iteration, now called a "down-iteration," with an "up-iteration," i.e., starting with $t(n) := b(n)$, iterate again but now with $i = n-1, n-2$, and so on until $i = 1$. This step is completely symmetrical to the down iteration, with the role of **z** and **t** interchanged. It was even shown in [CaW77a] and [CaW79] that the amount of work compared to the Gauss-Seidel method is reduced by 50%. Unfortunately, this method is inefficient for parallelization because it suffers from a different type of the Haydn

effect. When an $x(i)$ in slave k is calculated, vector $\mathbf{z}$ is updated only in slaves k, $k+1$ down to p, but slaves 1 to $k-1$ do nothing. The reverse is true for the up-iteration and vector $\mathbf{t}$.

3. Note that at the end of the iteration as described by Eqs. (6-64) to (6-69), a new vector $\mathbf{t}$ is known and therefore another down iteration can be started. This is the method programmed in Sec. 9-4.

The speedup of this method can be computed as follows: The initialization step does not have to be considered, since it is a single step and there may be many iterations. The sequential step requires four binary operations ω, and the transfer τ of two values to all the slaves; both have first to be transferred from the slave to the master. Altogether the number of required operations is

$$t(s) = 4 * \omega + 4 * \tau \tag{6-71}$$

In the parallel step, each slave except the one in which $x(i)$ is calculated needs $4*n$ operations for each of its h rows. The slave where $x(i)$ was calculated needs $4*n$ operations for only $h-1$ rows. If $h-1 \simeq h$ then, for each slave, the number of operations is

$$t(p) = h*n*4*\omega = 4*n^2*\omega/p; \ h = n/p \tag{6-72}$$

There is one synchronization per iteration. Collecting the terms and noting that for sequential execution $t(1) = 2*n^2*\omega$ yields the time ratio

$$\rho = 1/p + 2/(n^2) + (2*\tau)/(n^2*\omega) + \zeta/(2*n^2*\omega) \tag{6-73}$$

If τ and ζ are short and n is large, then all terms can be neglected compared to the first—therefore, the optimal speedup is achieved. If τ and ζ are large, then this algorithm would result in a low efficiency.

The next example is that of directly solving a tridiagonal set $\mathbf{A}*\mathbf{x} = \mathbf{b}$ by, say, the recursive doubling method [Sto73] and the cyclic reduction method [LaV75]. The recursive doubling method is designed for a parallel processor such as Illiac-IV [Wan81]. (Actually, a similar method was already developed in 1970 in [EaW70].) The cyclic reduction method is more effective on a vector computer. The method of [Wan81] can be applied to both SIMD and pipeline computers. Another method for a MIMD system was published in [Hea83]. These methods are summarized in [OaV85] and were developed in [Hoc65, Hel76, Sto73]. In the next section an additional method, especially suited for ASP systems, is developed. We exemplify the tridiagonal system by

$$
\begin{vmatrix}
b(1) & c(1) & 0 & 0 & 0 & 0 & 0 \\
a(2) & b(2) & c(2) & 0 & 0 & 0 & 0 \\
0 & a(3) & b(3) & c(3) & 0 & 0 & 0 \\
0 & 0 & a(4) & b(4) & c(4) & 0 & 0 \\
0 & 0 & 0 & a(5) & b(5) & c(5) & 0 \\
0 & 0 & 0 & 0 & a(6) & b(6) & c(6) \\
0 & 0 & 0 & 0 & 0 & a(7) & b(7)
\end{vmatrix}
*
\begin{vmatrix}
x(1) \\ x(2) \\ x(3) \\ x(4) \\ x(5) \\ x(6) \\ x(7)
\end{vmatrix}
=
\begin{vmatrix}
r(1) \\ r(2) \\ r(3) \\ r(4) \\ r(5) \\ r(6) \\ r(7)
\end{vmatrix}
\tag{6-74}
$$

The solution for any i may be calculated from

$$x(i) := [r(i) - a(i)*x(i-1) - c(i)*x(i+1)]/b(i) \qquad (6\text{-}75)$$

This equation shows that the values of $x(i-1)$ and $x(i+1)$ are needed in order to compute $x(i)$. This indicates that the calculation may be difficult to parallelize.

In the *odd-even reduction* we start by eliminating the odd-numbered variables from the even-numbered equations. In Eq.(6-74) the four values of *odd* i are:

```
x(1)  := (r(1)-a(1)*x(0)-c(1)*x(2))/b(1);  (a(1)=x(0)=0)
x(3)  := (r(3)-a(3)*x(2)-c(3)*x(4))/b(3);
x(5)  := (r(5)-a(5)*x(4)-c(5)*x(6))/b(5);
x(7)  := (r(5)-a(7)*x(6)-c(7)*x(8))/b(7);  (c(7)=x(8)=0)
```

Inserting these four x's yields for $x(2) := b(2) - a(2)*c(1)/b(1)*x(2) = r(2) - a(2)*r(1)/b(1) - c(2)*r(3)/b(3) - a(2)*a(1)*x(0)/b(1) - c(2)*c(3)*x(4)/b(3)$ or $b'(2)*x(2) = r'(2) - a'(0)*x(0) - c'(4)*x(4)$ and similarly for $x(4)$ and $x(6)$. Dropping the quotes and renaming yields

$$\begin{vmatrix} b(2) & c(2) & 0 \\ a(4) & b(4) & c(4) \\ 0 & a(6) & b(6) \end{vmatrix} * \begin{vmatrix} x(2) \\ x(4) \\ x(6) \end{vmatrix} = \begin{vmatrix} r(2) \\ r(4) \\ r(6) \end{vmatrix} \qquad (6\text{-}76)$$

The new elements are calculated (with $j = 2*i$) according to

```
a(j)  := -a(j-1)*a(j)/b(j-1);  c(j) := c(j)*c(j+1)/b(j+1)
b(j)  := b(j)-a(j)*b(j-1)/b(x-1)-b(j)*a(j+1)/b(j+1)
r(j)  := r(j)-a(j)*r(j-1)/b(j-1)-c(j)*r(j+1)/b(j+1)

In the next step: a(4) := 0; c(4) :=0;
b(4)  := b(4)-a(4)*c(2)/b(2)-c(4)*a(6)/b(6)
r(4)  := r(4)-a(4)*r(2)/b(2)-c(4)*r(6)/b(6)
```

Since the only equation left is $x(4) = r(4)/b(4)$, we back-substitute and get $x(2)$ and $x(6)$, which lead to $x(1)$, $x(3)$, $x(5)$, and $x(7)$. In general, k steps (where $n = 2**k - 1$) lead to a single equation. A back-substitution process produces then all the unknown $x(i)$'s.

It has been noted [He76b] that the elimination steps may be applied to every equation, not just to the even-numbered ones. This results in an algorithm known as *odd-even elimination*. This algorithm leads after k steps to a diagonal matrix so that the solution may be obtained in a single parallel step; the back-substitution is unnecessary. Because the elimination is applied to every row for $\log(n)$ steps, the computational complexity is $O[n*\log(n)]$. This algorithm is not consistent with the sequential algorithm; therefore, it should not be applied on VPs.

It so happens that this algorithm can be applied on other PPSs. The calculations are reordered in such a way that extra work is done in each step. Since it is done by processors that would otherwise be idle, no additional time is required. Therefore, both odd-even reduction and odd-even elimination require $\log(n)$ steps and are consistent. However, odd-even reduction requires back-substitution or additionally $\log(n)$ steps, whereas odd-even elimination does not. Thus, odd-even elimination is superior on some PPSs.

We discuss next the *recursive doubling* algorithm. For this, let us rewrite Eq. (6-14) in factored form for $n = 3$ and tridiagonal equations:

$$\begin{vmatrix} 1 & 0 & 0 \\ L(2) & 1 & 0 \\ 0 & L(3) & 1 \end{vmatrix} * \begin{vmatrix} d(1) & t(1) & 0 \\ 0 & d(2) & t(2) \\ 0 & 0 & d(3) \end{vmatrix} * \begin{vmatrix} x(1) \\ x(2) \\ x(3) \end{vmatrix} = \begin{vmatrix} b(1) & c(1) & 0 \\ a(2) & b(2) & c(2) \\ 0 & a(3) & b(3) \end{vmatrix} * \begin{vmatrix} x(1) \\ x(2) \\ x(3) \end{vmatrix} = \begin{vmatrix} r(1) \\ r(2) \\ r(3) \end{vmatrix}$$

Multiplication shows that $t(i) = c(i)$ so that only the lower matrix L and the diagonals $d(i)$ of the upper bidiagonal matrix have to be calculated. Using the same approach that was used in Sec. 6-2 yields

$d(1) := b(1); \; L(2)*d(1) = a(2); \; L(2) := a(2)/d(1) = a(2)/b(1);$
$L(2)*c(1)+d(2) = b(2); \; d(2) := b(2)-L(2)*c(1); \; L(3)*d(2) = a(3);$
$L(3) := a(3)/d(2); \; L(3)*c(2)+d(3) = b(3); \; d(3) := b(3)-L(3)*c(2).$

$$L(i) := a(i)/d(i-1) \tag{6-77}$$

(To check it, note that $L(1) = 0$ because $a(1) = 0$; $L(2) = a(2)/b(1)$, etc.)

It is more difficult to calculate the diagonal elements. Insertion of $L(2)$ in $d(2) := b(2)-L(2)*c(1)$ and $L(3)$ in $d(3) := b(3)-L(3)*c(2)$, yields $d(2) := b(2)-a(2)*c(1)/d(1); \; d(3) := b(3)-a(3)*c(2)/d(2)$

$$d(i) := b(i)-[a(i)*c(i)]/d(i-1); \tag{6-78}$$

Equation (6-78) is a recurrent equation because $d(i)$ is a function of $d(i-1)$. It seems to lend itself poorly to parallelization, except by the following way. Define first: $q(0) := 1; \; q(1):=b(1);$

$$q(i) := b(i)*q(i-1)-a(i)*c(i-1)*q(i-2) \text{ for } i \geq 2 \tag{6-79}$$

In the case of $n = 3$, we would have $q(2):= q(1)*b(2)-a(2)*c(1)*q(0)$, which is $b(2)*b(1)-a(2)*c(1) = q(2)$ and $q(3) := b(3)*q(2)-a(3)*c(2)*q(1)$, which is $b(3)*b(2)*b(1)-a(2)*c(1)*b(3)-a(3)*c(2)*b(1)$. The importance of the q's lies in the fact that having computed all $q(i)$'s, the hard to get elements $d(i)$ result from

$$d(i) := q(i)/q(i-1); \; i = 1, \ldots, n \tag{6-80}$$

Checking Eq. (6-80) for $n = 3$: $d(1):=q(1)/q(0) = b(1);$
$d(2) := q(2)/q(1) = [b(1)*b(2) - a(2)*c(1)]/b(1) = b(2) - a(2)*c(1)/b(1);$
$d(3) := q(3)/q(2) = [b(3)*q(2) - a(3)*c(2)*q(1)]/q(2) = b(3) - a(3)*c(2)/d(2)$
which is $b(3) - L(3)*c(2)$, as it should be.

Calculation of the $q(i)$ factors from Eq. (6-79) looks sequential, but we may rewrite them using a matrix F as

$$\mathbf{Q}(i) = \begin{vmatrix} q(i) \\ q(i-1) \end{vmatrix} := \begin{vmatrix} b(i) & -a(i)*c(i-1) \\ 1 & 0 \end{vmatrix} * \begin{vmatrix} q(i-1) \\ q(i-2) \end{vmatrix} = \mathbf{F}(i) * \begin{vmatrix} q(i-1) \\ q(i-2) \end{vmatrix} \tag{6-81}$$

The second row is the identity $q(i-1) = q(i-1)$ and the first is Eq. (6-79). The equation reduces to $\mathbf{Q}(i) = \mathbf{F}(i)*\mathbf{Q}(i-1)$. Checking, we find for the first row of Eq. (6-79):

$$q(2) := \begin{vmatrix} b(2); & -a(2)*c(1) \end{vmatrix} * \begin{vmatrix} q(1); & q(0) \end{vmatrix}^T = b(2)*b(1) - a(2)*c(1)$$
$$q(3) := \begin{vmatrix} b(3); & -a(3)*c(2) \end{vmatrix} * \begin{vmatrix} q(2); & q(1) \end{vmatrix}^T = b(3)*q(2) - a(3)*c(2)*q(1)$$

This shows that

$$\mathbf{Q}(1) = \begin{vmatrix} b(1) \\ 1 \end{vmatrix}; \ \mathbf{Q}(2) = \begin{vmatrix} q(2) \\ q(1) \end{vmatrix} = \mathbf{F}(1)*\mathbf{Q}(1); \ \mathbf{Q}(3) = \begin{vmatrix} q(3) \\ q(2) \end{vmatrix} = \mathbf{F}(3)*\mathbf{F}(2)*\mathbf{Q}(1) \qquad (6\text{-}82)$$

$$\begin{vmatrix} q(i) \\ q(i-1) \end{vmatrix} = [\Pi \mathbf{F}(j)]*\mathbf{Q}(1); \ j\Pi = i, i-1, \ldots, 2 \qquad (6\text{-}83)$$

The problem reduced itself to that of computing the products

$$h(i,j) = \Pi f(j); \ j\Pi = j, j-1, \ldots, i \qquad (6\text{-}84)$$

where, by definition, $h(1,1) = b(1)$. For $n = 8$, these products are computed as follows (with scalars replacing matrices Q):

$$\begin{vmatrix} b(1) \\ b(2) \\ b(3) \\ b(4) \\ b(5) \\ b(6) \\ b(7) \\ b(8) \end{vmatrix} * \begin{vmatrix} 1 \\ b(1) \\ b(2) \\ b(3) \\ b(4) \\ b(5) \\ b(6) \\ b(7) \end{vmatrix} = \begin{vmatrix} h(1,1) \\ h(1,2) \\ h(2,3) \\ h(3,4) \\ h(4,5) \\ h(5,6) \\ h(6,7) \\ h(7,8) \end{vmatrix}; \ \begin{vmatrix} h(1,1) \\ h(1,2) \\ h(2,3) \\ h(3,4) \\ h(4,5) \\ h(5,6) \\ h(6,7) \\ h(7,8) \end{vmatrix} * \begin{vmatrix} 1 \\ 1 \\ h(1,1) \\ h(1,2) \\ h(2,3) \\ h(3,4) \\ h(4,5) \\ h(5,6) \end{vmatrix} = \begin{vmatrix} h(1,1) \\ h(1,2) \\ h(1,3) \\ h(1,4) \\ h(2,4) \\ h(3,6) \\ h(4,7) \\ h(5,8) \end{vmatrix}; \ \begin{vmatrix} h(1,1) \\ h(1,2) \\ h(1,3) \\ h(1,4) \\ h(2,5) \\ h(3,6) \\ h(4,7) \\ h(5,8) \end{vmatrix} * \begin{vmatrix} 1 \\ 1 \\ 1 \\ 1 \\ h(1,1) \\ h(1,2) \\ h(1,3) \\ h(1,4) \end{vmatrix} = \begin{vmatrix} h(1,1) \\ h(1,2) \\ h(1,3) \\ h(1,4) \\ h(1,5) \\ h(1,6) \\ h(1,7) \\ h(1,8) \end{vmatrix}$$

The entire calculation consists of multiplying a vector by a shifted vector. The shift is by one, two, four, . . ., log (n) positions and *is therefore suitable for execution on a vector processor*. (We multiply by 1 in order to use vectors of constant length.)

Having computed the $L(i)$ and $d(i)$ factors of Eqs. (6-77), (6-78), we solve the set by a forward and backward substitution:

$$L(i)*y(i-1) + y(i) = r(i) \qquad (6\text{-}86)$$

$$d(i)*x(i) + c(i)*x(i+1) = y(i) \qquad (6\text{-}87)$$

The computational complexity of the sequential and of the cyclic reduction algorithms is $O(n)$ for n-by-n matrices—the two algorithms are *consistent*. Cyclic reduction is often used on VPs.

Thus, we have seen that good parallel algorithms can be ignored if one relies solely on computational complexity as a guideline. In particular, we must look for ways to perform extra computations in parallel on otherwise idle computers, if it will reduce the number of steps required, or the time of communications.

6–6 OTHER PARALLEL METHODS

6–6.1 Synchronized and Asynchronous Algorithms

Algorithms can be classified according to whether they need synchronization or not. *Synchronized algorithms* are those in which tasks are not executed unless other tasks have completed some of their stages. For example, if $(\mathbf{A}*\mathbf{B}*\mathbf{C})-(\mathbf{D}*\mathbf{E})$ is to be computed, then it could be done by two tasks $T(1)$ and $T(2)$. Task $T(1)$ consists of a single stage computing $\mathbf{F}:=\mathbf{A}*\mathbf{B}*\mathbf{C}$, while task $T(2)$ consists of two stages: compute $\mathbf{G}:=\mathbf{D}*\mathbf{E}$ and then $\mathbf{H}:=\mathbf{F}-\mathbf{G}$. Clearly, the activation of the second stage of $T(2)$ cannot occur before $T(1)$ is complete.

Depending on the hardware and software of the system, synchronization may be an expensive overhead. As indicated in Sec. 5-3, when discussing barrier synchronization, it takes the OS about 500 machine cycles to manipulate the flags. On the C.mmp system it was found that sometimes up to 30 mls are wasted on one synchronization. Also, PEs that have finished earlier must wait idly for those that have not yet finished. The question is whether the number of synchronizations can be reduced or eliminated completely. In some cases it can.

Recall the formulation of the Laplace problem (Fig. 6-3). For every point of the area, the potential u is calculated according to Eq. (6-23), with i being the number of the iteration. Clearly, this algorithm requires synchronizations since values at iteration $i+1$ can be computed only after the values at iteration i are known.

Asynchronous computation is based on the simple idea that one takes for the values on the right of Eq. (6-23) those values that exist and not necessarily from a previous iteration. This was originally called "chaotic relaxation" [CaM69].

The properties of asynchronous algorithms are not well understood. In some cases, it was found that if the values on the right of Eq. (6-23) are taken often enough from recent iterates then the algorithm will converge. Obviously, the same conditions needed for convergence of the sequential algorithm (e.g., diagonal dominance) must be fulfilled also in the asynchronous algorithm. Unfortunately, in some asynchronous methods the values of the iterates may diverge wildly. Another difficulty is in the debugging of such programs, since the values may not be reproducible due to the fact that the order of computations may have changed. This makes isolation of errors very difficult. Some experimental studies on the C.mmp comparing the performance of various asynchronous methods with sequential ones indicate that the asynchronous methods perform well, but the sequential methods were not among the best available.

Even if the program itself is based on synchronization of its processes, a tightly coupled SM like the C.mmp may introduce fluctuations in the speed of processes [Ole82] because of the following:

1. The multiprocessor may include processors with differing speeds (e.g., the PDP-11/20 and PDP-11/40 of the C.mmp). A process running on an 11/20 would take more time than if it runs on an 11/40.

2. The individual processors may be asynchronous.

3. A process may be delayed because of memory conflicts.

4. There is no master in the system, so any CPU may assume this role at any given time. This involves a time-costly context-swap, and the stage of the task that was interrupted is either taken over by another CPU or suspended for an unknown, indefinite time.

6–6.2 Macropipelining or "Chasing"

Let us solve the Laplace problem for the area of Fig. 6-15(a). If Eq. (6-23) is applied to every one of the 30 inside points, Table 6-4 results [WaK88]. It will be called "example-a" and is similar to Eq. (6-25).

Suppose we solve Eq. (6-25) by the reordered Gauss-Seidel algorithm of Sec. 6-4. In this case, the elements of the vectors **t** and **z** are

$$t(k) = r(k) - c(k)*x(k+1); \quad z(k) = a(k)*x(k-1) \qquad (6\text{-}88)$$

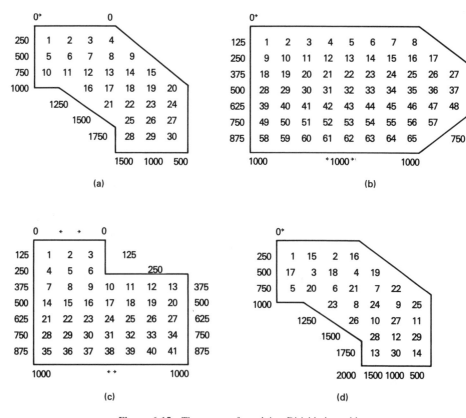

Figure 6-15   Three cases for solving Dirichlet's problem

TABLE 6-4 THE MATRIX FOR CASE (A) OF FIG. 6-15

	1	2	3	4	5	6	7	8	9	10	11	12	13	14	15	16	17	18	19	20	21	22	23	24	25	26	27	28	29	30	*	u	=	b
1	-4	1			1																											1		250
2	1	-4	1			1																										2		0
3		1	-4	1			1																									3		0
4			1	-4				1																								4		0
5	1				-4	1				1																						5		500
6		1			1	-4	1				1																					6		0
7			1			1	-4	1				1																				7		0
8				1			1	-4	1				1																			8		0
9								1	-4					1																		9		0
10					1					-4	1					1																10		1750
11						1				1	-4	1					1															11		1000
12							1				1	-4	1					1														12		0
13								1				1	-4	1					1													13		0
14									1				1	-4	1					1												14		0
15														1	-4						1											15		0
16										1						-4	1				1											16		2250
17											1					1	-4	1				1										17		0
18												1					1	-4	1				1									18		0
19													1					1	-4	1				1								19		0
20														1					1	-4					1							20		0
21															1	1					-4	1			1							21		2750
22																	1				1	-4	1			1						22		0
23																		1				1	-4	1			1					23		0
24																			1				1	-4				1				24		0
25																				1	1				-4	1		1				25		1500
26																						1			1	-4	1		1			26		0
27																							1			1	-4			1		27		0
28																								1	1			-4	1			28		3250
29																										1		1	-4	1		29		1000
30																											1		1	-4		30		500

269

Any $x(k)$ can still be computed from

$$x(k) := t(k) - z(k) \text{ where } \mathbf{t}, \mathbf{z} \text{ are of iterations } i-1, i \text{ respectively.} \qquad (6\text{-}89)$$

Counting the number of operations required for updating the $\mathbf{t}$ and $\mathbf{z}$ vectors, for calculating the new $\mathbf{x}$, the r's, and the sum of their squares, leads to

$$t(1) = 7*n*\omega \qquad (6\text{-}90)$$

The speedup would be low because while in the general case, there is a lot to do in the parallel step and only very little in the sequential step, in the present case, there is only one multiplication for $\mathbf{t}$ and one for $\mathbf{z}$, so that the parallel step is as short as the sequential one. The granularity is too fine and another method is needed.

As "example-d," take the case of $n = 90$ and three slaves $p = 3$. Each of the slaves can store 30 equations. Slave 1 can solve successively equations 1 to 30, starting from known or assumed values of $\mathbf{x}$. Slave 2 would have to start from the equation for $x(31)$, which for $\mathbf{A}*\mathbf{x} = \mathbf{r}$ is

$$x(31) := r(31) - A(31)*x(30) - c(31)*x(32) \qquad (6\text{-}91)$$

It seems wasteful to use the assumed value of $x(30)$; it is better to let slave 2 wait for $x(30)$ until it is calculated by slave 1. In the same way, slave 3 will wait until slave 2 calculates $x(60)$. The values of $x(30)$ and $x(60)$ have to be transferred from a slave to its "successor slave" and this is normally done through the master in a sequential step. The timing picture of the first few iterations is shown in Fig. 6-16(a). Starting from iteration 4, all three slaves work in parallel. Note that if slave 1 is in iteration i, then slaves 2 and 3 are in iterations $(i-1)$ and $(i-2)$ respectively. If many iterations are required—and this is usually the case—then this time shift is insignificant. Note also that, say for $x(30)$, the equation is

$$x(30) := r(30) - A(30)*x(29) - c(30)*x(31) \qquad (6\text{-}92)$$

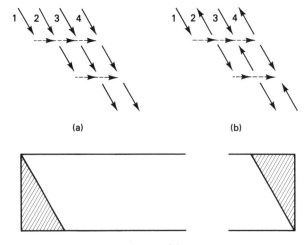

(a)   (b)

(c)   **Figure 6-16** "Chasing"

The sequential step involves transfer of $x(30)$ to slave 2, calculation of $x(31)$ and transfer of this value back to slave 1. The same applies to other slaves. If the master stores the a, b, c, and r elements of the "boundary areas," then it can compute those values (of $x(30)$, etc.) and transfers them, thus saving time.

Because the iterations proceed in each slave in direction "down," this algorithm is called "dodo" for down-down.

At the beginning of iteration 2, slave 1 could calculate the x's "upward" i.e., as $x(29)$, $x(28)$, . . . , $x(2)$ and $x(1)$. In iteration 2, slave 1 will iterate "down," slave 2 will iterate "up." From iteration 3 on, all three slaves are used [Fig. 6-16(b)] either as up or down. The algorithm is therefore called "doup."

For the doup algorithm and tridiagonal matrices, the count of operations leads to $10*n*\omega$ *for two iterations*. If the total number of iterations is the same, the computational effort was reduced by a factor of $10/16 = 62.5$ or by 37.5%. This speedup applies to a single computer working on all n equations. On an ASP, the transfer of information among the slaves during the sequential steps has to be accounted for. A simulation of example-d for an ASP with $p = 3$ and $\epsilon = 0.0001$ is shown in Table 6-5. It shows the number of iterations $i(1)$, $i(2)$, and $i(3)$; the operations count $\Omega(s)$ and $\Omega(p)$ and the speedup $\sigma = \Omega(s)/\Omega(p)$.

It would seem that the dodo algorithm has a higher speedup. This is misleading since the overall operations count $\Omega(s)$ is much higher. In terms of time, doup is faster by a factor of $5880/4900 = 1.2$. This is primarily the result of the lower number of iterations for convergence.

In addition to problem-a of Fig. 6-15(a), cases b and c, called here example-b and example-c were run. The results are summarized in Table 6-6. For example-a, the simulation resulted in 46 and 86 iterations respectively and a speedup of 1.887 for the doup algorithm. Comparing this with the optimal speedup of 3 is still slightly depressing. Both algorithms, the dodo and the doup, may be called *macropipelined* because of the

TABLE 6-5 RESULTS OF SIMULATING EXAMPLE (D)

	i_1	i_2	i_3	Ω_1	Ω_3	σ
do-up	10	9	8	12490	4900	2.549
do-do	12	11	10	15262	5880	2.596

TABLE 6-6 RESULTS OF SIMULATING EXAMPLES (A, B, AND C)

	Example a	Example b	Example c
i of do-do	86	57	42
i of do-up	46	32	24
σ of do-up	1.887	1.786	1.754

way they proceed; see Fig. 6-16(c). Especially note the "filling" and "draining" of the pipeline. The time ratio is

$$\rho = [2*nv*\tau + \zeta + n*(3*\mu + 2*\alpha)]/[n*(3*\mu + 2*\alpha)] \qquad (6\text{-}93)$$

where nv is the number of elements in a vector. Since $nv < n$, $\tau < \omega$, $3*\mu + 2*\alpha \simeq 5*\omega$, the second term can be neglected, and

$$\rho \simeq 1/p + \zeta/(5*n*\omega) \qquad (6\text{-}94)$$

The speedup depends on the time of synchronization ζ (we will see in Chap. 8 that it can be made relatively short). A better speedup can be achieved as follows.

Consider Fig. 6-15(d). It is identical to Fig. 6-15(a) except that the points are renumbered from the "natural" to a "red-black" order. The set of equations that follows this ordering is shown as Table 6-7.

Note that the equations for nodes 1 to 14 depend *only* on the x's of nodes 15 to 30 and vice versa. This leads to the following algorithm.

Assuming $p = 3$ and that potentials $x(15)$ to $x(30)$ are known, slaves 1, 2, and 3 calculate $\{x(1),. . .,x(5)\}$, $\{x(6),. . .,x(10)\}$, and $\{x(11),. . .,x(14)\}$ independently of each other and thus simultaneously. If these potentials are next transferred en-block to the master and retransmitted back to *all* three slaves, then potentials $\{x(15),. . .,x(20)\}$, $\{x(21),. . .,x(25)\}$, and $\{x(26),. . .,x(30)\}$ can be calculated *independently* and thus concurrently by all three slaves. This enables the start of the first half-iteration, etc.

The speedup is calculated as follows. If the dodo scheme is employed, then each half-iteration requires $7*n*\omega/2$. This can be done independently on all p slaves. For an iteration, $7*n*\omega/p$ operations are therefore needed. Two synchronizations and the transfer of n values are also required. Altogether, for every iteration:

$$t(p) = 7*n*\omega/p + \zeta + n*\tau \qquad (6\text{-}95)$$

Since $t(1) = 7*n*\omega$, the inverse of the speedup is

$$\rho = 1/p + (\zeta + n*\tau)/(7*n*\omega) \qquad (6\text{-}96)$$

The speedup approaches the ideal speedup of p if τ, ζ are small.

The next question is whether a doup scheme would improve the speedup even more. Results of simulations showed this not to be the case.

A simulation for $n = 30$, $p = 3$, $\zeta = 10$, $\tau = 1$, and $\omega = 120$ resulted in $\sigma = 2.713$. If the operation time ω is changed in the range from 50 to 120, but ζ and τ remain the same, then the results are as summarized in Table 6-8.

As expected, the lower the ratio $(\zeta + n*\rho)/\omega$, the higher is the speedup. It was also verified by simulations that the larger the number of equations n, the higher will be the speedup. For $n = 41$ and $n = 65$ of examples b and c, the corresponding speedups were 2.814 and 2.913 respectively, and for $n = 143$ in example-a, the speedup for $p = 3$ was 2.967.

Conclusions. Block-tridiagonal matrices can use both doup and dodo iterations. The speedup of the red-black algorithm on ASP is very high—it approaches the optimum

TABLE 6-7 THE MATRIX FOR RED-BLACK ORDERING OF CASE (D)

	1	2	3	4	5	6	7	8	9	10	11	12	13	14	15	16	17	18	19	20	21	22	23	24	25	26	27	28	29	30
1	−4														1		1													
2		−4													1	1		1												
3			−4													1	1		1											
4				−4													1	1		1										
5					−4													1	1		1									
6						−4													1	1		1								
7							−4													1	1		1							
8								−4													1	1		1						
9									−4													1	1		1					
10										−4													1	1		1				
11											−4														1		1	1		
12												−4														1	1		1	
13													−4														1	1		1
14														−4														1	1	1
15	1	1													−4															
16		1	1													−4														
17	1		1	1													−4													
18		1		1	1													−4												
19			1		1	1													−4											
20				1		1	1													−4										
21					1		1	1													−4									
22						1		1	1													−4								
23							1		1	1													−4							
24								1																−4						
25									1		1														−4					
26										1		1														−4				
27											1	1	1														−4			
28											1		1	1														−4		
29												1		1															−4	
30													1	1																−4

$$
*
\begin{bmatrix}
u_1 \\ u_2 \\ u_3 \\ u_4 \\ u_5 \\ u_6 \\ u_7 \\ u_8 \\ u_9 \\ u_{10} \\ u_{11} \\ u_{12} \\ u_{13} \\ u_{14} \\ u_{15} \\ u_{16} \\ u_{17} \\ u_{18} \\ u_{19} \\ u_{20} \\ u_{21} \\ u_{22} \\ u_{23} \\ u_{24} \\ u_{25} \\ u_{26} \\ u_{27} \\ u_{28} \\ u_{29} \\ u_{30}
\end{bmatrix}
=
\begin{bmatrix}
250 \\ 0 \\ 0 \\ 1750 \\ 0 \\ 0 \\ 0 \\ 0 \\ 0 \\ 0 \\ 0 \\ 3250 \\ 500 \\ 0 \\ 0 \\ 0 \\ 0 \\ 1250 \\ 0 \\ 0 \\ 2250 \\ 0 \\ 0 \\ 2750 \\ 0 \\ 1500 \\ 0 \\ 1000 \\ \ \\ \
\end{bmatrix}
$$

TABLE 6-8   SPEEDUP AS FUNCTION OF SIZE OF THE MATRIX

ω	50	60	70	80	90	100	110	120
σ	2.692	2.698	2.702	2.705	2.708	2.710	2.711	2.713

value of $\sigma = p$ if τ and ζ are negligible. The same algorithms can be applied to MP multiprocessors (Chap. 10).

6–6.3 Noisy Sort, etc.

This algorithm was introduced in [Dea88][†] from which we next quote:

> It is often the case that reflecting on problems with an eye towards parallel computation will suggest a new algorithm, in many instances one which is better than traditional ones even on a sequential machine. It seems useful, then, to reflect on ways of approaching problems that limit the size of dependence chains, in some way or another.
>
>   At least three approaches have been suggested:
>
>   Find "profuse parallelism," that is, approaches where the dependencies dissolve and massive degrees of parallel, independent structure emerge.
>
>   Ignore dependence, and exploit statistical properties to guarantee convergence, as in simulated annealing, or other "chaotic computation," as considered [by [CaM69]. (Profuse is data-parallelism).]
>
>   Violate dependence, but in "synergistic" ways, that have better convergence properties than the original method. [Dea88][††]

"Noisy sort" of [Dea88] using *associative memories* is next reviewed.

> Let x be a list of N real numbers to be sorted. Consider x to be a column vector, and let $CP(x)$ be the collection of N! vectors, the permutation of x taken in some order, hereafter fixed. $CP(x)$ will also denote the $N \times N!$ matrix composed of these vectors, in that order, as columns. $CP(x)$ will be called a CP matrix (of x), that is a complete permutation matrix (of x). Let $x = (x^1, x^2, \ldots, x^N)$ be a sorted list of data, and let $x = CP(x)$. We call x^i the i-th principle component of X (x^i is the $(i,1)$ entry of X). Let y be the vector of integers $(1,2,\ldots,N)^T$, and let $Y = CP(y)$. The column y_i in Y is the destination address set into which the column x_i in X should be stored by sorting. . . . Sorting is a mapping $\tau : CP(x) - >CP(y)$. Equivalently, τ is a mapping of $\{x_i\}^{N!}$ onto $\{y_i\}^{N!}$ and $y_i = \tau(x_i)$, $i = 1,2,\ldots,N!$.
>
>   There exists an $n \times n$ matrix M such that $y_i = M * x_i$, $i = 1,2,\ldots,N!$ in the sense of least squares. [The reader will recall that we introduced the least squares method in Sec. 7-2]. M is given by

$$M = Y * X^+; \quad X^+ = X^T * (X * X^T)^{-1}$$

> Multiplication by M is an operational representation of table lookup by access to an

---

[†]C.C. Douglas, et al: "The interaction of Numerics and Machines," Informationstechnik, Vol. 30, No. 2, pp. 83–88.

[††]Reprinted with permission from R. Oldenburg Verlag, P.O. Box 801360 8000 Munich, 80, West Germany.

associative memory. This is a highly parallel operation, since the table look-up occurs in one memory access cycle.

[The authors then proceed with the following example.] Let $N = 3$. Then

$$X = \begin{vmatrix} x^1 & x^1 & x^2 & x^2 & x^3 & x^3 \\ x^2 & x^3 & x^1 & x^3 & x^1 & x^2 \\ x^3 & x^2 & x^3 & x^1 & x^2 & x^1 \end{vmatrix} \quad Y = \begin{vmatrix} y^1 & y^1 & y^2 & y^2 & y^3 & y^3 \\ y^2 & y^3 & y^1 & y^3 & y^1 & y^2 \\ y^3 & y^2 & y^3 & y^1 & y^2 & y^1 \end{vmatrix}$$

where $(y^1, y^2, y^3) = (1,2,3)$. We suppose that data are sorted into ascending order; if in descending order, $y = (3,2,1)$. In principle, any of the six permutations could be the first column of Y. Then

$$X(+) = \begin{vmatrix} z^1 & z^2 & z^3 \\ z^1 & z^3 & z^2 \\ z^2 & z^1 & z^3 \\ z^2 & z^3 & z^1 \\ z^3 & z^1 & z^2 \\ z^3 & z^2 & z^1 \end{vmatrix}$$

Here, $z^j = \{s^3 - t^2*(2*x^j - s)\}/\{6*s^2*(3*t^2 - s^2)\}$, $j = 1,2,3$ where $s = x^1 + x^2 + x^3$, $t^2 = (x^1)^2 + (x^2)^2 + (x^3)^2$. M is given by

$$M = \begin{vmatrix} a & b & b \\ b & a & b \\ b & b & a \end{vmatrix}$$

where
$a = 2*(y^1*z^1 + y^2*z^2 + y^3*z^3)$
$b = y^1*(z^2 + z^3) + y^2*(z^1 + z^3) + y^3*(z^1 + z^2)$

Consider a numerical example for $N = 3$. Y, X, X^+, and M, respectively, are given by

$$Y = \begin{vmatrix} 1 & 1 & 2 & 2 & 3 & 3 \\ 2 & 3 & 1 & 3 & 1 & 2 \\ 3 & 2 & 3 & 1 & 2 & 1 \end{vmatrix}$$

$$X = \begin{vmatrix} 0.9067 & 0.9067 & 3.5211 & 3.5211 & 6.1482 & 6.1482 \\ 3.5211 & 6.1482 & 0.9067 & 6.1482 & 0.9067 & 3.5211 \\ 6.1482 & 3.5211 & 6.1482 & 0.9067 & 3.5211 & 0.9067 \end{vmatrix}$$

$$X(+) = \begin{vmatrix} -0.0478 & 0.0157 & 0.0794 \\ -0.0478 & 0.0794 & 0.0157 \\ 0.0157 & -0.0478 & 0.0794 \\ 0.0157 & 0.0794 & -0.0478 \\ 0.0794 & -0.0478 & 0.0157 \\ 0.0794 & 0.0157 & -0.0478 \end{vmatrix}$$

$$M = \begin{vmatrix} 0.4435 & 0.0619 & 0.0619 \\ 0.0619 & 0.4435 & 0.0619 \\ 0.0619 & 0.0619 & 0.4435 \end{vmatrix}$$

Suppose that the vector $a = [3.4316, 5.9832, 1.1080]^T$ is to be sorted. Multiplication $M*a$ produces $[1.9289, 2.9346, 1.0743]^T$. Rounding yields $[2, 3, 1]^T$ which indicates that 3.4316, 5.99832, and 1.1080 are the second, third, and first element of the sorted list. [Dea88]

Note that the memory is used very extensively.

Another method is described in [BCL88] and is based on a *chemical reaction metaphor*: "The computation is a succession of application of rules which consume elements of a multiset while producing new ones and inserting them in the initial multiset. The computation terminates when no rule can be applied. The application of rules is made in a nondeterministic way and a parallel interpretation of the model is straightforward [BCL88]. The particular algorithms of [BCL88] use set theory and are beyond the mathematical treatment in this book.

CHAPTER 7

SEQUENTIAL
PART
OF ADA

This chapter begins by examining the reasons for the development of Ada. Traditional Ada features are described by way of example programs in sections 7-1 through 7-9 and are summarized in section 7-10. The *objectives* of this chapter are:

Review the reasons for the development of Ada.

Describe the more traditional features of Ada.

Discuss in slightly more detail the packages and exceptions.

Summarize the sequential part of Ada.

7–1 INTRODUCTION

7–1.1 Embedded Systems

As early as 1974, the U.S. Department of Defense (DoD) became concerned about the high cost of producing and maintaining software. A comparison study of cost increases revealed that while hardware costs increased linearly, software costs increased quadratically. Based on these trends, it was projected that by 1990, software will cost about ten times more than hardware. An analysis of the budget showed that some 58% of software expenditures were for the development of embedded systems.

In an embedded system, the computer and its software are part of a larger system. For example, an avionics control system is embedded in the aircraft and interacts with both the plane's sensors and the pilot. Embedded systems are mostly real-time systems, which means that there exist fixed time constraints that must be met or the system fails.

Embedded systems have special requirements, including the following:

1. Control is required for separate system components which run in parallel. The need to control such interactions arises when information is to be exchanged or the progress of one process depends on another (synchronization). For SMs "monitors," for MPs features for message passing were proposed. Ada provides the *rendezvous* for message passing. It will be shown that semaphores (a part of monitors) can be simulated by rendezvous.

2. The time for an action must be specified in absolute terms, and actions may need to be synchronized, as in the case of communication. The language must include such real-time facilities.

3. As a real-time system, accuracy and timeliness of results are extremely important. A ballistic missile defense must calculate a hostile missile's target before the missile completes its flight.

4. Real-time systems require the ability to interact with the environment (Input and Output I/O registers). In avionics, taking measurements and viewing the surrounding air-space are both extremely important to the safety of crew and passengers.

5. Default actions must be available in the case of erroneous behavior of hardware or software. The language must allow continued program execution during abnormal conditions.

6. In a commercial system, fixing a few errors after delivery is normal practice; embedded systems should be delivered error-free, because lives may depend on the reliability of the programs. The language must allow extensive testing and produce robust programs.

7. The problem is complicated by the fact that software packages of embedded systems

tend to be very large. It was determined by the DoD that 90% of the costs are for maintaining old programs, while only 10% go toward developing new programs. The reasons are their (large) size, longevity (10 to 20 years), and the proliferation of computer languages. The problems of large programs are studied in "Software Engineering" and Ada was designed according to its principles.

a. Emphasis was placed on program's readability rather than how it is written. English-like phrases are preferred to cryptic ones.

b. Strong typing of code allows the compiler to find more errors. "Exceptions" handle run-time errors so corrective action can be taken without the program being interrupted.

c. Data abstraction and encapsulation are helpful in achieving aims 1 to 5 above. Packages and generic packages enable the decomposition of large programs, making the writing of such programs more economical and safe. Separate compilation enables isolated testing, debugging, and library management.

The DoD wanted a single language that would meet all these requirements. To this end and in particular for a, b, and c, Ada was designed. In addition, Ada allows multitasking, the single most important requirement of parallel processing systems. Multitasking is discussed in Chap. 8 while other more traditional features of Ada are covered in this chapter.

7–1.2 A Program

Traditional features of Ada will be discussed by way of example programs which the reader can compare to those in a language he/she knows. The first program is shown as Code 7-1. It computes the least number of coins (pennies, nickels, dimes, and quarters) to be given as change for a dollar. Since the comments are too long, they are numbered and explained later; a comment starts on two minus symbols.

```
with TEXT_IO; use TEXT_IO;                                       -- 1
procedure code71 is                                             -- 2
c25,c10,c5,c1,change,cost,cng: INTEGER;                         -- 3
begin                                                           -- 4
  PUT_LINE(" cost change quarters dimes nickels pennies ");     -- 5
    loop GET(cost)                                              -- 6
    if cost>100 then return; end if;                            -- 7
    change := 100-cost; cng := change;                          -- 8
    c25 := change/25; change := change-c25*25;                  -- 9
    c10 := change/10; change := change-c10*10;                  --10
    c5 := change/5; c1 := change-c5*5;                          --11
    PUT(cost); PUT(cng); PUT(c25);                              --12
    PUT(c10); PUT(c5); PUT_LINE(c1); NEW_LINE;                  --13
  end loop;                                                     --14
end code71;                                                     --15
```

Code 7-1

1. The two statements provide Input/Output or I/O capabilities, in this case, for reading and writing text. TEXT_IO is provided by an Ada library; we say that code71 *imports* it. (Actually, every compiler will have its way of importing I/O; we will leave this part open in all codes that follow.)

Words **with** and **use** are *keywords*. All keywords will be written using lower-case boldface letters. The keywords of Ada are:

abort	abs	accept	access	all	and	array	at
begin	body	case	constant	declare	delay	delta	digits
do	else	elsif	end	entry	exception	exit	for
function	generic	goto	if	in	is	limited	loop
mod	new	not	null	of	or	others	out
package	pragma	private	procedure	raise	range	record	rem
renames	return	reverse	select	separate	subtype	task	
terminate	then	type	use	when	while	with	xor

2. The program is a **procedure** (followed by ''name'' and **is**). Its name is code71—an *identifier*. The syntax of identifiers is as follows:

```
SR: IDENTIFIER ::= LETTER {[UNDERSCORE] LETTER_OR_DIGIT}
SR: LETTER_OR_DIGIT ::= LETTER | DIGIT
SR: LETTER ::= UPPER_CASE_LETTER | LOWER_CASE_LETTER
```

A syntax rule starts on ''SR:'' and uses ''::='' for 'is defined as,' ''{'',''}'' for 'any number of,' ''|'' for ''or,'' and ''['','']'' for 'an optional number of.' Thus, the first rule is equivalent to: 'An identifier is a letter followed by any number of letter-or-digit symbols preceded by an optional single underscore.' As seen, an identifier cannot contain two consecutive underscores nor end on one.

We will use upper-case letters for syntax definitions and items supplied by libraries, and lower-case letters and digits for identifiers.

3. Line 3 declares the *objects* of the program, which happen to be all of *type* INTEGER. Ada is a ''strongly typed'' language and all objects have to be declared. A misspelled variable name will be identified as an error, since it was not declared. The semicolon is used in other languages as a separator, but in Ada it *terminates* every statement. This enables insertion of a SEQUENCE-OF-STATEMENTS in place of a single statement, or use of **null** for documenting unused alternatives.

4. The procedure is enclosed by the *brackets* **begin** and **end**. (The last **end** is in line 15 and includes the identifier code71.)

5. Strings of characters are printed by PUT statements. The PUT_LINE will print a statement and move to the next line.

An object of type character has a ''value'' which is any printable character including the blank. A single character is enclosed in single quotes (e.g., 'x'). The quote symbol itself is represented by two quotes, as in ' ' ' ' with the two innermost quotes being the quote. A string of characters is enclosed in double quotes.

6. Keywords **loop** and **end loop** bracket a loop which would "go forever" unless left explicitly (such loops are needed in embedded applications). The integer, "cost," is input from the terminal.

7. This is the simplest CONDITIONAL-STATEMENT, bracketed by **if** and **end if**. A cost >100 would in this case indicate that the procedure should be left by the **return** (from the procedure) statement.

8. Symbol ": = " is used for assignment and is read: "is replaced by" or "becomes." Symbol " = " is reserved for testing for equality.

9. In Ada, *objects of different types should not be mixed*. Since change/25 divides two integers, it is an integer. If it were a real number it would have to be explicitly converted [by writing INTEGER(change/25.0)] in order to be assigned to integer c25. The advantage of this approach is that operation codes for arithmetic operations, which are different for different data types, are chosen on the basis of operand types.

9,10,11: These statements compute the number of quarters (c25), dimes (c10), nickels (c5), and pennies (c1). The use of ": = " makes it easy to understand their meaning. If the statement: change = change − c25*25 were used, " = " would be a test operator and the result would be false unless change = c25 = 0. With the symbol ": = " it is read "change is replaced by the (new) value computed by subtracting c25*25 from (the old value of) change."

12,13: These lines print the results. NEW_LINE directs the input to the next line. In code71 the output appears on the terminal.

7–1.3 Standard Data Types

The *choice of data representation* affects the computer algorithm. For instance, the height and weight of a person should not be measured in integers because it is a real number, but the social security number could. The person's name could be assigned a number, but a record with three strings of characters would be much better.

Certain operations are better suited for or only applicable to some data types. The only operation on a social security number is "accessing" it, the height and weight can be operated by say " + " and a substring extraction is all we want to do to a name.

A data type is a set of possible values of a variable and a set of operations that can be performed on them. The combination of the two sets is termed *encapsulation* of data and operators.

The predefined type BOOLEAN contains only two values, namely TRUE and FALSE. Boolean values can be assigned as in $a := $ TRUE. They may also result from *relations*, say $a > (b+c)$ where a, b, and c are integer values and the result is TRUE or FALSE. In addition to relation ">", Ada includes " = " for equality, "/ = " for inequality, "< = " for less-or-equal, ">" for greater, and "> = " for greater-or-equal. *The operands of a relation must be of the same type.* In Ada: FALSE < TRUE.

Boolean *expressions* combine objects using the operators **and, or, xor** or **not**. For equal precedences, a (Boolean) expression is executed left-to-right. There exist two so-called short-circuit forms: **and then** and **or else**. In both cases, two conditions are given. For **and then**, the second is checked only if the first is true, for **or else** the second is tested only if the first is false. For instance, "**if** $x/ = 0$ **and then** $10/x < 8$ **then** $a: = b/x$" checks if $x/ = 0$. If TRUE, the second is checked, but if FALSE (i.e., if $x = 0$) the second is not checked at all and the result is FALSE (from the first test). In "**if** $i/ = 0$ **or else** $j = k$ **then** $c := d$" no assignment is made if $i = 0$ or if $j/ = k$, but if any of these two conditions is true, d is assigned to c.

An INTEGER is defined as a whole number in some range. Commas are not allowed so that 3140 is, but 3,140 is not a legal integer constant. Spaces may not appear inside integers, but underscores may. This is convenient for large numbers, where it substitutes for commas, say in 123_456_789_000, which represents 123,456,789,000. Such large numbers may also use the "exponent notation" so that 4E6 is $4*10^6$ with E standing for "10 to exponent power of ..". Underscores may also substitute for hyphens in social security numbers and identifiers.

Bases 2 (binary) to 16 (hexadecimal) may be used. Thus, 2#0100# is 4 written in binary. Decimal 12 can be written as 2#1100# or 8#14# or 16#C#, and decimal 61.0 as 8#75.0# or 8#7.5#E1. Note that the base and the exponent are decimal numbers.

Operators " + ", " − ", "*", and "/" are predefined for integer and real numbers; they have their conventional meaning. For each of these operators, the operands and the result must be of the same type. Unary " − " has a high precedence, so it is advisable to use parentheses whenever unary " − " is used in ARITHMETIC-EXPRESSIONS. Operators "*" and "/" have higher precedence than " + " and " − ". Exponentiation $a**b$ can be applied if both a and b are integers, with b being non-negative. Exponentiation has a higher precedence than the other arithmetic operations.

The **mod** operator counts "modulo" some number so that 62 **mod** 5 = 2 since 60 **mod** 5 = 0. If the signs of integers a and b are the same, then a **rem** $b = a$ **mod** b. Otherwise, the sign of the result is that of the numerator or denominator for **rem** and **mod** respectively.

The REAL data types come in two classes: the *fixed-point* and *floating-point* numbers. With "d" being a decimal digit +d.dd or −ddd.dd or −dddd. exemplify fixed point numbers. "Fixed" means here a given number of digits on both sides of the (decimal) point. "Floating" point data represent numbers with a fixed number of significant digits and an integer exponent, e.g., d.ddE ± dd or dddd.ddE ± dd.

The declaration of the two types of real numbers is exemplified by

type a **is delta** 0.1 **range** − 50.0 .. 50.0; **type** b **is digits** 5;
$c:a;$.

The delta of 0.1 means that the numbers are − 50.0, − 49.9, . . . ,49.9,50.0. The step-size must be positive. The "range" − 50.0 .. 50.0 *must* always be included in the declarations. The precision is absolute. The 5 used to declare b specifies the number of decimal places to be used for the mantissa—the precision is relative. Floating-point numbers are predefined and declared as in d:FLOAT;.

In Ada, a test can determine if a number is in a prescribed range. For instance, "i **in** $a..b$" is equivalent to "$i > = a$ **and** $i < = b$". The test "i **not in** $a..b$" is equivalent to **not** (i **in** $a..b$), but is more readable. The membership tests **in** and **not in** are predefined for all types. The result is of type BOOLEAN.

Unlike the floating-point numbers, fixed-point numbers are evenly distributed—the precision is the same over the entire range.

The types introduced thus far were the *scalar types*:

SR: SCALAR-TYPE : : = INTEGER | FLOAT | BOOLEAN | CHARACTER

For the next section, the array is needed. An array is a *structured* data type; it is an ordered collection of objects all of the same type and accessed by an index. Matrices are arrays and can be defined as for example, in

a: **array** (1 . . 3, 1 . . 3) **of** INTEGER.

7–1.4 Precision (accuracy) of fixed-point numbers

The *type conversion* INTEGER of Ada truncates a real-type number (e.g., INTEGER(3.6) = 3) and FLOAT adds a decimal point and zero (e.g., FLOAT(15) = 15.0). More importantly, they change the internal representation of the number.

The floating-point number following 0.1234E2 is 0.1235E2, i.e., at a distance of 0.01, but 0.1235E6 and 0.1234E6 are at a distance of 100. There is more accuracy (precision) in using small floating-point numbers than large ones. The advantage of floating-point numbers is that very small and very large numbers can be represented.

Numbers are represented in computers in the binary notation. A binary fraction like 0.1011 is

$$1/2^1 + 0/2^2 + 1/2^3 + 1/2^4 \ = \ 1/2 + 0/4 + 1/8 + 1/16 \ = \ (1 + 2 + 8)/16 \ = \ 11/16$$

and could have been computed as the integer 1011 divided by $2^4 = 16$. To convert a fractional part into decimal base we use the algorithm of repeatedly multiplying the fractional part by two and writing down the integer part. Thus, 10#0.25# is 2#0.01# (as left below).

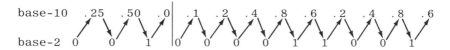

Some decimal numbers have no exact binary equivalent, e.g., 0.1 has no binary equivalent and is the irrational number 0.0001100110011.. (see right above). The nearest representation to decimal 0.1 with four bits is 2/16 or 0.0010 = 1/8 = 0.125—a 25% difference! Of course we may use more bits, but the point is that computers have fixed number of bits and therefore can only approximately represent some decimal numbers.

A decimal *literal* (constant) occurring with a decimal point is treated as fixed-point with precision determined by the number of digits following the decimal point. Since numbers are represented in binary form, a fixed-point decimal constant of the form $0.d_1 d_2 d_3 . . . d_d$ has precision $2**(-b)$ where b is the smallest integer such that $2**(-b)$

$\leq 10**(-d)$. For example, the constant 2.3 has precision determined by $2**b \geq 10**1$ and since $2^3 = 8$ but $2^4 = 16$, b is 4, which means that the precision is $1/2^4 = 0.0625$. On the other hand, 2.3000 has precision determined by $2**b \geq 10**4$ or $b = 14$ so that the accuracy is 0.00006103515625.

In a computer with 16 bits, the constant 2.3 might be represented by 00000000 00100101 with an implied binary point between the fourth and fifth bits from the right. However, the equivalent constant 2.3000 will be represented by 10010011 00110011 with the implied binary point between the 14th and 15th bit from the right. These two constants are not the same fixed point type (i.e., they have different precisions) and as a result may not have the same effect when used in an arithmetic expression.

In general, the compiler will allocate a single word (say 16 bits) for a variable if $2**x/p\_actual < 2**w$ where

$$p\_actual = \text{the actual precision used.}$$

$$x = \text{number of bits required for the integer part determined from}$$
$$2**x \geq (|\text{ range\_min }|, |\text{ range\_max }|)$$

$$w = \text{number of bits in the target machine word if the value of the variable is not}$$
$$\text{negative, but the number of bits minus one if the value may be either}$$
$$\text{positive or negative.}$$

Suppose we declare

type FX1 **is delta** 0.01 **range** 0.00..3.00;

The desired precision is 0.01, so $p\_actual = 1/2**b$ forces b to be 7 (since $2^6 = 64 < 100$; $2^7 = 128 > 100$). The actual precision $p\_actual = 1/2^7 = 0.0078125$ so that $2^2/0.0078125 = 2^9$ and since $9 < 16$, a single word is adequate and a variable of fixed-point type will be allocated by the compiler.

Suppose we declare

type FX2 **is delta** 0.01 **range** 0.00..1000.00;

In this case, $x = 10$ from $2**x = 1024 \geq 1000$ and $2**x/p$ actual $= 2**17$, which indicates that 17 bits would be required for a variable of type FX2. The compiler would issue an error message if such a definition were encountered.

When assigning a number, e.g., $a:=c$;, the precision may not match. If c has the higher precision, then some digits will have to be dropped to fit the lower precision of a. The result is a loss of digits and a *truncation* error.

Consider three common errors concerning fixed-point numbers of the type declared as

type F **is delta** 0.01 **range** −100.00..100.00:

1. Suppose we declared tenth: F:=0.1; As seen earlier, the computer will represent tenth as either 12.0/128 or 13.0/128, producing an error in both cases.

2. The product of two numbers of type F is likely to overflow the range of F and therefore, cannot, in general, be considered of type F anymore.

3. If a and b are two positive decimal fractions accurate to n significant figures, then the sum $a+b$, product $a*b$, and quotient a/b are also accurate to approximately n significant figures. However, $a-b$ may be accurate to less than n significant figures. For example $a = 0.142857 \approx 1/7$ and $b = 0.142142 \approx 142/999$ are both accurate to six significant figures, but $a-b = 0.00715$ is accurate to only three significant figures.

7–2 CONTROL STRUCTURES

7–2.1 Conditional Statements

The syntax and semantics of the IF-STATEMENT are:

```
SR:    IF-STATEMENTS ::=                    Semantic explanation:
       if CONDITION then            The condition is tested. If it is true
         SEQUENCE-OF-STATEMENTS     this sequence of statements is executed.
   {   elsif CONDITION then         If one of these conditions are true, then
         SEQUENCE-OF-STATEMENTS}     this sequence of statements is executed.
   [   else                         If none of the above conditions are true,
         SEQUENCE-OF-STATEMENTS]     this sequence of statements is executed.
       end if;
```

Note that the number of **elsif**s is arbitrary—possibly even none, and that the **else** is optional (and can be used only once). Writing **if** . . . **else** . . . **else** . . . is not permitted.

Let us exemplify the conditional statement by first calculating the absolute value abs(x) as: **if** $x < 0$ **then** $x := -x$; **end if**; with no **else**, but with the required bracket **end if**. Next, Euclid's method of calculating the greatest common divisor (gcd) of two positive integers x,y is shown as Code 7-2, and is based on the following statements:

- If $x=y$ then either x or y is gcd(x,y)
- If $x>y$ then gcd(x,y) = gcd($x-y,y$), but
- if $x<y$ then gcd(x,y) = gcd(x,y,x).

Note that the IF-STATEMENT allowed the choice to be made during run-time and thus can be based on data.

In Code 7-3, the IF-STATEMENT and the library function SQRT for extracting a square root of a positive number are used to solve the quadratic equation $a*x^2 + b*x + c = 0$. In high school, it was probably written as $x = (-b + \sqrt{b^2 - 4*a*c})/(2*a)$. It is more efficient to solve it by writing $x = (d) + \sqrt{d^2 - c/a}$; $d = -b/(2*a)$ since only three instead of four multiplication or division operations are required.

```
procedure code-2 is
x, y, v, w : INTEGER; -- v and w are temporary variables for x and y.
begin
  PUT_LINE ("The two numbers and their divisor are: ");
  GET (x); GET (y); v := x; w := y;  -- The temporary storage of x and y.
  <<lab>>                            -- The label supplies a return point.
    if v=w then                      -- The gcd(x, y) was found, is printed,
      PUT (x, y, v); return;         -- and Code72 is thereby completed.
    elsif v>w then                   -- In this case v should be reduced
      v := v-w; goto lab;            -- and processing resumed at label lab.
    else                             -- Otherwise, w should be reduced and
      w := w-v; goto lab;            -- processing resumed at label lab.
    end if;
end code72;
```

Code 7-2

```
with TEXT_IO, SMATHLIB; use TEXT_IO, SMATHLIB; -- These two packages
procedure code73 is -- are needed for I/O and to use function SQRT.
a, b, c, d, dis, im, re : FLOAT;
    -- The conditionals result from the following cases:
    -- a=b=0. This is a degenerate equation; print a statement.
    -- a=0, b/=0. Print that the only root is -c/b.
    -- a/=0, b/=0, c=0. Print that the two roots are -b/a and 0.
    -- In all other cases, the results are two real numbers or a complex,
    -- conjugate pair of real numbers.
begin                          -- The label <<lab>> is for a return address
  <<lab>> GET (d); GET (a); GET (b); GET (c);            -- Read data
  if d=1.0 then              -- d/=1 indicates that the job is completed.
    PUT_LINE ("The three numbers and the marker are: ");
    PUT (a); PUT (b); PUT (c); PUT (d); -- Data should always be verified
    if (a=0.0) and (b=0.0) then
      PUT_LINE ("This is a degenerate case ");
    elsif (a=0.0) then
      PUT ("The root is "); PUT (-c/b); NEW_LINE;
    else PUT (" The normal case "); NEW_LINE;
      re := -b/ (a+a); dis := re*re - c/a;
      im := SQRT (abs (dis));       -- The square-root is computed for the
      if dis>0.0 then             -- absolute value of the discriminant dis.
        PUT ("Real roots: "); PUT (re+im); PUT (re-im);
      else        -- Since there are no composite characters, "+ or -"
        PUT ("Complex roots "); PUT (re);                -- are used.
        PUT (" + or - j*"); PUT (im); NEW_LINE;
      end if;
    end if;
    goto lab;
  end if;      -- It will be shown later how to write libraries like
  end code 73; -- SMATHLIB (Ada does not provide them automatically).
```

Code 7-3

Note that the conditions in the program are tested *in the given order*; the first which is true is executed, the others are not. Also note that if no other condition remains to be checked, the **else** provides an "escape hatch" and that every **if** bracket ends on the matching **end if**, but **elsif** or **else** do not. This leads to a "comblike" structure that with proper indentation produces more readable programs.

The equation $x^2 - 44*x + 1 = 0$ has the roots $x(1) = 22 - 483 = 22 - 21.977 = 0.023$, and $x(2) = 22 + 21.977 = 43.977$. The square root was extracted with an accuracy of five digits, but only two digits of $x(1)$ are known. Information was lost because two nearly equal values were subtracted. We can produce a more accurate $x(1)$ by recalling that $x(1)*x(2) = c$ (in the present case $c = 1$). From the known $x(2)$ we calculate $x(1) = 1.0/43.977 = 0.022739$ with all five digits. It is from such tricks that some of the numerical work derives its fun.

The IF-STATEMENT is an example of a *compound statement*, that is, a statement that may contain other statements nested inside it. It frequently has the form

```
if      a=val1 then SEQUENCE-OF-STATEMENTS 1;
elsif   a=val2 then SEQUENCE-OF-STATEMENTS 2;
        -------------------------------
elsif   a=valn then SEQUENCE-OF-STATEMENTS n;
endif;
```

Instead of testing the conditions sequentially, the results of the test may be used to direct the program to one, specific path out of many. This is the CASE-STATEMENT exemplified by

```
case a is          -- The value of a is determined. According to this value:
  when 1 =>        -- Some action. The expression (1), is called a choice
  when 2|8 =>      -- Another action for the two alternatives: 2 or 8.
  when 3..7 =>     -- Still another, range of alternatives.
  when others=>    -- Others is an escape hatch for an error action.
end case;
```

For "do nothing," the NULL-STATEMENT, **null**, could have been used, thus indicating that the choice has not been simply overlooked, but that indeed no action was necessary. Additionally note that

1. The CASE-STATEMENT selects and executes only one statement out of all alternatives. The order is immaterial, but **when others** must be last.
2. No **begin** is needed but an **end** should match every **case**. A bracket **case. . .end case** is used around a SEQUENCE-OF-STATEMENTS.
3. If in the statement **case** item . . . **end case** with alternatives 1,2,. . . ,9 the "item" evaluates to be neither of these numbers, the CASE-STATEMENT is undefined. This is why **when others** is used. If the number of cases has changed, the CASE-STATEMENT can remain as it was because **when others** will take care of the additional cases.

To exemplify the use of the CASE-STATEMENT, a program to compute real estate tax is shown in Code 7-4.

```
with TEXT_IO; use TEXT_IO; -- The procedure will compute real-estate tax
procedure code74 is  -- from a table inside the CASE-STATEMENT.
category: INTEGER;   -- This is one of four possible tax categories.
value: FLOAT;        -- This is the assessed value of the real-estate.
rate, tax: FLOAT;    -- The tax rate of 3 to 6% and the actual amount.
begin GET(value); NEW_LINE; -- Get the value of the real-estate.
  loop
    if value>0.0 then          -- Terminate if value is zero or negative.
      category:=INTEGER(value/1000.0); -- The REAL number is converted.
      case category is                 -- to the INTEGER category.
        when 0 . . 1 => rate := 0.03;  -- For houses of 00000 to $19999.
        when 2 . . 3 => rate := 0.04;  -- For houses of 20000 to $39999.
        when 4 . . 5 => rate := 0.05;  -- For houses of 40000 to $59999.
        when others=>rate := 0.06;     -- For houses of $60000 or more.
      end case;
      tax := value*rate;
      PUT("Assessed value of house is      ");  PUT(value);  NEW_LINE;
      PUT("The tax-rate for this house is ");   PUT(rate);   NEW_LINE;
      PUT("The tax to be paid is           ");  PUT(tax);    NEW_LINE;
      GET(value);                -- Get the value of the next house.
    else return;                 -- Return from the procedure if value<0.
    end if;                      -- End of the IF-STATEMENT.
  end loop;                      -- From here, return to LOOP to compute
end Code74;                      -- the tax on the next house.
```

Code 7-4

Because there are four possible tax rates, a CASE-STATEMENT was used to select the appropriate rate. Since the assessed value could presumably be any positive number, at first glance it seems that a large number of possibilities will have to be listed in the case list. Even if the possibilities such as 20001, 20002, . . . ,39999, etc., would all be listed, there is no upper bound to houses above $60000. This problem was solved by dividing the value (an integer) by 10000 and by the use of **others**. The first yields 0,1, . . . and the second takes care of expensive houses.

The same problem could have been solved by the IF-STATEMENT.

```
if    value =< 19999 then rate := 0.03;
elsif value =< 39999 then rate := 0.04;
elsif value =< 59999 then rate := 0.05;
else rate := 0.06;
end if              -- but the CASE-STATEMENT is preferable.
```

7–2.2 Loops

A remark was once made that problems without loops do not warrant a solution by a computer—a pocket calculator will suffice.

The sine function can be computed from the following series:

$$\sin(x) = x - x^3/3! + x^5/5! + \ldots = \Sigma[(-1)**h]*(x**h)]/h! \qquad (7\text{-}1)$$

where $h = 2*i - 1$ and $h!$ is defined as $h*(h-1)*\ldots*2*1$. Figure 7-1(a) shows a flowchart corresponding to Eq. (7-1). *Initialization* consists of $s: = 0.0$; $i: = 0$; and is followed by the loop. Figure 7-1(b) is the additional loop required for calculating $h!$

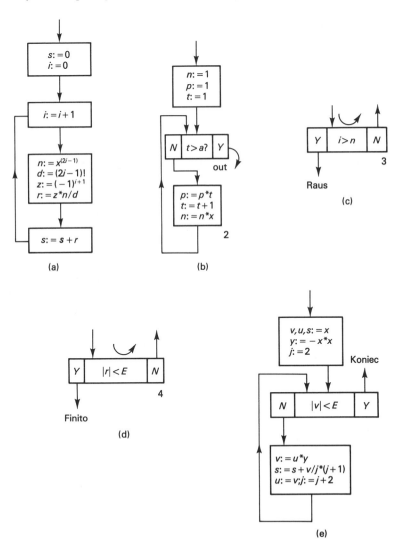

Figure 7-1   Parts of algorithm for calculating the sine

The following assignments result for $h = 3$:

$$n := 1; p := 1; t := 1;$$

$$t < h : p := 1*1, t := 2, n := x$$

$$t < h : p := 1*2, t := 3, n := x^2$$

$$t = h : p := 2*3, t := 4, n := x^3 \text{ and ``out''}$$

This provides not only $p = h!$ but also $n = x**h$.

The flowchart for calculation of sines contains the following intentional inefficiencies and errors (we do learn by mistakes).

1. Since $2*i - 1$ appears twice, $h = 2*i - 1$ should be computed once and used twice: first in $x**h$, then in $h!$

2. Although the loop for $h!$ is correct, its use is inefficient. For instance, the program loops 23 times to compute 23!, but since 21! is already stored, 22 loops can be saved by calculating $23*22*(21!) = 23!$

3. $n := x**h$ was calculated by multiplying x by itself h times. It is better to update it through $x**(2 + h) := (x**2)*(x**h)$.

4. The most inefficient step is in reversing the sign according to $z := (-1)**(i+1)$ each time through the loop. If z is initially 1, assigning $z := -z$ each time around the loop is sufficient.

5. Last, but certainly not the least mistake is that the calculation would never stop; there is no way to leave the loop of Fig. 7-1(a).

The loop may be terminated after a given fixed number of times [Fig. 7-1(c)], say, $n = 8$ times. In the case of computing the sine, this would be wrong since for angles approaching 90 degrees, the terms for $n = 9, 10, . . .$ are substantial and cannot be neglected. It is better to use a variable-length loop [see Fig. 7-1(d)] checking $abs(r)$ against some accuracy ϵ entered at initialization time.

To sum up the first four points, note that each successive term may be computed from the previous by multiplying it with $-x^2$ and updating the denominator so that instead of $(h+2)!$ we calculate $(h+2)*(h+1)*h!$. The resulting flowchart of Fig. 7-1(e) is implemented in Code 7-5.

There are a number of LOOP-STATEMENTS in Ada. Their syntax is

```
SR:  LOOP-STATEMENT ::= [ITERATION-CLAUSE] BASIC-LOOP ;
SR:  BASIC-LOOP ::= loop SEQUENCE-OF-STATEMENTS end loop
SR:  ITERATION-CLAUSE ::= while BOOLEAN-CONDITION |
                          for IDENTIFIER in [reverse] DISCRETE-RANGE
```

The basic-loop: "**loop** . . . **end loop**" will go on "forever" (i.e., as long as the computer is operating). This is useful for system programming when defining a scheduler

```
procedure code75 is
j : INTEGER; deg, dif, eps, rad, s, sn, u, v, x, y, : FLOAT;
begin rad := 57.2957795; GET (deg);
  x := deg/rad;   j := 2;                                      -- rad converts degrees to radians.
  eps := 0.001; sn := SIN(x);                                  -- The series starts with its second term.
                                                               -- sn is the sine computed by a library
                                                               -- routine and used to check accuracy; eps is the
                                                               -- allowed error size. Initialization.

  u := x; s := x; y := x*x; dif := s-sn; deg := 1.0;           --
  PUT ("x dif sn", x, dif, sn); NEW_LINE;
  PUT (" j u v dif s");          NEW_LINE;
  while abs(dif) > eps loop                                    -- Loop according to the algorithm.
    v := u*y; deg := deg/FLOAT(j*(j-1));                       -- deg is now the denominator.
    s := s+v/deg; dif := sn-s;                                 -- s and dif are updated
    PUT (j, u, v, dif, s); u := v; j := j+2;                   -- and so are u and j.
  end loop;
end code75;
```

Code 7-5

and in embedded real-time systems. Such loops may be left by an EXIT-STATEMENT. There are four possibilities of exits. With lab as the loop's name, i.e., written as lab: in front of the loop, they are:

```
exit;                 -- Exits innermost loop.
exit lab;             -- Exits loop named "lab".
exit when condition;  --Exits innermost loop only if condition is TRUE.
exit lab when condition; -- Exits loop lab if condition is TRUE.
```

The EXIT-STATEMENT can be used at the beginning, end, and inside of a loop, but in no other statement except in a loop:

```
loop                    | loop                    | loop
  exit when CONDITION   |   --- calculation       |   --- part-1.
  --- Calculation       |   exit when CONDITION   |   exit when CONDITION
end loop;               | end loop;               |   --- part-2
                        |                         | end loop;
```

Note: -- is a comment, --- is a pseudoinstruction!

The first is called a pre-test, while the second is a post-test loop identical to what some other languages use when the loop has to be traversed at least once. Pascal for instance uses the REPEAT . . . UNTIL; Fortran always traverses a loop at least once.

Next is a solution of $r = \sqrt{x}$ by the Newton-Raphson method: $r(i+1) := (r(i) - x/r(i))/2$ which we developed in Sec. 6-2. The problem is to select an accuracy criterion. Writing abs$(x - r^2) < eps$ is wrong since for very large numbers, the above implies an accuracy above that of most computers. It is better to use abs$(x/r^2 - 1) < eps$ which will guarantee that the result is accurate to within a small eps for any x. Code 7-6 uses instead a library function.

```
procedure code76 is
x,sq,r,tr,dif,eps : FLOAT;
begin -- The accuracy is assumed as 0.01, sq is needed for checking.
  eps := 0.01; GET(x); sq := SQRT(x); r := x/2.0; -- Initialization.
  PUT(" trm root sq difference "); SKIP_LINE; dif:=0.0;
  while dif < eps loop
    trm := 0.5*(r-x/r); r := r-trm; dif := ABS(sq-r);
    PUT(x); PUT(trm); PUT(r); PUT(sq); PUT(dif);
  end loop;
end code76;
```

Code 7-6

Code 7-7 reads student grades and stores them in a vector "grades(i)." Having finished reading, an average is computed by dividing the sum of all grades by the number of students, *ns*. Finally, the grades are printed as is the percentage "standing" of the student in this exam. We use the FOR-LOOP: **for** *i* **in** 1..*ns* **loop** . . . **end loop**;.

The FOR-CLAUSE implicitly declares an iteration variable, here *i*. The range must be discrete so that it can be counted as integers, Booleans, or characters, etc. The bounds are evaluated only once, ahead of the loop. An iteration variable is considered to be constant inside the loop; it should be used but not changed (assigned to) inside the loop; it cannot be changed outside the loop, or terminate abnormally.

```
with TEXT_IO; use TEXT_IO;
procedure code77 is
i,ns,stud: INTEGER; grades:array(1..100) of FLOAT;
gr,average,sum,standing: FLOAT;
begin GET(ns); SKIP_LINE; sum := 0.0;
  for i in 1..ns loop
    GET(gr); grades(i) := gr; SKIP_LINE;
    sum := sum+gr;              -- Accumulate the sum of grades in "sum".
  end loop;                     -- For computing the average, ns has to be
  average := sum/FLOAT(ns); -- converted to a floating-point number.
  PUT_LINE(" No.  grade  average  standing "); NEW_LINE;
  for i in 1..ns loop           -- The student number is incremented.
    standing := 100.0*grades(i)/average;   -- The percentual standing
    PUT(i,2); PUT(grades(i),6,3,0);        -- of student i.
    PUT(average,6,3,0); PUT(standing,6,3,0); NEW_LINE;
  end loop; -- The numbers 6,3,0 were used to print nicely.
end code77;
```

Code 7-7

The **for** and the conditional **exit** are exemplified by a loop which searches if a given key "*k*" appears in array ar(1..*n*), and if so, at which index:

```
for i in 1..n loop     -- Index i is declared implicitly by the for.
  found: = i;          -- This index must be stored in "found" to be
  exit when ar(i)=k;   -- recovered outside of the loop.
end loop;
```

The loop index *i* could also be changed in reverse which for the above means that the loop is written as **for** *i* **in reverse** 1..*n* **loop**.

The FOR-STATEMENT **for** *i* **in** 15..1 **loop** is a NULL-STATEMENT and is executed zero times. To make sure that the programmer does not do it inadvertently, the range (i.e., the two limit values) are evaluated *before* executing the loop and cannot be changed inside the loop.

As a summary, it is seen that whereas **while** is testing when to leave the loop, **for** is counting how many times to execute it.

7–3 SUBPROGRAMS

There are two types of subprograms, namely *functions and procedures*. They are similar and will be discussed together.

The functional notation (e.g., $a = b + f(x)$ where $f(x)$ is the *value* of function "f" for a given value of the *parameter* x) can be used in Ada. It is exemplified by the calculation of an area (see Sec. 6-2).

```
z : = h*[0.5*(f(a)+f(b)) + Σf(i)] for iΣ=1, . . . ,n−1
```

The values of $f(x)$ for $x = a,b$ and $n-1$ intermediate values of x are to be computed. Writing a straightline program with the entire code for computing $f(x)$ in $n+1$ places is out of the question. Even writing it for $f(a), f(b)$ and once inside a loop on i is too tedious. It is better to *declare* a function $f(x)$ once so that each time it is *called* with a different *argument* x, it delivers the value of $f(x)$ for this particular x. The program is shown in Code 7-8.

Note the following:

1. Up to now, statements followed each other sequentially, except if a **goto** or **exit** changed the control structure—and the use of gotos is discouraged. In code78, there is a jump to a function definition each time $f(x)$ is written. Moreover, the program "remembers" to return to the instruction immediately following the *call*.
2. Suppose the function changes, say to $f(x) = \sin h(x)*\log(x)$ or any other complicated function. In order to use code78, only the statements defining the function $f(x)$ have to be changed, but the rest is left as is. Thus, the program represents a general, albeit a simple-minded solution to the calculation of an area for any $f(x)$.
3. The part of the program starting with **function** . . . is a function declaration, because it declares the function. It must appear directly after the declarations of the variables. A function declaration consists of an identifier (the name of the function), the names of its parameters (the formal parameter list), **return** followed by the type of the result, **is**, the declaration of any variables *local* to the function, and a SEQUENCE-OF-STATEMENTS which form the body of the function and are enclosed in **begin** . . . **end** brackets.
4. No actual computation is performed as a result of declaring a function; for this to happen, the function must be *called* by writing the name of the function. When a function is called, the *actual arguments* replace the *formal parameters*. Control is then transferred to the first executable instruction of the function. When the return statement of the function is encountered, the execution returns to the statement following the point at which the function was called.

```
with TEXT_IO; use TEXT_IO;
procedure code78 is
a,b,c,h,s,x: FLOAT; n: INTEGER; -- These variables are local to and
  -- will be assigned memory locations each time code78 is called.
  function f(x: FLOAT) return FLOAT is -- x is a "formal" parameter.
    loc: FLOAT;              -- This function will return the value f(x)
    begin                    -- for a given x in the local variable loc.
      loc:=5.0+0.1*x*x;      -- Any other function could have been chosen.
      return loc;            -- This is the entire calculation in this case.
    end; -- This is the end of the declaration of the function f(x).
begin                        -- This is where the main program starts.
  GET(a); GET(b);            -- Read the input values and initialize the
GET(n);
  s := 0.0; h := (b-a)/FLOAT(n); -- values of the area s, height h as
  c := b-h; x := a+h;        -- well as the start x and stop c of the loop.
  while x=<c loop            -- This loop accumulates the sum of the areas
                                 from a+h
    s:=s+f(x); x:=x+h;       -- to c. Calling f(x) supplies the value f( )
  end loop; -- for the given argument x. Next f(a) and f(b) are added
  s:=h*(s+0.5*(f(a)+(b))); --to s and the value of the area calculated.
  PUT(n,3); PUT(h,3,3,0); -- Print out the values.
PUT(s,5,3,0);
end code78;
```

Code 7-8

5. The order of the entire program, namely its heading, declarations, function declarations, and program body, must be adhered to.

6. Suppose the function above was declared as function $f(x,y$: FLOAT). Calling it by $f(a,b)$ employs the positional notation because a and b replace x and y according to their position. It could employ the named notation, say as $f(a=>y, b=>x)$ which is especially useful when the names convey some meaning e.g., $f(\text{abscissa}=>y,$ ordinate $=>x)$.

7. The variables of the main program are called *global*; those of the function are *local* (to them). The *scope* of the global variables is the entire program unless they are redeclared. The scope of a local variable is the body of the function in which it was declared.

8. One of the reasons for writing functions is to group sequences of closely related instructions into program "modules" and build the program from these modules.

This makes the program more easily understood, easier to maintain, and enhances *program correctness*. The functions can be tested independently of the main program and used after having been tested thoroughly. The entire testing procedure is thereby made simpler, and the cooperation between workers on a large program made easier. It was once argued that the number of errors of a program is proportional to the 2.7-th power of its length. A short function may thus have fewer errors.

9. The name of the function is called its "designator." It can also be an operator symbol, provided the correct number of parameters is used:

function "*" (a:MATRIX; b:MATRIX) **return** MATRIX **is . . . end** "*";
could be called as
"*"(x,y : MATRIX) or in infix notation as x*y.

The use of the same name (here *) for more than one item is called *overloading*. The compiler can distinguish between the cases by checking the parameters. Thus, if the parameters are integers, integer multiplication is used; if they are floating-point variables this is used (and for instance the exponents are added); and if they are matrices, the multiplication is done according to the body of the function so that $c: = d*e$; will multiply the two matrices d and e.

Overloading of words is used extensively in natural languages; otherwise the number of words would have to be enormous. However, it often leads to ambiguities resolved in the minds of the speakers (and listeners). Actually, overloading exists also in all computer languages: we use "*" for multiplication of integers and floating-point numbers, but the compiler has to activate two different machine-language procedures for them. The resolution of any ambiguities is left to the compiler. Therefore, overloading should only be used if similar actions on different parameters are to be done. Otherwise a connection is implied which doesn't exist.

Most of this applies to procedures as well. The differences are:

1. Functions return a value and can thus be used as parts of expressions instead of variables. Like variables, a function has to indicate the type of value it will return by declaring it following the **return** in the function line. Every call to a function must return a value, so that every function must be terminated by a RETURN-STATEMENT.

2. A procedure provides services for other units, but may return many or no specific values. It may be terminated by a **return** (without the parameter), or if it does not have the **return** in its procedure line it may be terminated by arriving at its end point.

3. Ada considers the set of values of the individual items to constitute the *state* of the program unit. The execution of a procedure changes the state of the unit because

procedures have *side effects* in the sense that they change the value of external, nonlocal variables. The execution of a function delivers a result. Functions should not have side effects; they change the environment by returning one or more values.

4. There is a difference in the way parameters are passed. Since procedures usually perform more general services, the rules for passing parameters are more flexible. The mode of parameters is discussed next.

The parameters of a procedure may have the mode **in**, **out** or **in out**. The difference between them can be exemplified as follows:

Suppose you talk to your bank clerk. If he looks into the file and copies the balance on a note, he can use the note while talking and make a deposit, but when the talk is over, the amount in your file was not changed—only the note indicates that the balance changed. If the clerk brings the file with him and updates it while talking to you, the balance may be changed during the conversation and will be different when returned to the file cabinet. The first is sometimes called a transfer by ''value,'' the second a transfer by ''variable.''

In Ada these two are called **in** and **out** parameters respectively. As seen in the example, the **in** parameter is really initialized as a copy of, say, the balance. The actual balance (parameter) is inaccessible to the procedure (it is in the file cabinet) and will not be changed by this procedure (the clerk). There are two distinct variables: one within the subprogram (the copy) and the other outside (in the file cabinet).

When using **out** parameters, the formal parameters are *replaced* by the actual arguments. Only the actual parameter exists and therefore will be changed by the procedure; the formal parameter is just a placeholder. Even though the actual and formal parameters may have two different names, both refer to the same item and memory location (The file).

The general rule for *choosing* parameter modes is to use **in** modes to pass values into a subprogram and **out** modes to return them. Since **in** parameters work on a copy, they do not allow the value of the actual parameter to be changed. They should be used when the value of the actual parameter must be protected from accidental or intentional change. However, this same feature means that results cannot be transferred back to the calling program through **in** parameters. On the other hand, **out** parameters can be used for returning results. However, because a return path is possible, the protection of actual parameters is lost and changes to the formal parameters will cause corresponding changes to the actual parameters. Stated simply: If the name appears only on the right of the replacement operator '': = '', the mode is **in**, if it appears only on the left, the mode is **out**, and if it appears on both sides, the mode is **in out**. An **in out** parameter is initialized as if it were an **in** parameter, but loads the memory as if it were an **out** parameter. Since side effects are not allowed for functions, their parameters can only be **in** parameters.

Code 7-9 exemplifies the mode of parameters. It swaps the value of two variables ''*a*'' and ''*b*'' and will be used in Code 7-10 to effect the sorting of a list.

Suppose that the mode of old and nnew is **in**. In that case, the swap procedure makes temp : = 10, then old : = 20, and finally nnew: = temp will make nnew = 10.

```
with TEXT_IO; use TEXT_IO;
procedure code79 is
a, b: INTEGER; -- The values of a and b will be swapped or exchanged.
  procedure swap (old, nnew: in out INTEGER) is -- Note the mode used.
  temp: INTEGER := old;      -- This is the way to both declare a local
  begin                              -- variable "temp" and initialize it.
    old := nnew; nnew := temp;   -- old and nnew were swapped here.
  end;
begin
  a := 10; b := 20;          -- Instead of input, the two objects
  PUT (a, 3); PUT (b, 3);    -- were initialized and printed
  swap (a, b);               -- This call should exchange the two values.
  PUT (a, 3); PUT (b, 3);    -- To check it, they are printed again.
end code79;
```

Code 7-9

Unfortunately, all these operations are made on the "copies"; the *a* and *b* outside of the swap procedure are not affected by it and the second print would be *a* = 10 and *b* = 20—nothing was exchanged. Since old and nnew are on both sides of ": = " they should be **in out** parameters.

The bubble sort is shown in Code 7-10.

```
with TEXT_IO; use TEXT_IO;
procedure code10 (a: in out VECTOR) is -- The list to be sorted is stored
first, last: INTEGER; x, y: FLOAT; -- in a (vector) array "VECTOR".
  procedure swap (old, nnew: in out INTEGER) is
  temp: INTEGER := old;
  begin
    old := nnew; nnew := temp;   -- In case you wondered why nnew was
  end;                            -- used, recall that new is a keyword
begin                             -- of ADA. Please, add a Boolean
  first := 1; last := n-1;        -- variable and a while to repeat the
  for i in first . . last loop    -- loop as long as necessary.
    x := a(i); y := a(i+1);
    if x>y then swap (x, y); end if;
  end loop;
end code10;
```

Code 7-10

As a final example of a subprogram we calculate the "zero" of a polynomial $p(x)$, i.e., that x for which $p(x) = 0$. Since this is similar to finding a zero of any $f(x)$, we will again use Newton's iterative method $x(i+1) := x(i) - p[x(i)]/p'[x(i)]$. $p[x(i)]$ and $p'[x(i)]$ are abbreviated to $p(i)$ and $p'(i)$ respectively. For simplicity we will calculate $p(i)$ and $p'(i)$

$$\text{for } p(x) = a(4)*x^4 + a(3)*x^3 + a(2)*x^2 + a(1)*x + a(0).$$

The polynomial can also be written according to "Horners rule" as

$$p(z) = a(0) + z*(a(1) + z*(a(2) + z*(a(3) + z*a(4))))$$

where $x = z$.

This recurrent rule involves about half the original number of multiplications, and is simpler to program, since each new term is the result of multiplying the previous term by z (or x) and adding it to $a(i)$.

To use the Newton-Raphson method, the derivative is required:

$$p'(z) = a(1) + z*(2*a(2) + z*(3*a(3) + 4*z*a(4))0$$

Use the linear part of $x^4 - 10*x^3 + 37*x^2 - 60*x + 36 = 0$ for calculating the initial value: $-60*x + 36 = 0$; $x \simeq 0.5$. Next use Horner's rule for finding $p(x)$ and $p'(x)$ for $x = z = 0.5$. Since $p(z) \simeq 14$ and $p'(z) \simeq -30$, the next best value of z is $z(1) \simeq 0.5 + 14/30 = 0.96$.

No indices are needed to calculate $p'(z)$; it is called c in Code 7-11, which implements this method.

7-4 DIVERSE LANGUAGE ISSUES

7-4.1 Blocks and Scope of Variables

Ada carefully distinguishes between declarations and instructions. Declarations introduce objects; instructions don't. When both exist, e.g., in subprograms, declaration of objects must precede their use.

The simplest structure which includes both declarations and a body is a *block*. It encloses a SEQUENCE-OF-STATEMENTS in **begin**, and **end** brackets. An optional DECLARE-STATEMENT may introduce variables which then apply within the block but not outside of it. In this way, blocks associate local names with a SEQUENCE-OF-STATEMENTS.

When entering a block, the local variables are assigned memory locations and may be initialized to objects outside of the block. When leaving the block, *the variables cease to exist*. For instance, the swapping procedure used earlier can be rewritten as a block with "temp" existing only inside the block (i.e., between **declare** and **end**).

```
declare
temp: INTEGER := a;   -- This is a local, temporary variable. Any
begin                 -- attempt to use it outside the block is
  a := b; b := temp;  -- illegal. The swap requires no parameters.
end; -- The scope of temp is inside the block; it is visible there.
```

```
procedure code11 is
i,j,k,lim,n : INTEGER; c,d,eps,x,z : FLOAT;
a,b : array(0 .. 10) of FLOAT;
begin GET(n,eps,lim);   -- Read the order of the polynomial, run-limits
for i in 0 .. n loop get(a(i));   end;   -- and constants of the polynomial
for k in reverse 2 .. loop   -- Each root is calculated separately.
x := -a(0)/a(1); i := 0;                         -- Initial values for x, for
loop i := i+1; b(k) := a(k); c := 0.0;           -- b(k) and c.
   for j in reverse 0 .. k-1 loop                -- This loop calculates values of
   z := b(j+1); b(j) := z*x+a(j); c := c*x+z;    -- p(x) as b(0) and c.
   end loop;                                     -- The exit will occur if number of
d := -c/b(0); x := x+d;
d := ABS(b(0));
   exit when ((i>lim) or (d<eps));               -- iterations>lim or abs(b(0))<eps.
end loop;
for j in 0 .. k-1 loop a(j+1) := b(j+1); end loop;
   -- Shifting the coefficients of the polynomial for the next lower zero.
   PUT(x);                                        -- Print result.
end loop;                                         -- End of loop on k.
end code11;                                       -- End of code 11
```

Code 7-11

Large programs are usually written by teams of programmers. If each team has used the same name for different purposes, these names must use different locations in memory. An identifier declared in a block is internal, or *local* to the block in which it is declared and *global* to all inner blocks nested in it, provided they are not redeclared in these inner blocks. Redeclaring a variables means that a separate memory location is provided for it and is thus different from the global object. (Variables of a subprogram are also local.)

Blocks can be nested and identifiers are interpreted according to the innermost enclosing block. Thus, in the block structure below inner *b* hides outer *b* in the inner block. The *scope* of the outer ''*a*'' is the entire outer block, but ''*b*'' is not visible in the inner block because it was redeclared.

```
<<outer>> declare    -- A declaration is visible in those parts of
a,b: INTEGER;        -- the program where its identifiers can be
begin                -- used. Since a block may have a name (label),
  -- outer a,b.          declaration, and is a SEQUENCE-OF-STATEMENTS
  <<inner>>declare   -- enclosed by begin and end, it is similar to
  b,c: INTEGER;      -- a procedure. The only thing missing are
  begin                   -- the formal parameters. Because of this,
  -- outer a, inner b,c    procedures and functions can be considered
  end inner;              -- to be blocks.
  -- outer a,b valid.      Blocks can be nested inside procedures and
end outer;               -- used in parallel programs.
```

Variables are associated with storage locations, and block structures lead to an efficient technique for storage management. The fact that a variable is not known outside the block in which it is declared means that storage for objects in a block need only be allocated during the execution of the block. Thus, storage for the variables is obtained when the block is entered and released when the block is left. This is the basis for *sharing of storage* between blocks.

7–4.2 Enumeration Types

The standard, predefined types are INTEGER, FLOAT, BOOLEAN, and CHARACTER. Ada allows programmers to introduce their own data types, declared as:

type SOMENAME **is** its definition ;

The simplest new datatype is the enumeration (list) defined by

```
SR: ENUMERATION_TYPE_DEFINITION ::=
    ( ENUMERATION_LITERAL { , ENUMERATION_LITERAL } )
SR: ENUMERATION_LITERAL ::= IDENTIFIER | CHARACTER
```

For example, the colors of paint may be declared as

type COLOR **is** (black, blue, brown, green, red, white, yellow);

This definition shows that enumerations contain any finite number of identifiers or characters separated by commas and enclosed by a pair of parentheses.

Enumerations are useful in defining variables which range over finite value sets such as colors, directions, weekdays, truth values, etc. Enumeration types are discrete types with an ordering determined by the order in which the variables are listed in the type declaration.

The type of a variable is its constant property (e.g., integer variables are only whole numbers). The type also specifies which operations are permissible for variables of that type. Each type therefore *encapsulates* a set of values which objects of that type may assume with the set of operations that may be performed on them.

A color declared above could have the *values* black, blue, etc., but arithmetic operations on them are meaningless. Still, if the programmer wants to declare a function say '' + '' for mixing colors, he/she may do so.

The set of elements of an enumeration is considered to be ordered. They have successor and predecessor functions (defined later). The predecessor of brown is blue and its successor is green. There is no successor to yellow and no predecessor to black.

Suppose the days of the week and months are needed in a program. They could have been defined as numerical constants, e.g., as

sun = 1; mon = 2; tue = 3; wed = 4; thu = 5; fri = 6; sat = 7;
jan = 1; feb = 2; .... dec = 12;

or as enumerations:

type DAYSOFWEEK **is** (sun, mon, tue, wed, thu, fri, sat);
type MONTHS **is** (jan, feb, mar, apr, may, jun, jul, aug, sep, oct, nov, dec);

Next, some objects of these types can be declared, e.g.,

m, wn: MONTHS; w, m: DAYSOFWEEK; carcol : COLOR;

A variable, say carcol, can be assigned a value carcol : = black. In Ada, objects of different types should not be mixed. Hence, assignment of values (e.g., $m := w$) for days-of-week is valid, but $w := wn$; is illegal because a month was assigned to a day.

Next is an algorithm to calculate the days of the week for a given date, e.g., that May, 14, 1975 was a Tuesday. First, ''a'' is computed:

a : = d + 2*m + 3*m/5 + y + y/4 - y/100 + y/400 + 1

with the date being m,d,y (month, day, year) and the months numbered as

jan$=13$, feb$=14$, mar$=3$, . . . , dec$=12$. For $5, 14, 1975$ a is:
  a := $24 + {}^{15}\backslash_5 + 1975 + 493 - 19 + 4 + 1 = 2481$.

The remainder of dividing a by 7 is the number of the day, with Sunday being numbered 1. In the present case: ${}^{2481}/_7 = 354.3$, so that May,14,1975 was a Tuesday. The program is shown in Code 7-12.

```
with TEXT_IO; use TEXT_IO;
procedure code12 is
type DAY is (sun, mon, tue, wed, thu, fri, sat); -- DAY is an enumeration in
a, d, j, j2, j3, k, m, y: INTEGER;                    -- which sun is numbered 0.
aday: DAY; itoday: array (1 . . 7) of DAY; --itoday stores the days in an array.
begin aday := sun; itoday (1) := sun; -- Its first element is sunday, the
  for i in 2 . . 7 loop -- other six elements are inserted in this loop by
    aday := DAY'SUCC (aday); itoday (i) := aday; -- the successor function.
  end loop; --Next read and print the date, and change january, february
  GET (m); GET (d); GET (y); PUT (m); PUT (d); PUT (y); -- to 13 and 14 resp.
  if m<3 then m := m+12; end if;
  a := d+m+m+3*m/5+y+y/4-y/100+y/400+1;              -- Compute a and
  PUT (" a is "); PUT (a, 4); NEW_LINE;              -- print it.
  aday := itoday ((a mod 7)-1); PUT (" The day-of-the-week is a ");
  case aday is -- -1 was needed because sun is not numbered 1 but 0.
    when sun =>  PUT (" sunday ");
    when mon =>  PUT (" monday ");
    when tue =>  PUT (" tuesday");
    when wed => PUT ("wednesday");
    when thu =>  PUT ("thursday");
    when fri =>  PUT (" friday ");
    when sat =>  PUT ("saturday");
    when others => PUT (" An error has occurred ");
  end case; NEW_LINE;
end code12;
```

Code 7-12

The statement **type** DAY **is** (sun, . . . ,sat) is a *selector*. If the expression in the CASE-STATEMENT is "sun," the program transfers to the first **when**; if it is "mon," to the second, etc. A list of labels could be used instead of a single label, e.g., **when** sun | sat => PUT("weekend").

The types CHARACTER and BOOLEAN are predefined as enumerations, e.g.,

type BOOLEAN **is** (FALSE, TRUE); -- so FALSE < TRUE.

Enumeration types may be used as the range of iterations of a for-loop or as the index-range of an array. Thus, the two loops:

for m **in** COLOR **loop** and **for** m **in** black..yellow **loop**

are equivalent.

7–4.3 Subtypes and Derived Types

It is sometimes desirable to create types that are identical to some known or predefined types but whose values are constrained to some range. This could enable re-using the software on another computer or constrain subscripts to some range. Such types are called "subtypes" and are declared for example as: **subtype** INDEX **is** INTEGER **range** 0..100; or **subtype** WEEKDAY **is** DAYSOFWEEK **range** mon..fri; which would exclude the weekend. Objects can then be declared as

sub: INDEX; workday; WEEKDAY; i: INTEGER; d: day; etc.

The declaration of "sub" defines it as a *subtype* of *base type* INTEGER by placing a constraint on it in the form of a range. Should an INDEX be outside the range of 0..100, an error will occur at runtime. A subtype is not a new type and may be mixed with its base type. This may lead to run-time errors because $i := $ sub; is always correct, but sub $:= i$ is not necessarily correct.

A new type can be defined so that its characteristics are *derived* from a "parent" type (e.g., **type** WKDAY **is new** DAYSOFWEEK):

SR: DERIVED-TYPE-DEFINITION ::= **new** SUBTYPE-INDICATION

A derived type creates a new type incompatible with the parent type but with all of its characteristics. Derived types provide additional means of protection against mixing of types in an expression. For instance, if a person's weight, age, and social security number were all declared of type INTEGER, expressions such as weight + age or age*socsec are allowed, but if they were all defined like **type** AGE **is new** INTEGER; etc., then a: AGE; w: WEIGHT; s: SOCSEC; would make $w+$a or $a*s$ illegal.

A derived type can be converted to its parent type and vice versa, by prefacing it with the name of the type to which the conversion is made. For instance, if the declarations: **type** LENGTH **is new** INTEGER; **type** AREA **is new** INTEGER;*lf,ls*:LENGTH; *a*:AREA; are used to calculate an area, this is done by writing: **return**(AREA(INTEGER(*lf*)*INTEGER(*ls*))); where *lf* and *ls* were converted into integers, multiplied, and the result converted into the type "area."

7–4.4 Attribute Enquiries

The Reference Manual of Ada lists 45 attributes of data. For example, using the declaration of DAY in code 7-12 we have the attributes

```
DAY'FIRST          -- The first element of day is "sun".
DAY'LAST           -- The last element of day is "sat".
DAY'SUCC(tue)      -- The successor to tuesday is "wed".
DAY'PRED(tue)      -- The predecessor to tuesday is "mon".
DAY'POS(sun)       -- Position of "sun" is 0, so this is the value here.
DAY'VAL(1)         -- The value of object 1 is "mon".
```

The attribute IMAGE returns the string which represents its argument. Thus, DAY'IMAGE(1) returns the string "mon" and not the object mon of type day. The syntax is

```
SR: ATTRIBUTE ::= NAME'ATTRIBUTE-DESIGNATOR
SR: ATTRIBUTE-DESIGNATOR ::= ATTRIBUTE-NAME [(EXPRESSION)]
```

To prompt a user for, say a day, one could declare

```
subtype WEEKDAY is DAY range mon..fri;
PUT(WEEKDAY'IMAGE(DAY)); PUT(" ? ");
```

write this, and then wait for the input.

7–5 STRUCTURED DATA: ARRAYS AND RECORDS

An array is an ordered collection of objects all of which have the same type. The TYPE-DECLARATION **type** VEC **is array**(1..5) **of** INTEGER; (or FLOAT) defines a *template*. The declaration *v*: VEC; declares an object (in this case a one-dimensional array—a vector).

Arrays can also be declared without first defining their types:

```
st: array(1..80) of CHARACTER; str: array(1..80) of CHARACTER;
```

These are called *anonymous types* since there are no specific type-declarations and the compiler has to provide them. Since the programmer does not know what these are, *st* and *str* are considered to be of different types and could not be mixed in expressions. They could be so mixed if they were declared as follows:

```
type S is array(1..8) of CHARACTER; st, str: S;
```

Two arrays *a,b* can be assigned *a*:=b. For arrays of discrete elements there are relations $<, <=, >, >=$ which describe the lexicographic order. Concatenation of two vectors is written as vector1 & vector2.

In other languages, initiating values of an array is done mostly in loops e.g., **for** *i* **in** 1..10 **loop** *a(i)* := 0; **end loop**; In Ada, the aggregate is used frequently for initialization of constant arrays, say the number of hours worked during the week:

```
constant WEEKDAY : = (mon|wed => 9, tue => 10, others => 8);
or . . . : = (9,10,9,8,8) or . . . thur ..fri => 8);
```

Bounds for declaring objects in an array with unspecified bounds can be taken from an initialization. Hence, the statement

```
v: VEC : = (2,4,6,8,10); initializes v(1) : = 2, . . . ,v(5) : = 10
```

and makes the bounds of the index to be 1..5.

The **others** part, if used, should be the last in the aggregate. Positional and named associations should not be mixed in an aggregate.

Attribute enquiries for vector types and objects include, among others:

```
VEC'FIRST     -- Lower bound of the index for the vector (type).
VEC'LAST      -- Upper bound of the index for the vector (type).
VEC'LENGTH    -- Number of components of the vector (type).
```

and the same for objects: v'FIRST, v'LAST and v'LENGTH.

Consider two different declarations of a 20-by-20 matrix:

```
type MATRIX is array(1..20,1..20) of FLOAT;
type VECTOR is array(1..20) of FLOAT;
type MAT is array(1..20) of VECTOR; a:MATRIX; b:MAT;
```

Both a and b have $20*20=400$ elements, but a can access only single elements [e.g., $a(3,5)$] while b may access an entire row as in $b(6)$.

For some concurrent programs, it is important to deal with contiguous parts of arrays called *slices*. If v is a one-dimensional vector and i,j are in the v'RANGE then the subvector $v(i..j)$ consisting of the elements i to j is called a "slice" of v. For array b above, $b(6..10)$ would be a slice of 5 rows.

Code 7-13 sorts vector "a" into descending order by finding the maximum of successive slices $a(i..a$'LAST$)$ of a. It calls the function max to find the index of the greatest element in a slice and the procedure "swap" to exchange the first and the largest element of successive slices:

```
procedure code13(a: in out VECTOR) is
j,k: INTEGER;                    -- Local variables of code13.
begin                            -- Since i is increasing, the loop below
  j : = a'RANGE-1;               -- is for 1..j, 2..j, etc. The range may
  for i in 1..j loop;            -- not be known ahead of code13. For i in
    k:=max(a(1)..a(a'LAST));     -- the range of the slice, find the index
      swap(a(i),a(k));           -- of the largest element in
end loop;                        -- a(i)..a'LAST.
end Code13;                      -- Exchange the two elements and repeat.
```

Code 7-13

For indices of arrays with multiple dimensions, an attribute inquiry is subscripted (e.g., MATRIX'FIRST(k) for the k'th index).

The indices of arrays must be constrained or be of discrete types, but the specification of the range may be delayed until the variable is declared. Thus, **type** AMOUNT **is array**(INTEGER **range** <>) **of** FLOAT; uses "<>" to mean that the range will be specified later and the type is called unconstrained. The symbol "<>" is called a "box." The advantage of such specifications is that only as much storage is assigned as is needed, but it makes the work of a compiler more difficult.

Enumerations are useful as indices of arrays. The enumeration "DIRECTION" **is** (N,E,S,W)") could imitate clockwise rotation by declaring

constant array (DIRECTION) **of** DIRECTION: = (N=>E, E=>S, S=>W, W=>N) ;

Sets can be realized by arrays of Boolean elements: **type** SET **is array** (discrete) **of** BOOLEAN; Operators **and**, **or**, and **not** can then be used for their set counterparts (see Sec. 7-10.2).

Next we show how to multiply efficiently two matrices. The type of matrix is usually declared as a two-dimensional array: **type** MATRIX **is array**(subscript,subscript) **of** FLOAT; but the memory of a computer is not two-dimensional. Hence, the matrix is stored in the memory as a vector, so that matrix(i,j) is accessed by the compiler as follows: matrix(1,1) is stored in location $m(b)$, where m signifies "memory"; the first row in locations $m(b)$ to $m(b+n-1)$, the second row in locations $m(b+n)$ to $m(b-1+2*n)$, and so on. Row j is stored in locations $m(b+(j-1)*n)$ to $m(b-1+j*n)$; Element (i,j) is therefore stored in location $m(b+(j-1)*n+i)$ and to *accesss* it, the compiler has to do two additions α, and one multiplication μ (assuming that b is added initially). Thus, writing the following program for matrix multiplication:

```
for i in 1..n loop
  for j in 1..n loop
  c(i,j) := 0.0;
    for k in 1 . . n loop
      c(i,j) := c(i,j)+a(i,k)*b(k,j);
    end loop;  -- of k.
  end loop;    -- of j.
end loop;      -- of i.
```

would require $4*n^3$ accesses (or $8*n^3*\alpha + 4*n^3\mu$) to arrays a,b and c, as well as $n^3*\alpha + n^3*\mu$ in the loop on k. For 100-by-100 matrices, this amounts to $9,000,000*\alpha + 5,000,000*\mu$. It is therefore more efficient to write the innermost loop as follows:

```
sum := 0.0;
for k in 1..n loop
  sum := sum+a(i,k)*b(k,j);
end loop;   -- on k.
c(i,j) := sum;
```

Array c is not accessed inside the loop, but matrices a and b are accessed n^3 times. The program is therefore rewritten as follows.

Suppose we store matrix "a" row-wise as a vector {i.e., $a(1,1..n)$ in $m(1..n)$), then $a(2,1..n)$ in $m(n+1,2*n)$ and so on until $m(n*(n-1)+1..n*n)$. Element $a(i,k)$ is then stored in $a(i-1)*n+k$. The point is that the next higher element in the same row is stored one location away. Likewise, matrix "b" is stored column-wise and the elements accessed consecutively. Code 7-14 uses such storage and requires only $3*n*\alpha+n*\mu$ for the inner loop. For 100×100 matrices we need only 3 and 1 instead of 9 and 5 million operations respectively! The program may be made even more efficient if one notes that variable k used to update elements of a and b can be used also for updating "jj."

```
procedure code14 is
size: constant : = 8;
order: constant : = 10;
subtype SUBS is 1..size;
subtype ARR is array(SUBS) of FLOAT;
subtype VEC is array(SUBS) of FLOAT;
ii,jj,ji,k,n,nn,nm1: INTEGER: sum: FLOAT;
a,b,c: VEC;

begin
  PUT("The real size of the matrices");
  GET(n); nm1 : =n-1; k: =n*n;
  PUT("Read matrix a row-wise");
  for i in 1..k loop
    GET(a(i));
  end loop;
  PUT("Read matrix b column-wise");
  for i in 1..k loop
    GET(b(i));
  end loop;

  nn: =0; ii : =1-n;
  for ki in 1..n loop      -- This loop is the entire calculation.
    ii: =ii+n; jj: =1-n;
    for ji in 1..n loop
      jj: =jj+n; sum: =0.0;
      for k in 0..nm1 loop
        sum: =sum+a(ii+k)*b(jj+k);
      end loop;
      nn: =nn+1; c(nn): =sum;
    end loop;
  end loop;
end code14;
```

Code 7-14

Suppose that an employee is characterized by

type FIELDS **is** (name, nmb, street, city, zip, salary).

Then, one can declare table: **array**(name..salary) **of** STRING; and refer to the zip code not by table(5) but by table(zip). This might be nicer, but it is better to use records instead.

An old-style punched card is an example of a record. A punched card may look like: 1234 "Wallach" 8.35 5.14 21.25, for the following record:

```
type PCARD is record           -- This is a new data structure.
  employee: INTEGER;           -- The employee's number
  name: STRING(8);             -- The employee's name
  atime,dtime,rate: FLOAT;     -- Arrival, departure time; hourly rate
  gross: FLOAT;                -- Gross income
end record;
pay: PCARD;                    -- This declares pay an object of type pcard.
```

Note the following:

1. Objects of *various types*, namely integers, real numbers, and strings of characters, are included on the pay-card. Since arrays collected only items of identical types, they cannot be used to store cards like this. It is records that collect data of different types.

2. Every component or *field* of a record can be selected using the dot notation (e.g., pay.rate where pay is the record object and rate is one of its fields).

3. pay.name was declared as a string of eight characters. An assignment could read it, and a PUT statement could print it.

4. Records may serve as basic types of arrays, so that the company may have records like paylist: **array**(1..999) **of** PCARD; in which an index points to the record of every employee. Conversely, a record may include an array so that the gross-field may be changed into:

```
gross: array(1..31) of FLOAT;  -- for the 31 days of a month.
```

Suppose that n employees are on the payroll with a PCARD for each. At the end of a month, the gross pay could be computed by:

```
for j in 1..n loop             -- j is the index to a file of an employee
  g := 0.0;                    -- The gross pay of a month will be Σg(i)
  for i in 1..31 loop
    g := g + pay(j).gross(i);
  end loop;                    -- Having accumulated the pay for all 31
  pay(j).gpay := g;            -- days "i" in g, assign it to the gpay-
end loop;                      -- field of employee "j".
```

Next is a program that uses the previously defined record. Remarks which replace comments follow this program (Code 7-15).

```
with TEXT_IO; use TEXT_IO;
procedure code15 is
type STR is array(1..8) of CHARACTER;
type FIX is delta 0.01 range 0.00 .. 24.00;
type PCARD is record
  employee: INTEGER; name: STR;
  atime, dtime, rate: FIX; gross: FLOAT;
end record;
pay: pcard; ta, td, i: INTEGER;
ma, md, tim, tim2, over1, over2: FIX;
begin
  PUT(" Type-in the card, please "); PUT_LINE;
  GET(pay.employee); pay.name := "Yehuda ";
  GET(pay.atime, pay.dtime, pay.rate);
  PUT(pay.employee, pay.name, pay.atime, pay.dtime, pay.rate);
  ta := INTEGER(pay.atime); td := INTEGER(pay.dtime);
  ma := pay.atime-FIX(ta); md := pay.dtime-FIX(td);
  PUT_LINE("Arrival and departure hours and minutes," ta, td, ma, md);
  if td>12 then td := td+12; end if;
  if md<ma then td := td-1; md := md+0.60; end if;
  PUT("Again", ta, ma, td, md); PUT_LINE;
  tim := md-ma+FIX(td-ta); -- The calculation of the time.
  if tim>8.0 then
    over1 := tim-8.0;
    if over1>1.0 then over2 := over1-1.0;
    else over2 := 0.0;
    end if;
    over1 := over1-over2; tim := tim+over1-over2;
  end if;
  pay.gross := (tim+1.2*over1+1.5*over2)*pay.rate;
  PUT("Card: ", tim, over1, over2, pay.gross); PUT_LINE;
end code15;
```

Code 7-15

1. In the declaration of the variables, *ta* and *td* were the hours of arrival and departure respectively. They are both INTEGERS and are computed as *ta*:=INTEGER (atime) and *tb*:=INTEGER(dtime). The minutes of arrival and departure are *ma* and *md*. Two decimal places after the decimal point are used for minutes. Conversion may prove difficult especially since $\frac{1}{60} = 0.01666...$, $\frac{2}{60}$, etc., are irrational numbers and cannot be properly represented. Since *ta* is an integer, it has to be converted to a fixed-point representation, and the number of minutes *ma* can be

computed as pay$a$.$a$time-FIX(ta). The calculation is in real numbers and the results assigned to real numbers.

2. Variables *tim* and *tim*2 are needed to store the time and overtime which result when the arrival time is subtracted from the departure time. The variables *over*1 and *over*2 are overtime for the first hour and for the remaining time.

3. Whenever employees leave in the afternoon, the card shows the time as for instance, in 5.14, so that *td* = 5. In order to compute the time of work *tim*, 12 should be added to *td* (for *td* ≥ 1*pm*).

4. If the number of minutes at departure time is less than the number of minutes at arrival, then their difference would be negative. To prevent this, the departure hour is decremented by 1 and the minutes of *td* are incremented by 0.60. Thus, the time *td* = 5, *md* = 0.14 is changed into *td* = 16 (or 4 p.m.) and *md* = 0.74.

5. The calculation proceeds as follows: *tim*: = *md* − *ma* + FIX(*td* − *ta*); computes the time of work as a real number. If *tim* > 8.0, then the overtime is *tim* − 8.0. For the first hour of overtime, 1.2 times the normal rate and for the remaining overtime 1.5 times the normal rate will be paid.

Records are a type of data and as such must be attached to some specific operations (Encapsulation of data and operations). Ada provides (for entire records) only assignments and testing of relations. For example, complex numbers can be declared as

```
type COMPLEX is record
  realp, imagp: FLOAT;
end record;
```

Suppose that *a*,*b*: COMPLEX; is declared. Records can be initialized as *a*.real*p* := 2.5; *a*.imag*p* := 3.5; or *a* := (2.5, 3.5); or even by name association *a* := (imag*p* = >3.5, real*p* = >2.5). The operations on fields can be performed but only in the context of their data types. For *a* and *b* above, *a**b has no meaning, but multiplication *a*.real*p**b.real*p* is correct. The way to define multiplication and other operations on complex numbers will be discussed in Sec. 7-7.

Arrays of records are often used. As an example, consider how to input a tabulated function. This could be done as follows:

```
type ORDINATE is delta 0.10 range 0.00 .. 100.00;
type ABSCISSA is delta 0.05 range 0.00 .. 50.00;
type POINT is record            -- Each point has an abscissa and
  x: ORDINATE; y: ABSCISSA;     -- ordinate of a given type and
end record;                     -- range. The table is an
table: array(1..nmb) of POINT;  -- array of points, each indicated
for i in 1..nmb loop            -- by its x and y coordinates.
  GET_LINE(table(i).x, table(i).y);
end loop;                       -- End of reading the table.
```

Records are defined *recursively* (i.e., in terms of themselves). This means that a record can be a field of another record. For instance, a student file can be declared as follows:

```
type PERSONALDATA is record
  firstname: STRING(1..10); lastname: STRING(1..15);
  address: STRING(5..50); socsecnm: INTEGER;
end record;
type STUDENTREC is record
  pd:PERSONALDATA; -- This record is a field
  dept: STRING(1..4); -- in the student's record
  year: INTEGER range 1900 .. 2000;
end record;
```

The type of a record field *must not* be a new or anonymous type. It is therefore illegal to declare

```
type ILLREC is record
  a: array(1..100) of FLOAT;
end record;
```

Records can use parameters for referring to the existence, constraints, and initial values of some fields. Such parameters are called *discriminants*. They are used in cases where the information within a record may be missing or where it may vary according to some additional information. For such cases, there are records with *varying structure* exemplified by Code 7-16.

This record structure is set up with variant fields and a CASE-STATEMENT to specify the circumstances under which each variant is used. Each variant has associated with it a list of components, and each component has a type. The components and their types are enclosed in parentheses, and all the variants are listed after the invariant portion of the record structure. Component names should not be duplicated, even in different variants.

A record type with a variant part has a special component called a tag and a selection mechanism to supply the various substructures for possible values of the tag. Variant records, while useful, raise some difficulties in implementation. First, there is the question of assignment to the tag field. The value of the tag is set when the record object is created. While the program must be able to assign values with an ordinary statement to components of the record, assignment of a new value to a tag is a very different question because to change the tag really implies a change in the structure of the record. From the implementation point of view, this could imply a change in the amount of storage required for the record. Therefore, Ada specifically forbids assignment to tags.

Second, even in the simple case of a constant tag as above, the cases were so different for single, married, widowed, and divorced persons that it is difficult to assign memory to the record.

```
type NAME is array(1..20) of CHARACTER;
type GENDER is (male,female);
type STATE is (single, married, widowed, divorced);
type MONTH is (jan,feb,mar,apr,may,jun,jul,aug,sep,oct,nov,dec);
type DATE is record
  mo: MONTH; day: INTEGER range 1..31; year: INTEGER range 1900..2000;
end record;
type PERSON(sex:GENDER;st:STATE) is record -- sex is the discriminant.
  socsecnmb: INTEGER;
  last, first: NAME;
  case sex is
    when male=>colorblind: BOOLEAN;-- Females are not color blind.
    when female=>maidenname; NAME: -- Males do not carry maiden names.
  end case; -- Note that the two fields were completely different.
  identnmb: INTEGER;
  case st is
    when single => null;
    when married => spouse: INTEGER; -- Is the socsecnmb;
                    children: INTEGER;
                    wedding: DATE;
    when widowed | divorced => since: DATE;
  end case;
end record; --This record provides a description of a person.
```

Code 7-16

7–6 RECURSION AND LIST PROCESSING

7–6.1 Recursion vs. Iteration

Let us start by defining the factorial as $n! = 1*2*3*...*n$ for any integer $n \geq 0$ and $0! = 1! = 1$. This is called an iterative definition.

The factorial function can also be defined recursively with $n!$ defined as $n*(n-1)!$, i.e., in terms of a factorial function.

It is easy to compute recursively defined functions in Ada, e.g., $n!$ could be computed by the function fact in Code 7-17.

```
function fact(n: INTEGER) return INTEGER is    -- Since fact is a function, its
begin                                          -- parameter is an in parameter.
  if n=1 then                                  -- The first part of defining n!
    return(1);                                 -- The recursive part of the
  else return(n*fact(n-1));                    -- definition, namely
  end if;                                      -- n! = n*(n-1)!
end;
```

Code 7-17

Let us follow this program for $n = 4$. When called as fact(4), the function will substitute 4 for n and activate fact:$= 4*$fact(3). The two problems are how to store the number 4 for later use, and how to call the same function while it is still being processed.

Calling "fact" while executing it is called a recursive call. In a more literary way: "I came, I saw, I conquered (veni, vidi, vici)" is iterative because "I conquered" does not depend on "I saw" etc., but "You said, he thinks, I am mad" is recursive because each one is linked to the previous. Because fact(4) $=$ $4*$fact(3) and thus is linked to fact(3), we called it recursive.

Iteration is the repeated execution of a computational task (routine) until some condition is met. Each routine is computed, then the condition is checked and, in case it is not satisfied, the routine is restarted. By contrast, recursion involves self-nesting. The computation of the routine may be interrupted during its execution by repeated calls on the same routine again and again. The check occurs during (or within) the routine and the routine may be called as a subroutine of the uncompleted, previous (identical) routine.

To proceed with the computation of fact(4), an additional, recursive call on "fact" results, for we cannot compute fact(3) unless we store 3 and recursively call fact(2). This in turn results in fact:$= 2*$fact(1) requiring the storage of 2 and a call on fact(1). This last call is not recursive and results in fact(1):$= 1$.

Function "fact" was called recursively for $n = 4$, 3, and 2. These calls must next be completed and the intermediate results multiplied out.

Suppose we store the values in a *stack* working similar to a pile of dishes in a cafeteria (see Fig. 7-2). If we remove the stored numbers starting from the top and multiply them out we get 4! $= 1*2*3*4 = 24$. This is the correct result but it seems to be very inefficient since we had a lot of items to remember and to call "fact" repeatedly without leaving it first. An iterative solution is shown as Code 7-18.

```
function factorial(n: INTEGER) return INTEGER is
m : INTEGER;
begin
  m:=1;
  for i in 1..n loop
    m:=m*i;
  end loop;
  return(m);
end factorial;
```

Code 7-18

There is nothing to remember here or to store and no stack is needed. For $n = 4$ the loop produces iteratively m: $= 1*1$; $m:= 1*2 = 2$; $m:= 2*3 = 6$; $m:= 6*4 = 24$ and returns the result factorial:$= 24$.

Somebody once remarked that "Everything you recourse, I can iterate and do it

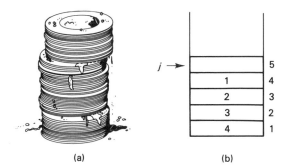

$j \rightarrow$

	5
1	4
2	3
3	2
4	1

Figure 7-2 The stack (and the analogy to a stack of plates)

(a)   (b)

better.'' This is not true in all cases, as was shown by simple examples taken from the area of compilation [Wal73].[†]

An expression like $((((6+3)/(8-5))*2)+1)$ is called *fully parenthesized* since every ordered triple: ''number, operator, number'' is enclosed in a pair of parentheses. To evaluate it numerically, one has to find the innermost pair of parentheses, perform the indicated operation, replace the triple and its enclosed pair of parentheses by the result and start all over again. How can a computer do it?

In a method proposed long ago by Rutishauser, weights were attached to variables, numbers, left parentheses, operators, and right parentheses, namely $w = +1$ to the first three and $w = -1$ for the remaining two symbols. Adding these weights consecutively results in a picture of *hills* as in Fig. 7-3(a) for the above expression.

Reduction of the expression can proceed according to the ''highest hill.'' Thus, the subexpression $(6+3)$ being located on the highest hill yields 9 and the expression is reduced to $(((9/(8-5))*2)+1)$. Next, $(8-5)$ leads to $(((9/3)*2)+1)$ and reducing the expressions on the highest hills leads consecutively to $((3*2)+1)$, $(6+1)$, and finally to the result, in this case 7.

It seems obvious that in the above procedure only the parentheses play any role in locating the highest hills. We may slightly modify Rutishauser's method by attaching a weight $w = +1$ to a left parenthesis, $w = -1$ to a right parenthesis, and $w = 0$ to all other symbols. The evaluation [Fig. 7-3(b)] proceeds similarly.

Let the number of symbols in the fully parenthesized expression be n and the total sum of weights up to symbol k be

$$p(k) = \Sigma w(i); \ i\Sigma = 1,2,\ldots,k$$

It may be verified for a correct fully parenthesized expression that $p(n) = 0$ and for $1 < i < n$, $p(i) > 0$ (since the number of left parentheses must be larger than that of right parentheses). It follows that any correct fully parenthesized expression has at least one maximum (but may have more) and this maximum corresponds to the innermost pair of parentheses, say *pmax*. This forms the basis for the following algorithm:

[†]Y. Wallach: ''Study and Compilation of Computer Languages,'' Gordon and Breach Science Publ., New York, 1974. Reprinted by permission.

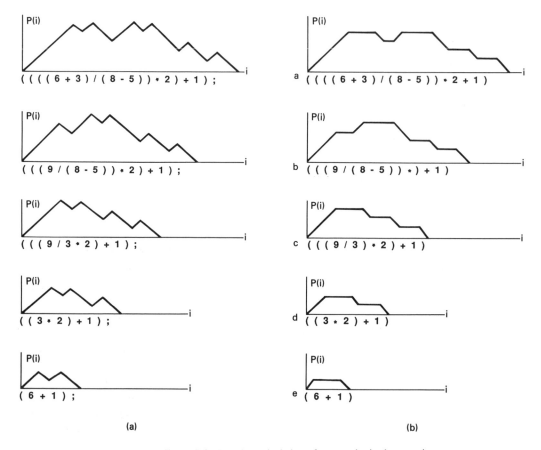

Figure 7-3 Iterative calculation of a parenthesized expression

1. Make an initial scan summing weights and calculating *pmax*.
2. Scan the expression left-to-right summing weights in say p. Whenever $p = pmax$, one of the innnermost pairs has been located and may be reduced. The expression is then recopied from this position up to the final symbol and the scan continued.
3. With the scanning complete, reduce *pmax* by 1. If the new $p$max is 0 then the evaluation is complete. Otherwise restart at 2.

Code 7-19 corresponds to the iterative algorithm for single-digit operands and binary operators. Reviewing this program shows that it has the following disadvantages:

1. It requires too much memory space since the entire expression has to be stored.
2. It requires a complete scan to determine the initial $p$max, thus wasting time. In the scan the expression itself remains unchanged.
3. It requires frequent copying within the expression, wasting time.
4. The program is relatively long and therefore error-prone.

```
with TEXT_IO; use TEXT_IO;                      -- Code 7-19
procedure iter is
type OP is (add,sub,mlt,dvd);                   -- Enumerating operators.
ch:array(1..30) of CHARACTER; c:OP;             -- Storing the expression.
a,b,j,m,p,pmax,x:INTEGER; sym:CHARACTER;        -- Variables

procedure schreibe is                           -- Printing procedure
begin
  PUT_LINE(" Schreibe ");
  for i in 1..m loop PUT(ch(i)); end loop;
end schreibe; NEW_LINE;

begin m:=0; p:=0; pmax:=0;                       -- Starting loop to read
  loop GET(sym);                                 -- the symbols and to
    if sym=' ' then null;                        -- accumulate pmax.
    elsif sym='(' then
      p:=p+1;
      if p>pmax then pmax:=p; end if;
      m:=m+1; ch(m):=sym;
    elsif sym=')' then
      p:=p-1; m:=m+1; ch(m):=sym;
    else
      m:=m+1; ch(m):=sym;
    end if;
    exit when sym=';';
  end loop;
  for n in reverse 1..pmax loop                  -- For each pmax down to 1
    PUT(" pmax = "); PUT_LINE(n,3);
    schreibe; NEW_LINE;
    p:=0; j:=1; sym:=ch(1);
    while sym/=';' loop                          -- perform this loop.
      if sym='(' then p:=p+1;
      elsif sym=')' then p:=p-1;
      end if;
      if p=pmax then                             -- Highest hill found.
        a:=INTEGER(ch(j));                       -- Change characters to
        c:=OP(ch(j-1));                          -- integers a and b, but
        b:=INTEGER(ch(j-2));                     -- make c an operator.
        case c is                                -- Perform the operation
          when add => x:=a+b;                    -- according to value of c
          when sub => x:=a-b;
          when mlt => x:=a*b;
          when dvd => x:=a/b;                    -- Next shift remaining
        end case;                                -- expression to left.
        ch(j):=CHARACTER(x); j:=j-4;
        for i in j+1..m loop
          ch(i):=ch(i+4);
        end loop; schreibe;
      end if;
      j:=j+1; sym:=ch(j);                        -- Go on scanning.
    end loop;                                    -- End of the while loop
  end loop;                                      -- End of the main loop
end iter;                                        -- End of the procedure
```

Code 7-19

```
procedure rec is
type OP = (add, sub, mlt, dvd);
ch: array(1..30) of CHARACTER; c: OP;
a, b, j, x: INTEGER; sym: CHARACTER;
procedure khtov is
begin PUT_LINE(" khtov ");
  for i in 1..m loop PUT(ch(i)); end loop;
end khtov;

begin j:=0; GET(sym);
  while sym/=';' loop            -- Loop until encountering an ';'
    if sym=')' then              -- Perform an operation
      a:=INTEGER(ch(j));         -- First operand
      c:=OP(ch(j-1));            -- Operator
      b:=INTEGER(ch(j-2));       -- Second operand
      case c of
        when add => x:=a+b;
        when sub => x:=a-b;
        when mlt => x:=a*b;
        when dvd => x:=a/b;
      end case;                  -- Next store the result on top
      j:=j-3; ch(j):=CHARACTER(x); -- of the stack.
    else                         -- For any symbol except ')'
      j:=j+1; ch(j) :=sym;       -- just copy.
    end if;
    GET(sym); khtov              --Prepare the next element.
  end loop;                      -- End of the while-loop.
end rec;                         -- End of a rather short program.
```

Code 7-20

Most of these disadvantages may be removed by using a stack *s* with pointer *j*. A provision must be made that both input and output are through the *top* location of the stack. Thus, with *j* being the index of the top location, only three operations may be performed with elements of a stack:

1. Input of an element *a* into the stack by: $j := j + 1$; $s(j) := a$;

2. Output of an element *b* from the stack by: $b := s(j)$; $j := j - 1$;

3. Erasing the top element of the stack by: $j := j - 1$;

A stack is best visualized as in Fig. 7-2(a)(b) where the pointer *j* indicates the present *height*. It also explains the stack's other names like LIFO for Last-In, First-Out, or

Push-Down store. Note that information stored (mostly only temporary) in a certain order, is available in a strictly reversed order.

The recursive algorithm is very simple: Transfer every input element into the stack until ')' is encountered. At this point, remove the three top-most elements from the stack, perform the indicated operation and replace the top-most element ('(') by the result. Proceed with these two steps until encountering a semicolon.

In Code 7-19, the expression was processed from its first to last character for each *pmax* and was therefore called iterative. In Code 7-20, the processing is done each time a right parenthesis is encountered even if a previous left parenthesis was not yet processed and is therefore called recursive.

The recursive program is considerably more efficient than the iterative evaluation. As a matter of fact, it has the following advantages:

1. Sequential reduction of pairs of parentheses is made during a single left-to-right scan.
2. The memory, in this case the stack, holds only intermediate results of already reduced subexpressions and "below" them the elements of operations not yet executed. This leads to two advantages:
3. Optimum utilization of the working storage space.
4. Removal of recopying and shifting, i.e., a safer and faster program.
5. The program is shorter and may therefore have fewer errors.

7-6.2 List Processing

Items of a list can be stored as a vector, but moving data in or out of such lists is very cumbersome. It is better to use *lists*. Unlike a sequential representation where successive items of a vector are located a fixed distance apart, a list allows these items to be placed anywhere in memory. Another way of saying this is, in a sequential array we have to store the entire vector, while a list stores only needed elements. It grows and diminishes dynamically.

To access elements in the list in the correct order, we store with each element the *address* (location) of the next element in that list (and not its index). This is the *pointer or link* to the next item. In general, a node is a collection of data, $d1,. . .,dn$ and links $l1,. . .,lm$. Each item in a node is called a *field*. A field contains either a data item or a link.

Suppose we have a list of two-letter items NS,IS,NT,OR,NS,NA,NT. It could be stored using pointers as in Fig. 7-4 by Code 7-21.

The elements may be of any data type, the pointers point to an element or to the "ground" (by being assigned pnt: = **null**).

```
with TEXT_IO; use TEXT_IO;      -- Code 7-21 inputs, saves a list,
procedure 1st is                -- and finally prints it.
type ELEMENT;                   -- This is an incomplete declaration.
type POINTER is access ELEMENT;   -- Pointing to an unknown element.
type ELEMENT is record          -- The record ties these declarations.
  next: POINTER;                -- ELEMENT has a POINTER next and
  da, db: CHARACTER;            -- two CHARACTERs of data.
end record;                     -- Look in the text for the use of
base, p, pa, pm: POINTER;       -- these pointers.
d1, d2: CHARACTER;              -- The d1, d2 are auxiliary data.

begin                                -- The compiler does not make the
  p: =new ELEMENT; p.next: =null;    -- pointer null, so we do it here.
  GET (d1); GET (d2);                -- Input of the first two letters,
  p.da: =d1; p.db: =d2;              -- insertion into element p, and
  base: =p; pm: =p;                  -- initialization of two pointers.
  while p.next=null loop             -- Loop as long as new elements are
    GET (d1); GET (d2);              -- input. When the list is complete
    exit when d1='0';                -- i.e. it is 00, exit the loop.
    p: =new ELEMENT; p.next: =null;  -- This creates a new record,
    p.da: =d1; p.db: =d2;            -- inserts the data into it, points
    pm.next: =p; pm: =p;             -- from the last node to it, and
  end loop;                          -- TRANSFERS pm.

  pm: =base; PUT ("The output:");    -- Start printing the list by
                                     --   making
  while pm/=null loop                -- pm point to base. The last node
    PUT (pm.da, pm.db);              -- was null. Print the 2 characters.
    pm: =pm.next;                    -- THIS IS THE OPERATIVE STATEMENT
  end loop; NEW_LINE;                -- shifting pm.
end 1st;
```

Code 7-21

Notes.

1. "ELEMENT" is declared before it is defined. "POINTER" links it to ELEMENT, so it also is undefined (Ada allows breaking the question of who is first: the chicken or the egg). "ELEMENT" is then defined as being a record which includes a pointer "next" and two characters. It can therefore be pictured as in Fig. 7-4(a). Objects *base* and *p* as well as the "moving" pointer *pm* are declared as pointers.

2. The program starts with $p := $ **new** ELEMENT which will generate an element and its pointer p. After reading, we have Fig. 7-4(b), and by making $pm: =p$; base: $=p$; we have Fig. 7-4(c).

3. In the **while** loop we first generate a new element, thereby shifting *p* to point to it (with *pm* and *base* still pointing to the previous element). Next we read and print the data to be stored and then do the following:

4. The statement *pm.next:* = *p* lets "next" of the previous element (as still identified by *pm*) to point to the new element and finally, since we don't need *pm* any more, *pm:* = *p* will shift it so that Fig. 7-4(d) results. When we have completed the loop, the entire list is stored with *pm* and *p* pointing to the last element. [Fig. 7-4(e))].

5. Next we print the list. First, we restore pointer *pm* to base (*pm* is the moving, base is the starting, and *p* is the end-pointer). The assignment *pm:* = *pm.next* shifts the moving pointer to the next element in the list because *pm.next* points to it. This goes on until **null** is encountered.

We now use lists for sorting in a (binary) tree structure. For instance, with an input 3,5,4,3,1,6,2,4,3,0, Code 7-22 produces the tree of Fig. 7-5. In the tree, the numbers on the left are smaller, on the right larger than in a given node. Since an item may appear any number of times, we use a counter "cnt." Code 7-22 has enough comments to be self-explanatory.

Such programs are even more applicable for listing the words in a book (a concordance). The words can be ordered by comparing characters so that they are

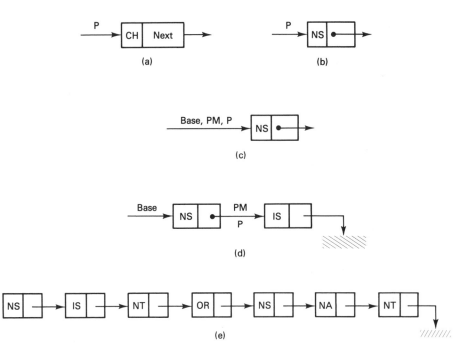

Figure 7-4   Setting up a list

```ada
with TEXT_IO; use TEXT_IO;          -- Code 7-22 creates a binary
procedure sorttree is              -- tree of numbers, sorts it
subtype POS is INTEGER             -- and prints it out.
  range 0..999; type NODE;         -- NODE represents a number.
type PNT is access NODE;           -- pnt is a pointer to a node
type NODE is record                -- of the binary tree. "cnt"
  cnt, nmb: POS;                    -- counts the numbers nmb.
  left, right: PNT;                 -- There are two pointers,
end record;                        -- the left and right pointer.
root, cp, pp: PNT;                 -- The root, the current and the
n: POS;                            -- previous pointers: cp and pp.

function newnode (nn: POS)         -- This function creates a new
        return PNT is              -- node to which p will point.
p: PNT;                            -- It then initializes cnt to 1,
begin                              -- inputs positive number nn and
  p:=new NODE;                     -- grounds the two pointers.
  p.cnt:=1; p.nmb:=nn;             -- The number nn is inserted
  p.left:=null;                    -- into the tree.
  p.right:=null; return p;         -- Pointer p to the new node
end newnode;                       -- is returned.

procedure traverse (p: in PNT) is  -- This procedure moves over
begin                              -- the binary tree recursively,
  if p/=null then                  -- printing first the
    traverse (p.left);             -- left part
    PUT ("The count and number");
    PUT (p.cnt, 3); PUT (p.nmb, 4); -- and then
    NEW_LINE; traverse (p.right);  -- the right subtree.
  end if;
end traverse;

procedure leftcreate (nn: POS,     -- This procedure creates
        pp: in out PNT) is         -- a left node,

qq: PNT;
begin                              --provided it
  if pp.left/=null then            -- was not grounded.
    PUT_LINE ("Cannot create left");
  else qq:=newnode (nn);
    pp.left:=qq;
  end if;
end leftcreate;

procedure rightcreate (nn: POS,    -- This procedure creates
        pp: in out PNT) is         -- a right node.
```

322

```
qq : PNT;
begin
  if pp.right/=null then
    PUT_LINE ("Cannot create right");
  else qq:=newnode (nn);
    pp.right:=qq;
  end if;
end rightcreate;


begin                               -- START OF THE MAIN PROGRAM.
  PUT ("Enter the first number");
  GET(n);  PUT(n,3);
  root:=newnode (n);                -- Create the node for the root.
  GET(n);  PUT(n,3);                -- We indicate the end of the
  while n/=0 loop                   -- list of numbers by making n=0.
    cp:=root;                       -- Point with cp to the root.
    while cp/=null loop             -- Loop until encountering null.
      pp:=cp;                       -- Update previous to current
      if n<pp.nmb then              -- pointer. If the number is
        cp:=pp.left;                -- smaller then go left,
      elsif n>pp.nmb then           -- if the number is larger
        cp:=pp.right;               -- then go right. If the two
      elsif n=pp.nmb then           -- numbers are equal, increase
        pp.cnt:=pp.cnt+1; exit;     -- the counter and exit.
      else PUT_LINE ("Something wrong");
      end if;                       -- If relations >,<,= are not
    end loop;                       -- sufficient, then something
    if n<pp.nmb then                -- is wrong.
      leftcreate (n,pp);            -- Create a left node,
    elsif n>pp.nmb then
      rightcreate (n,pp);           -- or a right node, or
    elsif n=pp.nmb then             -- if the two numbers are equal
      PUT ("equal");                -- don't create any node.
    else PUT_LINE ("What happened?");
    end if;
    GET(n);  PUT(n,3);
  end loop; NEW_LINE;
  PUT_LINE ("The sorted, counted tree");

  traverse (root);                  -- THIS RECURSIVE PROCEDURE MOVES OVER

end sorttree;                       -- THE ENTIRE TREE AND PRINTS IT OUT.
```

Code 7-22

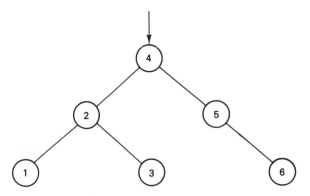

Figure 7-5 Setting up a tree using lists

arranged in a binary tree similar to that of Fig. 7-5. The number of times a particular word is used is kept in counters (an array of cnt).

The reader is encouraged to use the input and follow the assembling of the tree and the printing of it. This is the best way I know to learn list processing.

7–7 PACKAGES

Each conversation with devotees of Fortran leads to the statement: "But Ada doesn't have complex numbers and operations, which Fortran provides." Ada can in fact provide them as will be shown below.

Complex numbers are Abstract Data Types, *ADTs*. Actually, even the integers are ADTs since, as far as the computer is concerned, the only data type it recognizes is bit strings of word length. Thus, if we declared a,b: INTEGER; and written $a := b + 14$; the compiler assigns locations to a, b and 14 and calls some machine-language subroutines to perform the required operations. The details of *data representation and implementation* (the procedures) are a matter for the compiler; this is called *information hiding*. It is necessary in order to be able to treat complex numbers for what they are namely ADTs, but to hide the gory details of the implementation. Another note: Suppose we have declared an array of integers. The abstraction of an integer was *nested* inside the abstraction array.

In Sec. 7-5 we declared complex numbers to be records similar to RECT in Code 7-23 below. If complex numbers are needed in a number of programs, then each could have the declaration of the type RECT (for rectangular coordinates of a complex number) and then declare objects such as for instance, a,b: RECT;.

Normally, it is desirable that *all* programs be able to use complex numbers without having to declare them *each time*. This can be achieved by declaring *once* these numbers collectively as a *package* like in Code 7-23 and using them in *all* programs. Since the types (and objects) are considered "resources," packages are used as vehicles for providing resources to users.

The computational resources provided by a package may, and often will, include some programs (actions, verbs) in addition to the data (static, nouns). What good is having the type RECT if the operations on it are not defined? Recall that *each data type is distinguished by the set of operators that may be applied to it.* It is therefore imperative that, when declaring new *data types*, the operations that can be performed on them are also *encapsulated* with them. An important example of encapsulation is that for ADTs (e.g., complex numbers, sets, lists, trees etc.) which are treated as abstract quantities while the programmer concentrates on their mathematical properties.

```
package COMREC is              -- SPECIFICATION OF COMREC
  type RECT is record          -- It provides the type
    re, im: FLOAT;             -- RECT,
  end record;
  i, j: INTEGER;               -- two local variables,
  function "+" (v, w: RECT) return RECT;   -- and functions for
  function "-" (v, w: RECT) return RECT;   -- adding, subtracting,
  function "*" (v, w: RECT) return RECT;   -- multiplying and
  function "/" (v, w: RECT) return RECT;   -- dividing complex
end package;                   -- numbers.

package body COMREC is         -- BODY OF COMREC
c : RECT; -- All other local items should be declared here.
function construct (x, y: FLOAT) return RECT is
begin                          -- This function constructs a complex
  c.re := x; c.im := y;        -- number from two floating-point
  return c;                    -- numbers x and y
end construct;
function "*" (v, w: RECT) return RECT is
begin                          -- This function multiplies two complex
  c.re := v.re*w.re-v.im*w.im; -- numbers v and w according to:
  c.im := v.im*w.re+v.re*w.im; --     (v.re+j*v.im)*(w.re+j*w.im) =
  return c;                    --     (v.re*w.re-v.im*w.im) +
end "*";                       -- j * (v.im*w.re+v.re*w.im)
--- Functions "+", "-", and "/" should be declared here.
end COMREC;
```

Code 7-23

The package COMREC is shown in Code 7-23. Its specification declares the operations on complex numbers, but does not elaborate how they are done. Does a user need to know how they are implemented? Certainly not. On the contrary, everybody is better off if users don't know them, since they might be tempted to change and ''improve'' them. Other users of the same data types and operations may then find unexpected results which they cannot explain.

One of the advances of Ada was to recognize this fact with the result that a package has a "visible" or *interface* part and (if needed) a "hidden" part, called the *body* of the package. These two parts may be written by two different programmers and even be separately compiled. Thus, the *specification* makes certain resources (data, functions etc.) available to users, the *body* describes the actions to be implemented. The body may be replaced by a better one without having any effect on the programs that use the package. If only data items are included in the specification, no body is needed. Parenthetically, the mode (procedure or function), name, parameter-list and (for functions) the type of the result of a subprogram may be considered its interface with the remaining part being its body.

An Ada package can therefore be visualized as in Fig. 7-6. The visible part of a package is like a display in a bakery. The merchandise is shown (specification, interface) so that the customer knows what can be bought. It is inside the bakery (body) that bread or cookies are made. The buyer doesn't have to know how the cookies are made to enjoy them.

The package makes the type *visible* to the users of the package by a USE-STATEMENT. Any program that needs to refer to complex numbers can then do so as follows, without having to repeat the declarations:

```
declare use COMREC;
begin
  a, b: RECT;
  -- A program which uses data such as a.xcoor may be inserted.
end;
```

The keyword **use** removes the front item of a name. Thus, if a program starts without **use** COMREC; multiplication of a with b would have to be written as COMREC."*"(a,b). It is obviously preferable to write it as $a*b$ which is legal if **use** COMREC; precedes $a*b$; the qualifier COMREC may be dropped and, as seen earlier, the infix operator used. (Sometimes, it is better to leave the full name at least in large programs so that the meaning and ancestry of the name are known to programmers.) A USE-CLAUSE can occur only as the first statement in a declarative part. The USE-CLAUSE may contain the names of several packages.

The statement **use** COMREC; makes available all data types, objects, and subprograms defined in the specification part of the package. It is as if these were declared to be part of the user's program. Another statement, **with** COMREC, would cause the compiler to fetch the *precompiled code* and link it to the user's program. The WITH-STATEMENT must always precede the USE-STATEMENT. This is the way that the TEXT_IO was used in all the programs up to now: writing **with** TEXT_IO; **use** TEXT_IO; linked the precompiled code of this I/O package to the program so all objects and functions of it could be applied.

The above use of a package helps in making the language *portable*. For instance GET(ch) will use different machine-language subroutines in the body for reading a character on different computers, but no change is needed when the same program is used on different computers.

Figure 7-6   Hiding the "cookies" in a bakery

Another advantage of packages is that they may be *separately compiled*. Programs are written as "compilation units" (i.e., packages) preceded by WITH and USE-STATEMENTs, compiled separately and then joined together. Therefore, packages can be used in order to divide large programs logically into manageable units. Also, separate compilation makes it possible to test a new package, together with the units mentioned in its CONTEXT-CLAUSE (the USE and WITH-STATEMENTS), separately from the rest of a program. All this is in line with software engineering principles and makes programming less error-prone. Note though that if something in the body is changed, only the body has to be recompiled, but if anything in the specification is changed, both it and the body have to be recompiled. This is so because the specification declares what is available and must then provide it.

A queue (of a brokerage house) was introduced in Sec. 6-3. Assuming that the largest number of customers (*nc*) is known, and a CALL is the known type of information to be stored, the declarations for setting up the queue *without using a package* would be as listed in Code 7-24.

The callers can now add and remove messages. Unfortunately, there is no way in which to give the user access to procedures "add" and "remove" *without* making the waiting list also accessible. Since customers have access to the waiting list (or the functions of COMREC), they can change somebody else's message (call). For instance, a user could reduce *nc*, thereby automatically removing some waiting calls, or make other unauthorized and often wrong changes. *This is not desirable*. The internal structure of the queue is visible to the user, which may therefore operate on it not only with insert and

```
subtype SUB is INTEGER range 1 .. nc;
type AR is array (SUB) of CALL;
type CALLQU is record
  queue: AR;                          -- The array of waiting calls.
  head: SUB := 1;                     -- Head and tail are initialized
  tail: SUB := 1;                     -- to 1, and since no calls are
  nmb: INTEGER range 0..nc-1 :=0;     -- waiting, their nmb is 0.
end record;                           -- Next is the list of waiting
wlist: CALLQU;                        -- calls and procedures for
 procedure add(c: in CALL) is         -- adding and removing calls.
begin
  if wlist.nmb < nc+1 then                --If the queue has space
    wlist.queue(wlist.head) :=c;          --then add call c,
    wlist.head := (wlist.head+1) mod nc;  -- advance pointer head
    wlist.nmb := wlist.nmb + 1;           -- and the number of
  end if;                                 -- waiting calls.
end add;
procedure remove(c: out CALL) is
begin                                 -- If at least one
  if wlist.nmb >0 then                 -- call is waiting, then
    c := wlist.queue(wlist.tail);     --assign it to c and update
    wlist.tail := (wlist.tail+1) mod nc;
    wlist.nmb := wlist.nmb-1;         -- the tail pointer and the
  end if;                             -- number of waiting calls.
end remove;
```

Code 7-24

remove operations. The integrity of the queue is compromised, so we need a different method.

There are two items of programming without packages we need to improve. (1) If a program declared **use** COMREC; a:RECT; then it is entirely legal to write $a.xcoor + 5.4$ (i.e., treat object a as a floating point number). This is wrong since a should be treated as a complex number in the abstract sense. (2) If the implementation is modified, *all programs* must be checked to see whether the change has an effect on the way the objects are used. Experienced programmers know that it is very hard to check all places of usage and almost impossible to keep track of where these places are located in all the programs written for the system.

To solve both problems, *private types* should be used. For instance, package COMREC may be rewritten as

```
package COMREC is
type RECT is private;
unit: constant RECT := (0.0, 1.0);
function "+" (a, b: RECT) return RECT;
-- The same for functions "-", "*" and "/".
private type RECT is record
  xcoor, ycoor: FLOAT;
end record;
end COMREC;
```

The declaration **type** RECT **is private** makes the record definition inaccessible to the user *except* inside the package. Complex numbers can then only be manipulated by the functions that were declared for them in the body of the package. On the other hand, the compiler has to know that complex numbers are represented as records in order to allocate proper storage—hence the full record declaration is a part of the package specification.

Package COMREC is used as before, but now it is impossible to perform any unauthorized operation on RECT objects. We have made the data structure visible to the programmer, but we have restricted his ability to meddle with the package. Thus, if the representation of complex numbers is changed from rectangular to polar coordinates, this should not and will not affect the users.

A private type declaration automatically provides the operations of assignment and testing of relations (e.g., equality or inequality). To remove them, **limited private** is used. The broker's waiting list is shown in Code 7-25. The notes explain some of its features.

Note 1.   In a first attempt, this package could have been written in the same way as previously, declaring *nc*, *ar*, and CALLQU in the body. Since the call-queue is then "hidden," the only way it can be accessed is through, say, the procedures "add" and "remove." This makes the queue itself an *abstract object* since the user is not aware of how the queue is implemented—as an array or a list.

The information on CALLQU types are protected from being tampered with and users are allowed to declare a number of queues by using **private**. The assignment and relation testing operations should be removed, since they are ambiguous. When are two queues equal? If they have the same values stored in the same order or if their basic data type, the record, is the same? The user probably assumes the first, while the language defines it in the second way. The **limited** was used to eliminate these operations.

Note 2.   Parameter *q* of add is **in out** because it appears on both sides of an assignment. Therefore, add cannot be a function. However, a function could have been added as follows:

```
package queuepack is
type CALL is record
   account : idnmb;          -- Identification number.
   password: STRING(8);      -- Each customer has a password.
   transact: enm;            -- Is purchase, sale or quotation.
   amount : INTEGER;         -- The amount in whole dollars.
end record;
type CALLQU is limited private:                        -- Note 1.
procedure add(q: in out CALLQU; c: in CALL);           -- Note 2.
procedure remove(q: in out CALLQU; c: out CALL);
function empty(q: CALLQU) return BOOLEAN;              -- Note 3.
function full(q : CALLQU) return BOOLEAN;
private nc: constant INTEGER := 100; --100 is an arbitrary constant.
subtype SUB is INTEGER range 1 .. nc;
type AR is array(SUB) of CALL;
type CALLQU is record
   queue: AR;
   head: SUB := 0; tail: SUB := 0;
   nmb: INTEGER range 0 .. nc := 0;
end record;
end queuepack; -- Is the end of the specification.

package body queuepack is
   procedure add(q: in out CALLQU; c: in CALL) is      -- Note 4.
   begin
     if not full(q) then
     q.ar(q.head) := c;
     q.head := (q.head + 1) mod nc;
     q.nmb := q.nmb + 1;
     end if;
   end add;
   procedure remove(q: inout CALLQU; c: out CALL) is
   begin
     if not empty(q) then
         c := q.ar(q.tail);
         q.tail := (q.tail + 1) mod nc;
         q.nmb := q.nmb - 1;
     end if;
   end remove;
   function empty(q: CALLQU) return BOOLEAN is
   begin
     return q.nmb = 0;                                 -- Note 5.
   end empty;
   function full(q: CALLQU) return BOOLEAN is
   begin
     return q.nmb = nc;
   end full;
end queuepack; -- End of the body of queuepack.
```

Code 7-25

```
function "=" (qa, qb: CALLQU) return BOOLEAN is
begin
  for i in qa.tail .. qa.head loop
    if qa.ar(i) /= qb.ar(i) then
      return FALSE;
    end if;
  end loop;
  return TRUE;
end "=";
```

Equality of two queues is defined here in the way the programmer wants it and since CALLQU is declared to be **limited private** this is the only way function '' = '' can be used on call-queues.

Encapsulation of data types with operations on them was already mentioned. Data type CALLQU is such an item; it is also abstract. A user can declare abstract objects of type CALLQU and can use operations defined by the package, namely ''add,'' ''remove,'' and '' = ''. Note that no other operation on the queue is allowed, the CALLQU being **private**.

Note 3.   Since the queue is hidden, the user of the package does not know its state. A record may then be added erroneously to a full queue, or removed from an empty queue. Functions ''full'' and ''empty'' were added to indicate by TRUE that the queue is full or empty respectively.

Note 4.   If the number of items in the queue is less than nc, a call is added by $q.ar(q.\text{head}) := c$; to the head of the queue. The head pointer is then incremented (modulo nc) and the number of records in the queue is updated. Similar operations are included in ''remove.''

Note 5.   If the queue is empty, $q.nmb = 0$; returns TRUE. If it is not empty, it returns FALSE. This is precisely what ''empty'' was to provide. Similarly $q.nmb = nc$; is used in the function ''full.''

The final example is that of the ''Fibonacci'' numbers defined as: 0,1,1,2,3,5,8,. . . Starting with the third element, ''fibel(3),'' each of them is computed as: fibel(i) := fibel($i-1$) + fibel($i-2$);.

Suppose that the next fibel is to be produced with each call to a function ''fib.'' The array fibel is not needed since only the last two elements have to be remembered. If they are called min1 and min2 (where min stands for ''minus''), then function fibon is as in:

```
procedure fibon is
  neew, min1, min2, calc: INTEGER;
  function fib return INTEGER is
  begin
    neew:=min1+min2; min2:=min1; min1:=neew; return neew;
  end fib;                -- Next is a program which uses function
  begin                   -- fib. What will happen if min1 is set
    min1:=1; min2:=0;     -- initially to 0?
     loop                 -- This loop calculates and then calls
    calc:=fib;            -- fib to calculate a new value of fibel
    ---Rest of calculation. What happens if min1 and min2 are
    end loop;             -- changed above?
  end fibon;
```

The problem with this code is that variables neew, min1, and min2 can be changed in "fibon" outside of "fib" (see comments) without the programmer being aware that anything was changed in fib. Also, the fact that the initial values of min1 and min2 are 1 and 0 respectively should be hidden from the user. To improve both points, the above procedure is rewritten as a package in Code 7-26.

```
package packfib is
  function fib return INTEGER; -- Note that
end packfib; -- min1,min2 were not included in the interface.
package body packfib is -- Package bodies may contain items not
  min1: INTEGER := 1;    -- mentioned in the specification, but
  min2: INTEGER := 0;    -- declared local to the body like here.
  neew: INTEGER; -- Their scope is that of the body, so that they
  -- may not be used outside of the body. This "hiding" of the
  -- information inside the body, protects users from changes
  -- in the implementation of the package. A user of "packfib"
  -- can use function "fib" and any of the items declared in the
  -- specification, but cannot refer to them outside the body.
  function fib return INTEGER is
  begin
    neew:=min1+min2; min2:=min1; min1:=neew;
    return neew;
  end fib;
end; -- End of the body of packfib.
```

Code 7-26

The advantages of using this package are that min1, min2, and neew are local to this package body. The user cannot access and change them *except* through the function "fib"; this is an example of encapsulation. Initialization of min1 and min2 are implementation details hidden from the users. Hence, if the algorithm changes, this will not change the specification, which can be used as if nothing happened.

A variable declared in the body of a package is only visible, and consequently, its value can only be changed within the body of the package. The values of min1 and min2 remained unchanged between calls issued from outside the package to subprograms possibly declared in the specification of the package. Objects within a package body *retain* their values between calls to subprograms within the package.

7–8 EXCEPTIONS

Unexpected situations may occur while the program is running. They are called exceptions because they depict exceptional conditions, not normally present. Such conditions, e.g., array subscripts out of bounds, division by zero, hardware faults, etc., represent errors which require special handling. This is very important in process control or other real-time programs which may be executed on a parallel processing system. In computer-center environments, the operating system will stop the program and report to the user that a fault occurred. Real-time programs cannot afford such luxury: The operating system is rudimentary, the program should not be interrupted, and an alternative action should replace the procedure in which the fault was detected. Proper error handling should restore the system quickly to a consistent state and then continue its normal operation.

One way of catching exceptional conditions would be to insert in various places IF-STATEMENTS. If the anticipated error occurs, the subprogram branches to some place where an error message is printed or some other action initiated.

This approach has two disadvantages: It clutters the healthy program with too many IF-STATEMENTS and the action is normally to abandon the subprogram or even the main program. In real-time processing, it is very important not to do that, but instead to continue with the program even in the presence of errors—maybe through a different "path."

Ada provides facilities for dealing with exceptions. An *exception* is an event that causes suspension of normal program execution. Drawing attention to the event is called *raising* the exception. To raise an exception is to abandon normal program execution. Executing some action, in response to raising an exception, is called *handling* the exception. There are thus three items to be discussed: how to declare, how to raise, and how to handle an exception.

An exception *declaration* declares a *name* for an exception. This name can be used only in raise-statements, and exception-handlers. Thus, in the *specification* of the package "queuepack" isfull,isempty : **exception**; could have been added. The first could be used in procedure add, the second in remove. The main program is now free of these functions. These declarations are similar to those for objects, but exceptions are not objects. Rather, they indicate (exceptional) conditions.

Both user-defined and system-defined exceptions exist. The language defines among others the following exceptions:

CONSTRAINT ERROR generally corresponds to a range error.
NUMERIC ERROR corresponds to arithmetic errors (e.g. division by 0)
STORAGE ERROR corresponds to running out of storage.
PROGRAM ERROR corresponds usually to an attempt to violate a program
    structure. For instance if the end of a function is encountered
    instead of the return statement, program error occurs.

To detect an exception and alert the calling program is called to *raise* an exception. In the queue, following the **begin** of the procedure add, we may add:
if q.nmb> =nc **then raise** isfull; **end if**;.

When "add" is called, it will first check if there is space in the queue to add a call. If so, it will add it, but if not, it will raise exception "isfull' and thereby complete the processing of "add." Note that the execution will not return to the point of call; an exception is not a subprogram. When the exception is raised, the execution transfers to the particular exception *handler* and the processing of the called "add" is considered complete.

The response to one or more exceptions is specified by an exception handler. It is written at the end of a *frame* which is either a block statement or the body of a subprogram, package, or task unit.

```
begin
   SEQUENCE-OF-STATEMENTS;                -- of the frame.
   exception                              -- For matrix inversion, we
     when singular | NUMERIC ERROR =>     -- need an exception in case
       PUT("The matrix is singular");     -- the matrix is singular.
     when others =>                       -- and should not
       PUT("Fatal error ");               -- be inverted.
end;
```

The exceptions denoted by the exception names and choices must all be distinct. The exception choice **others** is only allowed for the last exception handler of a frame; it stands for all exceptions not listed in previous handlers of the frame.

An exception may be raised explicitly as in: **raise** NUMERIC ERROR; or implicitly as in $a := b/0$; with the same result. All user-defined exceptions must be explicitly raised by tests included in the program.

When an exception is raised, normal program execution is abandoned and control is transferred to the exception handler. *The sequence of statements of the handler replaces the rest of the frame.* Because of this, goto's are not allowed in handlers. Additional rules are that exception handlers are placed at the end of a frame and have access to all items declared in the frame. Exceptions cannot be declared as arrays of exceptions, cannot be components of records, parameters of subprograms, etc. In short, exceptions are conditions, not items, and therefore cannot be manipulated as items.

Propagation of exceptions: An example from [ARM] exemplifies the propagation possibilities by the "program" of Code 7-27.

```
procedure p is
  error: exception;
  procedure q is;
  begin
    r; -- Is a call on procedure r.
    --- Error situation No. 2 occurs here in the program.
    exception
      --- . . .
      when error => -- Handler of No. 2 is here.
      --- . . .
  end q;
  procedure r is
  begin
    --- Error situation No. 3 occurs here in the program.
  end r;
  begin -- This is the begin of procedure p.
    --- Error situation No. 1 occurs here in the program.
    q; -- Is a call on procedure q.
    --- . . .
    exception
      --- . . .
      when error => -- Handler No. 1 is here.
end p;
```

Code 7-27

The following situations can arise:

1. If the exception error is raised in the sequence of statements of the outer procedure *p*, then handler No. 1 inside of *p* is used to complete the execution of *p*.

2. If the exception ''error'' is raised in the sequence of statements of ''*q*'' then handler No. 2 within *q* is used to complete the execution of *q*. Upon completion, control is returned to the point where procedure *q* was called (in procedure *p*).

3. If the exception ''error'' is raised in the body of ''*r*'' called by *q* then the execution of *r* is abandoned and the same exception is raised in the body of *q*. Handler No. 2 is then used to complete the execution of *q*, as in situation 2.

Note that in the third situation, the exception raised in *r* results in (indirectly) transferring control to a handler that is part of *q* and hence not enclosed by *r*. Note also that if a handler were provided within *r* for the exception choice **others**, then situation 3 would cause execution of this handler rather than direct termination of *r*.

Finally, if ''error'' had been declared in *r*, rather than in *p*, handlers No. 1 and No.

2 could not provide an explicit handler for "error" since this identifier would not be visible within the bodies of p and q. In situation No. 3, however, the exception could be handled in q, providing a handler for the exception choice others.

Example No. 1 (of using an exception).   The square root $\sqrt{r}$ is computed by the recursive application of $sq := 0.5*(sqp - r/sqp)$; where sq and sqp are the new and the previous values of $\sqrt{r}$. The calculation has to be prevented whenever $r = 0$, $r < 0$, and if the process does not converge in, say, "max" iterations, it has to be completed. The program is Code 7-28:

```
with TEXT_IO; use TEXT_IO;
procedure sqroot is
number : FLOAT;
  function sqt(r: FLOAT) return FLOAT is
  diverged: BOOLEAN;        -- The process has converged if FALSE.
  sq, sqp: FLOAT;
  max: INTEGER :=30;        -- Is an arbitrary number.
  eps : FLOAT := 0.00001;
  negative, zero, noncon: exception; -- This declares the three
  begin                            -- exceptions. The first two
    if r<0.0 then raise negative; end if; -- are raised next.
    if r=0.0 then raise zero;     end if;
    sq := a/2.0; sqp := sq;       -- Initial values for result
    for i in 1..max loop          -- The loop of up to max times
      diverged := FALSE;          -- starts by assuming it is done.
      sq :=0.5*(spq-r/sqp):                -- The calculation of sq.
      exit when abs(r/(sq*sq)-1.0)<eps;          -- Exit criterion.
      diverged:=TRUE; sqp:=sq;          -- Otherwise shift sq and
  end loop;                                         -- proceed.
  if diverged then raise noncon; end if; -- Has not converged in max
  exception                       -- iterations, so sq is its
                                  value.
    when noncon =>
      PUT("The approximate value is "); return sq;
    when negative =>      -- Call the function recursively.
      PUT("The square root of -r is ");
      return sqt(-r);
    when zero =>
      PUT("The square root of zero is "); return 0.0;
end sqt;                                   -- Next is the main program.
begin
  GET(number);
  PUT(sqt(number));
end sqroot;
```

Code 7-28

Example No. 2 (of using an exception).   Package queuepack is rewritten with no functions "empty" or "full," but with two exceptions replacing them. The body is as in Code 7-29.

```
package body queuepack is
procedure add(q: in out CALLQU; c: in CALL) is
begin
  if q.nmb = nc then
    raise full;      -- Thereby moving to the end of the package.
  else q.ar(q.head) :=c;          -- Add call c to head of list.
    q.head := (q.head+1) mod nc;   -- Update head pointer,
    q.nmb := q.nmb + 1;            -- and the number of calls in
  end if;                          -- the queue.
end add;
procedure remove(q: in out CALLQU; c: in CALL) is
begin
  if q.nmb = 0 then
    raise empty; -- Thereby moving to the end of the package.
  else c := q.ar(q.head);    -- Remove call c from tail of list.
    q.head := (q.head+1) mod nc;   -- Update head pointer,
    q.nmb := q.nmb - 1;            -- and the number of calls in
  end if;                          -- the queue.
end remove;
exception -- Here, the user is only notified.
  when full => PUT("The queue was full. Please, call again ");
  when empty => PUT("The queue was empty. No call received ");
end queuepack; -- End of its body.
```

Code 7-29

7–9 GENERIC PACKAGES

Consider a stack to be declared as the following record type:

```
type STACK(n: INTEGER) is record
  size: INTEGER range 1..n;
  st: array (1..size) of INTEGER;
end record;
```

This stack can only hold integers. Using stacks whose elements are declared by: **generic type** TP; would allow it to use other types.

The stack requires a procedure to add an element to the top of the stack. In the procedure below, the generic type TP is used.

```
procedure addelement(el: in TP; j: in INTEGER) is
begin
  j := j+1;        -- Increase the stack-pointer.
  if j<m then;     -- m is the maximum size of the stack.
  st(j) := el; end if;
end addelement;
```

Generic procedures cannot be directly called since the generic type is not known. They must be first *instantiated*, as in:

```
procedure addint is new addelement(INTEGER, INTEGER);
```

where procedure addint was declared to be a new instance of addelement with the two parameters being both integers.

Assembly-language programmers look for *macros* in high-level languages. A macro may be viewed as a procedure which, when called, is copied with its formal parameters replaced by the names of the actual parameters. A call on a macro does not produce a result but an additional text.

A procedure is stored in a single block of memory locations, but each call requires additional access time for parameter passing. A macro is "expanded" for each call so that it requires storage for new text, but no additional time is wasted.

```
            -- In Ada we may declare subprograms and packages to be generic. Like
generic                     -- other program units, generic units have two
-- Formal parameters              -- parts: a specification and a body. The
package sort is             -- formal parameters which appear between the
-- Interface                -- word generic and the specification, include
end sort;                   -- objects, types, and subprograms. A generic
package body sort is            -- is thus a template and defines an entire
-- The body of sort             -- class depending on the formal parameters
end sort;                                          -- of the generic
```

Generic types can be used in packages, with the added advantage of being able to encapsulate data and operations. A common form of data encapsulation is where a data type is associated with a set of basic operations that applies to objects of that type. Often, the access to the data should be only through the supplied operations. The two forms are exemplified by generic packages for stacks (the program in Code 7-30 is copied from the Language Manual, [ARM], the comments are mine).

Basically, the generic unit is a template for program units that can be created by instantiating the generic unit. Instantiation of package STACK above will be identical to

```
generic SIZE : POSITIVE;            -- POSITIVE is known at this point
generic type ITEM is private;       -- ITEM is hidden.
package STACK is                    -- This generic unit is useful if
  procedure PUSH(E : in ITEM);      -- STACK, PUSH and POP are defined
  procedure POP (E : out ITEM);     -- independent of the type of ITEM.
  OVERFLOW, UNDERFLOW ; exception;  -- No items can be added to a full
end STACK;                          -- or removed from an empty stack.


package body STACK is
  type TABLE is array (POSITIVE range <>) of ITEM;
  SPACE : TABLE(1..SIZE);           -- This stack is an array; it could
  INDEX : POSITIVE := 0;            -- have been an array of records.

procedure PUSH(E : in ITEM) is
begin
  if INDEX >= SIZE then             -- Making sure there is no
    raise OVERFLOW;                 -- overflow.
  end if;
  INDEX := INDEX+1;                 -- Set position for the new element
  SPACE(INDEX) := E;                -- and insert it.
end PUSH;

  procedure POP(E : out ITEM) is
begin
  if INDEX = 0 then                 -- Making sure the stack is not
    raise UNDERFLOW;                -- empty.
  end if;
  E := SPACE(INDEX);                -- Remove the element from top of
  INDEX := INDEX-1;                 -- the stack and decrease the index
  end POP;
end STACK;
```

Code 7-30

writing a new package. If sort were a procedure or package, it would have to be written with a separate specification and body. The relationship between a generic unit and its instantiations is similar to that between a data type and its corresponding data objects. For instance, new packages can be obtained from STACK as follows:

```
package STACK_INT is new STACK (SIZE =>200; ITEM =>INTEGER);
package STACK_BOOL is new STACK(100, BOOLEAN);
```

Thereafter, the procedures of the instantiated packages can be called as follows: STACK_INT.PUSH(N) ; STACK_BOOL.PUSH(TRUE);.

Instantiation works like a macro; we can think of it as having copied the text of, say, addelement, with INTEGER replacing TP. We could have also instantiated it with FLOAT or some fixed-point data type and in all cases use "addelement." The result is a "generator" of procedures for adding elements to a stack without the specification of the type of the element. The program must supply the type. The generator is not an ordinary procedure—rather, it generates ordinary procedures.

The keyword **new** was used in Sec. 7-4 to produce a new (derived) type. Here, it produces a new stack: both the two operations and the type of elements it stores. In short, it produces a new package. As seen, in all cases, **new** signifies the generation of a new from an existing item.

Alternatively, a generic formulation of type STACK can be given as in Code 7-31 (package body is omitted);

```
generic type ITEM is private;
package ON_STACK is
  type STACK(SIZE : POSITIVE) is limited private;
  procedure PUSH(S : in out STACK; E in ITEM);
  procedure POP (S : in out STACK; E out ITEM);
  OVERFLOW, UNDERFLOW : exception;
  private type TABLE is array (POSITIVE range <>) of ITEM;
  type STACK(SIZE : POSITIVE) is
  record SPACE : TABLE(1..SIZE);
    INDEX : NATURAL :=0;
  end record;
end;
```

Code 7-31

To use such a package, it must first be instantiated and then stacks of the corresponding type can be declared:

```
declare package STACK_REAL is new ON_STACK(REAL); use STACK_REAL;
  S : STACK(100);
begin
  . . .
  PUSH(S,2.54);
  . . .
end;
```

The formal parameter of a generic should not be confused with formal parameters of procedures, functions, or packages. In these last units, the parameters can only be objects, whereas in generics they can also be types and subprograms and used in generating new units instead of parametrizing existing units.

In generics, an object should not have mode **out**, because it could not be instantiated. Generic type parameters give generic units much of their power and flexibility. This was shown in the case of stacks for various types of elements. These types could also have been arrays, access and private types with the associated sets of operations appropriate to the type.

7–10 ADDENDUM

7–10.1 Summary of Ada

Ada seems to be so much a "nicer" language—isn't it nicer to be able to write $a*b$ for multiplying the two complex numbers a and b, than to write a.real: $= \ldots$ as we would have needed in other languages? And even suppose we have defined a procedure "mult(a,b,c)", $c := a*b$ is still nicer than mult(a,b,c). With d being another complex number, $d := a*b*c$ is certainly easier to read, than mult$((a$,mult$(b,c$,temp$)),d)$. But there is much more to the language than being "nice"—it is a "shell" language, which means that it includes features for a variety of various uses. (In a "core" language, each new feature is added to the core as an extension of the language.) We sketch next some of the intended uses of Ada.

The design process of a program consists essentially of taking a proposed solution and successively refining it until an executable program results. The initial solution may be expressed in English or some form of mathematical notation. At this level the formulation is said to be *abstract* because it contains no details regarding the representation or manipulation of objects. If possible, the designer attempts to partition the solution into logical subtasks. Each subtask is similarly decomposed until all tasks are expressed within a programming language, e.g., by blocks. This method of program design is called *top-down*. There exists a *bottom-up* method in which the designer might solve different parts of the problem directly in the programming language and then combine these pieces into a complete program. To give an example from everyday life: the architect who first consults a brick catalog is designing the house bottom-up, while one who starts by overall sketches designs it top-down. Experience suggests that the top-down approach should be followed when creating a program.

The top-down approach and some of the newer techniques of *software engineering* started with the goto controversy centered on the question of whether gotos are needed. There exists a proof that the GOTO-STATEMENT is not needed—hence we will treat it briefly. Code 7-32 is a program of "bubble-sort" which uses the **goto**; a different version of the program was shown earlier.

```
with TEXT_IO; use TEXT_IO;
procedure bub is
n: INTEGER; fin: BOOLEAN; -- fin indicates that sorting is complete.
a: array(1..100) of INTEGER;   -- This is the array to be sorted.

procedure swap(old,nnew: in out INTEGER) is
temp: INTEGER := old;
begin  old := nnew; nnew := temp; end;

begin
  GET(n); PUT(n,3); -- n is the number of elements to be sorted.
  for i in 1..n loop -- This loop inputs and prints all n elements
    GET(a(i); PUT(a(i),3);     -- of array a.
  end loop; NEW_LINE;
<<beg>> fin := TRUE; -- It will be false if an additional swap
  for i in 1..n-1 loop          -- is necessary.
    if a(i+1)<a(i) then -- Next swap the two elements and indicate
      swap(a(i),a(i+1)); fin := FALSE; -- that another sweep
    end if;                            -- is necessary.
  end loop; -- This loop made a sweep over the entire array.
  for i in 1..n loop PUT(a(i),3); end loop; NEW_LINE;
  if not fin then goto beg; end if; -- This is the goto mentioned.
end bub;
```

Code 7-32

The label has to be in the same frame as the **goto**; it is not permitted to goto a label from outside the frame in which it appears, or into IF-, CASE-, or LOOP-STATEMENT. Gotos are not really needed in Ada: **exits** and **returns** permit leaving a loop or subprogram respectively, and even for exceptional cases, for which gotos are used in other languages, Ada has the exceptions. As a case in point, it is suggested that the readers rewrite procedure bub for bubble sort without having to use the goto.

The book *Software Engineering Concepts* [Fai85] mentions the following modern programming language concepts: type-checking, scoping-rules, verification and validation, portability, data-encapsulation, separate compilation, exception handling, and "various mechanisms for concurrency." Some of these were already mentioned, others will be mentioned next or (in case of concurrency) later.

The writing of a large software project is usually not done in a single step. Already in the initial stages, components and their interaction are identified. These subproblems are then discussed and finally coded. They are combined only after all components are tested and found to work satisfactorily.

A project is normally done by a team. Since the components require different times of writing, the state of the entire project is such that:

1. The problems and interfaces of the components are known, i.e., it is known which data are needed or supplied by the various components.
2. The solution to some of the problems already exists.
3. The codes to some of the problems already exist.

Separate compilation is provided in Ada in order to facilitate the integration of the components. The so-compiled components allow:

1. The separation of the project into self-contained units;
2. The simplification of program development;
3. The re-usability of the components;
4. A rational division of labor among the team members;
5. The hiding of implementation details (see packages above); and
6. A cost reduction.

If one of the components is changed, only it and the components that depend on it have to be recompiled (in Pascal, the entire project would have to be recompiled). This reduces the cost but requires management of a *library* (by the overall system). On the other hand, units of such a library can be used in different projects. Since Ada has not yet fully specified the management of a library, we refer the reader to [ARM]. This is also the place to look for predefined program environments, e.g., the packages of I/O, etc.

7–10.2 A Package for Sets

Another summary is presented here in the form of a package for sets; it will be needed in Chap. 9. A set is a collection of elements drawn from a universe; it may not contain duplicates.

The following *operations* are defined for sets:

1. *Union*: Given two sets, form a set containing the items that are members of the first *or* the second set.
2. *Intersection*: Given two sets, form a set containing the items that are members of the first *and* the second set.
3. *Difference*: Given two sets, form a set containing the items that are members of the first *and not* of the second set.
4. *Equal*: Return TRUE if the two given sets are identical.
5. *Member*: Return TRUE if the given element is a member of the set.
6. *Empty*: Return TRUE if the set contains no elements.

7. *Copy*: Copy the elements of one set to another set.

8. *Insert*: Insert a new element as a member of the set.

9. *Delete*: Remove a member from a set.

The *Exceptional conditions* are for

1. union, intersection and difference: the resulting set is not large enough to hold new elements,

2. equal, member and empty: the result is neither TRUE nor FALSE,

3. copy: the destination set is not large enough to hold the source set,

4. insert: the element is already a member of the set, and

5. delete: the element is not a member of the set.

The following *exceptions* are implemented: *overflow* when the destination set cannot grow large enough to complete the desired operation; *inset* when the element is already a member of the set; and *notinset* when the element is currently not a member of the set.

```
package SETS is   -- This package is similar to list processing
   node: INTEGER;   -- and encapsulates well known operations.
   type SET is private; -- PLEASE FOLLOW THE PACKAGE CAREFULLY.
   procedure union(ofset: in SET; andsetin SET; toset: in out SET);
   procedure insec(ofset: in SET; andset: in SET; toset: in out SET);
   procedure diff(ofset: in SET; andset: in SET; toset: in out SET);
   function equal(first: in SET; second: in SET) return BOOLEAN;
   function member(elem: in INTEGER; ofset: in SET) return BOOLEAN;
   function empty(theset: in SET) return BOOLEAN;
   procedure copy(from: in SET; to: in out SET);
   procedure insert(elem: in INTEGER; toset: in out SET);
   procedure delete(elem: in INTEGER; fromset: in out SET);
   overflow: exception; inset:exception; notinset:exception;
   private type ELEMENT;
         type SET is access ELEMENT;
end SETS;

package body SETS is
  type ELEMENT is record
    elem: INTEGER; next: SET;
  end record;

  procedure union(ofset: in SET; andset: in SET; toset: in out SET) is
  temp1: SET := ofset; temp2 : SET; totop : SET;
  begin
    toset := null;
    while temp1 /= null loop
```

```
      toset := new ELEMENT'(elem => temp1.elem, next => toset);
      temp1 := temp1.next;
   end loop;
   totop := toset; temp1 := andset;
   while temp1 /= null loop
     temp2 := totop;
     while temp2 /= null loop
       if temp1.elem = temp2.elem then exit;
       else temp2 := temp2.next;
       end if;
     end loop;
     if temp2 = null then
       toset := new ELEMENT'(elem=>temp1.elem, next=>toset);
     end if;
     temp1 := temp1.next;
   end loop;
   exception
     when STORAGE_ERROR => raise OVERFLOW;
end union;


procedure insec(ofset: in SET; andset: in SET; toset: in out SET) is
temp1: SET := ofset; temp2 : SET;
begin
   toset := null;
   while temp1 /= null loop
     temp2 := andset;
   while temp2 /= null loop
       if temp1.elem = temp2.elem then exit;
         toset := new ELEMENT'(elem => temp1.elem, next => toset);
         exit;
       else temp2 := temp2.next;
       end if;
     end loop;
     temp1 := temp1.next;
   end loop;
   exception
     when STORAGE_ERROR => raise OVERFLOW;
end insec;


procedure diff(ofset: in SET; andset: in SET; toset: in out SET) is
temp1: SET := ofset; temp2 : SET;
begin
   toset := null;
   while temp1 /= null loop
     temp2 := andset;
     while temp2 /= null loop
       if temp1.elem = temp2.elem then exit;
```

```
        else temp2 := temp2.next;
         end if;
      end loop;
     if temp2 = null then
        toset := new ELEMENT'(elem=>temp1.elem, next=>toset);
     end if;
     temp1 := temp1.next;
  end loop;
  exception
     when STORAGE_ERROR => raise OVERFLOW;
end diff;

function equal(first: in SET; second: in SET) return BOOLEAN is
count1 := NATURAL := 0; count2 := NATURAL := 0;
temp1: SET := first; temp2 : SET;
begin
  while temp1 /= null loop
     temp2 := second;
     while temp2 /= null loop
        if temp1.elem = temp2.elem then exit;
        else temp2 := temp2.next;
        end if;
     end loop;
     if temp2 = null then
        return FALSE;
     else count1 := count1+1; temp1 := temp1.next;
     end if;
  end loop;
  temp2 := second;
  while temp2 /= null loop
     count2 := count2+1; temp2 := temp2.next;
  end loop;
  return (count1 = count2);
end equal;

function member (elem: in INTEGER; ofset: in SET) return BOOLEAN is
temp : SET := ofset;
begin
  while temp /= null loop
     if elem = temp.elem then return TRUE; end if;
     temp := temp.next;
  end loop;
  return FALSE;
end member;

function empty(theset: in SET) return BOOLEAN;
begin
  return (theset = null);
end empty;
```

```
procedure copy(from: in SET; to: in out SET) is
temp1: SET := from; temp2 : SET;
begin
  if from = null then to := null;
  else
    to := new ELEMENT'(elem => temp1.elem, next => null);
    temp2 := to; temp1 := temp1.next;
    while temp1 /= null loop
      temp2.next := new ELEMENT'(elem=>temp1.elem, next=>null);
      temp2 := temp2.next; temp1 := temp1.next;
    end loop;
  end if;
  exception
    when STORAGE_ERROR => raise OVERFLOW;
end copy;

procedure insert(elem: in INTEGER; toset: in out SET) is
temp : SET := toset;
begin
  while temp /= null loop
    if temp.elem = elem then
      raise inset;
    else temp := temp.next;
    end if;
  end loop;
  toset := new ELEMENT'(elem => elem, next => toset);
  exception
    when STORAGE_ERROR => raise OVERFLOW;
end insert;

procedure delete(elem: in INTEGER; fromset: in out SET) is
origin : SET; temp : SET := fromset;
begin
  while temp /= null loop
    if temp.elem = elem then
      if origin = null then
        fromset := fromset.next;
      else
        origin.next := temp.next;
      end if;
      return;
    else
      origin := temp; temp := temp.next;
    end if;
  end loop;
  raise notinset;
end delete;

end SETS;
```

7–11 PROBLEMS AND PROJECTS

7–11.1 Sequential Cases

1. Write an Ada program for any or all of the following: linear search, binary search, Fibbonacci search, selection and improved selection sort, bubble sort, cocktail-shaker sort, card player's sort, quicksort, and binary-radix sort.

2. Write an Ada program for solving a linear set using elimination, LU-decomposition, and/or the Gauss-Seidel iterative method.

3. Write a program for calculating $x = \sqrt{r}$ using bisection. Add exceptions.

4. Write a package for using complex numbers expressed in polar coordinates.

5. Write a generic package for complex numbers which would include a "reduce" operation changing $2 + j*4$ into $1 + j*2$ (only for integer elements). Use it then for testing equality of two complex numbers. Alternatively write a generic package for fractions. (Such packages are discussed in [Fel85], but don't seem to be generic).

6. A *prime number* is a positive integer that is exactly divisible only by 1 and itself. The first few primes are: 2 3 5 7 11 13 17 19 23 29 31 37 41 43 . . .

   The oldest method of generating prime numbers is the *sieve of Eratosthenes*, which can be summarized as follows: Remove from the list of numbers 3. .n all even numbers since they are all divisible by two. Then remove all integers divisible by 3, 5, 7, etc.

   Write a program for generating prime numbers. Compare it with the program on pp. 113–14 of [Dro82] and add a program to compute the prime factors of an integer ([Dro82] pp. 118–19).

7. Write a generic package that can be used for list processing.

8. Rewrite the set package as a generic package.

9. The way older compilers worked is quite similar to the tree program of Sec. 7-6. There is even a complete program for it in [Wal73] written in PL/I. If you care to learn it, rewrite it in Ada using the list package of problem 7.

10. Write a generic package for matrix calculations.

11. If you know or are willing to learn about *quaternions*, then write a generic package for operating on them.

12. The method of Horner to calculate the value of a polynomial for a given value of x (called z) is recursive. Write a recursive function to compute it. The first line may be:

    function HORNER (z : FLOAT, i : NATURAL; a : VECT) **is**

7–11.2 Concurrent Cases

13. Write programs for parallel execution of image processing as described in Sec. 6-2. Characterize the difficulties you have while changing the sequential algorithms in the "area" cases.

14. During the second world war, Dirichlet problems were solved by the method of Southwell (see some of the older literature) in which a pointer was kept to the coordinates of the point with the highest residual in order to reduce it by averaging with its four neighbors. Suppose you do the same but keep pointers to p subareas to be computed on p PEs. Note that points near the

"borders" between the subareas require special treatment. Write a program in Ada to simulate the way your program would run on a PPS.

15. In most books on numerical analysis, you can find a collection of formulas for integration which go by the name of Newton-Cotes (one of them is the formula by Simpson). Simulate the running of these and change the division of labor between the PEs. Evaluate whether this influenced the speedup. Also, replace the rectangles in Fig. 6-5 by trapezoids, rewrite the programs, and calculate the errors.

16. Write an Ada program for the "Fast Gauss-Seidel" method and run it with data. Count the number of operations for steps that can be done in parallel on a PPS separately and calculate the speedup.

17. Do the same for the Jacobi method. Is it easier to parallelize the recursive or the Gauss-Jordan algorithm?

18. Assuming a "block-bordered" matrix of super-dimension 5 in Fig. 6-14(b), develop an Ada program for solving it in parallel on a PPS of your choice.

19. Develop a program in Ada for the three methods discussed in connection with tridiagonal sets. (If you have any trouble, [OaV85] will refer you to pertinent literature, although not using Ada.)

20. Let **M** be an n-by-n matrix. The *determinant* of **M**, denoted by $\det(M)$, can be defined recursively as follows: If $M[i,j]$ denotes the matrix obtained from **M** by deleting the i-th row and j-th column, then $\det(M) = \Sigma(-1)^{**}(j+1)^{*}A(1,j)^{*}\det(M[i,j]); j\Sigma = 1,\ldots,n$. If $n = 1$, then $\det(M) = A(1,1)$.

   Write a program to compute determinants up to $n = 5$. Prove that for this program, $\mathbf{O}(n!)$ operations are required. Use the Gauss-Jordan algorithm to calculate the determinant and prove that only $\mathbf{O}(n^3)$ operations are required. (Note the difference: if $n = 8$, then $n! = 8^{*}7^{*}6^{*}5^{*}4^{*} 3^{*}2 = 8^{*}42^{*}120 = 960^{*}42 = 40,320$, while $8^3 = 512$. The higher n, the greater the difference.)

21. The algorithm for Singular Value Decomposition is explained in [Wal86] to the point of giving a program for it. The second part of the algorithm centers on Fig. 6.16 and can be done by macropipelining. Develop such a method.

CHAPTER 8

ISSUES
OF USING ADA
IN MULTIPROCESSORS

The *objective* of this chapter is to show how Ada can be used on various multiprocessors. In particular:

For inquiry (database) applications, the problems of critical sections, deadlocks, and others are solved mostly by semaphores. We discuss critical sections in Sec. 8-1, the use of ''Fetch-and-add'' operations for them in Chap. 11.

Section 8-2 describes multitasking facilities. Critical sections and other examples of using multitasking are discussed in Sec. 8-3.

Language features relating to the use of Ada in process-control applications are discussed in Sec. 8-4.

In Chapters 9, 10, and 11 all these language features will be used in programming various parallel processing systems.

8-1 PROBLEMS OF PARALLELIZATION

8-1.1 The Example of a Brokerage Company

The problems of deadlock, critical section, and starvation mentioned in Sec. 4-2 occur mostly in the shared-memory multiprocessors, SMs. If used as *real-time* systems, they interact with the external world concurrently and asynchronously (see Chap. 1). They are redefined next for PPSs using the example of the brokerage company (see Sec. 6-3).

Brokers are called asynchronously by customers and work concurrently with others except at points where they occasionally synchronize. The single memory in which the database is located may be (time) shared by many brokers and this may lead to problems of the critical sections, of deadlock, and of starvation (recall Sec. 4-2).

Whenever a call for buying or selling stock arrives, one of the brokers takes it, investigates the status of the customer, and if possible executes the transaction. The "investigation" means to access the database, and that is a *critical part*. For instance, suppose that two customers want 100 shares each and two brokers find that 150 shares are available. They could both sell 100 shares each, so that 200 shares were sold, but only 150 were available. There must be *mutual exclusion* in updating the database: A broker updating the database excludes for this time all other brokers from accessing it.

Definitions. *Mutual Exclusion* is the mechanism by which a task gains exclusive access to a shared resource. A *Critical Section* is a SEQUENCE-OF-STATEMENTS of a task that must be executed excluding others.

A broker may be called by a number of customers and faster than service can be provided. Therefore, a *queue* (Fig. 6-9) is associated with each broker and waiting customers are processed on a "first come, first serve" basis. Each time a customer is accepted, one job is removed from the queue. The queue, or *buffer*, is also a critical section in that access to it must be by mutual exclusion.

The work of a broker consists of repeatedly "preprocessing" followed by accessing the database (the critical section) followed by some "postprocessing." Preprocessing and postprocessing may be combined because they always follow each other in the loop representing the working day.

8-1.2 Critical Sections

In 1968, E. W. Dijkstra published a solution [Dij68] to this problem using a sequence of graduated examples, each having some fault except the last. Since it exemplifies the problems and their solutions, it will be rewritten in Ada.

Suppose there are two brokers. To enter the critical section, broker-1 should first ask if the database is "busy" and access it only if it isn't. The programs for two brokers are shown in Code 8-1 typed side by side to indicate concurrency.

```
procedure code81 is
base: (busy, free);                                  -- Is an enumeration.
  procedure first is            procedure second is
  begin                         begin
    loop                          loop
      while base=busy loop          while base=busy loop
        null;                         null;
      end loop;                     end loop;
      base: =busy;                  base: =busy;
      cris;                         cris; --The critical section
      base: =free;                  base: =free;
      remain1;                      remain2; --Remaining parts.
    end loop;                     end loop;
  end first;                    end second;

begin                           -- The main (master) program begins.
  base: =free; first; second;   -- Both brokers proceed simultaneously
end code81;                     -- because two CPUs are assumed.
```

Code 8-1

This solution is obviously wrong since, if for any reason the two brokers arrive at the while-loop simultaneously and find database to be busy, they would wait forever: a deadlock occurs. In a second solution, before a broker tries to access the database, he/she may consult a variable, say "turn." If it is 1 then it is the turn of broker-1 to access the database; otherwise broker-1 waits. When finished, broker-1 makes turn: = 2 so that broker-2 may access the database. This solution corresponds to Code 8-2.

This solution has the following features:

1. It satisfies *mutual exclusion*, since the two brokers cannot be in the critical section (*cris*) at the same time. Broker-i may enter cris only if turn $= i$ and makes turn/ $= i$ only *after* leaving it.

2. A *deadlock* would exist if both brokers would simultaneously be looping in their while-loops. This is impossible since turn would have to be 1 and 2 at the same time.

```
procedure code82 is
turn: INTEGER;
  procedure first is              procedure second is
  begin                          begin
    loop                           loop
      while turn=2 loop              while turn=1 loop
        null;                         null;
      end loop;                     end loop;
      cris;                         cris;
      turn: =2;                     turn: =1;
      remain1;                      remain2;
    end loop;                      end loop;
  end first;                     end second;
begin                            -- The main (master) procedure starts.
  turn: =1; first; second;            -- First and second proceed
end code 82;                     -- simultaneously.
```

Code 8-2

3. The waiting is simulated by the WHILE-LOOP since nothing is done in the loop itself except a repeated check on "turn." This is the "lock" which was used earlier for the "busy waiting" loop.

4. Unfortunately, there may also be *too much synchronization*. In the main procedure, turn was made 1, so that broker-1 starts and broker-2 may follow only after broker-1 has left the critical section. Broker-1 can again interrogate the common database after broker-2 has left the critical section. In short, the critical section is visited strictly in the sequence: broker-1, broker-2, broker-1, broker-2, etc. This in turn may lead to *starvation* as follows: If broker-1 is sick and did not appear for work, broker-2 will never get a chance, but if broker-2 is sick, broker-1 will visit the database once and never get a second chance. In both cases, one of the brokers is starved (for work).

In order to remove starvation, two keys may be given to the two brokers. If one is using the database, his/her key is inserted and the second broker is prevented from entering the critical section. On the other hand, if one broker is sick, the other may use the key all day.

The program would then be as shown in Code 8-3.

```
procedure code83 is
key1, key2 : INTEGER
  procedure first is              procedure second is
  begin                           begin
    loop                            loop
      while key2 = 1 loop             while key1 = 1 loop
      end loop;                       end loop;
      key1 : =1;                      key2 : =1;
      cris;                           cris;
      key1: =0;                       key2 : =0;
      remain1;                        remain2;
    end loop;                       end loop;
  end first;                      end second;
```

Code 8-3

Actually, we went from bad to worse since not even mutual exclusion is guaranteed. The following scenario is possible:

	key1	key2
Initially	0	0
first checks key2		is 0
second checks key1	is 0	
first sets key1	1	
second sets key 2		1

This program is wrong: once broker-i found that key-j ($j/=i$) is not used, he/she charges right into the critical section and sets key-i to 1, too late for broker-j to be prevented from also charging. No mutual exclusion exists.

This may be corrected by setting key-i *ahead* of the busy-loop (**while**) as a *signal* by broker-i that he/she is ready to use the critical section. Since the busy-wait follows, broker-i will be unable to use the critical section as long as broker-j has not returned key-j (i.e., set it to 0). The program is shown as Code 8-4.

Again, there is a possible (bad) scenario:

	key1	key2
Initially	0	0
first sets key1	1	
second sets key2		1
first checks key2		is 1
second checks key1	is 1	

```
procedure code84 is
key1, key2: INTEGER
  procedure first is              procedure second is
  begin                           begin
    loop                            loop
      key1 : = 1;                     key2 = 1;
      while key2 = 1 loop             while key1 = 1 loop
      end loop;                       end loop
      cris;                           cris;
      key1 : = 1;                     key2 : = 1;
      remain1;                        remain2;
    end loop;                       end loop;
  end first;                      end second;
```

Code 8-4

The two brokers will never cease checking the other broker's key and are hopelessly *deadlocked*; they are waiting forever.

We may improve this if busy-waiting and setting of keys is reversed back to what it was in Code 8-2 and if additionally the brokers are a little more considerate. Instead of doing nothing during the busy-wait, they may—at least for say a minute—let the other broker gain access to the critical section, by relinquishing the key (see Code 8-5).

```
procedure code85 is
key, 1 key2: INTEGER
  procedure first is              procedure second is
  begin                           begin
    loop                            loop
      key1 : = 1;                     key2 : = 1;
      while key2 = 1 loop             while key1 = 1 loop
        key1: = 0;                      key2: = 0;
        delay: = 60. 0;                 delay: = 60. 0;
        key1: = 1;                      key2: = 1;
      end loop;                       end loop;
      cris;                           cris;
      key1: = 0;                       key2: = 0;
      remain1;                        remain2;
    end loop;                       end loop;
  end first;                      end second;
```

Code 8-5

Unfortunately there is such a thing as being too considerate. In Code 8-5 it is possible for both brokers to follow the lines below, each of which corresponds to some time *t*.

First sets key1: = 0	Second sets key2: = 0
First waits 60 seconds	Second waits 60 seconds
First sets key1: = 1	Second sets key2: = 1
First repeats the while-loop	Second repeats the while-loop

This is an (indefinitely blocked) deadlock with two idle brokers.

There exists a correct solution [Pet81] which involves entry and exit protocols.

```
procedure Peterson is
  key1, key2: INTEGER : = (0,0); turn: INTEGER: =1; -- 2 for second.
  procedure first is              procedure second is
  begin                           begin
    loop                            loop
      key1: =1; turn: =2;             key2: =1; turn: =1;
      while key2=1 and turn=2         while key1=1 and turn=1
      loop                            loop
      end loop;                       end loop;
      cris;                           cris;
      key1: =0;                       key2: =0;
      remain1;                        remain2;
    end loop;                       end loop;
  end first;                      end second;

begin              -- of the main procedure.
  first; second;   -- Both are called simultaneously.
end Peterson;
```

Code 8-6

8–1.3 Semaphore Solutions
for SM-Multiprocessors

The solution above is cumbersome. Dijkstra proposed to use *semaphores* to solve this problem by suspending tasks. A *queue* is associated with each semaphore and a task that cannot enter the critical section is "put into the queue" and suspended. For instance, if the broker is not permitted to access the database, he puts a customer (a task) on hold. The broker (a processor) is then freed and may do some useful work for another customer. If at some later time it is the turn of the task to enter the critical section *and* a broker is free, then the "suspended" task is removed from the queue and re-activated.

Semaphores are defined as integer variables, e.g., s with only two permitted operations and four characteristics:

wait (s):   If $s > 0$ then $s: = s - 1$, else the execution of the task that called wait(s) is suspended (put on hold in a queue).

signal (s):   If some task T has been suspended by a previous wait(s) on this s, then wake-up T, else set $s: = s + 1$.

1. We will deal only with *binary* semaphores which can assume the values of 0 or 1. General semaphores which can take arbitrary nonnegative values were also implemented.

2. The two operations are considered to be *indivisible* and *primitive* (i.e., to exclude each other). Hence, if a wait and signal (or two waits or two signals) occur simultaneously, they are executed one at a time, but no order is implied. Being primitive indicates that interrupts are disabled while they are executed.

3. The use of semaphores removes "busy-waiting" since the process (customer) is put on hold and the processor (broker) is free to do useful work instead of just waiting.

4. The definition of signal does not specify which process is reactivated if more than one process has been suspended on the same semaphore. A FIFO (First in, first out) policy is assumed.

Semaphores could solve the problem of critical sections not only for two, but for any number (nt) of tasks (see Code 8-7).

```
procedure Dijkstral is
nt: INTEGER constant : = 5; s: semaphore;        -- Five is an arbitary
  procedure task(i: in INTEGER) is               -- value; semaphores are
  begin                                          -- assumed to have been
    loop                                         -- defined earlier.
      wait(s); cris; signal(s);                  -- critical section i.
      remain;                                    -- Remainder of job i.
    end loop;
  end task;

begin
  --- Set s: =1 and call (simultaneously) all nt tasks task(1), ...
end;
```

Code 8-7

As seen, a task starts by wait(s). If $s = 0$, then this particular task is put in the waiting queue else s is made 0 and the task goes into the critical section. Since s was made

0, no other task can enter the critical section and mutual exclusion is ensured. When the critical section is complete signal(*s*) sets *s*: = 1 and one of the waiting tasks may enter the critical section. There can be no indefinite blocking because processors are not busy-waiting. If task (*i*) is not active, then others can work, so there is no starvation either.

The activity of the brokers is either to read or update (write into) the common database (possibly the buffer). The example of *Readers and Writers* is an extension of the brokers problem. A *reader* task reads the shared data, but does not update it. The previous solution prevented a number of brokers from reading the data concurrently. There is no harm if all of them *read* at the same time and thus reduce the waiting time of the customers—this is why the parallel solution was proposed in the first place. On the other hand, a *writer* task should have exclusive access to the database. This leads to the strategy of *many reading or a single writing broker*.

The problem with this strategy is that a steady stream of readers may block, or *starve* the writers from ever accessing the database. If writing has a higher *priority* than reading, then once a broker indicates the wish to write, he/she will get it as soon as the readers have finished (reading should not be interrupted). The problem here is the reverse, namely that the writers may starve forever the reading brokers.

Starvation may be prevented by the following *policy*: If there are readers waiting, they should get access to the database once the single writer has completed and before other writers are allowed to access the database.

Semaphores can not only solve the mutual exclusion problem but also provide *condition synchronization*, e.g., in buffers when the conditions that the buffer is not empty (full) synchronize (or delay) the removal (insertion) of messages.

Another proposed solution would be *monitors* [AaS83]. In terms of Ada, a monitor encapsulates the shared data and the procedures that access it. The procedures are written so that mutual exclusion is guaranteed. It is left as a problem to determine if monitors can be written by using packages.

Finally, synchronization can be based on message passing and since this is the way it is done in Ada, we discuss it closer.

8–2 MULTITASKING

Ada provides multitasking to simulate parallel and in particular inquiry systems. Multitasking can be summarized as follows: The processes are called *tasks*, each of which has a specification defining a number of *entry* points. These entries, which are syntactically similar to subprogram specifications, define the services that the task can provide. For instance, a broker (task) can open a new account, reply to an inquiry, accept a payment, access the database, etc. An entry describes the external appearance of the task; its internal behavior—what it does and how—is part of its *body*.

The activities of the brokerage house are organized as a collection of callers and acceptors. A task like that of a customer is always a caller, never an acceptor. A random number generator could simulate the behavior of customers, since their calls are completely random as far as the company is concerned. This leads to the simple declaration:

```
task customer;
```

A customer (caller) initiates service by an *entry call*, the server indicates readiness to provide the service by an *accept statement*. For the duration of the service, the so-called *rendezvous*, the two are *synchronized*, but once this phase is over they go their separate ways.

For the broker-task to provide diverse services, there must be *select* statements to enable customers to choose from the various services.

The summary above and in particular the italicized items are discussed next in more detail using as an example a broker trying to access the database DB.

Tasks may be first declared as *task types* with the specification containing *only ENTRY and REPRESENTATION-CLAUSES*. The latter will be used for interrupt services and will be described in Sec. 8-4. A single character buffer could be used at first incorrectly as in Code 8-8.

```
task insert;              -- A task consists of a declaration (this line)
task body insert is       -- and a body which in this case is a block.
  ch: CHARACTER;          -- ch is a local variable, inaccessible from
begin                     -- the outside.
  loop                    -- Embedded systems work in a never-ending loop.
    GET(c);               -- Read one character from the input.
    ch : = c;             -- Insert this character into the buffer ch.
  end loop;
end insert;               -- This completes the body of task insert.


task remove;              -- Task remove is similar to task insert.
task body remove is
  ch: CHARACTER;          -- ch is a local variable, inaccessible from
begin                     -- the outside.
  loop                    -- Embedded systems work in a never-ending loop.
    c : = ch;             -- Remove one character from the buffer
    PUT(c);               -- and print it.
  end loop;
end remove;               -- This completes the body of task remove.
```

Code 8-8

The above program is incorrect because no synchronization exists that would ensure that remove is waiting for insert to put a character into the buffer. Nothings prevents the removal of a character that is not even in the buffer, or insertion of a second character into a one-character buffer (overwriting). Additionally, mutual exclusion is not secured. This could be done by using the *rendezvous* of two tasks which access a single data-base, DB (type) as shown in Code 8-9.

```
task type DB is
   entry insert(c: in CHARACTER);    -- Note that only entries exist
   entry remove(c: out CHARACTER);   -- and that c is a buffer
end DB;                              -- for a single character.

task body DB is
   ch: CHARACTER;  --ch is local, inaccessible from outside.
begin
   loop              -- Embedded systems work in a never-ending loop.
     accept insert(c: in CHARACTER) do
       ch := c; -- Inserts character c into the buffer ch.
     end insert;
     accept remove(c: out CHARACTER) do
       c := ch; -- Removes character c from the buffer ch.
     end remove;
   end loop;
end DB;          -- End of the body of the DB type.
```

Code 8-9

Task "customer" was declared earlier without first using the type. It was an anonymous task type and an object of this type. It is better to declare tasks of a known type, say in buf: DB.

A task can communicate with any other program unit only through an entry call. Any subprogram or package declared inside of the task body is local to it and cannot be accessed by any other unit.

The entries are called similarly to procedures in packages, namely using the dot notation. A broker would call buf.insert(*a*) or buf.remove(*b*); these are the *calling tasks*. The ACCEPT-STATEMENTS are the *called entries*. We will use *caller* and *acceptor* respectively. When a caller is accepted, i.e., when the buffer is ready to *accept* the character, a rendezvous occurs, during which a character is inserted into the buffer. The broker is idle, during the rendezvous (and the rendezvous would be better kept as short as possible so as not to idle the brokers too much). The synchronization of the two tasks is *implicit*.

A *package* almost identical to DB could have been written and in both cases, a new character would have been entered into the buffer by buf.insert(char); with the character *ch* hidden inside the body. The differences are as follows:

1. In the case of the task, because "insert" precedes "remove," a call to insert *must* precede a call to remove. This ensures that a character is in the buffer before it is removed. In the case of the package, no such ordering is implied and an exception is necessary. (Is there overwriting if two inserts follow each other in the task?)

2. The package cannot control the simultaneous execution of both insert and remove or any one of them by more than one external task.

The rendezvous mechanism needs a run-time support from the Real-time Operating System. To the programmer, this system is invisible—the rendezvous will invoke it automatically in a way transparent to the programmer. This improves the *portability* of the language since it makes it independent of the OS of a particular computer.

Before a task is running, it has to be activated or made *executable*, i.e., the declarative part of the task body must be elaborated. Tasks are not compilation units so the only way a task can be compiled is if written in the declarative part of a frame which is a block, subprogram, or package. A frame is called a *parent* if it creates tasks (its children). The body of a child task is *automatically activated* when control reaches the active code of the parent, i.e., reaches its **begin**. This means that the declarative part of their body is *elaborated*; it doesn't mean that they are running, since the tasks may be waiting to be *accepted*. When the tasks execute, they run concurrently with their parent and children. If several tasks (*siblings*) are declared by a parent, they are activated concurrently. All siblings must complete activation before their parent begins to execute the *body* of its task.

Figure 8-1 shows the timing for the case of two siblings being declared inside of a parent. Dotted line L1 indicates elaboration of the declarative part of the parent. For the siblings, this is the activation stage: L2, L3. The dashed line indicates that a task exists (has been elaborated), but is blocked, or has terminated. Finally, a solid line shows a task executing. Note that the parent is executable during L4, but not yet running, waiting for the children to complete elaboration (L5, L6).

A task is elaborated in the declarative part of its parent and begins its activation, i.e., the elaboration of its declarative part. Notice the distinction between the *elaboration of the task* and the *elaboration of the declarative part of the task body*. We will return to this item again; remember the chain: elaboration - activation - execution.

Synchronization is achieved by the rendezvous mechanism, communication is achieved via parameters which transfer data between tasks. They are defined in the entry specification, e.g., c:CHARACTER of entries insert and remove which were part of the DB task (Code 8-9).

The modes of the parameters of entries are similar to those of procedures, namely, **in**, **out**, and **in out** with **in** again being the default mode. Unlike a package, names cannot be shortened by a USE-CLAUSE.

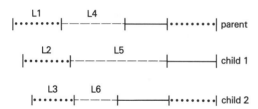

Figure 8-1 Activation of children by their parents

In the case of the brokerage company, there are *nb* brokers, so that an *array of tasks* is needed. For this, first a **type** of tasks is declared and then an array of this particular type follows:

```
    task type BROKER is -- Types CUSTID, STOCK and STATUS are known.
entry purchase       (id: CUSTID; amount: STOCK; stat: out STATUS);
entry sale           (id: CUSTID; amount: STOCK; stat: out STATUS);
entry quotation  (id: CUSTID; amount: out STOCK; stat: out STATUS);
entry update     (id: CUSTID; amount: out STOCK; stat: out STATUS);
    end task;
```

```
brokers: array(1 .. nb) of BROKER;
```

This declared *nb* brokers each of which may be called as, say, brokers(1).sale(11,222,*s*). Each broker has the following entries:

Entry "purchase" accepts the identification number *id* of the customer, how much stock is to be purchased (amount), and the status of the customer. It will provide the information of whether the customer has not exceeded the credit limit, and also confirm that enough stock is available. (Entry "sale" is similar.) Entry "quotation" provides information about the stock. Entry "update" checks the customer orders, so that the present status can be updated and quoted.

The task body may contain local declarations of objects. They cannot be changed by the calling task.

In order to communicate, synchronize, and exchange information, a caller must be *accepted*, thus leading to a rendezvous. For each and every entry in a task specification, there *must* be at least one *identical* ACCEPT-STATEMENT in the body of this particular task. For instance, if BROKER is used, there must exist:

```
accept purchase(id: CUSTID; amount: STOCK; stat: out STATUS)
do ... end;
```

in the corresponding task body (but there may be more). Such an ACCEPT-STATEMENT specifies what actions are to be taken whenever the entry is accepted. Between its **do** and the corresponding **end** there is a SEQUENCE-OF-STATEMENTs which may include not only simple statements, but also subprogram calls, entry calls, accept statements, and inner blocks. (The SEQUENCE-OF-STATEMENTs between **do** and **end** of an **accept** is the critical section discussed earlier.)

Note that if there is no **entry** in the interface then there is no **accept** in the body. Therefore, tasks appear similar to packages, except that packages are passive, while tasks are active—they are processes.

Types were templates for data objects, tasks are templates for process objects. Tasks are called asynchronously and work concurrently with other units except at points where they synchronize.

An entry may be called by a number of tasks and faster than it can process the calls. Therefore, *a single queue is associated with each entry*. Waiting tasks are mostly processed on a "First Come First Serve" basis: each time an entry is accepted, the task at the head of the queue is removed. There may be a number of ACCEPT-STATEMENTs for the same entry, but only a single queue for every entry. A task may be in only one queue at a time. For example, in DB a character must be inserted into the buffer before it can be removed from it. There are only two queues and the broker could possibly be waiting in one of the queues. A number of entries may call the same accept.

There exists an asymmetry in naming, namely that the caller must specify the name of the acceptor, while the acceptor does not specify or know the name of the caller. Another difference is that a caller can wait in only one queue, while an accept may have many queues. It follows that Ada will not allow a caller to issue more than a single call and wait for whichever is accepted first. A customer can therefore wait for only one task provided by a broker, while the broker can accept once a purchase, then a sale, etc.

Each entry has the attribute "Count" which provides the number of tasks waiting in the queue of this entry. The number of tasks waiting for sale is sale'count.

The use of the ENTRY and ACCEPT-STATEMENTS is exemplified by the broker example in Code 8-10.

```
with TEXT_IO; use TEXT_IO;
procedure transaction is -- This is the main program, the parent.
  task customer;   -- The caller has no entries; it is a signal.
  task broker is   -- Broker has an entry which will be called as
    entry receive(ch: in CHARACTER); -- broker.receive(char).
  end broker;
  --- Function "processing" is declared here and used later.
  task body customer is
    ch: CHARACTER;              -- The customer produces messages,
    begin loop random(ch);     -- character by character, one here.
      broker. receive(ch);     -- It then sends it to the broker,
    end loop;                  -- and prepares the next character.
  end customer;                -- End the body of consumer.
  task body broker is
    chr : CHARACTER;           -- chr is needed to replace ch.
    begin                      -- The tasks synchronize at the accept
      loop                     -- statement and exchange information.
        accept receive(ch: in CHARACTER) do -- Copying is all
          chr := ch; --that is done in the accept statement,
        end receive;--so that it does not tie up the broker.
        --- The broker is "processing" here.
      end loop;
    end broker;
  begin                        -- This starts the main procedure, which
    random(ch);                -- leaves all processing to the tasks.
  end transaction;
```

Code 8-10

Most applications use tasks to *communicate* (to pass information asynchronously) or to coordinate, *synchronize* activities. The two concepts are linked since synchronization may be considered as contentless communication, and some types of communication require prior synchronization. When a caller is accepted, there is a rendezvous between the two tasks. The rendezvous concept unifies synchronization and communication between tasks. *Synchronization occurs when the caller is accepted by the acceptor.* During the rendezvous, the execution of the caller is suspended while the acceptor executes statements which among others may prepare the exchange of information. The picture of the execution is therefore as in Fig. 8-2. Initially, the broker must wait for the customer to create *ch*, following which they meet forming a single thread of control. If the customer has another transaction, and there are at least two processors, the customer and the broker could work concurrently producing a new *ch* and transferring the previous *ch* to the memory. Recall that ACCEPT-STATEMENTS should include only the necessary part of processing the acceptor. Everything else should follow its end so as to be done concurrently with the caller. Hence, processing of *ch* is not part of the rendezvous (Fig. 8-2).

For real-time parallel programs, the time is important since some decisions will have to depend on the timing of the tasks. The Ada Reference Manual [ARM] defines a library package CALENDAR which may be used for this purpose (see Fig. 8-3). Note that TIME is an abstract data type. Its implementation is hidden from the user.

The current time is returned by the function CLOCK. It can be used in order for instance to test if some time-critical SEQUENCE-OF-STATEMENTS executes in a given time *dt*, as follows:

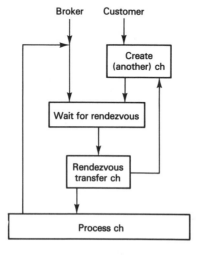

Figure 8-2 Concurrent work of a broker with customers

```
package CALENDAR is
  type TIME is private;

  subtype YEAR__NUMBER    is INTEGER   range 1901 .. 2099;
  subtype MONTH__NUMBER   is INTEGER   range 1 .. 12;
  subtype DAY__NUMBER     is INTEGER   range 1 .. 31;
  subtype DAY__DURATION   is DURATION  range 0.0 .. 86__400.0;

function CLOCK return TIME;

  function YEAR     (DATE : TIME) return YEAR__NUMBER;
  function MONTH    (DATE : TIME) return MONTH__NUMBER;
  function DAY      (DATE : TIME) return DAY__NUMBER;
  function SECONDS (DATE : TIME) return DAY__DURATION;

  procedure SPLIT   (DATE      : in  TIME;
                     YEAR      : out YEAR__NUMBER;
                     MONTH     : out MONTH__NUMBER;
                     DAY       : out DAY__NUMBER;
                     SECONDS : out DAY__DURATION);

  function TIME__OF (YEAR      : YEAR__NUMBER;
                     MONTH     : MONTH__NUMBER;
                     DAY       : DAY__NUMBER;
                     SECONDS : DAY__DURATION := 0.0) return TIME;

  function " + "    (LEFT : TIME;       RIGHT : DURATION) return TIME;
  function " + "    (LEFT : DURATION; RIGHT : TIME)      return TIME;
  function " – "    (LEFT : TIME;       RIGHT : DURATION) return TIME;
  function " – "    (LEFT : TIME;       RIGHT : TIME)      return DURATION;

  function "<"     (LEFT, RIGHT : TIME) return BOOLEAN;
  function "< ="   (LEFT, RIGHT : TIME) return BOOLEAN;
  function ">"     (LEFT, RIGHT : TIME) return BOOLEAN;
  function "> ="   (LEFT, RIGHT : TIME) return BOOLEAN;

  TIME__ERROR : exception; – can be raised by TIME__OF, " + ", and " – "

private
  – implementation-dependent
end;
```

Figure 8-3   Package CALENDAR of Ada

```
declare start, completion : TIME;
interval : DURATION := dt; -- Interval is a constant, say dt.
begin
  start := CLOCK;                  -- This sets the time the job starts.
    --- Here should be the sequence of statements to be executed.
  completion := CLOCK; -- It measures when the job was completed.
  crit_time := completion-start;     -- The time it took the job.
end;     -- to complete. If too high, something should be done.
```

For real-time programs, the function **delay** may also be useful. For instance, writing **delay** 45.0; will cause the suspension of the executing task for *at least* 45 seconds. When

45 secs. are over, the task may resume operations *if* it is free to do so and is not busy. Otherwise it is suspended waiting for some event to happen so that it can be activated again. Therefore, the delay will be increased. The resumption may depend on other tasks and is asynchronous.

The **delay** may also use more convenient units declared for instance as: minutes : constant := 60.0; hours : constant := 3600.0; and even mls by declaring millisecs : constant := 0.001;.

As an example, take a loop to be repeated every "interval" seconds on the average ([ARM 9.6]). The program part is as follows:

```
declare use CALENDAR;
next_time : TIME := CLOCK+interval; -- Interval is declared globally.
begin
  loop
    delay next_time-CLOCK; -- The approximate delay.
    --- some actions
    next_time := next_time+interval;
  end loop;
end;
```

Two tasks, task1 and task2, were written in DB to indicate that the second can be processed *only* after the first was accepted. When a nondeterministic selection between a number of alternatives is called for, the SELECT-STATEMENT is used. It is exemplified by

```
select
  accept entry1 do ... end entry1; ... ;
or
  accept entry2 do ... end entry2; ... ;
or
  accept entry3 do ... end entry3; ... ;
end select; -- Only one of these is chosen by the select.
```

When execution reaches this select, the three queues are inspected:

1. If no calls are waiting, then execution of this body is suspended. The first caller is accepted, the rendezvous takes place, and then the code following the **end select** is run.
2. If only one task is waiting, then it is accepted immediately.
3. If more tasks are waiting then the scheduler decides which to accept.

Note that an ACCEPT-STATEMENT can only appear in the SEQUENCE-OF-STATEMENTS of the body of a task in which it was declared, that such a body can include more than one ACCEPT-STATEMENT for the same entry, and that a task can

call its own entries. (In the case of a simple rendezvous, this would lead to a deadlock.)
An or-alternative can be a **delay**. If we write

```
select
  accept aaa do ... end aaa;
or
  delay 5.0; --- Sequence-of-Statements-1;
end select;
```

then *aaa* will wait only 5.0 seconds: If during this time *aaa* is called, a rendezvous occurs;
if not then the Sequence-of-statements-1 is executed.

Suppose that instead of the accept line we had written:

```
bbb.xxx; --- Sequence-of-Statements-2;
```

Here, if the called task *bbb.xxx* is ready in 5.0 seconds, a rendezvous occurs, the
Sequence-of-Statements-2 is executed, and the **select** is left. Unless a rendezvous occurs,
the task is delayed at least 5.0 seconds. If there is more than one **accept** alternative, the
first rendezvous that is possible prior to the expiration of the **delay** proceeds immediately.
If no rendezvous is possible prior to the expiration of the **delay**, then the **delay** is selected
and Sequence-of-Statements-1 is executed.

Sometimes a rendezvous is requested conditionally (i.e., so that if it cannot be
accepted then an alternative SEQUENCE-OF-STATEMENTS is to be processed instead
of waiting). This is done using **else** as follows:

```
select
  accept entry-call do ... end; ... ;
or -- Other accepts.
  else SEQUENCE_OF_STATEMENTS; -- Often a NULL-STATEMENT.
end select;
```

In the absence of the **else** part, the caller could have been suspended until it can be
accepted. This could take a long time and in some cases may even lead to a deadlock. By
using **null** for the SEQUENCE-OF-STATEMENTS, we have a way to prevent the task
from being suspended. This can be important for real-time systems.

Sometimes a *conditional selection* is needed. It may be as follows:

```
select                    -- This select provides a multiple choice.
  when condition1 =>             -- This is called a "guard."
    alternative1;                -- Usually, an ACCEPT-STATEMENT.
    --- SEQUENCE-OF-STATEMENTS;
  or when condition2 =>
    --- It may also be a delay or terminate statement.
  else SEQUENCE-OF-STATEMENTS;
end select;
```

The program part above included *guards* starting with the keyword **when**. On executing a select alternative, these guards are first evaluated *once* for each execution of the SELECT-STATEMENT. An alternative can therefore be either selected or not selected for *the current execution*. If the condition evaluates to TRUE then the alternative is said to be ''open'' and can be executed if there is an outstanding entry call for it. In that case, the rendezvous takes place, the SEQUENCE-OF-STATEMENTS which follows it is executed, and the entire SELECT-STATEMENT is thereby completed. However, if no open accept alternative exists or none has an outstanding entry call, then the **else** part will be executed. In each of these cases, control then passes to the statement following the **end select**. The **else** part could be a **delay**, or a **terminate** (see below). If no **else** exists then the task will be *suspended* on the **select** (i.e., put in a queue waiting to be reactivated by the entry call for which the alternative was open). For this to happen, an exception should be used, since Ada views this situation to be the exception, PROGRAM-ERROR.

Acceptors are more complex than callers. If a select is used, the acceptor does not know which of the guards will be open. (It is this indeterminacy which is useful since the acceptor may wait for many potential callers.) As seen above, the acceptor also has greater and more complex control over the rendezvous; the caller can either wait or meet immediately. Finally, by using the 'count attribute, the acceptor will know how many tasks are waiting to be accepted; the caller has no idea whether competition even exists.

Task types and task objects can be declared in any declarative part, even in the body of the task itself. Usually, the specification precedes the body, and the scope of the entries begins right after the task specification. The parent task plays a role in activating the ACCEPT-STATEMENT, with the following three possibilities:

1. If during the execution of a task an **accept** is reached *before* it has been called, then the execution of the task is suspended until the entry call has been issued.

2. If a parent issues an entry call before the corresponding **accept** has been reached in the body of the called entry, then the execution of the parent task is suspended until **accept** is received.

3. When the entry call finds the corresponding **accept** ready, then a rendezvous occurs. The SEQUENCE-OF-STATEMENTS between **do** and **end** is executed while the parent task is suspended.

This is shown in Fig. 8-4. At time $t(1)$, task B calls entry C but is not accepted because C is busy; likewise at time $t(2)$ when task A calls task C. At $t(3)$, task C is ready to accept either A or B and will accept B since B waited longer. During the rendezvous between B and C [i.e., from $t(3)$ to $t(4)$], B is suspended and C does the processing. Then Task A is accepted and completed by time $t(5)$. From $t(5)$ on, all tasks work in parallel. Note that *during any rendezvous only two tasks are involved*—one is processing, the other is suspended.

The model of tasking as developed up to now implies that each task has a separate CPU. Unfortunately, few systems will afford this luxury and, as a result, there are usually more tasks than processors. Therefore, it is necessary for the run-time system to choose which tasks to execute and which to delay, especially since deadlocks can occur.

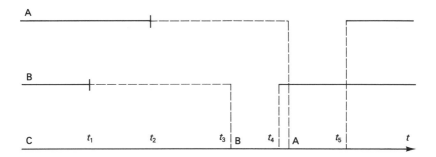

Figure 8-4   Activation and rendezvous of tasks

Priorities are needed to break the deadlock and to allow the run-time system to make better decisions regarding which tasks to run. They are assigned by an Ada construct called PRAGMA in a task specification, e.g.:

```
task types BUFFER is
  pragma priority(pr);
entry insert(i: ITEM);        -- The previously described task.
  entry remove(i: out ITEM);  -- ITEM is defined globally.
end buffer;
```

The particular priority *pr* is an integer constant and as such cannot be changed during the execution of a program. The range of priorities can be found in the library package SYSTEM. A low value of *pr* implies a low priority for the task. The Ada Manual [ARM] prescribes that the highest priority task will execute whenever the needed resources become available. If the number of PEs is lower than the number of tasks, this means pre-emptive scheduling: When a high priority task changes its state from blocked to ready, it immediately is changed to running. The tasks were put into the queue strictly first-come, first-serve.

A task is said to have *completed* its job if it has completed to execute the SEQUENCE-OF-STATEMENTS in its body or if an **exception** was raised, if it has no children tasks or they all have terminated. There is a rule concerning task execution which states: "A block statement or subprogram body that has been completed is not left until all its dependent tasks have terminated." A subroutine will not complete on a **return** if all tasks that depend on it have not terminated.

If there are no open alternatives other than a *terminate* alternative, that one will be chosen if the following conditions exist:

1. The parent of this task has completed;
2. Each sibling task has terminated or is able to terminate;
3. There is no queued entry call for any entry of the task;
4. The task has children tasks but all of them have terminated.

If the task takes the terminate alternative, it is said to have terminated. This is so because all tasks involved are of no further use (and the whole group of tasks, including the parent, terminates simultaneously). If these conditions are not met, the task is suspended waiting for an alternative to open for the conditions to be fulfilled.

The state of a parent that has completed its execution, but whose children have not completed, is called *completed*. If a parent has completed but its children have not terminated, then it will remain in the completed state until its offspring have all terminated. Only then will the parent terminate. The consequence of this rule depends on how the parent was activated: if by a subprogram, then control will not return to the caller; if by a block, control will not leave the block; if by a task, the task may not terminate; and it isn't defined if by a library package.

If an attempt it made to rendezvous with a task that has either terminated or completed, then the entry raises the TASKING-ERROR. Even if the caller has been placed on the entry queue of the task, it is possible for the acceptor to complete without accepting that particular call. In this case a TASKING-ERROR is raised.

An executable task can also be completed if an **exception** was raised either during its activation or during the elaboration of the declarations of its parent. In the first case, the task with the **exception** is completed, but the other tasks mentioned in the declarations proceed to execute. In the second case, all tasks in the declarative part become terminated. If an **exception** was raised during the elaboration of the parent, all its children become terminated. If an **exception** is raised during the activation of a task, that task becomes completed, while other tasks in the same declarative part are not affected; the parent though is affected since a TASKING-ERROR is raised immediately following the **begin** of the parent.

In general, a task waiting on a **select** with an open alternative may terminate if it depends on a parent that has completed its job. It can also terminate if each and every task that depends on that parent task is either already terminated or is waiting on an open alternative of a **select**. In this case, all tasks depending on that parent will be collectively terminated, after which the parent itself will terminate.

A task can be explicitly terminated either from inside the task by a **terminate** or from outside the task by **abort** task1, . . . , taskm;. The latter causes the unconditional and immediate termination of all *m* tasks mentioned and *all tasks for which these m are parents*. Even if such a task has not yet been activated and is waiting in a queue, it will be removed from the queue. If it is being delayed, the **delay** is canceled. Finally, if it is engaged in a rendezvous, the partner will be notified of the abortion by an exception. The aborted tasks become *abnormal*.

An ABORT-STATEMENT: **abort** task1, task2, . . . , taskm; will make all of those *m* (*m* may be 1) tasks *abnormal*. Moreover, all nonterminated tasks that depend on this abnormal task will themselves become abnormal, but the particular task that activated the **abort** will itself continue. A task can even abort itself.

The states of a task (and exceptions) are shown in detail in [BLW87] and in abbreviated form in Fig. 8-5. The state is:

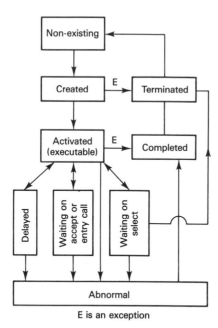

E is an exception

Figure 8-5   The states of a task

1. Created: It has not yet been activated, even though its specifications have been elaborated.

2. Active (Executable): The task is executing or is waiting for the elaboration of the declarative part of a package body. It may be delayed or waiting either on an entry call or on an **accept**. Having finished, it moves to the active or to an abnormal state.

3. Completed: Execution of the task has reached the **end** of the task body, or it stopped being abnormal.

4. Terminated: The task has completed and all its children tasks have terminated, or it has reached an open alternative, its parent has completed, and all its children have either terminated or are waiting on open terminate alternatives. If terminated, the task relinquishes all its resources.

5. Abnormal: An abnormal task obeys the following conditions:

   5.1 No further rendezvous is possible with such a task.

   5.2 If suspended (on a **delay**, **accept**, or **select**) then it becomes completed.

   5.3 If it has not yet been activated, it becomes completed.

   5.4 Nothing happens if an attempt is made to abort a task that is already abnormal, terminated, or completed. If the calling task becomes abnormal during a rendezvous, the rendezvous is completed normally and the called task is not affected.

If none of the above situations apply, then the abnormal task must become completed before it reaches:

- the end of its activation
- a SELECT or DELAY-STATEMENT
- The activation of another task
- an exception handler or another ABORT-STATEMENT
- the start or end of an ACCEPT-STATEMENT

The rationale for task abortion is the need to control wayward tasks, e.g., in order to break a deadlock. However, Hoare has remarked that "its successful use depends on a valid process aborting a wild one before the wild one aborts a valid process—or does any serious damage. The probability of this in negligible. If processes can go wild, we are much safer without aborts." The ABORT-STATEMENT is really controversial. For instance, if used in an SM multiprocessor and if a task is updating a shared variable when aborted, then the value of this variable becomes undefined. This and similar cases result in the warning contained in [ARM 9.10.10]: "An abort statement should be used only in extremely severe situations requiring unconditional termination."

Tasks can be used for three distinct purposes:

1. To model co-exsiting objects, the so-called "active tasks."
2. To provide synchronization services, the "synchronization tasks."
3. To define parallel algorithms, the "parallelization tasks."

These three types of tasks should be used as follows:

1. Active tasks communicate with each other by buffers (i.e., through synchronization tasks). They contain no entries but call (directly or indirectly) the entries of synchronization tasks.
2. Synchronization tasks are usually defined within packages and control access to various hardware and software resources. They do contain entries and process entry calls.
3. Parallelization tasks should be contained within functions or procedures and should terminate "normally."

8–3 EXAMPLES OF MULTITASKING

8–3.1 Replacing Semaphores

There are two ways to restrict access to a resource. In Ada, requests are not accepted unless they can be met. If semaphores (and monitors) are used, all requests are accepted, but any task whose request cannot currently be met is suspended in a queue. Ada though can simulate semaphores as follows:

```
task type semaphore is
  entry wait; entry signal;
end;
task body semaphore is
bs : INTEGER := 1;
begin
  loop
    select
      when bs = 1 =>
        accept wait do
          bs := bs-1;
        end accept;
    or
      when bs = 0 =>
        accept signal do
          bs := bs+1;
        end accept;
    end select;
  end loop;
end body; -- And the rest as in the semaphore program.

s: semaphore;
```

Code 8-11

A critical section would then be programmed as follows:

```
semaphore.wait; -- The critical section; semaphore.signal;
```

All previously described solutions can be used in the same way. We could also combine the semaphore with the other Ada features. For instance, in the above call on the critical section, even if the wait is successful, the task is moved from the suspended to the ready state and then must wait for the resources before the start of execution. We could use a procedure nowait (and a similar one for nosignal):

```
procedure nowait is
begin
  loop                        -- This loop is iterated repeatedly,
    select                    -- selecting first the semaphore.
      semaphore.wait;         -- If wait can be effected, then
      return;                 -- we achieved our purpose,
    else                      -- but if it cannot be done, then
      return;                 -- the call is canceled.
    end select;               -- Note that following the successful wait
  end loop;                   -- and the rendezvous, the return moves the
end nowait;                   -- program back to the calling environment.
```

It was shown in Sec. 4-2 that even for only two tasks the results depend on the timing and are thus *not reproducible*. These are called *race conditions*, namely a set of circumstances in which the relative speeds of the tasks influence the results. To make the program work correctly, the semaphore operations should be indivisible (atomic), as were the lock-operations in Sec. 4-2.

The semaphore solution was devised with an Operating System (OS) and multiprogramming in mind. The OS then changes the state of a process from blocked to ready, etc., when a semaphore is indicating that an event has occurred. In a PPS this may be unnecessary if a PaM is free to do the job: the state can then be changed from blocked to running. In Ada this is achieved easily since tasks are concurrent, asynchronous processes, each with possibly a separate PaM. Both the synchronization and communication are done by the mechanism of the rendezvous; an OS underlies the tasking model, but it is invisible to the user.

The critical section problem can be solved in Ada simply by using the ACCEPT-STATEMENT. The program would then use a variable *s* (call it "semaphore") and be correct for any number of brokers identified by the parameter *q*. It is shown in Code 8-12.

```
procedure Dij is
nt: INTEGER constant := 10;          -- Ten is an arbitrary number.
  procedure brok(q: in INTEGER);
  begin
    loop
      accept(s: INTEGER) do
        cris;                        -- The (short) critical section
      end accept;
      remainofq;                     -- Remainder of work of q.
    end loop;
  end brok;
end Dij;
```

Code 8-12

In the solutions with semaphores, shared variables are used for communication between tasks. In Ada, synchronization and communication are inseparable and should be catered to by the single mechanism of the rendezvous. Therefore, no semaphores or other means of ensuring the safe use of shared variables are supported in Ada. Shared variables of SM multiprocessors should therefore be used with considerable care. Only when it can be shown that two or more tasks are not updating the shared variables at the same time should such use be permitted. In any case, the following rules for use of shared variables in SM multiprocessors should be enforced.

  1. If a task reads a shared variable, then no other task should be permitted to write into it.

2. If a task updates (writes into) a shared variable, then no other task should either read or update it simultaneously.

If these rules are obeyed, shared variables can be used. On the other hand, Ada features are also appropriate for MP-Multiprocessors. Since the processors are supposed to wait in queues for jobs assigned by the scheduler, an ACCEPT-STATEMENT can be used.

8–3.2 A Circular Buffer

In the broker example, the customers produced requests, the brokers processed them. This is a common situation in which some tasks produce information (mostly by calculations), while others consume it (e.g., by putting it into the database). The interaction between them may be as shown in Code 8-13.

```
task type producer is
  --- Calls consumer.ininfo whenever it has the information.
end producer;
task type consumer is
  entry ininfo(item: ITYPE);    -- Input of information.
end consumer;

task body producer is
item: ITYPE;                      -- The item of information.
begin
  --- Produce the item of information, say, by random(item).
  consumer.ininfo(item);    -- Call task ininfo of consumer.
  --- Additional code.      -- Reply to a customer.
end producer;

task body consumer is
it: ITYPE;
begin
  --- Code preceding the transfer of information.
  accept ininfo(item in: ITYPE) do -- When the consumer accepts the
    consumer.it. := item;          -- item, it stores (consumes) it.
  end accept;
  --- Additional code.
end consumer;                       -- The buffer had one item.
```

Code 8-13

The rendezvous of the producer with the consumer means that if one of them is early, the other will have to wait. This limits the time in which the producer and consumer could work in parallel. It also makes the producer the caller and the consumer the acceptor (which is not always best). It is much better to put a *buffer* between the producer and the consumer.

The producer deposits the item in the buffer and proceeds to produce additional items without waiting for the consumer to pick up the item; this may be done later. Unfortunately, if the buffer has space for only a single item, the producer cannot deposit the second item if the first was not picked up. The consumer also has to wait sometimes, namely if the single-item buffer is empty. What we need is a buffer with as many spaces as possible. Its work can be described as follows.

Several tasks (the ''producers'') wish to transfer a number of characters to other tasks (the ''consumers''). In order for producers and consumers to be independent, a *buffer* is used. Producers then insert characters (unless the buffer is full), while consumers remove them (unless the buffer is empty). Tasks can be active or passive with passive tasks providing services for active tasks. In this case, the producers and consumers are the active, the buffer is the passive task that will accept calls from the other tasks. The p producers and c consumers as well as the buffer work all independently and concurrently. All of them are activated when the **begin** of the parent frame is reached.

It is assumed that the buffer can contain a fixed number of messages, say m, and that the message type has been previously declared. There are two pointers *iin* and *oot* (Fig. 6-9 with changed pointer names). Whenever a message is to be added to the buffer, *iin* is incremented first; whenever a message is to be removed from the buffer, it is removed from the slot pointed to by *oot* and this pointer is incremented. Since the buffer is circular, incrementation must be modulo m.

Accessing the buffer is a critical section since addition or removal of messages should exclude each other. Additional problems posed by the buffer are that no message should be removed from an empty buffer and no message added to a full buffer. The program is shown in Code 8-14.

The SELECT-STATEMENT ensures that the messages are appended to and removed from the buffer in the order in which they arrive provided the buffer is not full when a message is ''sent'' or empty when a message is to be removed. For $0 < s < m$ (normal circumstances), both accepts are considered ''open'' and the send/receive calls are accepted on a first-come, first-serve basis. The critical sections between **do** and **end** prevent a new call from being accepted until an active rendezvous is over.

Since the buffer cannot at the same time be both empty ($s = 0$) and full ($s = m$), at least one ACCEPT-STATEMENT will be open. If the buffer is full, the first alternative is closed and messages can be removed (''read'') from the buffer, decreasing the number of messages s in the buffer. When the buffer is empty, only the first alternative is open and

```
task body BUFFER is              -- Only the task body is interesting.
m: constant INTEGER : = 100;     -- m is the arbitrary size of the buffer.

buf: array(1 . . m) of MESSAGE;  -- "MESSAGE was declared earlier.
iin,oot: INTEGER range 0..m-1: =0; -- This is the initialization.
s: INTEGER range 1..m : = 0;     -- s counts the number of messages in
begin                            -- the buffer and starts with 0.
  loop                           -- The program is an infinite loop.
    select                       -- consisting of a single select.
      when s<m =>                -- If the buffer is not full, a
        accept send(min: in MESSAGE) do -- MESSAGE min is accepted
          buf(iin) : = min;      -- and if possible,
        end accept;              -- added to the buffer.
        s : = s+1;      -- The number of messages increases by 1.
        iin : = (iin rem m)+1;   -- The iin pointer is adjusted.
    or-- The or provides mutual exclusion, since only one when
      when s=0 =>  -- can be active. If the buffer is not empty,
        accept rec(mout: out MESSAGE) do -- Remove a MESSAGE mout
          mout : = buf(oot);    -- from buffer at position oot
        end accept;
        s : = s-1;               -- and reduce the number of messages.
        oot : = (oot rem m)+1;       -- The oot pointer is adjusted.
    or
      terminate;                 -- Terminate if neither possible.
    end select;
  end loop;
end buffer;
```

Code 8-14

messages can be accepted (''write''), but no messages can be removed. The rec(eive) entry waits in a queue. The **or** prevents both accepts from being active at the same time and *provides mutual exclusion*.

Tasks will often have priorities, but only a single queue for every entry. For the above example and the insert entry, a priority type is declared:
type PRIORITY **is** (hi,med,lo); and used as in Code 8-15.

There are now three queues and the guards make sure that the inserts are accepted only according to their priority.

```
---
loop
  select
    accept send(min: in MESSAGE, hi: INTEGER) do
      buff(iin) :=min;
    end accept:
  or when send(min,hi)'COUNT=0        -- No tasks waiting
    => accept send(min,med) do        -- on hi.
      buff(head) := min;
    end accept;
  or when send(min,hi)'COUNT=0        -- No tasks waiting
    and when send(min,med)'COUNT=0    -- on hi or on med.
    => accept send(min,lo) do
      buff(head) := min;
    end accept;
end loop;
```

Code 8-15

8–3.3 A Transducer (Relay) Program [Sch83]

The real problem with MIMD-systems is how to terminate jobs. Recall that in these systems a rendezvous occurs always between a *requestor and a server*. The general picture is exemplified by Fig. 8-6 in which there are three tasks: a PRODUCER of messages, a TRANSDUCER which transforms these messages, and a CONSUMER which consumes them. (The producer may be thought of as the input, the transducer as the PaM, and the consumer as the output device).

The basic cooperation between *any two* of these processes is:

- The *caller* (calling task) mentions a particular entry thereby requesting some particular service.
- The *server* (called entry) may accept a request carrying out the operations included in the service.

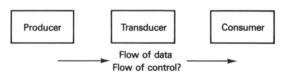

Figure 8-6 Flow of data/control between a producer and consumer

The *flow of information* in Fig. 8-6 is always from the producer to the transducer and then from the transducer to the consumer.

The relationship between caller and server is inherently asymmetric as far as the *flow of control* is concerned. The caller is active, the server is passive (without even knowing who the caller is). On the other hand, the caller is suspended until the server signals that the task is completed.

The first case to be discussed is that in which the flow of control and information are directed in the same way, and therefore, this case will be called a "straightforward producer-consumer control." The producers calls the entry receive of the transducer, which when accepted transfers an item *x*. The transducer calls the entry gett of the consumer, which when accepted, transfer an item *y*. The body of the producer will therefore include the entry call "transducer.receive(xx)." The body of the transducer includes both an **accept** receive(xx) and a call "consumer.gett(yy)." The consumer will have an **accept** gett(yy).

Before the bodies of the three tasks are designed, the initialization and termination should be discussed. In this case, *all three tasks will be initiated by virtue of being declared.* They will run concurrently exchanging information by rendezvous. Since a "parent" can shut down if and only if all its "children" shut down, there always exists the possibility that the entire system may become suspended forever waiting for a child-task to complete.

In the present case, the producer reads a file and signals completion whenever the end-of-file "eof" signal is detected. The body of the producer is therefore as shown in Code 8-16.

```
task body producer is
xx: XTYPE;
procedure read(x: out XTYPE) is ... end read;
-- Do not be misled by the single line above - it includes the entire
-- reading procedure and might be rather long in terms of time.
begin
  read(xx);
  while not eof loop             -- Send xx to the transducer and
    transducer.receive(xx);      -- read xx until the eof signal appears.
    read(xx);
  end loop;
end producer;                    -- The end of the body of the producer.
```

Code 8-16

The question is how to shut down the transducer and consumer tasks which do not read the eof symbol. As a matter of fact, both tasks will process the last item transferred by the producer and then wait (maybe forever) for more data to accept. This leads to an indefinite blocking or *deadlock* since the producer is also suspended, and none of the tasks is active (all waiting for something to happen). This is solved by sending an end-of-work *eow task* once an eof symbol is detected. The program is shown in Code 8-17.

```
procedure transmission is ..    -- This is the main program.

task producer;                  -- It will send "x" and when finished,
task transducer is              -- an eow task.
  entry receive(x: in XTYPE);   -- The transducer may receive x from the
  entry eow;                    -- producer or the eow signal. It then
end;                            -- sends the eow signal (task) to the

task consumer is                -- Consumer.
  entry gett(y: in YTYPE);      -- The consumer will accept items
  entry eow;                    -- y and will write them out.
end consumer;                   -- It then accepts the signal eow.

task body producer is
xx: XTYPE; -- Again don't be deceived; the next line is a procedure
procedure read(x: out XTYPE) is ... end; -- which acquires an item, but
begin                                   -- this may take a considerable
  read(xx);                             -- part of the overall time.
  while not eof loop
    transducer.receive(xx);   -- Ask the transducer to receive xx.
  read(xx);                   -- Read the next item from the input.
  end loop;
  transducer.eow; -- This is the signal that the task has finished.
end producer;

task body transducer is
xx: XTYPE; yy: YTYPE; --Next line has a procedure to transform x into y.
procedure transform(x: in XTYPE; y: out YTYPE) is ... end transform;
begin
  loop
    select
      accept receive(x: in XTYPE) do -- Item x sent by the producer
        xx := x;                 -- is accepted and assigned to the local
      end;                       -- variable xx, so as not to tie-up the
      transform(xx,yy);          -- producer for a long time. Local xx is
      consumer.gett(yy);         -- transformed into yy. This will take
    or                           -- most of the time. The yy is send to the
      accept eow; exit;          -- consumer. If the producer sends eow,
    end select;                  -- it will be accepted and an exit taken.
  end loop;                      -- Both select and loop are then left.
  consumer.eow;                  -- The signal of end of work is transferred
end transducer;                  -- to the consumer.
```

```
task body consumer is
yy: YTYPE;                                    -- yy is a local variable.
procedure write(y: in YTYPE) is ... ; end; -- A procedure to write y out.
begin                                         -- Begin of consumer body.
  loop                                        -- An endless loop in real-time.
    select
      accept gett(y: in YTYPE) do             -- If y is accepted then it is
        yy :=y;                               -- transformed into local yy and
      end accept;                             -- written out, but outside of
      write(yy);                              -- the accept so as not to lose
    or                                        -- time.
      accept eow; exit;                   -- Task eow completes the loop and thus
    end select;                           -- the consumer. This was a child of the
  end loop;                               -- transducer which is thus terminated. So
end consumer;                             - is the producer - ending all the work.
```

Code 8-17

The entry "eow" has no body and is therefore a *signal* to terminate. Summing up this flow of control: a selective wait, an ACCEPT-STATEMENT, and a signal eow were used to terminate the process.

Control also can move *backwards* (i.e., so that the consumer requests data from the transducer which itself requests it from the producer). The program is then changed as per Code 8-18.

Note that all entry calls and ACCEPT-STATEMENTS were reversed, reflecting the fact that control is now effected backwards.

The three tasks are initiated by virtue of being declared and are running concurrently. The main program consists of a NULL-STATEMENT. The producer reads a range of items and stops. As will be shown next, *the transducer and consumer are stopped by exceptions.*

When a task terminates, all pending and future calls to any of its entries will result in the raising of a built-in exception, TASKING-ERROR, for each caller. Exceptions usually serve to notify a calling task if an operation fails to complete successfully.

When an exception is not explicitly handled at some level by the caller, all of the exception's outstanding operations are successively terminated. This signal is thus propagated back not further than the level of the task for which the exception was raised (i.e., not to any embedding tasks).

When an unhandled exception reaches the level of the corresponding task body, the parent is exceptionally terminated. There is no further distinction between normal and exceptional termination of subtasks at the level of the immediately embedding task.

These conventions of Ada can be used as follows. Raising of the exception serves to

```
task body producer is
xx: XTYPE; --Procedures read, transform and write are predefined.
procedure read(x: out XTYPE) is ...; end;
begin
  for i in range loop            -- Next, the producer may accept
    read(xx);                    -- a call from the transducer,
    accept send(x: out XTYPE) do -- to send it an x. The call
      xx : = x;                  -- was accepted and item
    end accept;                  -- x was send.
  end loop;
end producer; -- body.
task body transducer is
xx: XTYPE; yy: YTYPE;
produce transform(x: in XTYPE; y: out YTYPE) is ... ; end;
begin
  loop
    producer.send(xx);           -- Ask the producer to please send
    transform(xx,yy);            -- item xx. Transform it and wait
    accept gett(y: out YTYPE) do -- for a call from the consumer to
      yy : = y;                  -- send it the transformed item.
    end accept;
  end loop;
end transducer; -- body.          -- Call the transducer to supply item yy.
task body consumer is                write(yy);
yy: YTYPE;
procedure write(y: in YTYPE) is
... ; end;
begin
  loop
    transducer.gett(yy);
-- Having received yy, dispose of it.
  end loop;
end consumer; -- body.
```

Code 8-18

---

signal the end of a given data stream and triggers termination of the receiving task when that event occurs. This is the effect desired to achieve graceful shutdown in our example. The requisite properties may be established by the following argument:

The *producer* process passes all input arguments that it receives to the transducer. When no more items are input, the producer accepts no further communication and *terminates normally*.

The *transducer* process delivers to the consumer a result for every argument it receives. The transducer requests further data from the producer but *terminates exceptionally*.

```
task producer;                      -- It does not require anymore any entries.

task transducer is
  entry send(x: in XTYPE);                          -- Send item x.
  entry gett(y: out YTYPE);                         -- Get item y.
  entry eow;
end transducer;

task consumer;                      -- It does not require entries.

task body producer is
xx: XTYPE;
procedure read(x: out XTYPE) is ... ; end;
begin
  for i in range loop
    read(xx);
    transducer.send(xx);            -- Ask transducer to accept xx.
  end loop;
  transducer.eow;                          -- Signal the end-of-work.
end producer;

task body transducer is
xx: XTYPE; yy: YTYPE;
procedure transform(xx: in XTYPE; yy: out YTYPE) is ... ; end;
begin
  loop
    select
      accept send(x: in XTYPE);              -- Accept an item or hang up.
        xx := x;
      end accept;
      transform(xx,yy); -- This is where most of the work is done.
      accept gett(y: out YTYPE) do -- Accept a call for the result.
        y := yy;        -- Note that this accept can only be accepted
      end accept;       --after the transformation is completed.
    or
      accept eow; exit;
    end select;
  end loop;
end transducer;

task body consumer is
yy: YTYPE;
procedure write(y: in YTYPE) is ... ; end;
begin
  loop
    transducer.gett(yy);            -- Ask the transducer to send item yy.
    write(yy);
  end loop;
end consumer;
```

Code 8-19

The *consumer* process disposes of every result received from the transducer, and always requests further data from the transducer but *terminates exceptionally*.

All processes of the system will complete action on the first item of information that enters the *pipeline* and will eventually terminate. Termination of the corresponding component tasks means that execution of the main program is also terminated, whereupon the entire system will shut down as required.

The relative simplicity of the solution obtained in this instance points to one of the primary advantages of backward directed control where data is effectively *pulled* rather than *pushed* downstream. When the receiving task is actively requesting the next item of information, it is in a position to be directly informed of the success or failure of that request even if the transmitted task has already terminated. This is to be contrasted with the opposite approach in which the receiver passively awaits the next item, and so must somehow be informed that it should not wait any longer.

The program discussed last was similar to the first without requiring a separate task for shutting down. The transducer and consumer attempt to communicate with the terminated producer. The failure to communicate synchronizes the shutdown.

A better solution might be to let the transducer ask the producer for data and send it (transformed) to the consumer. The producer would then be an input source, the consumer an output sink, and the *transducer the only active task*. The changed program is shown in Code 8-19.

In Code 8-19, a call transducer.eow indicates the end of work to the transducer. In the transducer-task, the **exit** essentially terminates the transducer and by the exception TASKING-ERROR terminates the consumer (which asks the shut-down transducer to send yy).

8–4 PROCESS CONTROL WITH ADA

8–4.1 Introduction

In Sec. 1-2, jobs were classified according to whether or not they were activated by interrupts. In particular, *real-time* systems for process control are activated by interrupts (through the Operating System, OS). Typically they interface with external devices reading signals from sensors and controlling devices. The definition of real-time systems can be extended as follows:

Real-time systems interact with the environment through sensors and *Status and Control Registers* (SCRs). They are *interrupt-driven* at a rate keyed to the time-scale of the process (instead of the CPU). Their response time must be shorter than the changes in the state of the process.

This definition leads to the following hardware features:

1. Since the CPU must follow real time, a clock is needed (see Sec. 8-2). Some even call real-time processing *clock-based computing*.

2. The state of the process is read from the various sensors which function as control registers. The sensors are also used in output. Some even call real-time processing *sensor-based computing*.

3. Interrupts of off-line computing are generated internally by the computer or its OS. In real-time computing, the interrupts are generated externally to the computer. Also, in off-line computing, interrupts occur seldom whereas in real-time computing they form the very basis on which the system works. Some therefore call real-time processing *interrupt-driven computing*.

4. Input/Output of single bits, registers (SCRs), and process-generated signals are required.

8–4.2 Device Drivers

High-level languages relieve the programmer from dealing with data-representation details. The declared data types specify the logical properties of objects of a given type. The declaration of objects specify allocated storage. Mappings between data types and bit-patterns and between object-names and storage-locations are left to the compiler. Thus, the declaration i:INTEGER; defines *i* as being of type integer and the compiler keeps track of how and where this variable is stored. Ada maintains this separation for SCRs with the program containing the definitions of logical properties of objects and separate statements defining their low-level representations. Such separation of the abstract properties of data provided by the programmer and implementation details provided by the compiler enhance the *portability* so that programs can be compiled for different computers and compilers select the best implementation in each case.

Virtually all input/output in real-time control is done at the machine level by manipulating bits in specific hardware interface registers. For instance, an analog-to-digital converter may be controlled through a two-byte register located at any two consecutive addresses and the format could be as in Fig. 8-7(a): Bits 0..3 of the right byte would have a channel number, bits 4 and 5 are not being used, the remaining 10 bits of the two bytes will contain the (digital) result transferred from the channel.

Starting the conversion of a particular channel is accomplished by writing its number to the low 4 bits of the register. Upon completion, the 10-bit result is stored in the 10 high-order bits of the register. The result must be obtained by reading the two bytes of the register separately (hardware requirement), the first to get the eight most significant and the second to get the least significant bits.

The data was stored in the register above ("interface" in general) in a form not normally used in Ada. In such cases, the representation details are absolutely necessary. Traditionally, system programmers use machine (assembly) code for this. Ada provides the means by which program variables can be *mapped* into such nonstandard structures.

Registers can be assigned to objects using statements called REPRESENTATION-CLAUSES. They form data-structures (analogous to an enumeration or packed record) which may be defined so as to mirror the format of specific hardware (e.g., the interface register above). A number of different *REPRESENTATION-CLAUSES* are next discussed.

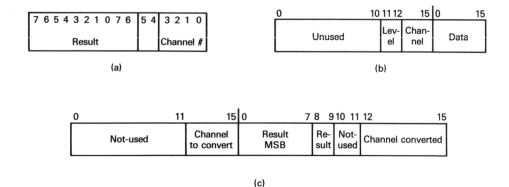

(a)

(b)

(c)

Figure 8-7 Status and control registers

The *LENGTH-CLAUSE* **for** . . . **use** . . . ; specifies the amount of storage to be allocated to a given type (or subtype), for the group of an access type, and for the working storage of a task type. For instance, we may indicate that "byte" occupies eight bits by

```
type BYTE is range 0..255; --Defines byte as integer in range 0..255.
  for BYTE'SIZE use 8;      --Attribute SIZE of byte is 8 bits long.
```

Note that the upper bound is specified for the *number of bits* to be allocated. *Storage units* could also be used for storage allocation. Thus, [ARM 13.4] lists the declaration of the following clauses:

```
type MEDIUM is range 0..65000;
type SHORT is delta 0.1 range -100.00..100.0;
type COLOR is (white, red, yellow, green, blue, brown, black);
BYTE: constant := 8; -- Byte will be used below as a storage unit
for COLOR'SIZE use 1*BYTE; -- Seven colors can be expressed by a byte.
for MEDIUM'SIZE use 2*BYTE; -- 2**16=64K or 65536 is sufficient.
for SHORT'SIZE use 15;-- The basic unit is still the bit.
```

The STORAGE_SIZE attribute provides the number of storage units to be reserved for an activation (not the code) of the task. As an example, we could use:
for a_to_d_conversion 'STORAGE_SIZE **use** 1024;

An *ENUMERATION-CLAUSE* specifies the internal code for enumeration types. For example an SCR, which transmits by single bits its status (off = 001, ready = 010, and on = 100) is defined as:

```
type SCR is (off, ready, on);
for SCR use (off=>1, ready=>2, on=>4);
```

As with other enumerations, the Successor, Predecessor, and Position functions are defined, e.g., SCR'Succ(ready) is on.

Another example [ARM] describes some machine instructions:

```
type Mix_code is (ADD, SUB, MUL, LDA, STA, STZ);
for Mix_code use (ADD=>1, SUB=>2, MUL=>3, LDA=>8, STA=>24, STZ=>33);
```

It shows that the representation of the values need not be contiguous.

Next, consider the seven-segment display used in computer terminals. The light-emitting diodes that are ''on'' for the ten digits and the ''truth-table'' are shown in Fig. 8-8.

The mapping can be obtained by declaring

```
type SVS is ('1', '7', '0', '3', '2', '4', '9', '5', '8');
for SVS use( '1'=>6, '7'=>7, '0'=>63, '3'=>79, '2'=>91,
    "4'=>102, "9'=>103, "5'=>109, "6'=>125, "8'=>127);
```

Note that the numbers are in strictly increasing order. If a variable, say ''dis'' of type SVS was declared, then dis: = '3'; will cause the digit (character) 3 to be displayed by the light-emitting diodes.

A *RECORD-CLAUSE* specifies the layout of components of a record type by providing their order, position, and size. It can be exemplified by an I/O register of Fig. 8-7.(b) as follows:

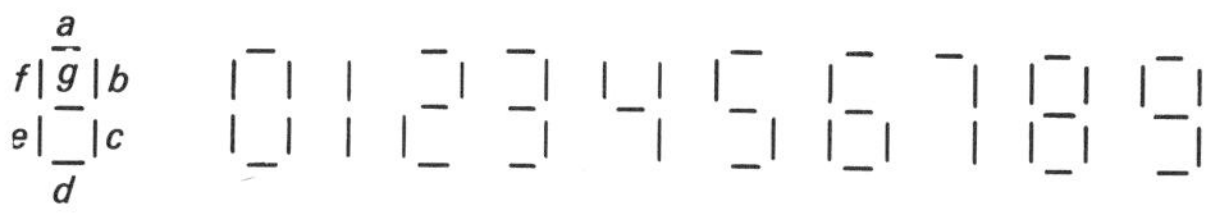

	1	2	4	8	16	32	64	
	a	b	c	d	e	f	g	dv
0	1	1	1	1	1	1	0	63
1	0	1	1	0	0	0	0	6
2	1	1	0	1	1	0	1	91
3	1	1	1	1	0	0	1	79
4	0	1	1	0	0	1	1	102
5	1	0	1	1	0	1	1	109
6	1	0	1	1	1	1	1	125
7	1	1	1	0	0	0	0	7
8	1	1	1	1	1	1	1	127
9	1	1	1	0	0	1	1	103

Figure 8-8 Activation of light-emitting diodes to display digits

```
type MODE is (low, high);
type IO_REGISTER is record
  unused_bits: INTEGER range 0..2047;    -- bits 0 to 10.
  code: MODE;                            -- 2 bits, namely 11, 12.
  channel: INTEGER range 0..7           -- Bits 13, 14, 15.
  data: INTEGER range 0..65535;          -- Another 16 bits.
end record;                              -- See Fig. 8-7. (b)
```

The above record defined a two-word, 32-bit register with the first word being the control and the second the data word.

Regardless of the machine address to which an I/O register is assigned, successive bits from most to least significant within each word are assigned to the fields in the given order.

Note.   Since the bits are assigned sequentially, it is necessary to label those bits that are unused in the device. The field-name unused-bits has no implicit meaning except to remind the programmer that the field is not used.

An *ADDRESS-CLAUSE* is used to:

1. Specify the starting address of an object in memory. With this mechanism, program objects can be associated with hardware objects such as device registers and hardware buffers.
2. Specify that a subprogram, package, or task is to be allocated starting at a specific memory location.
3. Associate a hardware interrupt with an entry (this cannot be an entire entry family, like an array of tasks).

The ADDRESS-CLAUSE has the form **for** name **use at** address; where "name" is the program entity that is being associated with the memory address.

A *DEVICE* in Ada is a data structure which may be defined to mirror the format of specific hardware interface registers [ARM 13.5.1].

To access a device register, one instructs the compiler, by means of an ADDRESS-CLAUSE, to allocate a program variable of an appropriate type at the hardware address corresponding to the device register. References to this variable translate into references to the device register. For example, the declaration:

```
printer_buffer : CHARACTER; for printer_buffer use at 8#177566#;
```

specifies that the buffer is actually located at address 177566 (octal).

The statement: **for** hardware_buffer **use at** 8#177562#; enables location 177562 (octal) to be accessed by the program-variable hardware_buffer. For Fig. 8-7(b) we have:

```
for IO_REGISTER use record
  unused_bits at 1 range 0..10;       -- 11 bits.
  code at 1 range 11..12; -- additional bits, numbered 11 and 12.
  channel at 1 range 13..15;          -- Bits 13, 14, 15.
  data at 2 range 0..15;              -- Another 16 bits.
end record;
```

Specific bits of a location in computer memory can be accessed by mapping a Boolean array onto a word. For example:

```
status: array(0..15) of BOOLEAN;
```

is mapped to the location 8#177564# and the compiler is told to use only 16 bits for it by means of the representation and length clauses:

```
for STATUS use at 8#177564#; for STATUS'SIZE use 16;
```

Bits of memory location 177564 (octal) are then accessed by STATUS(i).

As an example of a device, consider the type-identifier IO_REGISTER defined earlier [for Fig. 8-7(a)]. It has no hardware register address associated with it and as a result it represents a family of devices, each member of which is denoted by specifying an appropriate address in the declaration section of the program such as in:

```
a_to_d1: IO_REGISTER; a_to_d2: IO_REGISTER; a_to_d3: IO_REGISTER:
```

This form of DEVICE allows for situations where several distinct hardware devices all have the same format (i.e., the same data structure) for their I/O register, but are mapped into different memory locations.

Without a subsequent *ADDRESS-CLAUSE* defining where the variables are to be located in memory, the compiler will decide the location of *a_to_d1*, *a_to_d2*, and *a_to_d3*. This is not desirable since the obvious intended use of these variables is to control I/O from devices that are mapped to specific hardware-defined locations in memory. An ADDRESS-CLAUSE for the example above would thus be as follows:

```
for a_to_d1 use at 8#204#;  -- The registers will be located
for a_to_d2 use at 8#206#;  -- at addresses 204, 206 and 210
for a_to_d3 use at 8#210#;  -- (octal) respectively
```

The second form of REPRESENTATION-CLAUSE definition differs from the first form only in that it contains an ADDRESS-CLAUSE immediately following the object declaration. This address may be an expression, but it must evaluate to a constant at compile time. Because the resulting interface is implicitly associated with a single interface register, its definition will probably occur explicitly within an object-declaration section of a program. This is shown in the declaration of Code 8-20.

```
byte: constant:=1;                               -- The storage unit is 1 byte.
type io_register is
record
  result            : INTEGER range 0..1023;              -- Number
  unused_bits       : INTEGER range 0..3;                 -- range.
  channel_converted: INTEGER range 0..15;
end record;                          -- Next is the REPRESENTATION-CLAUSE
for io_register use
  record at mod 2;                   -- Note that 2 represents the number of
    result at 0*byte range 0..9;                 -- storage units.
    unused_bits at 1*byte range 10..11;          -- Bit positions.
    channel_converted at 1*byte range 12..15;
  end record;
  a_to_d: io_register;              -- Declare it to be of type register.
  for a_to_d use at 8#14#;          -- At location 14 octal.
```

Code 8-20

This declaration results in a single word at address 14 being allocated to the variable *a_to_d*. The field "result" is assigned to the ten most significant bits of the word, followed by two unused bits and four bits which are assigned to the field "channel_ converted." Access to the value of the field "result," such as in the statement:

```
temp:=func(a_to_d.result)*0.0015+2.1;
```

will cause the compiler to generate code to read a word (in addition to other code) to get all ten bits of the field. A "word read" is performed in this case because the field "result" overlaps a byte boundary. This information is significant only when a hardware restriction requires byte-reads to be made on an I/O register. The next REPRE-SENTATION-CLAUSE will deal with such a situation.

The body of a record type definition may consist of only fixed components, only a variant component, or a fixed part followed by a variant part. The variant part is identified by the CASE-CLAUSE which specifies the data-type of the labels used to discriminate between the different variants. Each variant is characterized by a list of the declaration of its components with each list preceded by a label.

An example of using a REPRESENTATION-CLAUSE with a variant record is shown in Code 8-21 for the two registers of Fig. 8-7(c).

This data representation contains two variants: one labeled read_a_to_d (for input of the A/D result) and the second labeled start_a_to_d (for controlling when a conversion is started and which channel is to be converted). Access to a particular field of the device is accomplished by using the field name in an expression or statement:

```
a_to_d.channel_to_convert := 3;
```

```
byte: constant:=1;                              -- The storage unit is one byte.
type FORMAT is (read_a_to_d, start_a_to_d);
type IO_REGISTER(i_or_o: FORMAT) is
  record
    case FORMAT is
    when read_a_to_d =>                                      -- Variant-1
      result_msb          : INTEGER range 0..255;
      result_lsb          : INTEGER range 0..3;
      not_used_r          : INTEGER range 0..3;
      channel_converted   : INTEGER range 0..12;
    when start_a_to_d=>                                      -- Variant-2
      not_used_s          : INTEGER range 0..4095;
    channel_to_convert    : INTEGER range 0..12;
    end case;
  end record;          -- Next is a record representation clause
for IO_REGISTER use
  record at mod 2
    result_msb          at 0*byte range 0..7;
    result_lsb          at 1*byte range 8..9;
    not_used_r          at 1*byte range 10..11;
    channel_converted   at 1*byte range 12..15;
    not_used_s          at 0*byte range 0..11;              -- Variant
    channel_to_convert at 1*byte range 12..15;              -- overlap.
  end record;
a_to_d: IO_REGISTER;
for a_to_d use at 8#4#;    -- a_to_d is at word address 4.
```

Code 8-21

This statement causes the value 3 to be written to the low four bits of the word at address 4, which in turn will cause the A/D conversion process to begin on channel 3. Note that Ada requires that field names within a record or a device be unique. This restriction allows the compiler to recognize which variant of a particular device is being utilized during any access (read or write) to a device register.

Due to hardware requirements, the 10-bit result of a conversion must be obtained separately from the two bytes in the interface register. That is, the two separate fields: result_msb and result_lsb (for the eight most and two least significant bits) must be used in a statement such as:

```
count :=a_to_d.result_msb * 4+a_to_d.result_lsb;
```

Since neither of the two result fields crosses a byte boundary, the compiler will generate byte reads for these accesses.

The amount of memory allocated for a device is determined by the total number of bits required to satisfy the fields that are defined in its declaration. Regardless of whether a single byte, a single word or multiple words are allocated, the most significant byte of the word is assigned first.

For example, the allocation rules for a 16-bit word computer could be:

1. A device requiring eight or fewer bits is allocated a single byte. Note that the word address of the byte will be that of the low byte regardless of what address is used in the device-declaration.

2. A device requiring more than eight but 16 or fewer bits will be allocated a full word at the address given in the declaration. This requires that the address be a word-address in order for the allocation to be performed correctly.

3. A device requiring more than 16 bits will be allocated successive words until all fields of the device has been assigned. The bytes of each word are assigned first the high-byte and then the low-byte.

This situation also requires that a word address be used in the declaration. Correct allocation will not take place if a nonword address is used.

It is the programmer's responsibility to use correct addresses in each of the above cases since the compiler does not issue error messages for mistakes of this type.

Bits are assigned successively from the most significant position of the byte to the fields of the device in the order of the occurrence in the fields. The result of this is that any unreferenced bits must be accounted for in the device-declaration by providing dummy fields.

8–4.3 Interrupts

Interrupts must be able to identify the source and type of the interrupt, perform enable and disable operations, and take into account priorities.

In Ada, an interrupt is considered to be a hardware caller to an acceptor which acts as its handler:

> An address clause given for an entry associates it with some device that may cause an interrupt; such an entry is referred to as an *interrupt entry*. If control information is supplied upon an interrupt, it is passed to an associated interrupt entry as one or more parameters of mode **in**; only parameters of this mode are allowed. [ARM13.5.1]

An interrupt is regarded as a rendezvous with an external task. The interrupt handler is a task that has an ACCEPT-STATEMENT for the entry associated with this particular interrupt. This association is brought about by including in the task specification an address for the entry. The general structure is then as in Code 8-22.

```
task name is        -- The name of the handler, say "break" is to be
entry ir;      -- supplied, as is the name, here ir, of the interrupt.
  for ir use at 16#A123#    -- Address of the interrupt "trap" is
end name; -- the first location of the task handling this interrupt.
task body name is   -- The actions to be taken by this interrupt.
begin               -- The entry would have had in-parameters to pass
  loop              -- information. An endless loop with an accept is
    accept ir do    -- typical for an interrupt. The same parameters.
                    --- if any, as in the entry. Here are positioned
                    --- the statements constituting the interrupt
    end accept;     -- handler i.e. the response to this interrupt.
  end loop;
end;
```

Code 8-22

To ensure that the interrupt is handled with the required urgency, such tasks are given a higher priority. They will therefore be processed ahead of other tasks and should be fast (i.e., include only those actions that must be treated immediately).

If a select statement contains both a terminate alternative and an accept alternative for an interrupt entry, then an implementation may impose further requirements for the selection of the terminate alternative in addition to those given earlier. *Example*:

```
task INTERRUPT_HANDLER is
  entry DONE;
  for DONE use at 16#40#; -- assuming that SYSTEM.ADDRESS is an
end INTERRUPT_HANDLER;    -- integer type.
```

Note 1.   Interrupt entry calls need only have the semantics described above; they may be implemented by having the hardware directly execute the appropriate accept statements.

Note 2.   Queued interrupts correspond to ordinary entry calls. Interrupts that are lost if not immediately processed correspond to conditional entry calls. It is a consequence of the priority rules that an accept statement executed in response to an interrupt takes precedence over ordinary, user-defined tasks, and can be executed without first invoking a scheduling action. [ARM 13.5.1]

Note 3.   The handler may enable and disable interrupts by modifying some SCRs.

Note 4.   The following deficiencies of the priority mechanism of Ada are mentioned in [BLW87]. ''First, the language does not discriminate between the hardware priorities of different interrupts . . . Second, there is no association between the software priority pragma (and hence the priority of interrupt handlers) and the hardware priority of the interrupts themselves . . . A further problem with interrupt handling in Ada concerns the passing of data from the handler to other consumer tasks. The normal means of communication is the rendezvous, but'' it leads to a number of problems. The concept of priority is weak and in particular: (1) All instances of the same task type must have equal priority; (2) A task cannot change its priority; (3) Tasks without a given priority may assume a low or high priority; (4) The queue on an ACCEPT-STATEMENT is strictly FIFO; and (5) The choice among open alternatives of a select statement is arbitrary.

As a summary, a program from [New82] is modified. The original program uses polling to wire up a home computer for burglar alarm, fire alarm, alarm clock, pulling up the window shades at a predetermined time, switching on the coffee machine, setting the code for the garage opener, etc. All inputs are supposed to be read from control-and-status registers. I/O is done through a Peripheral Interface Register (PIA) of the MC6800 (MPU). The MPU directs the PIA as it interfaces with external equipment. Each register of the PIA is accessed like a memory location, using the register's address. We will make two changes to the program in [New82]: Use Ada instead of the assembly language, and use interrupts instead of polling (and send activation signals through the PIA).

Each PIA has two addresses (Fig. 8-9) corresponding to the control registers A and B (CRA and CRB). The address assignments for these registers are:
CRA = 16#8005#; CRB = 16#8007#. CRA and CRB are nearly identical so what is said for CRA will be implied for CRB.

The PIA has two kinds of interrupt pins: input and output. Its input interrupt pins allow it to receive interrupts from peripherals, and its output interrupt pins pass an interrupt to the MPU.

A possible connection is shown in Fig. 8-9. This is a simple case where all four control lines are interrupt lines to the PIA. The PIA uses its control lines CA1, CA2, CB1, and CB2 to communicate with external devices regarding interrupts. A and B refer to the A and B sides of the PIA. PIA uses its interrupt outputs IRQA and IRQB to communicate with the MPU. A low signal on the IRQA means that side A of the PIA is requesting an interrupt; likewise for IRQB.

The RES line is usually connected to the Reset Button of the system along with the RES line of the MPU. Hence, when the MPU is reset, the PIA is also reset. Because the RESET automatically clears all registers of the PIA, it is important to reconfigure the PIA. This is done by configuring the PIA as part of the RESET service routine.

Bits 6 and 7 of the CRA [Fig. 8-9(b)] are interrupt bits. Bit 6 [7] is automatically set if there is an interrupt input to the PIA on line CA2 [CA1]. Hence, if device 2 [1] interrupted the PIA, bit 6 [7] is set. These two flags indicate which device has caused the interrupt.

An interrupt service routine is considered by Ada as an entry call. (When vectored interrupts are permitted, the task can be attached to the interrupt.) When an interrupt is

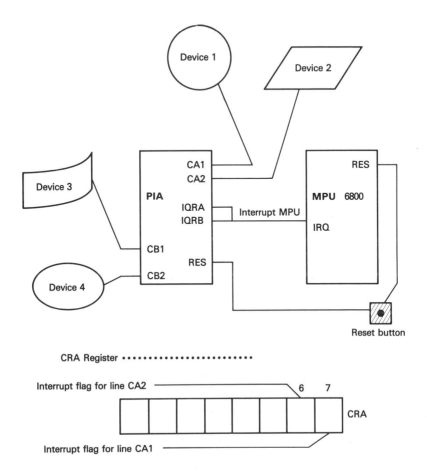

Figure 8-9   Connecting the PIA to the computer

received and the execution transfers to this location, the action is equivalent to calling the entry and acts as an interrupt service routine.

A portion of the interrupt code for the configuration of Fig. 8-9 is as shown in Code 8-23.

8–5 NOTES

Parallel algorithms require languages that can use parallelism. Since the 1960s, APL dealt with parallel numerical, and SQL with parallel data-based problems. Both were used on single computers. We need languages adapting parallel algorithms to parallel hardware.

A computer language may be defined as ''a formal notation for describing a computation to a computing engine. The computing engine is thought of as implementing

```
BYTE : constant :=8; WORD : constant := 1*BYTE;
type CONTROL_REGISTER is record at mod 2;
  DATA at 0*WORD range 0..5;
  C1 at 0 WORD range 6..6; C2 at 0 WORD range 7..7;
end record;
CRA, CRB: CONTROL_REGISTER;

task MONITORING_SYSTEM is
  entry HIGH_PRIORITY;
  for HIGH_PRIORITY use at 16#8005#;
  entry LOW_PRIORITY;
  for LOW_PRIORITY use at 16#8007#;
end MONITORING_SYSTEM;

task body MONITORING_SYSTEM is
begin
  loop
  accept HIGH_PRIORITY
     for CRA use at 16#8005#;
     if CRA.C1=1 then
       --- do whatever is necesssary for fire alarm.
     if CRA.C2=1 then
       --- do whatever is necessary for burglar alarm.
   end HIGH_PRIORITY;
   accept LOW_PRIORITY;
     for CRB use at 16#8005#;
     if CRB.C1=1 then
       --- do whatever is necessary for power alarm.
     if CRB.C2=1 then
       --- do whatever is necessary for moisture alarm.
   end LOW_PRIORITY;
  end loop;
end MONITORING_SYSTEM;
```

Code 8-23

the language.'' The language must ''be capable of implementation on computing machines without surprising limitations.'' Here are some of the most important reasons for using a parallel language in describing a computation.

1. ''The computation models a naturally concurrent system. The world is full of independent activity. Many computations are simulations and are most naturally expressed in a language based on the multiprocess model.

2. The data is replicated on a large scale. Data parallelism also reflects a property of the world.'' [Lak86].[†]

3. The computation is to be done in shorter time; a speedup is required.

4. Parallelism increases the reliability.

We have already discussed the last two points extensively. Data parallelism is normally treated with the ''dusty decks'' approach. What is meant is that all those large programs written in FORTRAN, LISP, and other well-known languages are adapted to PPSs. This is the approach taken by VPs and by cellular systems. As mentioned earlier, if Ada will establish itself as the dominant language, there is no reason why all these programs cannot be rewritten in Ada (maybe automatically). For others, we use multitasking.

The unit of concurrent computation, the task, has well-defined interfaces, is useful in managing multiple real-time asynchronous activities, and can be mapped to a PPS. Unfortunately, existing systems rely on a software implementation of tasks and have achieved execution times of only $\mathbf{O}$(mls) for a *send-receive-reply* cycle among tasks on the same processor. Communication between tasks on different nodes is typically several times greater. It was proposed in [Bea86] to change communication and let the hardware do it. The reasoning is as follows:

> The expense of existing implementations of tasks and task communication is a significant disincentive to their use. Consider the choice between implementing a particular facility either as a procedure or as a task. In existing systems, calling the procedural implementation would involve an overhead between one and two orders of magnitude less than communicating with the task implementations. [Hence, task implementation will probably be avoided. It is thought that] a number of existing applications could have been structured using many tasks, but were not, due to the (actual or perceived) inefficiency of existing tasks implementations. A parallel can be drawn with the evolution of architectural support for procedures. Procedures now universally accepted were much less popular before they were supported efficiently. Until recently, the IBM PL/I language reference manual warned programmers of the performance pitfalls of using procedures. [Bea86]

Tasks as implemented in hardware by using a specially installed *Taskmaster* coprocessor led the authors of [Bea86] to believe that such an architecture ''will enhance the efficiency of tasks and task communication. This efficiency will allow us to explore *the use of tasks at a smaller level of granularity* than is currently feasible.''

If successful, task masters may finally lay to rest the view that tasks are too time-consuming for efficient use.

All in all, the language is certainly suitable for all except maybe the SMs. One of the Butterfly systems [BBN87], the

---

[†]T. Lake: ''Languages for Parallel Processing.'' *Informationstechnik*, Vol. 30, No. 2, pp. 118–128. Reprinted with permission of Oldenburg Verlag, Munich, West Germany.

GP1000 supports the Butterfly Ada language, providing a high-performance, reliable compiler specifically designed for developing large-scale Ada systems. . . . Butterfly Ada features a production-quality compiler that fully complies with ANSI/MIL STD-1815A. The compiler maximizes compilation speed while providing an efficient runtime system for *full-featured tasking*, exception-handling, and I/O support. [BBN87]

I have italicized tasking because it shows that it can be used not only in Cubes, but also in an SM. As a matter of fact, [BBN87] mentions also that the message passing is possible.

The versatile shared-memory architecture of the Butterfly also supports a Message-Passing programming approach. This approach has several advantages, including clear problem partitioning, and support both for parallel and distributed processing such as that found in local area networks.

In message-passing systems, communication channels may be established between pairs of processor in the computer. Processors communicate and synchronize by passing data according to an established protocol. The protocol ensures the integrity of each process data, just as atomic operation ensure data integrity in a shared-memory approach.

Typically, a message-passing system consists of a single parent process and a number of child processes, each located on a different processor. The parent process begins the task by sending task-description messages to each child process. The child process then performs the required function and returns the result in a message to the parent process for further operation.

Synchronizing data-reads or writes is essential whenever two or more processors are operating simultaneously. Message passing readily handles this requirement with an implicit form of synchronization. When a process wants to read data from another process, it simply waits until the message arrives from the sender. If a message has already been written and sent to this processor, the data in the message is immediately read. If there is no message yet in transit, the reading processor waits until one is available. [BBN87]

This long quote was considered important because it shows that there may yet be convergence between MPs and SMs through the language used.

In Ada, the unit of decomposition and abstraction is the package and not the task. Packages are supported by separate compilation facilities, allow modular construction of programs, allow data to be encapsulated so that only the operations are visible, not the data itself. Packages can form library units and define abstract data types. Tasks are used only for control over concurrent processes, access to shared resources, buffering, and most of all, to transfer messages. They will therefore be most useful for Hypercubes and Alternating Sequential-Parallel, but less so for Shared-Memory and Array Processors.

8–6 PROBLEMS

1. Show why semaphores are needed.
2. Give an example of using REPRESANTATION-CLAUSES.
3. The MC68020 [Mot85] support both the TAS and compare atomic operations which can be

used to implement semaphores. The TAS was used in Chap. 4, here the compare should be used. It has three operands: a memory location M, a compare value C, and an update value U. The old value in M is compared with C; if they match, U replaces the value in M, if not then the value in M replaces C. Use this instruction to implement a semaphore.

4. In [Man79] a ''Register Transfer'' language is described for simulating and designing digital computers. Write an Ada package that will implement this language.

5. Rewrite the interrupt routine of Sec. 8-4.3 using [Wak89].

CHAPTER 9

PROGRAMMING VP
AND ASP
PROCESSORS

We have now studied various parallel (PPS) organizations in chapters 1 to 5, and both sequential and concurrent programming in Ada. In the next three chapters we discuss how to program various PPSs in Ada, and start with the simplest, the Array (Vector) Processors (VPs) and the Alternating Sequential-Parallel systems (ASPs). The objectives of this chapter are:

Discuss programming of array processors

Introduce programming of ASP systems. To be able to run these programs, we discuss in Sec. 9-2 how to transform an IBM Token Ring into an ASP.

Develop programs that solve organizational (mostly searching and sorting), and numerical (mostly matrix) problems.

9–1 PROGRAMMING ARRAY AND VECTOR PROCESSORS

As shown in Chap. 3, even though ARPs are architecturally different from VPs, from an algorithmic point of view they are quite similar. The basic difference between VPs and ARPs is how they slice the data-flow graph of the program (Fig. 9-1). For VPs the graph is sliced horizontally to provide the registers with long vectors, for ARPs, it is sliced vertically to eliminate communication between the ALUs. Thus, ARPs work on vectors distributed spacially whereas VPs work on vectors in (time) pipelines. They both have similar control and very similar instruction sets. Algorithms for ARPs are usually the same as those for pipeline computers since the objectives are the same for both cases. We discuss first programming of ARPs.

Array Processors (and especially the CM and MPP) are used primarily for data-parallel, fine-grained problems. Multitasking as discussed in Sec. 8-2 is not suitable for such systems, since a parent task (CU) would have to make a rendezvous with every of the very many children in turn, passing information through the entry parameters. Such an initialization loop would be an enormous waste of time, even if the context switch were done in hardware. Another method is preferred. If we denote the fact that the same operation is to be done on all n data points by writing **for** i **in** $1..n$ **loopar**, then we can write Ada "programs" for such problems (loopar is a loop on an array). For instance, brightening a picture of n-by-n pixels $p(i,j)$ could be represented by

```
for i in 1..n loopar
  for j in 1..n loopar
    p(i,j) := p(i,j)+konstant;
  end loopar;
end loopar;
```

Convolution, solution of the Laplace equation, etc. proceed similarly.

In a CRAY-1, the vector data must first be brought from the memory to one of the vector registers. The functional units operate on a register to register basis. The transfer of data to a vector register starts by loading the VL (vector length) register with the length (<65) of the vector, the A0 register with the first address of the vector, and another address register with the increment. The vector and the second operand are transferred, and then, the result register is chosen.

Assume that two independent vector operations are to be performed:

$$V1 := V1 + V2; \quad V3 := V4*V5 \qquad (9\text{-}1)$$

Once the first instruction is issued, CRAY-1 will attempt to process the second operation even while the additions go on. The problem is that both operations will use the same

for i **in** 1 .. 6 **loop**
    a(i): = d(i) ∗ e(i);
    b(i): = a(i) − f(i);
end loop;

(a)

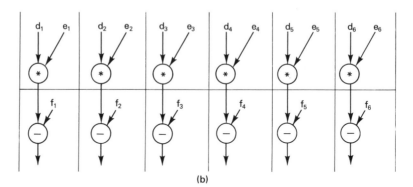

(b)

Figure 9-1 Slicing a program for VPs and ARPs

length register, so that only complete synchronization can be used. The loading of the two operands from the vector registers takes a single clock period, but the addition or multiplication may take different "function times." The above operations can be synchronized only if sometimes one of them is waiting. The result has to be transferred to the memory, so that the so-called "chain slot time" is the function time plus two clock times (load and store). If in Eq. (9-1) the second instruction reads $V3 := V1*V5$, then even if all registers are free, the two instructions cannot proceed in parallel since $V1$ may not be ready for the second instruction.

Assuming $VL := 64$, the following sequence of vector instructions is given in [Jor82] to illustrate the power of chaining in CRAY-1:

```
V0 = load from memory,
V2 = S1*V0,
V3 = V1 + V2.
```

The first instruction loads V0 from memory and is issued at clock period zero. The chain slot time for a memory read is nine clock periods; therefore the multiply of the scalar in register S1 times V0 is issued at clock period nine. The chain slot time of the multiply is nine clock periods, thus the add starts at clock period 18. The add completes in the time equal to VL (which is 64) plus the functional unit time of the add (which is six) plus 2 for a total of 72 clock periods. Because the add started at clock period 18, the entire sequence of instructions is completed in 90 clock periods [for 64 scalar multiplications and 64 floating-point additions.] [Jor82]

The vectorization of loops is so simple that it is sometimes done by the compiler:

The programmer writes a sequential program and the compiler adapts it for a vector processor. For instance, suppose that the loop at left below is rewritten as on the right:

```
for i in 1..4 loop          for j in 1..4 loop
   for j in 1..4 loop          for i in 1..4 loop
      b(i) := b(i) +a(i,j);       b(i) := b(i)+a(i,j);
   end loop;                   end loop;
end loop;                   end loop;
```

The first case would compute the b's according to Fig. 9-2(a):

$$b(1) := b(1)+a(1,1); \ b(1) := b(1)+a(1,2); \ \ldots \ ; \ b(1) := b(1)+a(1,4)$$

The second case is a simple vector addition [Fig. 9-2(b)] easily done on a VP.

$$b(1) := b(1)+a(1,1); \ b(2) := b(2)+a(2,1); \ \ldots \ ; \ b(4) := b(4)+a(4,1).$$

Changes in loops are part of the "Parallel Fortran Converter" (PFC) developed at Rice University [AaK84]. *Data dependence* determines when vectorization is safe. Two possibilities of dependence are distinguished by the two loops below:

```
for i in 1..n loop  │  for i in 1..n loop
   a(i) :=      ;    │     a(i) :=        ;    -- Statement S1.
        := a(i);     │          := a(i-1);    -- Statement S2
end loop;            │  end loop;
```

In the case at left, the dependence is independent of the loop, but not so in the case at right, because $a(i\text{-}1)$ must have been stored in the previous iteration.

As an example: On the left below is a matrix multiplication (Fortran) program, on the right, the PFC output. The three indices in C(I:J,K) represent the starting index, the ending index, and the stride.

```
DO 100 J=1,N                        DO 100 J=1,N
DO 100 I=1,N                        DO 100 K=1,N
DO 100 K=1,N                        C(1:N,J)=C(1:N,J)+A(1:N,K)*B(K,J)
C(I,J)=C(I,J)+A(I,K)*B(K,J)
100 CONTINUE                        100 CONTINUE
```

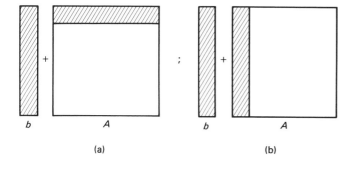

$b \qquad A \qquad\qquad b \qquad A$

(a)   (b)

Figure 9-2 Adding a vector to a matrix on a VP

As previously, loops have been interchanged and instead of the loop on i, there is a vector computation of the entire vector C.

Supercomputers are executing badly the **if** condition **then** $x := a$; **else** $x := b$; **endif**; where the condition and the two vectors assignments should be computed in parallel. Since the vector a (b) is evaluated only when the condition is true (false), either a and b are both computed for the length of the vectors and the result merged (as on the CRAY-1), or alternatively new compressed vectors are formed, computed separately, and then merged to form x. In either case, considerable extra work is performed that may make a vector calculation unprofitable in a pipeline computer.

Having discussed vectorization, we apply it to matrix problems, the first being the solution of $A*x = b$ with a lower triangular matrix A. It can be shown that

$$x := L^n * L^{n-1} * \ldots * L^1 * b \tag{9-2}$$

$$L^i = \begin{vmatrix} 1 & & & & & & \\ & \cdot & & & & \mathbf{0} & \\ & & \cdot & & & & \\ & & 1/A(i,i) & & & & \\ & & -A(i+1,i)/A(i,i) & & & & \\ \mathbf{0} & & \cdot & & \cdot & & \\ & & \cdot & & 1 & & \\ & & -A(n,i)/A(i,i) & & & 1 & \end{vmatrix} \tag{9-3}$$

The following vectors $y^1, y^2, \ldots, y^{n-1}$ are calculated using matrices L defined in Eq. (9-3):

$$y^{i+1} := L^i * y^i = [y^i(1), \ldots, y^i(i) /A(i,i), \ldots, y^i(n)-A(n,i)*y^i(i) /A(i,i)]^T \tag{9-4}$$

with $y^1 = b$ and the result achieved when $i = n-1$.

According to Sec. 6-2, the number of operations on a sequential computer would be $O(n^2)$. The reader may run (on paper or on a computer) the above algorithm to find that x is calculated in about $3*n$ steps, so that on a VP or ARP, this algorithm is $O(n)$, $\sigma \simeq n/3$, and $\eta \simeq 1/3$ if n steps or PEs are available.

Two sorting procedures are next adapted for vector computers. Sorting may involve elements $x(i)$ of a vector x stored in a non-orderly way in memory, so they must first be rearranged and stored in consecutive locations. The STAR computer is used because it has the GATHER operation required for it.

A typical vector operation like Eq. (9-1) will be executed on a Vector Processor in a time t measured in (minor) cycles:

$$t = s + k*l \tag{9-5}$$

where s is the startup time, l is the length of the vectors, and k is a small integer or fraction that depends on the operation. The following values are given in [Sto78] for vector operations on full-word floating-point operands in STAR: add and subtract is $94 + 0.5*l$, multiply is $154 + l$, divide is $154 + 2*l$, and an element-by-element compare it is $112 + 0.5*l$.

As seen, after paying the price of the start-up time, the results are produced at the rate of 0.5, 1, 2, or more per (minor) cycle. On the other hand, the load and store operations on scalars are very time-consuming: An item fetched is available in a machine register no sooner than 31 cycles after the instruction is initially executed. Interleaving memory access speeds things up, but even in the best case two items can be retrieved from memory, added, and the result stored in 54 cycles, as compared to one result every half (minor) cycle in vector mode. For short vectors the overhead of s becomes dominant, and in many situations the scalar mode is preferred.

Quicksort (Sec. 6-1) is redefined for vector execution. It uses recursively a procedure partition(x,first,last) that sorts the elements of an array x from x(first) to x(last). An index j is located so that:

1. x(first) is moved to position j, first $\leq j \leq$ last,
2. The elements between x(first) and $x(j-1)$ are all less than $x(j)$.
3. The elements between $x(j+1)$ and x(last) are all not less than $x(j)$.

Given the procedure partition, the following algorithm sorts an array x whose indices run from first to last. [Sto78][†]

```
procedure sort (x,first, last) is
j: INTEGER;
begin
  j:=partition(x,first,last);
  if j-first>1 then sort (x,first,j-1); end if;
  if last-j>1 then sort(x,j+1, last); end if;
end sort;
```

This algorithm was implemented on pages 118–119 of [Knu73] using the MIX language, and a stack was provided for recursion. It was then translated into STAR code and the time required to sort $n \geq 32$ items was

$$t(1) = 153*n1*ln(n1) + 132*n1 - 532.9; \; n1 = n+1 \qquad (9\text{-}6)$$

The vector version of this algorithm is given in [Sto78] as follows:

1. With a vector comparison operation, compare the scalar operand x(first) to $x(i)$, first$\leq i \leq$last, to create a 0,1-vector whose elements indicate whether or not x(first)$<x(i)$.
2. With a vector compress operation and the 0,1-vector produced in step 1, copy to a temporary vector all elements identified to be not less than x(first). The elements retain their relative order in the temporary vector.
3. With a vector compress, compress in place the elements identified to be less than

†H.S. Stone: "Sorting on Star," Trans. IEEE, Vol. SE-4, No. 2, 1978, pp. 464–72 (© 1978 IEEE). Reprinted with permission.

x(first). This moves all elements less than *x*(first) to the beginning of the subarray, while retaining their relative position in the array.

4. With a vector count operation, count the 1's in the 0,1-vector to find the number of elements moved to the temporary array.

5. With a vector copy operation, recopy the elements not less than *x*(first) from the temporary vector back to the original array starting with the first element beyond the subarray formed in step 3. The number of elements moved is determined from step 4.

We next describe Batcher's algorithm (see also [Fel85]). For its vector version we will need a mask(*i*) defined as having $2**k$ zeros followed by $2**k$ ones, e.g., {0,1,0,1, . . . }, {0,0,1,1,0,0,1,1, . . . }, etc. We also need two procedures "CE" for "Compare-Exchange" and "MERGE".

Procedure CE(*x*,mask,*cr*) has the following steps:

1. Split *x* into two halves *va, vb*, compare them by putting a 1 in *cr* if *va* > *vb*, but 0 otherwise. For *x* = (1,3,7,6,0,4,2,5): *va* = (1,3,7,6), *vb* = (0,4,2,5); *cr* = (1,0,1,1).

2. Create a new *cr* by appending its inverse: *cr* = (1,0,1,1, 0,1,0,0).

3. Set *cr* := mask + *cr*: mask = (0,1,0,1,0,1,0,1), *cr* = (1,1,1,0, 0,0,0,1).

4. Shuffle *cr* to get *cv*: *cv* = (1,0,1,0,1,0,0,1).

Routine MERGE(*x*,*cv*) merges vector **x** according to vector **cv**: If *cv*(*i*) = 0 then select an element from **va**, if 1 then from **vb**. The result is *x* = (0,1,4,3,2,7,6,5). The vector procedure is then as in Code 9-1.

```
procedure qsort (x,n) is
i,j,logt,logg : INTEGER;
  ce(x,mask(1),cv); merge(x,cv);
  logt := log2(n);
  for i in 1..logt-2 loop
    logg := logt-1-i;
    for j in 1..logg loop merge(x,mask(1)); end loop;
    for j in logt-1 loop
      ce(x,mask(j+i+1-logt),cv); merge(x,cv);
    end loop; -- on j.
  end loop;   -- on i.
  for j in 1..logt loop
    ce(x,mask(0),cv); merge(x,cv);
  end loop;
end; -- of the procedure.
```

Code 9-1

With the original x, $ce(x,\text{mask}(1),cv)$ yields va, vb, cr, cv, and
· $x = (0,1,4,3,2,7,6,5,)$, as above.

Next $\log t$ is computed to be 3, i is set 1, and for each j we get:

```
merge(x,mask(1): x := (0,2,1,7,4,6,3,5)
```

```
For j=2, CE(x,mask(1),cr) produces:
  cr := (0,0,0,1,1,1,1,0), mask(1) := (0,1,0,1,0,1,0,1)
  cr := (0,1,0,0,1,0,1,1), cv := (0,1,1,0,0,1,0,1)
  shuffle(x,cv) produces: x := (0,4,6,2,1,3,7,5)
```

```
For j=3, CE(x,mask(2),cv) produces:
  cr := (0,1,0,0,1,0,1,1), mask(2) := (0,0,1,1,0,0,1,1)
  cr := (0,1,1,1,1,0,0,0), cv := (0,1,1,0,1,0,1,0)
  shuffle(x,cv) produces: x := (0,1,3,4,7,6,5,2)
```

Next, i is set to 2 and for each j we get:

```
For j=1, CE(x,mask(0),cv) produces:
  cr := (0,0,0,1,1,1,1,0), mask(1) := (0,0,0,0,0,0,0,0)
  cr := (0,0,0,1,1,1,1,0), cv := (0,1,0,1,0,1,1,0)
  shuffle(x,cv) produces: x := (0,7,1,6,3,5,2,4)
```

```
For j=2, CE(x,mask(0),cv) produces:
  cr := (0,1,0,1,1,0,1,0), mask(0) := (0,0,0,0,0,0,0,0)
  cr := (0,1,0,1,1,0,1,0), cv := (0,1,1,0,0,1,1,0)
  shuffle(x,cv) produces: x := (0,3,5,7,1,2,4,6)
```

```
For j=3, CE(x,mask(0),cv) produces the sorted list as follows:
  cr := (0,1,1,1,1,0,0,0), mask(0) := (0,0,0,0,0,0,0,0)
  cr := (0,1,1,1,1,0,0,0), cv := (0,1,1,0,1,0,1,0)
  shuffle(x,cv) produces: x := (0,1,2,3,4,5,6,7)
```

The time for the vector version of Quicksort was estimated to be:

$$t(2) = 5.875*nl*ln(nl) + 101.875*nl - 294.2; \quad nl = n+1 \tag{9-7}$$

while the time for Batcher's algorithm was, according to [Sto78]:

$$t(3) = [ln(n)]^2*(7.268*n+883.5) - n*(4.125*ln+4.328) - 63.607*ln(n) + 1706.708 \tag{9-8}$$

This timing is clearly $O[n*\log(n)]^2$ as expected, but the term $883.5*(ln(n))^2$ dominates the expression until $n = 122$, at which point the term $7.268*n*(ln(n))^2$ becomes dominant. The former term accounts for the number of vector startups, and the latter term accounts for the number of fetches, stores, and comparisons. Terms of the other orders are negligible with respect to these terms for most values of n.

[Plots of $t(1)$, $t(2)$, and $t(3)$ appear in Fig. 9-3.] The data shown are absolute times computed with one minor cycle equal to 40 nns. We assume that there is sufficient memory

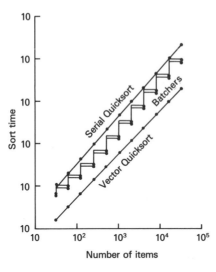

Figure 9-3 Results of sorting on the STAR. Courtesy of H.S. Stone: "Sorting on STAR," Trans. IEEE, Vol. SE-4, No. 2, pp. 464–72

available to sort the arrays in core, and note that the STAR is configured with one megaword of memory to make this assumption valid. . . . Note the "staircase" form of the plot in Fig. 9-3 to acknowledge the fact that the sorting time for i elements is identical for all i in an interval $2**m + 1 \leq i \leq 2**(m + 1)$. [Sto78]

Comparing the two algorithms, Stone mentions the following:'

1. Each algorithm was encoded by hand in STAR assembly language, and recoded into equivalent STAR Fortran.

2. The results for vector Quicksort agreed to within 2% with the estimates, but only 15% for Batcher's algorithm. This is accounted for in Fig. 9-3, where Batcher's (likely) results are also shown.

3. "Hence for all reasonable values of N, Quicksort sorts in *linear* time on STAR in spite of its asymptotic complexity of $N*lnN$.

4. The vector version of Batcher's algorithm is clearly faster than serial Quicksort for most file sizes up to 32768, the maximum vector size on a STAR. The interesting observation here is that the complexity of Batcher's algorithm is strictly worse than the complexity of serial Quicksort since the former is $O[N*(logN)^2]$ and the latter is $O[N*logN]$. Because the STAR is organized to do some operations extremely efficiently, it reduces the constant coefficient on terms that dominate complexity arguments. Consequently, complexity arguments that hold for large enough N are invalid for values of N of most interest to the programmer.

5. The most surprising aspect of this study is that Batcher's sort comes close to a vector adaptation of Quicksort, and is competitive with a serial version of Quicksort, yet it does not have minimum computational complexity $O(N*logN)$, but has computational complexity $O[N*(logN)^2]$ on Star. [The timing analysis shows] that the timing dependency on $N*(logN)^2$ has a very small constant coefficient because

this term is charged to operations for which the STAR is very efficient. Consequently, asymptotic estimates of relative timings are invalid for size of N of most practical interest.'' [Sto78]

9–2 INTRODUCTION TO PROGRAMMING ASP (AND LAN) SYSTEMS

9–2.1 Programming ASP systems

It is easy to program ASPs because they don't need the rendezvous for the active and synchronization tasks like other systems.

An ASP system includes a master and p identical slaves. Therefore, the main program (usually a procedure) represents the master. The p slaves perform identical tasks during any parallel step, so that they form an array, for example

```
task type TS is
  entry slave (lo,hi: in INTEGER);
end;
declare slatasks: array(1 ..p) of TS:
```

This will *create* all p slave tasks simultaneously, but they will become active when the master arrives at its **begin**. Even if active, they may be waiting in an accept queue. In most cases, the entries ''slave'' are programmed as follows:

```
task body TS is
--- Local variables are declared here, say k1 and k2.
begin
  accept slave(lo,hi: in INTEGER) do
    k1:=lo; -- Note that the accept follows directly the begin
    k2:=hi; -- since this is all the slave is supposed to do here.
  end accept;
  --- Here is the location where almost all of the task
  --- will be done, i.e., outside of the accept.
end;
```

The ACCEPT-STATEMENT is the critical section and is tying up the master and always one of the slaves. It is therefore *essential* that it be as short as possible. In most cases, it will—as above—only be long enough to transfer some parameters which will identify to the slave the part of the job this particular slave is supposed to do.

The next question is *how to start all p slave tasks simultaneously*. In some languages there is a special instruction for starting a number of concurrent processes, e.g., COBEGIN S(1), . . . ,S(n) COEND or splitting of the computational thread. A COBEGIN is particularly well-suited for ASPs since it terminates only when all the statements S(l), . . . ,S(n) have completed. In Topps, the activation was actually done by *broadcasting* a go-bit. Ada has no such facilities so that the closest way of starting the slaves simultaneously is the following:

```
for i in 1 .. p loop
  slatasks(i).slave(low(i),low(i)+h);
end;
```

Each task is called *in turn* with different parameters. These parameters are transferred to the slave by the ACCEPT-STATEMENTS. While the master has a rendezvous with slave 1, all remaining slaves 2 . . *p wait* in the queue to be accepted. The ACCEPT-STATEMENT was made very short, so that this time is not too long. When the end of the **accept** is reached in the first slave, this slave embarks on its real task, and slave-2 is accepted. This procedure is shown graphically in Fig. 9-4.

The master should resume when all slaves have finished. This happens automatically in Ada because of the rule that the parent task is completed or terminated only when all its children have terminated. Thus, the master waits until all slaves have terminated. Following this, a new part of the master's program is initiated as the next sequential step and so on.

As an example we take a procedure which forms both the product of all elements of two vectors of integers and their sum. This could be done by having a main procedure and two tasks as in Code 9-2.

```
type VEC is array(1..1000) of INTEGER;
procedure mult(a,b: VEC; sum,mm: out VEC) is
task type prod; m: prod; -- In the specification we have a (possibly
task type summ; s: summ; -- empty) list of the services offered by
                         -- the particular task - its entries.
task body prod is        -- In the body are the (hidden) details
begin                    -- of what is done by those entries.
  for i in VEC'RANGE loop
    mm(i) := a(i)*b(i);
  end loop;              -- mm(i) and sum(i) below should be printed
end prod;

task body summ is
begin
  for i in VEC'RANGE loop
    sum(i) := a(i)+b(i);
  end loop;
end summ;

begin    -- At this point, both tasks are activated and since
  null; -- there are no accept-statements, they start running.
end mult;
```

Code 9-2

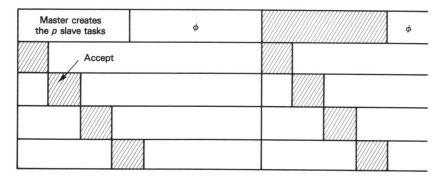

Figure 9-4   Activating slaves of ASP

In Code 9-2, the procedure itself consisted only of a NULL-STATEMENT and therefore can replace the second task as in Code 9-3.

```
procedure mult(a,b: VEC; sum,mm: out VEC) is
task type prod; m: prod;

task body prod is
begin
  for i in VEC'RANGE loop
    mm(i) := a(i)*b(i);
  end loop;
end prod;                    -- At this point, task "prod" is
begin                        -- activated and its body is executed
  for 1 in VEC'RANGE loop    -- because mult is a parent of prod.
    sum(i) := a(i)+b(i);     -- If prod is not completed at this point,
  end loop;                  -- mult can also not terminate.
end mult;
```

Code 9-3

In Code 9-3, the master assumes one of the tasks instead of being idle during the parallel step. We decided not to use such scheduling.

9–2.2 A Token Ring as an ASP, the RASP

The use of a ring as an ASP [YaW88][†] is based on applying the NETBIOS (Network Basic Input/Output System) software which allows computers to communicate over the (token)

[†]Most of the material in 9-2.2 is from the Ph.D. Thesis of Mrs. E. Yaprak [Yap89]. Quoted by permission.

ring. NETBIOS used as a high-level programming interface to IBM's LAN is a layer of software used to link a network operating system with specific hardware [St187].

NETBIOS provides an interface to various levels of International Standards Organization (ISO) protocols. Most NETBIOS services are provided at the session level. NETBIOS also provides a number of support functions; we use the "Datagram Support." It allows messages to be sent to or received from a PC, a group of PCs, or broadcast to the entire network. We will use the functions "send datagram" (SD), "receive datagram" (RD), "send broadcast datagram" (SBD), and "receive broadcast datagram" (RBD) to implement RASP in Token Ring Networks. Messages are limited in size from 0 to 512 bytes; messages of more than 512 bytes have to be sent as a number of datagrams.

The message is never acknowledged by the receiver's adapter, so it is up to the sender and receiver to agree on their own network protocols. For example, if PC(1) of Fig. 9-5(a) sends a datagram to PC(2) then PC(2) should have a "Received Datagram," RD, command outstanding at the time a "Send Datagram," SD, is issued by PC(1) in order not to lose the data.

The programming interface of NETBIOS uses Message Control Blocks (MCBs). Once a command is presented to the NETBIOS in the MCB format, a response is returned to the program in the form of a return code inside the MCB.

Let us assume that we have three PCs connected as a token ring [Fig. 9-5(b)], with M as the master, SL1 and SL2 as the slaves. Let us also assume that we need to add 130 values of cosines:

$$y = \Sigma\cos\,(x(\mathrm{i})) + \Sigma\cos(-x(i)); \; i\Sigma \; = \; 0, \; \ldots \; 64 \qquad (9\text{-}9)$$

Suppose we add concurrently the sum for positive x's on SL1, and of the negative values on SL2 (where $0 \leq x\,(i) \leq \pi/2$). The results of these two computations are then sent to the master to be added.

When the two slaves start, they both will have an RBD pending. When the master starts, it will broadcast an SBD to both slaves. The receipt of this message will start the slaves. As soon as the SBD message is sent by the master, the master issues an RD message and waits to receive a message. When one of the slaves (SL1) completes its calculation, it sends an SD message to the master. The master's RD will receive this message and the result of the sum on that slave. As soon as SL2 finishes its calculation, it will issue an RD message. *This message is needed for polling.* The SD from the SL1 triggers the master to poll the remaining slaves (in this case only SL2) for their results. The master then issues an SD message to SL2 which will be received by RD on SL2. Then, SL2 issues an SD message to the master and the master's second RD will receive the message and the second partial sum. At this point, the master adds the two partial results and the program is completed.

The summation [Eq. 9-9] was run on three PCs and the results are shown in Fig. 9-5(c). The delay (of 0.06 sec) in accepting the second sum is a result of polling.

The overhead time and the time for calculating the results are κ and Ω respectively. The overhead is mostly for communication between the PCs. Three different algorithms will be discussed in order to show the influence of the communication penalty $\pi \, = \, \kappa/\Omega$ on the speedup. They are:

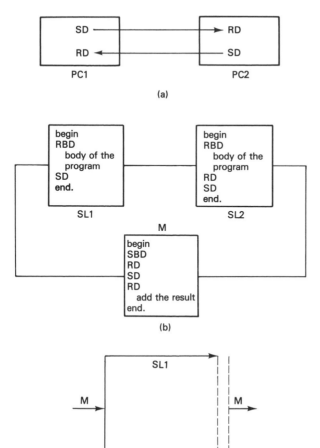

Figure 9-5 Activating slaves and running programs on RASP

a. *Image processing*: For "brightening" a picture, the image area is scanned and a constant added to get an improved appearance.

A program was run for an array of (0..101, 0..101) using a single PC. The same array was then divided by four according to Fig. 9-6(a) and a slice of that array (0..101, 0..25 including boundaries) was run on four PCs concurrently. The time of the run includes initialization, meaning that PC1 sends a broadcast message to all PCs to let them know when to start. When PC2, PC3, and PC4 receive this message, they should also have pending an RBD message. Then they all run in parallel.

b. In solving the *Laplace equation* we need neighborhood information in addition to the value of $p(i,j)$ in each point. To calculate a new value, we have [Fig. 9-6(b)]:

$$p(i,j) = 0.25*[p(i,j+1)+p(i+1,j)+p(i-1,j)+p(i,j-1)] \qquad (9\text{-}10)$$

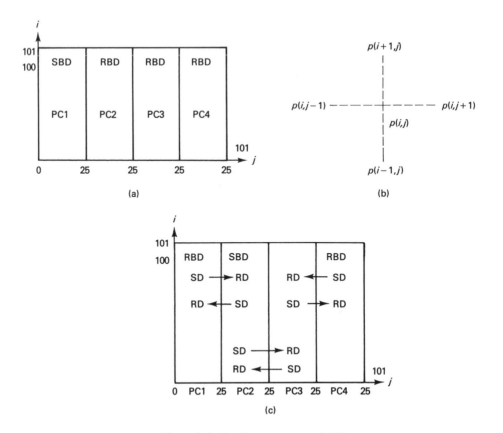

Figure 9-6 Running programs on RASP

This problem for an array of $(0..101, 0..101)$ was solved first on a single PC. Then, the same array was divided into strips of $(0..101, 0..25)$ and solved concurrently using four PC's [Fig. 9-6(c)].

For each strip we need the boundary values. For example, in strip PC2 $(j:1\text{-}25)$ to evaluate $j = 1$ we need values for $j = 0$ and $j = 2$. To get the value for $j = 0$, PC1 needs to send its $j = 25$ (corresponds in PC2 $j = 0$) to PC2. To get the value for $j = 26$, PC3 needs to send its $j = 1$ (corresponds to $j = 26$ in PC2) to PC2 and so on. Therefore, while each PC is sending or receiving the border values, some sort of synchronization is needed.

PC2 has been chosen (for no particular reason) to initiate this synchronization. Again we assume that by the time a PC receives a message, it should already have a pending "receive datagram." The algorithm is as follows:

   1. PC2 issues an SBD (send broadcast datagram).
   2. PC1 and PC4 receive this datagram (RBD). While PC1 sends its boundary data to PC2, PC4 sends in parallel its data to PC3.
   3. PC1 and PC4 now receive data from PC2 and PC3 respectively in parallel.

4. When PC1 and PC4 receive all the data, they run in parallel until they complete. In the meantime, PC2 and PC3 need more data from each other to finish the calculations.

5. While PC1 and PC4 are still working, PC2 sends data to PC3. Then PC3 sends data to PC2.

6. At this time all four PC's are working in parallel. Obviously, PC1 and PC4 will finish some time later because of communication delays.

   c. Quotient-difference algorithm (QD) is a method to determine all the roots of a polynomial without starting values [Cur78]. Given the n-degree polynomial

$$P(n) = a(n)*x^n + \ldots + a(2)*x^2 + a(1)*x^1 + a(0) \tag{9-11}$$

arrays q and e are formed as follows. Initialize $e(0) = e(n) = 0$ and set:

$$q(1) := -a(2)/a(1), \text{ all other } q\text{'s are zero} \tag{9-12}$$

$$e(i) := a(i+2)/a(i+1) \text{ for } i = 1,2, \ldots ,n-1 \tag{9-13}$$

The array starts as in Fig. 9-7(a). New rows of e's and new rows of q's are then computed as shown in Fig. 9-7(b), i.e., according to

$$q(i) := e(i) - e(i-1) + q(i); \; e(i) := e(i)*q((i+1)/q(i) \tag{9-14}$$

Let us now divide the array by two as in Fig. 9-7(c). To find q's and e's for each subrow, each PC requires information, e.g., for PC(1) the values of q and for PC(2) values of e are required to finish the calculation. Therefore, while they are running concurrently, at each step they have to transfer boundary values.

   The *results* obtained were as follows: For image processing there is no need for any communication between the PCs except for initialization. The sequential run on a single PC took 4.12 seconds while the parallel run took 1.05 seconds on four PCs. The speedup was

$$\sigma \simeq 4.12/1.05 = 3.92 \tag{9-15}$$

   For the Laplace problem, communication is needed only for sending data of boundary values. The sequential run took 13.4 seconds, while the parallel run took 3.68 seconds. The speedup was

$$\sigma \simeq 13.4/3.68 = 3.64 \tag{9-16}$$

   For the QD algorithm, much communication is needed in every step. To solve a polynomial of 14-th degrees sequentially took 5.71 secs (with 139 iterations) while the parallel run took 6.54 secs. The speedup was only

$$\sigma \simeq 5.71/6.54 = 0.87 \tag{9-17}$$

meaning that four PCs required more time than a single PC!

   Summing up.   It was shown that ASPs can easily be programmed in Ada and

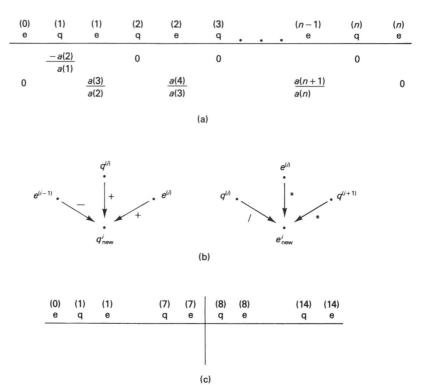

Figure 9-7   Running QD algorithms on RASP

that a LAN can be used to solve some problems in parallel. The examples show that the speedup strongly depends on the penalty ratio. A RASP provides some speedup, good fault detection, and availability at a very low (additional) cost. NETBIOS provides software which facilitates parallel programming (at least for ASPs).

9–3 SEARCHING AND SORTING WITH ASPs

9–3.1 Searching on an ASP

Searching was described as follows: A list holds "keys" and the index at which a given key, say "given," is located should be found. An example might be the search for the name and address in a telephone book, when the phone number is given. Since the phone book is ordered by letters, this means a search for the key, here the phone number.

Assume that "given" is always among the stored keys. If linear search is used, the search is conducted by checking the consecutive keys until key "given" is found.

For concurrency, the list is divided into two parts and the search is conducted with one task from the midpoint "down" and with the other task "up." The boundaries of the search-loop and the direction of search can be supplied to the two tasks through parameters—otherwise the two tasks are identical. This case requires that the two tasks be first declared as types and activated once as "up" and once as a "down" task.

The problem is how to terminate the two tasks. The task that finds the given key terminates normally, but how should the other task terminate? Obviously, it can't be allowed to go on until the end of the list since this would make the two tasks be of different duration, increase the waiting and synchronization time ζ, thus decreasing the speedup. Another way would be to use a global variable, but in ASP no global variables should be used, because this means accessing the master's memory. A third way would be to use an exception, but the way exceptions are propagated eliminates this possibility for ASP; the tasks are independent. We cannot use a TERMINATE-STATEMENT since it can be used only from the inside of a task, not from the other task. To terminate the task from the outside, the ABORT-STATEMENT will be used.

The program is shown in Code 9-5; notes to it are given first.

1. The specification of package "list" includes two subtypes and a function for the search after the given key. Note that nothing indicates how the search or "lookup" will proceed, in particular that it will be done by two tasks concurrently. The body of "list" includes the array in which the list of keys is stored, and the task liar ("*look in ar*ray") in which the entries find and result appear.

2. Function "lookup" calls entry liar.find. Having located the index in which the key is stored, it returns the key.

3. Task "psearch" waits until "search" is called by the task liar. A search can be conducted either "up" with start being the midpoint and dir (direction) being TRUE, or "down" with start being an element below midpoint and dir = FALSE. The delta of $+1$ or -1 and the end-index are set accordingly, and the *WHILE-LOOP* conducts the linear search. The result is then transferred to task liar.

4. Task liar uses a nested ACCEPT-STATEMENT. First, the call to search for the key has to be accepted. If and when it is accepted, and up-task and a down-task are spawned by liar. They start the search from the midpoint start: $= (n+1)/2$, [start -1], have directions TRUE, [FALSE], and a delta of $+1$, $[-1]$.

5. It is assumed that the given key is stored in the array, so that either up or down will locate it. When it does, it calls entry "result" with 'kfound" as the index where the given key was found. The problem is that having stored it in the running index "run," we must stop *both* tasks from further search, especially the one that might try to locate the key in vain. As mentioned, the ABORT-STATEMENT is used to terminate the execution of the task which would go on searching, by checking the index "run" for which the given key was located. The task that found the key will terminate normally, the other task will be aborted. The IF-STATEMENT which tests if run<start determines which of the tasks found the key.

```
generic arsize : INTEGER;

package list is                                          --Note 1.
   subtype KEY is INTEGER range 1 .. 1000;
   subtype INDEX is INTEGER range 0 .. arsize-1;
   function lookup(k: in KEY) return INDEX;         -- for the search.
   overflow : exception;
end list; -- End of the package specificiation.


package body list is
ar: array(0 .. arsize-1) of KEY;           -- This is the array of keys.


task liar is
   entry find(k: in KEY; i: out INDEX);
   entry result(kfound: in INDEX);
end; -- End of the specification of task liar.


task type PSEARCH is
   entry search(k: in KEY; start: in INDEX; dir: in BOOLEAN);
end;                        -- end of specification of the task type psearch.


function lookup(k: in KEY) return INDEX is              --Note 2.
tindex: INDEX;                             --This is a table index.
begin
   liar.find(k, tindex); -- A call which returns the (task) index.
   return tindex;
end;                                       --End of the function lookup.


task body PSEARCH is                                    --Note 3.
q: KEY; ind: INDEX; delta, endin: INTEGER;
begin                          -- It waits until called as liar.search.
   accept search(k: in KEY; start: in INDEX; dir: in BOOLEAN) do
      q := k; ind := start;
      if dir then delta := 1; endin := n; end;
      else delta := -1; ind := ind-1; endin := 1;
      end if;
   end accept;              -- The next line starts the search loop
   while ar(ind)/=given and ind/=endin loop
      ind := ind+delta;     -- It is assumed that the loop will consume
   end loop;                -- most of the time and therefore was put
   liar.result(ind);        -- outside the ACCEPT-STATEMENT.
end;                         -- End of the task body psearch.
```

```
task body liar is
start, run: index; dir: BOOLEAN;                          --Note 4.
begin
  loop
  accept find(k: in KEY; i: out INDEX) do -- If accepted then
    declare up, down : PSEARCH;          -- declare the two tasks
    begin
      start := (n+1)/2;
      up.search(k,start,TRUE);           -- Call of up with +1
      down.search(k,start-1,FALSE);      -- and down with -1.
      accept result(kfound: in INDEX) do -- Note 5.
        run := kfound;
      end; --of a very short accept.
      if run < start then abort up;
      else abort down;
      end if;
      i := run;
    end;
  end;                                 -- of the accept find statement
  end loop;
end;                                   --of the body of liar.
end;                                   -- end of the list program.
```

Code 9-4

Next we use the more efficient *binary search*. This sequential algorithm was already discussed and only its Code is given:

```
function bins(a,b,eps:REAL) return REAL is
m,fm:REAL; at:REAL:=a; bt:REAL:=b;            -- Temporary a and b.
begin                -- m and fm are the midpoint and function value at m.
  loop
    m:=(at+bt)/2.0;
    if abs(at-bt)<0.5*eps then return m; end if; fm:=f(m);
    if fm<=0.0 then at:=m; end if;
    if fm>0.0 then bt:=m; end if;
  end loop;
end bins;
```

Code 9-5

The program searches after a value x for which a given function f is zero [Fig. 9-8(a), i.e., where $f(x) = 0$. It assumes that $f((a)/= 0$ and $f(b)/= 0$ and is almost identical to searching for a value in a table.

A parallel search procedure for MIMD computers is described in [HaP83]. It is based on hash coding and uses a rather complicated way of termination. Another way is to adapt a method described in [KaM68]:

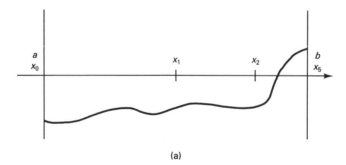

(a)

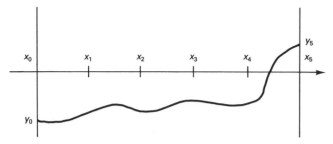

The results of sin $(x) - x/2 = 0.0$ running
on parallel with 4 slaves.

Figure 9-8   Searching for zero of $f(x)$ on
a RASP

(b)

Suppose there are four slaves ($p = 4$). The distance $a = x(0)$ to $b = x(5)$ will be divided by 5 (or $p + 1$). The values of the x'es [$x(1)$ to $x(4)$] are calculated by the master and broadcast to all the slaves. Each slave will receive its value of x and evaluate the corresponding $f[x(i)]$. (It is assumed that this evaluation will take most of the overall time.) The results are next polled by the master (in the way described earlier), and the master will check for $y(i)*y(i+1) < 0.0$. As soon as it is found [in Fig. 9-8(b), between $x(4)$ and $x(5)$], this defines the new interval to be searched. The distance $d = x(5) - x(4)$ is again divided by 5 and the same procedure is repeated until either $f(x) = 0$ (which happens very seldom) or the distance is less than some predetermined accuracy ϵ. As seen, the only difference to sequential search with a single computer [Fig. 9-8(a)] is that the distances are divided by $p + 1$ instead of by 2.

The speedup can be arrived at in the following way: the calculation is completed whenever $d/(2**i) \leq \epsilon$ in the sequetial, and $d/[(p+1)**i] \leq \epsilon$ in the parallel case. *Assuming the same accuracy ϵ and that in the parallel case s instead of i iterations are required,* we have

$$2**i = (p+1)**s, \text{ or } i = s*\log(p+1) \tag{9-18}$$

In each iteration on ASP, the times of φ and $p*\tau$ as well as a "synchronization" time ξ are required. Thus

$$1/\sigma = s*(\varphi + p*\tau + \zeta)/(i*\varphi) = s/i + s*(p*\tau + \zeta)/(i*\varphi) \tag{9-19}$$

If $(p*\tau + \zeta)/\varphi$ is much smaller than s/i, we may write

$$\sigma \simeq i/s = \log(p+1); \tag{9-20}$$

For, say, $p = 2, 3$, and 7, the speedup and efficiency would be only 1.6, 2, 3, and 80%, 67%, and 43%.

The function $f(x) = \sin(x) - 0.5*x$ has a zero between 0.5 and 100.0. It was programmed both for sequential and parallel execution (on a LAN with $p = 4$). The results are shown in Table 9-1. The sequential and parallel solutions required 13 and 6 iterations respectively. The speedup is therefore $\sigma \simeq 13/6 = 2.016$, while $\log(p+1) = \log(5) = 2.32$.

9–3.2 Sorting on ASPs

Recall from Sec. 6-1 that "Selection Sort" of a list of records (or keys) low, . . . , hih is done as follows: the first element is compared with the second, third, . . . , hih and wherever it is larger, the two are exchanged. Therefore, at the end of such a sweep, the element in "low" is the smallest of all. The second sweep does the same from low $+1$ to hih and places the second lowest element in position low $+1$. Next, sweeps are made over low $+2$, . . . , hih and so on until hih -1 is compared with hih and the list is sorted. This procedure can be parallelized similar to the search procedure of Sec. 9-3.1: The difference is that instead of searching, we sort a sublist. Since Selection Sort was not yet programmed, we do it next, using procedures instead of tasks.

Note that if a sublist is sorted, comparisons $ar(j)<ar(i)$ are all FALSE and no exchange is necessary. The particular slave will then complete its task much earlier than all the other slaves and will have to wait for the others to finish. This will reduce its utilization.

Having finished sorting p sublists, they are merged. Assuming for instance $n =$

TABLE 9-1 SPEEDUP AS FUNCTION OF SIZE OF THE MATRIX

	$i = 1$	$i = 2$	$i = 3$	$i = 4$	$i = 5$	$i = 6$
x[0]	0.500	0.500	0.500	1.296	1.774	1.869
y[0]	0.220	0.229	0.229	0.314	0.093	0.021
x[1]	20.400	4.480	1.296	1.455	1.805	1.875
y[1]	−9.200	−3.213	0.314	0.266	0.070	0.016
x[2]	40.300	8.460	2.092	1.614	1.837	1.882
y[2]	−19.635	−3.408	−0.179	0.192	0.046	0.011
x[3]	60.200	12.440	2.888	1.774	1.869	1.888
y[3]	−30.588	−6.346	−1.193	0.093	0.021	0.006
x[4]	80.100	16.420	3.684	1.933	1.901	1.895
y[4]	−41.050	−8.863	−2.358	−0.031	−0.004	0.001
x[5]	100.000	20.400	4.480	2.092	1.933	1.901
y[5]	−50.506	−9.200	−3.213	−0.179	−0.031	−0.004

1000 and $p = 8$, each sorted sublist has 125 elements and sublists 1 and 2 are merged on slave $q = 1$, sublists 3 and 4 on $q = 2$, sublists 5 and 6 on $q = 3$, and finally sublists 7 and 8 on slaves $q = 4$. As seen, the Haydn effect again reduces the speedup by $O[\log(p)]$.

Sorting of a sublist is done in Code 9-6 by "sort," merging of the sublists is done by procedure "merge."

```
package parsort is
   type ARR is array(1 .. 125) of INTEGER;
   procedure sort(low,hih : in INTEGER; 1st : in out ARR);
   procedure merge(low,hih,q1,q2: in INTEGER;
                     lst1,lst2:in ARR; list:out ARR);
end parsort;

package body parsort is

procedure sort(first,last: in INTEGER) is
local,m1,pl1: INTEGER;                        -- This is the procedure
begin m1 := last-1;                           -- promised in Sec.6-1.
   for i in first .. m1 loop
     pl1 := i+1;
     for j in pl1 .. last loop
       if ar(j) < ar(i) then
         local := ar(j); ar(j):=ar(i); ar(i):=local; -- The swap.
       end if;
     end loop;
   end loop;
end sort;

procedure merge(first,last,q1,q2: in INTEGER;
                  lst1,lst2:in ARR; list:out ARR) is
i1: INTEGER := lst1'FIRST;
i2: INTEGER := lst2'FIRST;
begin                                         Merging is done
  loop                                        -- according to the
    if lst1(i1) < lst2(i1) then               -- algorithm shown
      list(i1) := lst1 (i1); i1 := i1+1;      -- in Sec.6-1.
      if i1<lst1'LAST then
        for i in i2 .. lst2'LAST loop
          list(i) := lst2(i);
        end loop; return;
      end if;
    else list(i2) := lst2(i2); i2 := i2+1;
      if i2 > lst2'LAST then
        for i in i1 .. lst1'LAST loop
          list(i) := lst1(i);
```

```
      end loop; return;
    end if;
  end if;
 end loop;
end merge;
end parsort;

 --M A I N  P R O G R A M.

with TEXT_IO, parsort; use TEXT_IO, parsort;
procedure mainsort is
package intio is new INTEGER_IO(INTEGER); use intio;
-- This instantiates package INTEGER_IO as intio.
begin intio.GET(n); intio.GET(p); h := n/p;
  declare
    ar : array(1 .. n) of INTEGER; -- ar holds the entire list.
    slice: array(1 .. p, 1 ..h) of INTEGER;            -- p sublists.
    low := 1; hih := h;
    while hih =< n loop j := 1;
      for i in low .. hih loop
        intio.GET (slice(j)); j := j+1;
      end loop;
      low := low+h; hih := hih+h;
    end loop;
                    -- declare srt array(1..p) of srtask; might have
    begin           -- come above if sorting were done concurrently.
      sort; merge;
    end;
  end;
end;
```

Code 9-6

9–4 PROGRAMMING MATRIX PROBLEMS

9–4.1 Matrix Multiplication

Throughout the first part of this book, matrix multiplication was used to exemplify the way in which various architectures use parallelism. This is next programmed in Ada for an ASP.

With n the size of the matrices and p the number of slaves, we distinguish between the cases [Figs. 9-9(a) and (b)]. Both use slices whose width is $h = n/p$. In the first case, p^2 slaves are needed, in the second, only p. Since the same slice of **A** is to be multiplied

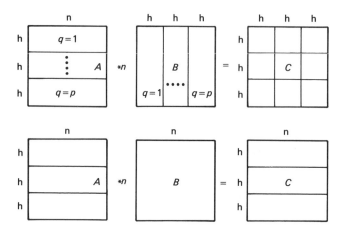

Figure 9-9 Different slicing of matrices for multiplication

by all p slices of **B**, even if we rotate (pipeline) the B slices, case a is time-consuming. In case b and for large and dense matrices, the memories of the slaves cannot store the entire matrix **B**. For the horizontal slice of **A** and a vertical slice of **B**, only $2*n^2/p$ storage locations are required. When, as is mostly the case, the matrices are sparse (case b), each slave easily stores a horizontal slice of **A** and the entire matrix **B**.

The main program, in this case procedure "matr," is called by the system. First it inputs matrices mta and mtb. Then it calls procedure "mn" with the parameters arranged so that $p1 = 1$, $p2 = h$, $p3 = h+1$, and $p4 = 2*h$, etc. After returning from "mn" the three matrices are printed and this completes the program.

Procedure "mn" starts by declaring a task of type "slice." This means that up to this point the program was sequential, but that from that point on, p tasks will be activated (by the loop on q). In the case of $p = 2$, the first will be from $p1 = 1$ to $p2 = h$, while the second will be from $p1 = h + 1$ to $p2 = n$. Having accepted each task, procedure "mm" is called and computes the product of a slice of **A** with the entire matrix **B**, or rather mta and mtb.

The speedup of this program is calculated next. Initially, every slave inputs a slice of matrix **A** that is $h*n = n^2/p$ data values and n^2 for the entire matrix **B**. If the slices have to be sent sequentially from the master, the entire matrix **A** is sent, but if the slaves each have a separate I/O device, the slices may be input concurrently on all p slaves. Assuming this to be the case, the required time is

$$(n^2 + n^2/p)*\tau = (1.0 + 1/p)*n^2*\tau \qquad (9\text{-}21)$$

where τ is the time to transfer a single word over the bus.

The actual multiplication of a slice of **A** by the matrix **B** requires n multiplications and additions or $2*n*\omega$ "operations" for calculating each of the $h*n = n^2/p$ elements of a slice of **C**. This means that each slave needs $2*(n^3/p)*\omega$ operations. Since this is done by all p slaves in parallel, this is also the entire time needed in this step.

The resulting slices have to be stored in the main memory and in this case it is not

```
package matmul is                                    -- Code 9-8, case b
   type ARR is array (1 .. 20,1 .. 20) of INTEGER;-- 20 is arbitrary.
   procedure mm(j1,j2: in INTEGER; mta,mtb: in ARR; mtc : out ARR);
   procedure mn(q1,q2,q3,q4: in INTEGER);
end matmul;


package body matmul is
   task type MS is
     entry st(low,hih : in INTEGER);
   end MS;
   procedure mm(j1,j2: in INTEGER; mta,mtb: in ARR; mtc: out ARR) is
   sum : INTEGER; -- Recall from Sec.7-5 that it can be done faster.
   begin
     for i in j1 .. j2 loop
       for j in 1 .. n loop
         sum := 0;
         for k in 1 .. n loop
           sum := sum + mta(i,k)*mtb(k,j);
         end loop; -- of k.
         mtc(i,j) := sum;
       end loop; -- of j.
     end loop; -- of i.
     return;
   end mm;



procedure mn(q1,q2: in INTEGER) is
   begin
     declare slice :MS;            -- This is the task !
     begin
       slice.st (q1,q2); -- Two st's will be called sequentially, so
       return;           -- it is important that they be very short.
     end;
end mm;


task body MS is
k1,k2: INTEGER;
   begin
     accept st(low,hih : in INTEGER) do
       k1 := low; k2 := hih; -- Only two substitutions are effected
       -- in this rendezvous; matmul is done outside of it.
     end;
     mm (k1,k2,mta,mtb,mtc);              -- This is where the multiplication
   end MS;                                          -- will be performed.
   end mn;
end;        -- of body of matmul.
```

425

```
-- M A I N   P R O G R A M   C A L L E D   matr.
with TEXT_IO, matmul; use TEXT_IO, matmul;
procedure matr is -- intio instantiates INTEGER_IO for this program.
package intio is new INTEGER_IO(INTEGER); use intio;
n, p, p1, p2: INTEGER; mta, mtb, mtc: ARR;
procedure getmat(mat: in ARR) is
begin
  for i in 1 .. n loop
    for j in 1 .. n loop
      intio.GET (mat(i,j));       -- Read matrix mat.
    end loop; -- of j.
  end loop; -- of i and of reading-in matrix mat.
end getmat;
procedure putmat(mat: in ARR) is
begin
  for i in 1 .. n loop
    for j in 1 .. n loop
      intio.PUT (mta(i,j));
    end loop -- of j.
  end loop; -- of i.
end putmat;
begin
  intio.GET(n); intio.GET(p);
  PUT_LINE (" The start of the program "); NEW_LINE;
  getmat(mta); getmat(mtb);        -- Input of matrices mta and mtb.
  h := n/p;                         -- h is assumed an integer number.
  for q in 1..p loop                -- Boundaries of slices are
    p1 := (q-1)*h+1; p2 := q*h;     -- computed in this loop.
    mn(p1,p2); -- This single call activates all p tasks in turn!
  end loop;        -- The rest of the program is only the output.
  PUT_LINE (" Printing the three matrices "); NEW_LINE;
  putmat(mta); putmat(mtb); putmat(mtc);
end matr;
```

Code 9-7

possible to use the services of the I/O devices and the entire matrix **C** has to be transferred to the main memory. Therefore, this step requires the time of $n^2*\tau$.

To compute the time ratio, the time of two synchronizations has to be added. Recall that sequentially, matrix multiplication requires $2*n^3*\omega$. The ratio is

$$\rho = [(1+1/p)*n^2*\tau + (2*n^3/p)*\omega + (n^2)*\tau + 2*\zeta]/2*n^3*\omega)$$

$$\rho = 1/p + [(2+1/p)*\tau]/(2^2 n*\omega) + \zeta/(n^3*\omega) \qquad (9-22)$$

The last term can certainly be neglected because of the very large term n^3 in the denominator.

If the time to transfer a word over the bus is relatively short so that $\tau < \omega$, $\tau \ll n*\omega$, and if $1/p$ is smaller than 2, then the ratio is

$$\rho \simeq 1/p \qquad (9\text{-}23)$$

and a nearly optimal speedup can be achieved. The program also demonstrates how easily ASP algorithms are expressed in Ada.

The program for the first case would be very similar except that the ranges of the loops would be smaller. The number of slaves would have to be increased and the speedup would be lower because the work done in parallel is relatively smaller, whereas the work done sequentially is relatively larger.

Concerning the data structure, note that there are two ways to number the slices. Each slice could be numbered as in the original matrices or the rows of each slice could be numbered from 1 to h. In this case, some renumbering will have to be done. Row i and therefore the first index of any slice will have to be computed as $h*(q-1)+1$ where q is the number of the slave. Thus, in slave -1 the rows are numbered from $h*(1-1)+1 = 1$ to $q*h = 1*h = h$, in slave -2 the rows are numbered $h*(2-1)+1 = h+1$ to $2*h$, and so on. This amounts to adding the constant $h*(q-1)$ to each index, and since this constant can be prepared beforehand, little time is added to the calculation and this solution is preferred. Recall that Ada provides slices of arrays.

Next, sparse matrices are considered. Their characteristics are:

a. Their density, i.e., the percentage of nonzeros, is $d \simeq 3$ to 5%.

b. The nonzero terms are distributed in a random way (very sparse but regular matrices such as those used in numerical solution of partial differential equations are discussed in Sections 6-2, 6-6.2).

c. All diagonal elements are nonzero.

Matrices A, B, C are shown in Fig. 9-10(a) and the corresponding storage scheme in Fig. 9-10(b). Zero elements are not stored. If A(3,1) is to be accessed, first $ia(3)$ is 6 so that $ja(6)$ is located. Since $ja(6)=1$, that is the second index, and element A(3,1) is located as A(6).

Multiplication of two matrices is based on the observation that it can be written as follows (indicating by . all indices of a column):

$$C(i,.) = \Sigma A(i,j)*B(j,.); \text{ for all indices such that } A(i,j)/=0 \qquad (9\text{-}24)$$

If written in full, this means that C(i,.) is a linear combination of those rows of **B** for which $A(i,j)/=0$. In the present case, for instance

$$C(1,1) = A(1,1)*B(1,1) + A(1,3)*B(3,1) + A(1,6)*B(6,1) \qquad (9\text{-}25)$$

and since B(3,1) cannot be found in the storage vector, the product involving it would be dropped (see also Sec. 10-2).

Obviously, in the case of irregularly sparse matrices, the speedup is better found from simulation studies. Such studies were run and for the matrices of Fig. 9-10 the result was

$$
\begin{bmatrix}
a_{11} & 0 & a_{13} & 0 & 0 & a_{16} \\
0 & a_{22} & 0 & 0 & a_{25} & 0 \\
a_{31} & 0 & a_{33} & a_{34} & 0 & 0 \\
0 & a_{42} & 0 & a_{44} & 0 & 0 \\
0 & 0 & 0 & 0 & a'_{55} & a_{56} \\
0 & 0 & 0 & a_{64} & 0 & a_{66}
\end{bmatrix}
*
\begin{bmatrix}
b_{11} & b_{12} & & & & \\
 & b_{22} & & b_{24} & & b_{26} \\
 & & b_{33} & & b_{35} & \\
b_{41} & & & b_{44} & & b_{46} \\
 & & b_{53} & & b_{55} & \\
b_{61} & & & & & b_{66}
\end{bmatrix}
=
\begin{bmatrix}
c_{11} & c_{12} & c_{13} & 0 & 0 & c_{16} \\
 & c_{22} & c_{23} & c_{24} & c_{25} & c_{26} \\
c_{31} & c_{32} & c_{33} & c_{34} & c_{35} & c_{36} \\
c_{41} & c_{42} & & c_{44} & & c_{46} \\
 & & & & c_{55} & c_{56} \\
c_{61} & & & c_{64} & & c_{66}
\end{bmatrix}
$$

RELEVANT INFORMATION OF A

INDEX	1		2	3			4	5	6		7
IA =	1		4	6			9	11	13		15
JA =	1	3	6	2	5	1	3	4	2	4	5	6	4	6
A =	1	1	1	2	2	3	3	3	4	4	5	5	6	6

RELEVANT INFORMATION OF B. SLICE: 1

INDEX	1		2	3
IB =	1		4	6
JB =	1	4	6	1	2
B =	10	10	10	20	20

RELEVANT INFORMATION OF B. SLICE: 2

INDEX	1	2	3
IB =	1	3	5
JB =	3	5	2	4
B =	30	30	40	40

RELEVANT INFORMATION OF B. SLICE: 3

INDEX	1	2	3
IB =	1	3	6
JB =	3	5	2	4	6
B =	50	50	60	60	60

THE PRODUCT MATRIX C ROW-WISE

20	20	30	0	50	60
0	40	60	80	100	120
60	60	80	120	150	180
40	80	0	320	0	480
50	0	150	0	250	300
120	0	0	240	0	720

Figure 9-10   Matrix multiplication on an ASP

$$t(p) = 14.8 + 124 + 8.6 = 147.4 \tag{9-26}$$

Assuming that $t(1) = n^3 = 216$, the speedup is $\sigma \simeq 1.465$, which for $p = 3$ leads only to an efficiency of $\eta \simeq 0.488$. This is a very misleading result since the matrices were very small, their sparsity therefore not representative of the real cases. For much larger matrices, the efficiency and speedup would have been higher.

9–4.2 Direct Solutions of Linear Sets

Two cases should be distinguished: that of dense and that of sparse matrices. In the first case, the assumption is that the matrices are not too large and that slices fit into the memories of the slaves.

As mentioned in Sec. 6-2, the method of Jordan is used more often for inverting a dense matrix. It produces a diagonal matrix and saves the back-substitution or in cases of inversion the n back-substitutions required by the elimination method by Gauss. The fact that it requires three times the work of elimination is immaterial in parallel environments, since this time would be wasted on a Haydn effect.

The outline of the program is:

```
for i in 1 .. n loop
  --- Call here a task which will normalize all rows in the slice
  --- of every slave i.e. do A(i,.) := A(i,.) / A(i,i).
  -- The dots indicate "all columns 1 to n" as earlier.
  for j in 1 .. n loop
    C := A(j,i); -- C is the chosen pivot.
    --- The pivot and the pivot row are send to each slave.
    --- Each slave performs elimination on its slice i.e.
    --- A(j,.) := A(j,.)-C*A(i,.) except that row i should not be
    --- eliminated. For this another task type should be used.
  end loop;
end loop;
```

Code 9-8

In many practical cases (e.g., electronic or power system networks), the matrices are very large (on the average 2,000 by 2,000), but extremely sparse (only 10 to 20 nonzeros in a row). For such cases, the "Optimally Ordered Factorization" *OOF* is normally applied. An efficient method based on the work by Markowitz [Mar57] was developed by George and Liu [GaL81], but it can be applied only to positive, definite systems. The method of [Wal82] is suggested because it does not have this constraint and can be parallelized easily. It is applicable to "zero-symmetric matrices" which exhibit a symmetrical pattern of zeros. In these matrices, if $A(i,j) = 0$ then also $A(j,i) = 0$, but if $A(i,j)/ = 0$, then $A(j,i)$ may have any nonzero value.

The main idea of the algorithm is that, for zero-symmetric matrices, basic Gaussian steps, called bag (i,k) and bag(j,k), are commutative operations provided $A(i,j) = 0$. For sparse matrices (Fig.9-11), this will enhance parallelism by enabling a large number of pivots to be applied simultaneously. This is now pursued in a more rigorous way.

Theorem 1: In a zero-symmetric matrix, bag(i,k) and bag (j,k) commute if $A(i,j) = 0$ (bag (i,k) operates with row i on row k).

Proof: Let i,j be two pivots and k a "row" to be operated on. If bag (i,k) is applied first and bag (j,k) later, the result for $m > 1$ is

$$A'(k,m) := A(k,m) - A(i,m)*A(k,i)/A(i,i); \text{ following bag}(i,k) \qquad (9\text{-}27)$$

$$A''(k,m) := A'(k,m) - A(j,m)*A'(k,j)/A(j,j); \text{ following bag } (j,k) \qquad (9\text{-}28)$$

The assumption was that $A(i,j) = 0$, so that for running index m, if $m = j$ then Eq. (9-27) results in $A'(k,j) = A(k,j)$. Substituting this and Eq. (9-27) into Eq. (9-28) yields

$$A''(k,m) := A(k,m) - A(i,m)*A(k,i)/A(i,i) - A(j,m)*A(k,j)/A(j,j) \qquad (9\text{-}29)$$

The indices i,j of this equation may be interchanged. Hence, the operations may also be performed in the reverse order. Q.E.D.

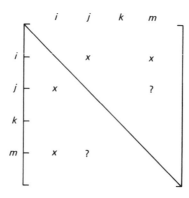

Figure 9-11 For the proof of the Theorem

Theorem 1 shows the condition for a number of pivots to act interchangeably and thus simultaneously on the same row. Obviously, elimination of rows j and k by pivot i are also independent operations.

Theorem 2. If after bag (i,m); $m > i$, both row and column i are discarded, the symmetric pattern of zeros is retained.

Proof: Suppose that $A(k,i) = 0$, but $A(m,i)/ = 0$ and $A(j,i)/ = 0$ (Fig. 9-11). Since $A(k,i) = 0$, the zeros in row and column k will not be changed. Element $A(m,j)$ will be changed, but so will $A(j,m)$. The zero-symmetry is thus retained. Q.E.D.

Corollary. If a matrix **A** is zero-symmetric and $A(i,j) = 0$, then all operations using pivots i and j may be performed independently and simultaneously and the matrix which remains after row and column i and j are eliminated is also zero-symmetric. In an obvious way, this result applies to a set of indices $\{i,j, \ldots \}$.

The problem is therefore: given the matrix, find an independent submatrix with the largest number of pivots. This is known to be an NP-complete problem, which has no known, efficient solution. An enumerative "brute force" approach seems to be the best, but would require an inordinate amount of work and time.

Another, much more practical approach is to suggest a suboptimal (instead of optimal) policy. Such policy is arrived at in a heuristic way, that is by trial and error. The following policy is recommended for the posed problem:

1. The node with the least number of links (i.e., the row with the least number of nonzeros) is given index 1. If there are several, one is selected arbitrarily.
2. Assume nodes 1 to k have been chosen already. Next, index $k+1$ is assigned to the node that has the least number of links and is not directly connected to any of the first k nodes.
3. When rule 2 cannot be applied any more (with $k = m$), number the remaining nodes $m + 1$ to n arbitrarily.

The algorithm, called *POOF* for "Parallel Optimally Ordered Factorization" which uses the renumbering policy described above, is best exemplified by a concrete example—Figs. 9-12(a)–(c) and Tables 9-2(a)–(c). (In order to exemplify the characteristics of POOF, matrices of at least 100-by-100 should be used, otherwise, it is difficult to have meaningful sparsity. The network of Fig. 9-12(a) is therefore only intended for description of the algorithm. Experimentation with larger matrices is reported in [Wa182].)

The initial renumbering step-by-step [Fig. 9-! a)] leads to:

1. Node 1 is chosen as the first node.
2. Nodes 2, 6 are "crossed out," 9 is chosen as pivot, 10 is crossed out, 3 is chosen as pivot, 4 and 5 are crossed out, and finally 7 and 11 are chosen as pivots. Pivots are encircled in Fig. 9-12(a).
3. The renumbering of the original network and the resulting adjacency matrix are shown in Table 9-2(a). As seen, the rows and columns corresponding to the chosen five pivots form a diagonal block.

According to the corollary, all five pivots may next be eliminated simultaneously. For example, if two slaves work in parallel, the first could eliminate pivots 1 and 2 at the same time that the second slave eliminates pivots 3, 4, and 5. The network which corresponds to the nodes not yet eliminated is shown in Fig.9-12(b), its renumbering and adjacency matrix in Table 9-2(b).

Figure 9-12(c) and Table 9-2(c) show the next stage of elimination. The elimination of the two remaining nodes completes the algorithm.

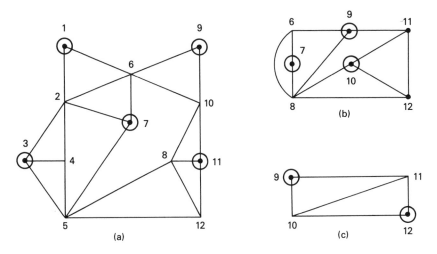

Figure 9-12   Reduction of matrices in the Poof program

TABLE 9-2(a) REDUCTION OF THE MATRIX IN THE POOF PROGRAM

old	new		1	2	3	4	5	6	7	8	9	1()	11	2
1	1	1	X					X		X				
2	6	2		X							X		X	
3	3	3			X			X	X	X				
4	7	4				X		X		X	X			
5	8	5					X					X	X	X
6	9	6	X		X	X		X	X		X			
7	4	7			X			X	X	X				
8	10	8			X	X		X	X			X		X
9	2	9	X	X		X		X			X		X	
10	11	10					X			X		X	X	X
11	5	11		X			X				X	X	X	
12	12	12					X			X		X		X

TABLE 9-2(b)

old	new		6	7	8	9	10	11	12
6	9	6	X			X	X		
7	6	7		X		X	X	X	
8	10	8			X	X	X		X
9	7	9	X	X		X	X		
10	8	10	X	X	X	X	X		X
11	11	11		X	X			X	X
12	12	12		X		X		X	X

TABLE 9-2(c)

old	new		9	10	11	12
9	9	9	X		X	X
10	11	10		X	X	X
11	12	11	X	X	X	X
12	10	12	X	X	X	X

This algorithm may be rephrased in more mathematical terms as follows: [Wa187]:[†]
Define the data as a vector "noofadj(i)" and a vector of sets showing which nodes are adjacent to node i. For Fig. 9-12(a) its is shown in Table 9-3. Note that only nonzero elements need be stored.

For the node with the smallest number of adjacents, here $i = 1$, the "pivotset" is started as $ps := \{1\}$ and using always the node with the smallest remaining noofadj's, compute $ps \wedge$ adjnodes (i). ($\wedge$ is the intersection of "and" operator of the SETS package

---

†Y. Wallach: "Solution of Linear Equations . . . ," *Journal of Pascal, Ada, and Modula 2*, Vol. 6, No. 2, 1987, pp. 3–19 (© 1987 Wiley). Reprinted by permission of John Wiley & Sons Inc.

TABLE 9-3 STORAGE OF THE MATRIX FOR THE POOF ALGORITHM

$i(=$ node)	1	2	3	4	5	6	7	8	9	10	11	12	12
noofadj	2	5	3	3	5	5	3	4	2	4	3	3	3
adjnodes	2,6	1,3,4,6,7	2,4,5	2,3,5	3,4,7,8,12	1,2,7,9,10	2,5,6	5,10,11,12	6,10	6,8,9,11	8,10,12	8,10,12	5,8,11

in Sec. 7-10.) If the result is the empty set $\{\phi\}$ then add i to ps; otherwise do nothing. For example above. this leads to

i=9: ps Λ adjnodes (9) $= \{1\} \Lambda \{6,10\} = \{\phi\} \div$ ps $:= \{1,9\}$.
i=3: ps Λ adjnodes (3) $= \{1,9\} \Lambda \{2,4,5\} = \{\phi\} \div$ ps $:= \{1,3,9\}$.
i=4: ps Λ adjnodes (4) $= \{1,3,9\} \Lambda \{2,3,5,\} = \{3\} \div$ 4 is not a pivot.
i=7: ps Λ adjnodes (7) $= \{1,3,9\} \Lambda \{2,5,6,\} = \{\phi\} \div$ ps $:= \{1,3,7,9\}$.
i=11: ps Λ adjnodes (11) $= \{1,3,7,9\}\Lambda\{8,10,12\}=\{\phi\} \div$ ps$:=\{1,3,7,9,11\}$.

For $i = 12,2,5,6,8,10$ the result of $ps\Lambda$adjnodes $(i)/=\{\phi\}$, so that none of these nodes is a pivot. The result is identical to Table 9-2(a).

The program of GAussian DIrect elimination or *GADI* is shown as Code 9-9. It is based on storing the entire matrix in the local storage of every slave. This will not require excessive storage, since essentially only nonzero elements are stored (3% to 5% of n^2). Obviously, each slave works only on ''its'' slice of matrix.

```
with SETS, TEXT_IO; use SETS, TEXT_IO;          -- The master program

procedure gadi(noofnodes,p,h: in INTEGER) is    -- is called "gadi".
type NODENOS is 1 .. noofnodes;                 -- Package SETS was
type CONSET is SET of NODENOS;                  -- slightly modified.
type MXTYPE is array(NODENOS,NODENOS) of FLOAT; -- Intersection and
type NODEREC is record                          -- Union were denoted
  nodenum, noofadj: INTEGER;                     -- by * and + resp.,
  adjnodes         : CONSENT;                   -- empty denotes the
end record;                                      -- entire empty set.
type NODETYPE is array(NODENOS) of NODEREC;     -- It starts with null
adjmx: MXTYPE; node: NODETYPE; pivotset: CONSET;
il, jl, m, noofpivots, nrem, nrows, startrow: INTEGER;
procedure renummx(adjmx: in out MXTYPE; node: out NODETYPE;
  n,il: in INTEGER; noofpivots: out INTEGER; pivotset: out CONSET) is
  -- This procedure renumbers the matrix according to equations above.
  -- It represents a sequential step of the algorithm.
tempentry, temp: FLOAT; i,j,k,minpos,np1 : INTEGER;
tempnode: NODEREC; diag: array(NODENOS) of FLOAT;
begin
  np1 := n+1;                              -- n plus 1 will be used a number of times.
  for i in il .. n loop
    diag(i) := adjmx(i,i);
    node(i).nodenum := np1;
```

```
        node(i).noofadj := 0;
        node(i).adjnodes := null;
      end loop;
      for i in il .. n loop
        for j in il .. i-1 loop
          if adjmx(i,j) /= 0.0 then
            node(i).noofadj := node(i).noofadj + 1;
            node(j).noofadj := node(j).noofadj + 1;
            end if;
          end loop;                        -- end of the loop on j.
        end loop;                          -- end of the loop on i.
        for i in il .. n-1 loop            -- Set all elements of upper
          for j in i+1 .. n loop           -- triangle to zero.
            adjmx(i,j) := 0.0;
          end loop;
        end loop;
        noofpivots := il-1; pivotset := null
        for i in il .. n loop
          minpos := il;
          for j in il .. n loop
            if (node(j).noofadj<node(minpos).noofadj) and
               (node(j).nodenum=np1) then minpos := j;
            end if;
          end loop;
          if (node(minpos).adjnodes*pivotset) = empty then
            noofpivots := noofpivots + 1; -- Above * corresponds to Λ.
            node(minpos).nodenum := noofpivots;
            pivotset := pivotset + {minpos}; -- The + cooresponds to or.
            node(minpos).noofadj := node(minpos).noofadj + n;
          else
            node(minpos).nodenum := 0;
            node(minpos).noofadj := node(minpos).noofadj + n;
          end if;
        end loop; -- of i.
        k := noofpivots;
        for i in il .. n loop
          if node(i).nodenum = 0 then
            k := k+1; node(i).nodenum := k;
          end if;
        end loop;
        for k in il .. n loop
          node(k).noofadj := node(k).noofadj - n;
        end loop;
        for i in il .. n loop
          tempnode := node(i); tempnode.adjnodes := null;
          for j in il .. n loop
            if j in node(i).adjnodes then     -- in is the ∈ operation.
              tempnode.adjnodes := tempnode.adjnodes+{node(j).nodenum};
```

434

```
        if i<j then
          temp := adjmx(j,i);
        else
          temp := adjmx(i,j);
        end if;
        if node(i).nodenum<node(j).nodenum then
          adjmx(node(i).nodenum, node(j).nodenum) := temp;
        else
          adjmx(node(j).nodenum, node(i).nodenum) := temp;
        end if;
      end if;
    end loop;                           -- end of the loop on j.
    node(i) := tempnode;
  end loop;                             -- end of the loop on i.
  for i in il .. n loop
    adjmx(i,j) := diag(node(i).nodenum);
  end loop;
  for i in il+1 .. n loop
    for j in il .. i-1 loop
      adjmx(i,j) := adjmx(j,i);
    end loop;                           end of the loop on j.
  end loop;                             -- end of the loop on i.
end renummx;

procedure sortnodes(node: in out NODETYPE; n, j1 in INTEGER) is
-- This procedure sorts the nodes placing the pivoted rows first.
minpos: INTEGER; tempnode : NODEREC;
begin
  for i in il .. n-1 loop
    minpos := i;
    for j in i+1 .. n loop
      if node(i).nodenum<node(minpos).nodenum then
        minpos := j;
      end if;
    end loop;
    tempnode := node(i);        -- Node(i) and node(minpos) are
    node(i) := node(minpos);    -- swapped with the help of tempnode.
    node(minpos) := tempnode;
  end loop;
end sortnodes;                  -- end of sortnodes procedure.

task type ELIMINATE is
  entry slice(start, stop : in INTEGER);
end ELIMINATE;                  -- task type, one for each slave.

task body ELIMINATE is
mul, term :FLOAT; k,num,picol,row : INTEGER;
begin
  accept slice(start,stop: in INTEGER) do
    startrow := start; stoprow := stop;
  end accept;
```

```
    for row in startrow .. stoprow loop
      for picol in 1 .. noofpivots loop
        if adjmx(row,picol) /= 0.0 then
          mul := adjmx(row, picol) / adjmx(picol,picol);
          adjmx(row,picol) := 0.0;
          for k in noofpivots+1 .. noofnodes loop
          if adjmx(picol,k) /= 0.0 then
            term := adjmx(row,k);
            term := term - mul*adjmx(picol,k);
            adjmx(row,k) := term; adjmx(k,row) := term;
          end if;
        end loop;
      end if;
    end loop;              -- end of the loop on the pivot column picol.
  end loop;                -- of all rows in the slice.
end ELIMINATE;             -- end of the body of ELIMINATE.

declare
  for i in 1 .. p loop           -- This loop declares and therefore generates
    el(i): ELIMINATE;                   -- all p slave tasks "eliminate".
  end loop;
  begin      B E G I N  O F  T H E  M A I N  P R O G R A M
    getmat(adjmx,noofnodes);  -- This procedure was not declared.
    --It inputs the matrix adjmx of size noofnodes-by-noofnodes.
    --Next is the initialization. It is sequential, done by master.
    il := 1; jl := 1;
    renummx(adjmx, node, noofnodes, il, noofpivots, pivotset);
    while il<noofpivots loop
      m := noofnodes - noofpivots;
      noofnodes := m mod p;
      nrem := m rem p;
      start := noofpivots + 1;
      sortnodes(node, noofnodes, il); -- All slaves are activated
      jl := il, il := noofpivots + 1; -- in the loop concurrently.
      for i in 1 .. p loop
        if nrem>0 then
          num := nrows+1; nrem := nrem-1;
        else
          num := nrows;
        end if;
        stop := start+num-1;
        el(i).slice(start,stop); -- T H E  C O M P U T A T I O N.
        start := stop+1;
      end loop;              -- end of the loop on i.
    end loop;               -- end of the while loop.
  end;                     -- end of the declare block.
end;                       -- of procedure gadi = GAuss DIrect method.
```

Code 9-9

9–4.3 Iterative Methods

The Gauss-Seidel algorithm was reordered in Sec. 6-5. It used vectors **z** and **t**. Since they are updated in the slaves, the following possibilities indicated in Fig. 9-13 exist:

a. If $i = lb$ (the lower bound of the slice) then only the **z** vector is to be updated. This is also true if $i > ub$.

b. If $i = ub$ (the upper bound of the slice) then only the **t** vector is to be updated. This is also true if $i < lb$.

c. If $lb < i < ub$, i.e., i is in the range between lb and ub, then both vectors **t** and **z** have to be updated.

The time ratio was computed to be

$$\rho = 1/p + 2/(n^2) + (2*\ \tau)/(n^2*\omega) + \zeta/(2*n*\omega) \tag{9-30}$$

For $2 \ll n^2$, $2*\tau \ll n^2*\omega$, and $\zeta \ll 2*n^2*\omega$, i.e., for a sizable n, all terms can be neglected compared to the first, so that the optimal speedup is achieved. The program for this algorithm is shown in Code 9-10, with comments explaining the various steps.

Iterative methods for general matrices were programmed on the SMS201. At first a modification of the Jacobi algorithm and then the Gauss-Seidel method were run. It is important to note at the outset that the results will not be very encouraging precisely because, as mentioned in Chap. 5, synchronization and data transfer are effected on SMS201 by the master's operating system (calls to its interrupt-handling routines). Thus $\zeta = 770$mls, $\tau = 370$mls for broadcast from the master, and $\tau = 280$mls from a slave. *These are extremely large times indeed.*

The Jacobi method [Nag79] showed low speedups also because each slave stored only a single row of **A** and calculated a single $x(k)$ which it then broadcast to all the slaves. Each slave checks all flags and stops the computation only if *all flags were set.*

It is easily seen that the parallel step is very short compared to the sequential step which leads to a low speedup. Still, even this version of the iterative methods had advantages: simpler programming and faster execution for lower accuracy for nonlinear equations, because each iteration can start with the results of an earlier solution of the linearized problem (solved with lower accuracy).

The Gauss-Seidel method was run for various matrices of dimension n, and the

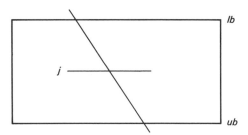

Figure 9-13   The three possibilities for pivot position

```
with TEXT_IO; use TEXT_IO;
procedure gait(n,p,h,numiter in INTEGER; eps:=in FLOAT) is
-- This is the main procedure for the Gauss iterative method.
type AR is array(1..n,1..n) of FLOAT;
type VEP is array(1..p) of INTEGER;
type VEC is array(1..n) of FLOAT;
a: AR;         -- The matrix a to be used is read independently
t,z,x: VEC; -- Vector b will be stored on the diagonal after matrix a
lo,hi: VEP; -- is normalized i.e. when all a(i,i)=1.0.
lb,ub: INTEGER; e,diag,r,y: FLOAT;


begin       -- Next is the initialization step done by the master.
  lo(1) := 1; hi(1) := h; -- Vectors lo and hi define the slices of
  for i in 2 .. p loop     -- matrix a to be processed by a slave.
    lo(i) := lo(i-1)+h;   -- Each slice has h=n/p rows to process.
    hi(i) := hi(i-1)+h;   -- If h is not an integer, add rows of
  end loop;                -- zeros so that it is.
  for i in 1 .. n loop      -- Reading data could have been distributed
    for j in 1 .. n loop    -- among the p slaves, if they have
      GET(a(i,j));          -- independent I/O equipment.
    end loop;
    diag := a(i,i);
    for j in 1 .. n loop    -- This loop on j normalizes matrix a.
      a(i,j) := a(i,j)/diag;
    end loop;
    GET(a(i,i)):            -- Reading-in the right hand side b.
  end loop;                 -- End of reading the data.

  for i in 1 .. n loop      -- Initializing the unknown vector x to 1.0.
    x(i) := 1.0;            -- Other values could have been used.
  end loop;
  for i in 1 .. n loop      -- Initializing vector t.
    t(i) := a(i,i); ip1 := i+1;
    for j in ip1 .. n loop
      t(i) := t(i) - a(i,j)*x(j);
    end loop;
  end loop;
  -- This completes the initialization step. Next, p identical tasks
  -- are activated and used inside a loop which is completed either
  -- when the error is less than eps or the number of iterations
  -- "numiter" is exceeded.

  iter := 0;
  while iter<numiter loop
    e := 0.0;                -- e will accumulate the total error.
    for i in 1 .. n loop    -- The sequential step includes:
      z(i) := 0.0;           -- Initialization of all z to 0.0
    end loop;

    for i in 1 .. n loop    -- and calculation of:
```

```
y := t(i) - z(i);     --      the new value of x(i),
r := y - x(i);        --      the residual r,
e := e + r*r;         --      the error, and
x(i) = y;             --      the new value of x(i).
-- Actually, this x(i) should be broadcast to all p slaves
begin declare         -- Here begins the parallel step.
  task type SLICE is
    entry compute(i, lb, ub: in INTEGER);
  end SLICE;
  task body SLICE is
    procedure zupdate(lb, ub: in INTEGER) is
    begin
      for k in lb .. ub loop
        z(k) := z(k) + a(k, i)*x(i);
      end loop;
    end; -- of procedure which updates the z values.
    procedure tupdate(lb, ub: in INTEGER) is
    begin
      for k in lb .. ub loop
        t(k) := t(k) + a(k, i)*r;
      end loop;
    end; -- of procedure which updates the t values.
    begin -- of body of task slice.
      if i=lb then zupdate(i+1, ub);
      elsif i<lb then zupdate(lb, ub);
      elsif lb<i and i>ub then
        zupdate(i+1, ub); tupdate(lb, i-1);
      elsif i=ub then tupdate(lb, i-1);
      elsif i>ub then tupdate(lb, ub);
      else null;
      end if;
    end;
    for sl in 1 .. p loop
      comslice(sl): slice; -- Declaration.
    end;
    for sl in 1 .. p loop
      lb := lo(sl); ub := hi(s1);
      accept comslice(s1).compute(i, lb, ub: in INTEGER) do
        null;
      end accept;
    end;
  end;
end;
end;                     -- of the loop on i which computes
iter := iter + 1;     -- all x's and updates all t's.
exit when e<eps or iter<numiter;
end;
end;
```

Code 9-10

times $t(s)$, $t(e)$, $t(p)$ for sequential (and synchronization) exchange of data and parallel steps were measured. The hardware utilization was calculated according to

$$v = t(p)/[t(s)+t(e)+t(p)] = t(p)/t \qquad (9\text{-}31)$$

Time $t(s)$ was constant for a given n and is shown in Table 9-4, other times and v in Table 9-5. Since theoretically, for $\xi = 770$mls, $\tau = 370$ mls we have:

$$t(s) = (3.4 + 0.77n)mls; \; t(e) = (0.067 * p + 0.314*n)mls;$$
$$t(p) = 20n^2/p + 3(2 + 1/p)n$$

we can compare the calculated and measured, total times (Fig. 9-14).

$$t' = 0.067*p + (20n^2 + 3*n)/p \qquad (9\text{-}32)$$

Time t' is the portion of the time dependent on the number of slaves p. The increase in the exchange times $(0.067*p)$ is negligible if compared to the reduction in the parallel time (about $20*n^2/p$). Therefore, it may be concluded that all 128 slaves should be used.

The results prove a number of points. First among them is that calculated and measured results are very close (Fig. 9-14). The hardware utilization factor is over 95% and this disproves the notion that the bus or exchange of information are in any way the bottlenecks of the program. This is the more encouraging, since in the case of the Gauss-Seidel method, the parallel steps are extremely short and data is exchanged much more often (n times more often) than in the Jacobi method.

The results are even better if for the transfer of information and for synchronization *the operating system is not used*. The Gauss-Seidel method was programmed in the assembly language of the MC68000 and ran on the TOPPS system. Typical results such as those of Fig. 9-15 show that for large matrices, the efficiency approaches 100%.

The *conclusion* is that ASP and RASP can be used for various problems providing speedup, fault-detection, and availability at a very low (additional) cost.

9–5 PROBLEMS

(1, 2, 3 for ARPs, the rest for ASPs)

1. Use loopar and shift(i) where i is North, East, West, or South respectively for a program to solve the Laplace equation on an ARP. Calculate the speedup for a square with 128*128 internal points. Using language constructs of Sec. 9-1, solve by recursive doubling a tridiagonal set on a VP.

2. The LU-factorization of a tridiagonal matrix [Eq. (6-74] produces lower **L** and upper bidiagonal matrices so that the upper diagonal of **U** is the original diagonal **c**, the diagonal of **L** is l, and the remaining lower diagonal **e** of **L** and diagonal **d** of **U** are

$$d(1) := b(1); \; d(i) := b(i) - a(i)*c(i - 1)/d(i - 1); \; e(i) := a(i)/d(i - 1); \; i = 2..$$

TABLE 9-4 SPEEDUP AS FUNCTION OF SIZE OF THE MATRIX

n	15	30	60	128	256	512	1024
t_s	14.95	26.50	49.6	101.96	200.52	397.64	791.88

TABLE 9-5 RESULTS OF RUNNING PROGRAMS ON THE SMS

T_{ex}	T_A	T	P	v_2
4.777	4635.000	4654.727	1	0.996
4.911	1605.000	1624.861	3	0.988
5.045	999.000	1018.995	5	0.980
5.715	393.000	413.665	15	0.950

T_{ex}	T_A	T	P	v_2
9.487	18270.000	18305.990	1	0.998
9.554	9225.000	9261.055	2	0.996
9.621	6210.000	6246.121	3	0.994
9.755	3798.000	3834.255	5	0.991
9.822	3195.000	3231.322	6	0.989
10.090	1989.000	2025.590	10	0.982
10.425	1386.000	1422.925	15	0.974
11.430	783.000	820.930	30	0.954

T_{ex}	T_A	T	P	v_2
18.907	72540.000	72608.500	1	0.999
18.974	36450.000	36518.570	2	0.988
19.041	24420.000	24488.640	3	0.997
19.108	18405.000	18473.710	4	0.996
19.175	14796.000	14864.770	5	0.995
19.242	12390.000	12458.840	6	0.994
19.510	7578.000	7647.109	10	0.991
19.644	6375.000	6444.242	12	0.989
19.845	5172.000	5241.445	15	0.987
20.180	3969.000	4038.780	20	0.983
20.850	2766.000	2836.450	30	0.975
22.860	1563.000	1635.460	60	0.956

T_{ex}	T_A	T	P	v_2
40.259	328832.000	328974.200	1	1.000
40.326	164800.000	164942.300	2	0.999
40.460	82784.000	82926.440	4	0.998
40.728	41776.000	41918.690	8	0.997
41.264	21272.000	21415.220	16	0.993
42.336	11020.000	11164.300	32	0.987
44.480	5894.000	6040.441	64	0.976
48.768	3331.000	3481.728	128	0.957

T_{ex}	T_A	T	P	v_2
80.451	1313024.000	1313305.000	1	1.000
80.518	657280.000	657561.100	2	1.000
80.652	329408.000	329689.200	4	0.999
80.920	165472.000	165753.400	8	0.998
81.456	83504.000	83786.000	16	0.997
82.528	42520.000	42803.050	32	0.993
84.672	22028.000	22313.190	64	0.987
88.960	11782.000	12071.480	128	0.976
97.536	6659.000	6957.055	256	0.957

T_{ex}	T_A	T	P	v_2
160.835	52467488.000	5248046.000	1	1.000
160.902	2625280.000	2625839.000	2	1.000
161.036	1314176.000	1314735.000	4	1.000
161.304	658624.000	659182.900	8	0.999
161.840	330848.000	331407.500	16	0.998
162.912	166960.000	167520.600	32	0.997
165.056	85016.000	85578.690	64	0.993
169.344	44044.000	44610.980	128	0.987
177.920	23558.000	24133.560	256	0.976
195.072	13315.000	13907.710	512	0.957

T_{ex}	T_A	T	P	v_2
321.603	20980740.000	20981860.000	1	1.000
321.670	10493440.000	10494550.000	2	1.000
321.804	5249792.000	5250906.000	4	1.000
322.072	2627968.000	2629082.000	8	1.000
322.608	1317056.000	1318170.000	16	0.999
323.680	661600.000	662715.600	32	0.998
325.824	333872.000	334989.700	64	0.997
330.112	170008.000	171130.000	128	0.993
338.688	88076.000	89206.560	256	0.987
355.840	47110.000	48257.720	512	0.976
390.144	26627.000	27809.020	1024	0.957

Write a parallel version of it based on

$$d^0(i) := b(i); \text{ and } d^j(i) := b(i) - a(i)*c(i - 1)/d^{j-1}(i - 1); i = 1, \ldots$$

3. Transducer programming (Sec. 8-3.3) is similar to a three-stage pipeline: the producer is the input device, the transducer is the PaM and the consumer is the output device. Using a generalization, write a package for running a five-stage pipeline.

4. Write a program to use the Fibonacci sequence for searching. A large number of optimization methods are mentioned in [Wil64]. Parallel programs for these algorithms can be developed.

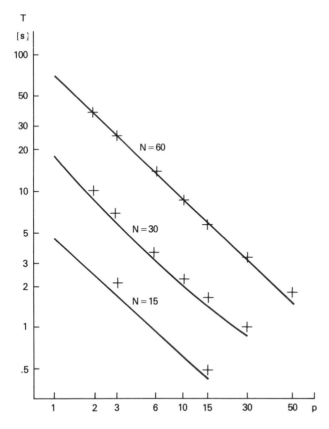

Figure 9-14 Results obtained on the Siemens computer

5. Change the parallel serch routines so that there are p tasks, all tasks are going in the same direction, say "up," and abort all tasks once one of them has located the given key.

6. Change the sorting routine in Code 9-6 into a parallel sorting program by using tasks. Change this sorting procedure so that p instead of two tasks is used. Calculate an average speedup and verify it by running a number of simulation studies.

7. Change the sorting procedure by using the bubble-sort, cocktail-shaker and especially, the quicksort procedure. In the last case, determine if the Haydn effect decreases the speedup.

8. Write a program for multiplying two dense matrices (the "first" case). Compare the storage requirements and the speedups achieved.

9. Program the Jordan elimination procedure. Use pivoting in a Gaussian elimination program. Use storage of diagonal vectors in any of the programs above. Calculate their speedup σ and communication penalty π.

10. Write a program based on the Poof algorithm.

11. Write a program based on the Jacobi iteration.

12. Write a program for multiplying sparse matrices on ASP.

13. An algorithm for solving linear sets viewed as recurrent relations is given in [CaW77]. Program it for ASP.

14. The sieve of Eratostenes was introduced in Problem 7-6. Write an ASP version of it in Ada.

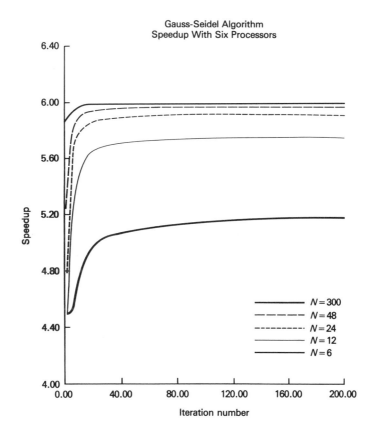

Figure 9-15   Results obtained on the TOPPS computer

15. Problems 13, 14, 15, and 21 of Chap. 7 described algorithms for image processing, those of Southwell, Newton-Cotes, and for calculation of a determinant. Write ASP versions for these algorithms.

16. Discuss the possibility of writing an ASP version of an inquiry problem, for instance the broker's example.

17. Given two Boolean matrices **A** and **B**, we define the Boolean product **A∧B** as a matrix whose (i,j) entry is $\Sigma(A(i,k)\wedge B(k,j))$ where Σ stands for a Boolean "or." The Boolean sum **A** $+$ **B** is defined as a matrix whose i,j element is $A(i,j)+B(i,j)$ ($+$ is an or).

The use of Boolean matrices to represent topologies has led to interest in matrix products such that matrix A′ is produced as follows: $A'=\Sigma A^{i}$, where we define $\mathbf{A}^{1}=\mathbf{A}$, $\mathbf{A}^{i+1}=\mathbf{A}^{i}\wedge\mathbf{A}$ and $i\Sigma=1,\ \dots\ ,n-1$.

An efficient algorithm for calculation of **A**′ was developed in [War62], and its program [Flo62] in Ada would be as follows:

(ARR is a Boolean array declared in an enclosing block. Initially $M(i,j)$ is TRUE if individual i is a parent of individual j. At completion, $M(i,j)$ is TRUE if i is an ancestor of individual j. That is, at completion $M(i,j)$ is TRUE if there are k,l, etc. such that initially $M(i,k),M(k,1),\ \dots\ ,M(p,j)$ are all TRUE.)

procedure ancestor (M **inout**: ARR, n **in** INTEGER);

```
begin
  for i in 1..n loop
    for j in 1..n loop
      if M(j,i)=true then
        for k in 1..n loop
          if M(i,k) = true then M(j,k) : = true; end if;
        end loop k;
      end if;
    end loop j;
  end loop i;
end ancestor;
```

It can be seen that each iteration $i+1$ produces a new matrix $\mathbf{M}^{i+1}$ in which $\mathbf{M}^i$ is set to TRUE if and only if there exists a k such that $\mathbf{M}^i(j,i)$ and $\mathbf{M}^i(i,k)$ are both TRUE. The rows of $\mathbf{M}^i$ can be checked simultaneously for descendency, since the descendents of one element have no effect on, nor are they affected by, the descendents of another element. Therefore, the new TRUE values of $\mathbf{M}^{i+1}$ can be determined simultaneously. However, the entire matrix $\mathbf{M}^i$ is needed at the start of the iteration. The descendants of a given element are also descendents of the ancestors of that element.

This algorithm can be parallelized for an ASP as follows:

1. $\mathbf{M}^0$ is the original matrix.
2.   **for** i **in** $1..n$ **loop** on steps 3 to 5:
3.   Main task sends TRUE values of $\mathbf{M}^{i-1}$ to each of p tasks running on p slaves.
4.   Each task produces, *in parallel*, the new TRUE values for a range of rows in $\mathbf{M}^{i-1}$ and sends the new values to the master task.
5.   The master task produces $\mathbf{M}^i$ using the new values. It consists of the new TRUE values set during this iteration plus any existing TRUE values of $\mathbf{M}^{i-1}$.

   Program this algorithm for an ASP, and try the same for a VP.

   Below are test results for $p = 4$, based on Boolean matrices of the type as produced by:

```
for i in 1..n loop M(i1):=TRUE;    end loop i;
  for i in 1..n loop M(1,i):=TRUE; end loop i;
```

n	$t(1)$	$t(4)$	σ	η	ρ
50	2	3	0.67	0.17	1.50
100	15	12	1.25	0.31	0.80
150	50	32	1.56	0.39	0.64
200	117	58	2.01	0.50	0.50
250	228	100	2.28	0.57	0.43

As the matrices become larger, the computation time Ω becomes larger compared to the overhead (communication κ and synchronization ξ times). Therefore, the communication penalty π decreases, the speedup σ and efficiency η increase, and the time ratio ρ decreases.

CHAPTER 10

PROGRAMMING HYPERCUBES

The *objectives* of this chapter are:

Determine the mapping of the problem to the architecture, the ratio of communication to computation time, the loading, and the language features required for programming the Cubes.

Develop programs for solving linear equations, for searching and for sorting on the Cubes.

Provide (sometimes rather extensive) problems and projects.

10–1 INTRODUCTION

10–1.1 On the Communication Penalty

In Cubes, the degree of concurrency depends on the way that tasks are distributed among the nodes. For a low penalty, it is important that the tasks be computationally significant and the granularity at least medium sized. They should also be of approximately equal size for balanced loading. For higher concurrency, the more tasks the better, but the more tasks we have, the lower is the granularity, the larger the amount of communications between the more numerous nodes, the higher the communication penalty π and the lower the efficiency η. The two conditions lead to contradictory requirements, and must be decided upon case by case. As will be seen below, particular problems may require special methods for solving these contradictory requirements.

We have seen in Chap. 5 that the iPSC/2 uses circuit-switching. In the present chapter we assume that the more traditional "store-and-forward" packet switching is used. A packet may have to pass several PEs and be stored at any one of them waiting for some resource. This means that the queuing time may be non-negligible and complicates seriously the analysis of the communication penalty π.

Some general principles are deduced in [Fea88][†] using the example of Fig. 10-1(a). It shows a simple picture digitized as a square array of pixels. This two-dimensional image can be decomposed for a 16-node Cube as a 4-by-4 two-dimensional mesh with each node holding an 8-by-8 pixel subarray. A real image-processing problem might involve a 4096-by-4096 pixel array with a large number of possible intensity or color values associated with each pixel. However, basic ideas can be illustrated with this example. For instance, we will use convolution, which calculates

$$p(i) = \Sigma w(j)*p(j); \text{ where } j \text{ is over } i \text{ and the 8 neighbors of } i \qquad (10\text{-}1)$$

according to Fig. 10-1(b). Since the new pixel value at any point depends on its previous value as well as of those pixels that are adjacent in the array, this is a two-dimensional *nearest neighbor* algorithm.

As seen, each node solves the same subproblem as a sequential machine solving the whole problem. The differences are that the node needs only to update the 64 pixels assigned to its subdomain, rather than the full 1024 of the sequential case, and that the 22 pixels on some edges need special treatment.

Each of these "special" pixels requires information contained in other nodes in order to complete the convolution. Thus, the key features of the software in this example are:

[†]Fox/Lyzenga/Otto/Salmon/Walker, *Solving Problems on Concurrent Processors*, Volume I, © 1988. Reprinted by permission of Prentice Hall, Englewood Cliffs, N.J.

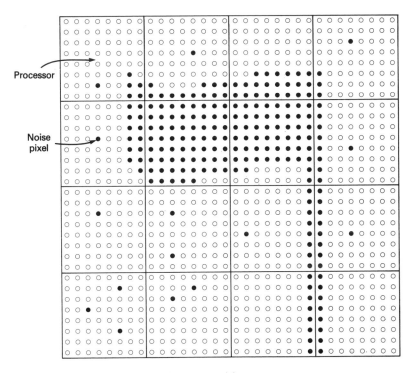

(a)

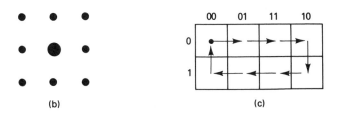

(b)   (c)

Figure 10-1   Solving problems on the Cube

- The algorithm is identical to that of a sequential machine except that each node has special geometry constraints corresponding to the restriction of the algorithm to the grain contained in the given node.

- At the edges of the cell contained within each node, there occur "unusual" boundary conditions. In Fig. 10-1(a), these boundary conditions on the north, south, and east edges amount to an instruction of the form: "Please communicate with a neighboring node to perform the convolution for an edge pixel."

- [Note that the convolution of an edge pixel can be done only *after* the information from the neighbors arrives. Therefore, this algorithm is driven by communication. A common characteristic of such examples is that] each node runs identical code but at any given time different nodes will typically be executing different instructions, because of data-dependent branches. This kind of branching occurs in the boundary condition phase of the image processing example, and for some convolution algorithms in the basic pixel update itself. [Fea88]

We have used ω to denote the time for a single arithmetic operation and τ for the transfer of a single word from one node to its neighbor. The magnitude of these two depends on the PaM, since for nodes with a floating-point co-processor, ω will decrease in relation to τ. The value of ω also depends on whether the operands are in the local memory, LM or in some registers of the PaM. τ depends on the type of switching: circuit or packet. For the NCUBE/TEN it was determined [RWS88] than an eight-byte message transfer between two directly connected processors (one hop apart) takes 42 times as long as an eight-byte real addition and 32 times as long as an eight-byte real multiplication.

There are $n*p$ pixels and to update each one of them, we need [Fig. 10-1(b)] $9*\mu$ and $8*\alpha$, or altogether $17*n*p$ operations. The number of words to be transferred is $4*(\sqrt{n}+1)$ since each node holds n pixels stored as a $\sqrt{n}$-by-$\sqrt{n}$ array. Each iteration requires a single "synchronization," so that the inverse of the speedup is

$$1/\sigma := t(p)/t(1) \simeq (17*n*\omega + 4*\sqrt{n}*\tau + \zeta)/(17*n*p*\omega) \tag{10-2}$$

$$1/\sigma \simeq 1/p + (4*\sqrt{n}*\tau)/(17*n*p*\omega) \tag{10-3}$$

The second term is the "fractional communication overhead" (we called it *communication penalty π*) which, for large n, takes the form

$$\pi \simeq (\text{constant}/\sqrt{n})*(\tau/\omega) \tag{10-4}$$

Equation (10-3) shows that the constant is in this case 4/17 and of principle relevance is the fact that it is a number of order unity.

The penalty π depends only on the hardware through the ratio κ/Ω which is shown in [Fea88] to be approximately 2 for the Caltech Cubes (κ is the communication, Ω is the computation time). The communication speed may increase in the future with optical communications, but so will the computational speed. π should remain where it is today.

The penalty π depends on the size of the domain through the grain size n. For fixed n, π is independent of the number of processors. *It does not grow with increasing number of processors.* This is important since it again points to the scalability of Cubes.

With d being the dimension, Eq. (10-4) can be written as

$$\pi \simeq \kappa*c/[n**(1/d)] \tag{10-5}$$

With small exceptions, $0.1 \leq c \leq 10$, and π represents a generalized surface-to-volume ratio which is always proportional to $n**(-1/d)$ for a grain size (volume) of n. *The choice of the grain size strongly influences κ and through it also the speedup σ.*

Consider changing the local algorithm illustrated in Fig. 10-1 to one in which the updated value of the pixel at any point is a function of all other pixels in the image. In this case:

$$\kappa = n*(n*p)*\tau \tag{10-6}$$

where n is the number of pixels in the node and $n*p$ the number of pixels in the image. The optimal implementation leads to a total communication time of

$$\kappa = n*(p-1)*\tau \qquad (10\text{-}7)$$

In Eq. (10-7), $n*(p-1)$ is the number of pixels stored outside the node. We find in this case that the communication penalty takes the form:

$$\pi = \kappa/\Omega \simeq (1/n)*(\tau/\omega) \qquad (10\text{-}8)$$

The comparison of Eqs. (10-4) and (10-8) illustrates an important point. The communication overhead π depends on the ratio of communication to calculation and not simply on the amount of communication. The nearest-neighbor algorithm leading to Eq. (10-4) involves a minimal absolute amount of communication but it also requires minimal calculation. As a result, π is not particularly small. The fully connected algorithm analyzed in Eqs. (10-6)–(10-8) involves much more communication, but even more calculation. Thus we find that the ratio π is very small.

. . . This approach to the analysis of communication overhead has shown the importance of two fundamental parameters of the complex system. One is the *size* of the problem as embodied in the grain size n when the problem is to be mapped onto a Cube. The second important parameter is the system dimension d. The value of d in systems comprising the problem and the computer are important determinants of the effectiveness of the computational mapping. Note that d can be equal to, greater than, or less than the natural topological dimension.[Fea88]

We have already mentioned other ways of reducing the communication overhead: Overlapping computations with communications and adjusting the dimension of a sub-cube to the problem at hand.

10–1.2 The mapping problem

The mapping of a problem requires the assignment of a set of parallel tasks to a set of nodes such that some performance criterion (e.g., σ or π) is optimized. In mapping the algorithm to a Cube, it is important how data are distributed across the LMs, how the computational load is balanced, and whether the program repeats identical computations.

1. Data is distributed because there is either not enough space in the LMs or because communication time is to be minimized. (In some cases it is possible to reduce interprocessor communication by replicating some or all of the data across some or all PaMs.) The size of the LMs limits the replication of data.

2. Often the workload is not known at the start of the program and is adjusted dynamically by averaging the load over neighboring nodes. To reduce the communication time of load-adjustment, sometimes the neighbors exchange data without bothering the manager.

3. On a unicomputer the time can be reduced by using computed values repeatedly instead of recomputing it [Code 10-1(a) vs. (b)]. On a Cube it may be faster to recompute rather than to broadcast a value [Code 10-1(c) vs. (d)].

```
(a)  y := f (x) ;                              (d)  if me=0 then
     for i in 1..n loop z(i):=g(i,y); end;          y:=f (x) ;
(b)  for i in 1..n loop z(i):=(i,f(x)); end;        broadcast y to
(c)  y:=f (x) ;                                      other nodes else
     r:=g(i,y) ;                              receive g(i,f(x)) into y; end;
```

Code 10-1

For various mappings, the standard ordering is based on (recursively defined) Binary Reflected Gray Code (BRGC). With one bit the BRGC sequence is 0,1. With two bits, take first this sequence, followed by the same sequence in reversed order: (01),(10). If you prefix the first with 0, the second with 1, you get the sequence for two bits, namely 00, 01, 11, and 10. In the same way, we get the two sequences

```
000, 001, 011, 010, 110, 111, 101, 100 decimal=(0,1,3,2,6,7,5,4)
```

Next, reverse this to get a second row, then prefix the first row by 0 and the second row by 1 to get

```
0000, 0001, 0011, 0010, 0110, 0111, 0101, 0100; 0 - (0,1,3,2,6,7,5,4)
1100, 1101, 1111, 1110, 1010, 1011, 1001, 1000; 1 - (4,5,7,6,2,3,1,0)
```

This can be summarized by defining $G(i)$ recursively as $G(1) = \{0,1\}$, $G(i) = 0\{GS(i-1)\}, 1\{GR(i-1)\}$ where GS and GR are the straight and reverse Gray codes and $k\{\ \}$ means to prefix each element of set $\{\ \}$ by k. Note in particular that in a Karnaugh map [Man79], the BRGC sequence is obtained [Fig. 10-1(c)] by following a closed path through the map.

The main attraction of these sequences is that consecutive elements differ in only one bit (see the Karnaugh map). If we interpret the terms in a BRGC sequence as node numbers, then nearest neighbors in the sequence will also be physical neighbors. This allows mapping a problem on a Cube using only nearest neighbor connections. The BRGC code has two additional advantages. First, it is periodic: the first and last element in the sequence also differ by just one bit. Second, two elements of the BRGC sequence that are a power of 2 apart differ in at most two bits.

Figure 10-2(a) shows how a Cube of $d = 3$ is mapped into a *ring* (as a problem, do the same for $d = 4$). For the convolution problem, the mapping should be to a *mesh*. Regular cases, e.g., Fig. 10-2(b), can be assigned to the PaM mesh of Fig. 10-2(c). The communication requirement is very regular—each task needs to communicate with each of its neighboring tasks. The outer periphery of the tasks does not exhibit this regularity. (The program is similar to an ASP program in that a communication phase follows each computation phase in each iteration.)

In general, if the problem mesh can be mapped straightforward into a node mesh as in Figs. 10-2(b) and (c), then the load is balanced. However, as shown in Fig. 10-2(d), if

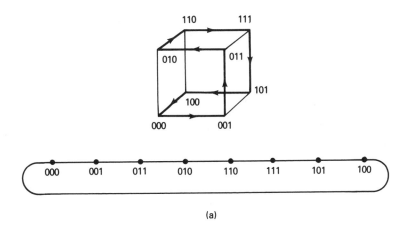

(a)

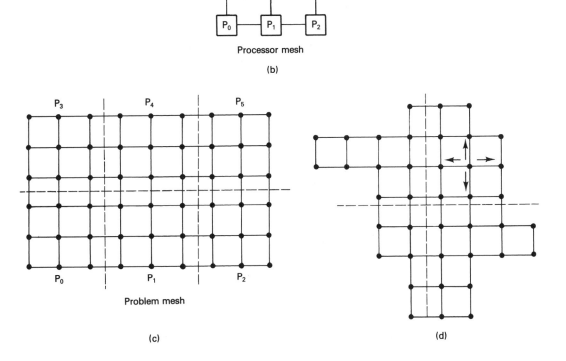

Processor mesh

(b)

Problem mesh

(c)

(d)

Figure 10-2 Various mappings of the Cube. Courtesy of K. Schwan et al: ''Mapping parallel Applications to a Hypercube''

the problem-mesh does not bear any simple relation to the node-mesh the load is not balanced. A mapping is required that will effectively map the tasks of the problem onto the nodes of the cube so that the computational load is uniformly balanced among the nodes and the overhead due to interprocessor communication is minimized.

> The speedup of the program corresponding to Fig. 10-2(b) can be estimated as follows: On a single computer we will need the time of $t(1) = n*\omega$ if there are n tasks and each of them takes time ω. The number of tasks mapped into node q is $T(q)$. The computation time for this node is $T(q)*\omega$. The amount of time spent by a processor for communication will depend on the number of values that need to be transferred to neighbor processors from processor q. For example, in Fig. 10-2(b) and (c), processor P(4) needs to communicate a total of nine values per iteration step: three to P(5), three to P(1), and three to P(3). If the communication time per iteration step for processor q is denoted $C(q)$, the iteration step completion time on the parallel processor system is given by[†]

$$t(p) := \max\{T(q)*\omega + C(q)\} \tag{10-9}$$

The best mapping would minimize $t(p)$, but it is difficult to accurately model the communication times (due to set-up times, time for forwarding through intermediate nodes, possible overlap of communication with computation etc.), and the determination of optimal assignment is NP-complete. Since, in practice, optimal assignments are not really necessary, near-optimal assignments are adequate.

Heuristic approaches to node mappings are used. They attempt

> to separately minimize the maximal $\omega*T(q)$ and $C(q)$ values among the processors (rather than minimizing the combined sum of the two) by:
>
> - trying to allocate equal number of processes to each processor, thus achieving minimal $\omega*T(q)$ through load-balancing.
> - trying to allocate processes among processors such that only nearest-neighbor communication is ever required (this is especially important with the Intel iPSC running under the Intel Node OS because of the very high message set-up times that are involved).
> - trying to collect physically close sets of processes into clusters with as small a perimeter/area ratio as possible, so as to minimize the number of values needing interprocessor communication at each step. [Sea7b]

An approach is next described to achieve the above objectives. First, the total number of tasks N is divided by the number of nodes p to determine the number of tasks to be allocated to each node processor in order to achieve uniform load distribution. In the example of Fig. 10-3, 48 processes need to be allocated among the six processors, i.e., eight processes per processor will result in perfect balancing of the computational load.

[†]K.Schwan et al: ''Mapping Parallel Applications to a Hypercube,'' in pp. 141–54 of M.T. Heath: ''Hypercube Multiprocessors,'' SIAM Press © 1987. Reprinted by permission.

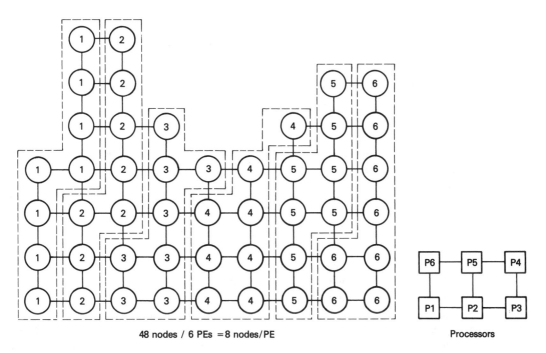

48 nodes / 6 PEs = 8 nodes/PE   Processors

Figure 10-3   A particular mapping. Courtesy of K. Schwan et al: "Mapping parallel Applications to a Hypercube"

In order that the method guarantees communication locality, the problem-mesh should satisfy the following condition: If the maximum number of process-nodes in any column is $N(C)$, and the maximum number of process-nodes in any row of the problem-mesh is $N(R)$, then

$$|N/p| > \min[N(C), N(R)] \tag{10-10}$$

The method groups processes from one or more adjacent rows (columns) into "strips" such that each process needs to communicate only with processes in the same strip or the (single) strip on either side. Starting at one corner of the problem-mesh, processes are counted off, either along the row [if $N(R) >= N(C)$] or along the columns [if $N(C) >= N(C)$] till all the processes in that row (column) have been selected. [MaV87]

To fill the quota, tasks are then picked from the next row(s) (column) and allocated to one of the processors. The next strip is formed by continuing to pick processes from the incompletely covered row (column). When that row (column) is complete tasks from the next row (column) are selected that require communication with any task already assigned to a node. Additional tasks are picked from the same rows (columns) so that they are contiguous to those already selected, and overflowing to the next row (column) if necessary.

Thus, groups of processes are selected in such "strips," each containing an optimal number of processes to uniformly balance the computational load. Each strip spans the width (length) of the problem-mesh, so that each strip has exactly one neighbor strip on either side of it. Thus the processes that any given process needs to communicate with will lie either on the same strip or on one of the neighbor strips. Strips are allocated to processors in such a way that neighbor strips are mapped onto adjacent processors, thus guaranteeing complete locality of interprocessor communication. [MaV87]

This mapping results in long strips and hence such that the ratio perimeter/area is high. Schemes have been derived to have a more square division [Aea86], but generally they fail to achieve perfect load-balancing.

10–1.3 Broadcast and Accumulation

In a Cube, broadcast is done using a "spanning tree" such as shown in Fig. 10-4(a) for broadcast from node 0 (binary 0000) to all nodes 1 to 15 (binary 1111). It can be seen that at each transfer a single bit is changed so that all communications between pairs of nodes take place along direct Cube links. Note also that since there are $d = \log(p)$ bits for $p = 2**d$, *the time for broadcast is proportional to log(p)*. If a long packet is to be broadcast, it could be segmented into smaller packets which would be sent in a pipelined fashion through the Cube.

Another tree is shown in Fig. 10-4(b).

(The broadcast from the root to all nodes takes d time units, which factor $(2**d-1)/d$ over the corresponding time of say a ring with $2**d$ nodes.) It is constructed as follows: First the 0. . .0 is changed so that one 0 in inverted. From this level on, the tree is constructed sequentially . . . by using the rules that the identities of the children of each node are obtained by inverting one of the zero bits of the identity of the parent that follow the rightmost unity bit [BaT89].

A global sum can be accumulated by following the spanning tree [Fig. 10-4(a)] in the reverse order. At the first step each of the nodes 8..15 sends their partial sums to the node above them which adds it to their partial sum, then nodes 4..7 send these to the nodes above them etc. The time is proportional to $\log(p)$. Broadcast and bottom-up tree operations are called fanout and fanin respectively.

10–1.4 Language Problems

A cube program consists of a *control task* which runs on the manager and p *node tasks*. The control task is similar to the program of the master in an ASP system. It coordinates, controls, and monitors the node (slave) tasks. Each of these runs on a single computer as a sequential program. As determined in ASP, the control task is usually shorter than the

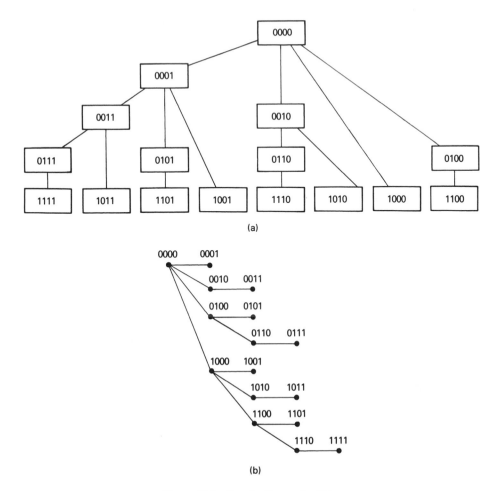

Figure 10-4   Broadcasting on the Cube

node tasks, so that a node could run it. Such a node is called a "workstation." Choosing it instead of the manager will improve the efficiency since the communication between the nodes is generally faster than between the nodes and the manager. We will use the name "manager" for both.

Cubes need routines for communication among the nodes and between the nodes and the manager. For this, they require only a few extensions to existing languages, namely those needed for opening a channel, closing a channel, sending a message, receiving a message, etc. Some of the operations for iPSC and iPSC/2 are listed in Table 10-1. Using them (and Ada), let us write Code 10-2 for calculating the area as defined in Fig. 6-5. The programs for the manager and each node are separated.

The last instruction is called a *global operation* and will produce in the manager a global sum (because of " + "), probably using the tree accumulation method. The Haydn effect may reduce the efficiency.

```
GET(n);                        -- The program of the manager starts here.
send(n,allnodes);              -- The manager broadcasts n to all nodes and waits.
recv(pi);                      -- It finally receives the value of pi and prints it.
PUT(pi);
                               -- Next is the program of a node.
open(man);                     -- Open the channel to the manager.
me := mynode(os);              -- Get the number of the node from the kernel
recv(n); h:=1.0/n;             -- Wait for the manager to sent n. Start the
sum := 0.0;                    -- calculation by setting h and the sum.
for i in me+1..n loop          -- i starts with me+1 because of next line
  x:=h*(FLOAT(i)-0.5);         -- For calculating x, see chapter 6.
  sum := sum+f(x);             -- It is assumed that f(x) is a known
end loop;                      -- function. For π it would be 4/(1+x²).
pi := h*sum;                   -- This completes the calculation of pi.
gop("+",pi,manager);
```

Code 10-2

Similar facilities are provided by an OS in the iPSC Cubes. The Caltech method [Fea88, Fea90] is to add application programs to the existing OS. The claim is that the communication is fast, since only short routines are called, but the full functionality of the OS is retained. The Caltech approach needs routines for: (1) Communication between the nodes, (2) Shift, broadcast, and combine operations, (3) Communication between the manager and the nodes, and (4) Mapping of the program topology onto the Cube.

We next define a *possible package for programming Cubes* along the lines of the Caltech approach, but using Ada instead of the C language.

Every node of a Cube has a number nn (from 1 to *p*) and *d* channels for communication with other nodes. The numbering of these channels may be such that they point to the node on the opposite end of the channel: If the channel connects nodes *i* and *j*, it has number *i* in node *j* and *j* in node *i*.

A node may, and probably will have more than a single process (task) executing concurrently. It is therefore necessary to distinguish between them, so that the messages are transferred to the correct task. Therefore, task numbers *tn* will be attached to messages.

TABLE 10-1 HYPERCUBE INSTRUCTIONS FOR MESSAGE PASSING

SEND	— Send a message to another task
RECV	— Receive a message from a task
GOP	— Execute a global operation
MYNODE	— The number of this node
NUMNODES	— How many nodes are there in the system.

An example might be send (type, buffer, size, node, task) in which the parameters are similar to those in the Caltech Cubes.

As a PROJECT, write a number of entries for a *package* "com." Two of them may be nrite(type,nbytes,buffer,node,process) and nread(type,nbytes,buffer). No node and task identifications are needed. The semantics are that invoking nrite will write (send) nbytes bytes from the "buffer" to "node" for "process." The message has a "type." A node may inquire as to its ID number by calling routine "whoami," and find out the number of nodes by calling "pnodes." Hence, "nread" does not need "node" and "process" parameters.

When nread is called by a program, the PaM checks if a message is ready in the buffer of the "node." If not, it will busy-wait until a message is available for reading. Note that if the "node" does not produce a message then the task calling "nread" is blocked and we may have starvation. The same behavior is shown by nrite. In both cases there is *synchronization* through the rendezvous. Incidentally, if two routines nread(11,20,*i*) and nread(11,20,*j*) are issued in node *j* and *i* simultaneously, we have a *deadlock*. It can be prevented if each nread is complemented by a corresponding nrite, and vice versa.

In a Cube, there may be no synchronization at all and the tasks may be blocked (i.e., put into a queue waiting for a message while the node is executing another task). Ada takes care of this case by providing a queue for every entry and the programmer has to make sure that a node works on multiple tasks—otherwise the entry node will wait idly. The tasks run *asynchronously* between calls on nrite and nread.

Most algorithms for Cubes are such that if a node is transmitting to its neighbor, so do *all* other nodes. We thus need an entry shift(type,sbytes,sstr,sn,dbytes,dstr,dn) which consists of a set of nreads and nrites from the sources to the destinations.

It was seen on a number of occasions how important *broadcast* is. In ASP it was always from the master to all slaves and was therefore easy to implement; not so in Cubes. Here, any node can be the source and the message may have to be passed to a subset of nodes on the Cube. To solve this problem, we may declare a d-dimensional array "nar" and use, say, a range to indicate which nodes should receive the message. The call would be bcst(type,sbytes,sstr,sn,nar,num) where num is the number of nodes stored presently in vector nar.

The inverse to bcst is "cmbn" which combines messages from *all* nodes and sends them to the manager. For this, it may have to concatenate, add, fill-in, etc., the messages. The particular function to be used is indicated by parameter *fn* of a call like cmbn(type,nbytes,str,"fn").

Next we turn to communication between the manager and specific nodes. One entry could be mtnrite(type,nbytes,str,nn) where *mtn* means "manager to node" (we could also have *ntm*) and which will write a message "str" of nbytes bytes from the manager to node nn. Obviously, we could use a loop over all nodes to implement broadcast, but the use of *bcst* is probably more efficient. Transfer of a message from node *nn* to the manager is by **entry** ntmrite(type,nbytes,str,nn).

In the same way we may declare the entries

```
mtnread(type,nbytes,str,nn)    for reading messages from the manager,
ntmread(type,nbytes,str,nn)    for reading messages from node "nn",
mtnbct for broadcast, ntmcbn   for broadcast and combining of messages
                               before they are sent to the manager.
```

All entries starting with shift are composed of writes and corresponding reads. For instance, in ntmrite it is not enough for node *nn* to have a message in *str*; the manager must be ready to accept the message for the transfer to actually happen.

We have indicated that each problem may have a best "problem topology" and that a Cube can be changed into a mesh, ring, spiral, tree, etc. We may envision routines of a package "top" (for topology) which will perform the *mapping* and provide the node number and consequently channel numbers required for the entries discussed above. Suppose we want to change $p = 2**d$ nodes of a Cube into a ring, with the manager or a particular node used as its number. The routine rinit(which,nar,pp,. . .) may be used for it.

Let us see how the codes above would rewrite Code 10-2 for *calculating the area*. The program might have in addition to declarations, etc., the instructions of Code 10-3.

```
GET(n); -- Manager program. n is the number of subintervals.
com.bcst(type,sbytes,sstr,sn,nar,num); -- Broadcast n to all nodes,
com.cmbn(type,nbytes,str,"+"); --and wait for all of them to arrive,
PUT(pi);                        -- add them up and print results.

pp := pnodes; -- pp is the number of nodes assigned to the problem.
me := whoami; -- me is the number of this node.
com.mtnread(type,nbytes,buffer,n); -- read n into this node.
h := 1.0/n;              -- h is the width of a strip in Fig.6-7
sum := 0.0;              -- one sum per node is initialized.
i := -p;                 -- prepares i to have a stepsize of p.
for j in me+1..n loop
  i := i+p;              -- i is the start-x of a rectangle in
  x := FLOAT(h*(i-0.5)); -- Fig.6-7, and x points to its midpoint.
  sum := sum+f(x);       -- Function f(x) is supposed to be known.
end loop;                -- The summation is as in Fig.6-7. with
pi := h*sum;             -- each node working on strips i,i+p etc.
ntmrite(type,nbytes,str,nn);      -- Write to the master which is
  -- waiting with com.cmbn(type,4,pi,"+") to perform the addition.
```

Code 10-3

10–2 MATRIX CALCULATIONS

10–2.1 Matrix Multiplication

Not every program is as simple as Code 10-3. The difficult parts are how to select the proper topology (mapping) for the problem and to distribute the data so that all nodes work at approximately the same time (balance) and how to minimize communication between the nodes. These *objectives* will ensure that nodes are not idle, that the communication penalty π is low (locality), and efficiency η is high. Matrix calculations provide good examples for these requirements.

The simplest case is to calculate the inner product of two vectors **x** and **y**: $z = \Sigma x(i)*y(i); i\Sigma = 1,\ldots n$. As in ASPs, the vectors are segmented into slices of equal (integer) length $h = n/p$. Each PaM(q) stores a slice of **x** and **y**, calculates the inner product w of these slices, and lets the root of a spanning tree accumulate

$$z = \Sigma w(j); j = (q-1)*h+1.$$

Assume first that the Cube was mapped into, say, a ring. The optimal choice for the root node is a "middle" node [Fig. 10-2(a)] that is at distance no more than $m = \lfloor p/2 \rfloor$ from every other node. The time to compute the inner product is then $h*\alpha + m*(\alpha + \tau)$. If we differentiate this expression for p, despite the fact that p is an integer, the approximate optimal number of PaMs is

$$p \simeq \sqrt{[2*\alpha*n/(\alpha + \tau)]} \tag{10-11}$$

Assume now that a Cube uses the spanning tree of Fig. 10-4(b). The total time to compute the inner product is then $n*\alpha/p + (\alpha + \tau)*\log(p)$ and the optimum number of processors is

$$p \simeq \alpha*n/(\alpha + \tau) \tag{10-12}$$

The optimal number of PaMs is much larger, and the time to solve the problem is much smaller than with a ring, because the communication using the spanning tree is much more efficient.

The next case is the multiplication of a matrix by a vector $\mathbf{A}*\mathbf{x} = \mathbf{b}$, e.g., of a 4-by-4 matrix **A** with a vector **x**:

$$\mathbf{x} = \begin{vmatrix} 1 \\ 2 \\ 3 \\ 4 \end{vmatrix}; \quad \mathbf{A}*\mathbf{x} = \begin{matrix} 1*A(1,1)+2*A(1,2)+3*A(1,3)+4*A(1,4); \\ 1*A(2,1)+2*A(2,2)+3*A(2,3)+4*A(2,4); \\ 1*A(3,1)+2*A(3,2)+3*A(3,3)+4*A(3,4); \\ 1*A(4,1)+2*A(4,2)+3*A(4,3)+4*A(4,4); \end{matrix} \tag{10-13}$$

As seen, column i of **A** is multiplied by $x(i)$, here simply by i. This shows that the product is a linear combination of the columns of **A** using the appropriate elements of **x**. This is almost trivial on a Cube were it not for problems of storage and broadcasting.

Suppose we have a matrix that is n-by-n and a vector that is n-by-1 with a large n which divides integrally by the number of nodes p (otherwise, a number of zero columns may be added). We will use numbering from 0 to $n-1$ or 0 to $p-1$ since this is consistent with the numbering of the Cube nodes.

There are two ways of storing the matrix columnwise: either each node stores p contiguous columns (*block*) storage or each stores columns $q+0, q+p, \ldots, n-p+1+q$ for $q = 0, \ldots, p-1$ (*wrap* storage). The second case resembles the way cards are normally dealt to players $0,1,2,\ldots,p-1$ and again players $0,1,2,\ldots,p-1$ until the list is exhausted. If two nodes are used, the first would store columns 1,2 in the block and 1,3 in the wrap storage, and the second would store 3,4 or 2,4 respectively.

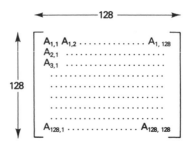

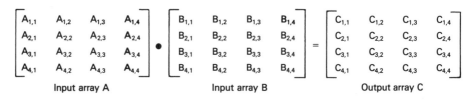

Figure 10-5 Solving matrix multiplication on the Cube

Reviewing Eq. (10-13) we see that for $n>>p$, most of the time required for computing the product will be in performing the combinations with each node computing its slice of the columns of **A**. There is good load-balancing since each node got the same number of columns and will operate on them independently and simultaneously. Initially, vector **x** has to be broadcast. Then, two communication steps are required: at the end of the first step the partial sums of products have to be received, in the second step they are accumulated by the manager or one of the nodes which participates in forming the combinations. As n grows with p remaining fixed, the *computation time* will increase more than the *communication time* since slices are getting "thick," but the communication requirements increase only slightly. We therefore expect π to be proportional to p/n approaching zero for increased n/p.

Next consider matrix multiplication $\mathbf{C} = \mathbf{A}*\mathbf{B}$. Suppose $n = 512$, but $p = 16$. The matrix [Fig. 10-5(a)] consists of 128-by-128 blocks ($512/4 = 128$).

Both the problem and node topologies are *meshes* (Fig. 10-5) but are easily changed into other types (e.g., a torus which will also be used). The submatrices (blocks) should be treated as single elements, so that the equation for any element is

$$C(i,j) := \Sigma A(i,k)*B(k,j); \; k\Sigma = 1, . . .4 \tag{10-14}$$

or for the elements of the first "row":

```
C(1,1)  :=  A(1,1)*B(1,1)+A(1,2)*B(2,1)+A(1,3)*B(3,1)+A(1,4)*B(4,1)
C(1,2)  :=  A(1,1)*B(1,2)+A(1,2)*B(2,2)+A(1,3)*B(3,2)+A(1,4)*B(4,2)
C(1,3)  :=  A(1,1)*B(1,3)+A(1,2)*B(2,3)+A(1,3)*B(3,3)+A(1,4)*B(4,3)
C(1,4)  :=  A(1,1)*B(1,4)+A(1,2)*B(2,4)+A(1,3)*B(3,4)+A(1,4)*B(4,4)
```

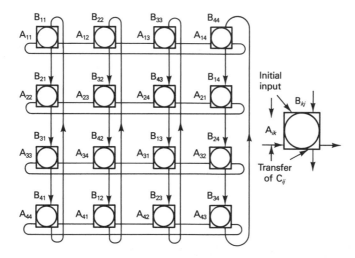

Figure 10-6 Solving matrix multiplication on the Cube

The number of operations for multiplying two 128-by-128 blocks is $\Omega = 2*n^3*\omega = 2^{22}*\omega$ or 2 million operations. This means that each node computes a sizable task before it communicates with its neighbors, ensures coarse granularity, and reasonable penalty.

No two identical products appear twice (e.g., the product $A(1,3)*B(3,1)$ appears only in the first equation and does not re-appear in any of the remaining 15 products). On the other hand, block $A(1,3)$ and others appear in all four equations. This shows that it might be a good idea to sequence $A(i,j)$ so that it is transferred from a block computing $C(i,1)$ to those computing $C(i,j)$ for $j = 2,3$, and 4. If we review the elements of the second "column" of C, e.g.,

$$C(2,2) := A(2,1)*B(1,2) + A(2,2)*B(2,2) + A(2,3)*B(3,2) + A(2,4)*B(4,2) \qquad (10\text{-}15)$$

then a shift is also required by blocks $B(i,j)$. This leads to data assignment, at least for reading, as in Fig. 10-6.

Examination of the equations reveals that elements $C(i,j)$ share elements of **A** and **B** between them. For example, $C(1,1)$ includes $A(1,2)*B(2,1)$, while $C(1,2)$ includes $A(1,2)*B(2,2)$. Therefore, the equations for $C(1,1)$ and $C(1,2)$ share element $A(1,2)$.

A mesh topology can exploit these relationships effectively. Each node can compute a partial product and add it to an accumulated sum. Because none of the partial products in a single equation share any **A** or **B** elements, they need not be retained for future iterations. Since equations for different indices do share **A** and **B** blocks, the nodes must not simultaneously use any of the blocks. Also, when a node is through using blocks $A(i,j)$ and $B(k,l)$, it must pass them to a neighboring node where it will be used next. Therefore, the proper mesh topology must allow a node to read two blocks *from its neighbors*, perform the multiplication and accumulation, and transfer the two blocks to its neighbors. Ideally, this transfer would be done in parallel with all 16 nodes making the same transfer (say, shift).

In a mesh, each point can communicate with its four neighbors. For the blocks on the periphery, four transfers must be possible, so that the final topology is a toroid shown in Fig. 10-6.

Figure 10-7 shows the four steps of the algorithm. As seen, each node computes at any time a different partial product. It reads the two blocks needed for it, from its west and

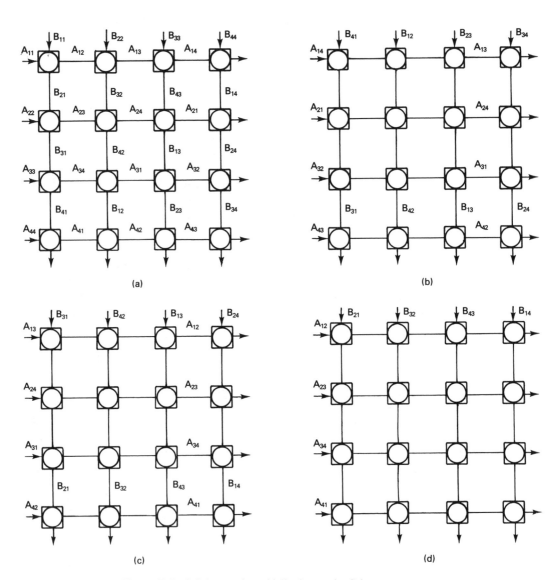

Figure 10-7 Solving matrix multiplication on the Cube

north neighbor. When finished, it transfers them to their east and south neighbors respectively. Initially, the blocks are read from the input as shown in Fig. 10-7(a). The reader is asked to follow the calculation through all four stages of Fig. 10-7 to see that it is conflict-free.

10–2.2 Factorization

The first method to solve $\mathbf{A}*\mathbf{x} = \mathbf{b}$ will be for a symmetric matrix $\mathbf{A}$ since then the factorization yields $\mathbf{A} = \mathbf{L}*\mathbf{L}^T$ ($\mathbf{L}^T$ is $\mathbf{L}$-transposed). No pivoting is required if $\mathbf{A}$ is positive-definite. For $n = 3$ we have

$$\begin{vmatrix} L(1,1) & 0 & 0 \\ L(2,1) & L(2,2) & 0 \\ L(3,1) & L(3,2) & L(3,3) \end{vmatrix} * \begin{vmatrix} L(1,1) & L(2,1) & L(3,1) \\ 0 & L(2,2) & L(3,2) \\ 0 & 0 & L(3,3) \end{vmatrix} = \begin{vmatrix} A(1,1) & A(1,2) & A(1,3) \\ A(1,1) & A(1,2) & A(1,3) \\ A(1,1) & A(1,2) & A(1,3) \end{vmatrix}$$

Note that A(1,1) = L(1,1)*L(1,1), A(2,2) = L(2,1)*L(2,1)+L(2,2)*L(2,2) and in general

$$L(i,i) = SQRT [A(i,i) - \Sigma L(i,j)*L(i,j)]; \; j\Sigma = 1,\ldots,i \qquad (10\text{-}16)$$

Matrix factorization is an interesting problem for Cubes because it poses two requirements which tend to inhibit efficiency. Precedence constraints require that some operations occur in a strict sequential order. As in the case of $\mathbf{A}*\mathbf{x}$, results computed by a node must be made available to *all* the other nodes. Both of these requirements tend to cause delays in which some nodes wait idly for some results to be either computed or communicated by other nodes.

Several algorithms for elimination and factorization on a HEP multiprocessor were developed in [GHL84]. Since HEP is a shared-memory multiprocessor, we mention only that they are all based on the following generic algorithm for Gaussian elimination:

```
for
  for
    for
      A(i,j) := A(i,j)-A(i,k)*A(k,j)/A(k,k);
    end; -- Factorization is the same with L on the left.
  end;
end;
```

A particular algorithm results by providing an order for the indices i, j, and k. It was found that from the six possible orderings

```
i,j,k;  i,k,j;  j,i,k;  j,k,i;  k,i,j;  and k,j,i
```

the best is the j,k,i order. "Best" is defined as the one that provides the highest number of possible parallel tasks and good load balancing.

A column-oriented factorization algorithm with **L** replaced by **A** is shown in Code 10-4. This algorithm [GLN87] is well suited for Cubes (and other PPSs that can apply medium- to coarse-granularity). In the inner loop, column j is modified by *each* previously computed k, an operation that may be denoted as $cmod(j,k)$. After column j is completely modified by all previous columns, it is first divided by $\sqrt{A(j,j)}$ to produce the final column j of **L**. We refer to this part as $cdiv(j)$. The two parts can be denoted as tasks and the algorithm is then as shown in Code 10-4.

```
for j in 0..n-1 loop                    --First part of Code 10-4.
  for k in 0..j-1 loop
    for i in j..n-1 loop
      A(i,j) := A(i,j)-A(i,k)*A(j,k);    -- is cmod (j,k).
    end;                                 -- end loop on i.
  end;                                   -- end loop on k.
  A(j,j) := SQRT(A(j,j));                -- See Eq. (10-16).
  for k in j+1..n-1 loop                 -- Starts cdiv(j).
    A(k,j) := A(k,j)/A(j,j);
  end;                                   -- end loop on k.
end;                                     -- end loop on j.

for j in 0..n-1 loop                    -- Second part of Code 10-4.
  for k in 0..j-1 loop
    accept cmod(j,k); end accept;
  end;                                   -- modification of column k.
  accept cdiv(j); end accept;            -- the division of column j.
end;                           -- end of index i and the entire computation.
```

Code 10-4

There is considerable potential for concurrency even if the concurrency within the two tasks is not used (because it would lead to a small-grained algorithm which is not suitable for a Cube). Note that $cdiv(j)$ cannot begin until $cmod(j,k)$ has been completed for all $k<j$, and column j can be used to modify subsequent columns only after $cdiv(j)$ has been completed (these are the precedence constraints referred to earlier). However, there is no restriction on the order in which the cmod tasks are executed, and cmod operations for different columns can be performed simultaneously. For example, after $cdiv(1)$ has been completed, all $cmod(j,1)$ for $j = 2, \dots$ could run concurrently.

Since in a Cube all memory is local (to the PaMs), each column computed in a node must be sent to the nodes that need it for updating their columns. Thus, broadcast is required which can be done in the way mentioned in Sec. 10-1. The algorithm is then as follows [GaH86]:[†]

[†]G.A. Geist, M.T. Heath: "Matrix Factorization on a Hypercube Multiprocessor," pp. 161–80 of M.T. Heath (Ed): "Hypercube Multiprocessors 1986," SIAM Press. Reprinted by permission.

for j **in** 0..n-1 **loop**
  --- if column j is one of "my" columns then *cdiv*(j).
  --- *communicate* globally j to all nodes which need it.
  --- for all my columns for which k>j do cmod(k,j);
end; -- of index j and the entire computation in a node.

In this algorithm the task *communicate* either sends or receives col-*j*, depending on whether the processor calling *communicate* is responsible for computing col-*j*. In either case, after returning from the *communicate* task, every processor now has a copy of col-*j* and uses it to modify any of its columns that may be affected. Note that the *cdiv* operation on a given column will be done only after all of its necessary modifications have taken place. Thus, the proper synchronization of the algorithm is implicit in the flow of completed columns through the network.

For simplicity we stated the message-passing Cholesky algorithm in a synchronous form: There is a strict alternation between computation and communication. It is possible to overlap the two, however, in an effort to mask some of the communication cost with computation. The philosophy here is to send out results at the earliest possible time in the hope that this will minimize any subsequent waiting for them. In particular, as soon as any column has had all of its modifications completed, the *cdiv* operation should be carried out immediately so that the broadcast of the resulting column of L can be started. Thus, a test is inserted into the *cmod* loop to detect completion of modifications to any column, in which case, the *cdiv* operation is carried out and the results transmitted before continuing with the remaining *cmod* operations. The effect of this strategy is to pipeline the computation of successive columns. [This increases the utilization of the nodes.]

The manner in which the matrix is mapped onto the processors will affect the communication requirements, the degree of concurrency, and the load balance among the processors. *We would like to minimize communication, maximize concurrency, and have a uniform work load across the processors. These objectives tend to conflict, however, and so we must weigh the trade-offs among them.* [GaH86] (Italics added by author.)

As for the choice between the block and wrap storage, once a PaM completes its slice, it remains idle for the balance of the calculation. From this point of view, the block storage is ineffective, since it keeps many PaMs idle; whereas the wrap mapping keeps them busy almost all the time. On the other hand, the block mapping has potentially smaller communication requirements, since each completed column needs to be sent only to higher numbered processors, rather than to all processors as in the wrap mapping. It was found experimentally in [GaH86] that when broadcast using the spanning tree is used, *the wrap mapping is consistently more efficient.*

Having factored matrix A into $L*L^T$, we have to solve the original set $A*x = b$, by first solving $L*z = b$ for z and then solving $L^T*x = z$ for x. The first part is not problematic since the matrix L can be preserved in its column mapping and the slices of z are then added. Unfortunately, if the "back-substitution" $L^T*x = z$ is executed, the matrix should be in the row mapped form. To preserve the mapping and thus reduce the amount of data movement, the use of the classical inner-product formulation is suggested [Rom87], namely:

```
for i in 0..n-1 loop
  for j in 0..i-1 loop
    b(i) := b(i)-L(i,j)*x(j);
  end;                              -- end of the loop on j.
  x(i) := b(i)/L(i,i);
end;                                -- end of the loop on i.
```

The j loop computes the inner product of row i of **L** with the first i elements of vector **x**. If we assume the columns of **L** distributed in the wrap mapping and the elements of **b** (and hence **x**) distributed to the nodes so that $b(i)$ is assigned to node $q = i \bmod p$, then the partial inner products $L(i,j)*x(j)$ can be executed in parallel. Next, these are added by the method discussed above; whereupon, $x(i)$ can be calculated by node q. The resulting pseudo-code is

```
for i in 0..n-1 loop
  s := 0.0;
  --- for all columns j<i in my slice do
  s := s+L(i,j)*x(j);
  --- add all values of s by the fan-in method into variable t.
  --- if b(i) is in my slice then
    x(i) := (b(i)-t)/L(i,i);
end;
```

This code is efficient inasmuch as the only communication required by it is contained in the summation, which is implemented using the spanning tree method that is $\log(p)$ long.

10–2.3 Elimination

Column storage, wrap mapping, broadcast (fanout), and summation (fanin) are assumed. To reduce a possible sequential bottleneck we should pivot and broadcast as soon as possible. While you work on a column and know this column is going to be the next pivot column, you should find the pivot immediately. To decrease the penalty π, a block algorithm could be used to produce fewer, but longer messages. The method is shown in pseudocode below paraphrased from [Mo186].[†]

> The outer loop of the algorithm involves k, the index of the variable to be eliminated. At the k-th step, the processor owning the k-th column of A assumes a temporary role as a root processor for that step. The root processor determines the pivot element and divides elements $k+1$ through n of the pivot column by the pivot to form the vector e of multipliers. During this time the other $p-1$ processors are logically idle, although some of them may actually be finishing the previous step. We refer to this part of the computation as the *sequential* portion of the algorithm since only one processor is active.
>
> After the root processor determines the multipliers, all the processors participate in the global send, so they all get copies of e. This is the *communication* portion.

[†]C. Moler: "Matrix Computations on Distributed Memory Multiprocessors," pp. 181–95 of M.T. Heath (Ed): "Hypercube Multiprocessors 1986," SIAM Press. Reprinted by permission.

```
m := 1;
for k in 1..n loop
  if myid = (k-1) mod p then
    --- find pivot in the m-th column of A.
    --- set vector e to (A(k+1..n,k)..A(n,k))/pivot;
    m := m+1;
    --- initiate broadcast of vector e;
  else
    --- participate in receiving vector e.
  end if;
  for j in 1..h loop -- h is, as usually, the width of a slice.
    s := A(k,j);
    for i in k+1..n loop
      A(i,j) := A(i,j)+s*e(i);
    end;                        -- end of the i-loop.
  end;                          -- end of the j-loop.
end;                            -- end of the k-loop.
```

Code 10-5

Most of the time is spent in the nested *j* and *i* loops, where each processor adds scalar multiples of *e* to each of its remaining active columns. This is the *parallel* portion of the algorithm since all the processors are active with arithmetic operations. Some of the processors may have one more active column than some of the others, but all the columns are the same length, so the load balancing is quite good. [Mo186].

Note the following:

1. We could have used all PaMs to determine the pivot. This would increase the utilization of the PaMs, since they all are active and none is idle. On the other hand, the order of the PaMs which compute vector *e* is determined ahead of the calculation and if the pivot is in the "wrong" PaM, the shifting would require too much time.

2. The operation **A**∗**x** is again useful.

3. The sequential and parallel steps correspond to those same steps when this algorithm is executed on an ASP.

4. Since the calculation is much more computationally expensive than the communication, the penalty ratio π should be low.

10–2.4 Sparsity

Next we discuss factorization of sparse matrices with a random distribution of zeros. For notational convenience, we collect the modification and division of column *j*: *cmod* (*k,j*) and *cdiv* (*j*) into a task *tcol*(*j*). An elimination tree like the one drawn in Fig. 10-8(b) for

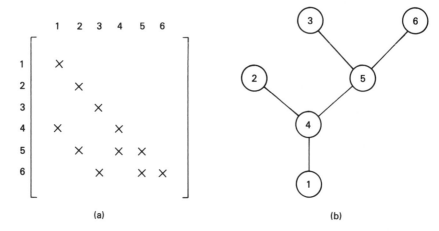

(a)   (b)

Figure 10-8   An elimination tree

the matrix of Fig. 10-8(a) is derived as follows: We start with node i on the diagonal and move vertically to the first nonzero element, from there move horizontally to the (always nonzero) diagonal and from there vertically to nonzero elements in columns not yet covered, and so on.

The main difference between the sparse and dense versions of the factorization algorithms is that for sparse $\mathbf{A}$, column j may no longer need to be modified by all columns $k<j$ of $\mathbf{L}$. Specifically, column j is modified only by columns k for which $L(j,k)/=0.0$, and following $cdiv(j)$, column j needs to be made available only to tasks $tcol(m)$ for which $L(m,j)/=0.0$. Thus, in Fig. 10-8, column 4 is to be modified only by column 1 and is not needed later. The elimination tree also provides precise information about the column dependencies. Specifically, we cannot execute $cdiv(i)$ until $cdiv(j)$ has been completed for all descendant nodes j of node i.

The elimination tree is used in an algorithm for elimination of sparse matrices described in [GLN87]. It uses "short and wide" elimination trees because they yield a low fill-in and low operation count. It was shown that such trees lend themselves well to parallel computation.

Specifically, in the elimination tree, if node i and node j belong to the same level of the tree, the tasks $tcol(i)$ and $tcol(j)$ can be performed independently so long as the tasks associated with their descendant nodes have all been completed. In order to gain high processor utilization, it is therefore desirable to assign, if possible, nodes on the same level of the tree to different processors. An overall tasks assignment scheme will then correspond to assigning the $tcol(i)$ tasks to successive processors in a breadth-first bottom-up manner from nodes of the elimination tree. [GLN87]

10–2.5 The Laplace equation

There are two ways to approach the solution of the Laplace equation on a Cube: either by using the odd-even reduction and odd-even elimination algorithms of Sec. 6-5, or directly from the geometrical basis of the problem. We have already discussed the first case, and shall deal next with the second.

We have seen in Sec. 6–6.2 that the "black-red" ordering leads to simple equations and an efficient algorithm. To achieve medium granularity, the algorithm should use the red-black ordering not to single points but to entire subareas like in Fig. 10-1 in which we color the squares alternately black and red. All points in the red areas can be updated first, and following node synchronization, black subareas are updated. The main structure of the pseudo-code is as follows.

Until a residual ϵ is small enough do steps 1 to 4 below:

1. Exchange edge values with neighboring PaMs.
2. Perform the update on all red subareas in parallel.
3. Exchange edge values with neighboring PaMs.
4. Update values in all black subareas in parallel.

Note that each PaM has a lot of calculations to perform in its subarea before it communicates the potentials on the boundary to its neighbors. The count Ω is therefore high enough and increases with greater subareas—but so does the amount of information to be transferred. The balance can be made almost perfect by making the subareas equal in size. This being so, the first step of exchanging edge values will be made in a "military" fashion: first each node sends values north, then all send information west, then south, and finally all send it east. The PaMs on the border of the region in which the equation is to be solved will be idle for some short time, but the loss is not significant and leads to simpler control.

The algorithm for the manager could be the following pseudocode:

```
--- Get data
--- Send it, including ε, to the nodes and start "update" procedures.
--- Wait for an indication that they have finished.
--- Receive the messages and deal with the output.
--- Terminate the program.
```

The algorithm for "update" is paraphrased from [Fea88] in Code 10-6.

As described earlier,

during the "red" phase of a cycle, edge data need only be received from neighboring black points, and need only be sent to neighboring points. The reverse is true during the "black" phase. In the illustrated implementation, we have skirted the issue that only half of the edge values need be communicated during any call to *edge*. An intelligent implementation of *edge* should be designed to recognize whether the current phase is red or black, and communicate only the needed values.

A function similar to *edge* was already discussed in Chap. 3. Each node program requires additional storage space for a single layer or "guard ring" of points from (to) a neighbor. These slots are to be filled with values supplied by interprocessor communication.

```
procedure update(eps) is
begin r := 1.0;              -- r will accumulate the residuals.
  while r<ε loop
    edge;                    -- The call to exchange values with neighbors
    for i,j in range     -- Range of the red subareas
      --- update by taking the average of each point.
      --- compute the sum of all residuals.
    end loop;
    edge;                    -- The call to exchange values with neighbors
    for i,j in range     -- Range of the black subareas
      --- update by taking the average of each point.
      --- compute the sum of all residuals.
    end loop;
    --- r is the sum of all residuals (or their squares, or maximum).
  end loop;                  -- end of the while loop.
end update;


direction := (north, west, south, east); -- This is an enumeration.

procedure shift (direction) is
begin
  --- Load edge values into the buffer of "direction"
  --- Send the buffer values to "direction" while accepting them from
                     --- the opposite direction ( (d+2) MOD 4).
  --- Store values from opposite direction for use in "update".
end shift;

procedure edge is
begin
  shift(west);
  shift(east);
  shift(north);
  shift(south);
end;
```

Code 10-6

In our rectangular decomposition geometry, the exchange is accomplished by four successive calls to *shift*. First, a processor's values falling along the right edge are copied into a communication buffer and sent to the right neighbor while complementary left edge data arrive from the left neighbor. These data are stored in the appropriate guard ring locations, and the "right-shift" pass is ended. This is followed by analogous "left," "up," and "down-shift" passes, after which the guard rings of all processors have been filled with up-to-date values. We have made use here of the ability of *shift* to transparently handle nonexistent neighbors in the case of processors with fewer than four two-dimensional neighbors. [Fea88]

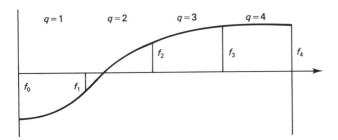

Figure 10-9   Searching on the Cube

Following the completion of the *edge* communication step, each processor independently performs a sequential update on its red points according to Fig. 10-1 (except that each point represents a square area). In this sequential process, each nodal value is immediately overwritten by its updated value. The communication step is then repeated, followed by an update of all black points.

10–3 SEARCHING AND SORTING

Searching on a Hypercube is very similar to that on an ASP, especially if we map the nodes into a ring. The algorithm as proposed in [FaJ86] starts with the sequential initialization of setting up the various *x* values and the number of iterations. The algorithm (see Fig. 10-9) has the following pseudocode:

1. Broadcast the *x*'es from start-node to all other nodes.
2. Node *i* computes the function $f(i)$ at the right end of its subinterval.
3. Pass this $f(i)$ to the right neighbor ($q = i + 1$, except for $q = 4$ in Fig. 10-9).
4. Each node *i* computes $f(i-1)*f(i)$. In node 2 it is negative, so $x(1)$ is the new start node. Generalizing: The subdivision is again divided into *p* equal parts and the algorithm repeated.

The transfer of a value to every "right" neighbor presents no problems on a ring. The broadcast assumes that all destination nodes must be ready to receive the information on any link. In particular, on the FPS T-series on which this program was run, this means that each node must actually receive something on every link; and hence each node must send something on every link. The transfer was organized so that all nodes pass dummy information until they have real information and then pass on the real information. Step 1 of the algorithm is therefore equivalent to

```
for i in 1..d loop
   hyp.send(real or dummy information on link i);
    accept hyp.recv(information on link i) do...end;
end loop; -- This is a parallel loop inside sequential step 1.
```

On the FPS T-series computer, it is possible to communicate simultaneously in both directions over the same link. This allows the use of tasks sending and receiving in parallel. Otherwise, procedures would replace tasks and sequential execution would replace the parallel execution of broadcast.[†] [FaJ86]

To calculate the speedup, the interval d is assumed to be normalized to 1 and reduced to $1/k$ in the end. The root of $f(x)$ will be determined with an accuracy of $1/k$. To make the analysis simpler, k is assumed to be a power of 2 (i.e., $2**d$ for some d). For i iterations $k = (2**d)**i$, we have that $i*d = \log(k)$. In each iteration only one function is evaluated. If this takes time φ then the time on a single computer is $d*i*\varphi$ or

$$t(1) = d*i*\varphi = \varphi*\log(k); \tag{10-17}$$

In the parallel case, each of the i iterations reduces the interval by $1/k$. Each slave has to be given the x for which it has to compute $f(x)$. This will take time τ where τ is the time it takes to transfer a word (by broadcast). Having computed $f(x)$, each slave sends the value of $f(x)$ to its "right" neighbor so that each can compute the products $f(x')*f(x'')$, etc. Altogether, the time is $t(p) = i*(\varphi+2*\tau)$. The inverse of the speedup is therefore

$$1/\sigma = (\varphi+2*\tau)/(\varphi*\log(k)) = 1+2*\tau/\varphi/\log(k) \tag{10-18}$$

If we assume that the time φ to compute the function is much higher than the transfer time τ, we have $\tau/\varphi \cong 0$ and

$$\sigma \cong \log(k) \tag{10-19}$$

Sorting. An argument can be made as to what is considered a sorted list.

Case (a): We may assume that the data is initially distributed (or input) into all p nodes and the sorted list also resides in all nodes, but in such a way that if the Cube is mapped into a ring, then the keys in node i are all lower (or all are higher) than those in node $i+1$. In this way, the data can be used for any further processing following the sorting of it.

Case (b): We may assume the data initially in a single node (mostly, node 0) and the sorted list also stored in the same node. Additional time is needed to distribute the list among the p nodes and collect it in node 0. We discuss first case (a) and then how to distribute and collect the lists for case (b).

The first algorithm, as proposed in [Fea88], is as follows. Divide the list to be sorted between the nodes into approximately equal parts and let each node sort its part of the list. The merging is now done by "fanin" of the sorted sublists in a manner similar to fanin addition. The two lists, each of size, say n, are merged into one sorted list of $2*n$ items (stored collectively in two nodes). For a simplified (and inefficient) version of comparing-merging, we introduce the notation ":" for "compare" and use parentheses to bracket the stored keys (either in the memory or a buffer). Sorting proceeds so that two sublists are merged as exemplified below for the list from Sec. 6-1 and $p = 2$

[†]J.M. Francioni, J.A. Jackson: "An implementation of a 2^d Section Root Finding Method for the FPS T-Series," pp. 495–500 of M.T. Heath: "Hypercube Multiprocessors 1987," SIAM Press. Reprinted by permission.

$$(2) : (1,5,6,8) \text{ and } (2,3,4,7,9) : (8)$$

i.e., the smallest element (2) from node 2 is transferred to node 1 where it is compared with the sorted sublist (1,5,6,8), while the largest element from node 1, namely 8, is sent to node 2 where it is compared with the largest element first. Note that the sublists were first internally sorted in the same way—both from low to high keys.

On a Cube the communication between any two nodes may proceed in both directions at the same time. While the smallest key in node 2 is sent to node 1, the largest is transferred from node 1 to 2. Then they are inserted into the proper position. When this has occurred, the following result is obtained:

$$(3) : (1,2,5,6) \text{ and } (3,4,7,8,9) : (6)$$

Elements 3 and 6 were swapped.

In this way, two more steps produce the sorted sublists:

$$(4) : (1,2,3,5) \text{ and } (4,6,7,8,9) : (5)$$
$$(5) : (1,2,3,4) \text{ and } (5,6,7,8,9) : (4)$$

There is nothing to merge anymore and this is taken as a sign that the two sublists are sorted. The problems with this sorting method are how to get the initial sublists into the nodes, how and where to store the sorted list, how to perform the above ''compare-exchange'' step, which of the sorting procedures to use for sorting inside the PaMs, and how to use buffers for larger lists. We will next discuss some of these items.

Let us improve the compare-exchange procedure. First, the new lists were constructed by actually copying the items from one memory location to another. If instead of sorting keys, we sort large records, we would not move them in the memory—we would use pointers to records instead and manipulate these. Also, sometimes one of the PaMs had to wait for the other, which leads to an unbalanced load and lower utilization. What is even more important, a single element was sent from one node to the other, so the communication penalty π may have been large. Loading can be made more balanced and the penalty may be decreased by sending more than a single element through the link. The exact number of keys to be sent depends on the size of the buffers—we will assume that two keys can be sent over. For the list above with key 0 added, the steps would be as below where '' $->\#$'' means '' stored in the new sublist.''

```
(0, 2) :  (1, 3, 5, 6, 8)  and  (0, 2, 4, 7, 9)  :  (8, 6)
1)   0 : 1 -> 0                          1)   9 : 8 -> 9
2)   2 : 1 -> 1                          2)   7 : 8 -> 8
3)   2 : 3 -> 2                          3)   7 : 6 -> 7
4)   buffer is empty, so finished        4)   4: 6 -> 6 buffer empty.
```

During the next communication phase the buffers are filled again.

```
   (4) :  (3) and (4) :  (5)
5)   4 : 3 -> 3              5)   4 : 5 -> 5
6)   buffer is empty; finished   6)   Output 4
```

In Code 10-7 we paraphrase the code of [Fea88].

```
procedure ceh is -- comp-exchange high; this PaM contains highest keys
nitems: INTEGER; -- the number of items in the sublist of this PaM.
nbuf : INTEGER;   -- the number of items to be kept in the buffer.
ar : array(0..n-1) of INTEGER; -- needed for declarations below.
buf(1..nbuf) of integer        -- Declaring the buffer.
oldlist, newlist : ar; nml: INTEGER;
    -- Note: This part appears at the head of the cel (compare-exchange
    --       low) below and will not be repeated.
    --- Divide oldlist into blocks of nbuf keys, with smallest key first
    --- Exchange first block of oldlist with block from the other node,
    ---         store incoming block in buffer buf.
  nml := i := nitems-1; j := nbuf-1;
  for k in reverse 0..nml loop
    if oldlist(i) >= buf(j) then
      newlist(k) := oldlist(i); i := i-1;
    else
      newlist(k) := buf(j);
      if j=0 then              -- all keys in buf have been processed.
        --- Exchange next block of oldlist with next block from the
        ---                    other PM, store incoming block in buf.
        n := nbuf-1;
      else
        j := j-1;
      end;          -- end of the inner if
    end;            -- end of the outer if
  end;              -- end of the for loop
end;                -- end of the procedure

procedure cel is --compare-exchange low: this PaM contains lowest keys
    --- The same declarations as in ceh.
    --- Divide oldlist into blocks of nbuf keys, with largest key first
    --- Exchange first block of oldlist with block from the other node,
    ---         store incoming block in buffer buf.
  i := 0; j := 0;
  for k in 0..nml loop
    if oldlist(i) =< buf(j) then
      newlist(k) := oldlist(i); i := i+1;
    else
      newlist(k) := buf(j);
      if j=nml then -- all keys in buf have been processed
        --- Exchange next block of oldlist with next block from the
        --- other PaM, store incoming block in buf.
        j := 0;
      else
        j := j+1;
      end;          -- end of the inner if
    end;            -- end of the outer if
  end;              -- end of the for loop
end;                -- end of the procedure
```

Code 10-7

A PaM trying to communicate must wait if the other PaM is busy. The number of times such PaM are idle will be lessened if we increase the buffer size. In the extreme limit, if the buffer size is set equal to nitems, only one exchange need take place per compare-exchange and no waiting occurs. This approach, however, means that many items (on average, half of them) are transferred unnecessarily. [Fea88]

The programs stop when each PaM has gone through the k-loop nitems times since then nitems keys were transferred to the newlist.

Quicksort can be used instead of Selection Sort. The difference to the sequential algorithm is that once a sublist has been divided once more into two halves, *each half is sent to a subcube*. Once d splits occur, there remain no further splits, and the algorithm continues by switching to an internal quicksort on each node.

A "Hyperquicksort" is described in [Wag87] as follows:

1. Distribute the items evenly to all of the nodes.
2. Each node sorts the items it has using quicksort.
3. Node 0 broadcasts its median key K to the rest of the Cube.
4. Each node separates its items into two groups: those whose keys are less or equal K and those whose keys are greater than K.
5. Break up the cube into two subcubes: the lower subcube comprising nodes 0 through $[2**(d-1)-1]$ and the upper subcube consisting of nodes $2**(d-1)$ through $2**d-1$. Each node in the lower subcube sends its items whose keys are larger than K to its adjacent node in the upper subcube. Likewise, nodes in the upper subcube send their items whose keys are less than K to their corresponding adjacent nodes in the lower subcube. When this step is completed, all items whose keys are less than K are in the lower subcube while all those whose keys are larger than K are in the upper subcube.
6. Each node now merges together the group it just received with the one it kept so that its items are once again sorted.
7. Repeat steps 3..6 on each of the two subcubes. This time, node 0 will correspond to the lowest numbered node in the subcube, and the value d will be one less.
8. Keep repeating steps 3..7 until the subcubes consist of a single node (i.e., a total of d times). At that point, the list will be sorted.

For an even, initial distribution of the keys of random order, with a reasonably good guess of the median key, and without counting the distribution and collecting of data, the time for quicksort was

$$\text{time(quicksort)} \;=\; \mathbf{O}(n*\log(n)+0.5*d^2+0.5*d+d*n) \qquad (10\text{-}20)$$

The term $n*\log(n)$ represents the serial sorting time. The term $0.5*d$ can be neglected. For a large n, Hyperquicksort will be efficient.

The time of distributing and collecting the data depends on channel start-up times and the length of messages. Additionally, the channels are multiplexed, so that in a Cube, like in the T-series which have only four links, the multiplexer can be used by only one channel at a time. The routing which was used by [SaZ87] is described by Fig. 10-10.

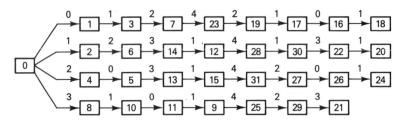

Figure 10-10   Routing for sorting on the Cube

Node 0 first sends the messages (subsequences) destined for nodes 18, 20, and 24 along links 0, 1, and 2 respectively. Nodes 1, 2, and 4 forward those messages to nodes 3, 6, and 5 while node 0 sends the messages destined for nodes 16, 22, 26, and 21 to nodes 1, 2, 4, and 8, and so on. All messages reach their destinations more or less concurrently at step 8. The collection of messages from the nodes is the inverse of this process. Note that the pair of links used by each node is not congruent mod 4 so that no pair shares the same multiplexer.ᵗ [SaZ87]

The assumption that the original complete list is stored in node 0 and a different algorithm for bitonic sorting appeared also in [SaZ87].

10–4 PROJECTS

1. Change the sorting routine into a parallel sorting program by using tasks. Change it further so that p instead of two tasks are used. Calculate an average speedup and verify it by running a number of simulation studies.

2. Change the sorting procedure by using the bubble-sort, cocktail-shaker and especially, the quicksort procedure. In this last case, determine by how much the Haydn effect will decrease the speedup.

3. Change the parallel search routines so that: There are p tasks, all tasks are going in the same direction, say "up," and abort all tasks once one of them has located the given key.

4. Use pivoting in a Gaussian elimination program. Calculate its speedup σ and communication penalty π.

5. Write a Cube program based on the Poof algorithm.

6. Write a Cube program based on the Jacobi iteration.

7. Instead of factoring $\mathbf{A} = \mathbf{L} * \mathbf{L}^T$ ($\mathbf{L}^T$ is L-transposed), we can also use a diagonal matrix $\mathbf{D}$ and factor according to

$$\mathbf{A} = \mathbf{L} * \mathbf{D} * \mathbf{L}^T \tag{10-21}$$

where matrix $\mathbf{L}$ now has 1's on the diagonal. This factorization results from $\mathbf{A} = \mathbf{L} * \mathbf{U}$ with $\mathbf{U}$ an upper triangular matrix as follows.

ᵗS.R. Seidel, L.R. Ziegler: "Sorting on Hypercubes," pp. 285–91 of M.T. Heath (Ed): "Hypercube Multiprocessors 1987," SIAM Press, 1987.

Multiply by $\mathbf{D}*\mathbf{D}^{-1}$ ($\mathbf{D}^{-1}$ is $\mathbf{D}$-inverse) to get $\mathbf{A} = \mathbf{L}*\mathbf{D}*\mathbf{D}^{-1}*\mathbf{U}$. Rename $\mathbf{D}^{-1}*\mathbf{U}$ as $\mathbf{Y}$ so that

$$\mathbf{A} = \mathbf{L}*\mathbf{D}*\mathbf{Y} \qquad (10\text{-}22)$$

Matrix $\mathbf{A}$ is symmetric, so that $\mathbf{A} = \mathbf{A}^T$, $\mathbf{L}^T = \mathbf{U}$, and $\mathbf{L} = \mathbf{U}^T$. By insertion we find that

$$\mathbf{Y}^T*\mathbf{D}*\mathbf{L}^T = \mathbf{U}^T*\mathbf{D}^{-1}*\mathbf{D}*\mathbf{L}^T = \mathbf{L}*\mathbf{D}*\mathbf{Y} \qquad (10\text{-}23)$$

With $\mathbf{L}^T = \mathbf{Y}$, this is an identity since both the right and the left sides of it are $\mathbf{L}*\mathbf{D}*\mathbf{L}^T$. Inserting $\mathbf{L}^T = \mathbf{Y}$ in Eq. (10-23) leads to Eq. (10-22). Program the Cholesky factorization with the diagonal matrix $\mathbf{D}$, and the Jordan elimination procedure.

8. The wave equation [Fea88], with t, z, and c being time, displacement, and a constant, respectively, is

$$(1/c^2)*(\partial^2 z/\partial t^2) - (\partial^2 z/\partial x^2) \qquad (10\text{-}24)$$

Inserting approximations for the partial derivatives, we get:

$$z(i,t+\Delta t) := 2*z(i,t) - z(i,t-\Delta t) + k^2*[z(i-1,t) - 2*z(i,t) + z(i+1,t)] \qquad (10\text{-}25)$$

where i is a nodal point in spacial discretization and $k = c*\Delta t/\Delta x$.
The algorithm suggested in [Fea88] for each PaM is:

  a. Initialize starting values.

  b. Identify neighbor communication channels required.

  c. Exchange end nodal values with neighbors.

  d. Perform update $z(i,t) - >z(i,t+\Delta t)$ on all nodal points.

  e. Goto (c); repeat until done.

Program the above algorithm. If you find it too hard, please consult Chap. 5 of [Fea88] and change the programs there into our notation or that of iPSC.

9. Rewrite all Cube programs for the iPSCs using Table 10-1.

10. Prepare as many parts of the package in subsection 10-1.3 and try to use them on any or all Cube programs developed. (This is an extremely large project, and the reader is advised to study first how it was done at Caltech [Fea88].)

11. The Cross III system is described in [Fea88] and [Fea90] in terms of the C-language. Rewrite the system using Ada. (This is a large project indeed and the reader is advised to study how it was done at Caltech.)

CHAPTER 11

PROGRAMMING
SM MULTIPROCESSORS

In this chapter, we discuss how to program the Shared-Memory multiprocessors (SMs) — the only organization that might be better programmed using semaphores, monitors, etc. The *objectives* are:

Review practical ways of synchronization in order to point to possible problems in running Ada programs.

Review the solution of some numerical problems on SMs, namely matrix multiplication, solution of sets of linear equations, of the Laplace equation and calculation of an area (integral).

Review sorting and searching.

Review an interrupt-driven program for process control.

Introduce problems and projects.

A large number of examples exist for these machines, e.g., an entire set of reports and results for the Butterfly [BBN87], and the book [Ole82] in which results of running a zero-finding routine on the C.mmp are reported. We will use some published solutions below.

11–1 SYNCHRONIZATION PROBLEMS

Shared variables are used in SMs for synchronization. Languages that include this form of synchronization must provide means for control of such data (Sec. 4-2) and synchronization primitives to operate on them. Ada has shared variables [ARM9.11] needed in SM programs, but no synchronization primitives (e.g., signal and wait) to protect them. It is the responsibility of the programmer to deal with mutual exclusion and so on. The programmer must therefore observe the following rules between synchronization points: (1) If a task reads a shared variable, no other task may update it; and (2) A task updates a shared variable excluding other tasks. The language provides some help through a pragma "shared" but restricts its use considerably. Unless an Ada compiler like the one for the Butterfly is available, simulation of semaphores and operations on them (Sec. 8-3) is suggested. As shown in Sec. 4-4 the F&A is more efficient than semaphores. In order to get better solutions for SM programs, we turn to the F&A instruction.

F&A instructions provide an efficient solution to the problem of initializing a number of identical tasks (recall the $q := 1..p$ loops), and to the potentially expensive termination for large numbers of tasks (recall the **abort** used). Ada was designed for solving problems on embedded systems, but the addition of F&A operators could make it quite suitable for SM multiprocessors. The challenge is to use the F&A primitive without extending Ada, and thus retain the *portability* of Ada programs even when written with SM implementation in mind.

> We incorporate the fetch-and-add into Ada without any extension to the language by defining a task type called *beacon*, which can be treated in a special way by the Ada compiler. A program using the *beacon* task type will execute correctly on any conforming Ada system and produce the same result as on the Ultracomputer. The *beacon* is defined as in [Code 11-1.]
>
> [This task type] synchronizes, reads, writes, and updates a protected variable v. As such, it subsumes many familiar synchronization mechanisms. In normal usage, a master task MT in which a *beacon* task T is created initializes the shared variable v by calling the entry T.init. After initialization, other subtasks of MT synchronize among themselves by performing rendezvous with entries of the *beacon*. The body of the beacon . . . [SaS85][2]

is also shown in Code 11-1.

[2] E. and E. Schonberg: "Highly Parallel Ada—Ada on an Ultracomputer," Proc. of the Ada Intl. Conf. 1985, pp. 56–68. Reprinted by permission.

```
task type beacon is
  entry init (e: in INTEGER) ;
  entry read (1: out INTEGER) ;
  entry write (e: in INTEGER) ;
  entry F_and_A (1: out INTEGER, e: in INTEGER) ;
end beacon;

task body beacon is
  v: INTEGER;
begin
  accept init (e: in INTEGER) do
    v := e;
  end init;
  loop
    select
      accept read (e: out INTEGER) do
        1 := v;
      end read;
    or
      accept write (e: in INTEGER) do
        v := e
      end write;
    or
      accept F_and_A (1: out INTEGER; e: in INTEGER) do
        1 := v; v := v+e;
      end F_and_A;
    or
      terminate;
    end select;
  end loop
end beacon;
```

Code 11-1

The precise transformation achieved by the use of beacon is as follows. A task type Tb of type *beacon* becomes a record T with four fields allocated in shared memory according to Code 11-2:

```
type beacon_struct is record
value : INTEGER;                        -- Stores the task variable.
  initialized : BOOLEAN := FALSE;       -- Two flags for being able
  completed : BOOLEAN := FALSE;         -- to call the task.
  initsync : INTEGER := 0;              -- Guarantees that only one
end record;                             -- task is allowed to initialize v.

T : beacon_struct;
```

Code 11-2

A task can read, write, and fetch-and-add the value field only if it is *initialized* and not *completed*. The task becomes *completed* when either it is aborted or the master task and all its descendants terminate. If a task tries to access the value when it is *completed* then TASKING-ERROR is raised by the caller.

More specifically, entry calls to Tb are transformed into accesses to the record T as [in Code 11-3, part 1. This code includes also] transformations to the *read, write,* and *F_and_A* entries of the beacon task. As before, the code obtained depends on whether the call is an ordinary call, a timed entry call, or a conditional entry call. In these transformations, *call* means either (i) *read(1)*, (ii) *write(e)*, or (iii) *F_and_A(1,e)*. The clause *code for call* used in the transformations stands for (i') 1:= T.value; (ii') T.value:= e;, or (iii') 1:=F&A(T.value,*e*); for (i), (ii), and (iii) respectively.

```
Tb.init(e) -- ==> This is Code 11-3 part 1.
  if T.completed then raise TASKING_ERROR; end if;
  --- num := F&A(T.initsync,1);
      if num /= 0 then
  --- Task Tb is already initialized.
  --- If this is a timed entry call,
  ---    wait for the stated time and then goto exitini;
  --- if a conditional entry call, goto exitini;
  --- else block until aborted or Tb is completed.
  --- ...
    end if;
    T.value := e; T.initialized := TRUE;
  <<exitini>>
Tb.call -- ==> This is code 11-3, part 2.
  while not T.initialized or T.completed loop
    if T.completed then raise TASKING_ERROR; end if;
  end loop;
  --- code for call
select -- ==> This is Code 11-3, part 3.
  Tb.call; --- [statement-1]
    if T.completed then raise TASKING_ERROR; end if;
else                        --- if T.initialized then
---[statement-2]            code_for_call [statement-1]
end select;                 --- else [statement-2] end if;
  end loop;
  --- code for call
select -- ==> dt := CLOCK+dt; This is code 11-3, part 4.
  T.call;           --- while not T.initialized or T.completed
  ---[statement-1]     loop
  or              --- if T.completed then raise TASKING_ERROR; end if;
    delay D; --- [statement-2]
end select; --- exit when CLOCK>dt and end loop;
            --- if CLOCK<dt then code for call;
            --- [statement-1] else [statement-2] end if;
```

Code 11-3

While at first glance it may seem that we have traded a rendezvous for a busy-wait in parts 2 and 4, in fact there should be very little busy-waiting. In normal circumstances, T.value will be initialized soon after master task activation, after which the while loop bodies of parts 2 and 4 will never be executed.

We now examine what happens if either a called *beacon* task Tb or the caller task is aborted. If task Tb is aborted, then its status becomes *completed*, and any calling task (which has not already entered the rendezvous code) will detect completion before accessing the value.

More complications arise if the caller is aborted. We must first of all ensure that the integrity of Tb is maintained if the caller is aborted during a rendezvous. Second, since the start and end of the rendezvous are synchronization points, we must be able to detect calls to abort that occurred both before and during the rendezvous.

Note that while the proposed transformation makes the *beacon* task itself disappear, the data structure that replaces it is in shared memory and independent of the tasks that call the beacon. Therefore, if any particular caller gets aborted, the other tasks that call the beacon still have access to it. We must also ensure that if the caller is aborted in the middle of executing the code for Tb (e.g., an F&A), then this execution is completed before the caller is actually aborted. This is guaranteed by the fact that the F&A, once initiated, is executed by the network and not actually by the caller.

If the calling task is aborted before the rendezvous is entered, then the code accessing T.value must not be executed. Therefore, a condition testing abortion must be included before the rendezvous code, which allows the calling task to disappear gracefully if aborted by someone else. This test simply interrogates a location in shared memory that holds the status of the calling task. This location is also accessed by the task that performs an abort. A similar test must be performed after the rendezvous code, to detect whether the caller was aborted during the rendezvous. In this fashion each task monitors its own status and recognizes when it has been aborted. The economy of this solution on the Ultracomputer also follows from the existence of fetch-and-add. [SaS85]

11–2 NUMERICAL PROBLEMS

11–2.1 Matrix Multiplication

A program for matrix multiplication [FCS82][†] shows the problems of using the rendezvous concept in an SM environment. (see Code 11-4).

Note 1. When the task was first run, the entry row_col led to an error which pointed to: "The parameters defined in the ACCEPT-STATEMENT of the task become undefined after the rendezvous is completed" [FCS82].

Note 2. There is definitely too much work inside of the **accept**. As repeatedly stated, the "body" of the accepts should be as short as possible. In the above case, not only is the entire inner product calculated, but even the matrix is transferred inside the **accept**.

---

†J.D. Fernandez et al: "Experience with Matrix Multiplication Using Ada Tasks," Ada Letters, Vol. II, No. 5, pp. 76–84. Reprinted by permission.

```
with TEXT_IO; use TEXT_IO;                    -- CODE 11-4
procedure matrix_multiply is                  -- The main procedure.
type MATRIX is array(1..2,1..2) of INTEGER;   -- The matrices should
m1: MATRIX := (1=>(2,3),2=>(4,5));            -- be general n-by-n and the in
                                                 put
m2: MATRIX := (1=>(1,2),2=>(3,4));            -- should be through GETs.
p:MATRIX;                                     -- p is the result matrix.
task type PROD is                             -- PROD calculates the inner-
  entry row_col(met:MATRIX);                  -- product of a row of m1 with
  entry result(temp: out INTEGER);            -- a column of m2. See NOTE 1.
end PROD;                         --The result is put into the scalar temp
task body PROD is                 -- which is returned to the main program.
  med: INTEGER;                   -- The body stores the result of the
  mat: MATRIX;                    -- inner product in the INTEGER med.
begin                             -- mat (an entire matrix) wastes space.
  accept row_col(met:MATRIX) do               -- The first rendezvous.
    mat:=met;                                 -- Please see NOTE 2.
    med:=mat(1,1)*mat(2 1)+mat(1,2)*mat(2,2);
  end accept;                                 -- It is not general enough.
  accept result(temp: out INTEGER) do         -- The second rendezvous.
    temp:=med;                                -- Entry variable set to
  end accept;                                 -- local and finished.
end PROD;                                     -- end of body of PROD.
-- The next line declares n² tasks - one per each element of p.
run: array(1..2,1..2) of PROD;                -- Is not general enough.
begin                                         -- Row i of m1 is moved to
  for 1 in 1..2 loop                          -- row 1 of matrix p.
    for j in 1..2 loop                        -- Column j of m2 is moved
      p(1,1):=m1(i,1); p(1,2):=m1(1,2); --to row 2 of matrix p.
      p(2,1):=m2(1,j); p(2,2):=m2(2,j);
      run(i,j).row_col(p);                    -- Please see NOTE 3.
    end loop;
  end loop;
  for i in 1..2 loop                          -- Entry result of task
    for j in 1..2 loop                        -- run is called n² times
      run(i,j).result(p(i,j));                -- each time returning one
    end loop;                                 -- result of an inner-
  end loop;                                   -- product calculation.
  for i in 1..2 loop
    PUT_LINE (INTEGER'IMAGE(p(i,1));          -- This type of output is
              INTEGER'IMAGE(p(i,2)));         -- suitable for terminals.
  end loop;
end;
```

Code 11-4

Note 3.   For each index i and j, the n^2 tasks are called sequentially. Each "call" receives a different row and column for inner-product calculation. This led to the following idea for improvement.

> Since the tasks and the main programs are potentially executing in parallel, it seemed appropriate to allow tasks to signal termination of their execution in such a way that the main program would be called when the inner product result was actually available. This approach, however, would depend on a symmetry of "accept" and "call" between the master (main) and the slaves (tasks). There is no apparent easy mechanism for the task to "call" the main to pass information. [FCS82]

Note 4.   A Boolean switch array, called sw, was added and initialized to all its elements (here 4) being FALSE. It is then used in the WHILE-LOOP to determine the order of task termination and acquire the result as soon as it is available. Code 11-5 is the modified code:

Note 5.   "Notice the more efficient rendezvous, the elimination of the second needless entry, and the use of the TERMINATED attribute to determine the order of termination. To make sure that the TERMINATED attribute worked properly, we delayed (delay 20.0) the first and third tasks and found that they terminated after the second and fourth tasks as expected. (This simple test is not included in" [Code 11-5].) [FCS82]

The program for matrix multiplication of Sec. 4-5.3 was developed for SMs but required n^3 processors and was based on the assumptions of no contention. It is only of theoretical value. We can program matrix multiplication for SMs as done for ASPs in Sec. 9-4: We copy slices of matrix **A** into each PE and multiply them with matrix **B** which resides in all PEs. The frequent copying from the shared to local memories makes such algorithms inefficient. We can also use $h*h$ PEs each storing a horizontal slice of **A** and a vertical slice of **B**. To compute a submatrix $C(i,j)$, a PE will use the two slices ($2*h*n = 2*n^2/p$ elements) and perform all n^3/p operations locally (at least in an SM like the Cm* which has local memory). The ratio of accesses to the shared memory to the number of operations is therefore $2/n$, which means a much smaller penalty π than in the first case.

A program like this was run [OHW82] on the Cm*. In the case of $n = 24$ and $n = 48$, the results (σ and η) were as in Table 11-1.

Note that both speedup and efficiency increase with n; for large matrices this SM multiprocessor should work fast. On the other hand, the efficiency decreases with an increasing number p of PEs. The algorithm is therefore fast but not very efficient—a "fast, fast" algorithm.

11–2.2 Solution of Linear Equations

We next discuss solving linear equations (or matrix inversion). In [Csa75] it was snown how the inverse is computed in time $\mathbf{O}(\log^2(n))$ with a bounded number of PEs ($<n^3$). The stability of this method is extremely sensitive to rounding errors, severe cancellation will occur, and a very large number of digits must be carried in order to obtain a reasonably computed value of $\mathbf{A}^{-1}$. It will not be further discussed except for quoting [Hel76.b]:

```
with TEXT_IO; use TEXT_IO;                          -- CODE 11-5
procedure matrix_multiply is                        -- The main procedure.
type MATRIX is array(1..2,1..2) of INTEGER;         -- The matrices should
m1: MATRIX :=(1=>(2,3),2=>(4,5));   -- be general n-by-n and the input
m2: MATRIX :=(1=>(1,2),2=>(3,4));   -- should be through GETs.
result:MATRIX;                                      -- The result matrix.
sw: array(1..2,1..2) of BOOLEAN :=                  -- Please see NOTE 4 above.
(1=>(FALSE,FALSE),2=>(FALSE,FALSE));
task type PROD is
  entry row_col(i,j:INTEGER);
end PROD;
task body PROD is
  L1,L2: INTEGER;                                   -- Two local variables.
begin
  accept row_col(i,j:INTEGER) do                       -- The first rendezvous.
    L1:=i; L2:=j;                                       -- Please see NOTE 5.
  end accept;
  result(L1,L2) := mat(L1,1)*mat(1,L2)+mat(L1,2)*mat(2,L2);
end PROD;                                              -- end of body of PROD.
-- The next line declares n² tasks - one per each element of p.
run: array(1..2,1..2) of PROD;
begin
  for i in 1..2 loop                                   -- Task run(i,j) is called
    for j in 1..2 loop                                 -- n² times, producing n²
      run(i,j).row_col(i,j);                           -- values of result(i,j)
    end loop;
  end loop;
  while not sw(1,1) or not sw(1,2)
    or not sw(2,1) or not sw(2,2) loop                 -- it means "do it".
    for i in 1..2 loop
      for j in 1..2 loop
        if run(i,j) terminated and not sw(i,j) then          -- NOTE 5.
          sw(i,j) := TRUE;
        end if
      end loop;
    end loop
  end loop;                                            -- end loop of the while
PUT_LINE("RESULT IS");
for i in 1..2 loop
  PUT_LINE (INTEGER'IMAGE(RESULT(i,1));
    INTEGER'IMAGE(RESULT(i,2));
end loop;
end;
```

Code 11-5

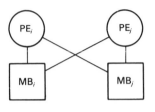

Figure 11-1 Interconnection of PaMs on the DIRMU

In summary, we have an excellent theoretical result, but it will be of little help in creating programs for real parallel computers. For this we must return to the standard elimination methods, which are known to be stable and which have enough inherent parallelism to allow efficient execution on parallel and pipeline computers. We suspect that there is a conservation law for linear systems, which states that if a stability criterion is to be met then a certain number of arithmetic steps must be performed. [Hel76b]

The Jordan ''in situ'' method of Sec. 6-2 [Eq. (6-20) and the numerical example] was programmed and run [Ott87] on an SM (the DIRMU connected in a ring). Every two PaMs were interconnected as in Fig. 11-1 and access each other's memory in the following ways:

- PaM(i) reads and PaM(j) reads
- PaM(i) writes and PaM(j) writes
- PaM(i) writes and PaM(j) reads

The last two cases require locks. The program used the notation signal(s) for setting semaphore s to TRUE, and wait (s) for waiting until $s = $ TRUE and then setting it to FALSE.

The PaMs are connected in a unidirectional ring with one serving as the master or slave-0. (This architecture is not an ASP since the memories are shared.) The master orders all slaves to read the data so that column slices reside in the memory (Fig. 11-2). Each PaM can only exchange data with its right neighbor. Determination of the pivots leads to problems, because each local pivot has to be compared with all other local pivots to find the global pivot. For ensuring that all PaMs have completed, this is done as a double synchronization:

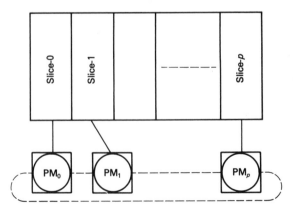

Figure 11-2 Storage of slices and pivoting on the DIRMU

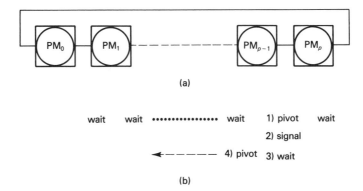

(a)

(b)

Figure 11-3 Synchronization of PaMs on the DIRMU

```
PaM(i):                    signal(s1); wait(s2);                  → t
PaM(j): wait(s1);                       signal(s2);
```

The data (local pivot) exchange proceeds then as in Fig. 11-3(a) whereupon the master computes the global pivot and sends it as well as the pivot column to all the PaMs as in Fig. 11-3(b).

Elimination is done in a similar way (back-substitution is described in [EaD83]). Both programs are left as projects.

We next discuss a program for solving Dirichlet's problem by the Gauss-Seidel overrelaxation method (Sec. 6-2) according to:

$$U(i,j):= \psi*[U(i-1,j)+U(i,j-1)+U(i+1,j)+U(i,j+1)-4*U(i,j)]+U(i,j) \qquad (11\text{-}1)$$

where the first three potentials U are from iteration $k+1$, the remaining four from iteration k. The rectangular region (Fig. 11-4) is divided into m points in a row and m in a column, and into n rectangles: one per task. The points (i,j) are numbered in row major order, with the potential vector being $U = [U(1),U(2),. . .,U(m*n)]$. The program was run on the C.mmp [Bau78] and published in [Hea83][†] from which we quote:

> The procedure we provide, *Parallel Relaxation*, takes the matrix U as a parameter. It is assumed that the outside edge of U has been initialized by the caller with the desired values. The procedure computes the values of U for the interior points. The procedure *Parallel Relaxation* also takes a parameter, *NumberOfRegions*, which indicates the number of Ada tasks to create (Fig. 11-4).
>
> In our implementation, the coefficient matrix is not present explicitly, rather, the coefficients are simply reflected in Eq. (11-1).
>
> Each Ada task works on a region of the matrix U. Each region is itself a rectangular matrix. A rectangular grid of such regions is laid out over the interior of matrix U. One Ada task is dedicated to each region.

[†]Hibbard, P. et al: "Studies in Ada Style," Springer Verlag, New York, NY, 1983. © Reprinted by permission.

Cols per region

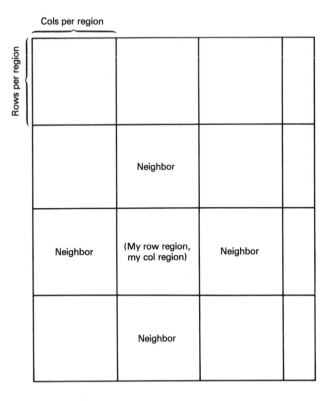

Rows per region

	Neighbor		
Neighbor	(My row region, my col region)	Neighbor	
	Neighbor		

Figure 11-4   Interconnection of PaMs on the DIRMU

Testing for convergence of the system as a whole must be done with care. To have convergence, each task must believe that its own region has converged, and furthermore, all tasks must hold this belief "simultaneously"; that is, they must reach a unanimous consensus on whether or not they all have converged. Observe that a task may decide prematurely that its region has converged, even though a change may soon occur in its region because of a change in one of its neighbors.

For each region task, there is a coordinator task that is used to assist in the communication between the region tasks. The communication consists of one region task, A, advising a neighboring region task, B, that A has not yet converged within its own region. Since A has not yet converged, no conclusion about the convergence of B can be reached, in spite of what B might believe locally. Thus, we can think of this message from A to B as a command to B to keep on going. To avoid deadlock and contention problems that would result if the region tasks did entry calls on each other directly, the message is actually sent by having A do an entry call on B's coordinator task. The consensus among the region tasks is achieved by passing messages to each other's coordinators, and by having a global counter of the number of unfinished region tasks. When a region task believes that it is done, it decrements the counter. When a coordinator task receives a message that its region could not really be done, it increments the counter. When the counter reaches zero, we know that all region tasks thought they were finished.

Each region task repeatedly executes the following actions. First, it computes one complete new set of values for the points in its region. If the region has not yet converged locally, the task advises its neighbor's coordinators to keep on going. If the region has converged locally, then the task decrements the global counter of unfinished tasks. If the counter is zero, we are done . . . and we may then return from the *Parallel Relaxation* procedure. If the counter is non-zero, the region task puts itself to sleep by calling an entry of its coordinator, *Wait*. The coordinator will wake it up by accepting the *Wait* entry call when a keep-on-going message is received; if such a message has already been received, the coordinator accepts the *Wait* entry call immediately. The coordinator merges multiple keep-on-going messages that have been received since the last *Wait* entry call into one message. Multiple keep-on-going messages will thus cause only one acceptance of the *Wait* entry.

When a region task discovers in the test above that the counter of the unfinished region tasks is zero, it must arrange to wake up any other region tasks that are sleeping on the *Wait* entries of their respective coordinators. This must be done because all tasks that are local to a block in Ada must terminate before we may exit the block [ARM9.4]. This waking up is handled by having another entry into the coordinator tasks, the *Finish* entry. After a *Finish* entry call is received, a coordinator will immediately accept any *Wait* entry calls. After a region task returns from the *Wait* entry call, it looks again to see if the global counter has gone to zero. If it has, the region task concludes that we are done and exit. [Hea83]

The program of [Hea83] less the solution of Eq. (11-1) is shown in Code 11-6.

```
package Protected_Counter_Package is      -- CODE 11-6
  task type Protected_Counter is          --This task type provides a pro-
    entry Initialize(Z in Integer);       --tected counter with operations
    entry Incr(Z: in Integer := 1);       --for incrementing and decremen-
    entry Decr(Z: in Integer := 1);       --ting; both are indivisible.
    entry Read(Z: out Integer);           --We surround the task with a
  end Protected_Counter;                  --package, so that it may be
end Protected_Counter_Package;            --separately compiled and placed.

package body Protected_Counter_Package is --in a library [ARM10.1].
  task body Protected_Counter is
    Counter: Integer;
  begin
  accept Initialize(Z: in Integer) do
    Counter := Z;
  end;
  loop
    select
      accept Incr(Z: in Integer := 1) do
        Counter := Counter + Z;
      end;
    or
      accept Decr(Z: in Integer := 1) do
        Counter := Counter - Z;
      end;
    or
      accept Read(Z: out Integer) do
        Z := Counter;
      end;
```

```
    or
      terminate;
      end select
    end loop
  end Protected_Counter;
end Protected_Counter_Package;
```

```
-- The procedure Parallel Relaxation determines the parameters
--- for the Region Tasks, initializes all U's to zero, etc.
```

```
procedure ParRelax_Inner_Proc is

  task type Region_Task is
    entry SetParameter(SetMyRowRegion,
                       SetMyColRegion: in Integer);
  end Region_Task;

  task type Coordinator_Task; is
    entry Wait; entry KeepOnGoing; entry Finish;
  end Coordinator_Task;

  Regions : array(1..RowRegions, 1..ColRegions) of Region_Task;
  Coordinators : array(1..RowRegions, 1..ColRegions) of
                                       Coordinator_Task;
  Unfinished_Counter:Protected_Counter_Package.Protected_Counter;

  task body Coordinator_Task is
    Head_KeepOnGoing: Boolean := False;
    Head_Finished: Boolean := False;
  begin
    loop
      select
        accept KeepOnGoing do
          if not Had_KeepOnGoing then
            Unfinished_Counter.Incr;
            Had_KeepOnGoing := True;
          end if;
        end KeepOnGoing;
      or
        when Had_KeepOnGoing or Had_Finish =>
          accept Wait do Had_KeepOnGoing := False; end Wait;
      or
        accept Finish do Had_Finish := True; end Finish;
      or
        terminate;
      end select;
    end loop;

  end Coordinator_Task;
```

```
begin -- The statements of ParRelax_Inner_Proc
--The count of unfinished tasks is initially all of the region tasks
  Unfinished_Counter.Initialize(NumRegions);
  for I in Regions'RANGE(1) loop      -- Set the parameters
    for J in Regions'RANGE(2) loop  -- of the region tasks.
      Regions(I,J).SetParameter(I,J);
    end loop; -- We next wait at the end of the
  end loop;    -- procedure for the tasks to terminate.
end ParRelax_Inner_Proc;

procedure All_Finish is
begin -- Calls the Finish entries of all the coordinators.
  for Rreg in Coordinators'Range(1) loop
    for Creg in Coordinators'Range(2) loop
      Coordinators(Rreg, Creg).Finish;
    end loop;
  end loop;
end All_Finish;
```

```
--- The task (body) of Region Task computes the U's according
--- to Eq. (11-1). Checking is done as follows:
```

```
  if not MyDone then
    if MyRowRegion /= 1 then
      Coordinators(MyRowRegion-1,MyColRegion).KeepOnGoing
    end if;
    ifMyRowRegion /= RowRegions then
      Coordinators(MyRowRegion+1,MyColRegion).KeepOnGoing
    end if;
    if MyColRegion /= 1 then
      Coordinators(MyRowRegion,MyColRegion-1).KeepOnGoing
    end if
    if MyColRegion /= ColRegions then
      Coordinators(MyRowRegion,MyColRegion+1).KeepOnGoing
    end if;
  end if;
  else
    Unfinished_Counter.Decr;
    Unfinished_Counter.Read(CurCount);
    if CurCount=0 then
      -- We are all done. Wake up everybody who's sleeping:
      ALL_FINISH; goto EndOfTask;
    else                -- Wait to hear of some change
        -- from my neighbors, or for all tasks to finish.
    Coordinators(MyRowRegion, MyColRegion).Wait; -- We were awakened.
    -- See whether this is because everybody was finished, or because
    Unfinished_Counter.Read(CurCourt); -- of a KeepOnGoing message.
    if CurCount=0 then goto EndOfTask;
```

```
    end if; -- See next if some other task has taken too many
    end if; -- iterations already and if so stop iterating:
    exit ItersLoop when DidNotConverge;
end loop ItersLoop; -- If some task has taken too many iterations,
  DidNotConverge := True; AllFinish; -- we set parameter to True and
  end Region_Inner_Block              -- return.
  <<EndOfTask>> null;
end Region_Task;
```

Code 11-6

The complete program is in [Hea83] and should be read. Note then in particular that some task types are *protected*.

11–2.3 Calculation of an Integral

The calculation of an area (integral) was extensively programmed in [Bab88] for the Butterfly, the Alliant FX/8, and the CRAY X-MP (all SMs). In addition, we list Code 11-7 written in Ada and simulating the programs of [DiN88] and [LPS88].

The main program accepts the input, calls a summation routine (in a loop) and prints the results. Each PE forms its partial sum and the main program then accumulates all partial sums.

```
procedure main is                      -- The area is stored in
area, penumb, p, nh: INTEGER;          -- the shared memory.
function f (x: in FLOAT) return FLOAT is -- The function uses a local
  loc : FLOAT;                         -- variable. The particular
  begin                                -- function for II is computed
    loc := 4.0/(1.0+x*x);             -- as integral of 4/(1+x*x),
    return loc;                        -- but can be changed into
end f;                                 -- other functions.
task type PE is                        -- Accumulates a subarea by
  entry work (q, nh, p);                -- calling task work for PE q=1..p.
end PE;
wope : array(1..p) of PE;              -- There are p tasks one for each PE. It
task body work (q, nh, p) is           -- is important that p is a parameter and
begin                                  -- not in the shared area since it must be
  sum, h, x: FLOAT;                    -- distinct for each of the parallel tasks.
  h := 1.0/nh; area := 0.0;
  istart := (q-1)*h+1;                 -- The starting slice of PE called q,
  istop := q*h;                        -- and the last slice.
  for i in istart..istop loop          -- Accumulate the subarea in this loop.
    x := FLOAT(i*h)-0.5;              -- Rectangular formula is used.
    sum := sum+h*f(x);                 -- Function f(x) = 4.0/(1.0+x*x) is
  end loop;                            -- declared in the main program.
end work;
```

```
GET(p,nh);          -- Usually the x-distance is needed; here it is 1.0.
for q in 1..p loop                                -- NOTE.
  accept wope(q) do      -- To make the time in the task as short as
    sum := 0.0;          -- possible, only the subarea is initialized.
  end accept;            -- The task wope computes the subarea.
  wope(q).work(q,nh,p);  -- At this point, a lock in the form of F&A
                         -- is needed because area is in the shared
  area := area+sum;      -- memory (critical section) and should be
end loop;           -- protected. At end, the lock should be unlocked.
```

Code 11-7

Note.   The program in [DiN88] is different because it is written in Fortran, and it uses a sequential loop to accumulate ''sum'' in a subroutine. In the parallel version this subroutine is in the main program. The determination of the times of various runs is possible.

Similar programs are shown in [LPS88] written in C for the Butterfly and in [Mod88] written in Fortran for the CRAY X-MP.

11–3 SEARCHING AND SORTING

The *search* algorithm proposed for SM multiprocessors is as follows: All slaves start searching for the key simultaneously in positions 1,2,. . .,p that is slave 1 in position 1, . . . , slave p in position p. If the key is not found by processors 1,. . .,p, the search proceeds to positions $p+1$, $p+2$, . . . $2*p$. Since the data is accessed in the common memory, this algorithm can be applied to SMs.

The subprogram called sear(q) is a straightforward linear search with p tasks, each having a step-size of p. To prevent unequal tasks occurring at the end of the run, a number of keys differing from the given key are added to the end of the list so that $n = k*p$. The program to be developed will use a list of 1,000 keys for $p = 8$ processors, with $k = 125$ keys for each processor. Since k is known beforehand, the search can be arranged as a loop on k which is left if the key was not found. On the other hand, if the key is located by one of the processors, all others have to be aborted. For this we subtract from the index where the key was found a multiple i of the number of slaves p, found $- i*p$. This is the processor which located the key (e.g., if the key was located in location 34, then $34 - 8*4 = 2$ and it was located by slave $q = 2$). The multiple index i is simply the for-loop counter.

The program in Code 11-8 is explained by its comments.

```
generic SIZE: INTEGER := 1000;    -- The arbitrary size of the list.
package list is                   -- This is the specification.
  subtype KEY is STRING(1..6);    -- Six letters to a name (key).
  subtype IND is INTEGER range 1 .. SIZE;
  function find(k: in KEY) return IND; --find is the search function
end list;
```

```
package body list is
-- It is assumed that the list "arr" is ready to be searched for k.
task main is -- Entry find is called by a user requesting a search.
  entry find(k: in KEY; f: out IND); -- Key was found in index f.
  entry rest(kf: in IND); -- This entry is activated by the search
end main; -- task that has located the key and reports this fact.

task type SEAR(q: INTEGER) is -- The number of the slave is q.
  entry search(k: in KEY, start: in INTEGER); -- Will be q.
end SEAR;

function find(k: in KEY) return IND is
g: IND;                          -- It uses main to order the search
begin                            -- and activate the p tasks.
  main.find(k,g); return g;      -- It returns a list index g.
end find;

task body main is
start, curr: IND;                -- The starting and current indices.
begin
  loop
    accept find(k: in KEY; f: out IND) do
      declare
      src: array(1..p) of SEAR; --Instantiation of p identical tasks.
      begin                      -- Loop q starts all p search
        for q in 1 .. p loop     -- tasks or processors
          search(k,q);           -- not really concurrently
        end loop;                -- since q is set sequentially
        accept rest(g: in IND) do -- to 1..p. Whenever the key
          curr := g;             -- was found in g, it is stored
        end rest;                -- in curr during the ACCEPT.
        for i in 1 .. 125 loop   -- Next, it is determined which
          gg := g-i*p;           -- processor found k.
          if (gg>0) and (gg<(p+1)) then
            for j in 1 .. p loop
              if j/=gg then
                abort src(j);
              end if;
            end loop;
          end if;
        end loop;
        g := curr;
      end; -- of the block.
    end accept;
  end loop;
end main;

task body SEAR is
lokey: KEY; locind: IND;
```

```
begin
  accept search(k: in KEY; start: in IND) do
    lokey := k; locind := start;
  end search;
  while arr(locind) /= lokey loop   -- This loop is the real search
    locind := locind+p;             -- and consumes most of the time.
  end loop;
  main.rest(locind); -- This call transmits the result to main
end SEAR;               -- and completes the search.
end;                    -- This is the end of package list.
```

Code 11-8

The disadvantage of this program is that there is much contention for memory; each CPU tries to get hold of the shared memory.

Next are two *sort* procedures for SM multiprocessors. The list is:

```
12 5 6 16 15 1 2 9 8 4 3 10 8 11 7 14
```

The first algorithm to sort this list with $p = 2$ is as follows: processor $q = 1$ compares keys $k(1)$ with $k(2)$, while CPU $q = 2$ compares $k(3)$ with $k(4)$. If needed, a swap is made. Arriving at the last key completes a *sweep*. After an entire sweep is made, the next sweep starts with $q = 1$ comparing $k(2)$ with $k(3)$, while $q = 2$ compares $k(4)$ with $k(5)$, etc. In order to show which parts are compared, commas are used below. The results for sweeps 2 to 14 are

```
5, 12 6, 16 1, 15 2, 9 4, 8 3, 10 11, 13 7, 14
5 6, 12 1, 16 2, 15 4, 9 3, 8 10, 11 7, 13 14
5, 6 1, 12 2, 16 4, 15 3, 9 8, 10 7, 11 13, 14
5 1, 6 2, 12 4, 16 3, 15 8, 9 7, 10 11, 13 14
1, 5 2, 6 4, 12 3, 16 8, 15 7, 9 10, 11 13, 14
1 2, 5 4, 6 3, 12 8, 16 7, 15 9, 10 11, 13 14
1, 2 4, 5 3, 6 8, 12 7, 16 9, 15 10, 11 13, 14
1 2, 4 3, 5 6, 8 7, 12 9, 16 10, 15 11, 13 14
1, 2 3, 4 5, 6 7, 8 9, 12 10, 16 11, 15 13, 14
1 2, 3 4, 5 6, 7 8, 9 10, 12 11, 16 13, 15 14
1, 2 3, 4 5, 6 7, 8 9, 10 11, 12 13, 16 14, 15
1 2, 3 4, 5 6, 7 8, 9 10, 11 12, 13 14, 16 15
1, 2 3, 4 5, 6 7, 8 9, 10 11, 12 13, 14 15, 16
```

This algorithm may appear to be inefficient since it requires 14 sweeps, but note that each sweep requires only n/p comparisons—here 8 instead of 16. Let us modify the algorithm with an algorithm in which the odd and even keys are compared:

```
6 12  2  8  3   13   7   15
 5   1  9  4  10   11  14   16
6  2  8  3  12   7   13   15
 1  5  4  9   10   11  14  16
2  6  3  8  7   12  13   15
 1  4  5  9  10   11  14   16
2  3  6  7  8   12   13   15
 1  4  5  9  10   11   14   16
```

This algorithm needs only two sweeps (so it seems more efficient). The first sweep produces 1 2 3 4 5 6 7 9 8 10 11 12 13 14 15 16

Actually, a number of similar algorithms could be formulated and the best chosen on the basis of either statistical considerations or simulation studies. What is of interest to us is that parallel algorithms for multiprocessors can be developed.

The contention will reduce the speedup considerably. It is better to use Quicksort (the fastest sort of Sec. 6-1), because it operates on disjoint subsets of the list. The sorting with Quicksort on an SM multiprocessor is discussed in [Coh82]. We have chosen to present the sorting program from [Bro86][†] including its remarks as Code 11-9. (For the algorithm, see Sec. 6-2.)

```
package SORT_PACKAGE is
  type VECTOR is array (NATURAL range <>) of INTEGER;
  type VECTOR_HANDLE is access VECTOR;     -- SORT arranges the elements
  procedure SORT (TABLE : inout VECTOR);   -- in TABLE in non-decreasing
end SORT_PACKAGE;                          -- order.

package body SORT_PACKAGE is
  task type SORTER is
    entry START (TABLE : in VECTOR);
    entry RESULT (TABLE : in VECTOR);
  end SORTER;
  function MERGE (LEFT, RIGHT : VECTOR) return VECTOR is separate;
  procedure SORT (TABLE : in out VECTOR) is
  begin
    if TABLE'LENGTH <= 1 then return; end if;
    declare -- Here if TABLE has at least 2 elements.
      LEFT_SORTER, RIGHT_SORTER : SORTER;
      FIRST  : NATURAL := TABLE'FIRST;
      LAST   : NATURAL := TABLE'LAST;
      MIDDLE : NATURAL := (FIRST+LAST) /2;
    begin -- Start the sorting of the two halves in parallel:
      LEFT_SORTER.START (TABLE (FIRST..MIDDLE));
      RIGHT_SORTER.START (TABLE (MIDDLE+1..LAST));
      -- get the sorted results:
```

[†]The sorting-with-tasking program was written by Benjamin M. Brosgol and is part of the Alsys *Ada Sampler*. It is reprinted in this book with permission of Alsys. Copyright 1988 Alsys, Inc.

```
      LEFT_SORTER.RESULT(TABLE(FIRST..MIDDLE));    -- Get the sorted
      RIGHT_SORTER.RESULT(TABLE(MIDDLE+1..LAST));-- results and
      TABLE:=MERGE(LEFT => TABLE(FIRST..MIDDLE),
                   RIGHT => TABLE(MIDDLE+1..LAST)); -- merge.

    return;
  end SORT;


  task body SORTER is
    HANDLE : VECTOR_HANDLE;
  begin
    accept START(TABLE : in VECTOR) do
      HANDLE := new VECTOR'(TABLE);
    end START;
    accept RESULT(TABLE : out VECTOR) do
      TABLE := HANDLE.all;
    end RESULT;
  end SORTER;
end SORT_PACKAGE;


separate(SORT_PACKAGE);
function MERGE(LEFT, RIGHT : VECTOR) return VECTOR is
  INDEX_L : NATURAL := LEFT'FIRST;
  INDEX_R : NATURAL := RIGHT'FIRST;
  RESULT : VECTOR(1..LEFT'LENGTH+RIGHT'LENGTH);
begin -- Assume that LEFT and RIGHT are sorted (non-decreasing order)
  for INDEX in RESULT'RANGE loop
    -- Check if we have exhausted either of the vectors : (Note:
    -- it cannot be the case that both vectors have been exhausted)
    if INDEX_L > LEFT'LAST then
      RESULT(INDEX..RESULT'LAST := RIGHT(INDEX_R..RIGHT'LAST);
      exit;
    end if;
    elsif INDEX_R > RIGHT'LAST then
      RESULT(INDEX..RESULT'LAST := LEFT(INDEX_L..LEFT'LAST);
      exit
    end if;
    -- Here if INDEX_L<=LEFT'LAST and INDEX_R<=RIGHT'LAST
    -- i.e., elements remain to be checked in both vectors.
    if LEFT(INDEX_L <= RIGHT(INDEX_R) then
      RESULT(INDEX) := LEFT(INDEX_L);
      INDEX_L := INDEX_L + 1;
    else
      RESULT(INDEX) := RIGHT(INDEX_R);
      INDEX_R := INDEX_R + 1;
    end if;
  end loop;
  return RESULT;
end MERGE;
```

```
with SORT_PACKAGE; use SORT_PACKAGE; -- The MAIN PROGRAM.
with TEXT_IO; use TEXT_IO;
procedure TRY_SORT is
  package INT_IO is new INTEGER_IO(INTEGER);
    use INT_IO; VALUES : INTEGER;
  begin
    MAIN : loop
      PUT_LINE("how many values will you input? ");
      PUT_LINE("Enter 0 or a negative number to terminate.");
      PUT_LINE(": "); GET(VALUES); SKIP_LINE;
      exit MAIN when VALUES <= 0;
      declare
        TABLE : VECTOR(1..VALUES);
      begin
        for i in 1..VALUES loop
          PUT("value " & INTEGER'IMAGE(i) & ": ");
          GET(TABLE(i)); SKIP_LINE;
        end loop;
        SORT(TABLE);
        PUT_LINE("The sorted vector is:");
        for i in 1..VALUES loop
          PUT("value " & INTEGER'IMAGE(i) & ": ");
          PUT(TABLE(i)); NEW_LINE;
        end loop;
        PUT_LINE("-------------------------");
      end;
    end loop MAIN;
end TRY_SORT;
```

Code 11-9

11–4 A PROCESS CONTROL APPLICATION

The application to be discussed is called *shaving*—a process used to produce gears (for automobiles, helicopters, etc.) at their ideal size. This is achieved by bringing a shaving cutter (tool) into mesh with the gear to be shaved and rotating them at a fast speed (300–1000 rpm). The shaving cutter has *sercations* on the face. These are grooves cut into the face of the tool so that as the tool traverses across the face of the gear, tiny shavings of metal are removed. This process is similar to a person shaving with a Trac-2-like razor (Fig. 11-5). As the tool and gear mesh and rotate, the sercations remove tiny amounts of metal. In addition to the rotational motion, the tool and gear are brought closer together by an amount called the *infeed*. The calculation of the infeed and the process of gear shaving (in a cell environment) is the purpose of Code 11-10.

To calculate the infeed (Fig. 11-6), the following are required:

1. Collect geometry information about the tool and gear (Inquire).
2. Determine the tool's tooth thickness (ToolThickness).

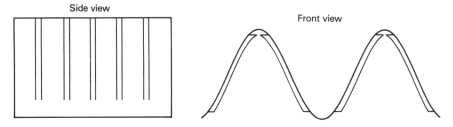

Figure 11-5 The shaving process of an SM

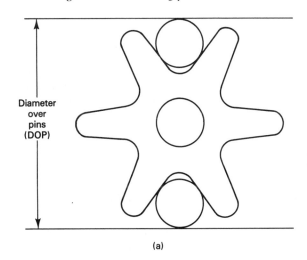

(a)

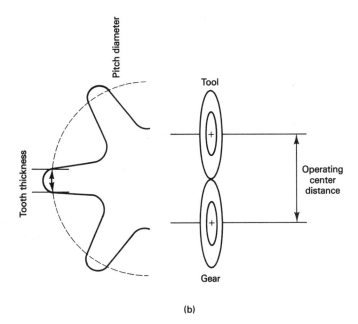

(b)

Figure 11-6 Calculation of the infeed

3. Determine the gear's tooth thickness. This will determine the rough gear tooth thickness (GearRghTk).

4. Same as step 3 but for gear's finish (ideal) size (GearFinTk).

5. Determine the gear's rough size operating center distance. This value, shown in Fig. 11-6(b), is the vertical distance between the center lines of the tool and gear (RoughDist).

6. Same as step 5 but for gear's finish size (FinDist).

7. The required infeed is the absolute value of the difference between the operating center distances calculated in steps 5 and 6 (ShavePart).

The parenthesized names are the modules (Fig. 11-7): Inquire is a procedure, 2–7 are tasks, and 7 calls tasks 3–7 to compute the required infeed. Steps 1, 2, and 7 are sequential, steps 3–6 are parallel, respectively. Note that steps 3–7 must be executed for every gear to be shaved.

Two items of information about the gear change dynamically (from part to part). These are the rough and finish Diameter Over Pin (DOP). The DOP is measured by a gage which inserts pins (cylinders) into the tooth spaces at opposite sides of the gear [Fig. 11-6(a)].

The process of gear shaving uses the following *equipment*:

1. Machine tool: determines infeed required and shaves the gear to its finished size.

2. Cell controller: sends an interrupt to the machine tool asking it to shave a part.

3. Pre-process gage: measures a gear's rough DOP.

4. Post-process gage: measures a gear's finish DOP and compares this measurement with the theoretical finish DOP.

The *physical path* of a gear being shaved can be described in the following three steps:

1. A gear is loaded into the preprocess gage to determine its rough size. The size of a gear is determined by measuring its DOP [Fig. 11-6(a). The rough size information is then sent to the machine tool via an interrupt. The gear is loaded into the machine tool's loader which holds up to 12 parts. When the machine tool receives this interrupt, it takes the rough size information and stores it into a circular queue.

2. The cell controller sends an interrupt to the machine tool to shave a gear. When the machine tool receives this interrupt, it calculates the infeed required as a function of current gear's rough size and the targeted finish size. *The required calculations are only simulated below.* The machine tool then shaves the gear and the gear is sent to the post-process gage.

3. The post-process gage measures the finished size of the gear. If that size varies from the theoretical finish size, then it will send a new target DOP size to the machine tool via an interrupt to compensate for this error.

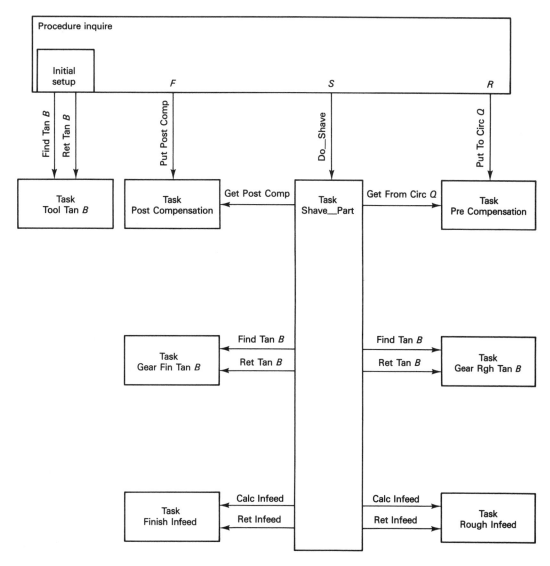

Figure 11-7 Steps of the gear-shaving algorithm

Note that these interrupts may not always occur in this order. Also note that the simulation of these interrupts in Code 11-10 will be performed in procedure Inquire. The program consists of the following *units*:

1. Procedure *Inquire* includes the initial gear and tool data as well as a call to the task ToolThickness which calculates the tooth thickness of the tool. Inquire also includes the simulation of the interrupts generated by the real-world devices (Fig. 11-7).

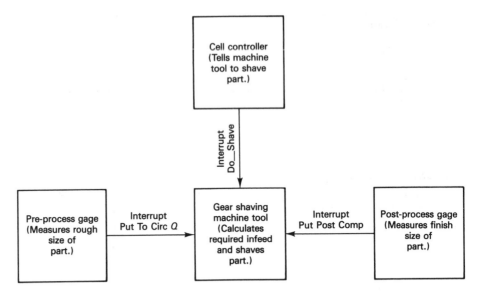

Figure 11-8   Gear-shaving process

2. Task type *Tks* calculates the tooth thickness given other geometry information. Note that tasks *ToolThickness, GearRghTk,* and *GearFinTk* are all of type Tks.

3. Task type *Distances* calculates the operating center distance between gear and tool. Tasks *RoughDist* and *FinishDist* are of type Distances.

4. Task PreCompensation contains a circular queue which holds the rough DOP at the gears to be shaved which are located currently in the Machine Tool's Loader.

5. Task PostCompensation contains the current target gear finish size to be used in determining the required Infeed.

6. Task ShavePart performs steps 1 to 7 as described above.

7. Since all of the units reside in package *Simulate*, a driver procedure named *Shave* is used to initiate this package.

Please follow the program execution in Fig. 11-8. It contains all the tasks mentioned above, the display of the interrupts, and the entry calls.

1. *The Pre-Process Gage Interrupt* is simulated by selecting ''R'' in the program menu. Once ''R'' is selected, the rendezvous is between procedure Inquire and task PreCompensation via PutToCircQ. The gear's rough DOP is sent to a circular queue in task PreCompensation to be read later by task ShavePart.

2. *The Post-Process Gage Interrupt* is simulated by selecting ''F'' in the program menu. Once ''F'' is selected, the rendezvous is between procedure Inquire and task PostCompensation via PutPostComp. The new finish DOP is sent to a buffer in task PostCompensation to be read later by task ShavePart.

3. *The Cell Controller Interrupt* is simulated by selecting "S" in the program menu. Once "S" is selected, the rendezvous is between procedure Inquire and task ShavePart via DoShave. The new task ShavePart gets the rough size of the gear to be shaved via a rendezvous with task PreCompensation through GetFromCirQ. Then task ShavePart gets the finish size of the gear to be shaved via a rendezvous with task PostCompensation through GetPOstCom. Next, *in parallel*, the base circle semi angles for both rough and finish sizes are obtained using FindTk and RetTk makes rendezvous with tasks GearFinTk and GearRghTk. After both angles have been returned, the operating center distances for both rough and finish sizes are obtained *concurrently* using the CalcDist and RetDist rendezvous. After both center distances have been obtained, the required infeed can be computed and the gear can be shaved.

```
with Text_IO; use Text_IO;          -- CODE 11-10.
package simulate is
  procedure Inquire;
end simulate;


procedure Inquire is
TTeeth, THelix, TNpa, TTpa, TDop, TPin, TBd, TPd : float := 0.0;
GTeeth, GHelix, GNpa, GTpa, GDopRgh, GDopFin, GPinRgh: float := 0.0;
TTk, TInvTpa, TBaseHelix, TNctt : float := 0.0; Ch : character;
GPinFin, GBd, GPd, GTkRgh, GTkFin, GInvTpa : float := 0.0
GBaseHelix,GNcttrGH,GNcttRgh,GNcttFin,GOpcRgh,GOpcFin:float:=0.0;
NewDopRgh, NewDopFin, InfeedRequired : float;

task type Tks is
  entry FindTk(Teeth,Helix,Npa,Tpa,Dop,Pin,Bd,Pd : in float);
  entry RetTk(Tk, InvTpa,BaseHelix,Nctt : out float);
end Tks;


task type Distances is
  entry CalcDist(GTk,TTeeth, THelix, TInvNpa, TPd, TPd, TBd,
    GTeeth, TBaseHelix, GBaseHelix, GBd, GInvTpa : in float);
  entry RetDist(OpCenterDist : out float);
end Distances;


ToolThickness, GearRghTk, GearFinTk : Tks;
RoughDist, FinishDist : Distances;


task PreCompensation is
  entry PutToCircQ(RoughInCompensation : in float);
  entry GetFrCircQ(RoughInCompensation : out float);
end PreCompensation;
```

```
task PostCompensation is
  entry PutPostComp (PostInComp : in float);
  entry GetPostComp (PostOutComp : out float);
end PostCompensation;

task ShavePart is
  entry DoShave;
end ShavePart;

task body Tks is
TempTeeth, TempHelix, TempNpa, TempTpa, TempDop, TempPin : float;
TempBd, TempPd, Tk, InvTpa, BaseHelix, Nctt : float;
begin
  loop
    select
      entry CalcDist (GTk, TTeeth, THelix, TInvNpa, TPd, TPd, TBd,
              GTeeth, TBaseHelix, GBaseHelix, GBd, GInvTpa : in float);
        TempTTeeth:=TTeeth; TempTHelix:=THelix; TempGBaseHelix:=
        GBaseHelix; TempGTk:=GTk; TempTpd:=Tpd; TempTNctt:=TNctt;
        TempTinvTpa := TinvTpa; TempTBd := TBd; TempGBd := GBd;
        TempGinvTpa:=GinvTpa; TempGBd:=GBd; TempGTeeth:=GTeeth;

      PUT_LINE ("Finding Operating Center Distances;
      OpCenterDist := 0.0;

  accept RetDistk, InvTpa, BaseHelix, Nctt: out float) do
      null;
  end accept;
      or
        terminate;
  end select;
  end loop
  end Tks;

task body Distances is
TempGTk, TempTTeeth, TempHelix, TempTNctt, TempTPd, TempTBd : float;
TempGTeeth, TempTBaseHelix, TempGInvTpa, TempGInvTpa, TempGBd : float;
TempGBaseHelix, OpCenterDist : float;
begin
  loop
    select
      accept CalcDist (Teeth, Helix, Npa, Tpa, Dop, Pin, Bd, Pd : in float) do
        TempTeeth := Teeth; TempHelix := Helix;
        TempNpa := Npa; TempTpa := Tpa; TempDop := Dop;
        TempPin := Pin; TempBd := Bd; TempPd := Pd;
      end accept; -- Next should be calculations; instead we have:
      PUT_LINE ("Finding Operating Center Distance");
      OpCenterDist := 0.0;
```

```ada
        accept RetDist(OpCenterDist : out float) do
          null;
        end;
      or accept RetTk(Tk, InvTpa, BaseHelix, Nctt : out float) do
        null;
      end accept;
    or
      terminate;
    end select;
  end loop;
end Distances;

task body PreCompensation is
CircularQueue : array(1..12) of float;
QueueHead, QueuTail : integer := 0;
begin
  loop
    select
      accept PutToCircQ(RoughInCompensation : in float) do
        QueuHead := (QueueHead mod 12) + 1;
        CircularQueue(QueueHead) := RoughInCompensation;
        PUT_LINE("Pushed Rough Compensation onto Circular Queue");
      end accept;
    or
      accept GetFrCirQ(RoughInCompensation : out float) do
        QueuTail := (QueueTail mod 12) + 1;
        RoughOutCompensation := CircularQueue (QueueTail);
        PUT_LINE("Popped Rough Compensation off the Circular Queue");
      end accept;
    or terminate;
    end select;
  end loop;
end PreCompensation;

task body Postcompensation is
CurrentPostCompensation : float;
begin
    loop
    select
      accept PutPostComp(PostInComp : in float) do
        CurrentPostComensation := PostInCompensation;
        PUT_LINE("Received Post-Process Gage Input");
      end accept;
    or
      accept GetPostComp(PostOutComp : out float) do
        PostOutComp := CurrentPostComensation;
        PUT_LINE("Requested Finish Compensation");
      end accept;
```

```
       or
          terminate;
       end select;
     end loop;
   end PostCompensation;

   task body ShavePart is
   begin
       loop
        select
          accept DoShave do null end;
          PreCompensation.GetFromCirQ(GDopRgh);
          PostCompensation.GetPostComp(GDopFin);
          GearRghTauB.FindTk(GTeeth, GHelix, GNpa, GTpa, GDopRgh,
                                            GPinRgh, GBd, GPd);
          GearFinTauB.FindTk(GTeeth, GHelix, GNpa, GTpa, GDopRgh,
                                            GPinRgh, GBd, GPd);
          GearRghTauB.RetTk(GTkRgh, GInvTpa, GBaseHelix, GNcttRgh);
          GearFinTauB.RetTk(GTkFin, GInvTpa, GBaseHelix, GNcttRgh);
          RghInfeed.CalcDist(GTkRgh, TTeeth, TNctt, THelix, TInvNpa,
            TPd, TBd, GTeeth, TBaseHelix, GBaseHelix, GBd, GInvTpa);
          FinInfeed.CalcDist (GTkFin, TTeeth, TNctt, THelix, TInvNpa,
            TPd, TBd, GTeeth, TBaseHelix, GBaseHelix, GBd, GInvTpa);
          RghInfeed.RetDist(GOpcdstRgh);
          FinInfeed.RetDist(GOpcdstFin);
          InfeedRequired := GOpcdstRgh - GOpcdstFin;
        or
          terminate;
       end select;
     end loop;
   end ShavePart;

   begin -- BEGIN OF PROCEDURE INQUIRE
   --- This section of pseudocode simulates the initial collection of
   --- tool and gear data. It must be collected prior to the start of
   --- the gear shaving. The following initialization substitutes
   --- for the trigonometric calculations which would have been done.
     TTeeth := 83.0; THelix := 15.0; TNpa := 20.0; TTpa := 20.6469;
     TDop := 7.305; TPin := 0.16; TBd := 6.00777; TPd := 7.1607;
     GTeeth := 111.0; GHelix := 0.0; GNpa := 20.0; GTpa := 20.0;
     GDopRgh := 9.55; GPinRgh := 0.16; GBd := 8.69215; GPd := 9.25;
     GDopFin := 9.5075; GPinFin := 0.16;
     NewDopRgh := GDopRgh; NewDopFin := GDopFin;
     PUT_LINE(" "); PUT_LINE("Processing Initial Setup");
     ToolTk.FindTk(TTeeth, THelix, TNpa, TTpa, TDop, TPin, TBd, TPd);
     ToolTk.RetTk(TTauB, TInvTpa, TBaseHelix, TNctt); -- Initialize
     PostCompensation.PutPostComp(GDopFin); -- target size with value
```

```
loop -- Simulates real-time interrupts via keyboard input.
  NEW_LINE(2); PUT_LINE("Enter simulated interrupt: ");
  PUT_LINE(" S = Shave Part Interrupt ");
  PUT_LINE(" R = Pre-Process Gage Input Interrupt ");
  PUT_LINE(" F = Post-Process Gage Input Interrupt");
  PUT_LINE(" E = End Simulation "); PUT_LINE(" ");
  GET(Ch);                        -- The delay is inserted because
  if ((Ch='S') or (Ch='s')) then  -- the Janus Ada suspends I/O
  PUT_LINE("Simulate Shaving");    -- of other tasks while GET(Ch)
  ShavePart.DoShave;               -- procedure is being executed.
  delay;             -- To demonstrate it, comment out this delay.
  elsif ((Ch='R') or (Ch='r')) then
    PUT_LINE("Simulate Pre-Process Gage Input: ");
    PreCompensation.PutToCircQ(NewDopRgh);
  elsif ((Ch='F') or (Ch='f')) then
    PUT_LINE("Simulate Post-Process Gage Input: ");
    PostCompensation.PutPostComp(NewDopFin);
  elsif ((Ch='E') or (Ch_'e')) then
    PUT_LINE("Simulation Completed..Bye!");
    exit;
  else PUT_LINE("Invalid Character received");
  end if;
 end loop;
end Inquire;
end Simulate;

with Simulate; use Simulate;
procedure Shave is
begin
 Inquire
end Shave;
```

Code 11-10

11-5 PROBLEMS AND PROJECTS

1. The *jik* factorization is described in general in [GHL84]. Program it using either semaphores or multitasking features of Ada.

2. The solution to the problem of Laplace was discussed above. Rewrite it using the F&A task (*beacon*). (If you have problems, [SaS85] may be consulted.)

3. Rewrite the programs in [LPS88] and [Mod88] using Ada.

4. Elimination as discussed and back-substitution (as described in [EaD83]) are to be programmed as projects.

5. Sorting by Quicksort was discussed in the book. Program it for an SM. (If you have problems, consult [Coh82].)

6. Change the sorting procedure of Sec. 9-3 by making the package generic and adding Exception Handling. ''As presently written, the program terminates with an unhandled exception if the user input does not correspond to an INTEGER value. Correct this by at least providing exception handlers in TRY_SORT that print out the nature of the input error before the program terminates'' [Bro86].

7. The stock broker example was now solved in stages. Change it into a banking problem and write a suitable program for an SM multiprocessor. You may want to consult [OaW83] where this problem is solved.

8. A large number of programs for the Butterfly was published by the Company (BBN) which builds it [BBN87]. They are mostly programmed in C, not in Ada, and use semaphores, not tasks. Study these programs and rewrite them in Ada, using F&A instructions and/or multitasking.

9. Implement *in parallel and in Ada* Moore's shortest-path algorithm. The program should find the shortest path from a specified vertex, the source, to all vertices in a weighted directed graph. ''weight(u,v)'' is the length of the edge from u to v. If no such edge exists then the weight is infinite. (If you encounter problems, see [Qui87]). The sequential algorithm is as follows:

```
ShortP( );
begin
  for i in 1..n loop
    initialize( );
  end loop;
  --- insert source into queue
  --- while queue is not empty loop
  SearchPath( );
  end while loop;
end ShortP;

SearchPath( );
begin
  --- Dequeue vertex u;
  --- For every edge (u,v) in the graph loop
    NewDistance := Distance(u)+Weight(u,v);
    if NewDistance<Distance(v) then
      Distance(v) := NewDistance;
      --- If v is not in the queue then enqueue vertex v.
    end if;
  end loop;
end;
```

APPENDIX 1

THE TRANSPUTER AND OCCAM[†]

A1–1 TRANSPUTERS

The transputer[†] is a small PaM that can be used as a building block with other transputers to construct a PPS. It derives its name from the words transistor and computer. The reasoning is that a transistor is a silicon component which is a building block used to make a computer, but a transputer is a building block used to make a larger computer.

The transputer [Fig. A1-1(a)] was developed by INMOS in 1984. Its primary purpose was to compete with other PaMs for use in fifth generation computers and Cubes. The transputer architecture defines a family of programmable VLSI components. A typical member of the transputer family is a single chip with a processor, memory, and four full-duplex interface links for interfacing with peripheral devices or with other transputers. The design philosophy of the transputer is different from its competitors in the following respects: (1) although the transputer is a PaM, i.e., a microprocessor with built-in local memory (*LM*), it also contains special high-speed communication links. These links are used to connect one transputer to another, or to other devices; (2) The transputer is a stack-based machine which uses its high-speed LM in place of registers and contains a reduced instruction set (RICS) of 64 instructions; and (3) a transputer can contain special circuitry and interfaces adapting it to a particular use such as a disk controller or graphics driver.

[†]G. Jones, *Programming in occam*, Prentice-Hall International, 1987.

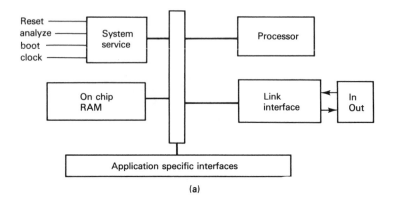

(a)

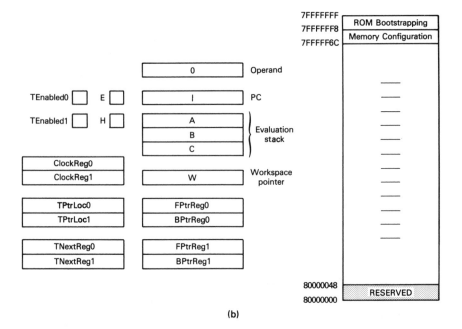

(b)

Figure A1-1   Organization of the transputer

The generic architecture of the transputer is shown in Fig. A1-1(a). We are next discussing its parts and in most cases refer specifically to the T800 transputer of INMOS. This T800 is a 32-bit transputer, with four channels, 4 KB of on-chip static RAM (the LM), 2^{32} or 4Gigabytes of directly addressable memory space and is supposed to provide 10 MIPs. It implements floating-point instructions using a special on-chip unit.

Memory.   The LM is used as stack space (see below) and by the compiler to hold the base addresses of arrays (recall the matrix-multiplication program of Chap. 7)

Although all transputers have high-speed static RAM on board, they can also access external memory (*EM*), but this decreases the speed of computation. The maximum data rate is 80 Mbytes/sec while the EM can be accessed at 25 Mbytes/sec. The access time of the LM is 50 ns. The transputer does not distinguish between these two memories except that it takes less to access the on-chip LM. The user should write the program so that the on-chip LM is used much more often than the EM. This is so because a program that fits into the LM will execute instructions in the fast cycle time of the transputer. An experiment conducted by INMOS showed that if the on-chip LM cannot hold both the program and data, the data should be placed in the on-chip LM, while the program be better placed in the external memory.

Registers.   The transputer has a number of registers [Fig. A1-1(b)]: an operand register O, an instruction counter I (similar to a program counter), a workspace pointer, W, and three registers A,B and C which form the evaluation stack mentioned earlier. Recursion is implemented by using the stack (recall compilation example in Chap. 7). Additional four registers are used for scheduling tasks running on the same transputer. For this, there are two priorities: the higher, or 0, and the lower or 1 priority. (Obviously, higher priority tasks should be kept relatively short in order to let other tasks also run on the transputer). The parallel tasks are in lists and the FPtrReg# and BPtrReg# point to the front and back of list with priority # (0 or 1). There is no condition code register; the result of a comparison is left on top of the stack (Register A). Error (E) and Halt-on-error (H) flags handle overflows. There are also clock and other support registers.

The use of the registers is exemplified in Fig. A1-1(b). Registers A,B and C form the evaluation stack, W tracks the address of the used data, I points to the next instruction, and O stores the operand. Since the instructions are one byte wide, but the word length is 32 bits, four instructions fit into a single word and are transferred simultaneously, thus saving memory access time.

Interfaces and channels.   What sets the transputer apart from other "Computers on a Chip", i.e., PaMs are its high-speed communication links. The links are used to interconnect one transputer with another. This allows transputer networks of some size and topology (say, a Cube) to be constructed. The T800 has four 10 Mbps bidirectional, DMA channels which transfer data between links, internal and external memory. The data paths to the memories are 32 bit.

The point-to-point communication links have many advantages over multiprocessor buses:

1. There is no contention for the communication mechanism, regardless of the number of transputers in the system.

2. The communication bandwidth does not saturate as the size of the system increases because the number of communications links increase with each transputer.

What this means is that while the bus can connect only a few PAMs, a crossbar maybe 16, and MINs up to say 100—all because the bandwidth or the MIP rate would be reduced, the use of transputers is not so limited. Because the number of channels increases linearly with the number of transputers, the MIP rate increases linearly too.

Each link provides two channels, one in each direction: a serial input and output, both of which carry data and link control information. Communication via any link may occur concurrently with communication on all links and with program execution. Synchronization of a link is automatic and requires no explicit programming.

A message is transmitted as a sequence of data packets. Each packet (Fig. A1-2) is transmitted as a one bit followed by another one bit followed by eight bits followed by a zero bit. After transmitting a data packet, the sending transputer waits for an acknowledge signal. The signal consists of a one bit followed by a zero bit. The receiving transputer can transmit an acknowledge as soon as it starts to receive a data packet provided that there is sufficient buffer space for another packet. Since each link is bidirectional, data and acknowledgment packets can be transmitted concurrently. This protocol enables transmission to be continuous and synchronizes the communication of each packet of data, ensuring that slow and fast transputers communicate reliably.

Figure A1-1(a) shows that the chip may include application specific interfaces. This leads to special purpose computers which—at least for graphics and disk drive control—were already produced.

ALU.   Although all transputers do contain some arithmetic logic functions such as add or multiply, all of them do not contain complete ALUs. In some transputers, a set of predefined procedures are provided to support the implementation of multiple length and floating-point arithmetic, while in other transputers a full 64 bit ALU can be found. The T800 has a floating-point unit (*FPU*) which performs addition, subtraction and multiplication of 32-bit floating-point words in less than 1 mcs, division in slightly more than 1 mcs. The FPU can run concurrently with the integer ALU.

Multiple transputers.   The transputer is actually a Reduced Instruction-Set Computer which has fewer instructions, but those it has execute faster. Since the development of programs for such computers is both tedious and error-prone, INMOS decided that the lowest language for programming the transputer should be occam, and did not release any assembly language. This has the additional advantage of portability, since the same program will run on a number of different transputers provided each has an occam compiler.

The instruction a: = 5*b will compile into

```
LDAL b      -- Load accumulator A with b from local memory.
LDBC 5      -- Load accumulator B with constant 10.
MUL         -- Multiply.
STOL a      -- Store result in local a.
```

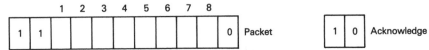

Figure A1-2   The packet and acknowledge signals

The first instruction requires two, the others only two cycles—altogether five cycles are required. Since the clock of the transputer works with a frequency of 20*10' cps, the cycle time is 50 nns. For the assignment statement 250 nns are required. This corresponds to 16 MIPs. Because of larger constraints, nonlocal addresses and more complex instructions, the figure quoted by the manufacturer is 10 MIPs. By way of comparison, note that personal computers run at approximately 1 MIPs, supercomputers at 1000 MIPs. As noted earlier, many applications require a high MIP rate. To increase the MIP rate, we may connect a number of transputers.

A (binary) number of transputers can be combined into various networks, e.g., the mesh of Fig. A1-3(a) or toroid of Fig. A1-3(b). It can also be combined into a Cube. For dimensions not greater than four the number of links is sufficient. For $d>4$, there exists a possibility of adding links to the four links that are standard. Rumors have it that the company is to produce transputers with as many as nine links, which would enable it to assemble a Hypercube with 512 transputers. Another trend is to buy meshes of transputers, making the parallel processing market even more competitive.

Another way to increase the power of a transputer-based PPS is to combine four transputers into a single, but more powerful one. As shown in Fig. A1-3(c), the number of

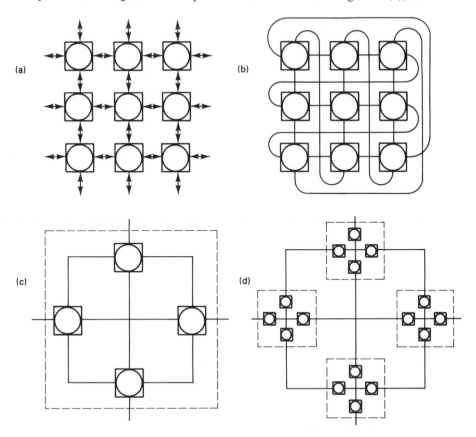

Figure A1-3 Combination of transputers

such nodes is a multiple of 4, 4^2, 4^3 etc. This has the following advantage: in a mesh-connected 4-by-4 PPS, a message may have to travel through up to six links, while if the same 16 transputers are connected as in Fig. A1-3(d), the longest distance is only three. Using more clusters may not be advisable on account of rather complicated wiring, and a Cube may be the better solution.

As already mentioned the power of transputer combinations increases linearly with their number, because all parts: CPU, memory and primarily the communication capability increase in the same proportion.

The interconnection of transputers may be solved in hardware. A mesh of transputers looks similar to the way in which chips are laid out on the wafer on which they are produced. It seems a waste of time and money to split these wafers, package individual chips and then interconnect them in a way in which they were originally produced. It would seem much more sensible to connect the transputers into meshes while they are still on the wafers. Unfortunately, this would connect some transputers which may be faulty, and produce too much heat on a single wafer. Still, some view such meshes as the PPSs of the future.

A1–2 NOTES ON FIRMWARE

We have used the Caltech and Intel approaches to programming Cubes. Actually, the additions needed for interprocess communication in Cubes were proposed first by C.A.R. Hoare [Hoa78] in his influential paper "Communicating Sequential Processes," CSP. His language model, the CSP is used in Occam[r] which may be considered an assembly language for Cubes. Programming in it is similar to Ada. The basic idea of CSP is that a number of purely sequential PaMs, each executing a sequential task, can by communicating through a network of self-synchronizing channels execute parallel computations.

As other microcomputers, transputers are "defined" by their "assembly language"—Occam. Transputers and Occam support the two essential features of real-time processing: *concurrency and communication.*

As mentioned above, the transputer is capable of processing both sequential and parallel tasks. These tasks work both on the local data, but also communicate with other tasks (in transputers) through the links.

A task cooperates with other tasks using point-to-point communication channels. A collection of tasks (processes) is itself a task. A hierarchy of tasks can be built-up to reflect the real-time structure of occurring events.

Tasks communicate through the ports. If two tasks are on the same transputer, they communicate by a memory-to-memory transfer not using the channels. If they are on different transputers, the channels will be used. In both cases, the tasks are synchronized, with the transfer happening when both the input and output tasks are ready.

Suppose a task is unable to output to a channel. This could lead to the receiver not being able to read. A chain reaction could then lead to a deadlock. Occam provides no assistance in preventing deadlocks.

The load should be distributed as equally as possible on a Cube. If we have three tasks taking the times of 1, 2, and 3 time units and divide them between three transputers, the job will be completed in 3 instead of 6 time units needed on a single computer. The speedup is approximately 2 and the efficiency is only 67%. If we split the third task into two tasks one running for 1 and the other for 2 time units, and run the job on four transputers, we get it completed in 2 time units, with a speedup of 3 and an efficiency of 75%. The tasks can be distributed among the transputers by using the PLACE operator of Occam. The main problem of programming is seen in dividing the job into tasks and assigning tasks to transputers. This is so because it is important to identify both the tasks and the communication pattern between them.

Every transputer includes a small *hardware kernel* (OS) to implement the (process) task model and the communication between the tasks. Communication is handled directly by Occam statements for passing messages, scheduling and de-scheduling tasks (see below). The kernel includes two levels of priority with the higher normally used for external events (interrupts) or for indirect message transfer.

The context switching required by interrupts is done in hardware, i.e., fast; most require only between 1 mcs and 2.5 mcs. The kernel gives a high-priority task unconditional control over the CPU preventing any low-priority task from using the transputer until the first task has completed. The transputer also has a hardware timer which can activate synchronous interrupts for time-critical tasks.

Each link has a DMA device built in so that if one end of a channel sends a message and the other one is ready to receive it, the message is transferred. While this takes place, the two tasks are de-scheduled, but the two transputers may work on other tasks that are not waiting for messages.

The transputer and the Occam language were designed at the same time by INMOS. Such hardware features as the links have been designed to support concurrency as practiced by Occam, while some features of the Occam compiler were tailored to the transputer hardware.

We have seen that designing a PPS means dealing with problems of task scheduling, synchronization, and communication between the PAMs. On the transputers, the majority of these problems are handled by the Occam language and the transputer itself.

A1–3 THE OCCAM LANGUAGE

The language takes its name from William of Occam who lived in England in the fourteenth century. William was credited with the Latin quotation: *Entia non sunt multiplicanda praeter necessitatem*, or "entities should not be multiplied beyond necessity"—in short, *keep things simple*. This is what the language is attempting to do by combining the performance of an assembly language with the readability, programmer productivity, and maintainability of higher level languages. It lacks such parts of higher level languages as recursion, pointers, and especially types of variables and constants. However, it includes the concepts of concurrency and communication needed for Cubes. A few language items are discussed below in terms of Ada. A more complete description of the language can be found in [Jon87].

Occam and Ada both support concurrency by using multitasking (tasks are called *processes* in Occam).

A new type of variable, called a "port," is added to the programming language. Whenever a value is needed from a node, the program mentions the port name followed by a question mark. If on the other hand a value is to be sent, the program contains the port name of the receiver preceded by an exclamation mark. For instance, if the two values of A and B are to be input and their sum transferred to port C, then the task would contain the instruction: !C : = A? + B? In evaluating this expression, the task waits until both input ports A and B contain the values, then adds them and finally sends the result to port C.

After having distributed the tasks among the transputers, we need to assign channels (of Occam) to links (of transputers). Suppose we measure the current of an electric generator in a "cur.sen" sensor. To assign this channel to link 1 we need to write: PLACE cur.sen AT 0: while in order to assign an external port st.reg (for status register) to memory location 17, we need to write: PLACE st.reg AT #0011.

All transputers incorporate a timer which can be used by a variable:

tim ? t reads the time into t.

Delayed inputs are of the form:

tim ? after t which reads the time after a delay.

Language features like assignments, conditional statements, procedures, input and output statements will be described shortly. First, let us discuss the three "constructors" of Occam, namely:

1. The sequential constructor (**seq**) causes its statements to be executed in a strictly sequential order, terminating when the last of them completes.
2. The parallel constructor (**par**) causes its parts to be executed concurrently, terminating when *all* its components have terminated.
3. The alternative constructor (**alt**) chooses one of its components for execution and terminates when this component completes.

Each of these constructors can be viewed as a block (of Ada). Occam uses indentation to distinguish between units of a program. Since we are used to (Ada) comblike structures, we will use comments to indent blocks. The three constructors will therefore appear as:

```
seq                    par                    alt
  --- statements         --- statements         --- statements
  --- statements         --- statements         --- statements
--end of seq.          --end of par.          --end of alt.
```

The following operators are used in Occam for calculating expressions:

```
Arithmetic:            +,-,*,/, and the remainder operator \
Modulo arithmetic:     plus, minus, times, divide
Boolean:               and, or, not
```

```
Relational:              = , > , < , <> , >= , <=
Bits:                    bitand, bitor, bitnot, and exclusive-or ><
Shifts:                  <<, and >>
```

To describe sequential processes, we write in Table A1-1 Ada statements alongside the corresponding Occam statements.

TABLE A1-1

	Occam	Ada
Assignment:	a := a + b	a := a + b;
For-loop :	**seq** i = [0 for n]	**for** i in 0. .n loop
	--- statements	---statements
	--end of loop.	**end loop;**
While-loop:	**seq while** a > b	**while** a > b **loop**
	--- statements	--- statements
	--end of while.	**end loop;**
If-statement:	**if** n < 0	**if** n < 0
	sign := −1	**then** sign := −1;
	n = 0	**elsif** n = 0
	sign := 0	**then** sign := 0;
	n < 0	**elsif** n < 0 --It is not an else.
	sign := 1	**then** sign:= 1;
	--end of if.	**end if;**

Declaration are as follows:

```
var a,b,c:   a,b,c : integer;
```

The statement **seq i** = 1 **for** *n* tasc(i) will loop *n* times, while the statement **par** i = 1 **for** *n* tasc(*i*) will create *n* tasks.

Ada is a strongly typed language: Occam has no types at all. On the other hand, while Ada depends on the OS for its I/O, and leaves no choice to the programmer, Occam allows free choice of I/O channels. Such channels can be declared, like in chan in, out, link, and used for example in ''in ? a ; b'' (''input variables *a* and *b* through channel in''), or in ''out ! a ; b'' (''output variables a and b through channel out'').

Procedures (called processes in Occam) are declared similarly to Ada, namely

OCCAM		ADA	
proc name ( )	and	procedure name (	)

with channels used as parameters in Occam. A procedure could end with skip: where skip has no effect and the colon terminates the procedure.

As an example of an Occam procedure we will code the ''swap''ping of two values *a* and *b*, used so much in sorting (see Code A1-1). The procedure is to be called as in Ada, e.g., swap(e,w,n,x,y,z).

```
proc swap (chan in, out, link, var a, b, c) =
seq                         ---The procedure is sequential
  link ? c                  ---Input c through a link, c is a condition
while c                     ---As long as c=true, run the loop
    var temp:               ---Temp is a variable for temporary storage
    seq                     ---The sequential process of swapping a<->b
      in ? a, b             ---Input the values of a and b
      temp := a             ---Store a temporarily in temp
      a := b                ---Replace value of a with previous value of b
      b := temp             ---Assign previous value of a to b
      out ! a, b            ---Output new values of a and b through "out"
      link ? c              ---Input a new condition c=true if to proceed
    --end of seq.
  --end of while.
--end of proc swap.
```

Code A1-1

Just as a list of actions can be specified to be executed strictly sequentially, so it can be specified to proceed concurrently (i.e., in any order), denoted in Occam as parallel. For instance, the following two assignments could proceed in the given order:

```
par
  b := a+2
  c := b-2
--end of par,
```

or with the two statements reversed. If a was initially 2, then in the first case: b := 4 and c := 2, whereas in the second case c cannot be assigned any value because b has none. Thus, for a parallel construct to be legal, no value used in any expression on the right should be changed in any other part of the par-construct.

If such mutual interference is not allowed, how then are concurrent processes to communicate? The answer is that they do so by input and output over channels. The output process: channel ! expression sends the value of the expression over the channel. Similarly, the input process: channel ? variable receives a value from the channel and stores it in the variable. Each of these communications waits for the other, so that an output does not happen until the corresponding input happens and vice versa. [Jon87]

The *rendezvous* of Ada transfers values between the sender and receiver. The above communication between the two channels corresponds to the rendezvous of Ada, since one of the channels will wait for the other to be ready and then exchange the information. This, incidentally, may lead to *deadlock* as in the case when tasks A and B run simultaneously and request input on channel a (b). Both will wait forever if each output should follow a successful input.

A par-construct terminates when *all* its components have terminated. Thus, we could use the previously declared procedure swap to sort a list in parallel on two transputers. It is assumed that half of the list is stored in firalf, the other half in secalf, and that the swap procedure is a part of a sort procedure sort. Then, the program might be:

```
par
   sort(ina,ota,firalf)  --ina is an input, ota an output channel.
   sort(inb,otb,secalf)  --inb is an input, otb an output channel.
--end of parallel sort. The sequential sort can be found in Chap. 7.
```

Decisions may also be distributed across several processes, using an alternative, which is similar to a conditional except in that the choice can depend on whether another process is performing an output. An alternative is written with the keyword alt above a list of components, each of which is either an alternative, or consists of a guard with, and a process which is indented a little further. A guard may be an input process, or skip, or either of these simple guards preceded by an expression and an ampersand sign, as for example in Code A1-2.

```
   alt
      red.selected & red ? x     -- If red selected, then read x from
                                 -- red
         out ! x                 -- and write x on the out-channel.
      --end of first alternative.
      green.selected & green ? x
         out ! x
      --end of the second alternative (for the green channel)
      not (red.selected or green.selected) & skip
         out ! default.value
      --end of the third and last alternative.
      --end of the alternatives.
```

Code A1-2

An alternative waits until there is a guard which is "ready." An input guard becomes ready when a corresponding output is possible; a skip guard is always ready; and a guard preceded by an expression can only become ready if both the value of the expression is true, and the process part of the guard is ready. When some guard has become ready, one of the ready guards is selected and executed, followed by the corresponding process. After this the alternative terminates. At most, one of the branches of an alternative is selected; if no guard ever becomes ready (for example, if there are no components in the alternative), then the whole alternative is deadlocked.

It is possible to associate priorities with alternatives by using **pri alt**. The alternatives are then checked in the lexical order and the first alternative with a ready guard is executed. The **skip** command terminates with no effect; thus

```
if
  (char = 'a') or (char = 'b')
    skip
  --end of first case.
  true                        --else can be written by using true.
    char := ' '               --insert blanks for characters a and b.
  --end of second case
--end of the if.
```

The two primitive constructors par and alt can be used with loops, as for example **par** $i = $ [0 **for** n] or **alt** $i =$ h [0 **for** n], but beware of the possibilities inside the loops.

The wait primitive is used to delay a process for some time. A wait process is defined to be ready to execute if its following condition evaluates to true. The condition must involve the clock. For example, wait delay>time delays the process until delay is greater than time. If two time values have to be compared, the primitive after can be used. For example, wait now after delay means the process continues execution when the time supplied by the local clock is larger than "delay"; now provides the value of a clock local to each process; after ensures that the delay is compared to now.

In order to synchronize the activities among channels the "any" primitive is used; for instance we may have as part of a program:

```
while c
  alt                         --do something with the amount input
    amount ? number           --through channel 'amount', but if none
    link ? any                --appears, then disregard the value on
      c := false              --channel link, and set c to false so that
    --                        --the while will not be executed any more.
  --end of the two alternatives.
--end of the while.
```

A1–4 EXAMPLES

First, we use Occam for two *image processing* problems: for transforming images by rotating and scaling them. Other transformations can be found in the abundant literature on image processing.

Given a point $[x(1),y(1)]$ in the x-y plane, its angle with the x axis according to Fig. A1-4 is β defined by $\tan(\beta) = y(1)/x(1)$. The rotation of this point by an angle θ yields:

$$\sin(\beta+\theta) = \cos(\beta)*\sin(\theta)+\sin(\beta)*\cos(\theta) = y(2)/d \qquad (A1-1)$$

$$d = \sqrt{x^2+y^2} \quad \text{(is the distance from the origin)} \qquad (A1-2)$$

$$x(2)=d*\cos(\theta)*\cos(\beta)-d*\sin(\theta)*\sin(\beta)=x(1)*\cos(\beta)-y(1)*\sin(\beta) \qquad (A1-3)$$

$$y(2)=d*\sin(\theta)*\cos(\beta)+d*\cos(\theta)*\sin(\beta)=y(1)*\cos(\beta)+x(1)*\sin(\beta) \qquad (A1-4)$$

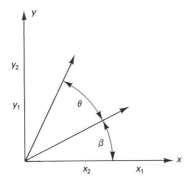

Figure A1-4 Transformation of coordinates

This transformation may be summarized as the matrix product

$$[x(2),y(2)] := [x(1),y(1)] * \begin{vmatrix} \cos(\beta) \ \sin(\beta) \\ -\sin(\beta) \ \cos(\beta) \end{vmatrix} \tag{A1-5}$$

Scaling an image can also be achieved by a matrix multiplication. For instance, if an image is to be doubled in the x-coordinate and remain the same in the y-coordinate, its points have to be premultiplied by

$$r := \begin{vmatrix} 2 & 0 \\ 0 & 1 \end{vmatrix} \tag{A1-6}$$

The two transformations can be combined into a single matrix multiplication.

Next we follow (in reduced form) one of the examples given in [Jon87]. The example is that of *matrix multiplication*, but for image processing. Rotation of coordinates {x(0), x(1), x(2)} and scaling it involves matrix multiplication, translation, and an addition of a constant:

$$y(i) := \Sigma a(i,j)*x(j) + k(i); \quad j\Sigma = 0,1,2 \tag{A1-7}$$

If the transformation is being applied once to an object with a view to printing an image on a slow, hard copy device such as a pen plotter, then the time taken to do the transformation is probably not important, and it does not matter much how the matrix multiplication is organized. On the other hand, if the image is being displayed on a cathode ray tube, and the observer is allowed to change his point of view from the console, then *speed is important*. Ideally, the transformation should be applied to every relevant point of the object as the position of that point is required for refreshing the display, so that the observer sees the effect of a change in the transformation as soon as possible.

If there are of the order of a thousand points in the representation of the image, then this means something of the order of a hundred thousand matrix multiplications in a second. For practical purposes, this requires that special hardware be dedicated to perform the matrix multiplications on a stream of coordinates on its way to the display. In such an arrangement, the time taken to perform the nine individual multiplications will dominate the time taken by all of the communications and additions involved. It is advantageous to arrange as many multiplications as possible concurrently.

The channels connected to a typical multiplier process are

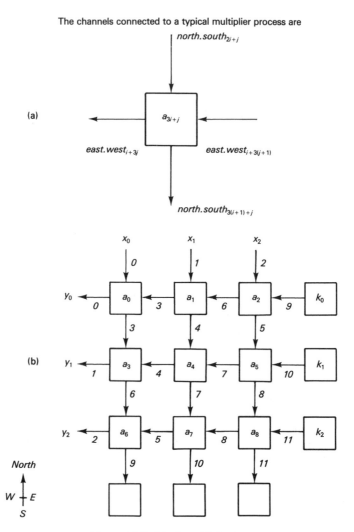

Figure A1-5   Matrix multiplication

A natural configuration of processors to perform this task is a square array, mimicking the matrix, one processor being responsible for each element of the matrix, and performing the multiplication by that element. [Jon87]

As seen in Fig. A1-5, the values of $x(i)$ stream into the embedded system from the north, the translation coordinates from the east, and the transformed coordinates emerge from the west. Each transputer has to input and output data as well as perform the multiplication. The only sequential constraints are that the transfers to the west and from north must come *after* other operations have been performed. Therefore, the program of a single multiplier is as in Code A1-3.

Since different components of a *multiplier* implemented in hardware would be used by the arithmetic and each of the communications, the branches of the **par** constructs naturally execute simultaneously.

Notice that the multiplier process does not need to know where it is in the array—it is independent of i and of j. This means that an implementation in hardware could use nine identical circuits.

In order to complete the matrix multiplier, a source of the k(i) offset values is needed along the eastern border, and a sink must be provided at the southern end of each column of multipliers to receive the redundant x(j) from the southernmost multiplier. [Jon87]

They appear as two procedures of Code A1-4.

```
proc multiplier(value aij, chan north, south, west, east) =
  var xj, atx, yi : -- atx stands for "a(i,j) times x(j)".
  seq
    north ? xj              -- Input a single xj from the north.
    while true              -- This while goes on "forever".
      seq                   -- It consists of two parallel blocks.
        par                 -- This is the first block.
          south ! xj        -- It outputs xj for a lower multiplier,
          atx := aij*xj     -- performs the multiplication and
          east ? yi         -- outputs yi - the three in any order.
        -- end of parallel construct.
        par                 -- The second block follows sequentially.
          west ! yi+atx     -- It adds atx to the previous value of yi,
          north ? xj        -- and inputs a new xj from the north.
        -- end of the second parallel construct.
      -- end of the sequential construct.
    -- end of the while loop.
  -- end of the sequential procedure.
: -- end of the procedure "multiplier.
```

Code A1-3

```
proc offset (value ki, chan west) =
  while true                -- This loop goes on "forever".
    west ! ki :             -- It inserts the offset value from west.
  -- end of the while loop
-- end of procedure "offset.

proc sink(chan north) =
  while true
    north ? any
  -- end of the while loop.
-- end of procedure "sink".
```

Code A1-4

"Although the *sink* does nothing with the values received, its input actions are necessary so that the corresponding output can happen in its neighboring *multiplier*" [Jon87].

If the channels and multipliers are numbered as in Fig. A1-5(a), then each multiplier has indices as indicated in Fig. A1-5(b), and the entire array of multipliers can be described as in Code A1-5.

```
def n = 3                          -- Dimension is three.
var a[n*n], k[n] :                 -- One dimensional arrays.
seq                                -- The main program.
  -- initialize a and k here        Next the ns=nort.east and ew=
  chan ns[(n+1)*n],ew[n*(n+1)] :   -- east,west channels are declared.
  par                              -- Main parallel construct.
    par j = [0 for n]              -- Producing x(j) values by
      produce.xj(j,ns[j])          -- a procedure.
    -- end of producing all xj values on the north-south channels.
    par
      par i = [0 for n]            -- Calling in parallel all n
        offset(k[i], ew[(n*n)+i])  -- offset procedures.
      -- end of par on the offset.
      par i = [0 for n]            -- Calling all multipliers
        par j = [0 for n]          -- in parallel.
          multiplier(a[(n*i)+j], ns[(n*i)+j],
          ns[(n*(i+1))+j], ew[i+(n*j)], ew[i+(n*(j+1))])
        -- end of par j.
      -- end of par i.
      par j = [0 for n]            -- Sinks on ns channels.
        sink(ns[(n*n)+j]
      -- end of par on sink j.
      par i = [0 for n]            -- Consumers of coordinates y(i).
        consume.yi(i,ew[i])
      -- end of par on consume.yi.
    -- end of matrix multiplier par.
  -- end of the main par construct.
--end of the main program.
```

Code A1-5

Another possible embedding for a straightforward matrix multiplication is shown in Fig. A1-6 and the "program" might be as in Code A1-6.

```
proc mult(chan up, down, left, right)=
var a, b, result;
seq; -- This is the first of three sequential processes.
  result := 0.0;
  seq i = [0..n]
    seq
      par;
        up?a;  -- Get the up value for a.
        left?b; -- Get the left value for b.
      -- parend;
      result := result + a*b; -- Perform the calculation.
      par;
        down ! a;  -- Transfer the a-value down.
        right ! b; -- Transfer the b-value right.
      -- end of the parallel step.
    -- end of the inner sequential step
  -- end of the outer sequential loop
-- end of the multiplication procedure.

-- In the main program, use the following:
chan vert(n*(n+1)); -- Open an array of vertical channels.
chan horz(n*(n+1)); -- Open an array of horizontal channels.
par;
  par i = [0..n]
    c := n*i;
    par j = [0..n]
      mult((vert(c+j), vert(c+j+1), horz(c+j), horz(c+j+1));
      -- This multiplies the elements.
      -- Input and output values on the border.
    -- end of the parallel loop on j.
  -- end of the parallel loop on i.
-- end par.
```

Code A1-6

Another example for an embedded hardware system is one which solves the Dirichlet problem. The program is very similar to that defined earlier except for the way of communicating the results near the borders to neighboring nodes. It can be summarized as follows:

1. Transfer the values of the potential to neighboring nodes and get them from the neighbors.
2. Update the edge and corner values upon receiving the information from the neighbors.

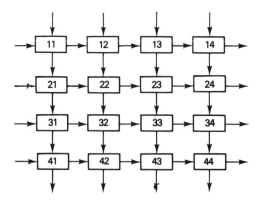

Figure A1-6   Matrix multiplication

3. Update all inner points of a subarea residing in a node.

4. ''Goto'' 1 for the next iteration or stop the computation.

Let us finish with listing some shortcomings of Occam: It does not support enumerations, records or some other data types, allows no dynamic memory allocation, and has no built-in recursion: a stack must be used for various recursive data structures like lists or trees.

APPENDIX 2

RELIABILITY
ASPECTS

A2–1 RELIABILITY AND SELF-TEST PROGRAMS

Reference [EaT73] mentions that the reliability of PEPE and similar parallel processing systems (PPSs) can be improved by using processing modules (PaMs). Paraphrasing the reference, it can be stated that: ''Even though a PPS contains a large amount of hardware, about 95% of that hardware is contained in the PaMs. Therefore, most faults will occur in the PaMs and element failures can usually be tolerated and frequently even ignored. Most other architectures, such as sequential or vector machines, do not exhibit this property; a hard failure anywhere in the processing unit cannot usually be ignored.''

Most contemporary PPSs discussed in Chapters 3–5 use PaMs. The use of PaMs allows the designer to choose the degree of fault tolerance appropriate for the particular application. The *fault tolerance* of a system is usually taken to consist of (hardware) reliability and its availability.

Fault-tolerant systems work essentially according to the four phases:

1. Each PaM runs a self-test program (STP). A faulty PaM is removed by placing a fault signal in a register accessible to other PaMs, or by letting a healthy PaM take part in the following steps.

2. Each PaM tests its immediate neighbors and produces an ''agreement'' or a ''disagreement.'' It is impossible to judge at this stage which of two differing PaMs

is working correctly. It is even possible (though improbable) that both may be faulty. At this point, each PaM assembles a table of results from these neighborhood tests. These results are further transmitted to fault-free neighbors, which in turn transfer them to other PaMs.

3. A common table is produced by all PaMs. From this table it is possible to deduct which PaMs are really faulty, since a faulty PaM must appear faulty to all PaMs. (If at **2** a new fault occurs, the table would not be identical for all PaMs.)

4. Assuming that points **1** to **3** produce a clear indication of which PaMs are faulty, a *reconfiguration* will occur. Faulty parts will be removed, the program distributed among the healthy PaMs, and restarted (rollback and restart).

The following two procedures were developed before the advent of PPSs to achieve high reliability and availability [Han86]:

1. Two systems are provided with only one "on-line." When this system is down, the stand-by system replaces it. The problem is: how is the fault detected?

2. Three systems are running simultaneously with 2-out-of-3 voting to decide which results are correct.

In both cases, but especially in the second case, the price we pay for "useful redundancy" is very high. In Parallel Processing Systems (PPSs) we can reduce this price increase of 100% or 200% substantially. The performance will obviously decrease when units are removed.

To illustrate the various possibilities available to the designer of PPSs, we will take a simple macropipeline configuration as an example. It is assumed that a continuous stream of data is fed into the first processor of the pipe, then processed in four pipeline stages, and finally the last processor is responsible for the output (Fig. A2-1).

Evidently the whole pipeline in Fig. A2-1(a) will fail as soon as one building block becomes defective. If continuous operation is required even with (not more than one) hardware failure in every stage of the pipeline, the Triple Modular Redundancy (TMR) in Fig. A2-1(b) can be used. All three processors in any stage execute the same task. A 2-out-of-3 voter (implemented in software) votes on data from the previous stage.

If short interruptions in case of a failure are acceptable, the configurations in Fig. A2-1(c) and A2-1(d) are proposed. In Fig. A2-1(c) each pipeline stage is duplicated, allowing the next stage to compare the results of the previous one (by software). However, in case of a mismatch, additional diagnostic techniques (e.g., self-test programs; see below) are necessary to decide which of the two building blocks is faulty. Only the results of the fault-free PaM are further processed.

Figure A2-1(d) shows a configuration having only one spare building block and some additional bypass links. Usually the spare is idle (perhaps executing some self-tests). Fault diagnosis techniques are used to detect and locate a faulty building block. Then the defective processor is bypassed and the spare activated. It is clear that recovery time is now much longer than in the other cases, because tasks have to be moved between building blocks.

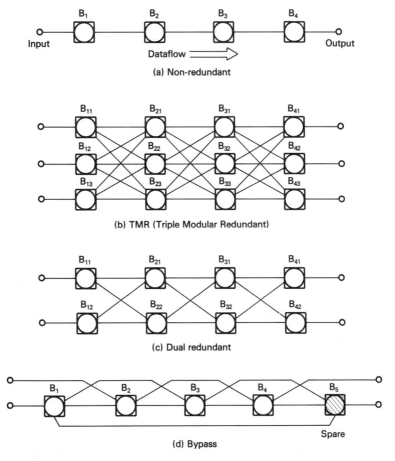

Figure A2-1   Reliability enhancements. Courtesy of E. Maehle: "Fault-tolerant DIRMU multiprocessor configurations," Computer Architecture Newsletter, IEEE Computer Society, June, pp. 51-56.

A common property of all the examples we have discussed so far is redundant building blocks, making such configurations rather expensive. However, for many applications, a degraded performance in case of a fault is fully acceptable. [Mae85b]†

We have already seen a number of such arrangements for PPSs. In Chap. 2, while discussing rings, hardware to handle a faulty unit was described. Multiprocessor configurations that allow degraded service are especially useful for problems that work on say n columns (e.g., linear sets, partial differential equations, image processing, etc.). Assuming $n \gg p$, we may work with $p, p-1, \ldots ,p-\mathrm{k}$ PaMs while the throughput or

†E. Maehle: "Systematischer Entwurf von Mikrocomputer-Selbstest programmer," 13 Fachtaging "Technische Fuverlassigkeit," Nuernberg, pp. 145–49; reprinted by permission.

speedup changes (almost) linearly. As a case in point, a ring could be used as shown in Fig. A2-2(a) or (b). For the case depicted in Fig. A2-2(b), the following procedure is advocated in [Mae85.a]:

> In the nonredundant ring a faulty block leads to a system failure. In order to achieve fail-soft operation, additional links are provided.
>
> If all PaMs are operational, only the outer links are used. All I/O is done by a MASTER, which has access to a disk and a terminal. The current state of the computation is checkpointed in regular, user definable intervals to disk. Besides the MASTER, another PaM (MASTER in spe) also stores checkpoints, otherwise it behaves like a normal SLAVE. In this way duplicate copies of each checkpoint are available.
>
> Let us assume that a SLAVE fails. This is detected by its immediate neighbors and triggers reconfiguration. Based on the results of the diagnosis, the MASTER remaps the ring structure onto the remaining fault-free configuration, making use of the additional links [Fig. A2-2(b)]. Then the MASTER restarts the program from the last checkpoint on its disk. Of course the system continues now with degraded performance, because the ring has shrunk by one PaM.
>
> All steps described above are executed automatically under software control. If the MASTER fails, basically the same steps are taken. The only difference is that the MASTER in spe executes the recovery procedures, using the checkpoints on its disk.
>
> Repaired PaMs are also detected by the self-diagnosis algorithms and are automatically *reintegrated* into the configuration. Note that in the example described above more than one faulty building block can be tolerated. If one MASTER survives, it always tries to find the maximum ring configuration that is still possible. No critical central components exist. [Mae85a]

In PPSs we may use *useful redundancy* of this sort in order to increase the fault tolerance and availability of the PPS. Moreover, whenever a PaM is "unemployed" and is not being used by its neighbors, it could perform a *Self-Test Program*, STP. On the other hand, an unemployed PaM could take a part of the job from an overburdened neighbor. This would help in providing the important balance (especially in Hypercubes).

The *ILLIAC* has extensive hardware and thus a high probability of system failure. Also, the failure of a single PE causes a complete system failure and because there are 64 of them, the probability of failure is high. TMR would be much too costly, but a dynamic scheme of enhancing the reliability was proposed in [BaL80]. In this proposal, a single PE is added, replacing any faulty PE (one of the 64). This small hardware redundancy enhances both the availability and the reliability of ILLIAC, also enhancing its fault tolerance.

The proposed technique would first detect a fault and then restart the program. If such "rollback" fails to correct the error, a permanent fault is assumed and the PE in which the failure was detected is removed (for repair). Unfortunately, ILLIAC's rigid interconnection scheme dislocates the entire MIN on the removal of a PE. If we label by x the PE that failed, removing x removes "neighbors" of the PEs labelled $x-1$, $x+1$, $x-8$, and $x+8$ (all modulo 64) and disturbs the routing interconnections in which PE took part. To restore the routing ability of ILLIAC, the spare PE is added and the PEs relabelled. Two relabelling schemes were proposed: Either the spare assumes the logical label x of the failed PE [Fig. A2-3(a)], or all PEs whose numbers are higher than x have

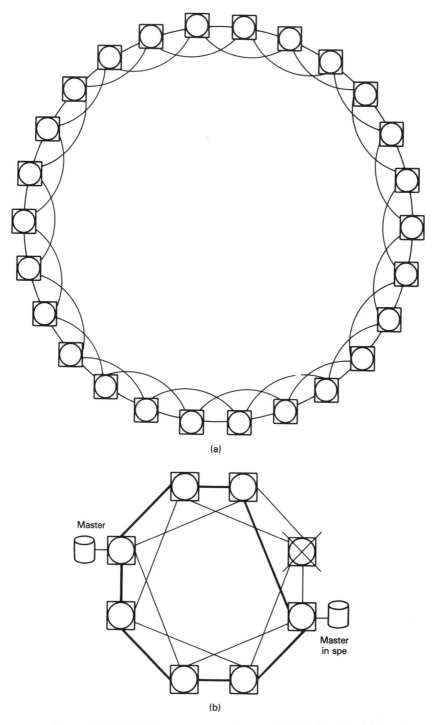

(a)

Master

Master
in spe

(b)

Figure A2-2 Reliability arrangements. Courtesy of E. Maehle: ''Fault-tolerant DIRMU multiprocessor configurations,'' Computer Architecture Newsletter, IEEE Computer Society, June, pp. 51-56.

their numbers reduced by one [Fig. A2-3(b)]. The "decoupling" network of Fig. A2-3 is needed in both relabelling schemes.

As mentioned in [Bal80], this scheme improved the reliability of ILLIAC by better than two orders of magnitude. Since only failures of the PEs were considered, the decrease of reliability due to the MIN, the Central Control Unit, host, etc., may be much higher. In fact, if any of these fail, the system is not available at all. Although the system should check itself periodically, it is virtually impossible to check the controller or host of ILLIAC.

Cellular computers are asymmetric. This may reduce their reliability—at least in the sense of the previous paragraph.

Self-Test Programs (STPs) should be designed so that as many faults as possible are located in minimum time and with the shortest program possible. STPs are more flexible than hardware solutions and can be added to PMs built as standard hardware. They consist of a CPU Test, a ROM Test, an I/O Test, and a RAM Test arranged in a hierarchical way as in Fig. A2-4. They can be executed as power-up tests or idle loop tests. The latter is appropriate for PPSs since a PaM waiting idly for a flag to clear might as well do an STP (transparent to the rest of the software). Discussion on CPU, ROM, and RAM tests is based on [Mae85b].

The STP programs reside in the memories of the PaMs. They start from a small core program (the tip of the triangle in Fig. A2-4) which is assumed to work properly. If that is not so, then it may safely be assumed that the TSP will not run at all. Additional hardware could be provided to watch over the reliability of the core program.

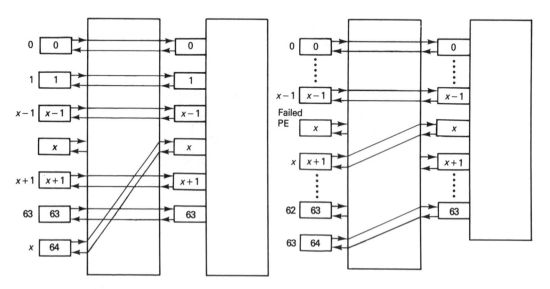

Figure A2-3   Reliability arrangements for the ILLIAC

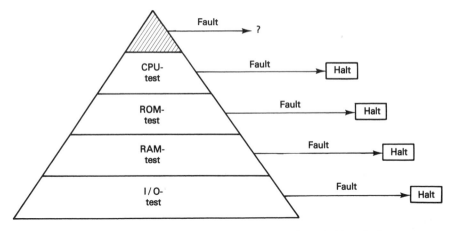

Figure A2-4   Hierarchy of Self-Test Programs. Courtesy of E. Maehle: ''Fault-Tolerant DIRMU multiprocessor configurations,'' Computer Architecture Newsletter, IEEE Computer Society, June, pp. 51-56.

The CPU tests.   Testing all the CPU's possible states is too cumbersome. A systematic test procedure therefore has to make assumptions about the faults (fault model). The CPU test usually proceeds as follows:

1. The CPU is divided into functional blocks and each block represented by its fault model.
2. All faults are located in the functional blocks by the fault procedures.
3. The block procedures are combined into an STP which begins with a minimal number of functions (core), builds up the number of blocks tested, and tests them all.

For most CPUs we can distinguish the following blocks: register array, register decoders, address logic, the ALU, and the instruction decoding logic. A test of any logic circuit will include correspondence checking with the truth table of the circuit and checking for short circuits between input and output units.

The following test is proposed in [Mae85b] for testing a register decoder. The following assumptions are made:

A register *rl* (e.g., the accumulator) is fault-free.

A conditional goto based on the content of *rl* is allowed.

The HALT instruction works fault-free.

Assuming that these conditions are fulfilled, the test procedure is

```
procedure testdecoder is
begin
  for m in 2..n loop
    r(m) := W0;                      -- This writes word W0 = 0,...,0 into r(m)
    for k in reverse 1..m-1 loop
      r(k) := W1;                    -- This writes word W1 = 1,...,1 into r(k)
    end loop;
    compare(W0,r(m));                -- This procedure is described below
    r(m) := W1;
    for k in reverse 1..m-1 loop
      r(k) := W0;                    -- This writes word W0 = 0,...,0 into r(k)
    end loop;
    compare(W1,r(m));
  end loop;
end testdecoder;
```

Command compare($Wx,r(y)$) means that the content of register $r(y)$ is tested to find out if it actually is the word Wx. If it is, then the test proceeds, else a fault is indicated and the testing HALTed. The content of $r(y)$ is first transferred to rl (which was assumed to work properly), then it is compared with Wx and a conditional goto executed if necessary.

The test of logical circuits makes the same assumptions and also that register rl (the accumulator) is connected to the I/Os of the ALU. Binary operations "#" (AND, OR, XOR, . . .) are then performed with the following operands:

$$1010...1010 \# 1010...1010 \quad | \quad 0101...0101 \# 1010...1010$$
$$1010...1010 \# 0101...0101 \quad | \quad 0101...0101 \# 0101...0101$$

The words W55 = 0101...0101 and Waa = 1010...1010 are sufficient for unary NOT operations. The result in register rl is then compared with the correct result and produces a fault signal in case they don't match.

Since all possible combinations exist for every bit, they can all be located by comparisons with truth tables. Faults "Stack-at 0" or at 1 can also be located because each bit is set to 0 or 1.

The tests of CPU functional blocks are similar. Having completed all these tests, the STP is produced by combining the results.

Memory tests.   Words in a *ROM* are supposed to be constant. They are divided into blocks of appropriate length and for each block a test-word is calculated. These words (often the checksum of all the words of a block) are then prestored in the ROM. The test algorithm consists of calculating the test-words and comparing them with the prestored values. A fault is indicated in case of disagreement.

All instructions used in the ROM test have already been found to work properly before they are used in the ROM tests. This is true if the ROM test is done only after a successful completion of CPU tests. The ROM test can be interrupted and proceeds at a later time, to allow the test to be transparent.

Transparent RAM tests split into elementary cycles, each of which is applied on a subset of words (working set) with other words not changed. The working set can be stored at the start of a cycle in the register array provided it is small enough. Following a successful outcome of a cycle, the working set is restored from the register array. Obviously a test should not be interrupted during an elementary cycle because the content of the RAM is changed by the test words. An interruption is allowed between two elementary cycles.

The test program below uses stack-at-0/1 tests for procedure T1 in the memory and data lines, T3 in the address lines, and for both on the outputs of decoders. For short circuits between data lines we use T1 and T2, between address lines we use procedures T3 and T4.

```
procedure T1 is
begin
  for i in 0..n-1 loop
    disable:                      -- This routine will disable the interrupts.
    save(r1,M(i));         -- This routine saves the content of the word at
    -- address i in register r1. Restore does the reverse: M(i):=r1;
    M(i) :=W55; Compare(W55,M(i));            -- M(i) = word in memory i.
    restore(r1,M(i)); enable;    -- This routine enables the interrupts.
    disable; save(r1,M(i));
    M(i) := Waa; Compare(Waa,M(i));
  end loop;
end T1;


procedure T2 is
begin           -- The hexadecimal words below mean that the length of the
  for w in #16#333,#16#0f0f,#16#00ff loop              -- words is 16 bits.
    disable;
    save(r1,any);                          -- any is here any address.
    any := w; Compare(w,any);
    restore(r1,any); enable;
  end loop;
end T2;


procedure T3A is
begin
  for i in 0..d(n)-1 loop     -- d(n) is the decoder line n.
    disable;
    save(r1,addr0(i));         -- addr0(i) has 0s in all bits,
    save(r2,addr1(i));         -- addr1(i) has 0s in all bits, 1 in bit i.
    addr0(i) := W0; addr1(i) := W1;
    Compare(W0,addr0(i));
    restore(r1,addr0(i));  restore(r2,addr1(i));
    enable;
  end loop; -- procedure T3B is as T3A with W0 exchanged for W1.
end T3A;    -- procedure T4 is as T3A but addr1(i) has all 1's
            -- and addr0(i) the same except for a 0 in position i.
```

The basic disadvantages of software tests are that hardware faults can be detected only *during* the running of the STPs and that only fixed faults are detected. To detect transient faults, special hardware is necessary.

Error detection and correction of TOPPS. Most system failures tend to occur due to the failure of the CPU, one of its controllers, or its memory. Because TOPPS is completely symmetric, any unit may be the master. This alleviates the problem considerably if not completely.

To replace a master by a slave requires two steps:

1. The detection of an error, and
2. The correction of the error.

Because of the availability of VLSI chips for implementing "Error Checking and Correcting Memory," it can be assumed, since most "soft" errors can be corrected, that any memory errors that remain will be "hard" errors which are normally processor failures. Once a hard error occurs, that processor may no longer be trusted and must be removed from the TOPPS. It is easy to detect these errors if they occur in memory, but it is not so easy to detect a "soft" or temporary failure of the CPU. For this, the CPU must be periodically "exercised" against a predefined calculation. In TOPPS [Ten82], this happens at system reset and at intervals when the various processors are "relaxing," i.e., during the sequential steps for the slaves and during the parallel steps for the master. The CPU exercises its instruction set in a predetermined sequence. The solution to this small, predetermined problem is loaded into a comparator which checks the performance of the CPU against the known, correct solution. If they agree, nothing happens, but if they disagree or if a memory error is detected, then an error recovery sequence is initiated. This allows the testing to proceed without slowing down system operation.

The test sequence is shown in Fig. A2-5 and includes five steps:

1. The system must know immediately about an error and halt any job in progress.
2. The failed processor must convey its number to other processors.
3. The failed processor must then amputate itself.
4. The remaining CPUs must reallocate the failed job among themselves.
5. The CPUs must reset themselves and start the job from scratch.

The *Error Handling Sequence* is as follows. Whenever a processor error occurs, the error flip-flop is set low (Fig. A2-6). Since this flip-flop is connected to an open-collector buffer, the error line on the master bus is pulled down. Simultaneously, the failed processor has its number clocked into a quad-register and this output is enabled for the error address bus lines.

Once the error line on the master bus goes low, all processors are immediately disabled via the ERROR line which is ANDed with the enable line on the mode-control PROM. At the same time, the RESET and HALT lines on each CPU are asserted. An RS

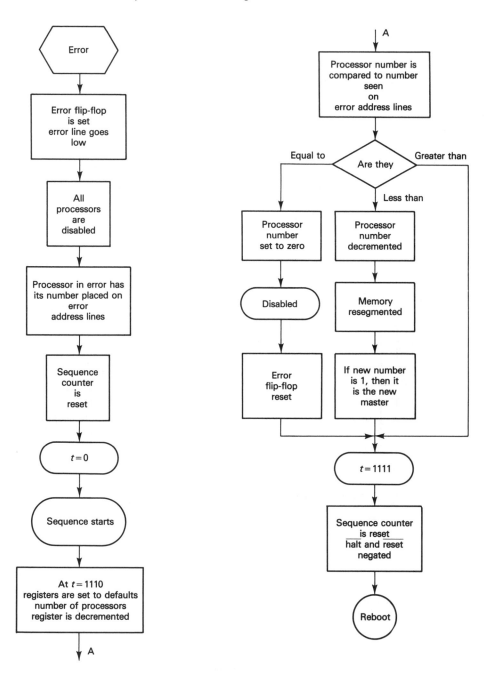

Figure A2-5 A test sequence for TOPPS

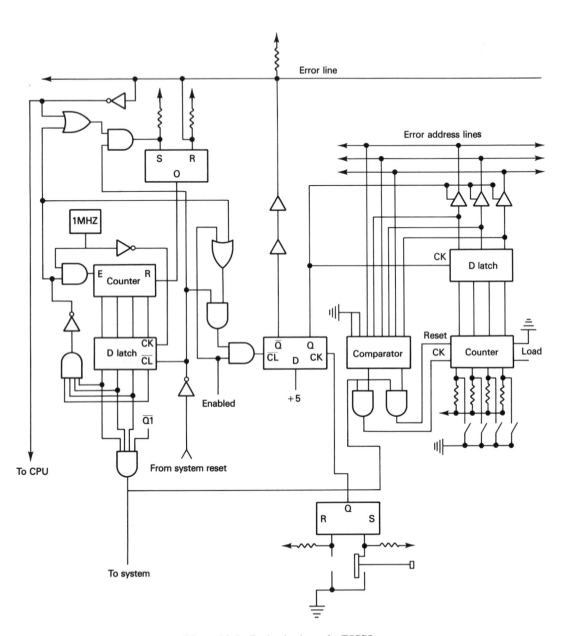

Figure A2-6   Testing hardware for TOPPS

flip-flop, which has its output connected to the reset pin of the error-sequence counter, is reset. This enables the counter whose output is buffered by a quad-register.

Each processor has its "A" error comparator inputs connected to the error address lines and its "B" comparator inputs to the output of the quad register "D" which contains its own number. From $t = 0$ until $t = 1101$ microseconds, the logic is allowed to reach the steady state and the error address comparator is allowed to finish the comparison of the failed processor number with its own number.

At $t = 1110$, the outputs from the comparator are enabled. If A>B is true, the processor-number register is set low, permanently disabling the processor. The error flip-flop is reset and this negates the ERROR line on the master bus. If A>B is true, then nothing happens. If A<B is true, the number register is decremented and its memory segment is reallocated. As an example, if the failed CPU was the master, CPU 1 becomes CPU 0 (the new master), CPU 2 becomes CPU 1, and so on.

At $t = 1110$, the following events also occur in all processors:

1. The slave wait/go register is cleared.
2. The mode register is set to the parallel mode.
3. The done/busy register is set to busy. This allows the processors to return from the error sequence gracefully. Since the sequence, as seen by the master, is asynchronous, the processors might not finish at the same time. After system reset, the master will therefore check the status of the done/busy line and wait until all processors have completed their jobs.
4. The number-of-processors register is decremented.
5. The DTACK counter is reset.
6. The slave subroutine-number register is reset.
7. The output port is cleared.

At $t = 1111$, the sequence counter is reset and the RESET and HALT lines are negated, allowing the system to reboot.

Since a report of the reliability of SMS201 follows, it might be proper to add here that the error detection and correction of TOPPS was checked and proved to fulfill the expectations.

A2–2 RELIABILITY OF SYSTEM HARDWARE

The (hardware) reliability of a system is usually taken to be the measure by which it conforms to the specification of its behavior. A failure is thus an event and the reliability is inversely proportional to the occurrence of failure events. For a single element, say a PaM, the reliability is usually expressed as

$$R_1(t) = \epsilon^{-\lambda t} \tag{A2-1}$$

$$\lambda = 1/MTBF \tag{A2-2}$$

where λ is the failure rate of the unit, and MTBF is the "mean time between failures." The problem here is to calculate the reliability of a system composed of p units.

Definition.   The reliability $R(t)$ of a system is given by the probability of survival for the time from 0 to t.

For calculating $R(t)$ we need the definition of *performance*. Let the performance of a single unit be $P(1)$ so that a PPS has a combined performance of $p*P(1)$. If r PaMs were removed because they were found to be faulty, the remaining performance is
$$p*P(1) - r*P(1)$$
The normalized performance is

$$\chi = (p - r)/p = 1 - r/p \qquad \text{(A2-3)}$$

It is plotted in Fig. A2-7 as a function of the number of removed units for systems with $p = 2$, 16, and 128. Obviously, with $p = 2$ if a unit fails, χ is reduced to 50% and the more units there are to begin with, the smaller is the loss of performance. Thus, according to [TaL80], the decrease in performance is insignificant if in the initial stage about a hundred modules or more are present. On the other hand, the more hardware there is, the more difficult it is to achieve high reliability. Finally, if this hardware is modular and there is little interaction among the hardware units, then they may be replaced easily.

The performance definition is not correct for pipeline computers, because the removal of a single pipeline unit results in a complete system-down. In the case of other PPSs, the removal of a single PaM reduces the performance by a factor of $(p - 1)/p$. Note that this is not a linear relationship. Thus, for $p = 2$, 5, 10, and 100, the performance would be reduced to 50, 80, 90 and 99%—χ "saturates." From this point alone it is not helpful to increase p more and more.

To calculate the reliability for a given system, we assume that

1. In the initial stage, p units are present.
2. At least $p - r$ units are required for minimal performance; failure and removal of more than r units is considered a system failure.
3. Unit failures are considered independent events.

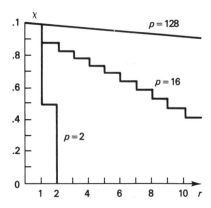

Figure A2-7   Reliability as a function of removal of units. Courtesy of Tomann, Liedl: "Reliability in a microcomputer array." Elsevier Science Publishers.

The reliability of a PPS can be expressed [May74] by

$$R(t) \; = \; \Sigma \gamma * R(1)^i * (1.0 - R(1))^{p-i}; \; i\Sigma \; = \; p-r, \; . \; . \; . \; ,p \qquad \text{(A2-4)}$$

where γ is defined as

$$\gamma \; = \; \binom{p}{i} \qquad \text{(A2-5)}$$

Thus

$$R(t) \; = \; \Sigma \gamma * \epsilon^{\lambda t i} [1.0 - \epsilon^{\lambda t}]^{p-i}; \; i\Sigma = p-r, \; . \; . \; .p \qquad \text{(A2-6)}$$

Instead of time, a relative unit κ will be used;

$$\kappa \; = \; \lambda * t \qquad \text{(A2-7)}$$

so that the reliability is

$$R(\kappa) \; = \; \Sigma \gamma * \epsilon^{-\kappa i} [1.0 - \epsilon^{-\kappa i}]^{p-i}; \; i\Sigma = p-r, \; . \; . \; .,p \qquad \text{(A2-8)}$$

Reliability is shown in Fig. A2-8 as function of κ for $p = 128$ and a parameter $\chi(i)$ where i is the number of units allowed to fail before the system is considered "down." The reliability $R(t)$ increases if a few slaves can be allowed to fail, i.e., if i in $\chi(i)$ is large.

Next, the expected time when the $p-r+1$ slave fails is calculated as

$$ET \; = \; \Sigma 1/(\lambda * i)), \; i\Sigma \; = \; p-r, \; . \; . \; .,p \qquad \text{(A2-9)}$$

The mean time between failures MTBF (denoted M below) or the expected time of the first failure $M(1)$ is

$$M \; = \; M(1) \; = \; 1/(\lambda * p) \qquad \text{(A2-10)}$$

The normalized mean time between failures m is defined as

$$m \; = \; M/M(1) \; = \; \lambda * p\Sigma(1/(\lambda * i)) \; = \; \Sigma(p/i) \qquad \text{(A2-11)}$$

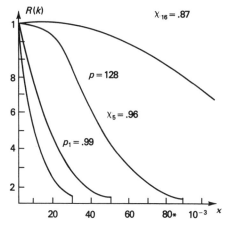

Figure A2-8 Reliability as a function of time. Courtesy of Tomann, Liedl: "Reliability in a microcomputer array." Elsevier Science Publishers.

Figure A2-9 shows that the more failed units were accepted (and p must be larger for this) the reliability can be increased significantly without additional redundancy or loss of performance.

The reliability of a PPS was seen to depend on λ and the M of the units of which it consists. The M of the SMS201 was calculated in [TaL80] and previously quoted in [Wal82]. It may be expressed by

$$M = 1/\Sigma(n(i)*\lambda(i)); \ i\Sigma = 1,\ldots,N \qquad (A2\text{-}12)$$

where $\lambda(i)$ is the failure rate of component i, $n(i)$ is the quantity of component i, and N is the total number of components.

Table A2-1 lists components utilized in the SMS201 boards and their failure rates $\lambda(i)$. Using Eq. (A2-12) and Table A2-1, the MTBFs of a computer module (a slave s) was found to be MTBF$(s) = 65,000$ hrs, and for the driver MTBF$(d) = 270,000$ hrs. The entire system may be viewed as a serial connection of the master (m), 8 drivers and $p = 128$ slaves:

$$1/M = 1/M(m) + 8/M(d) + 1/(M(s)*\Sigma(1/i)); \ i = 128 - r,\ldots,128 \qquad (A2\text{-}13)$$

where we have used already Eq. (A2-9).

In SMS201 the master is a single, large computer which is assumed to never fail: $1/M(m) = 0$. In the general case of an ASP, the master is identical to other CPUs so that only the summation in Eq. (A2-13) should be increased by one. In any case, the drivers have a large $M(d)$ so that $8/M(d)$ can be neglected and only the summation remains in Eq. (A2-13).

On a practical level, it was observed in [TaL80] that

> . . . the SMS201 has been working now for more than two years. After setting up the system, the failure rate decreased continuously until it became constant at the end of 1978.

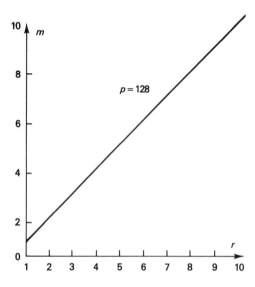

Figure A2-9 Mean time between failures as a function of removed units. Courtesy of Tomann, Liedl: "Reliability in a microcomputer array." Elsevier Science Publishers.

TABLE A2-1 FAILURE RATES OF COMPONENTS

	Failure rate	Device quantity	
		Computer module	Driver module
Components	Failure rate	Computer module	Driver module
8080 CPU and support IC's	0.2	13	4
4K dyn. RAM's	0.2	32	—
Other IC's (TTL)	0.1	64	29
Total failure rate		15.4	3.7
MTBF		65.000	270.000

For 1979 all observed failures are listed in Fig. A2-10. Without repair, the number of modules would have decreased from 128 to 116. This corresponds to an MTBF of about 730 hours. The loss of performance would have amounted to about 9% by the end of 1979.

Actually failing modules were replaced and no system failures were caused in 1979 by failures of the driver modules or by bus blocking.

By tolerating a few failing modules, the time intervals between necessary services can be extended without an essential loss of computational power. If a module failure occurs, the program is reloaded and the computation restarted. The rearrangement is done automatically. [TaL80]

A2–3 RELIABILITY OF MINs

In full-access Multistage Interconnection Networks (MINs) a unique path exists from any input port to any output port. The presence of a single failure among the Switching Elements (SEs) or the connecting links destroys the full access capability. Even though the failure rates of individual components may be very low, the failure rate of the large system consisting of many components can be quite high. Fault tolerance is therefore a necessary attribute of MINs.

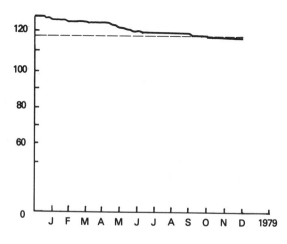

Figure A2-10 Number of units in 1979. Courtesy of Tomann, Liedl: "Reliability in a microcomputer array." Elsevier Science Publishers.

In a fault-tolerant MIN, a noncatastrophic fault should not force a complete shut-down of the PPS and the PPS should continue working with reduced capacity. A fault-tolerant MIN can tolerate faults to some degree and still provide reliable communication between the I/O ports.

A measure of fault tolerance has been described by a property called Dynamic Full Access (DFA) property. A MIN is said to possess DFA capability if, under a given fault set, each MIN input can be connected to any one of the MIN outputs, and the PPS continues to function with gracefully degraded service.

Fault tolerance is usually achieved by introducing redundancy (like the additional group of columns in the MPP of Chap. 3). By introducing hardware redundancy, more alternate paths are created among the ports of the MIN, thereby increasing its capability and fault tolerance. Hardware redundancy can be introduced into the MIN by:

- increasing the number of stages,
- using fault-tolerant switching elements, SEs,
- providing extra links.

Fault diagnosis is concerned with the detection and location of faults in MINs. The presence of a fault is detected first by applying a set of known inputs and comparing the actual outputs with expected values. Any mismatch indicates the presence of a fault. Once a fault is detected, additional tests may locate it.

The problem is approached [Wu978] (or [FaW81]) by generating suitable fault-detection and fault-location *test sets* for every fault in the assumed fault model. These test sets are then trimmed to minimal or nearly minimal sets. It is important to note that to conduct fault diagnosis, a fault model must be obtained so that it is known what faults to identify and locate. (This material is outside the scope of this book and may be found in the references, especially [FaW81].)

Fault diagnosis of MINs with a 4×4 SE will use the DEs and MINs of Sec. 2-4. We will deal only with some of the faults—the others should be looked up in [Sin87].[†]

In the fault diagnosis of this MIN, it is assumed that the terminal links are fault-free. This is a logical assumption and is justified because if a terminal link becomes faulty, the corresponding PE cannot be connected to the network and the line cannot be used for any data transmission. Additional stages will be of no help. The fault diagnosis is done in two phases:

1. In the first phase an input vector "V" with all its elements at logical 0 is applied in mode "0". If the network is fault free or the link fault is of the S-a-0 (Stack-at-zero) type then all the output terminals should be at the logical "0" value. In the second stage of this test, complementary logical values are applied as the input vector. Again, if the network is fault-free or the link fault is S-a-1 (Stack-at-one), then all output terminals will receive a logical "1" value.

2. In phase two, both the above tests are repeated while the network changes into mode "3."

[†]Reprinted from Dr. K. Singh's Ph.D. thesis, by permission of the author.

TABLE A2-2 DERIVATION OF LINK ADDRESSES

Link-level	Addresses of faulty links	Type of fault
1	000	S-a-0
1	110	S-a-1
1	213	S-a-0
1	333	S-a-1
2	001	S-a-1
2	103	S-a-0
2	223	S-a-1

Courtesy of Dr. K. Singh from his Ph.D. thesis.

Steps 1 to 5 below describe the first phase, steps 6 to 8 describe the second phase.

1. Set all DEs to mode "0."

2. Apply a test vector such that all the input terminals are assigned a logical value of "0." Observe the response at the output terminals.

3. Apply a complementary vector (i.e., a logical "1" at every input terminal). Again, observe the response at the output terminals.

4. Record the physical addresses of output terminals having identical output values in steps **2** and **3**. These are the output terminals having faulty response.

5. From the physical addresses recorded in step **4**, write down the addresses of links in all levels from level $(p - 1)$ to 1, that bring data to the recorded addresses of the terminals. The determination of such addresses [is similar to that done for 2×2 SEs.]

6. Change the control signals so that all units are set to mode "3."

7. Repeat steps **2** to **5** above.

8. Addresses of the links in different link-levels found in phase I and phase II are compared and common addresses are listed separately. Then this list of common addresses will be the list of faulty links.

[The following example is from (Sin87)]:
Consider the set of nonoverlapping arbitrary faults as shown in Table A2-2 and Figs. A2-11 and A2-12.

1. Set all DEs to mode "0" operation as shown in Fig. A2-11.

2. Apply the input vector "V" such that the logical value "0" is applied to all input terminals.
   In this case, S-a-0 faults will pass off undetected but S-a-1 faults will be reflected on the output terminals. For example, the S-a-1 fault of address 001 in link level-2 is reflected at output address 010 in link level-3. Observe the response at all output terminals. Now complement the input vector. In this case, S-a-0 faults will be reflected at the output terminals. Again observe the response at all output terminals. The addresses of the output terminals having identical response in both cases (i.e., logical values "00" or "11") are recorded and the corresponding link addresses in link level-2 and 1 are derived and shown in Table A2-3.

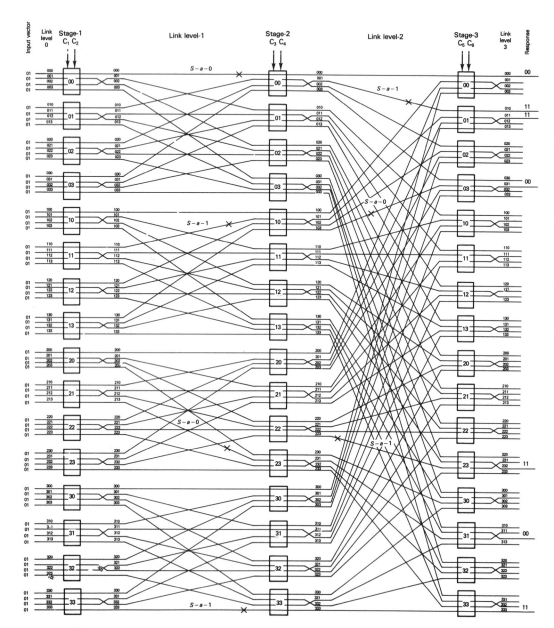

Figure A2-11 A three-stage faulty MIN with DEs in mode 0. Courtesy of Dr. K. Singh from his Ph.D. thesis.

   3. In phase II, the DEs are set to mode "3" operation (Fig. A2-12).

   4. Again, two test vectors as above are applied sequentially. The addresses of the output terminals having identical response in both cases (i.e., logical values "00" or "11") are recorded and the corresponding link addresses in link level-2 and 1 are derived and shown in Table A2-4.

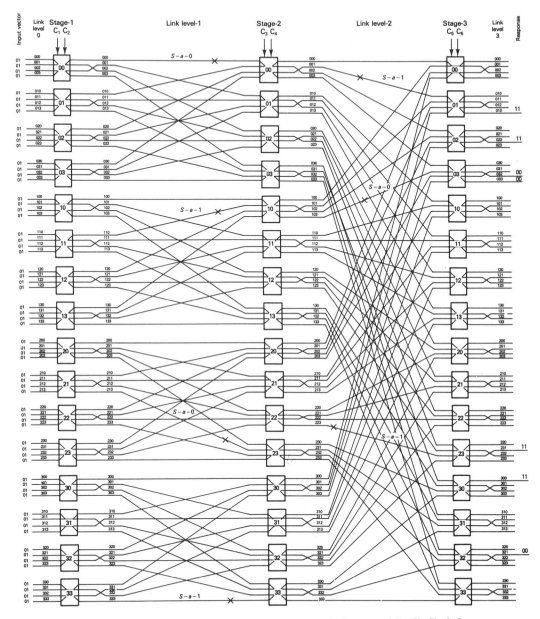

Figure A2-12 A three-stage faulty MIN with DEs in mode 3. Courtesy of Dr. K. Singh from his Ph.D. thesis.

5. Addresses of links in the above two phases are compared and the common links and their fault types are listed in Table A2-5.

6. The above results tally with the assumed arbitrary faults in the three stages of the MIN shown in Fig. A2-12.

TABLE A2-3 DERIVATION OF LINK ADDRESSES—LEVELS 1 AND 2

Output terminal		Corresponding link addresses in	
Addresses of faults	Type of fault	Link level-2	Link level-2
000	S-a-0	$(000)^0$	$(000)^0$
010	S-a-1	$(001)^1$	$(010)^1$
011	S-a-1	$(101)^1$	$(110)^1$
031	S-a-0	$(103)^0$	$(130)^0$
232	S-a-1	$(223)^1$	$(232)^1$
312	S-a-0	$(231)^0$	$(213)^0$
333	S-a-1	$(333)^1$	$(333)^1$

Courtesy of Dr. K. Singh from his Ph.D. thesis.

TABLE A2-4 DERIVATION OF LINK ADDRESSES—LEVEL 2

Output terminal		Corresponding link addresses in	
Addresses of faults	Type of fault	Link level-2	Link level-2
013	S-a-1	$(000)^1$	$(021)^1$
022	S-a-1	$(102)^1$	$(110)^1$
032	S-a-0	$(103)^0$	$(100)^0$
033	S-a-0	$(003)^0$	$(000)^0$
231	S-a-1	$(223)^1$	$(202)^1$
300	S-a-1	$(330)^1$	$(333)^1$
321	S-a-0	$(232)^0$	$(213)^0$

Courtesy of Dr. K. Singh from his Ph.D. thesis.

TABLE A2-5 DERIVATION OF THE COMMON LINKS

Addresses in link level-2	Type of fault
(001)	S-a-1
(103)	S-a-0
(223)	S-a-1

Addresses in link level-1	Type of fault
(000)	S-a-0
(110)	S-a-1
(213)	S-a-0
(333)	S-a-1

Courtesy of Dr. K. Singh from his Ph.D. thesis.

REFERENCES

[AaB85]   J. Archibald, J. L. Baer: "An evaluation of cache coherency solutions in shared-bus multiprocessors," Tech. Rep. 85-10-05, University of Washington, Seattle, WA, 98195.

[AaG89]   G. S. Almasi, A. Gottlieb: "Highly Parallel Computing," The Benjamin/Cummings Publ. Co..

[AaJ75]   G. Anderson, E. Jensen: "Computer Interconnection Structures . . . ," ACM Comp. Surveys, Vol. 7, pp. 197–213.

[AaK84]   J. R. Allen, K. Kennedy: "A parallel programming environment," Trans. IEEE on Software.

[AaS83]   G. R. Andrews, F. B. Schneider: "Concepts and Notations for Concurrent Programming," ACM Surveys, Vol. 15, No. 1, pp. 3–44.

[ABW85]   K. P. McAuliffe, W. C. Brantley, J. Weiss: "The RP3 Processor/Memory Element," Proc. Int. Conf. Parallel Proc., Chicago.

[Aea86]   C. Aykanat et al: "Parallel Computers for Finite Element Analysis," ASME International Conference on Computers in Engineering, Chicago, IL, ASME, Aug. 1986.

[Aea88]   S. Arshi, et al: "Application Performance Improvement on the iPSC/2 Computer, in [Hea88].

[Agr82]   D. P. Agrawal: "Testing and fault-tolerance . . . ," Computer, Vol. 15, No. 4, April, pp. 41–53.

[AJP86]   D. P. Agrawal, V. K. Janakiram, G. C. Pathak: "Evaluating the Performance of Multicomputer Configurations," Computer, Vol. 19, No. 5, pp. 23–37.

[Arl88]   R. Arlauskas: "iPSC/2 System: A Second Generation Hypercube," in [Hea88], 160284.

[ARM]   see [DoD83].

[Bab88]   R. G. Babb II: "Programming Parallel Processors", Addison-Wesley Publishing Co., Reading, MA.

[BaB88]   G. Brassard, P. Bratley: "ALGORITHMICS: Theory and Practice," Prentice Hall, Englewood Cliffs, NJ.

[BaF88]   A. Bode, R. Q. Feitosa: "Bewertung von Speicher-Konzepten," Informationstechnik, Vol. 30, No. 2, pp. 139–48.

[BaL80]   L. Baqai: "Reliability aspects of the Illiac-IV computer," Conference paper and NSF-Grant MC72-03633 A04.

[BaL81]   G. H. Barnes, S. F. Lundstrom: "Design and Validation of a Connection Network for Multiprocessor Systems," Computer, Dec., Vol. 14, No. 12, pp. 31–42.

[BaS76]   G. Bell, Strecker: "Computer Structures: . . . ," IEEE Computer Society, III Annual Symposium on Computer Architecture, Jan., pp. 1–14.

[Bat74]   K. E. Batcher: "STARAN . . . ," Proc. Nat. Comp. Conf., Vol. 43, AFIPS Press, pp. 405–10.

[Bat80]   K. E. Batcher: "Design of a Massively Parallel Processor," Trans. IEEE, Vol. C-29, No. 9, Sept., pp. 836–41.

[Bat82]   K. E. Batcher: "Bit-Serial Parallel Processing Systems," Trans. IEEE, Vol. C-31, No. 5, May, pp. 377–84.

[BaT89]   D. P. Bertsekas, J. N. Tsitsiklis: "Parallel and Distributed Computation," Prentice Hall, Englewood Cliffs, NJ.

[Bau78]   G. M. Baudet: "Asynchronous Iterative Methods for Multiprocessors," Journal of the ACM, Vol. 25, No. 2, pp. 226–44.

[BBN87]   BBN Advanced Computers Inc., 10 Fawcett St., Cambridge, MA 02238. From extensive literature we mention: "Butterfly Products, Overview," General Information . . . ," "Butterfly GP1000 Switch Tutorial."

[BCL88]   J. P. Banatre, A. Coutant, D. LeMetayer: "Parallel Machines for Multiset Transformation and Their Programming Style," Informationstechnik, Vol. 30, No. 2, pp. 99–109.

[Bea83]   I. M. Barron: "The transputer," Electronics, Nov., pp. 109–20.

[Bea85]   A. Bode et al: "A Highly Parallel Architecture Based on a Distributed Shared Memory," In: G. L. Reijns, M. H. Barton (Eds): Highly Parallel Computers, Proc. IFIP Working Conference, Elsevier Science Publishers B. V., pp. 19–28.

[Bea86]   F. J. Burkowski et al: "A Message-Based Architecture for High Concurrency," in [Hea86], pp. 27–37.

[Ben65]   V. Benes: "Mathematical Theory of Connecting Networks," Academic Press, New York.

[Ben82]   M. Ben-Ari: "Principles of Concurrent Programming," Prentice Hall, Englewood Cliffs, NJ.

[BLW87]   A. Burns, A. M. Lister, A. J. Wellings: "A Review of Ada Tasking," Springer Verlag.

[Bro85]   E. D. Brooks III: "Performance of the Butterfly . . . ," pp. 21–24 of Document
           0190-3918/85/0000/0021 $0.100 c 1985, IEEE.

[Bro86]   B. M. Brosgol: "Ada Sampler" in Alsys PC AT Ada Compiler, Alsys Inc. 1432 Main
           Street, Waltham, MA 02154.

[BYA89]   L. N. Bhuyan, Q. Yang, D. P. Agrawal: "Performance of Multiprocessor Interconnec-
           tion Networks, IEEE Computer.

[CaA79]   D. Calahan, W. Ames: "Vector Processors: Models and Applications," Trans. IEEE,
           Vol. CAS-26.

[CaF78]   L. M. Censier, P. Fautrier: "A New Solution to Coherence Problems in Multicache
           Systems," Trans. IEEE, Vol. C-27, No. 12, pp. 1112–18.

[CaM69]   D. Chazan and W. Miranker: "Chaotic relaxation," J. Lin. Alg. Appl., Vol. 2, pp.
           199–222.

[CaW77]   V. Conrad, Y. Wallach: "Scheduling of algorithms for concurrent execution," The
           Computer Journal, Vol. 20, No. 2, pp. 132–36.

[CaW77a]   V. Conrad, Y. Wallach: "A faster SSOR algorithm," Num. Math., Vol. 27, p. 371.

[CaW77b]   V. Conrad, Y. Wallach: "Interative solution of linear equations on a parallel processing
           system," Trans. IEEE, Vol. C-26, No. 2, pp. 838–47.

[CaW79]   V. Conrad, Y. Wallach: "Alternating methods for sets of linear equations," Num.
           Math., Vol. 32, No. 1, pp. 105–8.

[Cea81]   P. Y. Chen et al: "Interconnection Networks Using Shuffles," Computer, Vol. 14, No.
           12, Dec., pp. 55–64.

[Cea85]   W. Crowther et al: "Performance Measurements on a 128-Node Butterfly Parallel
           Processor," Proc. Int. Conf. on Parallel Proc., IEEE Computer Society Press, pp.
           531–40.

[Cha81]   A. E. Charlesworth: "An Approach . . . AP120B . . .'," Computer, Sept., Vol. 14,
           No. 9, pp. 18–27.

[Clo88]   P. Close: "The iPSC/2 Node Architecture," in [Hea88].

[Coh82]   N. H. Cohen: "Parallel Quicksort," Ada Letters, Vol. II, pp. 61–68.

[Csa75]   L. Csanky: "Fast parallel matrix inversion algorithms," contributed paper, 16th Ann.
           Symp. on Foundations of Computer Science (SWAT), Berkeley, Oct..

[Cur78]   G. F. Curtis: "Applied Numerical Analysis," Addison-Wesley Publ. Comp..

[DaB82]   M. Dubois, F. A. Briggs: "Effect of Cache Coherency in Multiprocessors," Trans.
           IEEE, Vol. C-31, No. 11, pp. 312–28.

[DaB85]   C. R. Das, L. N. Bhuyan: "Bandwidth Availability of Multiple-bus Multiprocessors,"
           Trans. IEEE, Vol. C-34, No. 10, Oct., pp. 918–26.

[DaH86]   J. J. Dongarra, A. Hinds: "Comparison of the CRAY X-MP-4, Fujitsu VP-200, and
           Hitachi S-810/20," Simulation 47:3, pp. 93–107.

[DaJ81]   D. M. Dias, J. R. Jump: "Packet Switching Interconnection Networks for Modular
           Systems," Computer, Vol. 14, No. 12, Dec., pp. 43–53.

[Daw87]   B. M. Dawson: "Introduction to Image Processing Algorithms," Byte, Mar., pp. 169–
           86.

[Dea88]   C. C. Douglas et al: "The Interaction of Numerics and Machines," Informa-
           tionstechnik, Vol. 30, No. 2, pp. 83–88.

[DeC89]   A. L. DeCegama: "The Technology of Parallel Processing," Prentice Hall, Englewood Cliffs, NJ.

[Den86]   P. J. Denning: "Parallel computing and its evolution," Comm. ACM., Vol. 19, No. 12, pp. 1163–67.

[Dig86]   Digital Equipment Corporation: "Introduction to Parallel Programming."

[Dij68]   E. W. Dijkstra: "Cooperating Sequential Processes," in *Programming Languages* edited by F. Genuys, Academic Press, New York.

[DiN88]   D. C. DiNucci: "Alliant FX/8," on pp. 27–42 of [Bab88].

[Dix87]   R. C. Dixon: "Lore of the token ring," IEEE Network, Vol. 1, No. 1, Jan. 1987, pp. 11–18.

[DoD83]   Department of Defense: "Reference Manual for the ADA Programming Language," Springer-Verlag, New York, NY.

[Dro82]   R. G. Dromey: "How to Solve it by Computer," Prentice Hall, Englewood Cliffs, NJ.

[EaD83]   D. J. Evans, R. C. Dunbar: "The Parallel Solution of Triangular Systems of Equations," Trans. IEEE, Vol. C-32, No. 2, pp. 201–4.

[EaT73]   A. E. Evensen, J. L. Troy: "Introduction to the architecture of a 288-element PEPE", Sagamore Computer Conference on Parallel Processing, pp. 162–68.

[EaW70]   R. K. Even, Y. Wallach: "On the Direct Solution of Dirichlet's Problem in Two Dimensions," Computing, Vol. 5, pp. 45–56.

[Erl86]   Erlangen University, Computer Sciences, Selected Publications on DIRMU, Erlangen, West Germany.

[Fai85]   R. Fairley: "Software Engineering Concepts," McGraw-Hill, New York.

[FaJ86]   J. M. Francioni, J. A. Jackson: "An Implementation of a 2^d-Section Root Finding Method for the FPS T-Series," in [Hea87], pp. 495–500.

[FaM87]   G. C. Fox, P. C. Messina: "Advanced Computer Architectures," Sci. Am., Vol. 257, Oct., No. 4, pp. 66–77.

[FaW81]   T. Feng, C. Wu: "Fault-diagnosis for a Class of Multistage Interconnection networks," Trans. IEEE, Vol. C-30, No. 10, pp. 743–58.

[FCS82]   J. D. Fernandez, H. Carlisle, and S. Sheppard: "Experiments with Matrix Multiplication Using Ada Tasks," Ada Letters, Vol. II, No. 5, pp. 76–84.

[Fea88]   G. C. Fox et al: "Solving Problems on Concurrent Processors," Prentice Hall, Englewood Cliffs, NJ.

[Fea89]   G. C. Fox et al: "Hands-On Parallel Processing," Byte, Oct., pp. 287–93.

[Fea90]   G. C. Fox et al: "Solving Problems on Concurrent Processors," Vol. 2, Prentice Hall, Englewood Cliffs, NJ.

[Fel85]   M. B. Feldman: "Data Structures with Ada," Reston Publ. Co..

[Fen72]   T. Y. Feng: "Some characteristics of parallel processing," Proceeding of Sagamore Conference on Parallel Processing, pp. 5–16.

[Fen77]   T. Y. Feng: "Parallel Processors and Processing," *Class Notes*, Wayne State University, Detroit, MI.

[Fen81]   T. Y. Feng: "A Survey of Interconnection Networks," Computer, Vol. 14, No. 12, Dec., pp. 12–27.

[Fer86]   S. Fernbach (Ed): "Supercomputers," Elsevier Science Publishers, New York, NY.

[Fly66]   M. J. Flynn: "Very High-Speed Computing Systems," Proc. IEEE, Vol. 54, pp. 1901–9.

[Fos76]   C. Foster: "Content Addressable Parallel Processors," van Nostrand Reinhold.

[GaH86]   G. A. Geist, M. T. Heath: "Matrix Factorization on a Hypercube Multiprocessor," in [Hea86], pp. 161–80.

[GaL73]   L. R. Goke and G. J. Lipovski: "Banyan networks for partitioning multiprocessing systems," Proc. 1st Ann. Comp. Arch. Conference, pp. 21–28.

[GaL81]   A. George, J. W. Liu: "Computer Solution of Large Sparse Positive Definite Systems," Prentice Hall, Englewood Cliffs, NJ.

[GaP85]   D. D. Gajski, J. K. Peir: "Essential Issues in Multiprocessor Systems," Computer, Vol. 18, No. 6, June, pp. 9–27.

[GaS82]   A. Gottlieb, J. T. Schwartz: "Networks and Algorithms for Very Large-Scale Parallel Computers," Computer, Vol. 15, No. 1, Jan., pp. 27–36.

[Gea83]   A. Gottlieb et al: "The New York University Ultracomputer . . . ," Trans. IEEE, Vol. C-32, No. 2, Feb, pp. 175–89.

[Gel87]   D. Gelernter: "Programming for Advanced Computing," Sci. Am., Vol. 257, No. 4, Oct., pp. 90–115.

[GHL84]   A. George, M. T. Heath, J. Liu: "Parallel Cholesky Factorization on a Multiprocessor," University of Waterloo, Waterloo, Ontario, Canada Research Report CS-84-49, Nov., 1984.

[Gla83]   R. L. Glass: "Real-Time Software," Prentice Hall, Englewood Cliffs, NJ.

[GLN87]   A. George, J. Liu, E. Ng: "Communication Reduction in Parallel Sparse Cholesky Factorization on a Hypercube," in [Hea87], pp. 576–86.

[HaB84]   K. Hwang, F. A. Briggs: "Computer Architecture and Parallel Processing," McGraw-Hill, New York, NY.

[HaJ81]   R. W. Hockney, C. R. Jesshope: "Parallel Computers," Adam Hilger Ltd., Bristol, United Kingdom.

[Han77]   W. Handler: "The Impact of Classification Schemes on Computer Architectures," Proc. International Conference on Parallel Processing, pp. 7–15.

[Han80]   W. Handler, H. Rohrer: "Gedanken zu einem Rechner-Baukastensystem," Elektronische Anlagen, Vol. 22, No. 1, pp. 3–13 (also in [Er187]), (in German).

[Han86]   W. Handler: "Multiprozessoren—Effizienz und Fehlertoleranz" in [Er187].

[Han86]   W. Handler: "Funfte Computer-Generation und zukunftige Rechner-Strukturen," BuW-fachtagung, Linz (Austria), Sept. 1986, pp. 38–61.

[Han88]   W. Handler: "Parallel Data-Processing," Informationstechnik, Vol. 30, No. 2, pp. 67–70.

[HaP83]   A. N. Habermann, D. E. Perry: "Ada for Experienced Programmers," Addison-Wesley Publ. Co. Inc., Reading, MA.

[HaS86]   W. D. Hillis, G. L. Steel, Jr.: "Data Parallel Algorithms," Comm. ACM, Vol. 29, No. 12, Dec., pp. 1170–84.

[HaZ81]   E. Horowitz and A. Zorat: "The Binary Tree As an Interconnection Network . . . ," Trans. IEEE, Vol. C-30, No. 4, Apr., pp. 247–53.

[Hea73]   F. E. Heart et al: "A New Minicomputer/Multiprocessor for the ARPA Network," AFIPS Conf. Proceedings, pp. 529–37.

[Hea83]   P. Hibbard et al: "Studies in Ada Style," Springer-Verlag, New York, NY.

[Hea85b]   W. Handler et al: "DIRMU Multiprocessor Configurations," 1985 ICPP, Aug., pp. 652–56, in [Erl86].

[Hea86]   M. T. Heath (Ed): "Hypercube Multiprocessors 1986," SIAM Press.

[Hea87]   M. T. Heath (Ed): "Hypercube Multiprocessors 1987," SIAM Press.

[Hea88]   M. T. Heath (Ed): "Hypercube Multiprocessors 1987," ACM Press.

[Hea86b]   M. T. Heath: "The Hypercube: A Tutorial Overview," in [Hea86] pp. 7–10.

[He76b]   D. Heller: "A Survey of Parallel Algorithms in Numerical Linear Algebra," Computer Science, Carnegie-Mellon University, Pittsburgh, PA 15213, Feb. 1976.

[Hel76]   D. Heller: "Some Aspects of the Cyclic Reduction Algorithm for Block Tridiagonal Linear Systems," SIAM J. Numer. Anal., Vol. 13, pp. 484–96.

[Her89]   F. Hertweck: "Vektor und Parallel-Rechner," Informationstechnik, Vol. 31, No. 1, pp. 5–22, (in German).

[Hil85]   W. D. Hillis: "The Connection Machine," Cambridge, MA: MIT Press.

[HMW85]   W. Handler, E. Maehle, K. Wirl: "The DIRMU testbed for high-performance multiprocessor configurations," Proc. of the first International Conference on Supercomputing systems, IEEE, Dec., pp. 468–75.

[Hoa78]   C. A. R. Hoare: "Communicating Sequential Processes," Comm. ACM, Vol. 21, No. 8, Aug., pp. 666–77.

[Hoc65]   R. Hockney: "A Fast Direct Solution of Poisson's Equation Using Fourier Analysis," J. ACM, Vol. 12, pp. 95–113.

[Hol76]   Holberger: "An Addressable Ring Conveyor," Dept. of Computer Sciences, University of Illinois, Champaign-Urbana, Jan..

[Hoc83]   R. Hockney: "Characterizing Computers and Optimizing the FACR(1) Poisson Solver," Trans. IEEE, Vol. C-32, pp. 933–41.

[Hos89]   T. Hoshino: "PAX Computer," Addison Wesley Publ. Co..

[HTW86]   A. Hopper, S. Temple, J. Williamson: "Local Area Network Design," Addison-Wesley.

[Hwa85]   K. Hwang: "Multiprocessor Supercomputers . . . ," Computer, Vol. 18, No. 6, June, pp. 57–75.

[Ili82]   J. K. Iliffe: "Advanced Computer Design," Prentice Hall, Englewood Cliffs, NJ.

[Int85]   Intel Scientific Computers: "Parallel Processing on Intel Concurrent Supercomputers," A Technical Seminar, 15201 NW Greenbrier Parkway, Beaverton, OR 97006, (503) 629-7629.

[Int88]   Intel Scientific Computers: "iPSC/2," Order Number 280110-001.

[Ive62]   K. Iverson: "A Programming Language," J. Wiley Inc., New York, 82.

[JaG80]   A. K. Jones, E. F. Gehringer [Eds]: "The Cm* Multiprocessor Project: A Research Review," Carnegie-Mellon University, Computer Science, July, CMU-CS-80-131.

[JaH79]   C. Jesshope, R. Hockney: "Supercomputers . . . ," Vol. 1 and 2, Infotech Int. Ltd., Maidenhead (UK).

[Jon87]   G. Jones: "Programming in occam," Prentice Hall International.

[Jor82]   T. Jordan: "A Guide to Parallel Computation and some CRAY-1 Experiences," in [Ro82], pp. 1–50.

[Jor88]   H. F. Jordan: ''Data Communication in Multiprocessors—Shared and Fragmented Memory,'' Informationstechnik, Vol. 30, No. 2, pp. 129–38.

[KaC81]   W. J. Karplus, D. Cohen: ''Architectural and Software Issues in the Design and Application of Peripheral Array Processors,'' Computer, Vol. 14, No. 9, pp. 11–17.

[Kah87]   R. E. Kahn: ''Networks for Advanced Computing,'' Sci. Am., Vol. 257, No. 4, pp. 136–43.

[Kai89]   R. Y. Kain: ''Computer Architecture,'' Vol. I and II, Prentice Hall, Englewood Cliffs, NJ.

[KaK79]   R. Kober, Ch. Kuznia: ''SMS—a multiprocessor architecture for high-speed numerical calculations,'' Euromicro-Journal, Vol. 5, No. 1, pp. 48–52.

[KaM68]   R. M. Karp, W. L. Miranker: ''Parallel minimax search for a maximum'' Journal of Combinatorial Theory, Vol. 4, No. 1, pp. 19–39.

[Kar82]   W. J. Karplus: ''Peripheral Array Processors,'' The Society for Computer Simulation, P. O. Box 2228, LaJolla, CA, 92038.

[KaS72]   D. J. Kuck, A. Sameh: ''Parallel Computations of Eigenvalues of Real Matrices,'' Information Processing 71, North-Holland Corp., pp. 1266–72.

[Kas82]   D. J. Kuck, A. R. Stokes: ''The Burroughs Scientific Processor (BSP),'' Trans. IEEE, Vol. C-31, No. 5, May, pp. 363–76.

[KaS83]   C. P. Kruskal, M. Snir: ''The performance . . . ,'' Trans. IEEE, Vol. C-32, Dec., pp. 1091–98.

[Kaw73]   K. R. Kaplan, R. O. Winder: ''Cache-Based Computer Systems,'' Computer, pp. 30–36, 138.

[KaW88]   D. Kaur, Y. Wallach: ''Parallel Methods for Tridiagonal Equations,'' Computing, Vol. 40, No. 3, pp. 267–72.

[KKK76]   R. Kober, H. Kopp, Ch. Kuznia: ''SMS-101 . . . ,'' Euromicro-Journal, Vol. 2, No. 1, pp. 56–64.

[KMP86]   Y. M. Kang, R. B. Miller, R. A. Pick: ''Comments on Grosh's Law Revisited: CPU Power and the Cost of Computation,'' Comm. ACM, Vol. 29, No. 8, pp. 779–81.

[Kni66]   Knight: ''Changes in computer performance,'' Datamation, Vol. 12, pp. 40–54.

[Knu75]   D. E. Knuth: ''Sporting and Searching,'' Addison Wesley, Reading, MA, Second printing.

[Kob76]   R. Kober: ''A fast communicating processor for the SMS multimicroprocessor system,'' Euromicro-Journal, Vol. 2, No. 3, pp. 183–89.

[Kob77]   R. Kober: ''The multiprocessor system SMS201—Combining 128 microprocessors to a powerful computer,'' COMPCON 77, Fall, pp. 225–30.

[Kow85]   J. S. Kowalik (Ed): ''Parallel MIMD Computation: HEP Supercomputer and Its Applications,'' MIT Press.

[Kun82]   S. Y. Kung: ''Why systolic architectures?'' Computer, Jan., pp. 37–46.

[Kun88]   S. Y. Kung: ''VLSI Array Processors,'' Prentice Hall, Englewood Cliffs, NJ.

[Kuz77]   Ch. Kuznia: ''Parallelrechner mit Mikroprozessoren,'' Carl Hansen Verlag, Munchen, pp. 63–68, (in German).

[LaC85]   B. H. Liebowitz, J. H. Carson: ''Multiple Processor Systems for Real-Time Applications,'' Prentice Hall, Englewood Cliffs, NJ.

[Lak88]   T. Lake: "Languages for Parallel Processing," Informationstechnik, Vol. 30, No. 2, pp. 118–28.

[LaM87]   G. J. Lipovski and M. Malek: "Parallel Computing," J. Wiley Interscience.

[LaV75]   J. J. Lambiotte, R. G. Voigt: "The Solution of Tridiagonal Linear Systems on the CDC STAR-100 Computer," ACM Trans. on Math. Software, Vol. 1, No. 4, pp. 308–29.

[LaV82]   T. Lang, M. Valero: "M-users, B-servers Arbiter for Multiple-Buses Multiprocessors," Microprocessors and Microprogramming, pp. 11–18.

[Law75]   D. H. Lawrie: "Access and Alignment of Data in an Array Processor," Trans. IEEE, Vol. C-24, No. 12, Dec., pp. 1145–55.

[Lee76]   R. B. L. Lee: "Performance Bounds for Parallel Processors," Stanford University, DSL Technical Report, No. 125, Nov.

[Lin82]   N. R. Lincoln: "Technology and Design . . . of a Modern Supercomputer," Trans. IEEE, Vol. C-31, No. 5, May, pp. 349–62.

[LMM85]   O. Lubeck, J. Moore, R. Mendez: "A benchmark comparison . . . ," Computer, Vol. 18, No. 12, pp. 10–24.

[LPS88]   A. R. Larrabee, K. E. Pennick, S. M. Stern: "BBN Butterfly Parallel Processor," on pp. 43–57 of [Bab88].

[MaC80]   C. Mead, L. Conway: "Introduction to VLSI Systems," Addison-Wesley, Reading, MA.

[Mae85a]   E. Maehle: "Fault-tolerant DIRMU multiprocessor configurations," Computer Architecture Newsletter, IEEE Computer Society, June, pp. 51–56.

[Mae85b]   E. Maehle: "Systematischer Entwurf von Mikrocomputer-Selbsttestprogrammen," 13 Fachtagung "Technische Zuverlassigkeit," Nuernberg, pp. 145–59, (in German).

[MaH78]   M. P. Mariani, E. J. Henry: "PEPE—A user's viewpoint; a powerful real time adjunct," National Computer Conference, pp. 993–1002.

[MaM61]   Morrison, Morrison: "Charles Babbage and his calculating engines," Dover Inc., NY.

[Man79]   M. M. Mano: "Digital Logic and Computer Design," Prentice Hall, Englewood Cliffs, NJ.

[MaP71]   M. Minsky, J. Papert: "On some associative, parallel and analog computations," in "Associative Information Techniques," ed. Jacobs, Elsevier, New York.

[Mar57]   H. M. Markowitz: "The elimination form of the inverse and its application to linear programming," Management Science, Vol. 3, pp. 255–69.

[May74]   Mayer: "Zuverlassigkeit von Systemen," Technische Rundschau, Bern, 5, 2.

[MaV87]   O. A. McBryan, E. F. Van de Velde: "Hypercube Programs for Computational Fluid Dynamics," in [Hea68], pp. 221–43.

[MHW87]   T. N. Mudge, J. P. Hayes, D. C. Winsor: "Multiple Bus Architectures," Computer, June, pp. 42–48.

[MMM84]   D. MacGregor, D. Mothersole, B. Moyer: "The Motorola 68020," IEEE Micro, Vol. 4, No. 4, pp. 101–18.

[Mod88]   K. B. Modahl: "CRAY X-MP," on pp. 59–72 of [Bab88].

[Mol86]   C. Moler: "Matrix Computation in Distributed Memory Multiprocessors," in [Hea86], pp. 181–95.

[Mot80]   Motorola Company: "MC68000 User's Manual," Prentice Hall, Englewood Cliffs, NJ.

[Mot85]   Motorola Company: ''MC68020 User's Manual,'' Prentice Hall, and ''MC68881 User's Manual,'' Prentice Hall, Englewood Cliffs, NJ.

[Moo59]   E. F. Moore: ''The shortest path through a maze,'' in Proceedings of the International Symposium on the Theory of Switching, Vol. 2, pp. 285–92.

[Nag79]   K. Nagel: ''Solving linear equations with the SMS201,'' Euromicro-Journal, Vol. 5, No. 1, pp. 53–54.

[New82]   S. B. Newell: ''Introduction to Microcomputing,'' Harper & Row, Cambridge.

[Nor84]   C. Norrie: ''Supercomputers—An Architectural Overview,'' Computer, Vol. 17, No. 3, pp. 62–74.

[Nug88]   S. F. Nugent: ''The iPSC/2 Direct-Connect Communication Technology,'' in [Hea88].

[OaV85]   J. M. Ortega, R. G. Voigt: ''Solution of partial differential equations on vector and parallel computers,'' ICASE REPORT No, 85-1, NASA Langley Research Center, Hampton, VA, 23665, Jan. 1985.

[OaW83]   E. W. Olsen, S. B. Whitehill: ''Ada for Programmers,'' Reston Publishing Company, Inc., Reston, VA.

[OHW82]   N. S. Ostlund, P. G. Hibbard, R. A. Whiteside: ''A Case Study in the Application of a Tightly Coupled Multiprocessor to Scientific Computations,'' in ''Parallel Processing,'' Academic Press, pp. 315–64.

[Ole82]   P. Oleinick: ''Parallel Algorithms on a Multiprocessor,'' UMI Research Press.

[Org83]   E. I. Organick: ''A Programmer's View of the Intel 432 System,'' McGraw-Hill, New York.

[Org83]   E. I. Organick: ''Algorithms, Concurrent Processors, and Computer Science Education,'' ACM SIGSE Bulletin, Mar., pp. 1–5.

[Ott87]   R. Otto: ''Inversion of dense matrix on the DIRMU multiprocessor,'' Ph.D. Thesis, Computer Science, University Erlangen, Feb. 1987, (in German).

[PaN85]   G. F. Pfister, V. A. Norton: ''Hot spot contention . . . ,'' Trans. IEEE, Vol. C-34, Oct., pp. 943–48.

[Pat78]   J. H. Patel: ''Processor-Memory Interconnections for Multiprocessors,'' Proc. of the 6th Ann. Symp. on Comp. Arch., pp. 168–77.

[Pat82]   J. H. Patel: ''Analysis of Multiprocessors with Private Cache Memories,'' Trans. IEEE, Vol. C-31, pp. 296–304.

[PaV81]   F. Preparata, J. Vuillemin: ''The cube-connected cycles . . . ,'' Comm. ACM, Vol. 24, pp. 300–9.

[PaZ86]   R. H. Perrot, A. Zarea-Aliabadi: ''Supercomputer Languages,'' ACM Comp. Surveys, Vol. 18, No. 1, pp. 5–22.

[Pea85]   G. Pfister et al: ''The IBM Research Parallel Prototype (RP3) . . . ,'' Proc. of 1985 Int. Conf. on Parallel Processing, (Chicago, Aug., pp. 764–71.

[Pel87]   A. Peled: ''The Next Computer Revolution,'' Sci. Am, Vol. 257, No. 4, Oct., pp. 56–65.

[Pet81]   G. L. Peterson: ''Myths about the mutual exclusion problem,'' Inform. Process. Lett., Vol. 12, No. 3, June, pp. 115–16.

[PFL75]   R. C. Pierce, J. A. Field, W. D. Little: ''Asynchronous Arbiter Modules,'' IEEE, Trans. on Computers, Sept., pp. 931–32.

[Pit87]   D. Pitt: "Standards for the token ring," IEEE Network, Vol. 1, No. 1, Jan. 87, pp. 19–22.

[Qui87]   M. J. Quinn: "Designing efficient algorithms for parallel computers," McGraw-Hill, New York.

[RaG87]   D. A. Reed, D. C. Grunwald: "The Performance of Multicomputer Interconnection Networks," Computer, Vol. 20, No. 6, pp. 63–73.

[RaL77]   C. Ramamoorthy, H. Li: "Pipeline Architecture," ACM Comp. Surveys, Vol. 9, pp. 61–102.

[RaP77]   D. Rohrbacher, J. L. Potter: "Image Processing with the Staran Parallel Computer," Computer, Vol. 10, No. 8, Aug., pp. 54–59.

[RaS84]   J. Riganati, P. Schneck: "Supercomputing," Computer, Vol. 17, No. 10, pp. 97–113.

[RaT86]   R. Rettberg, R. Thomas: "Contention is no obstacle to shared-memory multiprocessing," Comm. ACM, Vol. 29, No. 12.

[Rod82]   G. Rodrigue (Ed): "Parallel Computations," Academic Press, New York.

[Rom87]   C. H. Romine: "The Parallel Solution of Triangular Systems on a Hypercube," in [Hea87], pp. 552–59.

[Ros87]   F. E. Ross: "Rings are round for good," IEEE Network, Vol. 1, No. 1, Jan. 87, pp. 31–35.

[Rus78]   R. M. Russel: "The CRAY-1 Computer System," Comm. ACM, Vol. 21, No. 1, Jan., pp. 26–35.

[RWS88]   S. Ranka, Y. Won, S. Sahni: "Programming a Hypercube Multicomputer," IEEE Software, Sept., pp. 69–77.

[SaB77]   H. Sullivan, T. R. Bashkow: "A large-scale, homogeneous, fully distributed parallel machine," Proc. 4th Comp. Arch. Symp. 7, pp. 105–24.

[SaF83]   S. H. Saib and R. E. Fritz: "The Ada Programming Language: A Tutorial," IEEE Computer Society Press.

[SaM81]   H. J. Siegel, R. J. McMillen: "The Multistage Cube: A Versatile Interconnection Network," Computer, Vol. 14, No. 12, Dec., pp. 65–76.

[SaS85]   E. Schonberg, E. Schonberg: "Highly Parallel Ada—Ada on an Ultracomputer," Proc. of the Ada Intl. Conf., pp. 58–68.

[SaZ87]   S. R. Seidel, L. R. Ziegler: "Sorting on Hypercubes," in [Hea87], pp. 285–91.

[Sch80]   J. T. Schwartz: "Ultracomputers," ACM, Trans. Prog. Lang. Sys., Vol. 2, No. 4, Oct., pp. 484–521.

[Sch83]   S. A. Schuman: "Tutorial on Ada Tasking," pp. 346–407 of [SaF83].

[Sch84]   U. Schendel: "Introduction to Numerical Methods for Parallel Computers," Ellis Horwood Ltd., England.

[Sea62]   D. L. Slotnick et al: "The SOLOMON computer," AFIPS Fall Joint Computer Conf., Vol. 22, pp. 97–107, Spartan Books, Washington, D.C.

[Sea77]   R. J. Swan et al: "The implementation of the Cm* multi-microprocessor," Proc. Nat. Comp. Conf., Vol. 46, AFIPS Press, pp. 645–55.

[Sea87]   D. H. Schaefer et al: "The GAM Pyramid," in [Uhr87], pp. 15–42.

[Sea7b]   K. Schwan et al: "Mapping Parallel Applications to a Hypercube," in [Hea87], pp. 141–54.

[Sei85]   C. L. Seitz: "The Cosmic Cube," Comm. ACM, Vol. 28, No. 1, Jan., pp. 23–33.

[Sie79]   H. J. Siegel: "Interconnection Networks for Large-Scale Parallel-Processors: Theory and Case Studies," Lexington Books, Lexington, MA.

[Sie79]   H. J. Siegel: "Interconnection Networks for SIMD Machines," Computer, Vol. 12, No. 6, June, pp. 57–65.

[Sin87]   K. Singh: "Interconnection Networks," Ph.D Thesis, University of Roorkee, India, 1987.

[SLS82]   K. G. Shin, Y. Lee, J. Sashidhar: "Design of HM²p—a Hierarchical Multiprocessor," Trans. IEEE, Vol. C-31, No. 11, pp. 1045–53.

[Smi81]   B. J. Smith: "Architecture and Applications of the HEP Multiprocessor Computer System," Vol. 298 of Real-Time Signal Processing IV, by the Society of Photo-Optical Instrumentation Engineers, Bellingham, WA, pp. 241–48, M303 (also in [Kow85]).

[Smi82]   A. J. Smith: "Cache Memories," Computing Surveys, Vol. 14, pp. 473–530.

[Stl87]   W. Stallings: "Handbook of Computer Communications Standards—Local Network Standards," Vol. 2, Macmillan Press.

[Sta87]   C. Stanfill: "Communications Architecture in the Connection Machine™ System," Thinking Machines Corp., Technical Report Series, HA87-3, Mar., 17.

[Sto71]   H. S. Stone: "Parallel Processing with the Perfect Shuffle," Trans. IEEE, Vol. C-20, pp. 153–61.

[Sto73]   H. S. Stone: "An Efficient Parallel Algorithm for the Solution of a Tridiagonal Linear System of Equations," J. ACM, Vol. 20, No. 1, pp. 27–38.

[Sto78]   H. S. Stone: "Sorting on STAR," Trans. IEEE, Vol. SE-4, No. 2, pp. 464–72.

[Sto87]   H. S. Stone: "High-Performance Computer Architecture," Addison-Wesley Publishing Company, Reading, MA.

[Str69]   V. Strassen: "Gaussian elimination is not optimal," Num. Math, Vol. 13, pp. 354–56.

[Str87]   N. C. Strole: "The IBM token ring network—a functional overview," IEEE Network, Vol. 1, No. 1, Jan. 87, pp. 23–30.

[TaK77]   C. D. Thompson, H. T. Kung: "Sorting on a Mesh-Connected Parallel Computer," Comm. ACM, Vol. 20, No. 4, pp. 263–71.

[TaL80]   Tomann, Liedl: "Reliability in microcomputer arrays," Microprocessing and Microprogramming, Vol. 7, No. 3, pp. 185–90.

[TaO88]   B. Tangney, D. O'Mahony: "Local Area Networks and Their Applications," Prentice Hall International.

[TaW78]   S. Tolub, Y. Wallach: "Sorting on a MIMD-type Parallel Processing System," Euromicro-Journal, No. 4, pp. 155–61.

[Ten82]   J. Tenenbaum: "An Alternating Sequential Parallel Processor," Ph.D. Thesis, Wayne State University, Electrical and Computer Engineering.

[Thi84]   J. Thiebergen (Ed): "New Computer Architectures," Academic Press.

[Thi87]   Thinking Machines Corp.: "Connection Machine, CM2, Summary," Technical Report HA87-4.

[Tho86]   J. R. Thompson: "The CRAY-1, the CRAY X-MP . . . ," pp. 69–81 of [Fe86].

[Thu76]   K. J. Thurber: "Large Scale Computer Architecture," Hayden Book Company, Inc..

[TLL87]   S. L. Tanimoto, T. J. Ligocki, R. Ling: "A Prototype Pyramid Machine for Hierarchical Cellular Logic," in [Uhr87], pp. 43–83.

[Uhr87]   L. Uhr (Ed): "Parallel Computer Vision," Academic Press, Inc., Boston, MA.

[VaC78]   C. R. Vick, J. A. Cornell: "Pepe Architecture—Present and Future," National Computer Conference, pp. 981–92.

[Wag87]   B. Wagar: "Hyperquicksort . . . ," in [Hea87], pp. 292–99.

[WaF80]   C. Wu, T. Feng: "On a class of multistage interconnection networks," and "The reverse-exchange interconnection network," both in Trans. IEEE, Vol. C-29, the first on pp. 694–702, the second on pp. 801–11.

[Wak89]   J. F. Wakerly: "Microcomputer Architecture and Programming; The 68000 Family," John Wiley, Inc.

[Wal73]   Y. Wallach: "Study and Compilation of Computer Languages," Gordon and Breach Science Publ., New York, 1974.

[Wal74]   Y. Wallach: "Parallel processor systems in power dispatch," IEEE Summer Power Meeting, July, papers C74334-9 and C74335-6.

[Wal82]   Y. Wallach: "Alternating Sequential/Parallel Processing," Springer-Verlag, New York, NY.

[Wal86]   Y. Wallach: "Calculations and Programs for Power System Networks," Prentice Hall, Englewood Cliffs, NJ.

[Wal87]   Y. Wallach: "Solution of Linear Equations . . . ," Journal of Pascal, Ada, & Modula-2, Vol. 6, No. 2, pp. 3–19.

[Wan81]   H. H. Wang: "A Parallel Method for Tridiagonal Equations," ACM Trans. on Math. Software, Vol. 7, No. 2, pp. 170–83.

[War73]   W. Ware: "The Ultimate Computer," IEEE Spectrum, Vol. 10, No. 3, pp. 89–91.

[WaY88]   Y. Wallach, E. Yaprak: "Use of Local Area Networks as Alternating Sequential-Parallel Systems," Microprocessing and Microprogramming, Vol. 24, pp. 95–102.

[Wei72]   C. W. Weiss: "Bounds on the Length of Terminal Stuck Fault Tests," Trans. IEEE, Vol. C-21, Mar., No. 3, pp. 305–9.

[Wei80]   C. Weitzman: "Distributed Micro/Minicomputer Systems," Prentice Hall, Englewood Cliffs, NJ.

[WHB81]   Y. Wallach, E. Handschin, A. Bongers: "An efficient parallel processing method for power system state-estimation," Trans. IEEE, Vol. PAS-101.

[Wil64]   D. J. Wilde: "Optimum Seeking Methods," Prentice Hall, Englewood Cliffs, NJ.

[Wu978]   C. L. Wu: "Interconnection Networks in Multiple-Processor Systems," Ph.D. Dissertation, Wayne State University, Detroit, MI.

[YaA85]   S. Yalamanchili, J. K. Aggarwal: "Reconfiguration Strategies for Parallel Machines," Computer, Vol. 18, No. 12, pp. 44–61.

[Yap89]   E. Yaprak: "Use of Local Area Networks as ASPs," Ph.D. Thesis, Wayne State University, Detroit, MI.

[YaW88]   E. Yaprak, Y. Wallach: "Parallel Processing in Token Ring Networks," 31st Midwest Symposium on Circuits and Systems, St. Louis, MO, Aug..

INDEX

A